Presented with our compliments to

KARA CONTADINI

for participation in the

National PTA Reflections Project

A

1993

ANTARCTICA

ANTARCTICA

THE EXTRAORDINARY HISTORY OF MAN'S CONQUEST OF THE FROZEN CONTINENT

Published by Reader's Digest

Sydney London New York Montreal Cape Town

Second edition
Published by Reader's Digest (Australia) Pty Limited (Inc. in NSW)
26-32 Waterloo Street, Surry Hills, NSW 2010

Edited and designed by Capricorn Press Pty Ltd (Inc. in NSW)
3/9 Oaks Avenue, Dee Why, NSW 2099

National Library of Australia cataloguing-in-publication data

Antarctica, the extraordinary history
of man's conquest
of the frozen continent.

Second ed.
Includes index
ISBN 0 86438 167 0.

1. Antarctic regions – Discovery and exploration.
I. Title: Antarctica, great stories from the frozen continent.

919.8'904

MAJOR CONTRIBUTORS

K. Radway Allen, MA, ScD(Cantab)

Alice Alston

John Béchervaise, MBE, D.Litt.

Tony Bomford

Margaret A. Bradshaw, BSc(Hons)
Canterbury Museum, Christchurch

Ian Close, BA(Hons)

J. T. Darby
Assistant Director, Otago Museum, Dunedin

Ian Dear

Sir Ranulph Fiennes, Bt

Derek Hall

David L. Harrowfield
Canterbury Museum, Christchurch

R. K. Headland
Scott Polar Research Institute, University of Cambridge

Chris Hendy
University of Waikato, Hamilton

F. J. Jacka, PhD, FAIP
Director, Mawson Institute for Antarctic Research, University of Adelaide

P. G. Law, AO, CBE, MSc

Rod Ledingham
Antarctic Division, Kingston, Tasmania

David Lewis, MB, ChB, MSc

Ronald I. Lewis Smith, BSc, PhD
British Antarctic Survey, Cambridge

John Lilley

Desmond J. Lugg, AM, MD, Dip. Polar Studies
Antarctic Division, Kingston, Tasmania

John Manning

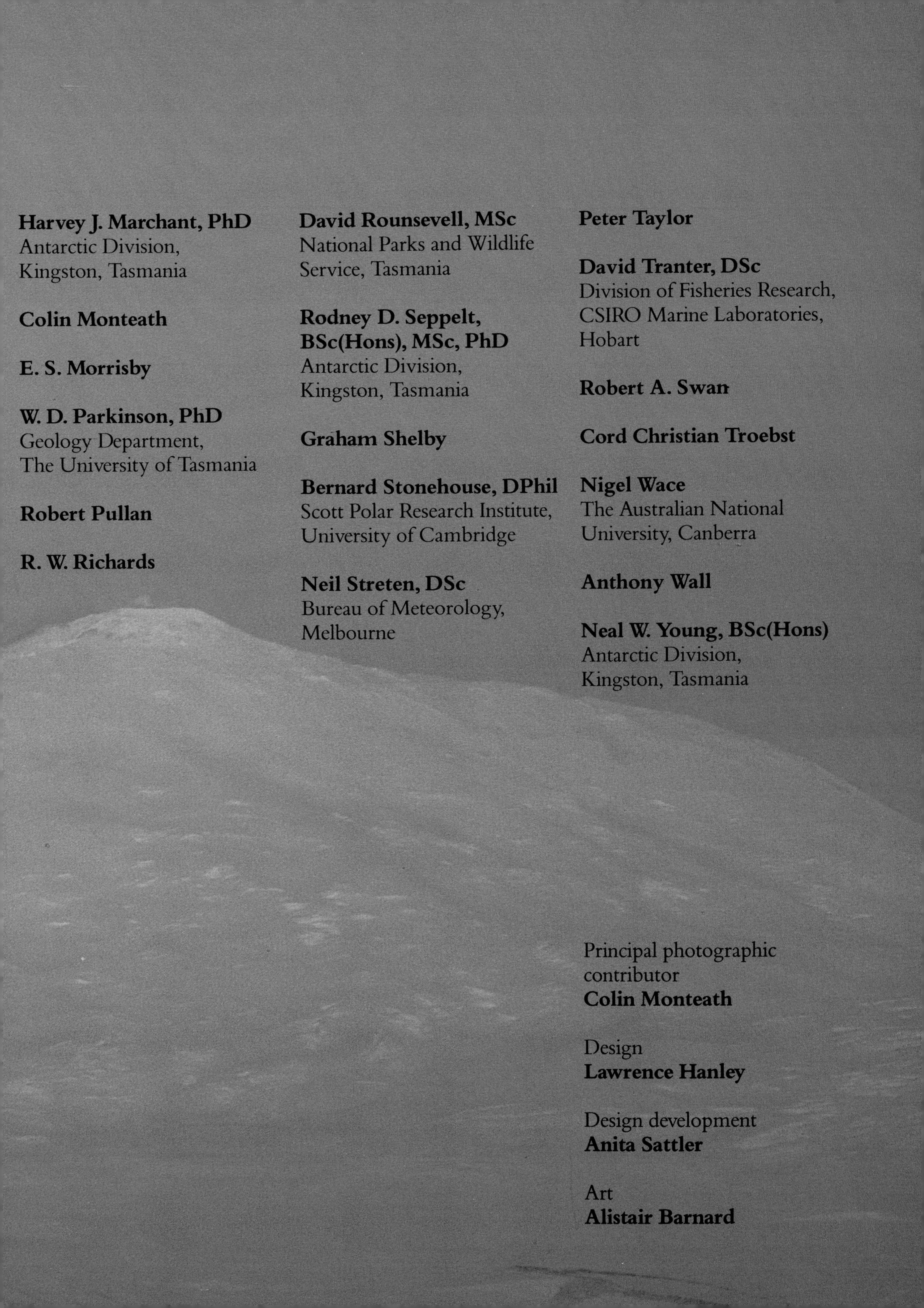

Harvey J. Marchant, PhD
Antarctic Division,
Kingston, Tasmania

Colin Monteath

E. S. Morrisby

W. D. Parkinson, PhD
Geology Department,
The University of Tasmania

Robert Pullan

R. W. Richards

David Rounsevell, MSc
National Parks and Wildlife
Service, Tasmania

Rodney D. Seppelt, BSc(Hons), MSc, PhD
Antarctic Division,
Kingston, Tasmania

Graham Shelby

Bernard Stonehouse, DPhil
Scott Polar Research Institute,
University of Cambridge

Neil Streten, DSc
Bureau of Meteorology,
Melbourne

Peter Taylor

David Tranter, DSc
Division of Fisheries Research,
CSIRO Marine Laboratories,
Hobart

Robert A. Swan

Cord Christian Troebst

Nigel Wace
The Australian National
University, Canberra

Anthony Wall

Neal W. Young, BSc(Hons)
Antarctic Division,
Kingston, Tasmania

Principal photographic
contributor
Colin Monteath

Design
Lawrence Hanley

Design development
Anita Sattler

Art
Alistair Barnard

CONTENTS

Special features

Antarctic atlas and chronology

THE LAST OF LANDS

Facts and figures about the least known continent on earth

For many people Antarctica is a great mystery — it often comes as a surprise to learn that the continent is so large, and that there are neither polar bears nor Eskimos at the southern extremity of the earth. These opening pages give a quick summary of Antarctic statistics — starting point for a voyage of exploration.

Antarctica is an island continent, almost completely covered by ice. If the ice were removed it would reveal a much smaller rocky land mass of some 7 million sq kilometres (2.7 million sq miles).

With its icecap, Antarctica is roughly circular with a diameter of about 4500 kilometres (2800 miles) and an area of 14 million sq kilometres (5.4 million sq miles). This makes it the fifth largest continent. It is larger than the USA (9.4 million sq kilometres; 3.6 million sq miles) and Europe (10.5 million sq kilometres; 4.1 million sq miles), but less than half the size of Africa (30.3 million sq kilometres; 11.7 million sq miles). Surrounding the continent is a frozen ocean that varies in area from about 2.65 million sq kilometres (1 million sq miles) in summer to 18.8 million sq kilometres (7.3 million sq miles) in winter.

Antarctica is separated from the other continents by the wide, stormy waters of the Southern Ocean. The nearest land mass is South America which is 965 kilometres (600 miles) away, while it is some 2500 kilometres (1550 miles) to Australia and 4000 kilometres (2500 miles) to Africa.

The vast icecap gives Antarctica the greatest average elevation of any continent at 2300 metres (7500 ft). The average elevation of North America is 720 metres (2362 ft) and of Australia only 340 metres (1115 ft). The highest point on the icecap is in east Antarctica where it rises to a height of 4100 metres (13450 ft). The continent's highest mountain is the Vinson Massif at 5140 metres (16859 ft).

Some 90 per cent of the world's fresh water is locked up in the icecap which covers all but about two per cent of the continent. This represents an enormous volume of water — roughly 24.5 million cubic kilometres (5.9 million cubic miles). If all this ice were to melt it would raise the level of the world's oceans by between 50 and 60 metres (160 and 200 ft). The thickest ice in the world is found reaching down 4800 metres (15700 ft) into some submerged basins in rock.

This cold, remote continent has produced the lowest temperature ever recorded on earth. This record was established at the Russian base Vostok, on the inland icecap, where the thermometer plummeted to −89.6°C (−129.3°F) in July 1983. Mean temperatures in the inland during the coldest month range from −40°C to −70°C (−40°F to −94°F), and in the warmest month from −15°C to −35°C (+5°F to −31°F). At the coast the figures are −15°C to −30°C (+5°F to −22°F) in winter, and 0°C (32°F) in summer.

Despite the persistent cold, some primitive forms of life still manage to eke out a precarious existence on the continent. A few microscopic animals survive in areas where the conditions are slightly more favourable than they are elsewhere — the continent's largest permanent inhabitant is a wingless fly. Primitive mosses and lichens are the most frequently found plants — one lichen even managing to grow on rocks just 400 kilometres (250 miles) from the South Pole. Some algae in the strange, ice-free dry valleys have taken to living inside rocks so they can escape the harsh conditions. There are, of course, numerous species of birds and seals to be found on and around the continent in summer, but only one, the emperor penguin, stays throughout the months of winter darkness.

The first person to see Antarctica was probably the Russian explorer Thaddeus von Bellingshausen on 27 January 1820, although it seems that he did not recognise his discovery for what it was. The first landing on the continent may have been made only a year later, in February 1821, by an American sealer, John Davis. There is, however, doubt about the exact spot where Davis landed and it may not have been on the mainland at all.

If Davis did not land on the continent, then the first landing was not made for another 74 years, until January 1895. In that year a party under the command of whaler Henryk Bull stepped ashore beneath Cape Adare.

Now some 2000 people live on Antarctica during the brief, busy summer months. They inhabit some 40 bases on the continent and its surrounding islands. In winter the human population of Antarctica drops to a mere 800 or so.

HOW THE BOOK IS ORGANISED

Antarctica is divided into three main parts. Part one, **The continent and.its wildlife,** explains the basic geology, geography, botany and zoology of the continent and the islands that surround it in the Southern Ocean. Much exciting work is being done in all scientific fields in Antarctica, and this section tells some of the fascinating tales that have emerged from this work.

Part two, **The explorers,** unfolds, in chronological order, the story of Antarctic exploration, starting from the earliest times and continuing up to the present day. Here are told some of the world's most exciting adventure stories – tales of extraordinary courage and daring. Interspersed between these stories are seventeen 'special features' which draw together threads that run through most of the explorers' tales. There are pages that cover such topics as entertainment, medicine, food and travel. The feature pages are distinguished by the grey border that edges them.

Part three, the **Antarctic atlas and chronology,** contains all the essential reference that is needed for a proper understanding of the rest of the book. Four full-page maps show the entire continent in vivid detail, with close-ups of important areas. These larger maps complement those on the explorers' pages. An Antarctic Time Chart places all the events in the book in their proper chronological order. In periods when there was great international interest in Antarctica, there were often four or five expeditions working simultaneously on the continent. It can be difficult to appreciate the order in which events occurred. All the principal figures involved in Antarctic exploration are detailed in the biographies that follow the Time Charts. It is interesting to know what happened to explorers after their Antarctic work was complete. This part of the book is rounded off with a comprehensive general index and a complete gazetter of the maps.

The sources of photographs, diagrams and information are included among the acknowledgments that appear on the last page of the book.

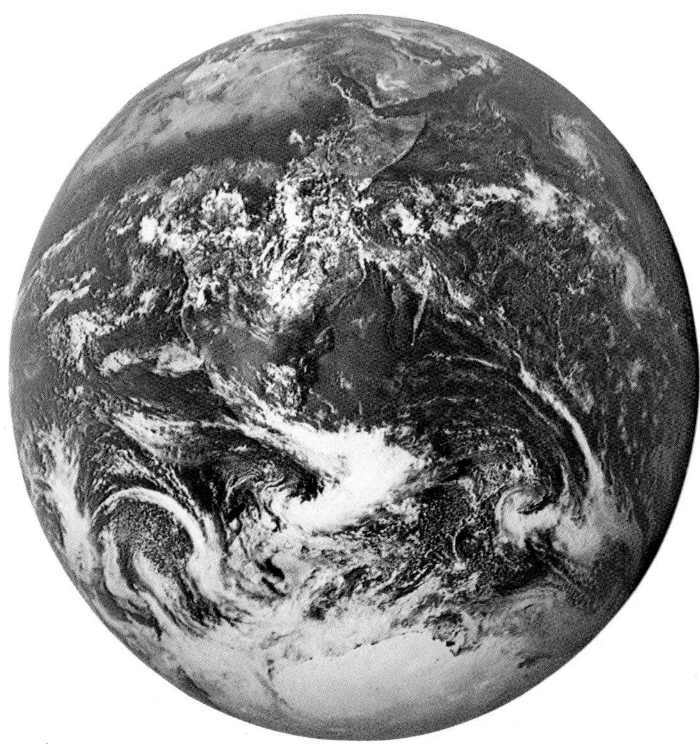

Cape Washington on the eastern shore of the Ross Sea, 300 km (186 miles) from Ross Island as seen from Landsat, 917 km (570 miles) in space. The large berg is about 40 km (25 miles) long.

A vast stretch of east Antarctica, from roughly Coats Land to Wilkes Land, is visible in this view of the earth taken by Apollo 17 astronauts. The indentation on the right is the Amery Ice Shelf.

A formidable tangle of mountains and glaciers separate the Ross Ice Shelf and the polar plateau.

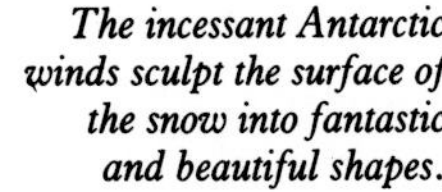

The incessant Antarctic winds sculpt the surface of the snow into fantastic and beautiful shapes.

The unearthly hues of an Antarctic dawn. In the distance the moon sets over the flanks of Mt Erebus, while in the foreground a finger of ice juts skyward.

PART ONE: THE CONTINENT AND ITS WILDLIFE

The bleak snow deserts that surround the South Pole are among the most inhospitable places on earth. Yet, despite the bitter cold, an unexpectedly large variety of plants and animals cling tenaciously to the rare rocky outcrops that fringe the all-enveloping ice. In contrast, the stormy Southern Ocean and its islands teem with life.

A UNIQUE CLIMATE

Antarctica and the world's weather

Continental Antarctica's climate is the result of its high latitude, perpetual snow cover, the great height of the ice plateau above sea level and the vast extent of its surrounding ocean. In many respects, it is the opposite of the north polar zone which, although at similar latitude, is essentially an ocean surrounded by land. Except for Greenland, and some smaller mountain areas, the Arctic does not have a permanent icecap.

The main, but not the only, reason for the low temperatures at the poles is that they receive very little short wave radiation from the sun, and what they do receive varies from season to season. Because of the tilt of the earth on its axis as it circles the sun the amount of radiation falling on any part of its surface changes according to the latitude, season, time of day and the amount absorbed by the atmosphere. At the poles there is a maximum in summer, a minimum in the winter, and quite rapid changes in spring and autumn. Because the earth's orbit is elliptical, the South Pole is closest to the sun in summer and so receives about seven per cent more radiation at the southern summer solstice than the North Pole does at the northern summer solstice. At midsummer it even receives more radiation than the equator does at any time throughout the year.

Why then does the temperature remain so low over Antarctica? Essentially the reason is that the continent's perpetual snow cover reflects back on average over 80 per cent of the incoming short-wave radiation, compared with five per cent over ice-free oceans and 15 to 35 per cent over snow-free land. Clouds also reflect back some radiation, and gases in the atmosphere absorb some more. In addition to reflecting short-wave radiation, snow is also efficient at radiating back to space at long wavelengths, further cooling the surface.

Throughout the year at the South Pole there is only a brief period in November and December when the ice surface receives more radiation than it loses to space. As the continent does not get progressively colder by this continual loss of heat it must acquire energy from elsewhere. This is mainly supplied by warmer air from the surrounding oceans, and from the process by which moisture in the atmosphere gives up some of its energy — latent heat — as it condenses out and freezes.

Antarctica cannot be looked at entirely in isolation. It plays an important role in global weather patterns. These are controlled by the motion of the atmosphere and oceans, which redistribute the heat received from regions of surplus heat energy (the tropics) to those of heat deficit (the poles). The process by which this redistribution takes place is still only partly understood.

Continental Antarctica is separated from the other continents by the wide expanse of the Southern Ocean. This is a region of strong westerly winds and the breeding ground of the great depressions, or low pressure centres.

These great weather systems, which typically last for about a week from birth to decay, move generally eastwards and polewards across the oceans, being guided by waves in the upper part of the troposphere. The general pattern of movement is similar at all times of the year. The depressions approach, and usually dissipate, near the coast of Antarctica where they help to cause a permanent ring of low pressure around the continent at about 60°S, known as the Antarctic Trough.

There is little change in the pressure pattern

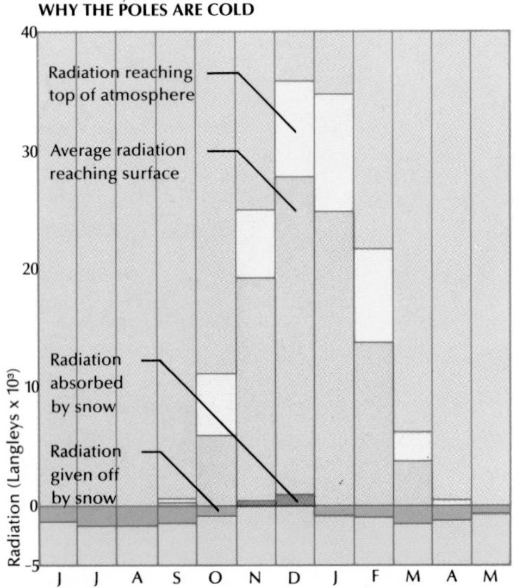

Heat from the sun
Only a small amount of the short-wave radiation from the sun that falls on Antarctica is actually absorbed by the surface. Some is absorbed by the atmosphere before it reaches the continent, some is reflected by clouds, but most is reflected back into space by the blanket of snow and ice. For most of the year, except for a brief period during midsummer, the centre of the continent actually loses more radiation than it gains from the sun. At the coast the situation is a little better, but over most of the continent for most of the year, more radiation is lost than is received.

Seasonal change
There are enormous differences in the temperature patterns over Antarctica between summer and winter. This is mainly because the continent has a period of continuous sunlight in summer and in winter a period of continuous darkness. The temperature does not get dramatically warmer in summer mainly because little of the energy that reaches the surface during the periods when the sun is shining is absorbed by the highly reflective snow surface. The final temperature patterns are closely linked to the height of the land, with the coast being much warmer than the high interior. As a result of the low winter temperatures, a huge area of the sea around Antarctica freezes — almost doubling the size of the continent. The sea ice also means that the coast is separated from the open sea for much of the year, and thus becomes more continental in climate. Of course, on any given day the temperature may not conform to the mean monthly pattern.

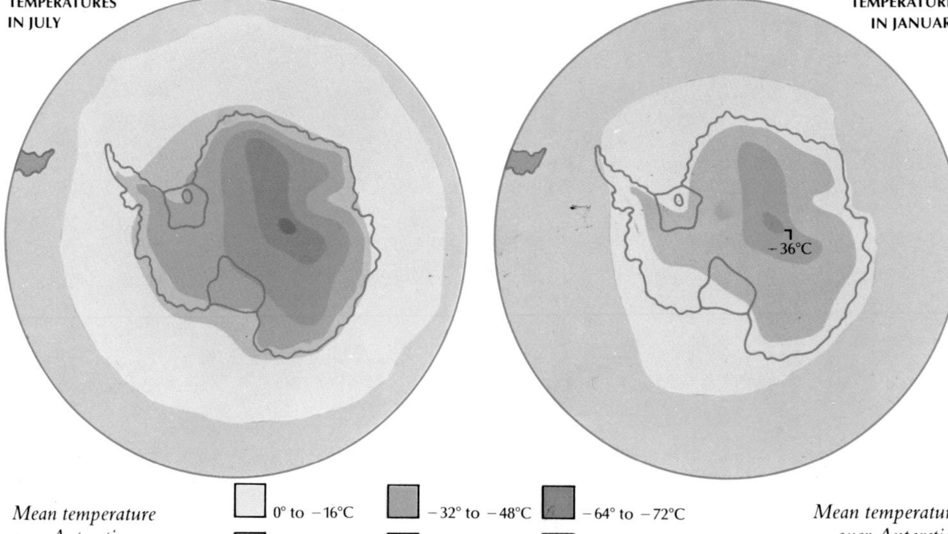

Mean temperature over Antarctica in winter.

Mean temperature over Antarctica in summer.

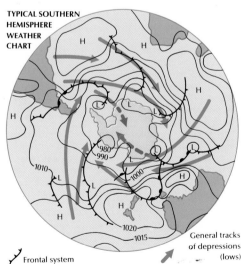

from month to month except that the trough moves slightly away from the continent and back towards it again on a half yearly cycle. As individual depressions approach the Antarctic coast they bring with them warmer and more humid air from over the ocean, particularly in summer and autumn when the edge of the sea ice is close to the coast. Cloud increases, the easterly winds get stronger and snow may fall. Most depressions decay near the coast, although several times per month they reach parts of the high plateau where they may cause some snow to fall before they decay.

The dramatically darkening sky heralds the approach of a depression. Most strike the Antarctic coast from the northwest.

Ships approaching Antarctica must pass through the Roaring Forties and Furious Fifties — regions of strong westerly winds that sweep almost unhindered right around the earth.

TYPICAL SOUTHERN HEMISPHERE WEATHER CHART

H H H H H H H L L L L L L L 980 990 1000 1010 1020 1015

Frontal system

General tracks of depressions (lows)

Global patterns

The oceans around Antarctica provide an almost uninterrupted corridor for circumpolar westerly winds which blow around the mid latitudes. These latitudes earned the nicknames of the Roaring Forties and Furious Fifties in the nineteenth century, when sailing ships used the winds for a fast passage around the earth. The westerlies extend through the entire depth of the troposphere (the lowest level of the atmosphere) and give birth to great atmospheric depressions. These depressions move around Antarctica and usually spiral in towards its coast.

A hole in the sky.

The earth's atmosphere is made up of many layers. One of these layers – between 10 and 50 km (6 and 30 miles) above the planet's surface – contains a large quantity of ozone, a form of oxygen. Ozone is produced when ordinary oxygen is exposed to sunlight, especially ultraviolet radiation. The ozone layer is of great importance because it absorbs almost all the ultraviolet radiation that reaches the earth from the sun – life as we know it could not exist without this protection. In the 1980s scientists working in Antarctica noticed that ozone levels were dropping at an alarming rate. In the spring of 1987 a record 'hole', as large as the USA and Mexico combined, appeared in the ozone layer over Antarctica. High-flying aircraft confirmed the ozone decline, but also found that it was mirrored by a proportional rise in the levels of chlorine monoxide. These findings confirmed a theory that chlorine from the gases (CFCs) used in refrigerators and as aerosol propellants was finding its way into the upper atmosphere, where it combined with ozone. Researchers now believe that in winter – when the air above Antarctica is isolated by circumpolar winds – chemical reactions that release active chlorine take place on tiny ice particles. When the sun returns in spring this chlorine combines with the ozone to destroy it, creating the 'hole'. International efforts are now under way to reduce the amount of chlorine being released.

Polar desert Only very small amounts of snow and ice crystals fall on the interior of Antarctica each year. The mean annual accumulation is equivalent to less than 50 mm (2 in) of water — slightly more than is received in the Sahara Desert. Much more falls on some coastal areas, particularly on the west of the Antarctic Peninsula and parts of east Antarctica. The northern end of the Antarctic Peninsula receives the equivalent of about 900 mm (35 in) of water a year. The vast amounts of snow and ice that have slowly been built up to create the icecap have been deposited over many millions of years.

ANNUAL ACCUMULATION OF SNOW

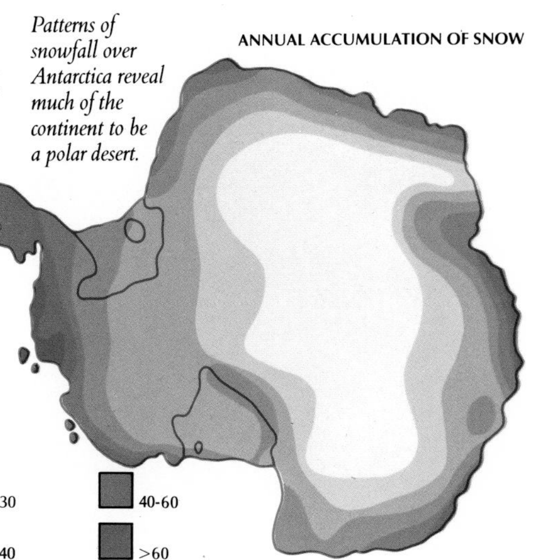

Patterns of snowfall over Antarctica reveal much of the continent to be a polar desert.

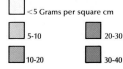

<5 Grams per square cm
5-10
10-20
20-30
30-40
40-60
>60

WEATHER AND PEOPLE

The effects of wind and cold

In the polar regions of the northern hemisphere, between 60° and 70°N, there are a wide range of climates, and these have created many different environments, such as the ice cap of Greenland, the forests of Scandinavia and the agricultural land of central Alaska. However, there are no such extreme contrasts in the climate of Antarctica.

A strange wind cloud looms over the horizon after a severe storm at Cape Crozier, on the tip of Ross Island. Field parties must be always alert for sudden changes.

Temperature and wind are the two elements of the weather that are of the greatest importance in the polar regions. They must be considered together because different combinations of the two characterise the regional climates of Antarctica.

Temperature decreases from summer to winter with increasing latitude, and also with height above sea level. Over most of the continent the mean temperature of the coldest month is around −15° to −30°C (+5° to −22°F) on the coast, and −40° to −70°C (−40° to −94°F) in the interior. The lowest temperature recorded in Antarctica was −89.6°C (−129.9°F) at Vostok in July 1983. In summer the mean temperature of the warmest month is around 0°C (32°F) on the coast [where maxima on individual days may reach + 7°C or +8°C (45° or 46°F), and as high as +10°C (50°F) on outlying islands] and -15° t o − 35°C (+5° to − 31°F) in the interior.

It is windspeed, however, which has the greatest effect on human activity. The winds over much of Antarctica are unlike those experienced in most other parts of the world. They are of a special type and their speed and direction are not primarily controlled by the overall pattern of atmospheric pressure, but rather by the shape of the icecap. These winds are known as katabatic (down flowing) winds. Their behaviour is not fully understood but, in simple terms, the cold air near the surface of the icecap tends to flow down the coastal slopes under the influence of gravity in a shallow layer — perhaps 300 metres (1000 ft) deep — with warmer air above. Many coastal stations experience very strong katabatic winds, usually from the southeast. In extreme cases they may resemble the amazing winds experienced by Sir Douglas Mawson's expedition at Cape Denison in 1911-14, where the annual mean windspeed averaged over 70 km/h (44 mph) — nearly twice that of other strong wind

Whiteout Under conditions when there are no shadows or contrasts between objects — when, for example, there is a uniformly cloudy sky over snow-covered terrain — a traveller can experience a loss of perception. The air may be very clear, but impressions of dips and rises in the snow surface are not conveyed to the brain of a traveller.

In a whiteout it is sometimes difficult to tell the difference between a small object nearby and a large object a long way off.

Even birds have difficulty seeing a snow surface while flying in a whiteout.

Aircraft pilots can crash as a result of disorientation.

Local weather
Antarctica has few of the variations in climate that occur in the north polar region. This is because the continent is essentially round and is encircled by a uniform expanse of ocean over which westerly winds blow for most of the year. Climates vary according to height above sea level and distance from the sea; otherwise differences are only slight, and usually result from local features in the landscape. The main characteristic of the Antarctic climate is its extreme severity, which has meant that only very few plants and animals are able to live there. Even man has only recently been able to establish himself on the continent with the help of advanced technology. Wind and temperature have the greatest effect on living conditions in Antarctica and the two are always considered together (see the windchill index on the right).

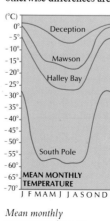

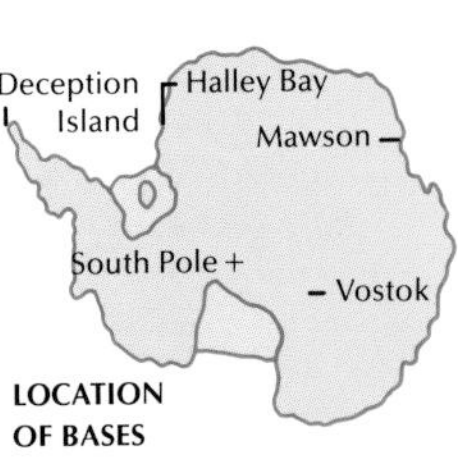

MEAN MONTHLY TEMPERATURE
(°C) 0° -5° -10° -15° -20° -25° -30° -35° -40° -45° -50° -55° -60° -65° -70°
Deception
Mawson
Halley Bay
South Pole
J F M A M J J A S O N D

Mean monthly temperature decreases dramatically at the pole.

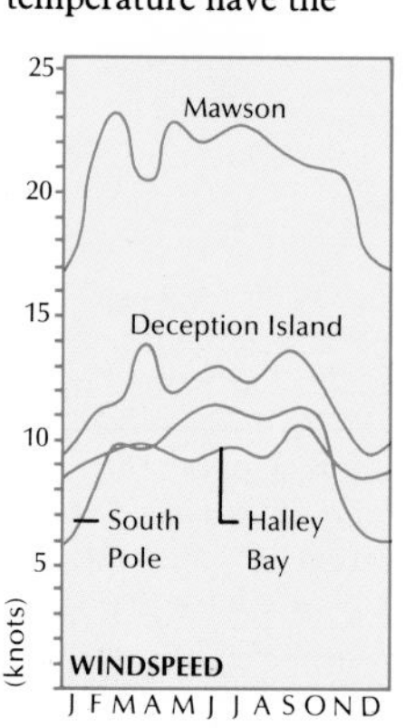

Coastal stations experience higher windspeeds than those on the polar plateau.

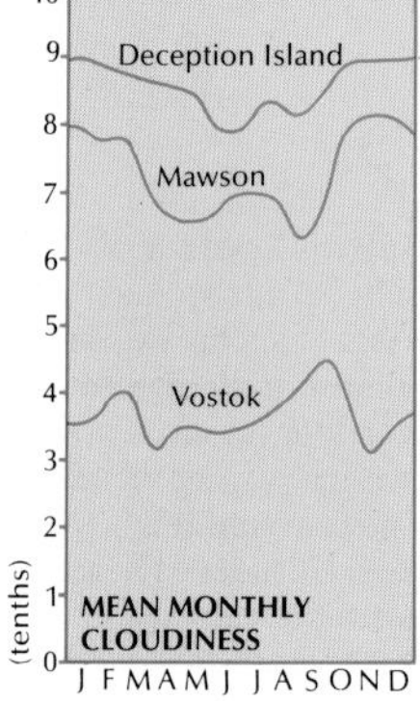

The skies are generally clearer over the centre of Antarctica.

Mock suns, or sun dogs, caused by the sun's light being reflected and refracted by ice crystals in the atmosphere. A similar effect is sometimes seen around the moon.

stations. Mawson aptly named the site of their hut: 'The Home of the Blizzard'.

Katabatic winds vary considerably at individual locations because of differences in the local landforms. Sometimes the winds may produce phenomena such as revolving whirlpools of cloud, and walls of drifting snow. The winds may also surge suddenly to high speeds, and stop in an instant.

Because of the low temperature in Antarctica, the absolute humidity (the amount of water vapour contained in a given volume of air) is always very low. By contrast, the relative humidity — the ratio, expressed as a percentage, of the amount of water vapour actually present to the maximum possible at the given temperature — varies a great deal, and may be over 95 per cent at times when there is a lot of drifting snow. The low absolute humidity of Antarctic air causes many things to dry and shrink. Imported wooden building materials can therefore become a great fire risk at an expedition base.

The Southern Ocean is very cloudy throughout the year, and the coastal regions around Antarctica are often cloudy as well, particularly where there are frequent onshore winds. Generally, there is less cloud over the interior. The low, thick stratocumulus cloud over the ocean and coast gives way to thinner, multi-layered ice crystal clouds over the continent. In summer cumulus cloud often forms locally over inland mountain ranges and isolated nunataks. The ice crystal clouds, which are common over Antarctica, often cause spectacular displays of optical phenomena called haloes as the sun's rays are refracted and reflected by ice crystals.

The most extreme weather conditions experienced in Antarctica are associated with blizzards. These are simply strong winds with falling snow or, more commonly, drifting snow picked up and driven along the surface. They may last for days at a time. In some cases it can be almost impossible to see, and it is not unusual for objects only a metre or so away to be hard to distinguish. In the field, expeditioners are confined to tents or caravans. A typical blizzard near the coast is usually associated with a nearby low pressure system, and conditions are usually worse in regions which normally have strong katabatic winds. The local winds are disturbed and strengthened by the winds of the low pressure system and wind speeds of 150 km/h (93 mph), with gusts exceeding 190 km/h (120 mph), are quite common. Temperatures during blizzards are often higher than normal. A full scale blizzard may last for several days and they occur with different frequencies at different sites — on average perhaps eight or ten times per year. There is often considerable damage caused after a blizzard, and scientific stations and their equipment must be specially constructed. On the high plateau, conditions are usually less severe, but locally intensified katabatic winds can still make travel impossible.

In fine weather visibility in Antarctica is usually excellent because of the clear air and the absence of dust and smoke. This may sometimes lead people to greatly underestimate the distance of objects. Mirages are also common in Antarctica. The polar type occur when there is a layer of cold air near the surface, with a layer of warmer air above it. Differences in the way light is transmitted in the two layers may produce complicated distortions. Distant features such as mountains or icebergs may seem to loom above the horizon, or appear as inverted images. These phenomena have led to many errors in polar exploration.

Windchill A windchill index links wind and temperature to show how heat is lost in various conditions. In still air at -20°C the index is around 550, very cool; at the same temperature in a one knot (1.9 km/h; 1.2 mph) wind the index is around 900, very cold; at the same temperature in a wind of 7.5 knots (14 km/h; 9 mph) the index is 1400 at which exposed human flesh starts to freeze.

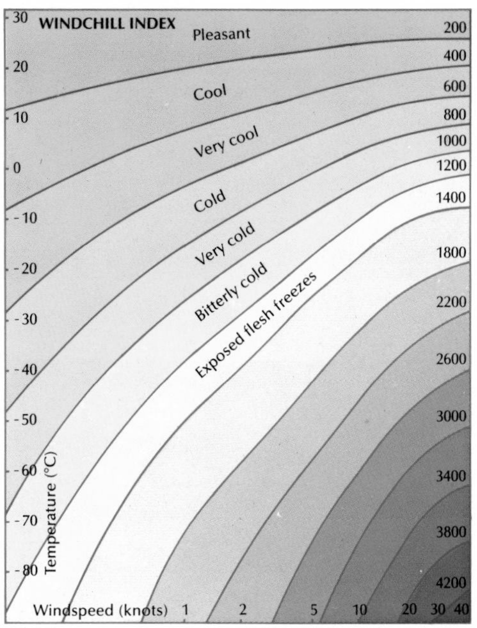

Blizzards are a combination of strong wind and falling or blowing snow. They bring all outside work to a halt and can cause considerable damage to unprotected machines and buildings.

A severe blizzard can cut visibility to less than one metre (three feet).

Variations in wind, temperature and visibility during a 7-day blizzard.

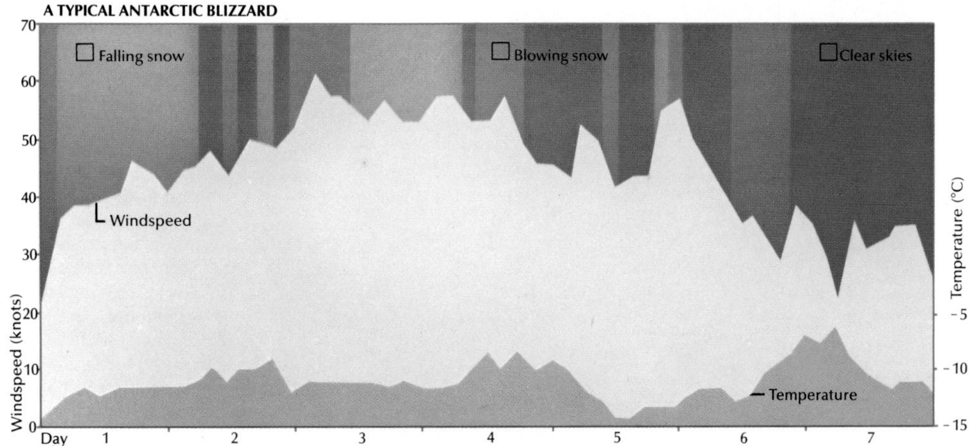

SNOW AND ICE

A landscape sculpted from water

The most abundant form of fresh water in the world is ice, with about 99 per cent of the world's surface fresh water locked up in snow, ice, glaciers and ice sheets that cover 10 per cent of the earth's surface. About 90 per cent of the world's ice is to be found in Antarctica.

Snow and ice crystals begin their journey as water molecules evaporated from the surface of the oceans. The water vapour is carried high into the atmosphere where ice crystals form about microscopic dust particles. Snowflakes grow by the addition of more water molecules, or by other crystals adhering to them. The most familiar shape is the branched form, but other shapes such as plates, needles and prisms are possible, depending on the temperature in the cloud.

Snow can form in the atmosphere anywhere over the globe, but it reaches the ground only when the temperature in the lower atmosphere and at the surface is cold enough. The surface of most of Antarctica is so cold that water only ever arrives there as snow or ice. Not that much moisture falls on Antarctica, which is the driest continent, mainly because very low temperatures limit the moisture-carrying capacity of the air. An average of only 120 to 150 mm (5 to 6 in) of water accumulates over the entire continent during a year. The highest rate of accumulation is near the coast where it is warmest. Large areas of the interior receive the equivalent of less than 50 mm (2 in) of water a year. In some areas the rate is as low as 20 to 30 mm (0.8 to 1.2 in).

Most of the snow falls in storms which move into the interior from the ocean. Some ice can also fall from a clear sky as 'diamond dust' — very fine crystals — which forms from water vapour in the air, in much the same way as fog or dew forms in warmer areas.

Liquid water is rarely found in Antarctica. Sometimes the snow surface melts in summer near the coast, but generally the water seeps into the snow beneath and refreezes. Only at low altitudes, and in extremely warm conditions, is there any surface runoff.

Once snow has fallen on the surface of the continent it is redistributed by the incessant winds, sometimes over great distances. The stronger the wind, the greater is its capacity to carry drift snow. As the crystals are buffeted they lose their shape and become rounded, making it more difficult for the wind to pick them up. They gradually become cemented to the surface, which becomes hardened as the snow is windpacked.

Wind-borne snow behaves in much the same way as sand. It builds up where the wind speed is low, such as behind obstacles, and erodes and shapes the surface where the wind is strong. In light winds snow dunes and ridges form, and in very faint breezes ripples are sometimes found on fresh surfaces.

Very rough surfaces can be found in winter when winds are strong and snowfall heavy, and these can make travel difficult. Sastrugi — a form of erosion that has been likened to frozen surf — and dunes often form belts many kilometres wide, and are most pronounced near the coast where strong katabatic winds occur. Sometimes two sets of dunes or sastrugi with different alignments are formed on top of each other; one shaped by katabatic winds, the other by periodic blizzards.

The strength and texture of the snow surface varies greatly across Antarctica. Inland, where it is cold and the winds are light, the surface can be quite soft, in some areas making travel slow and difficult. Where there is little snowfall and strong winds, the surface can be so

Drift snow is the bane of Antarctic travellers. With the consistency of talcum powder, it is constantly being blown about the continent by strong winds.

A night-time view of a drilling camp on the polar icecap. Drill cores reveal much about the remote history of Antarctica's ice and the world's climate.

Snow and ice Ice is the frozen, crystalline form of water. The crystals, composed of hydrogen and oxygen atoms, are built in layers with an inherent six sided symmetry. The crystals can take on many forms. Snow is one form of atmospheric ice made from supercooled water droplets which grow by the addition of more material.

Snow crystals are found in an infinite variety of six-sided shapes.

Large hoar frost crystals grow in the interior of caves and crevasses.

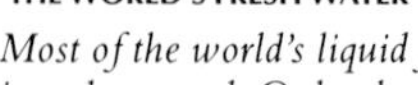

THE WORLD'S FRESH WATER

Most of the world's liquid fresh water is underground. Only about one per cent remains unfrozen in streams and lakes on the surface.

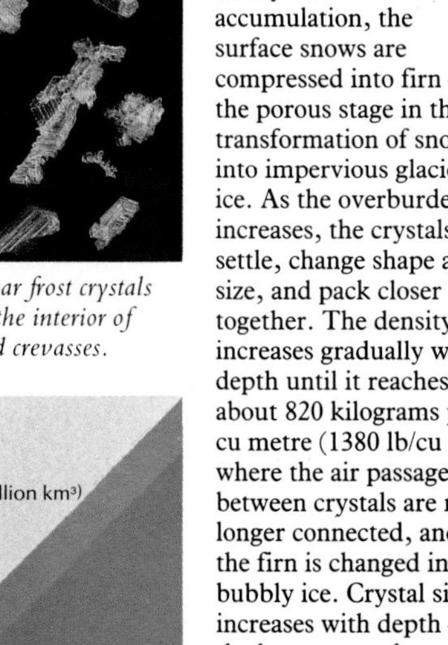

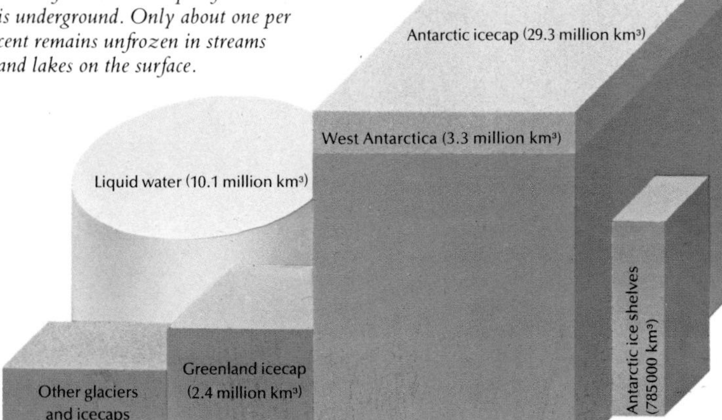

Crystal growth
Under the weight of each year's accumulation, the surface snows are compressed into firn — the porous stage in the transformation of snow into impervious glacier ice. As the overburden increases, the crystals settle, change shape and size, and pack closer together. The density increases gradually with depth until it reaches about 820 kilograms per cu metre (1380 lb/cu yd) where the air passages between crystals are no longer connected, and the firn is changed into bubbly ice. Crystal size increases with depth — the larger crystals growing at the expense of smaller ones. At the surface, crystals are generally less than 1 mm (0.04 in) across and they grow from there at a rate that depends on the temperature. The size can reach 30 to 50 mm (1.2 to 2 in), and even 100 mm (4 in) across.

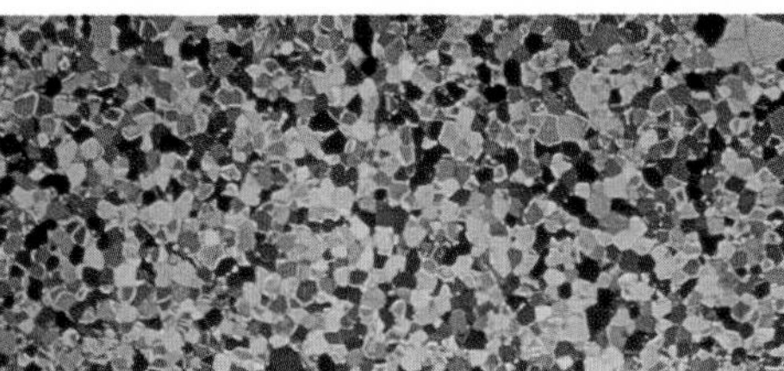

Ice crystals from a depth of 10 metres (33 ft) beneath the surface are about 2 mm in diameter.

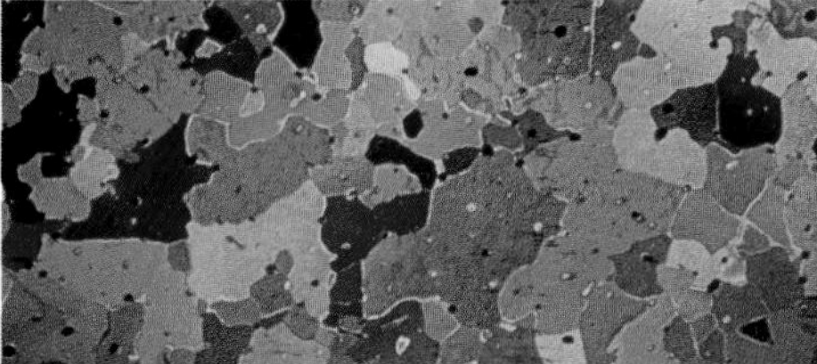

By 70 metres (230 ft) air bubbles (black dots) are visible in the 7 mm diameter ice crystals.

At 317 metres (1040 ft) the crystals from the base of this small icecap have grown to 28 mm across.

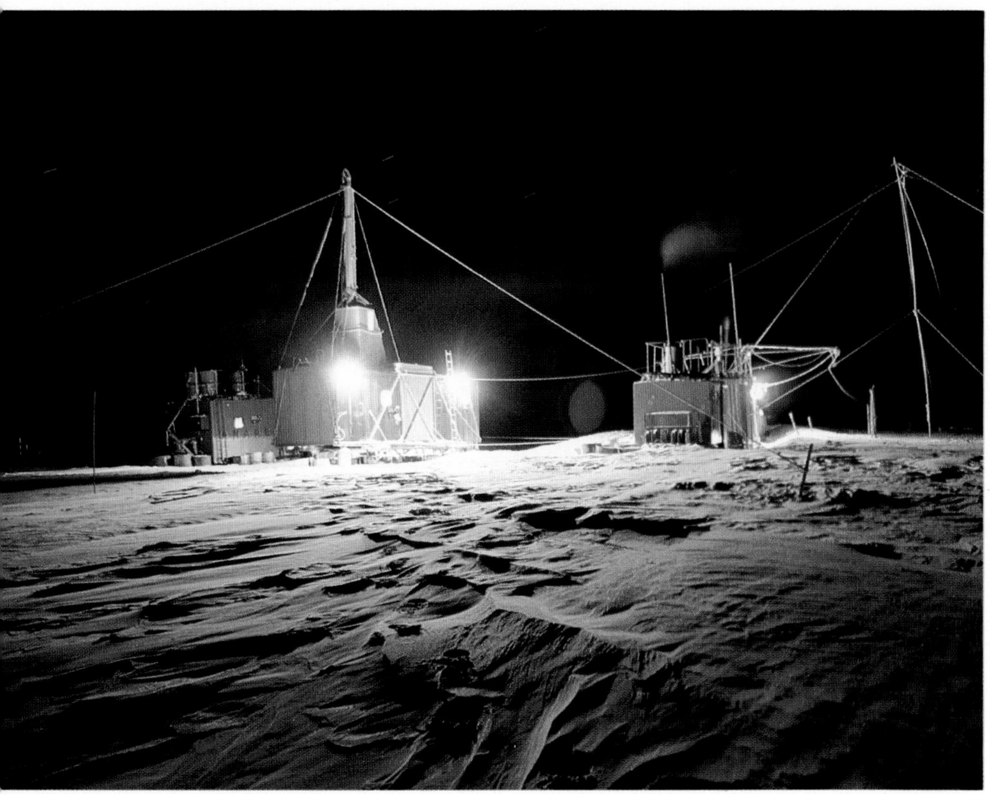

hard that heavy tractors barely make a mark on it, but snow surfaces will not generally support a heavy wheeled vehicle without it getting bogged. The load-bearing properties of snow can be improved, however, and experimental airstrips are being produced by grading and rolling snow to increase its density and hardness. A pavement about 0.5 to 1.0 metre (20 to 40 inches) thick is built up until it is strong enough to support an aircraft.

The density of freshly fallen snow can be as low as 100 kilograms per cu metre (168 lb/cu yd), but windpacking quickly increases that to 400 kilograms per cu metre (674 lb/cu yd). The increasing weight of snow accumulating on the surface compresses the material beneath, increasing its density. At a depth of between 70 and 100 metres (230 and 328 ft) the air passages trapped between crystals are closed, thus forming bubbly ice. By the time the snow has been buried to a depth of 1200 metres (3940 ft) there are no bubbles because the air has been compressed into the crystals.

Ice of very great age can be recovered by extracting cores from the ice sheet, and, when analysed, these cores reveal much about climates and environments in the past. Dust particles, gases, pollen, emissions from volcanoes and even fallout from nuclear bomb tests can all be found trapped in the ice.

The age of ice can sometimes be determined by measuring the relative concentrations of two different forms (isotopes) of oxygen — O^{18} and O^{16} — found in the ice. The lower the temperature at which the snow formed, the lower the proportion of the heavier O^{18} it contains. By measuring the ratio of the two isotopes of oxygen it is sometimes possible to decide whether the snow fell in summer or winter. By counting the seasons up to the surface, scientists can date a core, and thereby any trapped material it contains. It is not always possible, however, to use this technique.

Expeditions from a number of nations have been involved in drilling ice cores from Antarctica. In 1968 United States' engineers at Byrd station in east Antarctica drilled 2164 metres (7098 ft) right through the ice sheet for the first time. Other deep holes have been drilled at Dome C (905 metres; 2968 ft) and at the Russian base Vostok (2083 metres; 6832 ft). Because of the great thickness of the ice at these places, and the slow rate at which snow accumulates, the holes only penetrated the upper part of the ice sheet, but spanned a long period. At Vostok the deepest ice dated from perhaps 150 000 years ago.

The quantities of impurities found in the ice are so minute that they test current methods of analysis. However, as new techniques are developed, more and more will be learnt about past climates and how changes are related to variations in the amount of dust, carbon dioxide and other materials to be found in the air. This information may provide many valuable clues as to the way in which our climate could develop in future.

Frozen history The type of information revealed by analysis of ice cores is shown in the diagram below. This record of dust and gases trapped in a 905-metre (2968-ft) ice core drilled by French scientists at Dome C in east Antarctica stretches back for 33 000 years. It reveals the conditions that existed during the last great glacial maximum which occurred about 18 000 years ago when the northern hemisphere ice sheets reached their greatest extent, and then retreated during a warmer period. The decrease in the proportion of Oxygen[18] in the ice between 16 000 and 11 000 years ago shows that the climate warmed by about 7°C (13°F) and then cooled slightly again. During the last 10 000 years temperature variations have been small, although there was a warm period about 4000 years ago. There was a dramatic, 20-fold increase in atmospheric dust during the glacial maximum. This occurred during a major dry period which began about 26 000 years ago and ended 13 000 years ago. Stronger winds and more intense atmospheric circulation carried dust from the arid continents of the southern hemisphere. Chemical analysis of the dust shows that it did not come from volcanoes, which were once thought to have initiated ice ages. During the glacial maximum the amount of carbon dioxide in the atmosphere dropped to less than two-thirds of present values. Large variations have also occurred over shorter periods of time. The amount of carbon dioxide is thought to be a vital factor in determining climate, and the ice cores are perhaps the only reliable source of data over such long periods of time.

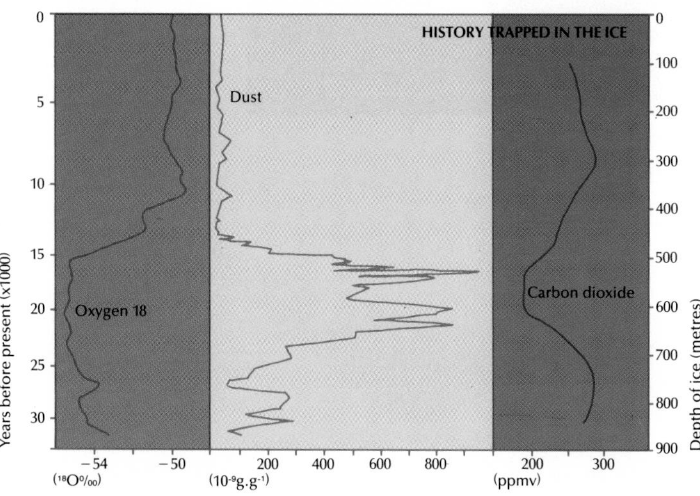

A graph showing variations in the amounts of oxygen, dust and carbon dioxide in a 905-metre (2968-ft) deep ice core from east Antarctica.

Surface features Wind-borne snow is deposited in the lee of obstacles to form snowdrifts. They can also build upwind of obstacles, eventually submerging them. Wind-borne snow is also a very abrasive material, eroding the surface to produce unusual shapes. Sastrugi, a common erosion form, are aligned along the direction of the prevailing wind and their size depends on the wind's strength.

Surface erosion has revealed this footprint once impressed in the snow. Explorers retraced their paths in this way.

The size of sastrugi varies with the wind's strength. They generally range from 150 mm to 2 metres (6 in to 6.6 ft) in height.

THE ANTARCTIC ICECAP

Storehouse for over half of the world's fresh water

Ice covers 98 per cent of Antarctica's continental area of 14 million sq kilometres (5.4 million sq miles). The ice sheet is the single largest body of fresh water or ice in the world, containing some 30 million cubic kilometres (7.2 million cubic miles) — about 90 per cent of the world's ice and 68 per cent of the world's fresh water.

Antarctica is the highest of all continents. Its average elevation is 2300 metres (7500 ft), compared with the average elevation of North America at 720 metres (2362 ft). The highest ice is in east Antarctica, above the submerged Gamburtsev Mountains, where it rises to 4100 metres (13 450 ft). The highest rock, 5140 metres (16 859 ft), is the Vinson Massif in the Sentinal Range, west Antarctica.

Early seismic exploration and aerial surveys with modern radio echo sounding equipment have revealed much about the structure of the ice sheet and the underlying bedrock. East Antarctica is an old continental shield with much of its concealed rock surface lying above sea level, except for Wilkes Land which is underlain by deep basins. The thickest ice is found there, descending to 4776 metres (15 669 ft), and large parts are between 4000 and 4500 metres (13 123 and 14 764 ft) thick. By contrast, west Antarctica is composed of a series of archipelagos and islands, with the deepest bedrock 2555 metres (8382 ft) below sea level. The present average rock elevation of east Antarctica is close to sea level, and of west Antarctica 440 metres (1444 ft) below sea level. If the ice were removed, and the rock allowed to rise to its original level (up to 1000 metres [3280 ft] higher) — a process that would take many thousands of years — then east Antarctica would be mostly above sea level, and the proportion of west Antarctica above sea level would remain largely unchanged.

Surveys show that the ice is distributed unevenly over the continent. The grounded ice sheet, which covers 12 million sq kilometres (4.6 million sq miles), contains most of the ice. The floating ice shelves occupy about 11 per cent of the area, but contain only 2.4 per cent of the volume because they are much thinner, ranging between 200 and 1300 metres (656 and 4264 ft) thick, with the thickest ice occurring where ice streams enter the shelves. There is also a large difference between the volumes of ice in east and west Antarctica, with 26 million cu kilometres (6.2 million cu miles) in the east and 3.3 million cu kilometres (0.8 million cu miles in the west. The remainder is in the Antarctic Peninsula and major ice shelves.

Of Antarctica's 32 000-kilometre (19 880-mile) coastline, about equal amounts — 44 and 38 per cent respectively — are ice shelves and grounded ice cliffs. Thirteen per cent of the coast is occupied by glaciers, and the remaining five per cent is rock outcrops.

The ice flows downhill from the high points of the icecap towards the coast under the influence of its own weight. The rate of flow varies from a few metres a year in the interior to 100 to 200 metres (330 to 660 ft) a year at the margins, and even faster in glaciers and ice streams. At the front of ice shelves, velocities can be as high as one to two kilometres (3280 and 6560 ft) per year. As the ice flows over buried mountains and valleys the surface takes on an undulating shape. The distances between undulations are between 5 and 15 kilometres (3.1 and 9.3 miles) and they are up to 50 metres (164 ft) or more high.

In a few areas the flow does not discharge into the ocean, but dams up behind mountain ranges where the surface is gradually worn away by wind and evaporation. With the ice comes all the material that has fallen onto the catchment area, and this is gradually concentrated at the surface. Large collections of meteorites have been found in such areas.

The ice sheet loses material — about 1450 cu kilometres (348 cu miles) a year — mainly as a result of icebergs calving away from the coastal margins. Most of the material comes from ice shelves, a large part from glaciers and ice streams and only a small proportion from the coastal cliffs of the ice sheet. Some 10 per cent of the annual loss melts from the bottom of ice shelves in contact with the ocean, and as a result of friction at the base of ice streams.

The loss of material from the ice sheet is offset by a build up of snow and ice at the surface, which is estimated to be 1700 cu kilometres (408 cu miles) per year. Some ocean water is also frozen to the base of ice shelves.

Past changes The size of the Antarctic ice sheet has varied a lot during its history. Large ice sheets have formed and disappeared in the northern and southern hemispheres a number of times in the past few hundred thousand years. At its maximum, ice covered nearly 30 per cent of the land surface of the earth and lowered the sea level by 120 metres (394 ft) or more.

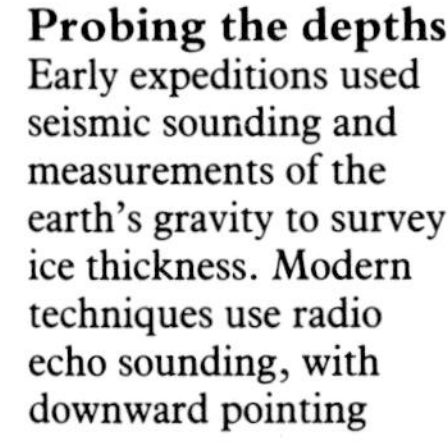

Probing the depths Early expeditions used seismic sounding and measurements of the earth's gravity to survey ice thickness. Modern techniques use radio echo sounding, with downward pointing radar. With the equipment mounted on a tractor or aeroplane, the shape of the surface and the bedrock can be recorded continuously. In some cases echoes are received from within the ice which are thought to represent layers of the same age. The shape of these layers show how the ice has been deformed as it has moved across the rough bedrock. About half of the ice sheet has been surveyed from aircraft using this method, and new techniques are being developed. These include the use of satellites with radar altimeters which can measure the elevation of the ice surface with great accuracy.

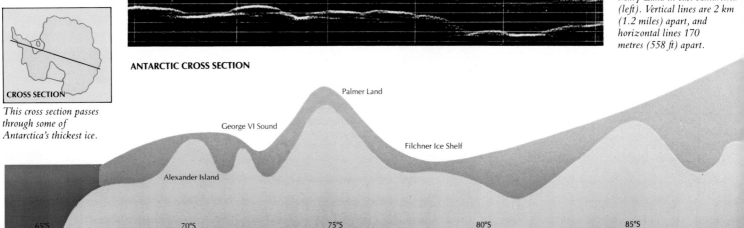

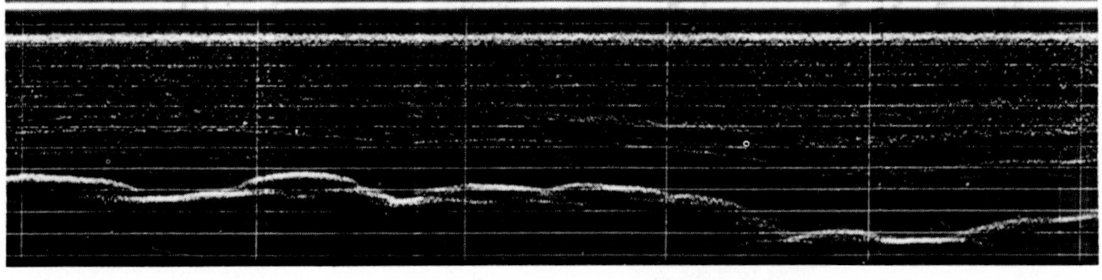

Traverse tractors (above) provide profiles of ice and bedrock, like this 2000-metre (6500-ft) deep echo sounding profile through Queen Mary Land in east Antarctica (left). Vertical lines are 2 km (1.2 miles) apart, and horizontal lines 170 metres (558 ft) apart.

CROSS SECTION

This cross section passes through some of Antarctica's thickest ice.

ANTARCTIC CROSS SECTION

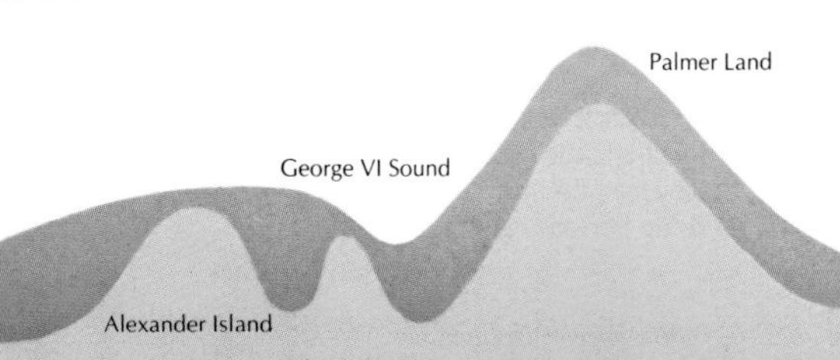

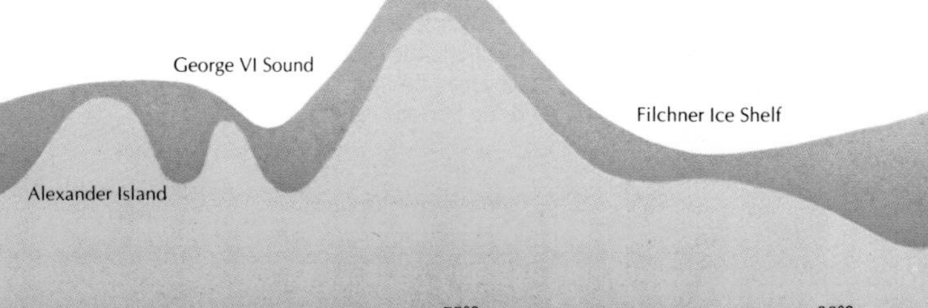

Clouds of powder snow billow from the tracks of a Russian tractor moving quickly across the polar plateau. Long-distance traverses by such vehicles provide much information about the ice surface and bedrock.

It is difficult to calculate whether the ice sheet is growing, shrinking or static, mainly because not enough measurements have yet been carried out. However, on present estimates, it appears that the continent is growing overall, but only very slowly. Detailed measurements in some areas show that the question of growth is very complex. In the Lambert Glacier basin, for example, almost twice as much ice is accumulating as is flowing out.

New technology, satellites and international co-operation have revolutionised the study of the Antarctic icecap. Using modern satellite systems it is now possible to measure the latitude, longitude and height of a point on the ice to within a metre in any direction. By remeasuring the same point after one or more years accurate estimates can be made of the rate at which the ice is moving. Satellites and aircraft are also used to determine other properties of the ice sheet. Complex mathematical models are gradually being built up to reconstruct the past history of Antarctica's ice, and to predict its future behaviour under a variety of possible circumstances.

Such programs are complex and costly and call for international co-operation to ensure the efficient use of resources and to prevent the duplication of research.

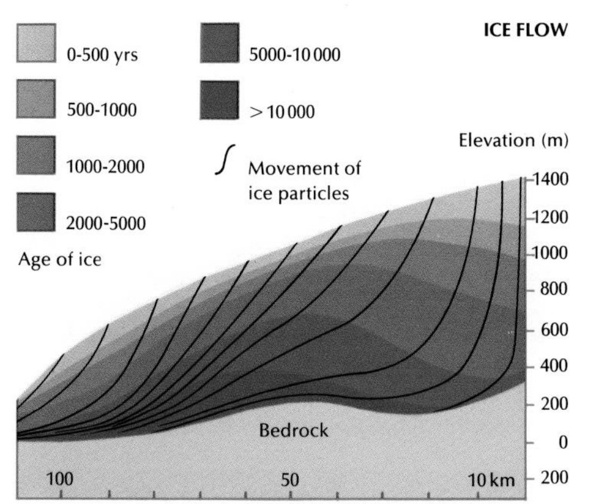

Gradual movement

Ice generally flows from the centre of the icecap out towards the edges, following the steepest surface slope. Flowline — lines following the motion of the ice — are drawn on the map (right). They show the flow converging into major streams, and spreading away from high points and ridges. The ice moves fastest at the surface and most slowly at the bedrock — deforming as though it were in many layers sliding over each other, like a deck of cards pushed sideways. Annual layers descend as snow accumulates.

A section through the Law Dome (left) showing the downward movement of annual snow layers.

Flowlines (right) show the direction in which ice descends from the interior of the icecap to the coast.

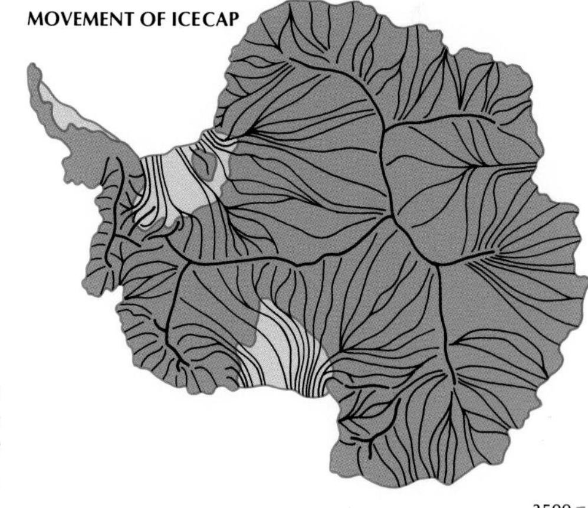

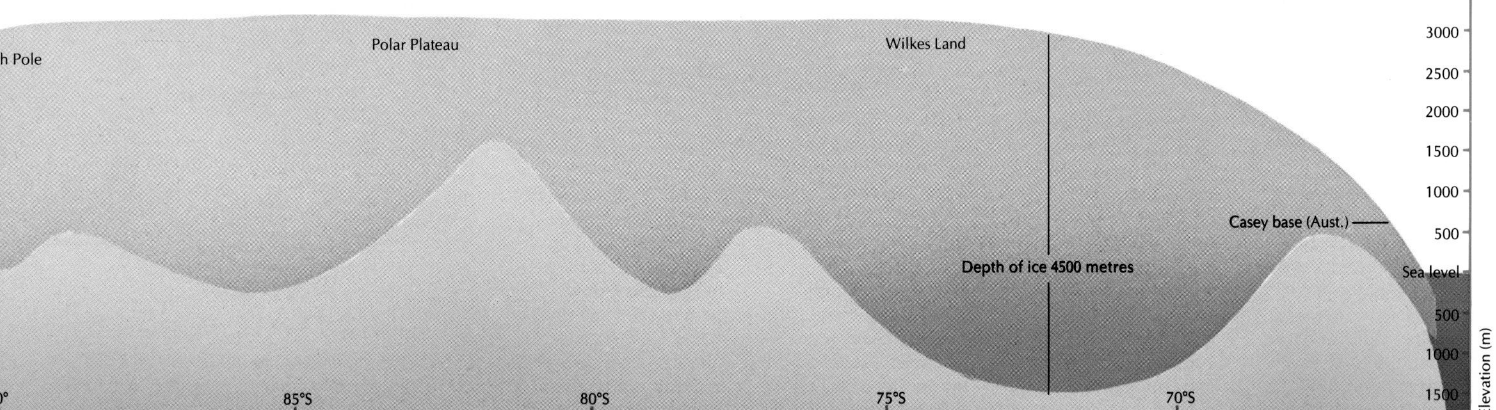

Rivers Of Ice

Frozen cataracts that drain the polar icecap

Where rivers channel water from the surfaces of more temperate continents, Antarctica is drained by vast systems of glaciers and ice streams. Studies of Antarctic ice movements may answer vital questions about the effects of long-term fluctuations in the earth's climate.

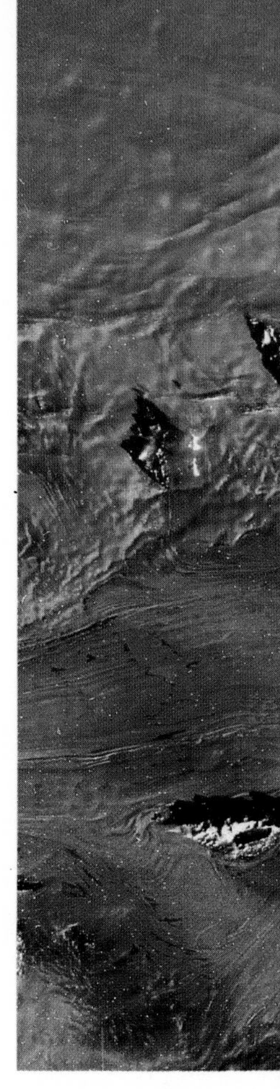

The giant Lambert Glacier flowing down to merge with the Amery Ice Shelf off the coast of east Antarctica. The area covered by this image is about 350 by 180 km (217 by 112 miles). This view was obtained by the United States' Landsat satellite on 16 March 1973, early in the Antarctic winter. More than 35 cubic kilometres (8.4 cu miles) of ice are discharged each year through this vast glacier system. More details about the Lambert Glacier are given below (right).

Most Antarctic glaciers occur around the edges of the ice sheet where they drain the interior of the continent. They often occupy depressions associated with major geological features, or have eroded a passage through some softer rock. The most spectacular glaciers pass through exposed mountain ranges, such as the Transantarctic Mountains, as valley glaciers. Even where the rock is hidden beneath the ice there are glaciers — deep streams moving much faster than the shallower ice alongside. Some of these streams are from 50 to 100 kilometres (30 to 60 miles) wide. There are also a number of small glaciers originating on the exposed mountains and islands around the coast.

Only a few Antarctic glaciers finish on the land, as they do in the dry valleys where the ice is melted and worn away by wind. Most glaciers flow through ice shelves or directly into the ocean. There they often form a floating extension — a glacier tongue — from which icebergs calve. Glaciers range in size enormously, from those a few kilometres long and a couple of hundred metres wide, to giants that can be hundreds of kilometres long. The Beardmore Glacier, which was the gateway to the high polar plateau for the early explorers, is 200 kilometres (124 miles) long, 23 kilometres (14 miles) wide and moves at about one metre (39 inches) per day. The fastest moving Antarctic glacier yet measured is the Shirase in eastern Queen Maud Land, which is moving at two kilometres (1.2 miles) a year.

The world's largest glacier is in Antarctica — the 40-kilometre (25-mile) wide Lambert which flows for over 400 kilometres (248 miles) through the Prince Charles Mountains, draining one million square kilometres (386 000 sq miles) of east Antarctica. At its lower reaches, the Lambert merges with the floating Amery Ice Shelf and flows for a further 300 kilometres (186 miles) to the seaward margin. It is moving at 230 metres (754 ft) per year at its entrance to the mountains, and nearly one kilometre (3270 feet) per year at the ice shelf front, where it is nearly 200 kilometres (124 miles) wide.

The speed at which glaciers and ice streams move depends on a number of factors. While the inland ice sheet moves by internal deformation, glaciers may move by sliding over their rocky beds. Friction between the ice and the glacier bed erodes the rock surface and generates heat which melts a little of the bottom ice, the meltwater providing lubrication which assists flow. Glaciers also flow faster and easier when their floors are below sea level. The pressure of water tends to buoy up the ice, reducing the load on the bed. Where the ice stream is floating, such as in the Amery Ice Shelf, the flow is restrained only at the sides of the embayment, or, when it is unconfined, by the natural resistance of ice to stretching.

The behaviour of Antarctic glaciers, and the size and shape of the ice sheet, is always changing in respose to global influences. During the last ice age the sea level was about 120 metres (394 ft) lower than it is at present. The ice shelves that now surround Antarctica were grounded, and glaciers could not move as fast.

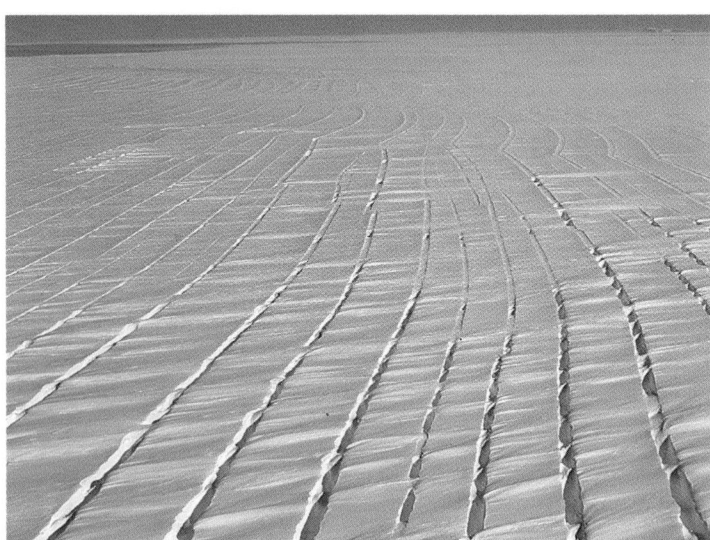

A pattern of crevasses caused by ice stretching in both directions as it flows over isolated humps in the bedrock hidden far beneath the surface.

Crevasses As glaciers move down their valleys they twist, stretch and deform. When the ice cannot keep up with the movement it cracks, and surface crevasses open up. Freshly formed crevasses have clean, straight sides and are usually from 30 to 40 metres (100 to 130 ft) deep, although in very active glaciers they can be deeper, and some tens of metres wide. Often snow will collect on each lip of a crevasse, building outwards until the opening is bridged. The crevasse may then become invisible — until a person or vehicle breaks through the snowbridge. In ice shelves the fractures can extend through the entire thickness to form rifts and chasms. Crevasses also form in the bottom of some ice shelves as they flex.

Moraines In Antarctica there are few visible moraines — rock trapped in the ice or left behind by glaciers. Rock debris from neighbouring mountains are quickly covered by snowfall and soon become incorporated into the ice sheet. They can be carried over very long distances, and on the rare occasions when they are exposed they can give clues to the types of bedrock concealed beneath the ice. Moraines are sometimes exposed in coastal ice cliffs, and often show the intense deformation and folding that the ice has undergone. Meteorites that fall on Antarctica are also carried by the ice in this way. Collections are sometimes found at places where movement of the ice is halted, perhaps by a mountain range. Occasionally a moraine from the sole of a glacier can be found in an overturned iceberg.

Rocks that fall onto the ice can be carried for hundreds of kilometres, usually in the heart of the ice sheet, and are sometimes exposed when the ice melts.

Debris exposed in a coastal ice cliff. Such material can reveal valuable information about the otherwise inaccessible bedrock of Antarctica.

This caused the ice sheet to grow outwards until it reached a new equilibrium. When the ice that covered much of the northern hemisphere melted, sea level rose and the Antarctic ice sheet retreated to its present size and shape.

Evidence of such fluctuations in the ice sheet can be found in parts of the Prince Charles Mountains where the tops of some peaks, 800 metres (2624 ft) above the present ice surface, show signs of having been covered by ice in the geologically recent past. In the Lambert Glacier basin the ice sheet is presently growing, suggesting that its size may fluctuate.

There is some concern that fluctuations, especially if global temperatures rise because of increased carbon dioxide in the atmosphere, may result in a collapse of the west Antarctic ice sheet. The base of the ice is below sea level, and if temperatures rise the ice shelves may break up, speeding up ice streams and causing an eventual decay of the ice sheet.

Such an event would cause a rise in sea level, although it is unlikely that this decay would take place in even 100 years. Once started, however, the process may be irreversible. A study of the west Antarctic ice sheet is now under way to find out if this is likely.

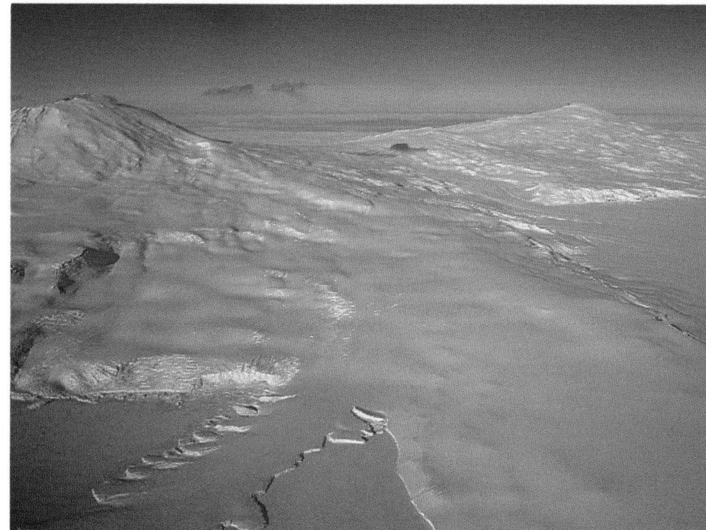

Most Antarctic glaciers discharge directly into the sea, where the ice breaks off into bergs. Sometimes ice tongues are formed, as (above) where the Erebus Glacier enters McMurdo Sound off the coast of Ross Island. Glaciers that finish on land, as they do in the dry valleys of southern Victoria Land (right), are rare in Antarctica.

Largest glacier The Landsat image above shows part of the world's largest glacier system — the Lambert in east Antarctica. The glacier flows from left to right and merges into the floating Amery Ice Shelf opposite Fisher Massif. The seaward edge of the ice shelf is 60 to 80 kilometres (37 to 50 miles) to the north (right) of this image, and the glacier can be followed 250 to 300 kilometres (155 to 186 miles) upstream through the Prince Charles Mountains to the south (left) of this scene. Other glaciers and ice streams merge with this system as it flows to the sea. The paths of these merging streams can be seen from the flow lines on the surface of the glacier, as, for example, at the point where the Charybdis Glacier flows into the ice shelf. Part of the Charybdis can also be seen to flow south into a depression

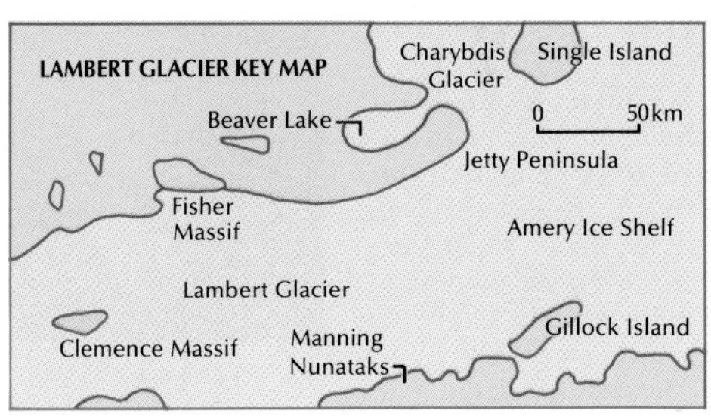

occupied by Beaver Lake, where it stagnates. Movement past objects such as Gillock Island disturb the flow causing crevassing in the wake of the island. Here, the crevasses form huge rifts in the ice shelf, some being several hundred metres wide and up to 40 kilometres (25 miles) long. These chasms are filled and bridged with snow, and are now lines of weakness along which sections of the ice shelf will in future crack off to form huge icebergs. Opposite Beaver Lake, where the ice shelf is 85 kilometres (53 miles) wide, the ice is 750 metres (2460 ft) thick and moving at 340 metres (1115 ft) per year. At the extreme right, where the surface of the ice shelf is partially covered by a layer of light cloud, the ice is 138 kilometres (86 miles) wide, 500 metres (1640 ft) thick and moving at about 750 metres (2460 ft) per year. The ice has its greatest thickness upstream, at the junction of the major tributary glaciers, where it is 2500 metres (8200 ft) deep. Altogether, some 35 cu kilometres (8.4 cu miles) of ice pass through the Lambert Glacier every year.

SEA ICE

Antarctica's treacherous frozen ocean

Icebergs, massive pieces of the Antarctic ice sheet, and sea ice, the frozen surface of the ocean, have a major impact on the circulation of the Southern Ocean, its interaction with the atmosphere, and thereby the climate and weather of the entire southern hemisphere.

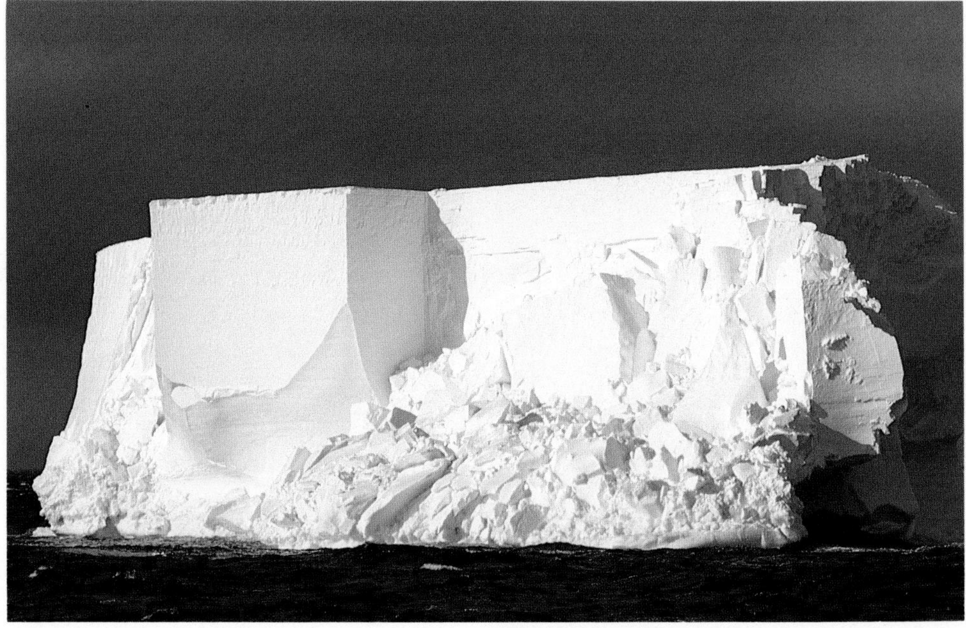

By the end of March each year, as temperatures start to fall after the brief summer season, the sea has begun to freeze around all of the Antarctic coast to form pack ice. The area covered by the pack ice increases until it reaches a maximum of about 19 million sq kilometres (7.3 million sq miles) in September or October, more than doubling the effective area of Antarctica. Thereafter, with warmer weather, the pack ice begins to decay and break up until it is dispersed by the wind and melts away. The pack is at its minimum in late February, although a small area of about 3 million sq kilometres (1.6 million sq miles) remains around the fringe of the continent.

This floating ice has a profound effect on the exchange of heat between the atmosphere and the ocean. Whereas open ocean reflects only about five per cent of incoming radiation, snow-covered pack ice reflects more than 80 per cent. Because the pack does not reach its maximum extent until September or October, when the effect of the sun's radiation is increasing, its presence delays normal warming and keeps the air over Antarctica cold.

The total area of pack ice, and its distribution around Antarctica, varies from year to year. On average it reaches as far north as 61°S, but in some areas, such as around South Georgia, it can be found at 52°S. The width of the ice belt ranges from 600 kilometres (370 miles) off east Antarctica to nearly 3000 kilometres (1860 miles) in the Weddell Sea. For most of the year this belt of ice prevents ships from reaching the coast of Antarctica.

Within the pack ice zone there is usually a mixture of open water and floating ice. Sometimes large areas of open water — known as polynyas — occur amongst the ice. The contrast between the very cold air and the warm ocean in polynyas, and around the fringe of the pack, has a strong influence on the development of Antarctica's weather.

The mixture of ice and open water also give the pack mobility, so that it is constantly mov-

How the sea freezes
As the ocean cools, and the surface begins to freeze, it takes on an oily appearance as frazil ice crystals start to form in the water. These float to the surface to create grease ice which is a soupy layer of ice spicules and plates. As the temperature continues to fall, the surface ice coagulates into a solid layer. Ocean swells and waves break this layer into irregular cakes, perhaps 500 mm (19.5 in) across, which collide with one another to form pancake ice. These pancakes may freeze together and break up several times before forming a solid cover. The ice thickens by water freezing to the base of it, by the addition of frazil ice, and by the accumulation of snow on its surface, where it acts as a thermal blanket. As the ice thickens, ocean swells break it into larger pieces.

The oily appearance of freezing ocean water.

The rounded forms of pancake ice.

Angular ice floes in a field of open pack ice.

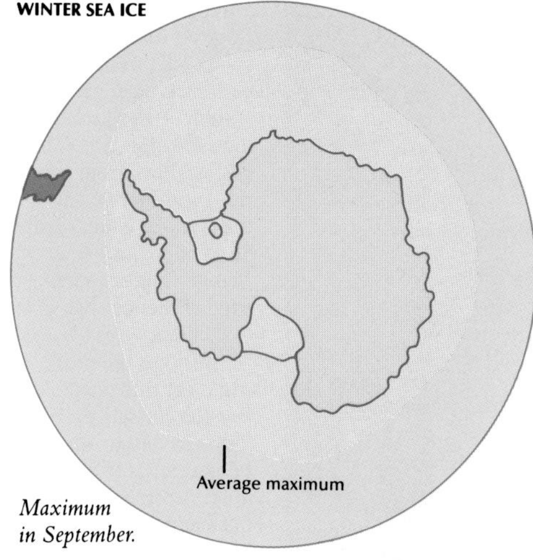

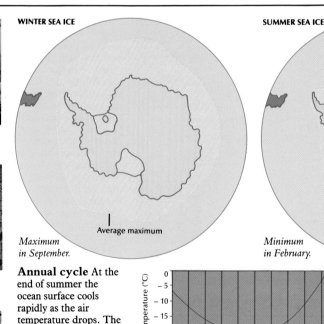

Maximum in September.

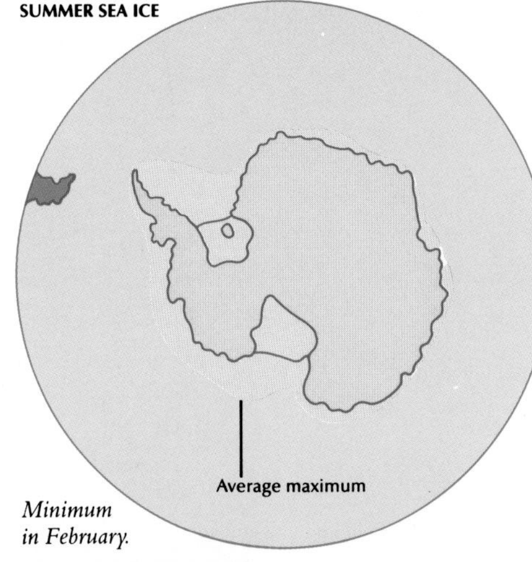

Minimum in February.

Annual cycle At the end of summer the ocean surface cools rapidly as the air temperature drops. The sea begins to freeze when the water reaches -1.8°C (28.8°F) and the ice grows quickly at first, reaching half its maximum thickness in a little over a month. Ice starts to form around the coast in late March and reaches its maximum extent in September, and maximum thickness near the coast in October. From November to January the ice cover weakens. Progressively it rots and is swept away by wind and waves. Final breakout near the coast is usually in January, and the ice reaches its minimum extent in late February each year.

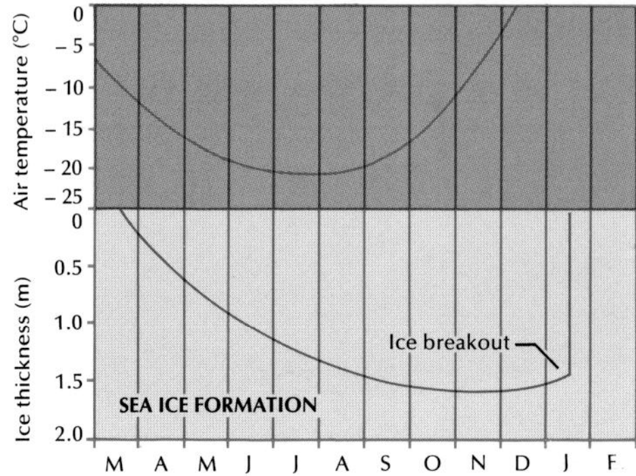

Icebergs occur in a multitude of shapes and sizes, ranging from those newly calved with sharp sides, to rounded, weathered forms. An average berg has a life of perhaps four years, during which time it will migrate to warmer seas. As they age, bergs split along lines of natural weakness and roll over as they become unstable. The most northerly sightings of icebergs in the South Atlantic and Indian Oceans have been at about 35°S, and in the South Pacific at 45°S. Icebergs are called bergy bits when they are between two and five metres (6.5 and 16 ft) across. Decayed fragments, smaller than two metres, are known as brash ice.

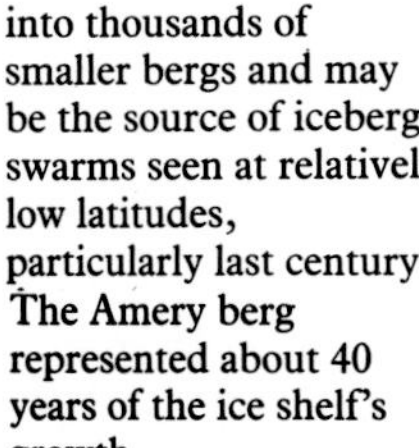

ing under the influence of ocean currents and winds. Offshore winds usually cause the ice to open up, while strong storm winds force it together, especially on a windward coast.

The mobility of the pack ice allows ships to penetrate it and has, from time to time, trapped and crushed vessels. The *Belgica* in 1898, the *Gauss* in 1901, the *Scotia* in 1903 and the *Deutschland* in 1912 were all trapped for various lengths of time. The *Antarctic* in 1901 and the *Endurance* in 1915 were both caught and lost after they were crushed in the ice. Modern vessels are usually much stronger and more powerful than those in the past, but they can still encounter problems. In 1972, a Russian ship, the *Ob*, was trapped for 100 days in pack ice off Victoria Land, and in 1981 the *Gotland II* was sunk. In some areas specialised icebreakers are used, the most powerful of which is the United States' ship *Polar Star*. Her engines can drive her at 3 knots (5.5 km/h; 3.4 mph) through ice two metres (6.6 ft) thick.

Although the pack ice is formed from sea water, it is not uniformly salty. As the ocean freezes in winter, ice is added to the bottom of the floating sea ice. Some brine remains in cells in the ice, but most is left in the ocean. If the ice survives for more than one year, much of the trapped brine drains away slowly until water obtained from this old ice is quite drinkable.

Perhaps the best known form of floating ice is icebergs, which are produced wherever the ice sheet meets the ocean — at grounded ice cliffs, glaciers or ice shelves. Large tabular bergs are calved from ice shelves which are usually 200 to 300 metres (650 to 1000 ft) thick. Bergs from this source have a freeboard of around 30 to 50 metres (100 to 160 ft), with most of their bulk below the water. As they age they lose their flat tops and become domed. Smaller, more broken and irregular bergs calve from glaciers and coastal cliffs. All bergs are swept westwards around the continent by circumpolar currents near the coast.

More than 1450 cu kilometres (348 cu miles) of icebergs are calved from Antarctica each year — a volume equivalent to about half the world's total water usage. A lot of thought has been given to ways of harvesting this vast source of freshwater but, although it may now be feasible to select and tow a suitable berg, many problems have yet to be solved. Towing times to southern hemisphere destinations would be about three to four months, by which time half of the berg would have melted. The main problem is that of devising some method of harvesting the remaining water from the berg. In many case the iceberg's huge draught would prevent it from being towed closer than about 30 kilometres (19 miles) to the coast.

Giant icebergs Occasionally a large section of the ice shelf breaks off to create a giant tabular iceberg, such as that formed in 1963 off the Amery Ice Shelf. This iceberg was carried around the coast by westerly currents until, in 1967, it collided with Trolltunga — a northerly extension of the Fimbul Ice Shelf at 0° longitude — to produce a second giant berg. Progress of the two giant bergs, which measured 110 by 75 kilometres (68 by 47 miles) and 104 by 53 kilometres (65 by 33 miles), was followed on weather satellite photographs as they passed through the Weddell Sea. Their movement was slowed occasionally when they were grounded for periods of up to a year, and the Amery berg was last sighted off the Antarctic Peninsula in 1970. The Trolltunga berg (map right) collided with the Larsen Ice Shelf in 1975, off the east coast of the peninsula, generating at least one more giant berg. It then entered the South Atlantic, heading east and to the south of South Georgia. Such giant bergs break up into thousands of smaller bergs and may be the source of iceberg swarms seen at relatively low latitudes, particularly last century. The Amery berg represented about 40 years of the ice shelf's growth.

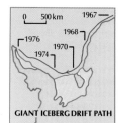

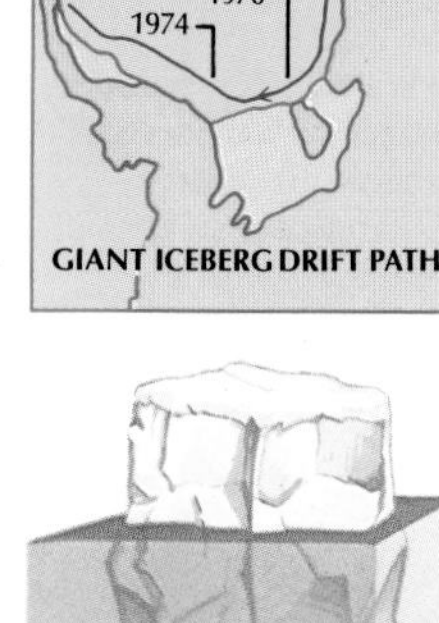

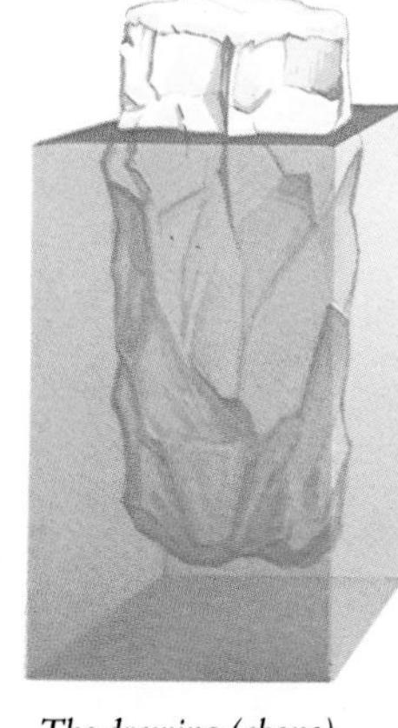

The drawing (above) shows approximately how much of the iceberg (left) would be beneath the water. Usually about four-fifths of an average berg are submerged.

Movements in the pack The pack ice moves gradually under the influence of ocean currents and winds, mainly travelling from east to west near the coast, in the opposite direction further north, and around great circular currents in the Ross and Weddell Seas. Wind can open the pack up and disperse it, waves and storm winds breaking up the floes. Conversely, wind can close the pack against a coast or other obstacle. Storms can put the pack under immense pressure, crushing and upending floes, rafting one on top of another and forming pressure ridges where the floes buckle. The resulting sea ice can be up to five or ten metres (16 to 32 ft) thick in places. The gradual movement of the pack past an obstacle, such as an island, will deform the ice.

Late afternoon sunlight highlights pressure waves in the sea ice as it is forced past the rocky shores of Ross Island by ocean currents and winds.

The junction between the ancient continental shield of east Antarctica and the more recent Beacon sediments can be seen clearly on this mountainside in the Ohio Range of the Transantarctic Mountains.

The rugged Sarnoff Mountains in Marie Byrd Land are made up of granite formed during a period of earth movements about 80 million years ago. The South American Andes were also being built at the same time.

ROCKS BENEATH THE ICE

Piecing together the history of a hidden continent

Despite the fact the the greater part of the rocky foundation of Antarctica is hidden beneath a thick ice sheet, enough can be seen along the Transantarctic Mountains, in the Antarctic Peninsula, and around the edges of the east Antarctic icecap, to be able to piece together a geological history of the continent, even though the details are far from complete.

Both geologically and physically there is a sharp contrast between east and west Antarctica. East Antarctica contains part of an ancient continental shield, overlain by younger rocks, whereas west Antarctica is continental material that has been joined to the east Antarctic shield late in its history.

The ancient continental core, or shield, of east Antarctica has a long and complex geological history going back at least 3000 million years. The rocks of the shield include granite and sedimentary layers that have been changed by high temperature. Facing west Antarctica, along one edge of the older shield and forming the foundations of the Transantarctic Mountains, is a belt of ancient folded sediments that were deposited in a trough beside the shield about 500-600 million years ago. A flat-lying sequence of unaltered sediments, known as the Beacon Supergroup, rests on these older rocks and was deposited during a stable period that lasted for 200 million years. The sediments are mainly sandy and are from 390 to 190 million years old. Fossils are rare and are mainly worm burrows, tracks and plants similar to those found in the other continents.

There are many examples of Antarctic rocks and fossils matching those found in other southern continents, suggesting that they were once joined together. Ancient crystalline rocks of the Antarctic shield, exposed along the east Antarctic coastline in the Enderby Land — Lützow-Holm Bay region, are remarkably similar to those along the east coast of the Indian peninsula and Sri Lanka. Fossils within the last sediments to be joined onto the east Antarctic shield, which are now exposed in the Transantarctic Mountains, are closely similar or identical to species found in Australia, New Zealand, China and Kazakhstan. But perhaps the most striking similarity is seen in sediments deposited about 280 million years ago when the world was experiencing a major ice age. Large ice sheets covered the land and sediments left by huge glaciers were deposited as the ice sheets retreated. These sediments, sometimes over 300 metres (1000 ft) thick, are found in Antarctica, Australia, India, South Africa and South America. If the continents had been in their present positions, the ice sheet covering them would have had to extend over more than half the globe — a situation

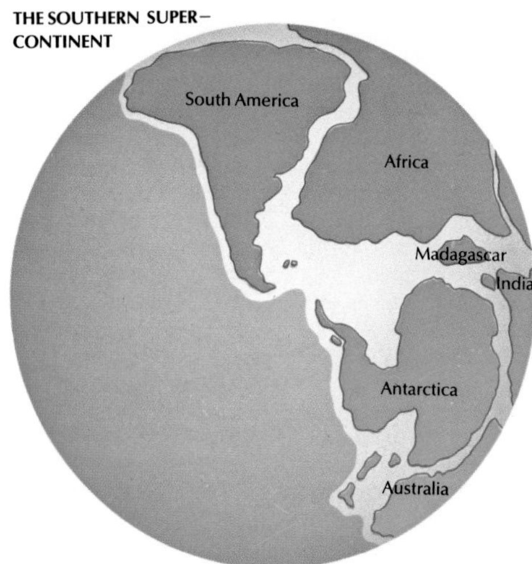

Drifting continents
Up until about 140 million years ago, east Antarctica formed the central block of a giant supercontinent called Gondwanaland. Africa, South America, peninsular India, Australia and New Zealand were all once joined to Antarctica, and have since drifted apart to their present positions. The reconstruction of Gondwanaland has been based on the best match between the edges of the different blocks, using the edge of the continental shelf, and reinforced by studies of the rocks on either side of the breakage line. The rough position of the fragments is well established, but there is discussion as to the fit of smaller blocks.

East versus west
If the ubiquitous ice was stripped from the surface of Antarctica, the land that was revealed below could no longer be considered a single unit. East Antarctica is an ancient land mass with a long geological history, dating back for at least 3000 million years. The rocks of west Antarctica are of far more recent origin. The present juxtaposition of the two halves is the result of recent continental drift. The Transantarctic Mountains may be the junction between the two parts of the continent, although the relationship between them is not clear.

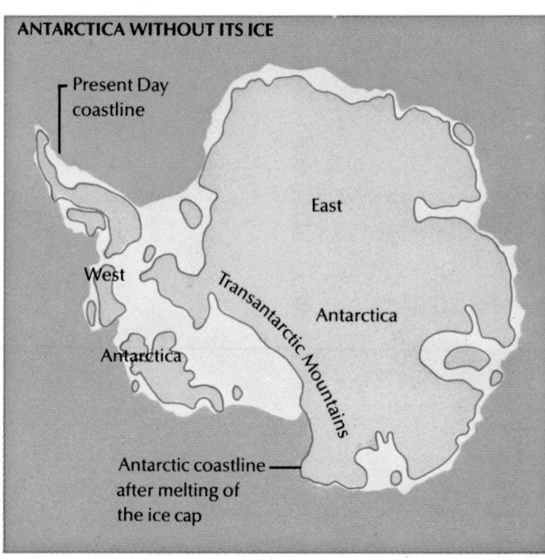

If the Antarctic icecap melted, the resulting rise in sea level would emphasise the basic physical differences between east and west Antarctica.

Mineral wealth
Many potentially valuable minerals are known to occur in Antarctica, such as gold, silver, beryl and graphite. However, no concentrations rich enough to be exploitable have yet been found. It seems more than likely that any rich deposits will be hidden beneath thousands of metres of ice. Coal is found in some parts of the Transantarctic Mountains, although it is of poor quality. Most interest centres around the possibility of oil discoveries.

An Antarctic coal seam. Although coal exists, there are as yet no plans to exploit it commercially.

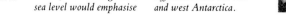

not supported by other evidence. However, an icecap covering the southern continents when assembled in a single mass is feasible, and consistent with the evidence. This super continent has been named Gondwanaland (see below).

After the glaciers retreated, the surface of Gondwanaland became covered by temperate plants, the most common of which was a deciduous conifer called *Glossopteris*. Conditions then were cold and humid.

Different plants appeared in the drier period that followed about 200 million years ago, and were again restricted to the southern hemisphere. The main plant then was a fern called *Dicroidium*, and identical species have been found in South America, South Africa, Australia and Antarctica. At about this time much of Gondwanaland was above sea level and inhabited by a variety of primitive reptiles and amphibians. Bones of these animals have been found in rocks about 200 million years old.

The stable period during which Beacon Supergroup sediments were laid down ended about 190 million years ago when there was a lot of volcanic activity, probably caused by the start of the break up of Gondwanaland. Erosion along the Transantarctic Mountains has revealed layers of once molten rock that formed deep below the active volcanoes which can be seen as dark coloured bands across the cliffs of Beacon sandstone.

The geological history of west Antarctica follows a completely different pattern to that of east Antarctica. West Antarctica appears to be made up of a number of distinct continental blocks covered by the present icecap. There is no ancient continental shield, although there are cores of older rocks, about 570 million years old, in the Antarctic Peninsula and Marie Byrd Land regions. The rocks of west Antarctica, and the Antarctic Peninsula, show similarities to those found in South America.

The history of the Antarctic Peninsula is of a succession of submarine troughs that stretched south from South America. Sediments began to be rapidly laid down in the troughs about 220 million years ago when 13 kilometres (8 miles) of material were deposited. These rocks were folded and worn away before the next layers of sediments were laid down about 180 million years ago in a second trough which developed next to the earlier one. This process continued until about 80 million years ago by which time six kilometres (3.5 miles) of sediments, rich in fossils, had been deposited.

Beginning about 80 million years ago there were a series of earth movements associated with extensive volcanic activity, and little new sediment was laid down. However, the small areas of sediment formed are rich in fossils and outcrops on Seymour Island contain fossil penguins far larger than those living today. Rocks produced during the period of volcanic activity are found in Marie Byrd Land and suggest that eruptions occurred below a thick icecap between 18 and 6 million years ago. Volcanoes erupting near the head of the Ross Ice Shelf 20-15 million years ago may be linked with the uplift of the Transantarctic Mountains.

In the area around McMurdo Sound a number of volcanic cones were formed about three million years ago that are now regarded as dormant. Mount Erebus is the only Antarctic volcano still active today near the mainland.

The relationship of east to west Antarctica is still not fully understood. The Transantarctic Mountains have developed along a major rift that runs from the Ross Sea to the Weddell Sea, and it is this line that separates east and west Antarctica. The rocks of the Ellsworth Mountains, which lie within west Antarctica, have features similar to some found in east Antarctica, although their structural grain lies at right angles to that of the Transantarctic Mountains. It is probable that the Ellsworth Mountains are a fragment of the earth's crust torn from east Antarctica and rotated along the dividing fracture line.

Warm past Antarctica has not always been covered by a sheet of ice. There is ample fossil evidence in Antarctic rocks of plants and animals living on the continent during periods when the climate was much warmer due to the absence of a polar icecap, and times when Antarctica was then positioned on a temperate part of the earth's surface. Similarities between fossil species found in Antarctica, and those on other continents, support the theory of continental drift. This is particularly so with animals like the reptile *Lystrosaurus* which is also found in Africa, the Indian peninsula, China and Southeast Asia. The fact that this, and related animals, lived on land and were incapable of crossing wide oceans makes their distribution difficult to explain by any means other than continental drift.

The Ohio Range is the only place in the Transantarctic Mountains where fossil-rich rocks from 390 million years ago are found. Sediments making up the cliffs on the right were laid down in seas teeming with life.

A reconstruction of the land reptile Lystrosaurus *which lived in Antarctica about 200 million years ago. Fossil bones have been found in sandstones that were deposited by ancient rivers.*

Fossilised remains of ancient ferns. The species Dicroidium *(left) was common in Antarctica 200 million years ago.*

Although there are no remains of fossil skeletons in the oldest Beacon rocks, there are numerous trace fossils such as these burrows preserved in sandstone, which indicate that life was abundant.

THE DRY VALLEYS

Desert landscapes on a continent of ice

On the eastern side of McMurdo Sound, opposite Ross Island, lies one of Antarctica's most intriguing areas — the dry valleys. Amid all the snow and ice, this strange desert landscape has remained virtually unaltered for millions of years — save for the action of the ceaseless winds.

A distant view of the dry valleys from Mount England, some 40 to 48 km (25 to 30 miles) away. This strange area was discovered by accident during an exploratory trip led by Robert Scott in December 1903.

Spanning Antarctica for more than 2200 kilometres (1370 miles) is one of the world's great mountain chains — the Transantarctic Mountains. Although many of its peaks exceed 4000 metres (13 000 ft), much of the chain is all but buried in ice, for it acts as a dam to the world's largest body of fresh water, the east Antarctic ice sheet. Great rivers of ice have carved deep glacial valleys through this barrier as they force their way to the sea. However, during the past 30 million years, uplift of the mountain chain has, in some places, exceeded the rate at which the glaciers cut their way down. Therefore the mountains at the head of a few of these valleys are now high enough to prevent the ice sheet from flowing through their former outlets.

However, these valleys still provide a passage for the cold dry air which accumulates on the great east Antarctic ice sheet. The air is warmed as it is compressed and descends up to 3000 metres (9800 ft) from the surface of the ice sheet to the valley floors as strong and extremely dry winds. These often exceed 100 km/h (62 mph) and because they have a relative humidity of less than 10 per cent, evaporate any snow brought into the valleys by the moist coastal easterly winds. Thus, deprived of through-flowing glacial ice and local snow, the valleys are the driest places on earth.

The discovery of the dry valleys extended over a period of 60 years, beginning with an accident on Robert Scott's first Antarctic expedition in 1901-04. Returning from a trip to the east Antarctic ice sheet, a party of three led by Scott were descending a glacier in heavy cloud, their food and fuel supplies exhausted. When they finally penetrated the cloud base they found that they were on the wrong glacier. Hoping that this glacier might also lead to McMurdo Sound and safety, Scott persisted on his route, eventually finding that it finished at a lake, beyond which there was a dry valley. Had they been equipped for backpacking, one day's walking would have enabled them to reach the coast. However, since all of his equipment was designed for sledging, they had no option but to retrace their steps.

Further exploration took place in 1909 when Ernest Shackleton sent Priestley, Armitage and Brocklehurst to examine the eastern end of the valley. However, the two ends were not linked until 1911 when Scott sent Griffith Taylor, the geomorphologist of the *Terra Nova* Expedition, to sledge up the Ferrar and down the Taylor Glacier. Taylor then made himself a pack, tramped 8 kilometres (5 miles) across Lake Bonney (named after one of Scott's dogs) and ascended to where a narrow pass, the Defile, enabled him to round the Suess Glacier. Here Taylor camped at the outlet of Lake Chad. On climbing a nearby hill, Taylor could see over the Canada and Commonwealth Glaciers to McMurdo Sound and his base at Cape Evans. The valley now bears Taylor's name.

The barren desert landscape of Garwood Valley, close to Scott base. The valleys are the driest places on earth — no rain has fallen there for at least two million years. The polygonal patterns on the dark hills are caused by constant freezing and thawing of the ground.

Although other smaller ice-free valleys were observed by sledging parties on the Koettlitz Glacier, further exploration had to await the passage of two world wars. Then aerial photographic reconnaissance during Operation

Strange lakes For a few short weeks in summer, glacial meltwater flows in some valleys. These ephemeral streams, the largest of which is the 48-kilometre (30-mile) long Onyx River, end in lakes. Although water flowing into the lakes is lost by evaporation, the small quantity of dissolved salts it brings into the valleys, and that released from the rocks during weathering, gradually build up. During the past 10 000 years enough salt has accumulated to make several of the lakes saltier than sea water. The depth of the lakes fluctuates as evaporation and inflow vary from year to year. Each time the lake evaporates, all of the dissolved salts are forced to the bottom of the basin where they form a dense brine, or crystallise into minerals. When wetter conditions return, fresh water flows in on top of the brine. The difference in the density of the two waters is too great to allow them to mix, except by the very slow process of diffusion. These layers of different density give the lakes unusual stability and enable them to act as giant natural solar heaters. In the case of Lake Vanda, solar heating has raised the temperature of the saltiest water at the bottom of the lake to 25°C (77°F), whereas at the top of the lake there is a permanent 4 metre (13-ft) thick floating cover of ice. Because the floating ice is constantly freezing at the bottom and evaporating from the top, all of the ice crystals are aligned vertically and act as light pipes which transmit sunlight down into the very clear waters beneath. The increasing density of the water towards the bottom of the lake prevents hot water from rising to the surface where the heat could escape. Therefore, water in parts of the lakes can reach a temperature of 45°C (113°F). The different densities of water in the lakes has a marked effect on their biology and chemistry. Large quantities of algae grow in the lakes, but in very thin layers, at depths where they receive optimum quantities of sunlight and nutrients for growth.

Garwood Glacier and a summer meltwater stream.

Four metres (13 ft) of strangely fractured ice cover the surface of Lake Vanda. The lake is 70 metres (230 ft) deep.

New Zealand's Vanda base in the Wright Valley.

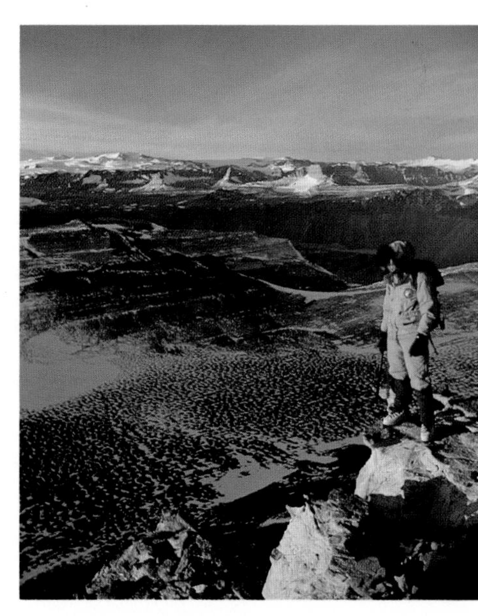

Midnight sun catches the distant peaks of the Olympus Range. Below, partly hidden in deep shadow, is the Wright Valley. Beneath the climber, who is on the summit of Peak Brunhilde in the Asgard Range, snow outlines the polygonal patterning on the valley floor, seen from another angle in the Garwood Valley (far left).

Highjump in 1946-47 revealed the presence of even larger ice-free valleys to the north, giving a total area in excess of 3000 sq km (1160 sq miles). Exploration of this area was started a decade later in 1957-58 by P.N. Webb and B.C. McKelvey, two geology students from Victoria University in Wellington. Examination of the valleys has now become an international enterprise, and in 1968 New Zealand established a base at Lake Vanda.

Cutting through the Transantarctic Mountains, the dry valleys provide a complete cross section of the rocks of central and southern Victoria Land. The bottom-most layer is 500-1500 million years old and on it was deposited a remarkable series of rocks — the Beacon Supergroup. These consist of spectacular yellow sandstones containing thick coal measures, and plant and animal fossils including freshwater fish, amphibians and reptiles. One fossil, *Lystrosaurus,* is particularly important since it was an animal not capable of swimming long distances. It has been found in rocks of similar age in Africa and India and provides evidence for the existence of the great super-continent Gondwanaland which once linked Antarctica, Africa, South America, India and Australia, with New Zealand forming part of the submerged continental shelf.

It is not known when glaciation started to gouge valleys through the Transantarctic Mountains. However, by 20 million years ago the valleys had been cut to more or less their present form. As the mountain chain was then lower, the valleys formed deep fjords so that their floors were covered by marine sediments. With the uplift they were raised above sea level and the glacial activity diminished.

Within the dry valleys are some of the most remarkable places on earth — deserts where in the past two million years at least, no rain has ever fallen. Temperatures range between −80° and +15°C (−112° and 59°F), and running water rarely occurs. As a result, rocks wear away extremely slowly and land surfaces are preserved for millions of years.

During the 25 years since the International Geophysical Year made Antarctica accessible, more than 1000 scientists have visited and worked in the dry valleys studying their geology, meteorology, biology and a host of other disciplines. The most ambitious expedition was the massive US-Japanese-New Zealand Dry Valley Drilling Project which drilled cores from depths of up to 300 metres (1000 ft) to study the geology and geophysics of the valleys. The most remarkable was sent by the United States' National Aeronautics and Space Administration to try to understand what a rainless desert on Mars might be like.

Natural sculpture Many of the valley floors are covered with rocks shaped and polished by windblown sand and snow. These ventifacts, as they are called, are often reduced to three- or four-sided pyramids, with faces sometimes curved and twisted. Coarser-grained rocks are eroded in a different way, by a process called cavernous weathering. Regardless of hardness they disintegrate, crystal by crystal.

Fine-grained rocks eroded for thousands of years by wind borne sand and snow — ventifacts — are carved into fascinating and intricate shapes.

Cavernous weathering may be the result of water expanding and contracting as it freezes and thaws in pores between individual crystals in the rock.

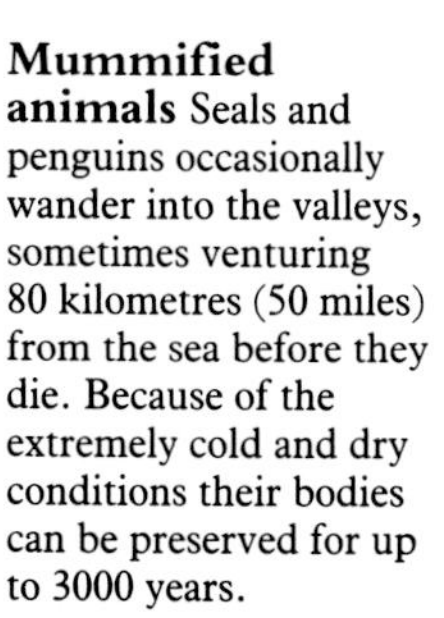

Mummified animals Seals and penguins occasionally wander into the valleys, sometimes venturing 80 kilometres (50 miles) from the sea before they die. Because of the extremely cold and dry conditions their bodies can be preserved for up to 3000 years.

A mummified seal head. No one is sure why these animals stray into the inhospitable dry valleys.

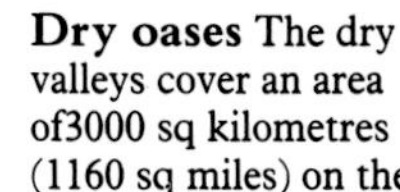

Dry oases The dry valleys cover an area of3000 sq kilometres (1160 sq miles) on the eastern side of McMurdo sound. Similar oases exist in the Bunger Hills, Wilkes Land; in the Vestfold Hills, Princess Elizabeth Land, and also on the peninsula.

SOUTHERN LIGHTS

Tracing the origin of the aurora australis

Perhaps the most spectacular natural phenomena to be seen in the polar regions are the aurorae — the aurora australis in the south and the aurora borealis in the north. Although much written about by early explorers, a complete explanation for the spectacular patterns of light that are seen in the night skies over the poles had to wait until modern times.

The diaries and journals of all polar explorers provide graphic accounts of the auroral lights that are to be seen over many parts of Antarctica.

In June 1911 Robert Scott described a particularly vivid display: 'The eastern sky was massed with swaying auroral light...fold on fold the arches and curtains of vibrating luminosity rose and spread across the sky, to slowly fade and yet again spring to glowing life.

'The brighter light seemed to flow, now to mass itself in wreathing folds in one quarter, from which lustrous streamers shot upward, and anon to run in waves through the system of some dimmer figure . . .

'It is impossible to witness such a beautiful phenomenon without a sense of awe, and yet this sentiment is not inspired by its brilliancy but rather by its delicacy in light and colour, its transparency, and above all by its tremulous evanescence of form.'

Another brilliant display was described by Edward Wilson during the night-time journey to Cape Crozier in July 1911. 'We had a magnificent display of auroral curtains between 7.30 p.m. and 8 p.m., during which four-fifths of the eastern half of the sky was covered by waving curtains right up to the zenith, where they were all swinging round from left to right in foreshortened, swaying curtains forming a rapidly moving whirl, constantly altering its formation. Some of the lower curtains were very brilliant and showed bands of orange and green and again orange fading into lemon yellow upwards. Bowers noted it as follows: "Remarkably brilliant aurora working from the N.E. to the zenith and spreading over two-thirds of the sky. Curtain form in interwoven arcs, curtains being propelled along as if by wind; the whole finally forming a vast mushroom overhead and moving towards the S.E. Colours lemon yellow, green and orange."

'It was such a striking display that we all three halted and lay on our backs for a long time watching its evolutions.'

The cause of the aurora was something of a mystery in Scott's time, although there were some theories about its origins. In 1901 Scott noted that, 'the luminosity of the aurora must be an electrical effect closely connected with the magnetism of the earth, it may be of some interest that in our observation it always appears in the south-east or away from the magnetic pole'. A complete explanation, however, had to wait for a better understanding of the structure of the earth's upper atmosphere and of events that occur beyond the earth, on the surface of the sun. This understanding has only come in recent years.

It is now clear that the aurora is initiated by the sun. Because of its very high temperature, the atmosphere of the sun, the solar corona, is forever expanding outwards at a velocity of about 400 km/sec (248 miles/sec), far beyond the orbit of the earth. This solar wind is very hot and is made up mainly of charged subatomic particles — mostly hydrogen atoms that have each lost their single electron. As it travels into space the solar wind carries with it a sample of the sun's weak magnetic field.

The earth too has a magnetic field and the electrical properties of the solar wind prevent it from crossing this field. The blast of the solar wind distorts the earth's field and creates a cavity surrounding the earth and its atmosphere, with a comet-like tail extending for perhaps a million kilometres (620 000 miles) out on the night side of the earth.

The outer fringe of the earth's atmosphere,

Atmospheric layers

The earth's atmosphere changes with increasing height, and is divided into layers according to the properties of each zone. Lowest is the troposphere which extends from the surface of the earth to a height of about 12 kilometres (7.5 miles). This layer contains about 75 per cent of the total mass of the atmosphere. Above that are successively: the stratosphere reaching to 46 kilometres (28.5 miles); the mesosphere reaching to 90 kilometres (56 miles); and the thermosphere reaching to about 700 kilometres (430 miles). Beyond is the magnetosphere which extends to a height of several thousand kilometres. Radiation from the sun is absorbed by the atmosphere at various levels, with the longest wavelengths penetrating to the greatest depth. Long wavelengths, absorbed at the surface of the earth, power the atmospheric 'machine'. High in the atmosphere short-wave radiation breaks up molecules and ionises atoms. The temperature of the atmosphere fluctuates between 200° and 300°K (−73°C; −100°F and 27°C; 80°F) beneath a height of 90 kilometres (56 miles), but above that height, in the thermosphere, it rises steadily. At times when the sun is quiet it can reach 700°K (427°C; 800°F), but during times of high solar activity, when there are many sunspots to be seen, it can rise as high as 2000°K (1727°C; 3140°F).

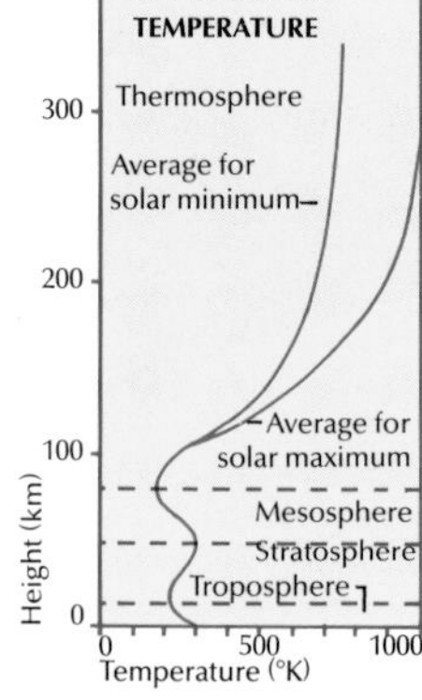

The temperature of the atmosphere rises rapidly from a height of about 90 km (56 miles).

The earth's magnetosphere (below), forced out of shape by the impact of the powerful solar wind.

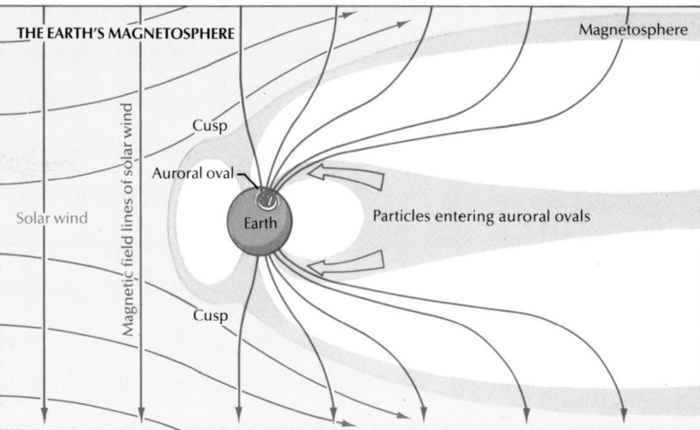

Auroral ovals

The auroral ovals are more or less continuous zones centred about the magnetic axis of the earth in each hemisphere. The size and width of the auroral ovals expands and contracts according to the level of solar activity, and the direction of the solar wind's magnetic field. The ovals are at their largest during times of greatest solar activity, and when the wind's magnetic field is pointing southwards.

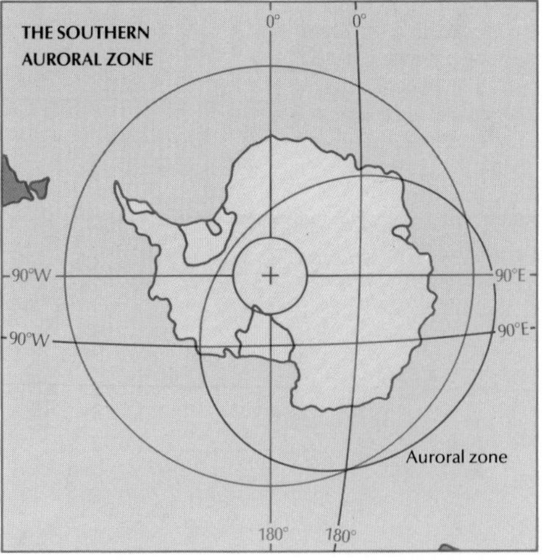

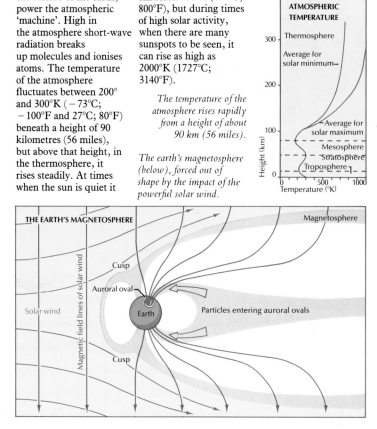

The southern auroral zone. Aurorae occur almost every night beneath the auroral zone — a path traced beneath the average midnight position of the auroral oval as the earth rotates on its axis.

A spectacular display of rayed bands and drapery over Mawson base. Aurorae are very difficult to photograph because they are very faint and moving rapidly. It is impossible to capture the full beauty and colour of the phenomenon on film.

known as the magnetosphere, is also made up mainly of subatomic particles and is ceaselessly changing in response to fluctuations in the solar wind. These changes are passed on to the lower, less conducting, layers of the atmosphere below.

The interactions between the solar wind and the earth's magnetic field vary in intensity according to the direction of the field carried by the solar wind. If the field is northwards, opposite in direction to the earth's, then the interaction is weak. If, however, the wind's field turns southwards (as shown below), then the interaction is very strong. The particles in the solar wind cannot cross the earth's magnetic field lines, but they can follow them and enter the magnetosphere at cusps centred near the noon meridian in each hemisphere.

These particles give rise to many complex reactions in the magnetosphere, some of which are still only poorly understood. Some particles travel down magnetic field lines into the lower thermosphere, and from there filter into the auroral ovals (see below). There they give rise to vast systems of electric currents, and also excite the polar aurorae.

The frequency and intensity of the aurorae is closely linked to the orientation of the magnetic field in the solar wind. If the wind's field has been reasonably strong and directed northwards for some time, then the aurorae almost vanish. If, however, the field turns southwards, or weakens, then greater numbers of particles are able to enter the earth's magnetosphere and a series of auroral substorms may be triggered off.

The colours of the aurorae are dictated by the atoms and the molecules that make up the thermosphere — violet for nitrogen, red and green for atomic oxygen, for example. The intensity of the aurorae is determined by the energies of the subatomic particles which excite those atoms. The colour and intensity of aurorae can thus reveal information to researchers about conditions in the upper atmosphere and the solar wind. A high intensity red colour, for example, is caused by large numbers of low energy particles which cannot penetrate below about 200 kilometres (124 miles). A green emission indicates more-energetic particles which excite oxygen atoms at a height of about 100 to 110 kilometres (62 to 68 miles), a little above the typical lower border of the aurorae.

Measurements of the spectra of aurorae can also be used to provide information about the composition, temperature and wind velocities of the thermosphere. Systems are now being developed to map temperature and wind patterns in the thermosphere over the whole sky. It is hoped that these studies will lead to a better understanding of the effects of heat generated by the vast electrical currents that are associated with aurorae, and which have a marked effect on the earth's magnetic field in the polar regions.

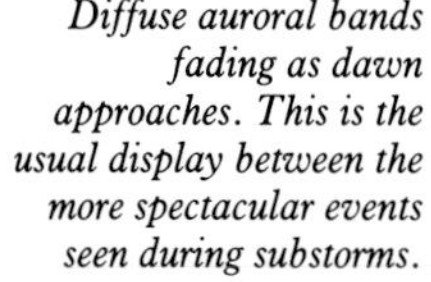

Diffuse auroral bands fading as dawn approaches. This is the usual display between the more spectacular events seen during substorms.

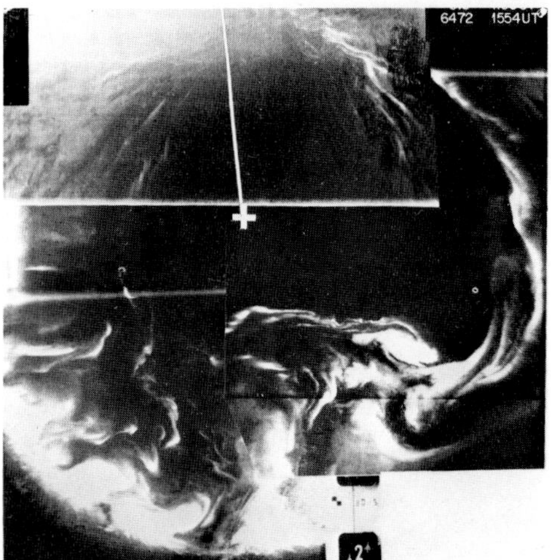

A satellite view (above) of the southern auroral oval at the peak of development of a substorm in the winter of 1975. The white cross marks the magnetic axis of the earth.

The disc of the earth and the northern auroral oval (left), during a quiet period, as seen from a satellite at a height of 9500 km (5900 miles).

Spectacular displays

Seen from the ground, the aurora takes on a great variety of appearances from quiet, barely visible arcs low in the sky to spectacular rayed, moving draperies of red, violet and green which fill the sky and recede and fade, leaving diffuse patches as dawn approaches. The details of a display depend on where the observer is — whether on the equator side of the auroral oval, under the oval, or towards the pole — and on local time. The most spectacular displays are caused by auroral substorms which occur when large numbers of subatomic particles from the solar wind enter the earth's magnetosphere and find their way into the auroral ovals. The average midnight positions of the auroral ovals define the auroral zones, along which aurorae occur overhead almost every night.

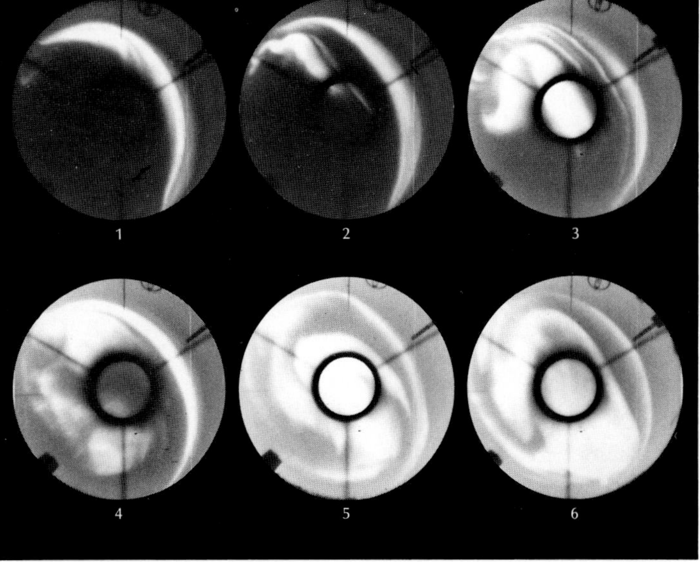

A series of photographs taken at one-minute intervals with an all-sky camera, showing the development of an auroral substorm above the Australian Mawson base on the coast of Mac.Robertson Land. The all-sky camera photographs the entire sky from horizon to horizon in all directions — the horizon appears around the perimeter of the photograph. At its greatest development (6), the auroral pattern fills about 80 per cent of the sky. Typical storms take between 10 and 30 minutes to develop, and the display disintegrates slowly into patches over a period of about an hour or so as the stable pre-storm pattern of quiet arcs is re-established. Such displays take place in the thermosphere at a height of about 150 km (93 miles) above the surface of the earth, and may on occasions exceed the full moon in brilliance.

Surviving The Cold

Strategies that preserve life in Antarctica

The adaptations that Antarctic plants and animals have had to make to survive the extreme cold are generally not unique. Their techniques for dealing with the difficult environment they live in are similar to those adopted by creatures in other stressful areas of the world.

Plants and animals living in Antarctica have two basic strategies for surviving the extreme low temperatures. Warm-blooded animals strive to maintain their core temperature by insulation and by changes to their behaviour and metabolism. Plants and cold-blooded animals are adapted to avoid or minimise the damaging effects of freezing. All favour sites where the local climate is less harsh than in the surrounding area.

The most damaging effect of low temperature is the formation of ice within the cells and tissues of both plants and animals. Ice disrupts living tissue in a number of ways. The outer membrane of the cells can be ruptured, in the same way that a frozen water pipe will burst, and at a sub-cellular level, the delicate machinery of the cell is irreversibly damaged.

Many organisms can be exposed to low temperatures provided ice crystals do not form inside them. There are several ways of preventing this from happening. Many species lose water as they become colder, thereby increasing the concentration of sugars, salts and other constituents of their cells and tissues. The extreme cold-resistance of Antarctic plants such as lichens and mosses, and the eggs and larval stages of some insects, is almost certainly due to their ability to dehydrate, and to recover rapidly when the temperature rises.

Some species, such as ice fish, produce substances in their bodies that prevent the formation of ice. These anti-freezes become linked to the ice crystals as they start to form and stop further water molecules from becoming attached. The concentration of anti-freeze in these fish has become fixed by evolution and does not vary if the fish are transferred to warmer water. Two fish have been found which lack any anti-freeze. One survives in a rare layer of warm water, the other by remaining super-cooled in very deep water.

Antarctic ice fish also have a number of other interesting adaptations for cold conditions. Their enzyme systems are highly efficient and allow them to remain active at low temperatures — their activity in water at 0°C (32°F) is close to that of a temperate water fish at 20°C (68°F). They also lack red blood cells for carrying oxygen around their bodies. These are not needed because oxygen is highly soluble in cold seawater. This lack of red blood cells gives the fish's gills and internal organs a creamy white colour. One result of not having red blood cells is that their blood is much thinner than it would be otherwise, and this means that the fish's metabolism can be much lower, again conserving vital energy.

All warm-blooded animals living on or around Antarctica — penguins, other sea birds, seals and whales — rely on thick layers of blubber to insulate them from their cold surroundings. The layer of blubber beneath the skin of a Weddell seal can be up to 100 mm (4 in) thick. This excellent insulation can present problems on summer days when the temperature rises above 0°C (32°F).

Only one warm-blooded animal remains on the Antarctic continent during the bitter winter — the emperor penguin, which is too large to cram its breeding cycle into the brief polar

A bedraggled Adélie penguin. When young, the birds are very vulnerable to a sudden drop in temperature, or to unseasonable snow fall.

A summer snowstorm transforms an Adélie penguin rookery. Groups of young chicks huddle together in scrums for warmth and protection.

Finding a niche Despite the low temperatures that occur on the Antarctic continent and in the seas surrounding it, living things, both plants and animals, occur in considerable numbers. Antarctica can be divided into four main ecological areas — the sea, coastal lakes, ice-free land and the icecap. The sea freezes at about −2°C (28°F) and never rises above 0°C (32°F) in coastal areas. It is, however, a rich environment and many types of microscopic floating plants (phytoplankton) live there. These plants are the base of a food chain that ascends through krill, fish, squid, penguins, other sea birds, seals and whales. On land the conditions are particularly difficult for life. Not only does the air temperature rarely rise above freezing, but the daily summer temperature fluctuates between about −20°C and +20°C (−4°F and 68°F) in the poorly developed Antarctic soils. Because temperatures are low, humidity is low as well, and there is little liquid water available. Despite the harsh conditions, plants such as algae, lichens and mosses manage to grow in sheltered areas. Among these simple plants, live tiny animals such as nematodes, tardigrades and mites. Some organisms even manage to live in the coastal lakes around Antarctica. Not only does the temperature in the lakes drop very low, down to −20°C (−4°F), but the water is also extremely salty. The only living organisms to inhabit the Antarctic icecap are some algae, fungi and bacteria that live in the water film that sometimes develops between ice and snow crystals in summer.

Hardy plants Simple plants such as lichens and mosses occur in ice-free areas. To survive they hug the ground where the wind speed is lower. They have also adapted in a number of ways to the Antarctic. Very often they are dark coloured which helps them to trap warmth; also outer layers are thick and tough to reduce water loss and to resist wind. Some live inside tiny pores and cracks in rocks.

A small rock split open to reveal green algae growing in a crack. There is sufficient light, warmth, moisture and shelter to sustain life.

Lichens are one of the hardiest of plants. Some species can remain active at temperatures as low as −20°C (−4°F).

Simple organisms The coastal ice-free oases of Antarctica, such as the dry valleys, contain lakes, some of which are up to 10 times saltier than sea water. The freezing point of salt water is lower than fresh water and as a consequence some of these lakes freeze at less than −20°C (−4°F). Some microscopic organisms have adapted to these conditions and remain active at temperatures as low as −14°C (7°F). In order to do this they contain high concentrations of molecules known as polyols, sugar alcohols and other organic molecules which are able to stop ice forming.

The Antarctic alga Pyramimonas gelidicola *is 0.015 mm (0.0006 in) long. It can remain active at −14°C (6.8°F).*

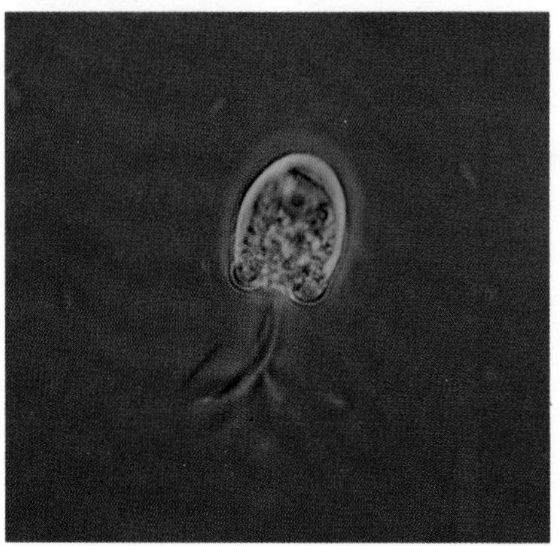

summer. These birds have developed a number of interesting adaptations which permit them to survive the cold.

The females each lay a single egg in June and then leave the colony to spend the winter at sea. The males take the eggs and place them on their feet where they are covered and kept warm by a flap of abdominal skin. They now spend nine weeks without food, incubating the eggs through the coldest part of the winter.

During this incubation the males lose about half their original body weight. With the temperature dropping to between −40°C and −60°C (−40°F and −76°F), they must rely on each other to conserve heat and energy. Huddled together, their backs to the wind, they stand in groups of as many as 6000 individuals. This technique of huddling reduces the surface area exposed to the biting cold and can reduce heat loss by one sixth. Experiments have shown that an isolated bird must maintain a body temperature of 37.9°C (100.2°F) to survive, while a bird in a large group only needs a body temperature of 35.7°C (96.3°F). The eggs hatch at about the same time that the females return, so she may take over the egg or small chick.

A juvenile ice fish, about 600 mm (23.6 in) long. These creatures need no red blood cells and are therefore almost completely colourless.

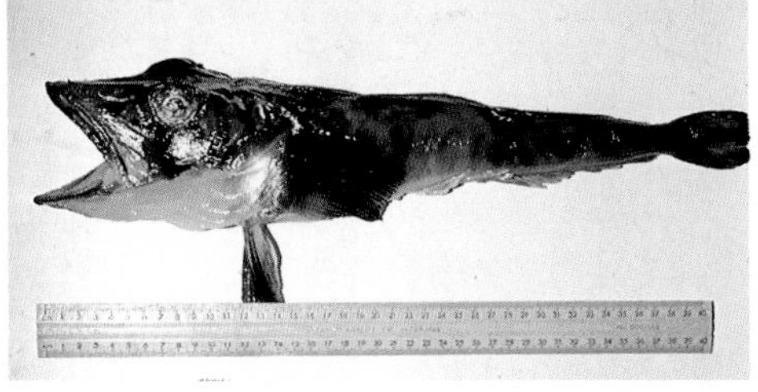

When fully grown, ice fish acquire external colouring, although gills and internal organs remain white.

Cold-blooded creatures Marine organisms such as crabs, snails and bivalve molluscs accumulate salts and organic compounds such as glucose and amino acids, which lower the freezing point of their body fluids. Some Antarctica fish accumulate sodium, potassium or chloride ions or urea. Others contain so-called anti-freezes (glycoproteins) which inhibit the growth of ice crystals. They become attached to the developing water-ice crystal lattice, and block the incorporation in them of further water molecules.

Warm-blooded animals Marine Antarctic animals, such as whales and seals, have thick deposits of fat under their skins which insulate them from cold water. In addition to their excellent insulation, they produce their own heat by metabolic activity. Antarctic birds, like marine mammals, have a thick layer of insulating fat under their skins. They also have extensive fat deposits throughout their bodies which can be drawn on as a source of energy in times of fasting. The birds' feathers provide excellent insulation, with a layer of down close to the skin, and an outer layer of closely overlapping feathers. Assisted by preen oil, secreted by a gland near the tail and spread on the feathers with the bill, a waterproof surface is produced. This combination ensures that little heat is lost.

The closely overlapping feathers on penguins — this is a king — produce a totally waterproof insulating layer.

A Weddell seal pokes its head through water on the verge of freezing. Thick blubber protects these warm-blooded animals from their surroundings.

ANTARCTIC PLANTS

A few primitive species cling tenaciously to a barren land

Only about two per cent of Antarctica's 14 million square kilometres (5.4 million square miles) is free of ice. Apart from snow algae, plant life is limited to those ice-free areas where they can grow on or in sand, soil, rock, the weathered bones and feathers of dead animals, or other plants. Despite the fact that humans have been visiting Antarctica for nearly 100 years, there are still gaps in what is known of Antarctic plants. Best studied are the mosses, liverworts and lichens, but little is known about the algae, fungi and bacteria.

Antarctic lichens growing in the Vestfold Hills — a snow-free oasis on the Ingrid Christianson Coast.

Antarctic plants must make the best use of whatever habitats are available. Lichens and mosses grow in any favourable niche they can find in the barren Vestfold Hills (right).

By growing in dense turfs, Antarctic mosses make the best use of scarce moisture.

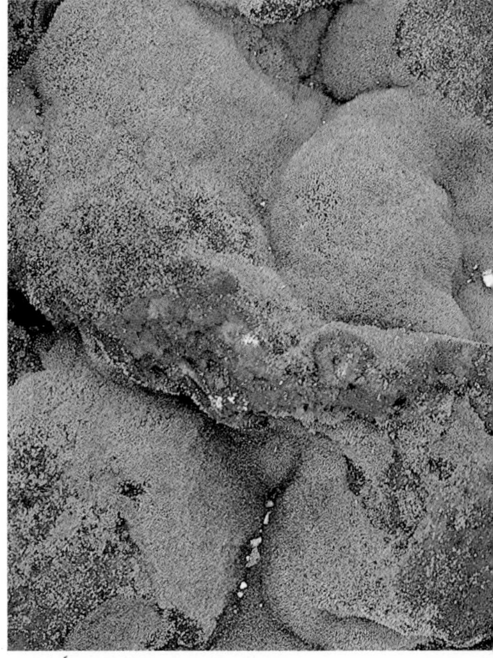

The distribution of plants is controlled by a number of factors such as temperature, the availability of water, wind, heat from the sun, material to grow on, and the influence of animals such as birds and seals. In coastal areas salt spray from the sea also has an effect on plant growth. The effects of human activity are mostly seen around bases, where fragile plant communities are frequently destroyed. Some introduced bacteria and microscopic fungi have also been found in the soil around major stations and field camps.

The severe Antarctic climate limits the number of land plants that are able to grow. Only two native vascular plants — a grass *Deschampsia antarctica* and a cushion-forming pearlwort *Colobanthus quitensis* — survive south of 56°S. Both have been found on Neny Island (68°12′S), on the western side of the Antarctic Peninsula. The grass extends further south, to Refuge Islet (68°21′S). This is in marked contrast to the Arctic regions where nearly 100 flowering plants are found at 84°N.

At the southern limit of their range, both of these vascular plants occur only occasionally, and then often together and with bryophytes (mosses and liverworts) and lichens, in moist, north-facing sites. The grass is more widespread and grows in patches that are usually less than 25 sq metres (270 sq ft) in area.

The most common large plants found around Antarctica are mosses and lichens. These are distributed chiefly around the edge of the continent, as well as on the Antarctic Peninsula. Mosses have been reported from as far south as 84°42′S and lichens from 86°09′S, at a height of 1980 metres (6500 ft). About 85 mosses, 25 liverworts and 150 lichens have been reported from the maritime Antarctic, which includes the western side of the Antarctic Peninsula and islands of the Scotia Arc. From the eastern side of the peninsula, which has a more severe climate, and continental Antarctica, only 30 mosses, one liverwort and 125 lichens have been found.

Peat banks are found on Signy Island in the South Orkneys and Elephant Island in the South Shetlands. These banks are up to three metres (10 ft) deep and as they build up at a rate of between 0.25 and 2.0 mm (0.009 and

Higher plants Only two vascular plants — those with vessels to circulate fluids — live in Antarctica. One is a grass and the other a pearlwort. Both can tolerate very cold and dry conditions. They continue to function at freezing point, when the rate at which they convert sunlight into chemical energy (photosynthesis) drops to about 30 to 40 per cent of that reached during the most favourable conditions.

*A clump of Antarctica's only grass—*Deschampsia antarctica. *It is found as far south as 68°.*

Moss Only a small number of moss species are found in Antarctica. Extensive fields occur in a few places on the continent and these are rarely more than 100 mm (4 in) deep, even in the most favourable areas where there is shelter and plenty of water. Short moss turf and cushion moss are found most frequently on sandy and gravelly soils. There are no extensive peat formations to be found.

Lichens Of all the plants, lichens are best adapted to survive in the harsh polar climate. Some lichens have even been found at 86°09′S, only about 400 km (250 miles) from the South Pole. In contrast to mosses, which can begin to function almost as soon as they thaw out, lichens recover very slowly following winter, and photosynthesis and respiration do not reach ideal levels until late in the spring.

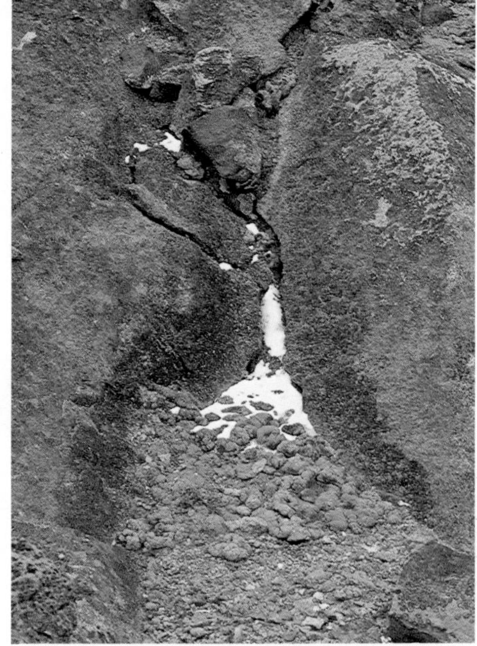

A typical convoluted moss bed on the Bailey Peninsula (left). Such beds accumulate slowly.

Mosses and lichens (orange and yellow) (above) take advantage of a damp corner.

after a prolonged period of freezing, and almost immediately following short periods.

Lichens are also well adapted to the Antarctic environment being able to function at lower temperatures, and with less light and water than other plants. The high concentration of pigments and lichen acids in the body of the plant prevents it from freezing until at least −10°C (14°F). Limited photosynthesis may still occur at these temperatures.

The ability of lichens and microorganisms to survive and colonise in extremely harsh conditions is emphasised by the presence of blue-green algae and lichens in the dry valleys of Victoria Land. In these dry valleys, the summer air temperature ranges between −15°C and 0°C (5°F and 32°F) and winter temperatures may be as low as −60°C (−76°F). Relative humidity is low at between 16 and 75 per cent and much of the snow which falls may vapourise without melting. Some lichens are adapted to live in fissures and cracks in rocks, and even to inhabit spaces between the grains.

0.08 in) each year, they must be between 1500 and 12000 years old.

Only one liverwort, *Cephaloziella exiliflora*, has been found on the Antarctic continent. Tight cushions or small turves are formed by the small, minutely leaved and densely packed shoots. It is widespread on rocky outcrops around the Australian Casey Station in Wilkes Land, and has also been found in the Larsemann Hills at 69°26′S, the most southerly record for a liverwort.

Most of these simple Antarctic plants grow in compact turves, mats and small cushions. By gathering together in colonies they are able to collect and retain more water. They also lose less by evaporation, and show a marked ability to use water rapidly whenever it becomes available.

These plants have also become well adapted to the almost continuous light during the long days of a polar summer. One Antarctic moss, *Bryum argenteum*, produces more energy by photosynthesis in low light at 5°C (41°F) than it does at 15°C (59°F), or higher. Photosynthesis can start within a few hours of thawing

More than 300 species of non-marine algae (simple plants) have been found in Antarctica. Blue-green and other algae are found growing in damp sand and gravel around lakes and tarns, along meltwater streams or in low lying areas where snow drifts or seepage may collect. Algae are commonly found under stones, particularly light-coloured quartz stones, where the microclimate is more favourable than in the surrounding sand or soil. Many species of blue-green algae have been found amongst moss turves.

The last group of plants to be found in Antarctica — the fungi — have been little studied. Several mushrooms have been found on the west coast of the Antarctic Peninsula, and on the South Shetland Islands. A few of the fungi found in Antarctica are unique to the continent. The majority, however, are also found in most temperate areas.

Algae These very simple plants take many diverse forms and a few have become adapted to live in difficult polar environments. Some such as *Prasiola crispa*, can tolerate high levels of nutrients and are found near bird colonies. Others — the snow algae — may form extensive and spectacular red, yellow or green patches on areas of permanent snow. Recent studies have shown that some blue-green algae live inside rocks in the dry valleys. Together with lichens, they are the only living things in a barren landscape.

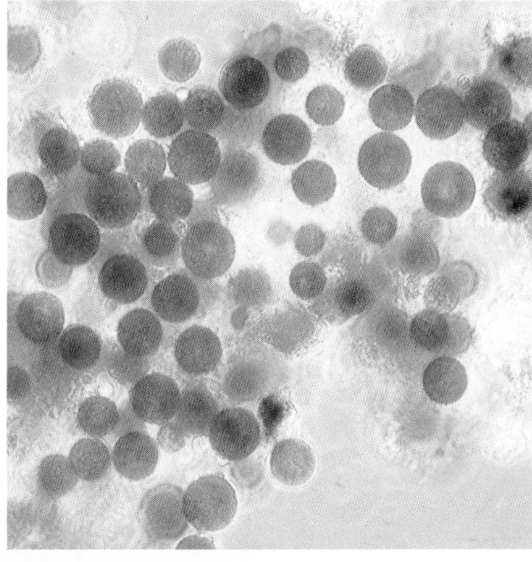

A variety of algae. Growths (left) of blue-green algae below a melting drift. Green algae (above) near a penguin rookery. Pink snow algae (below), and magnified (right).

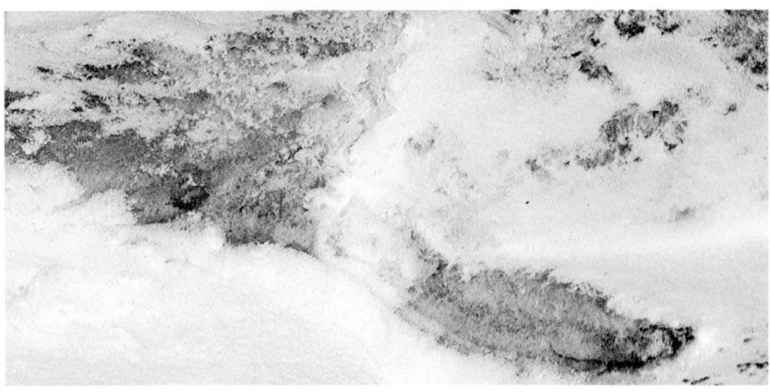

LAND ANIMALS

Only microscopic life survives throughout the year

A great variety of insects, birds and land mammals live in the high Arctic all year round. In contrast, only a handful of tiny invertebrates, and not one single land vertebrate, can survive the Antarctic winter. The southern continent's largest permanent inhabitant is a 12 mm (0.5 in) midge.

Fifty million years ago Antarctica had a temperate climate, evergreen forests, and many more kinds of animals than it has today. As the icecap slowly formed, most of these animals were obliterated. Today relatively few species live on the continent throughout the year. Some of those that do were probably left over from earlier times and survived on mountain tops that were never completely submerged beneath the ice.

Only invertebrate animals live year-round on the continent. No higher animals or flowering plants exist, and even birds and seals which breed on the coast (except for emperor penguins) leave during the 6 to 8-month-long winter. Even most invertebrates find the climate on the icecap and the few patches of rocks around the continent impossible for life during the winter. Most species are found on the Antarctic Peninsula and the islands of the Scotia Arc where the warming influence of the sea allows extensive lichen and moss beds, and two species of flowering plants to grow.

The Antarctic plants, which provide food for the majority of the animals, include about 1000 species of algae (land and freshwater), lichens, a few mosses and flowering plants and many kinds of microorganisms such as bacteria, fungi and yeasts. Algae and microorganisms are readily available in all the protected places that invertebrates favour — in the soil, under rocks, in bird nests, among moss or mats of algae at the bottom of lakes. Most of Antarctica's ice-free land lacks visible vegetation and the soils are a mixture of gravel and windblown sand. Organic soils develop only from guano deposited near penguin rookeries or beneath mats of moss growing in the warmer, damper climate of the Antarctic Peninsula. The lack of vegetation and the cold, dry, windy climate means that there are none of the animals available that help to create mature soils in more temperate regions.

Antarctica is the driest continent in the world and it is the lack of free water that imposes an absolute limit on the occurrence, distribution and activity of animal life. Most ice-free land receives the equivalent of only 50-150 mm (2-6 in) of rain each year, either as fallen or windblown snow. This does not melt to produce water until the spring thaw, and throughout winter the soil remains dry from the previous summer. The few animals that remain dormant in the soil during winter survive only because the humidity of the soil is maintained by a layer of permafrost. In winter the soil, moss beds and shallow glacial tarns containing mats of algae remain completely frozen for six to eight months. This long, cold period brings a halt to most activity.

Where the wind sweeps away all snow, such as in the dry valleys of southern Victoria Land, the soil receives virtually no moisture, and there is no life at all over large areas. Ice-free coastal lowlands such as the Vestfold Hills were once covered by the icecap and are still slowly accumulating animal species. Many small animals are probably carried from place to place by wind, or on the feet of birds.

Because of the short summer season there is limited time for growth and activity. Despite this, some animals with short life cycles multiply quickly and become very abundant. Those that reproduce by parthenogenesis — in which the unfertilised egg develops into a new

Few species The Antarctic land animals include moss- and soil-dwelling arthropods — about 50 species of mites, 20 species of collembola (springtails) and two species of midges; 28 species of metazoa, such as rotifers; 28 species of tardigrades (minute water-dwelling invertebrates); 51 species of nematodes (worms) and protozoa such as rhizopods and ciliates. Many of these creatures also live in meltwater ponds and lakes along with 12 species of crustaceans.

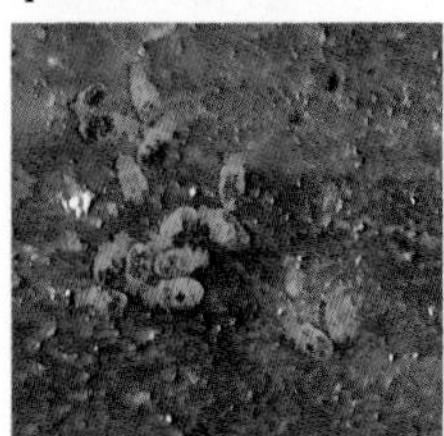

*Pink soil mites (*Nanorchestes antarcticus*) are among the most widespread of Antarctic animals.*

A matter of scale Almost all of Antarctica's permanent animal inhabitants can only be viewed through a magnifying glass or microscope. Largest is a wingless midge, *Belgica antarctica*, which grows to a maximum length of 12 mm (0.5 in). Most soil mites are barely visible, being only half to one third of a millimetre (0.02 to 0.013 in) long, although some larger mites are found on the Antarctic Peninsula. Rotifers are around one quarter of a millimetre (0.01 in) long and are only visible to the naked eye when they are present in large numbers — sometimes staining pools red. Tardigrades are about half as long as rotifers.

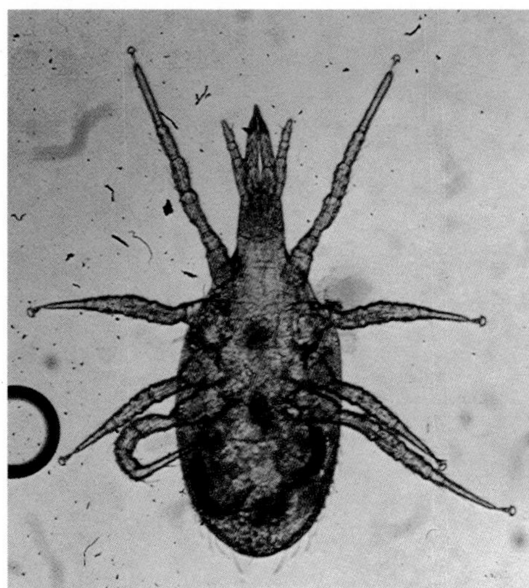

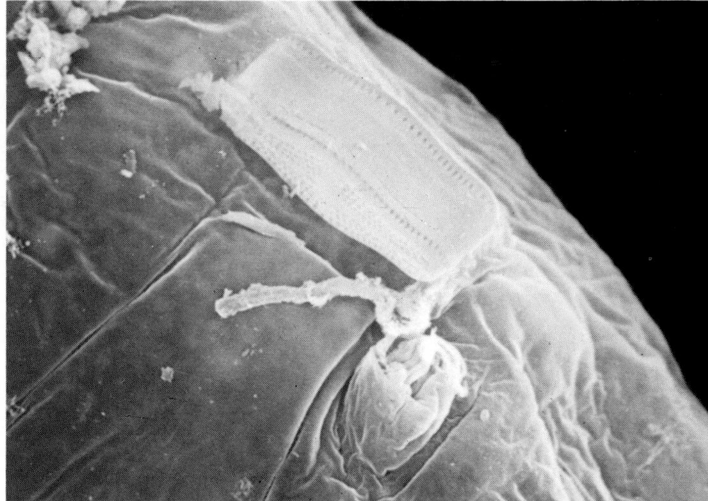

At left is a soil mite which is about 0.5 mm (0.02 in) long — just visible to the naked eye. On the right is a tardigrade which is usually found among algae and mosses. It is about 0.15 mm (0.006 in) long. Above is a diatom — which are eaten by some invertebrates — on the body of a tardigrade. It is about 0.000023 mm (0.0000009 in) long.

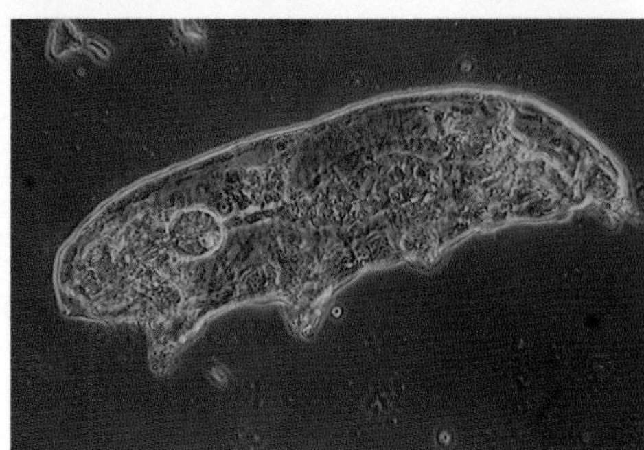

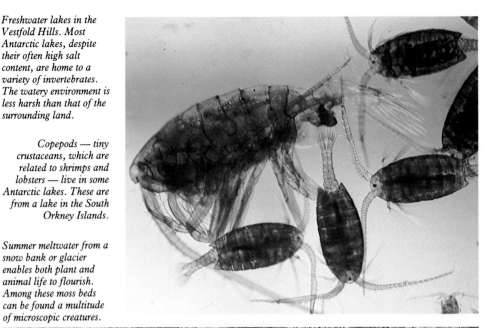

Freshwater lakes in the Vestfold Hills. Most Antarctic lakes, despite their often high salt content, are home to a variety of invertebrates. The watery environment is less harsh than that of the surrounding land.

Copepods — tiny crustaceans, which are related to shrimps and lobsters — live in some Antarctic lakes. These are from a lake in the South Orkney Islands.

Summer meltwater from a snow bank or glacier enables both plant and animal life to flourish. Among these moss beds can be found a multitude of microscopic creatures.

individual — have an advantage. Most species use sexual reproduction, a slower method of increase, although all the time available for growth can be used if the species can spend the winter dormant at various stages of its development. Some species of rotifers, which overwinter as eggs, are only able to develop and multiply by late summer. Few species synchronise their reproduction; most lay eggs throughout the summer. Tardigrades, nematodes and mites undergo numerous moults before reaching maturity and therefore take more than one year to complete a life cycle.

Surviving the cold

Ice damages cells and causes death. In order to survive the freezing temperatures of Antarctica, invertebrates must prevent or control the formation of ice in their bodies. Some, such as tardigrades and some rotifers, accomplish this by losing water and shrivelling up when the temperature drops, reabsorbing it when conditions are more favourable. Other rotifers lay drought-resistant eggs that can remain dormant for long periods, hatching only when conditions improve. A few insects, such as *Belgica antarctica*, can control the formation of ice in their bodies so that cells are undamaged. Most Antarctic land arthropods avoid freezing by making glycerol or other anti-freezing chemicals — in some species glycerol makes up one per cent of their blood.

Unique species

Some invertebrates found in Antarctica are found elsewhere in the world, although many are unique. Seventy five per cent of rotifer species are endemic.

A rotifer (below) Philodina gregaria *which is common in Antarctica. Large numbers (right) stain pond water red.*

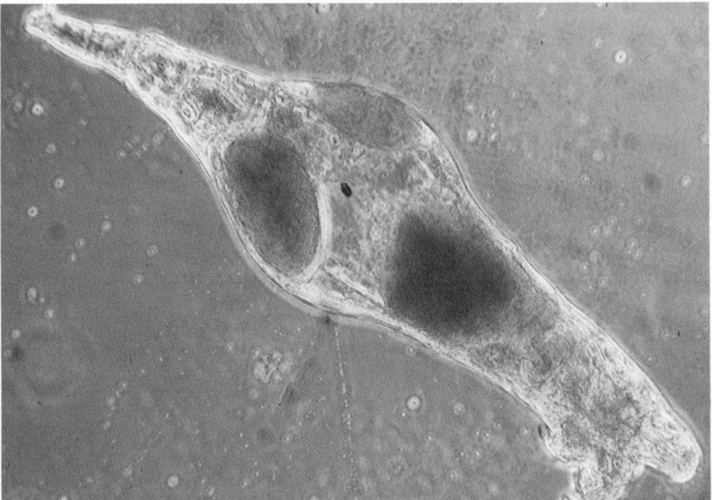

Living off others

Most of the invertebrate parasites found in Antarctica — 40 species of chewing lice, four species of sucking lice, nine species of feather mites, two species of nasal mites and two species of ticks — are all temporary residents which live only on their seal or bird hosts. They escape many of the difficulties associated with living in Antarctica that must be faced by any free-living species. Only one species of parasite, a flea, remains year-round in the nest of its bird hosts. Even entirely aquatic creatures like whales are hosts to a great variety of external parasites, such as lice, barnacles and water fleas.

A parasite, probably a worm, in the head of an Antarctic fish. Most Antarctic vertebrates are hosts to parasites which are thus able to avoid the worst effects of their hostile surroundings.

LIFE IN THE SOUTHERN OCEAN

The complex ecology of Antarctica's ice-covered waters

Life in the Antarctic is much more difficult on land than it is in the sea. The air temperature on the continent can fall as low as −70°C (−94°F) and most of the land is covered by ice and snow throughout the year. The only places available for plants and animals to grow and live are rocky coastal outcrops, and these are periodically swept by cold, fierce winds that roar down the coastal slopes from the high Antarctic icecap.

The pack ice would seem to be devoid of life, yet ice algae grow within it.

As soon as the temperature of sea water falls to freezing point, a layer of ice forms on the surface, insulating the water beneath. It is only near the shore, where more permanent ice scours the bottom, that living organisms find conditions as difficult as they are on land.

But the factor which has the greatest effect on life in the Southern Ocean is not temperature but light. There is no life without growth — except in certain most unusual cases — and there is no growth without photosynthesis. Photosynthesis is the process by which plants use light to convert carbon dioxide and water into food, and it is regulated by the length of the day. As the seasons progress from autumn into winter, the days get shorter and the nights longer. Eventually, a turning point is reached when more energy is lost by organisms at night than is gained by them in photosynthesis during the day. Then the whole Antarctic ecosystem runs on the reserves laid down during the previous summer.

Throughout the oceans of the world, growth takes place wherever there is enough light for photosynthesis and enough mineral nutrients in the water. The main algae of the Southern Ocean live in sunlit water (diatoms and dinoflagellates), near the shores of subantarctic islands (giant kelp), and on the undersurface and in the middle of the pack ice and snow (ice algae).

While there is sometimes a shortage of light around Antarctica, there are generally plenty of nutrients. Nowhere in the world are nearshore beds of kelp as luxuriant and prolific as they are in the surf zones around subantarctic islands. The subantarctic oceans, by contrast, are relatively poor in nutrients because surface waters are constantly being mixed by turbulent winds to a depth of 300–400 metres (1000–1300 ft), well beyond the 100 metres (330 ft) or so that light can reach. Only infrequently, when the westerly winds abate, are subantarctic phytoplankton able to find enough light for sustained growth. Conditions are more favourable for growth in the east-wind-drift. The winds are weaker there and the water column is more stable — partly the result of the layer of less-salty water formed by the melting pack ice. It is also an area where water is being brought up to the surface rather than drawn down. Because of this, there are sometimes huge quantities of phytoplankton there, particularly diatoms.

The third major area where algae can live in the Southern Ocean is the pack ice. A layer of algae grows in the ice during the autumn and spring, and is then released into the water during the summer thaw. The way in which the algae is thought to develop is explained in the box below.

There are therefore two different ecosystems in the Southern Ocean — one in the

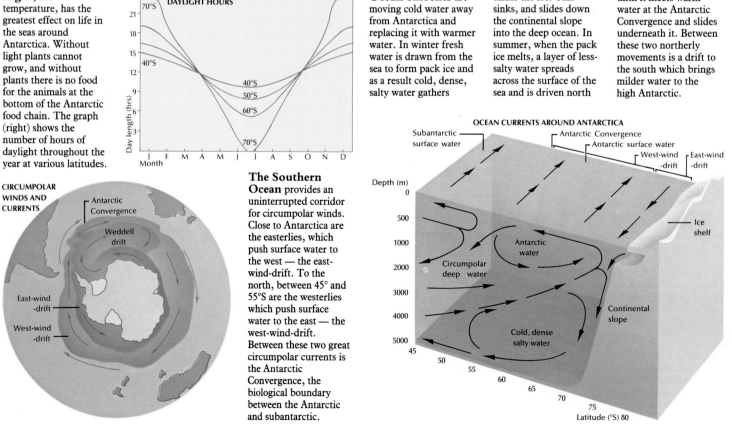

Light, not temperature, has the greatest effect on life in the seas around Antarctica. Without light plants cannot grow, and without plants there is no food for the animals at the bottom of the Antarctic food chain. The graph (right) shows the number of hours of daylight throughout the year at various latitudes.

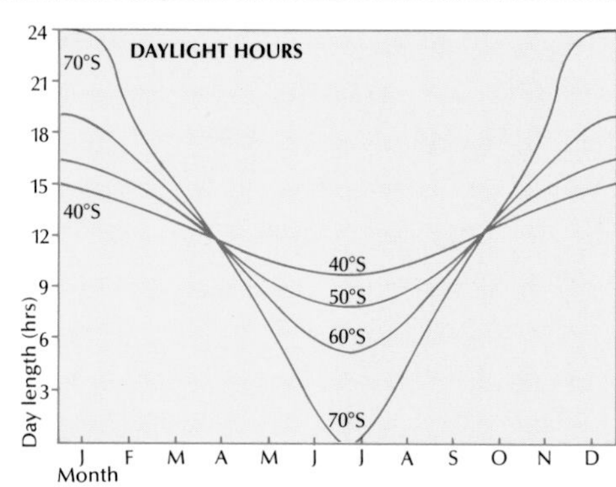

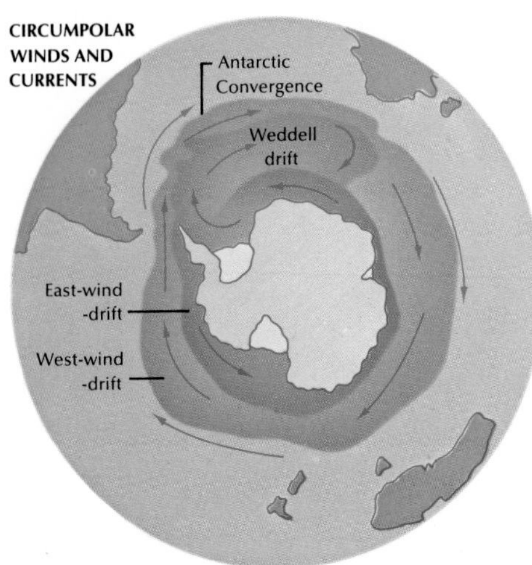
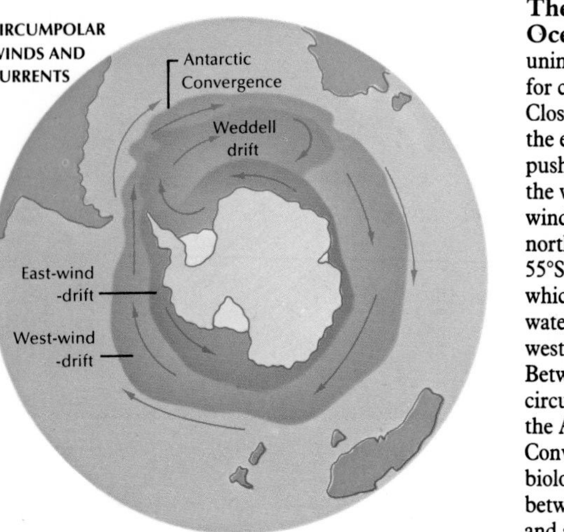

The Southern Ocean provides an uninterrupted corridor for circumpolar winds. Close to Antarctica are the easterlies, which push surface water to the west — the east-wind-drift. To the north, between 45° and 55°S are the westerlies which push surface water to the east — the west-wind-drift. Between these two great circumpolar currents is the Antarctic Convergence, the biological boundary between the Antarctic and subantarctic.

Ocean currents are moving cold water away from Antarctica and replacing it with warmer water. In winter fresh water is drawn from the sea to form pack ice and as a result cold, dense, salty water gathers under the ice. This sinks, and slides down the continental slope into the deep ocean. In summer, when the pack ice melts, a layer of less-salty water spreads across the surface of the sea and is driven north until it meets warm water at the Antarctic Convergence and slides underneath it. Between these two northerly movements is a drift to the south which brings milder water to the high Antarctic.

OCEAN CURRENTS AROUND ANTARCTICA

Subantarctic surface water
Antarctic Convergence
Antarctic surface water
West-wind -drift
East-wind -drift
Depth (m) 0 500 1000 2000 3000 4000 5000
Ice shelf
Antarctic water
Circumpolar deep water
Continental slope
Cold, dense salty water
45 50 55 60 65 70 75 Latitude (°S) 80

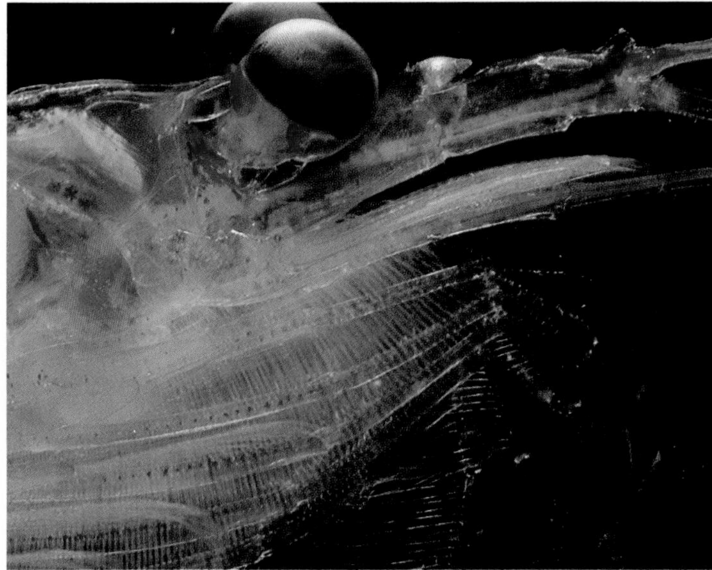

An Antarctic krill, Euphausia superba *(above). Vast swarms of this 65-mm (2.5-in) long crustacean live in the frigid ocean that surrounds Antarctica.*

west-wind-drift and the other in the east-wind-drift. The west-wind-drift ecosystem lies north of the limit of the winter pack ice, and is based entirely on phytoplankton which are eaten by tiny crustaceans in the plankton. These crustaceans are in turn eaten by lightfish, the lightfish by squid, and the squid by sperm whales.

The east-wind-drift ecosystem, on the other hand, is the more productive of the two. It draws its resources both from the phytoplankton in the water and from the algae in the pack ice. The main grazing organism there is the Antarctic krill (*Euphausia superba*), the most abundant animal in the world. This species is the largest representative of a group that was once thought to drift aimlessly through the ocean. However, schools of krill have recently been observed by Japanese trawlers to migrate southwards towards Antarctica in the summer, following the break-up of the pack ice. Such behaviour is more characteristic of animals such as fish.

Krill trap their food — minute drifting plants called phytoplankton — with their hair-covered thoracic legs (below) and then eat it.

Krill is the staple food of a wide range of Antarctic animals such as the baleen whales, crabeater seals, fur seals and Adélie penguins. The amount of krill now eaten by both crabeater seals and Adélie penguins probably equals that of all the remaining baleen whales. The numbers of both animals is now greater than it was before high seas whaling started. Although adult krill are found mainly near the surface of the sea, they are also eaten in large numbers by many bottom-living fish.

There is evidence that the numbers of creatures living in the east-wind-drift ecosystem are limited by the amount of food that is available. This is an important concept, because if it is true, then no one population can be managed effectively as a renewable resource unless its impact on all the other species is also taken into account. Evidence to support this theory is based on observations of the way in which populations of unfished krill-eating whales and seals have changed (see below). For example, the population of crabeater (krill-eater) seals has now increased to a point where they outnumber all the other seals in the world put together.

At present, Antarctic whaling is being phased out. A new industry is developing for harvesting Antarctic krill, but there is as yet no culling of either seals or penguins. Because of past and present practices, whale stocks are much reduced, and Antarctic fisheries show signs of over-exploitation. The current challenges are therefore to allow whale stocks to build up again, to control the intensity of fishing, and to find a way to harvest krill without damaging other parts of the Antarctic ecosystem. It is particularly important to understand the long term effects of krill fishing before the industry becomes too large.

Krill is the key species of the east-wind-drift ecosystem. These animals breed close to Antarctica and their eggs sink to the bottom to be carried northwards by cold, deep ocean currents. The developing larvae move up towards the surface of the water where the phytoplankton live that they feed on. They grow in summer, when there is abundant food, but it is not yet known how the later larval stages find food in winter when the water is covered in pack ice. Recent studies show that they may shrink in size in order to survive, drawing energy from their own bodies. Other studies suggest that they may be cannibals. Krill are now being exploited and may eventually be a source of food for humans. Dried, they are almost half protein and are also rich in vitamins. In 1981-82 over 500 000 tonnes were caught in Antarctic waters by Japanese and Russian trawlers. At that time Japan operated 14 krill trawlers in the Antarctic and Russia about 100.

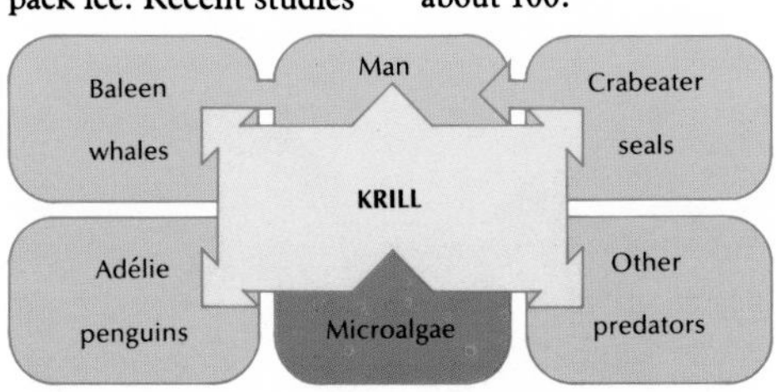

Krill occupy a central place in the Antarctic ecosystem. They consume micro-algae and are in turn eaten by penguins, seals, whales and now man. A reduction in the number of whales has meant that the populations of other animals have multiplied.

A delicate balance exists in many Antarctic food chains. Because a large proportion of the southern baleen whales were killed during 50 years of high seas whaling, the amount of krill (their food) increased enormously. Other krill-eating species — seals and penguins — were quick to exploit this surplus, and their numbers are now rapidly multiplying. In the seven years from 1966, the age of maturity of a group of crabeater seals was seen to drop from five to three years (graph, right) thus allowing them to breed more rapidly. It may be that it will be difficult for baleen whales to re-establish themselves.

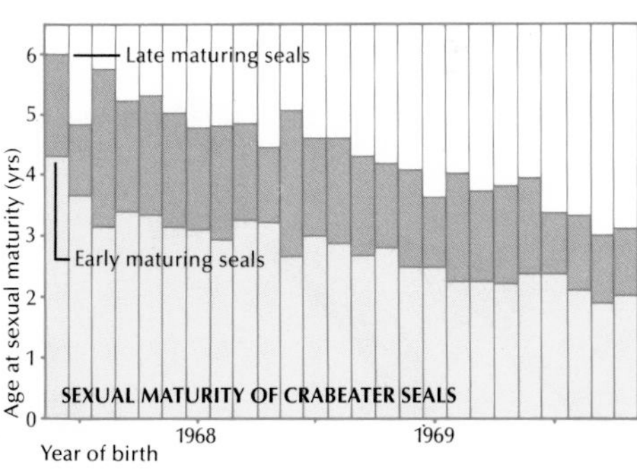

HOW ALGAE EXPLOIT AN UNLIKELY ENVIRONMENT

Pancake ice

Snow

Algae

Ice

As the water around Antarctica starts to cool in autumn, a layer of pancake ice starts to form on the surface of the sea. These pancakes gradually grow larger and soon collect a covering of snow which forces the ice down deeper into the water.

When the area between the ice and the snow reaches water level, sea water seeps between the layers, carrying nutrients and small algae which start to grow. Growth continues through autumn, but is interrupted during the winter darkness.

In the following spring, when the light returns, the algae in the ice grow very rapidly. The area of winter pack ice around Antarctica is so large that the crop of ice algae is nearly as great as that of the phytoplankton in the water below.

As the pack ice starts to break up in summer the entire annual crop of ice algae becomes available to animals, such as krill, which live in the water below the ice. However, it is not clear yet whether they, or any other species, use it for food or not.

Emperors are the largest of the penguins and the most truly Antarctic of all birds. There are only about two dozen colonies scattered around the continent with a population of perhaps 250 000 breeding birds. Emperors assemble in early autumn in sheltered bays around the coast to breed. The males remain on the ice incubating a single egg through the winter, while the females return to the ocean.

THE SOUTHERN PENGUINS

Flightless birds unique to southern waters

More active than seals, more personable than skuas or petrels, penguins are by far the most lively and interesting of Antarctic animals. They are found in all latitudes of the southern hemisphere, from the coast of Antarctica to the equator, with most species between 45° and 55°S.

Penguins evolved as sea birds of a much broader temperate zone in the early-to-mid Tertiary period (about 60 million years ago). Like petrels and other sea birds they were already adapted for living in cool water, and found themselves well equipped for life on cold lands. As the circumpolar region grew colder, they spread and diversified.

Their adaptations for cold are simple. Dense overall plumage, each feather overlapping its neighbours like tiles on a roof, combine with an underfelt of woolly down to keep out cold air, winds and water. A thick layer of fat provides additional insulation between the skin and the underlying muscles. Emperor and Adélie penguins have slightly longer plumage for their size, with shorter extremities — flippers, feet and head — that help to reduce heat losses. Their fat provides an additional bonus as an energy store.

Penguins are superb swimmers. The feet and stubby tail combine to form a rudder, and the flippers become powerful propellers on either side. Most species feed close to the surface, mainly on small fish and shrimp-like creatures of the plankton. The larger species dive deeper for their food: gentoos can dive to 100 metres (330 ft) or more; emperors to 250 metres

Emperor penguin
Aptenodytes forsteri
SIZE: 1 m (39 in) tall, weight 30 kg (66 lb).
DESCRIPTION: Cap black, neck blue-grey; ear patches brilliant orange; breast lemon yellow. Bill plates orange, pink, purple or lilac; rest of bill black and feathered. Eyes dark. Feet black. Juveniles: grey or yellow. Chicks: dense silver-grey down with black head.
VOICE: Male display call is a bray in musical cadences; in female a coo and cackle with a brief final note.
BREEDING: Late March to May in colonies in shelter of icebergs and coastal ice cliffs. No nest — single egg laid on ice and held on feet. Incubation period 60 days. Chick brooded 40 days, but is dependent for six months.

Short wings, useless for flying, now propel emperor penguins rapidly under water.

Adélie penguin
Pygoscelis adeliae
SIZE: 71 cm (28 in) tall, weight about 5.5 kg (12 lb).
DESCRIPTION: Cap and chin black; back black, tipped with blue. Eye-ring white. Feet grey-pink. Eyes dark red. Bill dark red, half feathered. Juveniles: chin white, eye-ring black, back blue-grey.
VOICE: A drum-like roll speeding to a gurgle. At sea, a single bark.
BREEDING: Nests a scattered pile of pebbles. Incubation 33 days, brooding 25 days.

Adélies have provided amusement for generations of Antarctic visitors.

In spring Adélies travel great distances over the sea ice to reach land.

Momentum gained from swimming quickly — up to 15 km/h (9 mph) — enables Adélie penguins to leap two metres (7 ft) vertically from the water onto ice floes. Penguins use this technique to escape from their chief predator — leopard seals.

Penguins usually travel upright, but in thick snow, or if alarmed and in a hurry, they drop down on their chests and toboggan — pushing their bodies forward with their flippers and toes. Travelling in this way they can outdistance a man.

(820 ft). For their size they swim fast; 10 to 15 km/h (6-9 mph).

Adélie penguins spend their winters in the pack ice, where air temperatures are always higher than on land. In early spring they turn south and head towards their colonies, navigating by the sun. Males usually arrive first, in late October, when they seek out and refurbish their nest sites of the previous year. Females arrive a few days later, often joining their mates of previous years and helping to rebuild and defend the pebble nests. The females lay two eggs, usually during the first or second weeks of November, then return to sea for eight to fifteen days, leaving the males to incubate the eggs. Separated from the sea by many kilometres of sea ice, the males have already starved for two or three weeks during nest building and courtship. A further spell without food during the first incubation watch, still in the biting cold of early spring, takes them to the physiological limit set by their fat reserves; on relief they are down to half their start-of-season weight.

By mid-November the sea ice is usually dispersing and food is available closer to the colonies. For the remaining three to four weeks of incubation the parents alternate at intervals of two or three days. After hatching they return at similar intervals, bringing back fish and plankton in their crops.

Chinstrap and gentoo penguins are two other species of small penguins that penetrate south of the Antarctic Convergence. Chinstrap penguins, similar and closely akin to Adélies, are widespread in the South Orkney, South Shetland and South Sandwich islands, and in the Palmer Archipelago off the western Antarctic Peninsula. Distinguished mainly by a narrow band of black under the chin, they breed two or three weeks later than Adélies, often on rougher, rockier ground. Gentoos, with their distinctive white head-flesh and orange bill, are the largest of the three pygoscelid penguins, with the widest breeding range. In the south they nest on bare, open ground, sometimes sharing colonies with chinstraps and Adélies. On the northern islands they nest in the shelter of tussock grass.

The small penguins that live south of the Antarctic Convergence all complete their breeding cycles well within the span of the polar summer. The problem is greatest in the far south, where summers are shortest and the summer abundance of food is to some degree restricted by sea ice. Adélie penguins breeding on mainland Antarctica can just complete their cycle by starting before the inshore ice disperses, and releasing their chicks before they are fully grown. Emperor penguins have a problem, for they are bigger birds and chick-rearing takes longer.

They solve their problem by gathering in the autumn, as soon as the new sea ice forms in sheltered bays of the continental coast. Laying in May or early June, they incubate for two months during the coldest period of the year, when temperatures may fall to −50°C (−58°F) and lower. Only the males incubate. Separated from the sea by many kilometres of fast ice, they would use up too much energy in regular exchanges of watch with the females. Instead they huddle together in heat-conserving scrums, with their single eggs balanced and kept warm on their feet.

The females return to the colony just as the chicks hatch out, and thereafter both parents cross the sea ice in turn to meet their chicks' ever-increasing demands for food. By January or early February the chicks moult and are ready for the sea; though less than fully grown, they are able to fend for themselves while there is still food for them in surface waters.

Gentoo penguin
Pygoscelis papua
SIZE: 76 cm (30 in) tall, weight 6 kg (13 lb).
DESCRIPTION: Breast white, rest of body black with white triangular flash across forehead from eye to eye. Bill plates red, rest of bill black. Eyes brown. Feet yellow-orange.
Juveniles: narrower head patch, white flecks near eye, mottled throat.
VOICE: Low double-note bray, or two notes trumpeted.
BREEDING: Nests of stones, moss and sea weed. Incubation 36 days, brooding 28 days.

Gentoo (above) and chinstrap (below) penguins are related to each other and to Adélies. All are about the same size.

Chinstrap penguin
Pygoscelis antarctica
SIZE: 76 cm (30 in) tall, weight 4 kg (8.8 lb).
DESCRIPTION: Black head, back and eye-ring. Cheeks white with narrow band of black-tipped feathers under chin. Bill black, unfeathered. Eyes red-brown. Feet pale flesh to yellow-orange.
VOICE: Medium-pitch, harsh cry.
BREEDING: Colonies on rocky ground. Nest platform of pebbles. Incubation 37 days.

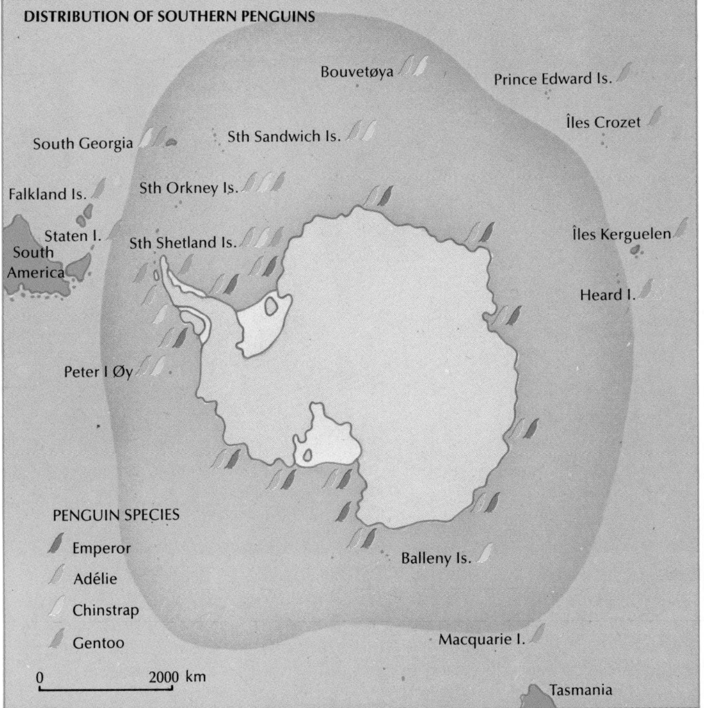

Distribution: Only emperor and Adélie penguins breed on the shores of Antarctica. Chinstraps breed on the islands around the continent and some are found on the islands close to the Antarctic Convergence. Gentoos have the widest range, being found from the cold peripheral islands to the cooler subantarctic islands.

THE NORTHERN PENGUINS

Birds of warmer shores

Moving north from Antarctica, away from the limit of the pack ice, winters become milder. One clear indication of this is the presence on islands of tussock grass and king penguins.

King penguins, the most colourful and spectacular of all the penguins, require the longest possible summers and mildest possible winters for the completion of their unusually complex breeding cycles.

Slightly smaller than emperors, with proportionately longer bill, feet and flippers, kings breed in colonies of several hundreds or thousands of birds on flat, slightly raised ground or gentle slopes close to an accessible beach. Often their beach is shared by gentoo penguins, but never the nesting grounds. Gentoos prefer steeper tussock-covered slopes, and will often climb steep hillsides to nest on grass-covered colonies at the top. Macaroni and rockhopper penguins that breed on the same islands seldom come into contact with kings or gentoos. Their preference is for open hillsides, scree slopes and steep rocky cliffs. With their lighter weight and hopping gait they climb with speed and agility that neither kings nor gentoos can ever emulate.

The small pygoscelid (Adélie, gentoo and chinstrap) and eudyptid (rockhopper and macaroni) penguins have no difficulty in fitting their breeding cycles to the regime imposed by the climate on these Antarctic fringe islands. Starting in September or October, they

King penguin
Aptenodytes patagonicus
SIZE: 94 cm (37 in) tall; weight 16 kg (36 lb).
DESCRIPTION: Dorsal feathers tipped with dark powder blue; shoulders and nape silver-grey; comma-shaped ear patches; orange leading to yellow band around the throat. Broad bill plates orange or red. Breast white. Chicks: Fine grey-brown down changing later to dense brown 'wool'.
VOICE: Loud bray.
BREEDING: In colonies on tussock flats. Laying begins in November. No nest — single egg held on feet covered by a fold of abdominal skin. Chick brooded 30 days, but is dependent for almost a year. Efficient parents raise two chicks every three years.

Two adult king penguins and a chick. These birds were ruthlessly hunted in the nineteenth century for their fat and plumage.

Rockhopper penguin
Eudyptes chrysocome
SIZE: 56 cm (22 in) tall, weight 3 kg (6.6 lb).
DESCRIPTION: Head, cheeks and throat black, rest of upper surface bluish-black. Head has long drooping silky tassels of straw-coloured feathers behind eyes and a yellow strip that extends forward to the bill. Under-surface of body white. Bill reddish brown. Feet white to flesh pink. Eyes red.
VOICE: Harsh, strident squawks.
BREEDING: Nest shallow. Laying September to November, two eggs, but only one raised. Incubation 35 days, brooding 26 days, fledging 70 days.

An adult rockhopper penguin (right), and a rockhopper penguin rookery on Macquarie Island (above right). These are the most aggressive of all penguins.

Part of a large king penguin colony at the Bay of Isles in South Georgia. Some colonies contain several hundred thousand birds. The brown-coated chicks need their thick plumage to protect them during the long and bitter subantarctic winter.

Penguins porpoising — leaving the water momentarily as they swim. This technique enables them to breathe without stopping their forward progress. Most can keep up a steady 24 km/h (15 mph) in this way. Some may reach 48 km/h (30 mph) in short bursts.

can court, build nests, lay, incubate and rear their chicks with ease by March or April, and even complete their own moult before the end of the season. King penguins cannot; like emperors they suffer the problem of size. It takes too long for their chicks to grow to a size that allows them independence — too long, therefore, for their breeding cycle to be fitted into a single summer. Where emperors set back their courtship into autumn and incubate through the polar winter — a device that allows the chicks time to mature before the end of summer — kings tackle their problem in a completely different way. They rear their chicks quite normally in the much longer spring and summer, then keep them in the colonies for the relatively short and mild winter, ultimately releasing them after a final period of fattening in the following spring.

On South Georgia the cycle of breeding starts in late October, when newly moulted adults return to the traditional colonies, pair off, mate, and produce their single eggs. These they incubate in turn, for almost eight weeks, holding them on their feet without the benefit of a nest. The first wave of breeders is made up of adults which, for one reason or another, failed to rear a chick during the previous season. They are surrounded during courtship and incubation by large chicks that have survived the winter, and are still being tended by the parents that hatched them up to a year before. As incubation proceeds the old chicks fatten, moult, and one by one leave the colony.

The new chicks of the early breeders hatch out from mid-January, growing rapidly in brown woolly down that protects them from the wind, rain, and snow flurries of the sub-polar summer. Fed by both parents, seeking mutual warmth and protection from skuas by banding together in créches, the new chicks grow rapidly. By mid-April they have reached weights of 10 to 12 kilograms (22-26 lb) and stand almost as tall as their parents. Meanwhile the parents of the mature chicks have moulted — a process taking over a month — and returned to the colony all ready to court, mate and lay again. This second wave of late breeders lays from February onward. By late April the colony is full, chicks of early and late breeders jostling with the last incubating birds, and a few new pairs trying to establish themselves. Then the pattern changes. The weather worsens, snow settles, and food becomes scarce in the sea. Courtship ceases, eggs are abandoned, and the smallest chicks die of hunger and exposure. The big chicks crowd together often in one single huge creche of 2000-3000 birds with only a handful of adults standing by. Parents that have lost chicks or eggs leave the colony altogether. Those with chicks to tend visit only at intervals of four to six weeks, staying just long enough to feed their offspring from the cropful of food they have brought back. Each chick is fed only by its own parents, receiving a meal once every two to three weeks. Nor surprisingly, they lose weight. Chicks that began the winter at 10 to 12 kilograms (22-26 lb) fall by September to 6 or 7 Kilograms (13-15 lb).

With the coming of spring in September and October food becomes more plentiful in the sea, and the surviving chicks — possibly 80 per cent of those that began the winter — receive food more frequently. Their weight increases, and in November or December they moult from their tired woolly down into smart juvenile plumage. Meanwhile the adults that lost their offspring in autumn and winter have undergone their prenuptial moult and taken up their positions in the colony as early breeders, and the cycle begins again. Thus a pair that breeds early in one season, and rears a chick to maturity by November or December, can become a late breeding pair in the following season, with a reasonable chance of rearing a second chick in succession.

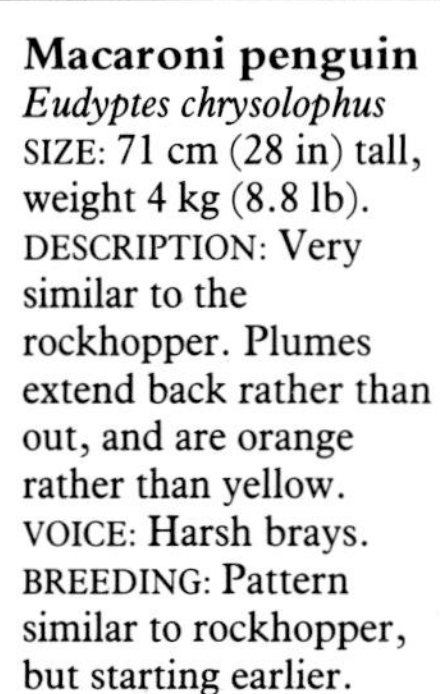

Macaroni penguin
Eudyptes chrysolophus
SIZE: 71 cm (28 in) tall, weight 4 kg (8.8 lb).
DESCRIPTION: Very similar to the rockhopper. Plumes extend back rather than out, and are orange rather than yellow.
VOICE: Harsh brays.
BREEDING: Pattern similar to rockhopper, but starting earlier.

A macaroni penguin. This species is similar in appearance to the rockhopper.

Other species There are altogether 21 species of penguins scattered throughout all latitudes of the Southern Hemisphere. The most species and biggest colonies occur in the cool temperate zone between 45° and 55°S. The northernmost penguins live on the Galápagos Islands.

Snares Island penguins racing ashore with a breaking wave.

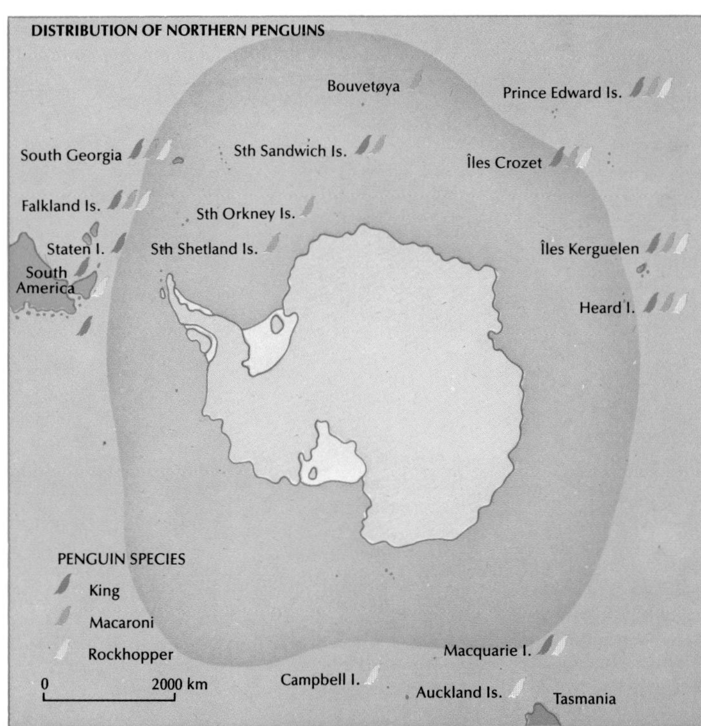

Distribution King, macaroni and rockhopper penguins all generally prefer to breed on the tussock-clad islands north of the limit of pack ice, and on many subantarctic groups. Macaronis are found breeding as far south as the South Shetland Islands, while no rockhoppers breed south of Heard Island which is at 53°S.

THE TRUE SEALS

Mammals adapted to cold Antarctic waters

The Antarctic coast, the sea ice surrounding it, and the subantarctic islands, are the home of five species of true or 'earless' seals — the ones without an external pinna or flap to their ears. Four species — the Weddell, Ross, leopard and crabeater seals — are all closely related to each other.

Carnivorous mammals, related to bears and otters, seals spend much of their life and catch most of their food in the water. Unlike whales, they are not entirely aquatic. Though excellent swimmers and divers, they breathe air and cannot stay long submerged. The larger species dive deep, but most live close to the surface, taking plankton, fish, squid and birds. Some, including Weddells of the Antarctic, mate in the water, but the pups are almost always born above high water mark. True seals have short, paddle-like flippers with hind limbs trailing. Their fur is bristly, and the thick layer of fat under the skin, which gives them their smooth, slug-like contours, is excellent insulation. On land or ice they are ungraceful, humping like fat caterpillars or slithering heavily with flippers at their sides. In the water they are agile, diving, rolling and turning with weightless ease.

Of all southern seals, the best known are probably Weddell seals of the inshore ice. Entirely a coastal species, these are the ones most often met. The sexes are similar, with females tending to be slightly larger.

In the cold sunless days of winter Weddells are not often seen. They stay below the sea ice, breathing through leads and cracks but seldom hauling out except when the weather is calm and still. As the sun returns to Antarctica in spring, and warm air drifts in from the sea, they emerge more often to lie out on the ice, struggling up through holes and along ramps which they maintain by sawing and grinding with their teeth. Not surprisingly, mature Weddell seals often have broken and abscessed teeth, worn down by several years' ice cutting.

While sunning themselves they are sleepy, inoffensive creatures, snoozing companionably in clubs of up to a dozen. In the water they are lively and alert. Males defend their breathing holes, fighting off other males but allowing small groups of females to share them. Silent on the surface (except for snoring) they are surprisingly noisy under water. Some of their hootings, trillings and groanings are thought to be social calls, others may help them to find food, and perhaps to relocate the all-important breathing holes in the dark after a long spell of swimming and diving under the ice. They may dive to 600 metres (2000 ft) or more in search of the fish which are their main food, and stay down for an hour at a time.

Weddell seals haul out in September and October; often groups of half a dozen or more pregnant females and a mature male form

A pair of fat, glossy Weddell seals (above) on the pack ice.

Weddell seal
Leptonychotes weddelli
SIZE: Three metres (10 ft) from nose to tail; weight up to 400 kg (880 lb). Sexes similar.
DESCRIPTION: Silver-grey coat spotted and blotched with black, slate-grey and white. In summer coat can bleach to grey-brown or fawn.
BREEDING: Groups of half a dozen pregnant females and one male gather on broken ice in spring. Single pups born between September and October. Grey pups weigh 25-30 kg (55-66 lb) at birth and are weaned after 6-8 weeks. Sexual maturity reached at three years.
FOOD: Fish and crustaceans.

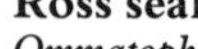

Ross seal
Ommatophoca rossi
SIZE: 2.3 metres (7.5 ft) long; weight 200 kg (440 lb).
DESCRIPTION: Dark uniform grey along the back and flanks, silver-grey to white underneath. Small head with large, prominent eyes, a short mouth, and needle-like teeth.
BREEDING: Not observed. Pups may be born in November.
FOOD: Squid, fish and krill.

Crabeater seal
Lobodon carcinophagus
SIZE: Up to 2.7 metres (8.8 ft) long; weight over 250 kg (550 lb).
DESCRIPTION: Dark grey along spine shading to fawn or tan-coloured sides and belly. Variable pattern of brown rings on sides. Coat can bleach almost to white in summer.
BREEDING: Because crabeater seals inhabit the pack ice little is known about their behaviour. Females may produce their pups in October and November, before the ice breaks up, but this is not certain. There is some evidence that they may be monogamous, although this is rare in seals.
FOOD: These seals feed only on krill, which are strained through their lobed teeth.

A section through the carcase of a Weddell seal showing 100 mm (4 in) of protective blubber.

Crabeater seals (below), once thought to be rare, now appear to be possibly the most numerous of all the world's seals.

The teeth of a leopard seal are clearly adapted for seizing and tearing flesh. Despite the fact that they are fierce predators, leopard seals have not been known to make unprovoked attacks on human beings.

A leopard seal snaps up its favourite meal — an Adélie penguin. The seals catch penguins by their feet and rump and beat them against the water to skin them before dismembering and eating them. Individual leopard seals often position themselves near penguin colonies to catch incoming and outgoing birds. Queues of wary penguins often wait at the water's edge for an individual to dive in so that they can see if there is a hungry leopard seal about.

around a breathing hole or lead in the ice, while young males live in separate clubs of their own. Rough, broken inshore ice is their favourite habitat, where cracks are plentiful and the uneven surface gives shelter from cold winds. The single pups are born in September towards the northern edge of their range, about a month later in the far south, where spring itself comes later. Expelled from the warmth of the mother's body which is about 37°C (99°F) a Weddell seal pup may find itself having to cope, in a matter of seconds, with an air temperature of −20°C (−4°F) or lower.

Weighing 25 to 30 kg (55-66 lb) and half as long as their mothers, the pups are covered at first with soft grey down, which they shed in favour of silver-grey fur during their third or fourth weeks. They grow quickly, feeding entirely on milk until five or six weeks old and by weaning they have more than doubled their birth weight. They swim readily on first entering the water, and probably reach independence in two to three months. At three years they become sexually mature, but like most other seals continue to grow slowly for several more seasons. The teeth, too, grow persistently; the large incisors especially carry a record of the seal's age in annual growth rings.

Ross, crabeater and leopard seals live mostly on the pack ice. Though leopard seals have a broader range, extending both north and south of the pack, Ross and crabeater seals are rarely found anywhere but on floating ice. Only young crabeaters approach the shores of the Antarctic continent. In the early days of Antarctic exploration these species were met with less often than Weddells, and so thought to be much rarer. But recent surveys with icebreakers and helicopters, penetrating deep into the pack ice, have shown crabeaters to be extremely abundant — possibly the most numerous of all the world's seals, with a population approaching five million. Ross seals too are more plentiful than was ever imagined, though mostly confined to the densest pack ice.

Crabeater seals grow as long as Weddells, though seldom as fat, with a fawn or tan-coloured coat. The key to their ecology is found in their complex, curiously lobed teeth. Crabeaters are filter-feeders, straining the rich summer plankton for krill — the small crustaceans which make up much of its bulk. Despite their numbers we know little of how they live. Small family groups — male, female and single pup — are sometimes seen together on the ice in September and October, suggesting a monogamous pattern of breeding that is rare among seals. Young crabeaters of two to three years seem to move towards the southern edge of the pack in summer, and are the ones most likely to be seen inshore among the Weddells.

Leopard seals, too, are surface feeders. Their molar teeth are lobed, though not so elaborately as those of crabeaters, and krill is an important part of their diet for some or all of the year. But they are also fierce predators with a taste for penguins and for other species of seals. Leopard seals breed almost exclusively in the pack ice — pups and yearlings are seldom seen.

Ross seals, too, are hunters, but their prey are mainly squid and fish, caught in midwater at depths below the pack ice. Their enormous eyes may be adapted for hunting in the dimly lit depths and their needle-like teeth are well suited to catching slippery prey. Slightly smaller on average than leopard and crabeater seals, with a small mouth and round head, they seem rarely to gather in large groups.

Killer whales are the main predators of all southern seals, with leopard seals a close second. Crabeater seals seem especially vulnerable. A high proportion of young ones carry open wounds or fresh scars in their skin and blubber — huge parallel gashes that tell of close encounters with one or other of their predators. Weddell seals, living closer inshore, have less to fear from killer whales except in summer, when the fast ice disperses. Though strong and agile swimmers, seals stand little chance against packs of killer whales if they cannot get out of the water. Even on floes they are not entirely safe.

Leopard seal
Hydrurga leptonyx
SIZE: Males to 3 metres (10 ft) long; weight about 350 kg (770 lb). Females 10 per cent larger than males.
DESCRIPTION: Various shades of grey shading from dark along the spine to pale on the belly. Conspicuous spots and patches on the head, neck and sides. Characteristic long sinuous body with head proportionally longer than with other seals.
BREEDING: Little is known about reproductive behaviour.
FOOD: Krill is an important part of the diet of leopard seals, which have lobed teeth for filtering, like crabeaters. They also hunt fish and squid, although penguins are their main food.

The sinuous body of a leopard seal. These usually solitary creatures are seldom seen in groups.

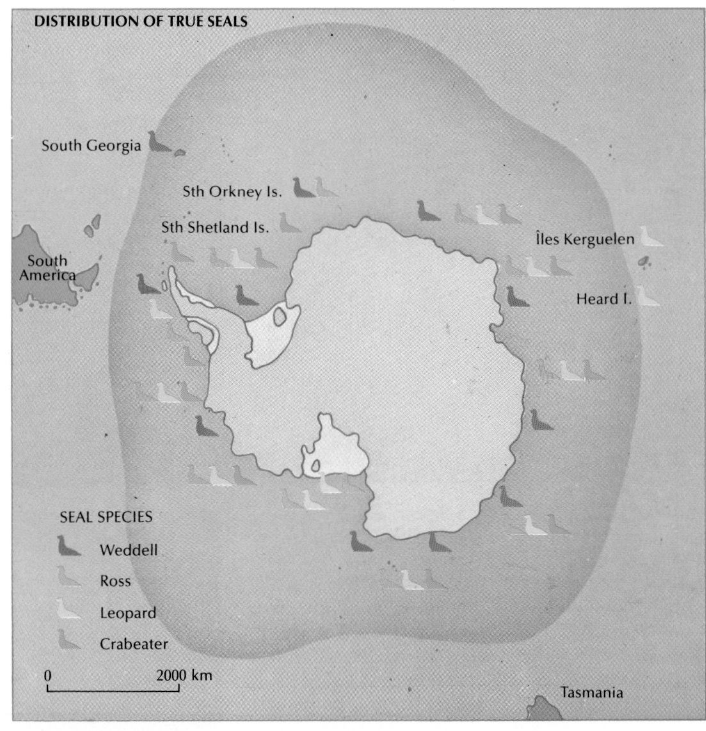

Distribution:
Weddell seals are found on fast ice all around the continent, and breed only as far north as South Georgia. Crabeaters inhabit the pack ice and rarely come inshore except in late summer. Leopard seals are common in the pack and throughout the Southern Ocean. Ross seals are also found in the pack.

ELEPHANT AND FUR SEALS

Two animals ruthlessly hunted by man

Many subantarctic beaches are shared by seals that represent two entirely different families. One is a true seal — the southern elephant — largest of its family. The other is the Kerguelen fur seal — a member of the family Otariidae, the so-called eared seals.

An adult Antarctic fur seal eyes the camera with disdain. The pinnae, or ear flaps, of fur seals and seal lions (family Otariidae) distinguish them from the true seals of the family Phocidae.

Largest and most spectacular of all southern seals are the southern elephant seals *Mirounga leonina* of the subantarctic. Grouped in a different family from the Antarctic species, these are the only true seals of the southern hemisphere in which the sexes show significant size difference. Both sexes are heaviest in early spring, about the time when the pups are born. Size may be related to feeding habits. Elephant seals take large fish and squid, and probably have to dive deep for them. The bigger the seal, the greater the economies in diving and hunting at depth.

Apart from their greater size, mature males are distinguishable by their 'trunk' or proboscis, a sac on the upper surface of the snout which, when fully inflated, overhangs the end of the upper jaw. Blown up during territorial disputes, the proboscis adds considerably to the appearance of the already massive head. Together with the open mouth it may also amplify the snorts and roars that accompany territorial battles. The proboscis first appears in the third or fourth year, but is not fully developed until the eighth or ninth year when the wearer first stands a reasonable chance of holding a territory and breeding.

Elephant seals breed on all the subantarctic islands, and on islands off southern South America. The biggest population — over 300000 strong — is based on South Georgia. Îles Kerguelen and Macquarie Island each have 100000 or more, and the total population of the southern oceans is estimated at 600000 to 700000. Few occur in the pack ice, but immature males are often found on the shores of Antarctica in summer.

Elephant seals begin their breeding in October, when mature bulls haul out onto the subantarctic beaches. Within a few days they are joined by the pregnant cows, which form closely packed groups of 20 to 30 around each bull. By mid-October most of the cows have given birth to their single pups. The bulls defend their harems vigorously from the attentions of interloping males.

Patrolling clumsily around the groups of cows and pups, the resident bulls or 'beachmasters' roar at rivals, mouth open and proboscis inflated. The interlopers roar back, often moving in and challenging ownership of cows and territory. If roaring fails to settle the dispute, the two may fight, rearing up and bashing each other solemnly with head and body until one or other retires exhausted. Fights often bring superficial damage, the blunt canine teeth cutting and ripping through the tough hide by the sheer weight of attack.

Newly born elephant seal pups measure just over a metre long (3.5 ft), weigh 34-41 kg (75-90 lb), and are covered all over in black woolly down. Three weeks later, when the

The head of a mature male elephant seal. The wrinkled skin on top of its nostrils can be inflated to form a trunk. This acts as a resonating chamber enabling the animal to produce a deafening roar when it is endeavouring to convince rivals to keep their distance.

Southern elephant seal
Mirounga leonina
SIZE: Males are 6-7 metres (20-23 ft) long; 3-4 metres (10-13 ft) in girth and weigh up to 4 tonnes. Females are seldom more than 3.5 metres (11.5 ft) long and may weigh 1 tonne.
DESCRIPTION: Males greyish brown with a paler belly; females dark brown. Mature males, 8-9 years old, have an inflatable trunk or proboscis.
BREEDING: Begins in October. Mature males have harems of around 20-30 females. Cows give birth to a single pup in mid-October. At birth pups weigh 34-41 kg (75-90 lb) and are 1 metre (3.5 ft) long, and covered in woolly down.
FOOD: Fish, crustacea, squid and octopus.

Elephant seals on a beach at King George Island in the South Shetlands. In the early part of the nineteenth century sealers stripped the beaches of these islands of most seals in a few short years.

Exploitation Stocks of southern elephant and Antarctic fur seals on islands of the Antarctic fringe are still recovering from the devastations of nineteenth century sealers. During the early years of the century virtually every island of the subantarctic, and all the seal-breeding islands south of the Convergence, were stripped of their fur seals by repeated visits from sealing ships. The South Shetland Islands alone, within four years of their discovery in 1819, yielded over 320000 fur seal skins to British and American sealers. When fur seals had been reduced to uneconomic levels, elephant seals were taken — not for their pelts, but for the oil contained in the thick layer of blubber beneath their skins.
Stocks of elephant seals may never have suffered such complete devastation as those of fur seals, but both were much reduced by the start of the present century. Oiling in the old-fashioned way continued on subantarctic Macquarie Island until 1919. On South Georgia a small seal oil industry was maintained until 1964. Total world population of southern elephant seals is estimated at 600000. World population of Antarctic fur seals is now estimated to have reached more than 300000.

A sealer's try pot, used for boiling down seal blubber to extract the oil. Relics of the sealers are found on many island beaches.

Alarmed at an apparent threat to his harem of eleven females, a large male elephant seal roars defiantly at the approaching human intruder. Males will fight vigorously to defend their territories and females.

supply of mother's milk ceases and the cows mate again, the pups have grown almost half a metre (20 in), quadrupled their birth weight, and shifted into sleek silver-grey fur. They enter the sea at four to five weeks, continuing to grow rapidly for the first year, then more steadily for the next 10 to 11 years. Females produce their first pup at three to four years. Males have little chance of breeding before their seventh year, and are unlikely to become territory holders until they have reached full length and weight.

Sharing the beaches on many subantarctic islands are seals of another family altogether — 'walking' seals of the family *Otariidae*. Otariids, commonly called 'eared seals' because of their small external ear-flaps or pinnae, include two sub-families, the sea-lions (Otariinae) and the fur seals (Arctocephalinae). Both are represented in the southern hemisphere, mostly in temperate latitudes. Both penetrate south to the warmer subantarctic islands, and one species — the Kerguelen fur seal *Arctocephalus tropicalis* — breeds on islands both north and south of the Antarctic Convergence. Small but significant differences in the pattern of their teeth, skull proportions and colour of fur separate stocks from northern and southern islands. Those breeding south of the Convergence on the South Orkney, South Shetland and South Sandwich Islands, South Georgia, Bouvetøya, Îles Kerguelen and Heard Island, form a separate sub-species of Antarctic fur seals, *Arctocephalus gazella*.

Like southern elephant seals, Antarctic fur seals show marked difference in size of the sexes. Adult males, almost two metres (6.5 ft) long from nose to tail, are stoutly built, with heavy neck and shoulders; their bulky appearance is enhanced by a striking mane or cape of long shoulder fur, and they weigh over 100 kg (220 lb). Females are only 1.5 metres (5 ft) long, more slenderly built, maneless, and weigh less than 50 kg (110 lb). Like all other fur seals and sea lions, but in marked contrast to true seals, they stand with fore and hind limbs under the body. Both hind flippers and elongate fore flippers point forward, with the tail curving down under the hindquarters. More agile than true seals on land, they run and walk briskly, scrambling over rocks and climbing even steep, tumbled scree slopes with great assurance.

A fur seal's fur consists of a dense velvety underpelt 2.5 centimetres (1 in) long, waterproof and virtually windproof, with an outer layer of coarse guard hairs. Sleek and wet when they emerge from the sea, a few violent shakes rid them of much of the water they carry among the guard hairs.

Antarctic fur seals breed in the late spring and early summer. Adult males haul out onto the traditional breeding beaches from September onward and stake out territories which they defend ferociously against each other. Three weeks to a month later the pregnant females appear, joining the bulls in harem groups of four or five. The pups, born in November and December, are less than half a metre (20 in) long at birth; weighing four to five kg (9-11 lb), they are swathed in black woolly fur which they keep throughout the summer. Though the mothers mate again within a few days of giving birth, they feed their pups for two to three months — far longer than true seals. To maintain their milk supply without losing condition they return to the sea during the feeding period. The pups find sheltered corners to hide in while their mothers are away, greeting them noisily with dog-like barking and whimpering on return.

Kerguelen fur seal
Antarctic fur seal
Arctocephalus tropicalis
Arctocephalus gazella
SIZE: Males two metres (7 ft) long; weight 100 kg (220 lb). Females: 1.5 metres (5 ft) long; weight 50 kg (110 lb).
DESCRIPTION: Dark grey along spine with distinctive yellow throat and chest; chestnut brown back from flippers. Mane on bulls.
BREEDING: Late spring. Males have harems of 4-5 females. Pups are born Nov.-Dec.
FOOD: Fish, crustaceans.

The dense, velvety fur of the fur seals almost led to their extinction. There was an insatiable demand from Europe and China for the skins at the end of the eighteenth century.

Fur seals, in this case Kerguelen fur seals, are much better at moving on land than the more clumsy true seals. They can run and walk, even over quite steep ground.

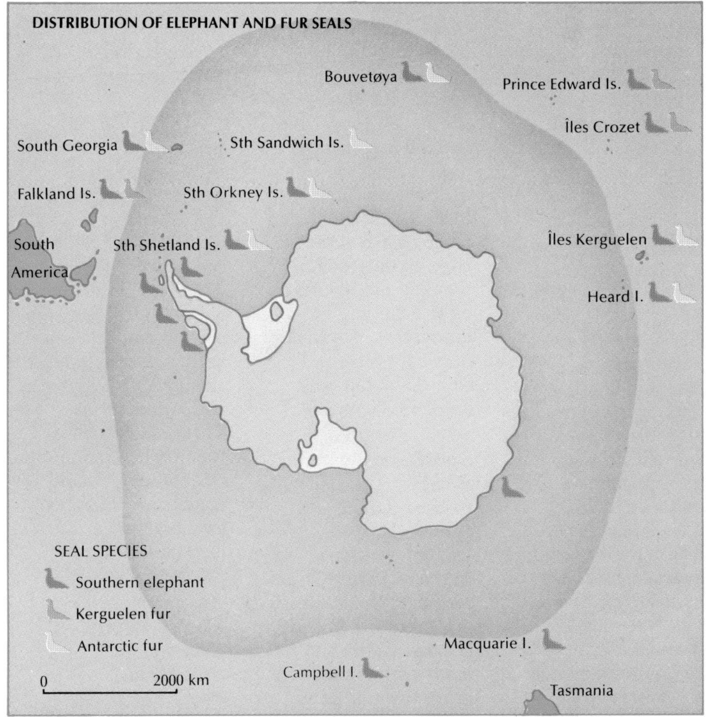

Distribution
Elephant seals breed on all subantarctic islands, with the biggest populations on South Georgia, Îles Kerguelen and Macquarie Island. Some immature males reach Antarctica in summer. Kerguelen fur seals breed both north and south of the Antarctic Convergence. Those to the south are a separate sub-species.

THE SOUTHERN WHALES 1

Survival of the world's largest animals in doubt

The largest animal that has ever lived on earth still survives today, although commercial hunting imposed a grave threat to its survival. This animal is the blue whale, which can grow to more than 30 metres (98 ft) in length.

With the other whales and their close relatives, the porpoises and dolphins, the blue whale is a mammal, belonging to the order Cetacea. Like all other mammals, it breathes air, develops its young internally and suckles them after they are born. In these essential features the cetaceans differ from the fishes. Their superficial resemblances in such things as streamlined shape and fins used for balancing and propulsion are secondary adaptations helpful to life in the water.

The Cetacea include about 75 species, of which about half are commonly called whales. There is, however, no scientific distinction which separates the whales from the others. In general the larger animals are called whales, while the smaller ones are mostly called dolphins and porpoises. The dividing line is roughly at an overall length of five metres (16 ft). The more important division is between those which have teeth, the Odontoceti or toothed whales, and those which have filtering structures, called baleen, in their mouths, the Mysticeti, or baleen whales.

The toothed whales include the great majority of the Cetacea — about 65 species as against 10 baleen whales. They include, however, only one large whale, the sperm whale, whose males can grow up to about 17 metres (56 ft) and females to 11 metres (36 ft). About 27 species are smaller whales ranging from some of the so-called beaked whales at about five metres (16 ft) to the killer and bottlenose whales at 10 metres (33 ft). The remainder are porpoises and dolphins, generally between two and five metres (6.5 and 16 ft) in length.

The baleen whales on the other hand are large animals ranging from the minke whale with a maximum size of 10 metres (33 ft) up to the blue whale. The only smaller species in the group is the rare pygmy right whale which grows to about six metres (20 ft).

Five of the baleen whale species are very similar in appearance, slender and highly streamlined. These, the blue, fin, sei, Bryde's and minke whales, are called rorquals. The other five species vary greatly in appearance.

The cetaceans, like all other mammals, are descended from small, four-footed terrestrial animals, which evolved from simple lizard-like reptiles, probably about 200 million years ago. Fossil remains have been found of large numbers of animals which represent stages in evolution of modern whales. The series is not yet sufficiently complete for the evolutionary chain to be reconstructed in detail.

In no part of the oceans of the world are cetaceans entirely absent, but individual species vary greatly in their distributions. Among the large baleen whales, two, the bowhead and the gray, are found only in the northern hemisphere. One, Bryde's whale, lives only in tropical and sub-tropical waters, and the right whale is restricted to temperate and cool-temperate seas in both northern and southern hemispheres. The remaining five species, the blue, fin, sei, minke and humpback, are almost universally distributed.

Among the toothed whales and dolphins only two are universally distributed, the sperm and killer whales. The other species show a variety in their distribution: some are widespread, others highly localised; some frequent the open oceans, others stay close to the coasts; some are found only in the tropics, others live

Six species of baleen whales are commonly found in southern waters. Most have been hunted and two, the blue and humpback whales, could be in danger of extinction.

Blue whale

Balaenoptera musculus
WEIGHT: 84 tonnes.
LENGTH: 24 m (79 ft).
The largest of all the whales. In their southern feeding migration, blue whales travel down to the edge of the ice and remain close to it for most of the southern summer. The northern migration takes place in the open ocean and their breeding grounds are still unknown. Blue whales in the Antarctic live almost entirely on krill. They were prime targets for whalers and by the 1950s had been reduced to negligible numbers. Only about 1000-5000 animals now survive, and it is not known if they are increasing.

Fin whale

Balaenoptera physalus
WEIGHT: 50 tonnes.
LENGTH: 20 m (66 ft).
The second largest of all the whales. Fin whales live and breed in the open oceans. They do not travel as far south as blue whales, and prefer to feed north of the ice edge. In the Antarctic they live almost entirely on krill and similar crustaceans. Fin whales have been protected since 1976, but only about 80 000 remain.

Southern right whale

Balaena glacialis australis
WEIGHT: 60 tonnes.
LENGTH: 15 m (50 ft).
Medium-sized whales that breed in herds in enclosed waters and bays, a habit that made them very vulnerable. A rewarding catch, they yield large quantities of oil and long baleen plates. They were the main support of the southern whaling industry until about 1850 by which time few remained. Their numbers may now be recovering.

Sei whale

Balaenoptera borealis
WEIGHT: 17 tonnes.
LENGTH: 16 m (52.5 ft).
Closely related to blue and fin whales, sei whales are smaller and more slender. They are oceanic and make long north-south migrations, although they only go as far south as about 55°S. Their numbers have been depleted since other whales became unavailable, and they have been protected in most parts of the Antarctic since 1978.

Minke whale

Balaenoptera acutorostrata
WEIGHT: 7 tonnes.
LENGTH: 8 m (26 ft).
Like their relatives, minke whales make north-south migrations, but little is known about the paths they take. When in the Antarctic they frequent the ice edge and feed mainly on krill. They were largely ignored by whalers until the early 1970s. From 1974-75 until the whaling moratorium in 1985, minkes were the principal baleen whale taken in Antarctic waters.

Humpback whale

Megaptera novaeangliae
WEIGHT: 31 tonnes.
LENGTH: 13 m (43 ft).
Humpback whales differ from the other baleen whales in that they are less slender and streamlined than the blue and other rorquals, and have very long flippers. While they resemble the others in making north-south migrations, they generally migrate close to coasts and breed in shallow water, often in lagoons among islands. Humpback stocks were reduced to only about 1000-3000 animals by the early 1960s.

Blue whale
Balaenoptera musculus

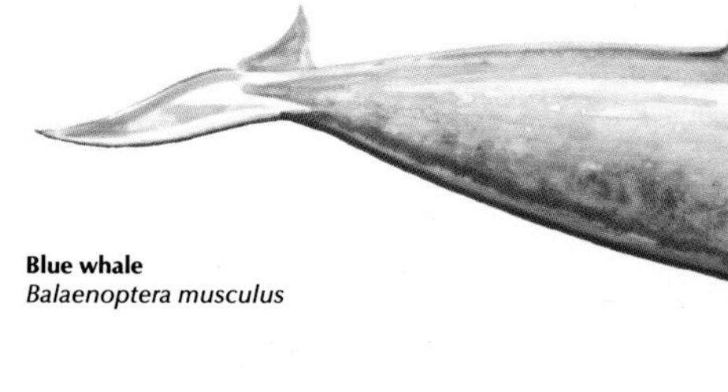

Southern right whale
Balaena glacialis australis

A humpback whale leaps from the water showing the extraordinary size of its water-filled mouth. Baleen whales fill their mouths with water and then squeeze it out through the baleen plates to filter out any food.

Tourists have replaced whalers on the waters of Lemaire Channel, off the west coast of the Antarctic Peninsula. A humpback whale obligingly dives beside the rubber dinghy to provide the occupants with photographs.

in cooler waters. Relatively few toothed whales inhabit the cold waters of the Southern Ocean. Only the sperm whale, two of the medium-sized whales, the killer and southern bottlenose, and two species of small dolphins are found there.

As would be expected from the nature of their mouths, there is a great difference between the feeding habits of the toothed and baleen whales. The toothed whales mostly have quite long jaws, often armed with a row of peg-like or cutting teeth. These teeth are well adapted for seizing or cutting up quite large and active prey, and these species feed mainly on fish and squid. The size of its prey varies with the size of the cetacean. At one extreme is the sperm whale which feeds mainly on squid and quite large fish; much of its prey consists of animals about one metre (3 ft) in length, but it is capable of tackling the giant squid with tentacles of 10 metres (33 ft) or more. The smaller beaked whales eat mainly small squid, and dolphins feed principally on small fish and squid.

The exception among the toothed whales is the killer whale. Although it may sometimes eat fish or squid it really prefers warm-blooded prey. This includes birds (penguins in the Antarctic), smaller cetaceans and seals. Packs of killer whales have been seen to attack fin and other whales larger than themselves, tearing mouthfuls of flesh from their living bodies.

The mouths of the baleen whales are equipped with curtains of several hundred triangular fibrous plates (really modified hairs) which hang from the sides of the upper jaw. These plates are called the baleen and form a filter with which the whales strain the water containing the small creatures on which they feed. The baleen plates are very large in the bowhead, up to four metres (13 ft) long, and in the right whales three metres (10 ft). In other species they are much smaller, well under one metre (3 ft) long even in the blue whale. The whales use their baleen in a variety of ways, but mostly by swimming through schools of their prey with their mouths open so that they skim out their victims; or by taking mouthfuls of water in which their prey is present and then squeezing out the water and swallowing the food left on the baleen. The food of baleen whales consists mainly of krill and other small crustaceans a few centimetres long, and of fish mostly up to about 20 centimetres (8 in) long.

All the cetaceans tend to live together in groups or schools, but the size of the schools varies greatly between species. The sperm whales have the most highly developed social structure. This is centred round the breeding herds which generally consist of 10-15 mature females, accompanied by their offspring of the last few years, and dominated by a large, mature male — the harem master. The young males leave the herds when they are a few years old and form schools with their own kind, but as they grow older they gradually disperse until by the time they are big enough to take command of a harem (when about 25 years old) they have become solitary.

The large baleen whales normally live in quite small groups, sometimes even singly. The groups generally include both sexes in more or less equal numbers, but it is not known whether any permanent pairing takes place, or whether they breed promiscuously.

The smaller toothed whales are generally seen in groups, but there is little evidence that they have an advanced social structure like the sperm whale. There is much variation in the size of the groups: the killer whale, for example, is generally found singly or in groups of up to 20, while the pilot whales form schools of 300 or more. Most of the porpoises living fairly close to the shore form quite small parties, but some of the oceanic dolphins are seen in schools of several hundred or even a few thousand. It is difficult to gain an understanding of the social structure of these animals because the groups are often unstable; the animals seem to split into small parties when travelling and then congregate in larger groups when sufficient food is found.

SOUTHERN BALEEN WHALES

The distinctive, shiny, black-and-white heads and sharp teeth of a pair of killer whales.

THE SOUTHERN WHALES 2

Many questions to be answered about whales

While quite a lot is known about some aspects of whale biology and behaviour, there are still huge gaps in our understanding of these extraordinarily complex creatures.

The pattern of reproduction in a wild animal species is difficult to study without examining large numbers of dead specimens. Therefore quite a lot is known about those large whales which have been extensively hunted during this century, and about a few species of dolphins such as those taken incidentally in fishing for tuna; but little or nothing is known about the others. There seems a surprising degree of similarity in the principal features between the different animals which have been studied. They all normally produce one young at a birth, with twins being very rare and larger numbers still more exceptional. The gestation period is about one year in most species, between 11 months in the large baleen whales and 16 months in the sperm; those dolphins which have been studied are between the two. The interval between births is generally two or three years and there is some evidence that it may become less if the population is depleted. Suckling commonly lasts about a year but in some species the young remain closely associated with their mothers for considerably longer periods. The females start to breed at five to eight years in baleen whales and some dolphins, at about 10 years in sperm whales; the males generally mature rather later.

Many cetaceans undertake quite long seasonal movements or migrations, but the most striking migrations are those performed by some baleen whales. In the Southern Hemisphere, the blue, fin, sei, humpback, and to some extent the minke whales, all migrate regularly between Antarctic and tropical waters. They spend the summer in the Antarctic feeding on the abundant supplies of krill, other crustaceans and small fish; then in the autumn they travel north to spend the winter in tropical waters, where they give birth to their young. Mating, and the conception of calves, takes place in the tropics, commonly a year after the preceding calf was born. Some of the smaller cetaceans have also been observed to move between cooler waters with abundant food in summer and warmer conditions, where breeding takes place, in winter.

A good deal is known about the migrating behaviour of a few species of whales which follow pathways close to shore and also breed in easily identifiable localities. The humpback, for instance, occurs worldwide but always follows the shorelines on its way from the Arctic or Antarctic to its breeding grounds on well-defined banks in tropical seas. The gray whale in the north Pacific breeds in summer in lagoons on the Mexican coast and then travels very close to the coast on its way north to the feeding grounds in the Bering Sea. Most of the other baleen whales, however, both travel and breed in the open ocean far from land and very little is known about routes they follow.

Being air-breathers, all the cetaceans, unlike fish, need to come to the surface at fairly frequent intervals to replenish their oxygen supply. Since they have to find their food below the surface, often at a considerable depth, their whole mode of life revolves around their ability to dive and remain submerged for quite long periods. Some of the fish-eating toothed whales in particular who find their food close to the sea bed, have to make very deep and prolonged dives. The sperm whale is outstandingly the best diver, descending to depths of 1000-2000 metres

SOUTHERN TOOTHED WHALES

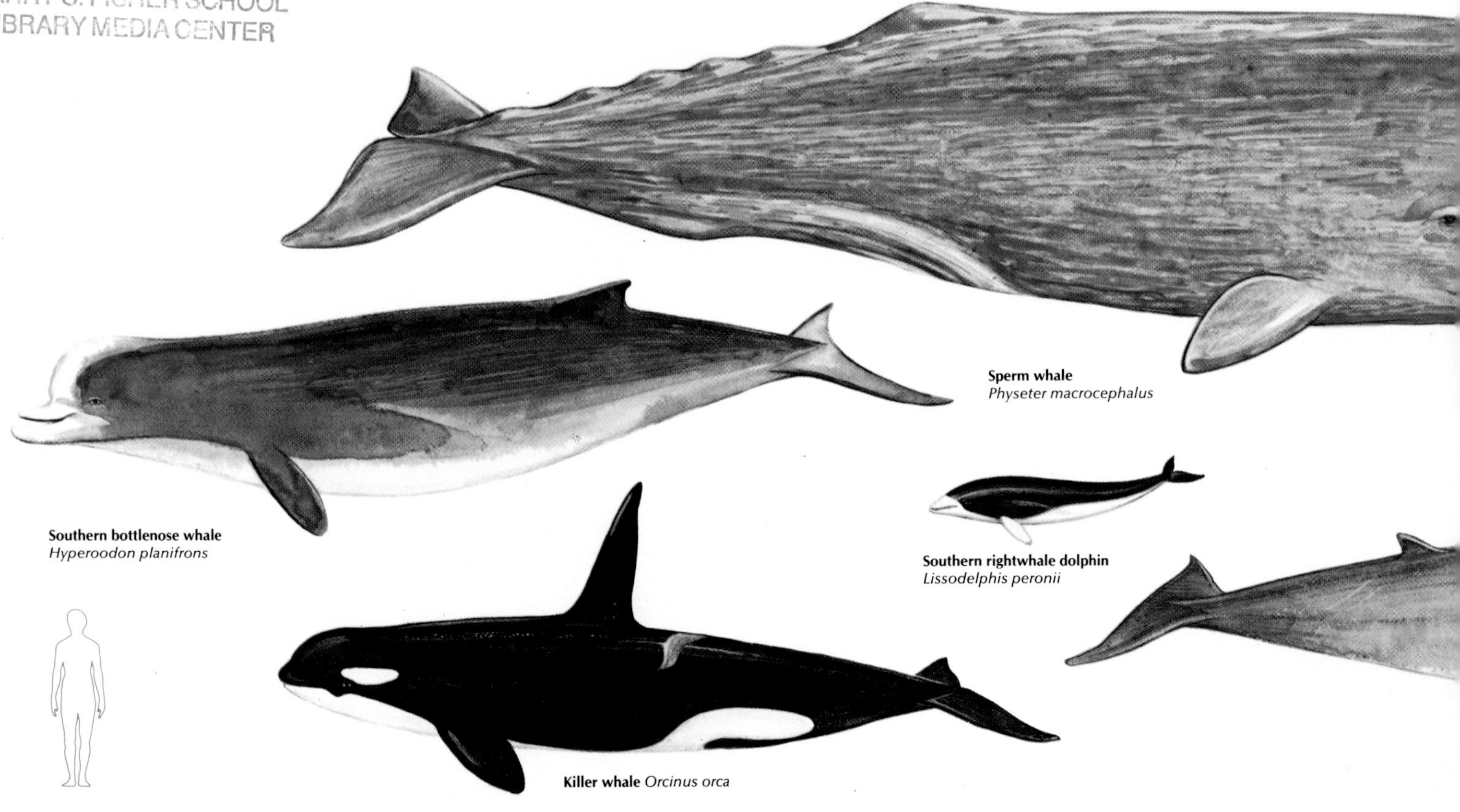

Sperm whale
Physeter macrocephalus

Southern bottlenose whale
Hyperoodon planifrons

Southern rightwhale dolphin
Lissodelphis peronii

Killer whale *Orcinus orca*

(3300-6600 ft) and remaining submerged for an hour or more. Some of the smaller toothed whales and dolphins also go down several hundred metres. The baleen whales, on the other hand, prey on plankton and small fish living in the surface layers of the ocean. They feed therefore mainly in the top 100 metres (330 ft) and their dives are correspondingly shallower and shorter.

The cetaceans, and particularly the sperm whale, have, during their evolution, acquired a number of special anatomical and physiological features which enable them to remain submerged for long periods and to resist the enormous pressures at great depths. The need to carry large quantities of oxygen down with them is met, not by having large lungs, but by special chemical characteristics in their blood which enable it to absorb much more oxygen than can, for example, human blood. The rate at which their bodies use up the oxygen is also reduced by closing down much of the circulatory system, so that the blood travels mainly between the heart, brain and lungs.

Living much of the time in almost total darkness, and even when near the surface often under conditions where vision is very limited, the cetaceans rely greatly on sound. All, or nearly all, species produce sounds: some, such as the dolphins, in great variety; others, such as some baleen whales, only a few. There is still much to learn about the uses to which these sounds are put, but they probably fall into two main categories. One group, mainly sharp clicks often produced in high-speed trains, may be used in a process of echo-location similar in principle to radar. In this way the animal may learn the distance to the sea bed or the surface, the presence of obstacles in its path or the position of prey.

Sounds in the other category may be used to pass information on to other individuals of the species. Some cetaceans, particularly among the dolphins, produce a great variety of sounds, but there is no evidence that any communication in a sophisticated or human sense occurs. The sounds probably mean little more than, for example, 'I am here' or 'I am frightened'. The much-publicised 'song' of the humpback whale is particularly interesting since it consists of a very complex series of sounds and may last for 20 minutes or more. At first hearing this could appear to be a sophisticated process of communicating information. However, research has found that in any one year all the humpbacks in an area are producing identical songs, and that next year the songs will be changed to some extent. It is difficult to imagine that, when all the songs are the same, any real interchange of information could be taking place.

There is still a great deal of debate among scientists as to the level of intelligence in the cetaceans. Some point to the large size and highly convoluted structure of cetacean brains, and the ease with which some species of toothed whales in captivity can learn quite complex behaviour as evidence of a very high level of intelligence. Some claim that it approaches that of humans. Other scientists believe that the large brains are required for the analysis of the sound signals which tell the animals about their environment. They are unimpressed by the evidence of learning ability as an indication of real intelligence and can find little sign of such intelligence in the normal behaviour of the animals in the wild.

Some scientists are seeking to communicate directly with the animals by trying to convey messages to them using the sounds they themselves use, and looking for any responses.

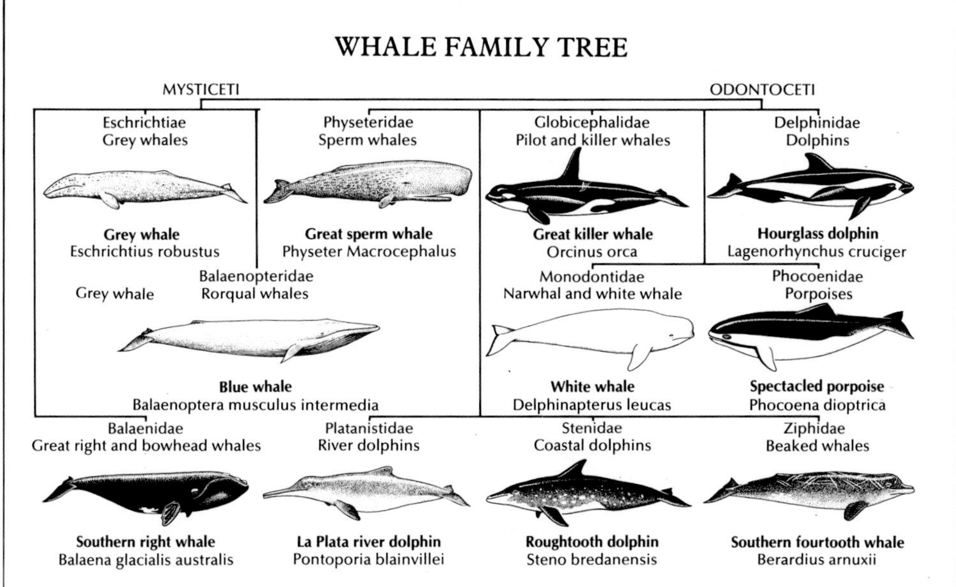

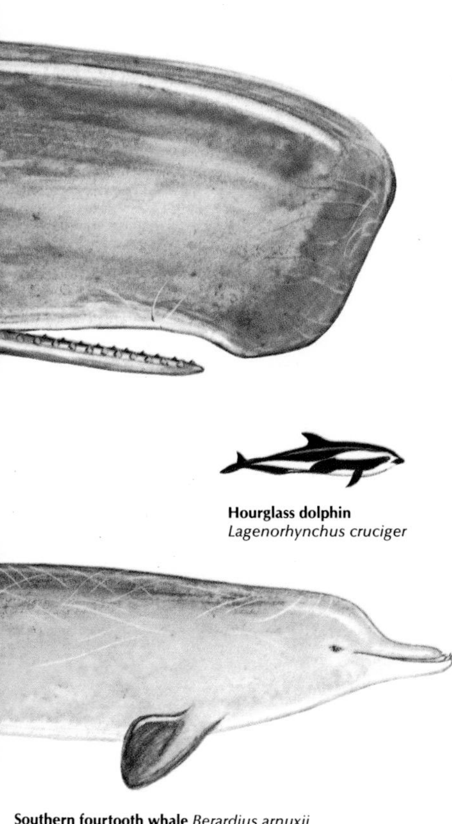

Hourglass dolphin *Lagenorhynchus cruciger*

Southern fourtooth whale *Berardius arnuxii*

Six species of toothed whales and dolphins are commonly seen in the waters around Antarctica. Most are much smaller than the baleen whales — only the sperm whale matches them in size. The sperm whale is also the only species to have been widely hunted.

Sperm whale

Physeter macrocephalus
WEIGHT: 30 tonnes.
LENGTH: 14 m (46 ft).
The largest of the toothed whales. Large herds of sperm whales were hunted in southern waters at the end of the 18th and the first half of the 19th centuries. In about 1860 the sperm whale fishery collapsed due to a decline in numbers of whales and fall-off in the demand for whale oil. Interest revived in the 1950s and about 5000 animals a year were caught from 1950-67. Declining numbers stopped hunting in 1979.

Killer whale

Orcinus orca
WEIGHT: 8 tonnes.
LENGTH: Males 7 m (23 ft); females 6 m (20 ft).
One of the most cosmopolitan of all whales, killers are found in all oceans from the tropics to the edge of the polar ice. They are common in the Antarctic waters where they feed largely on seals and penguins. Killer whales live mainly in small packs, which occasionally merge into large herds. The Antarctic population is estimated at about 200 000. In the Antarctic, whalers have shown little interest in killer whales, although about 900 were taken by Russian ships in 1978-79. Hunting was subsequently banned by the IWC.

Southern bottlenose whale

Hyperoodon planifrons
WEIGHT: 4 tonnes.
LENGTH: 8 m (26 ft).
There are two closely related species of bottlenose whales found in the northern and southern hemispheres respectively. The northern species is abundant, but the southern species is rarely seen. Bottlenose whales are characterised by their high, bulging foreheads and jaws in the form of a pronounced beak. They live in quite deep water and can stay submerged for an hour. They eat mainly squid. They are found quite close to the polar ice in summer but probably migrate, sometimes to tropical waters, in winter. Few of the southern species have been caught by whalers.

Southern fourtooth whale

Berardius arnuxii
WEIGHT: 8 tonnes
LENGTH: 11 m (36 ft).
The beaked whales are a large group, generally smaller than the bottlenose whales, with a less pronounced forehead. Only the southern fourtooth inhabits the Southern Ocean. It is very similar to the southern bottlenose whale and only an expert would be able to tell them apart. Little is known about it.

Dolphins

Only one species of dolphin is found throughout the icy waters around Antarctica — the hourglass dolphin (*Lagenorhynchus cruciger*). This animal is less than two metres (7 ft) long with striking black and white markings. They live in schools of from six to 40 animals, but little is known about their biology. The southern rightwhale dolphin (*Lissodelphis peronii*) sometimes enters southern waters, but it is essentially a warm water species. It is about 2.5 metres (8 ft) long.

THE ANTARCTIC PETRELS

Most numerous of all southern birds

Within the limits of the Antarctic Convergence breed 43 species of birds. Penguins are perhaps the group of Antarctic birds that everyone thinks of first. But despite their prominence, penguins take second place. Far more numerous are the petrels or 'tube noses'.

A traveller moving polewards across the tropical and subtropical zones of the southern oceans is passing through the maritime equivalent of deserts. The seas are azure or steely blue — always a sign of poor plankton. There may be flying fish, bonito and other game fish, perhaps a few dolphins and whales, but there will be very few sea birds, mostly isolated or in very small groups flying low over the waves. Pass through the temperate zones, through the Roaring Forties and Furious Fifties into the region of permanent pack ice, and you enter a different world. The seas are green-tinged with the reflections of millions of tiny plant cells, or reddened by shoals of krill and other crustaceans that swarm at the surface. Schools of whales, once numerous in this zone, are now rarely seen, though dolphins, almost untouched by commercial hunting, are still fairly plentiful. But the most prominent form of life among the pack ice of the Southern Ocean is birds.

Most numerous, in numbers and species, are the petrels which are found in all the world's oceans and all the climatic zones, though they are nowhere more prominent than in the far south. Common characteristics include their webbed feet, dense plumage, subdermal fat and tubular nostrils. The function of the tubes is uncertain, but petrels, like some other sea birds, secrete concentrated brine from glands above their eyes, and the tubes may help to drain it away. All petrels lay a single egg, large in proportion to their body size, and incubate for long periods. The smallest take 40 days or more, the largest 70-80 days. Superbly insulated against heat loss in waters far colder than their own body temperature, and equipped for taking food in a dozen different ways from the sea surface, petrels need few special adaptations for living south of the Antarctic Convergence. By breeding in spring and wintering at sea, they make the best possible use of their unpromising environment, avoiding the very low temperatures and thick snows of the land in winter, and using the brief summer and autumn — when food at sea is most plentiful — to rear their slowly growing chicks.

Largest of Antarctic petrels are the albatrosses. Breeding mainly on windblown slopes of tussock grass on islands north of the limit of pack ice, wandering, black-barred, grey-headed and light-mantled sooty albatrosses roam freely throughout the westerly wind belt, soaring and swooping in effortless gliding flight. They frequently appear also in the easterlies over the pack ice, venturing in summer to within sight of the Antarctic continent. Albatrosses feed by scanning the water, and settling to gobble fish, squid and plankton from the surface. Wandering albatrosses, which are solitary breeders, lay their eggs in mid-November, and keep their chicks in the nest for about a year. The smaller species, with wing spans of two metres (7 ft), lay in October or November. Black-browed and grey-headed albatrosses (also called mollymawks) breed colonially in vast hillside colonies. Light-mantled sooty albatrosses nest on solitary ledges. All manage to bring their chicks to fledging by April or May, completing breeding and moult before the onset of winter.

A light-mantled sooty albatross chick. Both parents leave to forage at sea when the chick is about one month old.

The great size of a fully grown adult albatross is best appreciated when it can be compared to a human figure.

Giant petrels, comparable in size with the smaller albatrosses, are strongly built scavengers of the Southern Ocean with a characteristic flapping and gliding flight. The two species, northern and southern, resemble

Antarctic birds It is no accident that most of the birds found in Antarctica are sea birds. Generally larger than land birds, with dense plumage that protects them against the chill of the cold ocean, sea birds were well adapted for living in cool marine environments long before the polar regions existed. With the development and spread of polar icecaps two to five million years ago, much of the habitable land in high latitudes disappeared under ice and snow. Trees and shrubs vanished, forests and grasslands were replaced by tundra and polar desert. As terrestrial habitats disappeared, so too did the land birds, leaving sea birds in sole possession of the remaining patches of habitable ground. Feeding at sea, using the coasts only for breeding, sea birds have flourished ever since.

A chick peers from beneath the tail feathers of a grey-headed albatross.

A colony of grey-headed albatrosses on the cliffs of South Georgia.

A black-browed albatross feeding its chick. Nests are often found on steep, windswept hillsides.

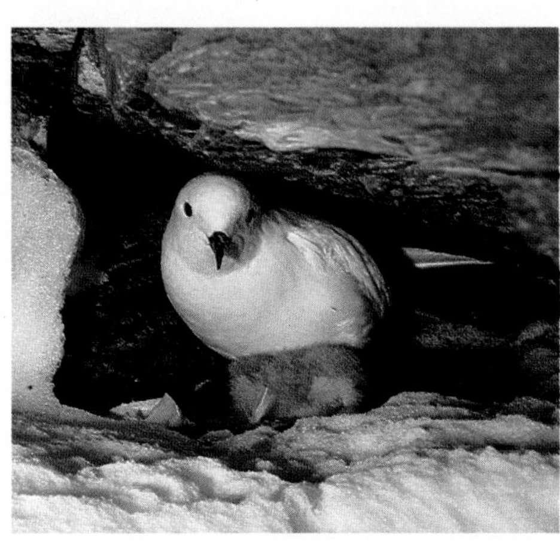

Snow petrel and chick. The pure white feathers of the adult conceal a black underdown that absorbs solar radiation.

Distribution Forty-three species of birds breed within the Antarctic Convergence, practically all of them marine birds that feed exclusively or mainly at sea. The seven species of penguins are dealt with on pages 40-43 and the twelve species of skuas, gulls, terns, cormorants and miscellaneous land birds that breed south of the Antarctic Convergence are on pages 54-55. The chart (right) shows the breeding distribution of the 24 species of Antarctic petrels (order Procellariiformes). Ranging in size from albatrosses with a wing span of 3 metres (10 ft), to storm petrels no bigger than thrushes, they include representatives of all the families of petrels. The southernmost breed on the continent itself, and many forage across the Southern Ocean.

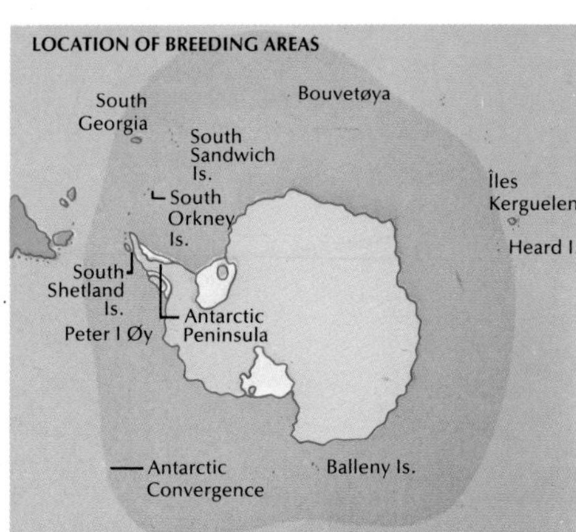

heavyweight mollymawks in manoeuvrability, with more massive bills. Feeding mainly on plankton and fish, they also attack and kill other birds. They even enter penguin colonies to gobble unwary chicks, and avidly clean up seal and whale carcases ashore and afloat. The darker northern species breed in the subantarctic and on Îles Kerguelen. Birds of the southern species, coloured light, intermediate or dark, breed mainly on islands south of the Convergence, but overlap with the northern form on several islands of the subantarctic.

The lesser fulmarine petrels of the Antarctic, all much smaller, nest colonially on bare ledges and in cavities of cliffs and scree slopes. Antarctic petrels — handsome brown or white birds often seen over the pack ice — breed only on continental Antarctica. Southern fulmars, snow petrels and the chequered Cape petrels breed on the continent and also on islands to the north, Cape petrels extending well into the subantarctic. They feed on plankton and small fish, settling on the water where food can be seen, and pecking busily. Snow petrels and Antarctic petrels are seldom far from floating ice. Southern fulmars prefer open waters, though they are mostly found within the pack ice zone. Cape petrels keep clear of heavy pack ice, but otherwise range very widely across the Southern Ocean from the shores of Antarctica to the Subtropical Convergence and beyond. Often they feed with other species in noisy mixed flocks numbering many thousands.

The great flocks of feeding petrels that are so much a feature of southern waters include both subantarctic and Antarctic breeding birds. Typically, the smaller petrels breed on open, windswept hillsides, in burrows deep among the roots of the tussock grasses. Within the Antarctic zone these conditions are found only to the north of the northern limit of pack ice, on South Georgia, Îles Kerguelen and Heard Island. A few species make do with burrowing in thinner, moss-covered soils, or even with deep crevices on bare, rocky hillsides. These can live on the colder islands that are surrounded by pack ice throughout the year. The small petrels seldom appear over land in daylight. Both burrowing and nocturnal habits protect them from the attentions of predatory skuas, which are usually present.

At sea they feed and fly together, benefiting from each other's ability to find rich patches of planktonic food, and avoiding competition by different methods of hunting. The shearwaters — grey petrels and white-chinned petrels — dabble for squid and krill at the surface but also dive and take their prey below the surface. The prions — three species which breed south of the Convergence — flutter delicately over the water, dabbling and filtering through tiny bill plates to trap fine particles of plankton. Differences in shape of bill between the species suggest that, even within the group, they seek different sizes and forms of prey, and the three have separate but overlapping feeding ranges. The gadfly petrels take squid, fish and other large prey by dipping, seldom settling on the surface. Tiny storm petrels patter over the water in search of smaller fish and crustaceans, while the diving petrels flutter above the waves and take their food in shallow dives.

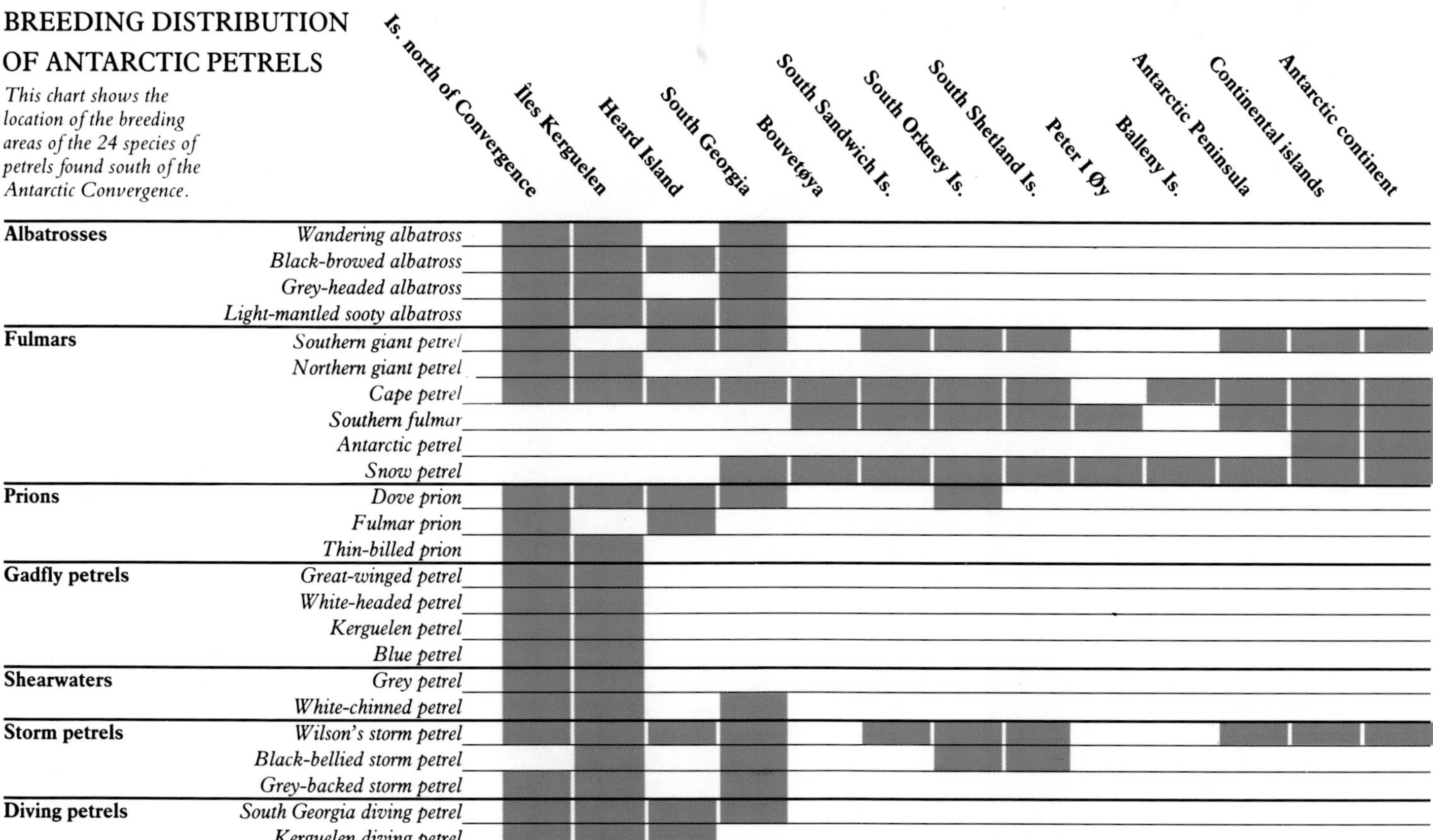

BREEDING DISTRIBUTION OF ANTARCTIC PETRELS

This chart shows the location of the breeding areas of the 24 species of petrels found south of the Antarctic Convergence.

		Is. north of Convergence	Îles Kerguelen	Heard Island	South Georgia	Bouvetøya	South Sandwich Is.	South Orkney Is.	South Shetland Is.	Peter I Øy	Balleny Is.	Antarctic Peninsula	Continental islands	Antarctic continent
Albatrosses	*Wandering albatross*	■	■		■									
	Black-browed albatross	■	■	■	■									
	Grey-headed albatross	■	■		■									
	Light-mantled sooty albatross	■	■	■	■									
Fulmars	*Southern giant petrel*	■		■	■		■	■	■			■	■	■
	Northern giant petrel	■	■											
	Cape petrel	■	■	■	■	■	■	■	■		■	■	■	■
	Southern fulmar					■	■	■	■	■		■	■	■
	Antarctic petrel												■	■
	Snow petrel				■	■	■	■	■	■	■	■	■	■
Prions	*Dove prion*	■	■	■	■			■						
	Fulmar prion	■		■										
	Thin-billed prion	■	■											
Gadfly petrels	*Great-winged petrel*	■	■											
	White-headed petrel	■	■											
	Kerguelen petrel	■	■											
	Blue petrel	■	■											
Shearwaters	*Grey petrel*	■	■											
	White-chinned petrel	■	■		■									
Storm petrels	*Wilson's storm petrel*	■	■	■	■		■	■	■			■	■	■
	Black-bellied storm petrel		■		■			■	■					
	Grey-backed storm petrel	■	■		■									
Diving petrels	*South Georgia diving petrel*	■	■	■	■									
	Kerguelen diving petrel	■	■	■										

Birds Of Land And Shore

Seabirds vastly outnumber those that live ashore

Alongside the countless millions of birds that inhabit the open ocean around Antarctica are a very much smaller number of inshore birds that catch most of their food in shallow waters, and the land birds that feed entirely ashore. These go about their business in solitary pairs or as small groups.

Largest and most colourful of the shore-living birds south of the Antarctic Convergence are the two species of cormorants or shags. By far the most common is the blue-eyed cormorant that breeds in small, widely scattered colonies throughout the Scotia Arc and along the western side of Antarctic Peninsula to Marguerite Bay. A closely related form, usually considered a sub-species, breeds on Heard Island. A similar but distinct species, the Kerguelen cormorant, is widely distributed on subantarctic islands, breeding only on Îles Kerguelen in the Antarctic zone.

Like coastal cormorants the world over these two species nest close to the sea, usually on cliffs or slabs of rock near sheltered water, in colonies of up to a few dozen pairs. They feed by diving and swimming underwater, in shallow channels and among reefs where they can take squid, bottom-feeding fish, and worms and molluscs from the mud. Sometimes they feed communally, a dozen or more in line across the water.

Blue-eyed and Kerguelen cormorants differ only slightly in appearance, and have similar breeding habits. Their nests are piles of seaweed and feathers cemented by guano. Their eggs, laid in a long season from October to January, take five weeks to hatch and the young birds — usually two, three or four to a nest — are ready for the sea by February or March. After April both young and adults disperse from the breeding colonies, though they do not travel far.

Only one species of true gull breeds in the Antarctic region — the large, black and white Dominican gull, which is widespread also throughout the subantarctic and a native of South Africa, South America and New Zealand. Dominican gulls breed on all the islands of the Scotia Arc, on the Antarctic Peninsula south to Marguerite Bay, and on Heard Island and Îles Kerguelen. Pairs nest alone or in small

Small niche The huge expanses of the southern oceans support enormous numbers of pelagic sea birds. In comparison, the areas of islands and coasts available for the birds to feed on are small and widely scattered. Hence the dense colonies of penguins, and vast cities and underground warrens where petrels crowd by the thousands for breeding each year. In temperate regions and the Arctic many species take up a shore-going way of life — sea ducks for example — and land-living birds form the great majority of breeding species over most of the world. But only a few kinds of birds have moved south to occupy similar niches.

A blue-eyed cormorant and chicks at Port Lockroy on the Antarctic Peninsula.

Birds that nest in Antarctica must be capable of surviving the savage polar climate.

A pair of sheathbills. These pigeon-like birds are often seen scavenging around penguin colonies.

Land birds Only three species of land birds manage to live permanently south of the Antarctic Convergence. South Georgia supports a pintail duck, closely related to the brown pintail of South America. Most common on marshy ground close to the coast, it breeds in November, usually managing to raise two or three chicks from clutches of five yellow-brown eggs. A similar, but unrelated pintail, of Indian origin, breeds on Îles Kerguelen. South Georgia also supports a resident species of pipit, a small songbird of lowland grasses and meadows. It feeds on insects, crustaceans and other tiny animals.

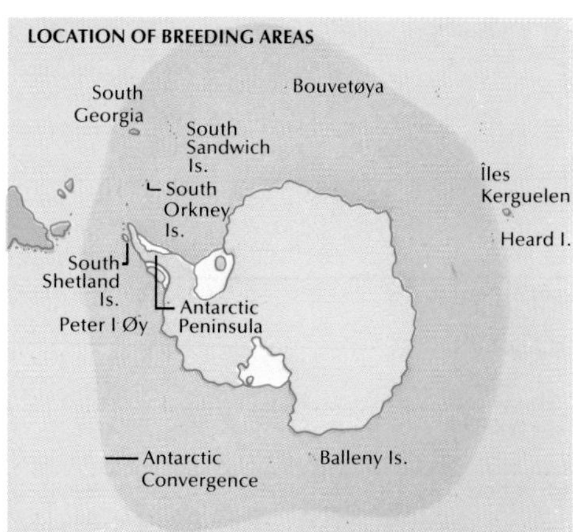

A map of Antarctica and its surrounding islands shows the location of breeding grounds south of the Convergence detailed in the chart (right).

A pair of great skuas attempt to make a meal of a young Adélie penguin chick, which seems to be quite capable of defending itself against these fierce predators. Sharp-witted and observant, skuas are constantly on the watch for food. Fish and plankton, caught close inshore, are important in their diet. They feed on beaches and among rocks at low tide, and will scavenge eggs or ailing and wandering chicks if they can. Other small skuas are attacked in flight, and they will tuck into carcases.

scattered groups, laying two or three mottled eggs in November or December. Typically of large gulls, the eggs hatch in less than a month, and the chicks reach independence in six to Kelp gulls are opportunists, and they feed Dominican gulls are opportunists, feeding where and when they can. On the Antarctic fringe they remain in residence throughout the year. Their southern breeding grounds are deserted for the winter months, and they are among the first to return in spring.

Antarctic terns are summer-breeding visitors to the Antarctic Peninsula, Scotia Arc islands, and most other islands in the Antarctic and subantarctic zones. A second, very similar species of black-capped tern breeds on Îles Kerguelen and neighbouring groups of islands in the Indian Ocean, where it is resident throughout the year.

Antarctic and Kerguelen terns nest in small colonies of up to a dozen pairs, usually on fine gravel or turf. Their one to three eggs, and the chicks that hatch out of them, match their background exactly. Intruders in a colony are mobbed severely by the parents, whose screaming and sharp, jabbing bills keep away gulls, skuas, and even wandering seals. During the breeding season terns catch their food in shallows just beyond the shoreline, even in rock pools when the tide is out. They dip delicately for tiny fish and particles of plankton, seldom settling for more than a second. After breeding they disperse, sometimes remaining in family parties for a few weeks. Kerguelen terns stay close to their islands in winter, but Antarctic terns disappear from the breeding grounds, probably wintering among the pack ice and open water beyond.

Call in at any Antarctic island or coastline in summer, and the first residents to notice your presence will almost certainly be skuas. Closely related to gulls, but brown, more heavily built, and far more aggressive, the two species of Antarctic skuas are very similar in habits of breeding, feeding and behaviour towards intruders. Great skuas, the more northerly form, breed throughout the subantarctic, the northerly Antarctic islands and the Scotia Arc. South Polar skuas, smaller, paler, with shorter bill and feet, breed entirely on the continent and southern Antarctic Peninsula.

Skuas spend their winters at sea. How far they travel is not known, but there are good records of great skuas as far afield as the West Indies, and of South Polar skuas off India, North America and Japan. They return to breed in the southern spring, taking up their traditional territories, building rough nests of pebbles, bones and moss, and laying two brown mottled eggs. Some skuas take inland territories, usually on hilltops within sight of the sea, and often where petrels are nesting. But most take up coastal territories, and may include within them part of a colony of penguins or petrels. Skuas defend their territories ferociously, swooping on intruders and hitting them with hard, leathery feet. They usually rear only one chick — the first to hatch out — and young and adults are ready to leave the breeding areas by April.

Sheathbills are small, white, pigeon-like birds with leathery facial wattles. There are two species, the larger wattled sheathbill breeding on the Antarctic Peninsula and the Scotia Arc, and the lesser sheathbill breeding on Heard Island, Îles Kerguelen, and subantarctic islands in the Indian Ocean sector. True land birds, with origins in coastal South America, the sheathbills scavenge entirely on land — on beaches, intertidal rocks, penguin and cormorant colonies, and even in seal wallows where they eat faeces, placentae and dead pups. They congregate in small groups wherever food is present, but breed in solitary pairs, laying two to four eggs in well-concealed nests, usually in crevices among rocks. Lesser sheathbills remain on their islands through the winter. Wattled sheathbills migrate from southern breeding grounds

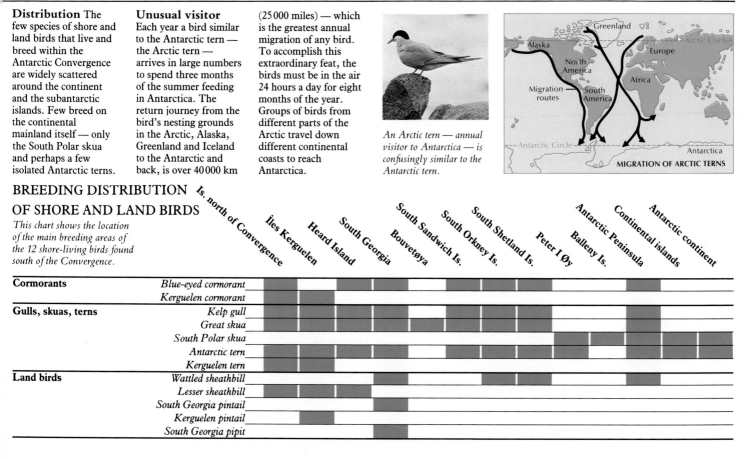

Distribution The few species of shore and land birds that live and breed within the Antarctic Convergence are widely scattered around the continent and the subantarctic islands. Few breed on the continental mainland itself — only the South Polar skua and perhaps a few isolated Antarctic terns.

Unusual visitor
Each year a bird similar to the Antarctic tern — the Arctic tern — arrives in large numbers to spend three months of the summer feeding in Antarctica. The return journey from the bird's nesting grounds in the Arctic, Alaska, Greenland and Iceland to the Antarctic and back, is over 40000 km (25000 miles) — which is the greatest annual migration of any bird. To accomplish this extraordinary feat, the birds must be in the air 24 hours a day for eight months of the year. Groups of birds from different parts of the Arctic travel down different continental coasts to reach Antarctica.

An Arctic tern — annual visitor to Antarctica — is confusingly similar to the Antarctic tern.

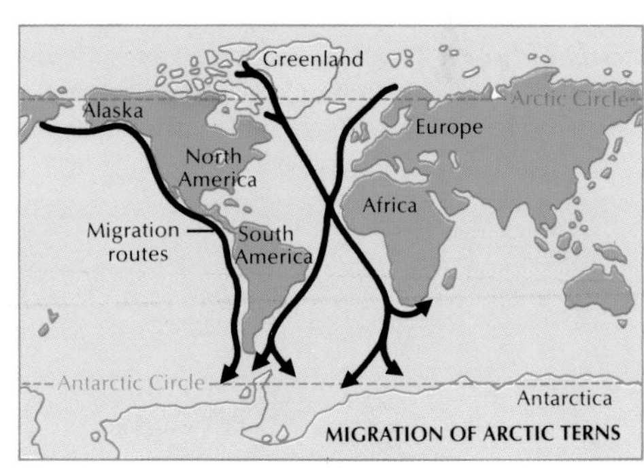

BREEDING DISTRIBUTION OF SHORE AND LAND BIRDS

This chart shows the location of the main breeding areas of the 12 shore-living birds found south of the Convergence.

		Is. north of Convergence	Îles Kerguelen	Heard Island	South Georgia	Bouvetøya	South Sandwich Is.	South Orkney Is.	South Shetland Is.	Peter I Øy	Balleny Is.	Antarctic Peninsula	Continental islands	Antarctic continent
Cormorants	*Blue-eyed cormorant*	■		■	■		■	■	■			■		
	Kerguelen cormorant	■	■											
Gulls, skuas, terns	*Kelp gull*	■	■	■	■		■	■	■			■		
	Great skua	■	■	■	■	■	■	■	■			■		
	South Polar skua									■	■	■	■	■
	Antarctic tern	■	■	■	■		■	■	■	■		■	■	■
	Kerguelen tern	■	■											
Land birds	*Wattled sheathbill*				■			■	■			■		
	Lesser sheathbill	■	■	■										
	South Georgia pintail				■									
	Kerguelen pintail		■											
	South Georgia pipit				■									

THE ISLANDS

Bleak outposts in the stormy Southern Ocean

Of all the continents, Antarctica is the most isolated from other lands. Pressed down by the weight of its icecap, its continental shelves are both narrower and deeper than those of other continents. It therefore has few offshore islands which have not been submerged beneath the sea on its depressed continental shelves, or else overridden by the outward-flowing ice sheets from the continental land mass itself.

Only along the Scotia Arc, between the eastern tip of Tierra del Fuego and the northern tip of the Antarctic Peninsula, is there an interrupted chain of islands and shallower seas linking Antarctica to another continent. Elsewhere, only a few remote and isolated islands pierce the surface of a deep ocean which forms an almost uninterrupted belt of water, 2500 kilometres (1550 miles) or more wide, separating Antarctica from other lands to the north. Between 40°S and the coast of Antarctica almost the entire surface of the planet is ocean. These broad stretches of the South Atlantic, South Pacific and South Indian Oceans which surround the Antarctic are known as the Southern Ocean.

From 46°S latitude to the Antarctic coast, the Southern Ocean includes only nine islands or island groups which are not situated in shallow seas close to the continent. A further five island groups lie in the Scotia Arc connecting South America to the Antarctic. Another five groups of islands to the east and south of New Zealand rise from the remnants of submerged continental land. To those 19, more or less isolated islands or island groups of the Southern Ocean, may be added a number closer to Antarctica itself. Some of these are now connected to the continent by permanent ice and do not therefore have many of the characteristics of islands. Islands lying near the coasts of South America, southern New Zealand and Tasmania are not considered here.

Except for the Falklands and South Georgia, and the islands lying near the Antarctic Peninsula, almost all the islands in the Southern Ocean are geologically young and volcanic. Some of these are still active — such as Bouvetøya, the South Sandwich, Heard and Peter I Islands — or have been active within the last few thousand years — such as Marion Island and Îles Crozets. Others are the remnants of older volcanoes situated on the Kerguelen and Campbell plateaux, and have long been extinct. The islands formed by the past activity of these older volcanoes include some sedimentary rocks, and are parts of now foundered fragments of continental land. The isolated mid-ocean islands on the flanks of the actively spreading mid-ocean ridges, are small, steep and mountainous with rocky coasts under continual attack from the ocean. None has any extensive sandy or muddy beaches. Their landscapes are young and have been moulded by constant wave erosion on their unsheltered coasts, by icecaps and glaciers that have affected most of them within the last 20 000 years — and which still cover those on the fringes of the Antarctic seas — and by the effects of wind, frosts and rain in their stormy climates.

The present climates of the islands are dominated by the characteristics of their surrounding seas. Most are under the influence of the cool, moist maritime air off the Southern Ocean: only those closest to the Antarctic come under the influence of dry, stable continental air masses. The position of the oceanic convergences — the zones where different water masses meet and mix — has a controlling effect on their climates. The westerly wind belt, in which most of the islands lie, is continually in violent motion. The islands therefore have cold, boisterous, squally, cloudy weather. Stable anticyclonic conditions are rare, and prolonged local heating or cooling are probably unknown away from the influence of Antarctica itself. Rain or snow falls throughout the year, and precipitation increases with the distance of the islands from the Antarctic coast. However, local terrain has a great effect on the amount of precipitation received at different places on the same island.

The islands of the Southern Ocean south of 46°S can be put into four categories according to their air temperatures at sea level and their vegetation. Antarctic coastal and maritime islands lie near the continent. They have climates dominated by their proximity to Antarctica, and to sea ice: these are true Antarctic islands. The subantarctic and temperate isothermal islands are less directly affected by the Antarctic continent, but more by the characteristics of their surrounding ocean waters.

Permanent research and weather stations which are supplied and relieved annually by sea have been established on all the cold, temperate isothermal island groups except the Aucklands, Snares, Bounty and Antipodes. None of the islands has an airstrip for long range fixed-wing aircraft, but airports are under construction on the Falklands and Îles Kerguelen. Surveillance of the krill-rich seas nearby and to the south of the Antarctic Convergence may lead to further airstrips being built in furture. Human use of the islands at present is mainly for scientific research, meteorology and environmental monitoring of the ocean and atmosphere, and continuing research on the huge populations of seabirds and mammals which breed ashore, and feed in the surrounding oceans. Conservation of native plants and animals, and control of imported species, is now an important consideration governing human activities on all islands.

THERMOISOPLETHS

The thermoisopleths on the right show the temperature to be expected at any season and at any time of the day or night. Mean hourly air temperature throughout the day (vertical axis) and throughout the year (horizontal axis) are plotted at 1°C intervals. Midday and summer are across the middle of each plot.

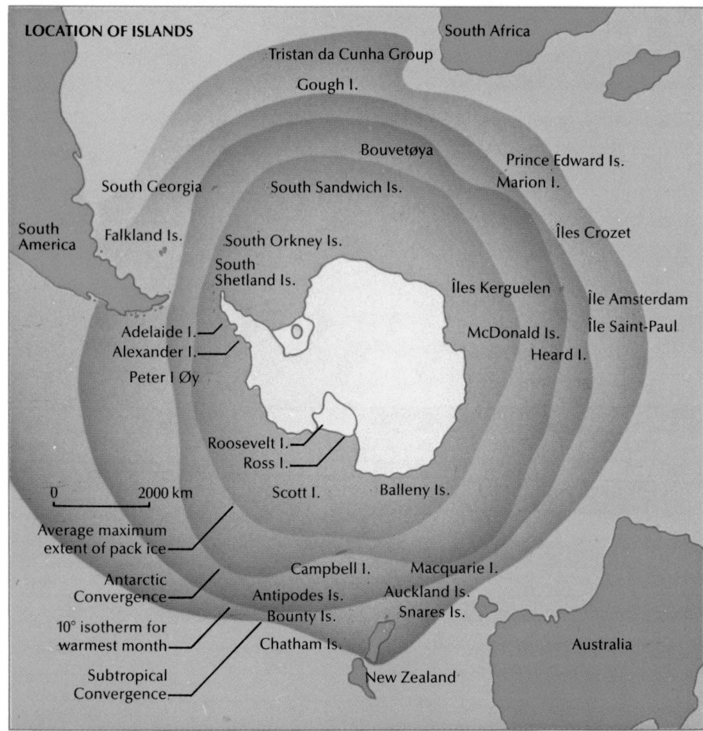

Distribution of islands around Antarctica. The shaded lines show a number of boundaries that influence climatic patterns and the distribution of plants and animals. The boundaries change from season to season

DIFFERENT HEMISPHERES

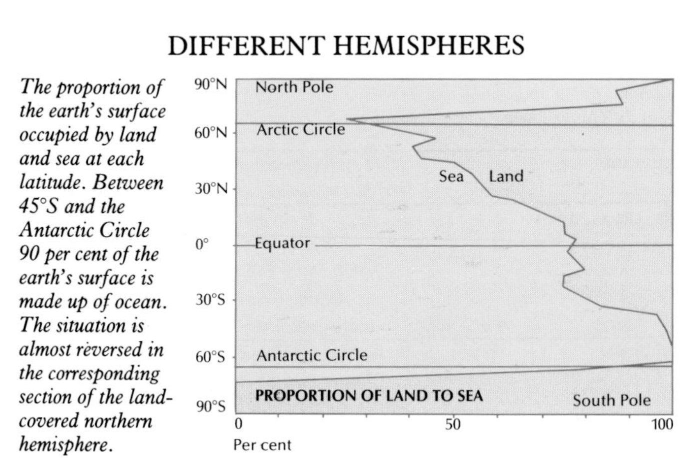

The proportion of the earth's surface occupied by land and sea at each latitude. Between 45°S and the Antarctic Circle 90 per cent of the earth's surface is made up of ocean. The situation is almost reversed in the corresponding section of the land-covered northern hemisphere.

Antarctic coastal islands

This group includes Alexander, Thurston, Ross, Roosevelt and Berkner Islands

These more or less ice-covered islands are beset by pack ice for much of the year, and are subject to the direct influence of cold, dry air from the Antarctic continent. Monthly mean air temperatures do not rise above freezing point even in summer, and mean annual air temperatures are −9°C (16°F) or lower. Precipitation falls as snow. Rain is unknown. Conditions on all these islands probably differ little from those on the nearby mainland. Little rock is visible and there are very few plants. Ice-free rocky areas attract large summer breeding colonies of sea birds and several species of penguins.

Ice links Alexander Island to the continent.

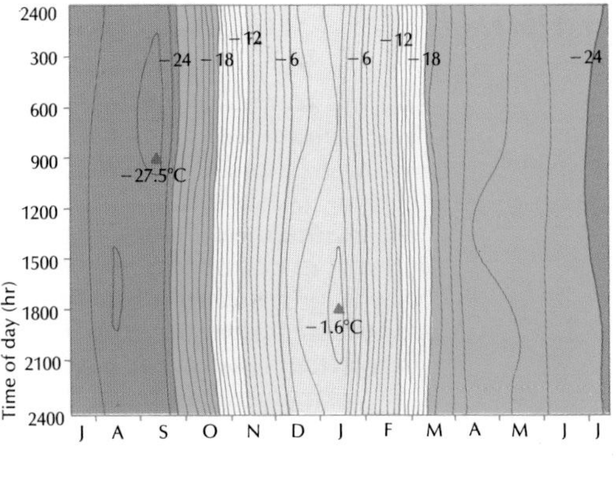

Thermoisopleth diagram for Ross Island.

Antarctic maritime islands

Bouvetøya, South Orkney, South Shetland, South Sandwich, Peter I, Scott and Balleny Islands

These islands are subject to the maritime influence of the Southern Ocean, and are surrounded by pack ice in winter. Mean monthly air temperatures rise above freezing for only short periods in summer, and mean annual air temperatures probably range from −7°C (19°F) to freezing point. Only two species of flowering plants are found among the few that grow on some of the islands near the peninsula which also have deep peat banks formed by slow moss growth. Some islands support huge numbers of breeding penguins and petrels. There are scientific stations on many of the islands near the peninsula.

Snow and ice cover most of King George Island.

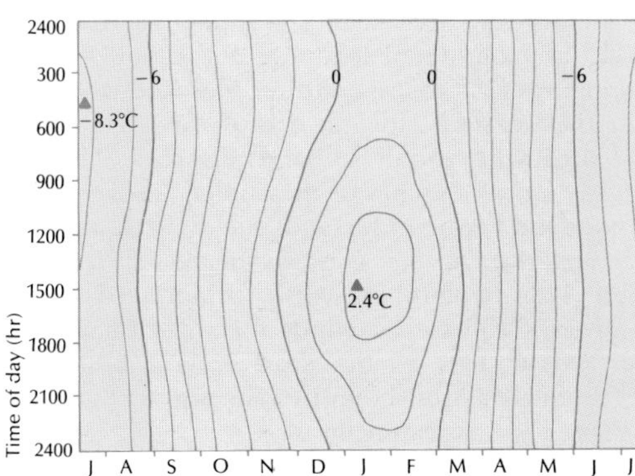

Thermoisopleth diagram for Deception Island.

Subantarctic islands

South Georgia, Heard and MacDonald Islands

These wet, windy islands lie near the Antarctic Convergence. Mean annual temperatures at sea level are between freezing point and 3°C (37°F). Coasts are seldom closed in by pack ice, but they have icecaps, and glaciers that descend to sea level. More than half of South Georgia and most of Heard Island is ice-covered and they experience furious katabatic gales. Native land vegetation consists of coastal tussock grassland, with limited areas of wet, peaty herbfields. Numbers of elephant and fur seals breed ashore in summer. There are no native woody plants. Attempts to establish cold-tolerant trees and shrubs on South Georgia have been unsuccessful.

Kerguelen cabbage on Heard Island.

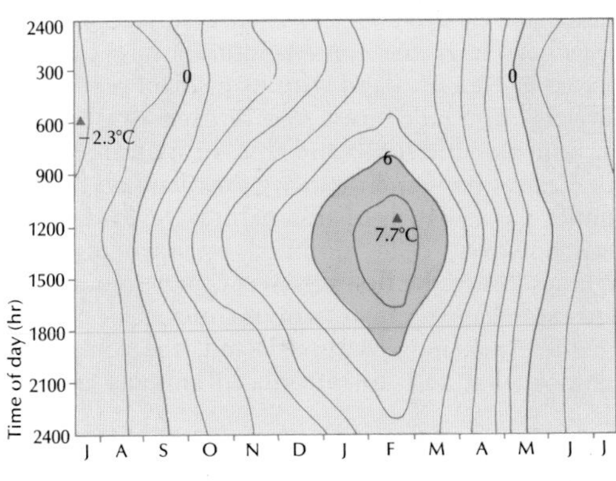

Thermoisopleth diagram for Heard Island.

Cold, temperate, extreme isothermal islands

Îles Kerguelen, Îles Crozet, Macquarie, Marion, Falklands, Diego Ramirez, Campbell, Auckland, Antipodes, Bounty and Snares Islands

All of these islands lie between the Antarctic and Subtropical Convergences, away from the influence of the dry, cold Antarctic air masses. They have extremely equable (isothermal), wet, stormy, cloudy climates. Mean annual temperatures range from 4°C to 10°C (39°F to 50°F). Macquarie Island has one of the most equable climates on earth. Kerguelen has a small icecap, but its glaciers do not descend to sea level. There is no substantial permanent snow or ice on the other islands. Most precipitation falls throughout the year as rain or sleet.

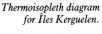

The three Indian Ocean island groups and Macquarie have very similar climates and vegetation of coastal tussock grass and treeless, peaty uplands. Both Diego Ramirez and the Falkland Islands are fringed by tussock grass, with uplands windswept and treeless — resembling the coast of South America. The islands near New Zealand are warmer.

The coasts of all these islands are ice-free and more or less surrounded by kelp. Land vegetation consists of a belt of coastal tussock grass, wet, peat-forming heaths and bogs, herbfields, and fellfields on the higher and more exposed parts. Extensive thickets of low, woody vegetation are found on the Campbell, Snares and Auckland Islands. Breeding colonies of seals and penguins are found above beaches on most islands.

The treeless slopes of Îles Kerguelen.

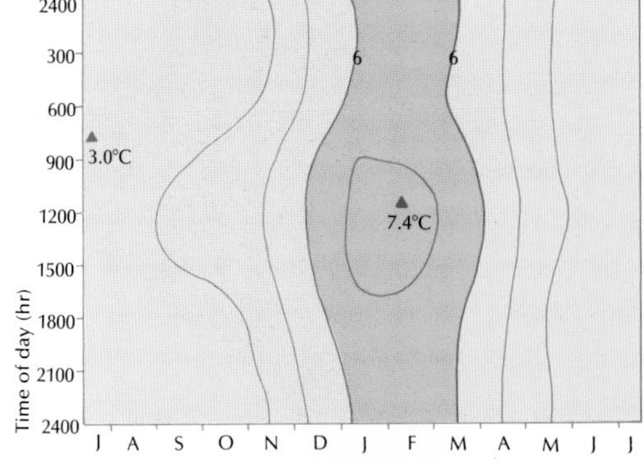

Thermoisopleth diagram for Îles Kerguelen.

Albatrosses dot an Auckland Island hillside.

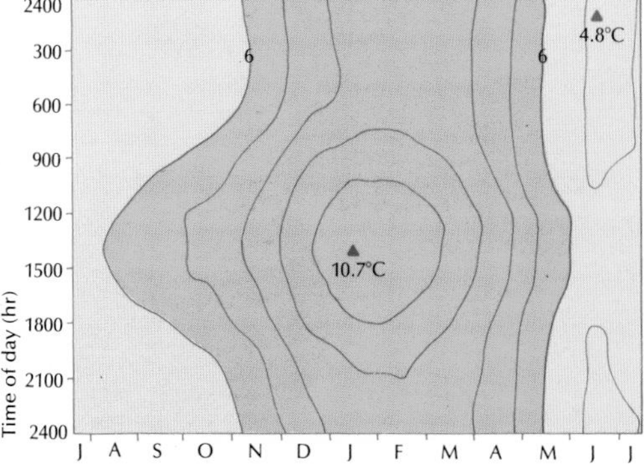

Thermoisopleth diagram for Campbell Island.

THE AUCKLAND ISLANDS

Windswept islands that defied settlement by man

Of the several subantarctic islands lying to the south of New Zealand, none has had a more romantic history than the Auckland Islands. First discovered in 1806, the islands were, for a time, the haunt of sealers and whalers and a bleak refuge for castaways. They were also the scene of a short-lived attempt at colonisation known as the Enderby Settlement. Today they are uninhabited and seldom visited, except by the occasional scientific expedition. They remain very much as they always were, for signs of human occupation quickly disappear in these stormy southern latitudes.

The Aucklands are a tiny group of one large and five smaller volcanic islands in the southern Pacific Ocean, about 400 kilometres (250 miles) south of New Zealand. On their eastern side the islands are deeply indented with pebble or sandy beaches. The thickly wooded slopes of these inlets display a unique and luxuriant blend of subantarctic and Pacific flora. On their western side 360-metre-high (1180-ft) cliffs present a forbidding and unbroken wall to the winds that rage for all but a few days of the year. It is a bluff, perpendicular, iron-bound coast, not without a rugged and awesome beauty.

Along the eastern and southern shores is a belt of rata forest with a low, dense, wind-flattened canopy of twisted trunks and branches. It is the same southern rata that occurs in New Zealand with its brilliant scarlet flowers. The rata forest slowly gives way to an impenetrable scrub and this, in its turn, to moor, peat bogs and tussocky grassland on the higher parts. Much of this natural vegetation has, however, been modified by introduced animals. Since the first discovery, pigs, rabbits and cattle have been, at various times, let loose on the Aucklands. Adams Island, the southernmost, has had no introduced animals and here can be seen the striking endemic plants in their original situations. One place in particular is unique throughout the subantarctic islands. It is known as Fairchilds Garden. As if laid out by a professional gardener, flowers and herbs grow in profusion in an area about as big as a bowling green. Bright yellow, red, green and white, they make a brave show against the inclement weather.

South Cape
ADAMS ISLAND
Cape Farr
Carnley Harbour
S.W. Cape
Cape Bennett
Cavern Peak
AUCKLAND ISLAND
SOUTH PACIFIC OCEAN
DISAPPOINTMENT ISLAND
0 10 km
N.W. Cape
EWING ISLAND
Port Ross
ENDERBY ISLAND
ROSE ISLAND
N.E. Cape
Auckland Islands

The islands are generally cold and wet. They lie in a belt of strong westerly winds which can gust up to 200 km/h (124 mph) over exposed areas. In the five months from November 1944 to March 1945 only 610 hours of sunshine were recorded at Port Ross. Rain falls there on between 22 and 28 days per month, with April being the wettest month when the mean rainfall is 178 mm (7 in). Because of the strong winds, the temperature does not vary much. The highest ever recorded at Port Ross was 19°C (66°F) and the lowest 3°C (37°F). The temperature of the sea around the islands varies between 7.2°C (45°F) and 10.5°C (51°F).

During the first two decades of last century the subantarctic islands were the great sealing grounds of the southern hemisphere. This trade had its headquarters in Sydney and Hobart and large fortunes were made. A year after the Auckland Islands were discovered in 1806 by Captain Bristow, 14 men were put ashore there. They gathered 11 000 skins. But this was just the beginning. Literally hundreds of thousands of seals were slaughtered and, so savage was the toll exacted, the industry collapsed fairly rapidly. It has taken 150 years for the seal population to recover. After the sealers departed the Aucklands were all but forgotten, although they were occasionally visited by whaling captains.

One of these, the captain of a French whaler, committed suicide there in the 1830s. He had invented a harpoon, which could be fired from a gun. Put to the test, it failed dismally. In despair he killed himself. Ironically all harpoons today are fired from guns. He was just before his time.

In 1841 it was suggested that the Aucklands might make a penal colony, but the Secretary of State for Colonies decided that it was too wet and damp. The following year the first permanent inhabitants arrived, a group of Maoris fleeing from the vengeance of the French corvette *L'Heroine*. They were still there when the Enderby settlers arrived eight years later. They had eked out a miserable existence by fowling and sealing and were able to grow New Zealand flax for clothing and potatoes for food. After the Enderby Settlement collapsed the Maoris stayed on for a few more years, but eventually they left for the Chathams, to the east of New Zealand.

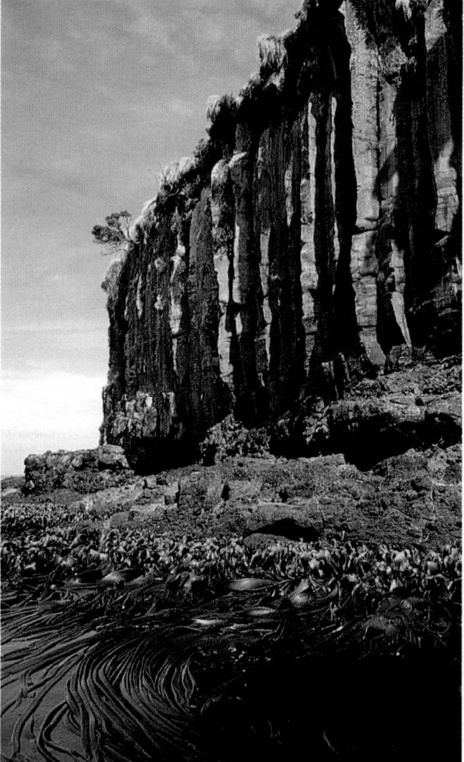

Charles Enderby's settlement at Port Ross was established in 1850 by 300 British colonists. The new colony's main industries were to be shore-based whaling, ship repair and refitting and the provision of fresh meat and vegetables. However, the settlers soon became disillusioned. The sun rarely shone, gales alternated with fogs, there was no arable land and the sour, peaty soil produced no crops. In 1851 two commissioners sent from England found the settlement to be a shambles and the following year the dejected settlers abandoned the colony and sailed for Sydney.

Despite the fact that sealers and whalers had been operating around the Aucklands for almost 50 years, no accurate charts or sailing

Seen from high on Adams Island the hills of Auckland Island sweep down to the Western Arm of Carnley Harbour.

Red-flowered rata (Metrosideros robusta) *adds some colour to dense bush that lines the shores of sheltered Erebus Cove in Port Ross.*

Luxuriant kelp beds fringe the rocky shores of Auckland Island. On the island's western coast the cliffs rise to a height of 360 metres (1180 ft).

directions to the islands existed. When the Great Circle Route from Australia to England round Cape Horn became popular a century ago the Aucklands soon acquired a sinister reputation. In succession the *Grafton*, *Invercauld*, *General Grant*, *Compadre*, *Dundonald*, *Anjou* and *Derry Castle* were wrecked there within a few years. The Aucklands had become a ships' graveyard.

After the survivors of the *General Grant* were rescued, caches of food were placed on the islands for shipwrecked mariners. Later, more substantial depots were built and serviced from New Zealand, but this ceased in 1929. By the time adequate charts were in existence the Great Circle Route had been abandoned, largely because of the popularity of steamships and the opening of the Suez Canal.

About 52 species of birds breed on the Aucklands. More than half of them are sea birds, including three species of penguins and 17 albatrosses. Of the land birds there is a subspecies of the red-crowned parakeet which is also found in New Zealand. The southern royal albatross was once plentiful on the islands, but hungry Maoris, sealers and castaways have much reduced their numbers. The survivors of the wreck of the *General Grant* used albatross for food and sewed with needles made from albatross bone. There are about seven endemic birds, including a shag, merganser, flightless teal, tit, rail, banded dotterel and snipe. The merganser has not been seen since 1904, and is probably extinct, but the teal is often seen running across the kelp.

During the last half of the nineteenth century several people applied for leases on the Aucklands, with the intention of turning them into a sheep run, but none succeeded. On the expiry of the last lease in 1934 the islands were made into a flora and fauna reserve. No one can land there today without the written permission of the New Zealand Offshore Islands Committee, and they usually restrict visits to scientific expeditions.

THE MYSTERY OF THE *GENERAL GRANT'S* GOLD

On 14 May 1866 the Auckland Islands were the scene of a bizarre shipwreck. The *General Grant*, an American vessel bound for London from Melbourne got off course and ran into a gigantic cavern in the 360-metre-high (1180-ft) cliffs on the western side of the islands. There were 83 people aboard, but only 15 survived the wreck. Four later lost their lives, attempting to reach New Zealand, and one died of scurvy. The remaining 10 were rescued on 21 November 1867.

The *General Grant* sailed from Melbourne on 4 May with a cargo of wool, hides and gold — 71 kg (156 lb) according to the manifest; nine tonnes, listed as zinc ingots, according to rumours.

The ship made good progress to begin with, but five days out of Melbourne the weather deteriorated. On the ninth day the wind and sea began to drop. They were unsure of their position and, that evening, they saw what they thought was fog dead ahead. It was no fog-bank, however, but the cliffs of the Auckland Islands.

The wind was so light that the ship had hardly any steerage way at all. The bottom was too deep to anchor and, although every stitch of sail was set, she was driven inexorably towards the cliffs. She struck head-on and an enormous surge carried her into a cave about 250 metres (820 ft) long. As the ship entered the cave, the masts struck the cave roof and snapped, showering the ship's deck with rocks and debris. The tide was falling and the doomed ship slid deeper into the cave. The mainmast then became wedged in a crevice in the roof and, as the tide turned, was forced through the bottom of the vessel. It was a case of every man for himself. Many jumped over the side and tried to get a foothold on the slippery walls of the cave. In the confusion that followed the longboat was lost, but two small ship's boats were successfully launched. Those who could, clambered aboard. In the morning the two boats left the scene of the wreck to row around the island to the other side. This took three days and, when they eventually got ashore, all they had were three pieces of pork, nine tins of bully beef and five matches.

The gold on the *General Grant* has never been recovered, although 18 salvage expeditions have attempted to do so over the past 100 years. It is even doubtful whether the right wreck, or the right cavern, have ever been found.

An imaginative reconstruction of the General Grant's *last moments, drawn by a magazine artist. In fact, only two of the ship's boats, carrying 15 survivors, managed to get clear of the doomed ship in the confusion.*

MACQUARIE ISLAND

One chapter in a sorry saga of exploitation

A small, isolated island surrounded by vast tracts of open ocean, Macquarie Island has a long history of exploitation. Elephant seals, penguins and fur seals were slaughtered here from the time the island was first sighted in July 1810 until commercial licences were finally revoked in 1919. Introduced animals such as cats and rabbits also took their toll of the native animals and plants, to an extent that appalled Douglas Mawson when he visited the island during his 1911-14 Antarctic expedition. Proclaimed a wildlife sanctuary in 1933, the island today hosts a permanent scientific station and steps are being taken to conserve what remains of the island's indigenous plants and animals.

'The island is dreadfully dreary to the ordinary observer, but to the naturalist it is full of fascinating interest', wrote J.R. Burton of Macquarie Island in the *Australasian* on 23 June 1900. Lying atop a submerged oceanic rise, approximately 1130 kilometres (700 miles) southwest of New Zealand and 1530 kilometres (950 miles) north of the Antarctic continent, Macquarie Island is 34 kilometres (21 miles) long and between 2.5 and 5 kilometres (1.5 to 3 miles) wide. It rises steeply from the sea to a plateau about 250 metres (820 ft) high in the north and 300 metres (1000 ft) high in the south, with peaks ranging from 370 metres (1213 ft) to 433 metres (1420 ft). The plateau is covered by glacial till and there are many lakes and tarns. Most of the exposed rocks are volcanic.

The climate is uniformly cold, wet and windy. The average monthly maximum temperature is 6.2°C (43°F), the average monthly wind velocity is 8.6 m sec^{-1}, and the average annual precipitation is 926 mm (36.5 in). It rains, snows or hails on 317 days of the year.

There are no shrubs or trees on the island. The coastal slopes are covered in tall tussock grass, a major habitat of introduced creatures such as the Stewart Island weka, rats and mice. The tussock-clad areas on the upper part of beach terraces are used by elephant seals.

The tall tussock grassland gives way to short tussock grassland dominated by short grasses and sedges. Numerous bryophytes (such as mosses) and lichens are found in this area. Nearly half of the exposed and windswept plateau is fellfield covered by cushion-forming mosses; the remainder, in terrace formation, is bare gravel with some vegetation. Mires and bogs predominate in the wetter areas.

This windswept island became the target of sealing gangs as soon as it was discovered. The elephant seal population was quickly reduced to the extent that the sealers had to turn to king and royal penguins for oil. One breeding colony of king penguins was wiped out. Fur seals, slaughtered for their skins, were also exterminated in large numbers.

Today, only rusting boilers, digesters, try pots and a few barrel staves remain as reminders of the carnage. The penguin and elephant seal populations have recovered. About 1000 fur seals land on the island each summer, but most of these are non-breeding animals, and fewer than 10 pups may be born in a season. The breeding animals, it was recently discovered, represent two species, the Antarctic fur seal *Arctocephalus gazella* and the New Zealand fur seal *Arctocephalus forsteri*.

A more permanent legacy of the sealers is the widespread distribution on the island of introduced animals. Mice and black rats came ashore from the numerous shipwrecks around the coast during the sealing days, or were brought ashore in boxes of provisions. The tussock grasslands are the favoured habitats of both mice and rats. Invertebrates and seeds provide the bulk of their food, but rats may also take the young of burrow-nesting birds, particularly prions and petrels.

Cats were introduced from shipwrecks or as sealers' pets. They had become feral by 1820. The major concentrations of cats are found near large breeding colonies of penguins. At least two bird species, a parrot and a rail, have been exterminated by cats. Estimates indicate that the adult population is between 250 and 500 animals; the availability of winter food is a major factor controlling the rate at which they can reproduce.

The European rabbit was introduced in the late 1870s, and large areas of the island have been denuded of their natural vegetation. Selective grazing, burrowing and scratching have considerably altered the vegetation patterns on many parts of the island. Rabbits provide a major part of the diet of the cats, but myxomatosis has been the main agent in the reduction of the rabbit population since the European rabbit flea, which carries the disease, was introduced to the island by man in 1959. In some areas the recovery of the native vegetation has been dramatic.

The Stewart Island weka, or rail, was introduced in 1867 as a food source for the sealers.

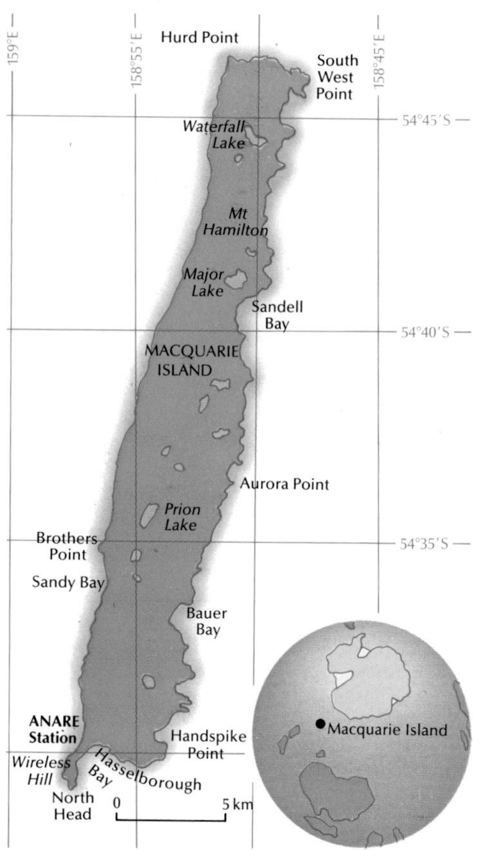

Elephant seals doze unconcernedly beside the rusting remains of digesters, at The Nuggets, that claimed so many of their kind.

A vast king penguin rookery at Lusitania Bay on the east coast. There are about half a million birds in this colony.

Protected lowland valleys — this is Finch Creek on the east coast — support quite luxuriant vegetation.

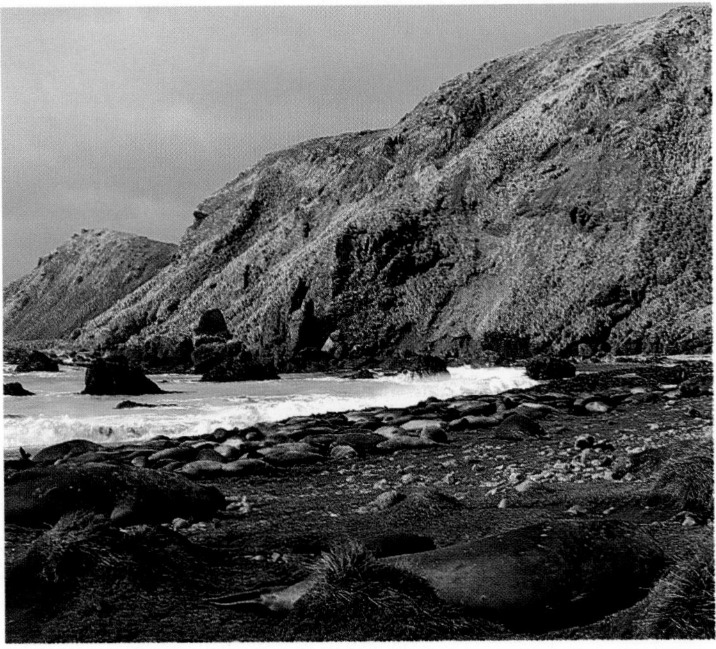

Like giant slugs, a group of elephant seals bask in weak subantarctic sunshine on a Macquarie Island beach. In the heyday of sealing, almost all the island's elephant and fur seals were killed. In a short time the industry became uneconomic.

The exposed, windswept plateau of Macquarie Island (left). Most of the vegetation is cushion-forming mosses. There are no shrubs or trees at all. Fine days are rare on the island, where mean total cloud cover is 83 per cent.

It has a range of prey similar to the cat and includes young rabbits and birds, rodents, invertebrates and probably some plant matter.

Domestic horses, donkeys, dogs, goats, sheep, cattle, pigs, ducks and chickens have been present on the island, usually only in small numbers, at one time or another since the early days of the sealers at the beginning of last century. None is now present.

Only four alien bird species — the European starling, the redpoll, the black duck and the mallard duck — have become established. But there is an impressive list of 35 transient visitors and vagrant bird species, despite the island's isolated position.

A number of vegetable and horticultural species and agricultural weeds have been deliberately introduced by man, but all are now confined to glasshouses or have been removed.

The first recorded collection of plants from Macquarie Island was made and forwarded to Kew Gardens for identification in 1824, probably by sealers. The first deliberate attempt to study the vegetation was made by J.H. Scott of New Zealand, who accompanied a sealing party to the island in 1880. In 1884 another New Zealander, A. Hamilton, collected most of the presently known vascular plant species.

The first long-term scientific study of the island was undertaken by the Australasian Antarctic Expedition of 1911-14, when H. Hamilton collected plants and made ecological observations of the vegetation. Douglas Mawson, the leader of the expedition, lobbied strongly on his return to Australia for the declaration of the island as a wildlife sanctuary. Sealing licences were revoked in 1916 and sanctuary status was conferred on the island on 17 May 1933.

In March 1948 a permanent scientific and meteorological station was established on a low, narrow isthmus connecting the small northern block with the main southern mass of the island. Extensive botanical and zoological collections and observations have been made since then, and scientific studies are continuing. Efforts are being made to eradicate, or at least control, the feral cat and rabbit populations, and the populations of seals, penguins and albatrosses are being monitored.

SOUTH GEORGIA

Island gateway to the Antarctic continent

South Georgia has played a vital role in the history of Antarctic exploration. First sighted in 1675, the mountainous island was claimed for Britain by Captain Cook when he landed there 100 years later. South Georgia subsequently became a haunt of sealers, then for much of this century it was the world's centre for whaling. From 1904, South Georgia served as the 'Gateway to Antarctica'.

South Georgia is the most mountainous of the Southern Ocean islands surrounding the Antarctic continent. On a clear day it appears as a sheer snow-covered range rising directly from the ocean. The island is roughly crescent shaped, with its mountainous spine rising to 2934 metres (9625 ft) at Mount Paget. Twelve other peaks exceed 2000 metres (6560 ft). Well over half of the island is permanently covered with ice and snow. The coastline is deeply indented with fjords carved by more than 150 glaciers.

The island has a complex geological history and its rocks are very old. Many of its mountains have steep, unstable scree slopes, a result of the frequent freeze-thaw cycles the rock is subjected to. Some of the few flat unglaciated areas have been used for whaling stations.

South Georgia's weather is wet, cold and very windy, although the central part on the northern side, in the lee of the mountains, is partly protected from these severe conditions. There has been a meteorological observatory at King Edward Cove since 1905, but as this is in the most protected part of the island its records are not truly representative. The minimum recorded temperature at the observatory is −15°C (5°F), the maximum is 22°C (72°F), and the annual average is 2°C (36°F).

Winds are frequent and often reach gale force. Föhn winds sometimes raise temperatures 10 degrees in as many minutes. Recent years have had an average of 198 days with rain and 183 days with snow; coastal snow depths may reach two metres (6.5 ft) in winter. During most winters the pack ice front does not reach South Georgia, but this is variable. Sea ice forms in the bays and fjords but is usually broken by powerful ocean swells.

Many of the areas near sea level are vegetated, with tussock grass, mosses and lichens.

The only indigenous land animals, other than birds, are invertebrates. But three introduced species of land mammals are established: reindeer, brown rats and mice. Reindeer were first brought from Norway in 1911, and about 2000 now inhabit the island. Their range is restricted by mountains, glaciers and fjords. Rats arrived over a century ago and are widespread. They have severely affected several species of smaller birds.

About 300000 southern elephant seals and two million Antarctic fur seals now breed on South Georgia. There is a small breeding col-

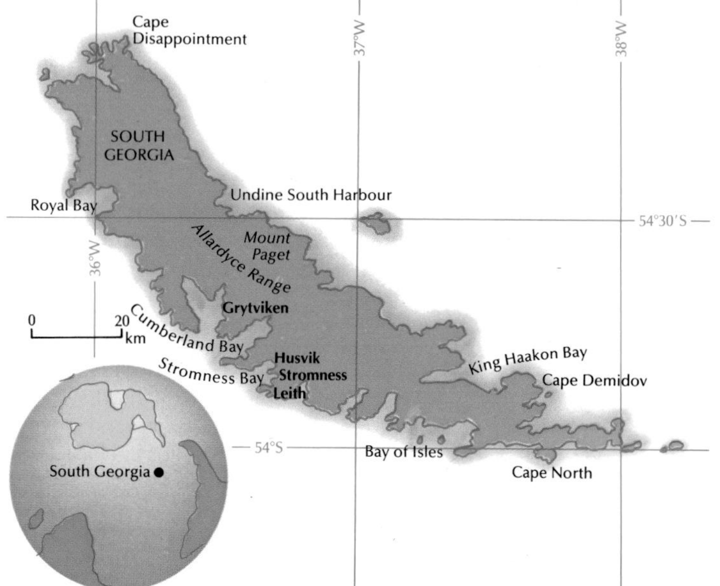

The high mountainous spine of South Georgia gives the island an impressive skyline. The tall peak is Mount Paget.

The ruined whaling station at Grytviken. Sir Ernest Shackleton is buried in the distant hillside cemetery.

ony of Weddell seals on the southern end of the island, and leopard seals are often seen but do not breed. Crabeater seals, Ross seals and Kerguelen fur seals are occasional visitors. Many of South Georgia's beaches have large seals populations during the breeding seasons and landings are difficult and dangerous.

The indigenous birds of South Georgia comprise 30 breeding and 27 non-breeding species. Most are sea birds and, as the island is the only breeding ground in a vast expanse of ocean, some species occur in huge numbers — 5.4 million pairs in the case of the macaroni penguin. It is a major breeding area for several large species of albatross.

South Georgia was the first land seen south of the Antarctic Convergence when, in 1675, a London merchant, Antonio de la Roché, was blown off course in a storm while rounding Cape Horn. He made no landing and recorded only a brief description of the island. A second sighting was made in 1756, also by a merchant vessel blown off course. Then Captain James Cook, circumnavigating Antarctica, landed on South Georgia in January 1775 and took formal possession of it.

The published accounts of Cook's voyage give many details of the island and include a description of the abundance of fur and elephant seals there. This information led to the next epoch in South Georgia's history: sealing, which lasted from about 1785 to 1913. The industry was rapidly depleting the population of fur seals in other areas, and the discovery of new sealing grounds was usually followed by a 'gold-rush' of sealers. This led to the virtual extermination of the fur seals of South Georgia by about 1810. Subsequent recoveries of their numbers yielded lesser fur sealing peaks in about 1820 and 1870. Elephant seals were also exploited for their oil over most of the period.

The first land-based scientific expedition to the island was the German contingent of the International Polar Year, who operated a station at Royal Bay from 1882 to 1883. The ruins of their huts can still be seen.

In 1894 the Norwegian Captain Carl Anton Larsen, aboard the *Jason*, made a short visit to the island while on his second Antarctic expedition for the development of whaling. In 1902 he was back on South Georgia as master of the *Antarctic,* with the Swedish South Polar Expedition.Larsen later discussed his ideas of whaling on South Georgia in Buenos Aires and received great support. He returned to Norway and purchased three vessels and other necessities for starting a whaling station. On 16 November 1904 Larsen landed at Grytviken, and so began permanent settlement and the island's modern whaling industry. Up to 1917 six shore-based stations and eight floating factories operated from South Georgia. During this period 175 250 whales were taken.

It was also at this time that South Georgia became the 'Gateway to Antarctica'. Two of Sir Ernest Shackleton's expeditions visited the island; on his second expedition to South Georgia, aboard the *Quest*, he died and was buried at Grytviken.

Concern about the increasing rarity of whales led the British Government to establish a scientific station on the island in 1925. The investigations yielded an enormous amount of information about both the island and Antarctica. Norwegian whaling at South Georgia finished in early 1962, but two of the stations were sub-leased to Japanese companies. By December 1965 these too had found the industry unprofitable and the stations closed, and have since fallen into disrepair.

The civil administration and settlement of King Edward Point were taken over by the British Antarctic Survey in 1969, and a large research station was established. Work at the station included zoological, geological and botanical investigations of the island, but this was interrupted by the Falklands War in 1982.

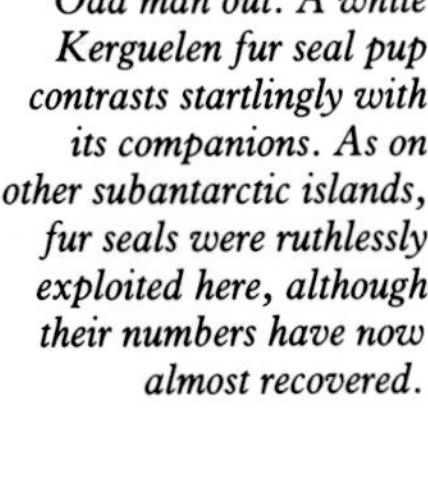

Odd man out. A white Kerguelen fur seal pup contrasts startlingly with its companions. As on other subantarctic islands, fur seals were ruthlessly exploited here, although their numbers have now almost recovered.

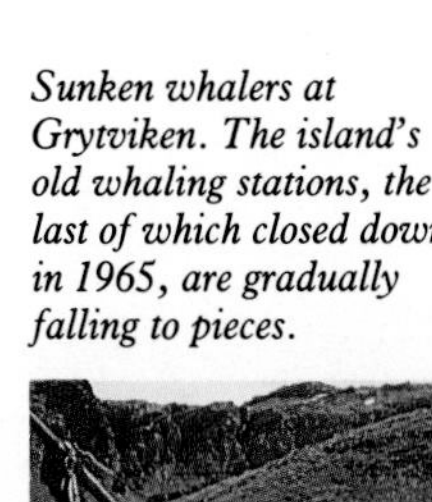

Tabular icebergs aground in Undine South Harbour on the deserted southern side of the island. The old whaling stations and modern settlements are on the more sheltered northern side. Tussock grassland and bogs are typical of the island's lower altitudes.

Sunken whalers at Grytviken. The island's old whaling stations, the last of which closed down in 1965, are gradually falling to pieces.

FIRST ANTARCTIC WAR

South Georgia has the unfortunate distinction of being the only part of the Antarctic region to have been directly involved in a war.

The island as one of the Dependencies of the Falkland Islands is administered by the Governor in Stanley. But British sovereignty has been disputed by Argentina.

The British claim to South Georgia dates from Captain Cook's proclamation of 1775. This was consolidated by Letters Patent in 1908 and 1917. Argentina regards the Falkland Islands (Islas Malvinas), and therefore its dependencies, as being their territory. The first indication of an Argentinean claim came in 1927, although this was not formally stated until 1938. In 1947 Britain proposed that the dispute be referred to the International Court of Justice, whose decision she bound herself in advance to accept. Argentina rejected this offer. Britain repeated the offer in 1951, 1953 and 1954, and met a similar response. In 1955 she made a unilateral application to the Court which Argentina countered by refusing to accept the Court's authority.

In 1979 a scrap metal dealer in Argentina obtained a contract to remove material from the abandoned whaling stations in South Georgia. This was at first believed to be a normal commercial transaction, but by late 1981 it was apparent that the Argentinean Navy had become closely associated with it. An Argentinean naval vessel with some scrap metal salvage workers arrived illegally at South Georgia on 18 March 1982, and an offical protest was made.

The naval presence was reinforced on 24 March and on 3 April 1982 two Argentinean naval ships with helicopters and over 200 troops attacked the scientific station at King Edward Point. After a two-hour battle 22 Royal Marines, who had landed from HMS *Endurance* on 31 March, surrendered. They and the scientific personnel were taken prisoner, removed from the island, and eventually released in Uruguay. Argentinean forces held Leith Harbour and King Edward Point. Four British field stations remained on the island with a total of 15 civilians. On 25 April the Royal Navy recaptured King Edward Point, and the Argentineans at Leith surrendered.

THE SOUTH SHETLAND ISLANDS

A remote archipelago shaped by fire and ice

The South Shetland group is the largest archipelago in the Antarctic. It forms a 540-kilometre (335-mile) chain of 11 main islands and many smaller islands, 900 kilometres (560 miles) south of Tierra del Fuego. In common with other islands of the region, the group has a history of exploitation by sealers and whalers. Today, the South Shetlands are the home of stations maintained by several countries, and in 1982 the first international conference in Antarctica was held at a Chilean base on King George Island.

All the islands of the South Shetlands are extensively covered by ice fields and glaciers, with many deep fjords. The coastline ranges from high, sheer cliffs of ice or rock to broad beach terraces. Most islands are mountainous, the highest peak being on Smith Island at 2105 metres (6906 ft). The largest islands are King George and Livingston Islands, both about 75 kilometres (47 miles) long and up to 25 kilometres (16 miles) wide.

The group does have a few large expanses of ice-free terrain, notably Byers Peninsula on Livingston Island, Fildes Peninsula on King George Island and on Deception Island. Some islands have shallow freshwater lakes.

Most of the islands of the South Shetlands are of volcanic origin. Deception Island is a horseshoe-shaped caldera, still active, with many hot springs, fumaroles and steaming beaches. It erupted at several places between 1967 and 1970.

The South Shetlands have a cold oceanic climate typical of the maritime Antarctic. The average annual temperature is about −3°C (27°F), with extremes occasionally reaching 15°C (59°F) and −30°C (−22°F). Rainfall is quite high, but snow and frosts may also occur throughout the year. To add to the general bleakness, the average daily sunshine is very low and most islands are usually shrouded by cloud; fog is common. The prevailing westerly winds are often very strong, sometimes gusting to hurricane force. In winter, sea ice surrounds most of the islands, while pack ice and icebergs are frequent in summer.

The vegetation of the South Shetlands is dominated by mosses and lichens, and the latter can be spectacular. Coastal cliffs are frequently covered with communities of orange lichens, their bright colour standing out at a distance of several kilometres. Antarctic hair grass *Deschampsia antarctica* occurs in many places, but is seldom abundant. The only other flowering plant is Antarctic pearlwort *Colobanthus quitensis* which is much less common and usually grows with the grass. The largest patch of this plant in the Antarctic was on Deception Island, but it was mostly destroyed by volcanic ash in 1967.

On Deception Island there are areas of geothermal activity where the ground is kept warm, and may exceed 50°C (112°F) a few centimetres below the surface. In a few such damp, heated places there are unique communities of mosses and liverworts, some known nowhere else in the Antarctic.

Although only 17 species of birds are found in the South Shetlands, most occur in very large numbers, notably some of the penguins and petrels. The most numerous penguins are the chinstraps, which total about 750 000 breeding pairs, with several rookeries on Deception and Clarence Islands exceeding 50 000 pairs. There are also about 50 000 pairs of Adélie penguins and 20 000 pairs of gentoo penguins. Macaroni penguins are at the southern extremity of their range in the South Shetland Islands; most of the 7000 pairs breed in the Elephant-Clarence Islands group.

Both fur and elephant seals were hunted to near extinction during the nineteenth century. Today there are many elephant seals, but their breeding population is still quite small. With the decline in the whaling industry, and the consequent surplus of krill, a massive increase in the number of fur seals has occurred on South Georgia since the 1960s, providing an overspill to the South Shetlands. A population of about 3000 has become re-established on some of the islands.

Weddell seals are also numerous, breeding on sea ice in coves in late winter, and crabeater seals, the most common species around the Antarctic continent, occur in large numbers on fast ice and later in summer in small groups on ice floes around the archipelago. They very rarely come ashore unless they are in ill health.

The South Shetlands are also inhabited by several forms of minute invertebrate animals, the most prominent being mites and springtails. There are two species of midge, but only

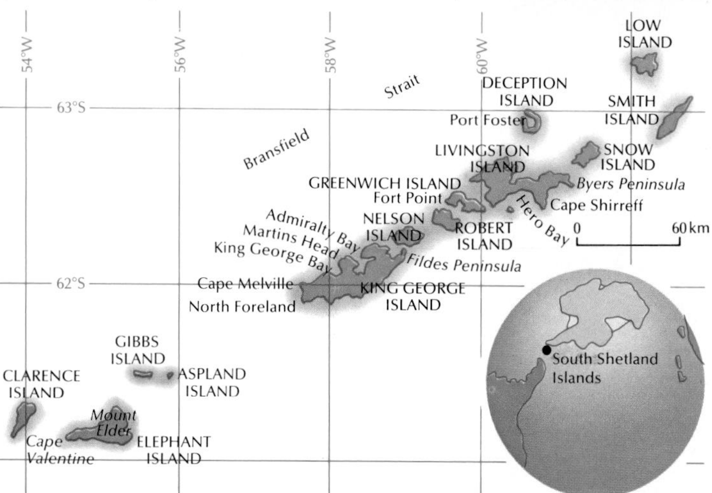

Vast numbers of chinstrap penguins dot the hills of Deception Island. The black ash beaches betray the island's volcanic origin. The last major eruption was in 1970 when Chilean and British stations were extensively damaged. Ships visiting the island often report considerable changes to the landscape and offshore islands.

A shrine at the Polish base, Arctowski, on King George Island. Several countries have permanent bases in the South Shetland Islands.

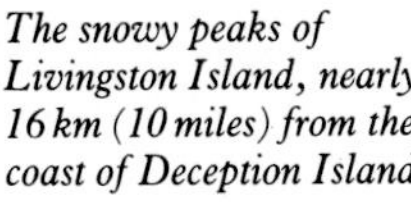

The snowy peaks of Livingston Island, nearly 16 km (10 miles) from the coast of Deception Island.

Volcanic heat makes the beaches steam at Whalers Bay on Deception Island. The sea is often warm enough to swim in. The surface water temperature frequently reaches 40°C (104°F) and on one occasion even blistered a ship's paintwork.

Elephant Island is bleak and mountainous. Most of it is covered by ice, and is seldom visited. In 1916 members of Ernest Shackleton's trans-Antarctic expedition camped on a narrow beach for several months.

one has wings; in Antarctica it occurs only on these islands. On rare calm, warm, sunny days in midsummer, small clouds of these flies dance above lake shorelines.

The discovery of the South Shetland Islands is attributed to the Englishman William Smith, master of the brig *Williams*, who was forced far to the south by stormy weather when rounding Cape Horn in February 1819. Later that year Smith returned and on 16 October landed and took possession of his new discovery for King George III. He named the land New South Britain, but amended this to New South Shetland shortly after. Between January and March 1820 Edward Bransfield, commanding the *Williams* with Smith as pilot, explored and charted the islands and harbours from Deception Island to Clarence Island, where he landed on 4 February.

After Bransfield's accounts of large numbers of whales and huge and potentially profitable numbers of elephant and fur seals, many sealers visited the islands. Within four years of their discovery, over 320 000 skins and 940 tonnes of elephant seal oil had been taken. The seals were almost exterminated and further visits were very few and unprofitable, except for a minor resurgence of the industry in the 1870s. Around the coast of Livingston and King George Islands are numerous relics of these sealing days — the remains of walled caves and stone walls of bothies, once roofed with timber, whalebone, sailcloth and canvas, where groups of sealers spent weeks or months ashore culling the seals for skins and oil.

After the Southern Ocean whaling industry began at South Georgia in 1904, whaling was extended to the South Shetlands. Up to nine factory ships and 29 whale catchers operated around the islands. The southernmost shore station in the world was established at Whalers Bay, Deception Island, in 1910 and operated until 1931 when the 21-year licence ended.

It was not until the 'scientific era' of Antarctica dawned that a new permanent settlement was established on the islands. A British station operated close to the former whaling station at Deception Island from 3 February 1944, but was destroyed by mud flows from the volcanic eruption of February 1969. There are now several permanently occupied stations, maintained by Argentina, Brazil, Chile, Poland and the Soviet Union on the islands.

Several areas in the South Shetland Islands have been designated Specially Protected Areas because of the diversity of plant and animal life and geological interest, while others are Sites of Special Scientific Interest and have restricted access. It is essential that these and other ecologically important areas are protected and managed in accordance with the conservation policies of the Antarctic Treaty. The growing tourist industry in this region, if allowed to develop without strict controls, poses a threat to the ecosystem. In this severe environment plants and animals are slow to recover from any form of disturbance.

PART TWO: THE EXPLORERS

In 1819 no human being had seen Antarctica: by 1958 this most inhospitable of all continents had been fully explored and mapped. In just 139 years a mere handful of men, members of some 50 major expeditions, had unlocked the secrets of the world's last wilderness. Here are their stories — some of the most extraordinary tales of courage and daring ever told.

In the 15th century, Europeans rediscovered the works of the Egyptian geographer Ptolemy. This map was published in an edition of his works produced in Ulm in 1486. Terra incognita, *linked to Africa, extends right across the world.*

TERRA AUSTRALIS INCOGNITA

Theories about a great undiscovered continent

The existence and size of a southern continent was a matter of intense interest to even the earliest civilisations, with the early Greek philosophers propounding the need for a southern landmass to 'balance' the weight of those lands known to exist in the northern hemisphere. And as the northern hemisphere lay under the constellation of Arktos, the Bear, so, Aristotle (384-322 BC) reasoned, the unknown land to the south must be Antarktikos — in other words, the total opposite.

As early as the sixth century BC Pythagoras was postulating that the world was round. Parmenides (450 BC) and Aristotle agreed, and Eratosthenes of Alexandria (276-194 BC) was probably the first to calculate its circumference.

Once it had become accepted that the earth was a sphere there came into being many theories about its nature. Parmenides, for instance, held that the globe was divided into five parallel climatic zones. The most northerly was a frigid zone. Then came a temperate zone which included the known Mediterranean world, then a torrid zone, then another temperate and frigid zone in the southern hemisphere. The two frigid zones and the torrid zone were thought to be uninhabitable.

Later Aristotle defined the northern temperate zone as being from the Tropic of Cancer to the Arctic Circle. The Egyptian geographer, Ptolemy (150 AD), while endorsing the classical Greek philosophy that the world was symmetrical — and must, therefore, contain a southern continent (*Terra Australis Incognita*) — held that this 'unknown southern land' was fertile and populous. However, he perpetuated the idea that it was cut off from the known world by the torrid zone, a region of fire and, some speculated, fearful monsters. It was an idea which persisted and grew, discouraging any exploration southwards for 1200 years.

During the Middle Ages, the geographical theories of the Ancients were all but lost to Europeans. Instead, the possibility of a southern continent became a matter of religious controversy. Speculation that inhabited countries existed on the opposite side of the world created awkward theological problems. How, it was asked, could such people be descended from Adam, and were there separate divine revelations and separate atonements for them? Such tricky debate was solved by denouncing as heretical the supposition that the world was round, and the flat earth theory was revived. This, of course, precluded a southern hemisphere and therefore an Antarctic continent.

Although the Middle Ages was a period of darkness so far as advancing man's knowledge of the world he lived in, Ptolemy's teachings had been preserved by the Arabs and from the tenth century onwards his theories began to filter into Europe via the Moors who had invaded Spain. These reawakened speculation that the world was, after all, round and that there were great unknown lands on the other side of it. Then in 1410 Ptolemy's works were translated into Latin and French and a new enlightened era began.

Philosophers' theories on the nature of the world were vital to stimulate man's curiosity. Equally important was the fact that they encouraged exploration to start once more, and the discoveries of men like Marco Polo, and the Portuguese under Henry the Navigator, fuelled practical interest in what lay beyond the bounds of the known world.

In 1488 Bartholomew Diaz reached the Cape of Good Hope, and a decade later Vasco da Gama rounded it and reached India. Both these voyages revolutionised the thinking of geographers, for it became immediately apparent that Africa was merely an extension of the known world, that Ptolemy's torrid zone was fictitious, and that his *Terra Australis Incognita*, if it existed, lay elsewhere. That it did so, and was connected, if not to Africa, then to that other great continent newly discovered across the Atlantic, was not doubted by contemporary map makers.

The theories of the geographers were backed up, or so they must have thought, by a Florentine seaman, Amerigo Vespucci, who in 1501 set out to explore the South American coastline. The Portuguese had probably known of this coastline for some years, but the visit there in 1500 by one of their countrymen, Pedro Alvarez Cabral, precipitated an expedition to confirm his discoveries.

In a letter describing his voyage Vespucci claimed to have penetrated far to the south and found a rocky coastline from which he was driven by extreme cold and high winds. For many years it was thought that he might have discovered South Georgia, or one of the other subantarctic islands, but it is now almost certain that he hugged the coastline and that the letter was a forgery. However, he probably sailed as far as 50°S, and it is conceivable that he found the Straits of Magellan. For when Magellan sailed for the area in September 1519 he seems to have known of its existence, as a passage from an account of his voyage shows: 'This strait was a circular place surrounded by mountains, and to most of those in the ships it seemed that there was no way out from it to enter the said Pacific Sea. But the captain-general said that there was another strait which led out, saying that he knew it well and had seen it in a marine chart of the King of Portugal, which a great pilot and sailor named Martin of Bohemia had made.'

Magellan sailed through the strait and into the Pacific, and although he was killed by natives there, one of his ships, the *Victoria*, returned to Spain. She was the first vessel to circumnavigate the earth, and the first to prove the theories, held since the early civilisations, about the spherical nature of the earth.

Magellan's voyage also dispelled the idea that *Terra Australis Incognita* was joined to South America. But it increased speculation that such a continent existed, for Magellan reported seeing land to the south of him as he approached the Pacific, land that became known as Tierra del Fuego. Map makers now charted *Terra Australis Incognita* as covering most of the South Pacific Ocean, with its coast running southwest from Tierra del Fuego. Francis Drake was sent to this coast in 1577.

Drake's mission has often been projected as piratical. No doubt he had every intention of securing booty and prizes if these could be found, but the orders given him by the group of merchants and ministers who provided the finance were quite plain. He was to enter the

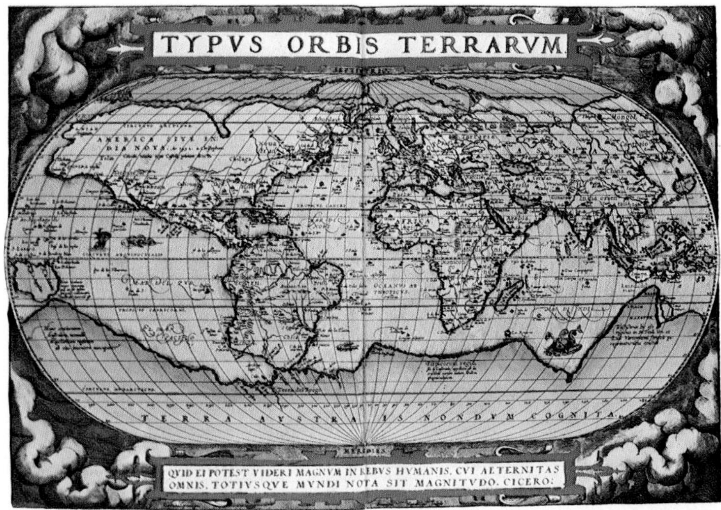

This map (left), drawn in Antwerp in 1570, shows the results of Magellan's voyage in 1519. Terra Australis *is now shown extending south from Tierra del Fuego, off the tip of South America. It was not until Drake's voyage in 1577 that this idea was proved to be incorrect.*

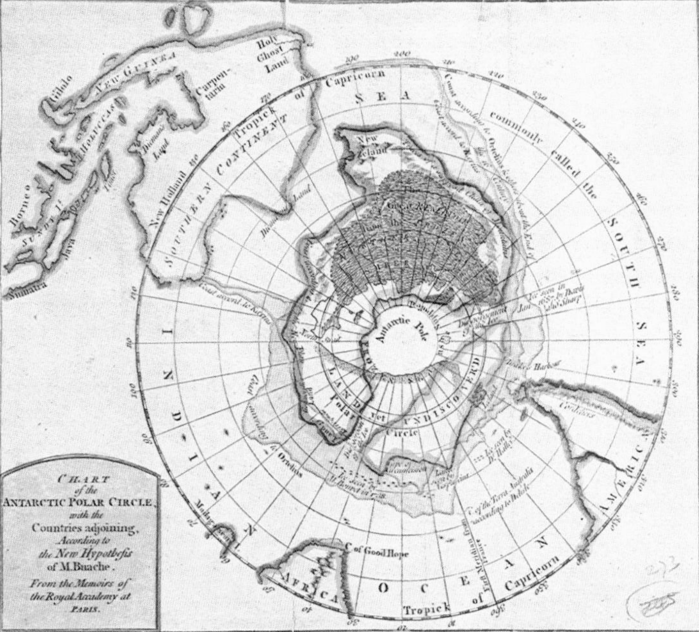

By 1763 (below), after the voyages of Davis, Gerritsz, de la Roche and Bouvet de Lozier, geographers were starting to narrow down the only possible location for an, as yet, undiscovered continent. This French map suggested an ice-filled sea surrounding the South Pole.

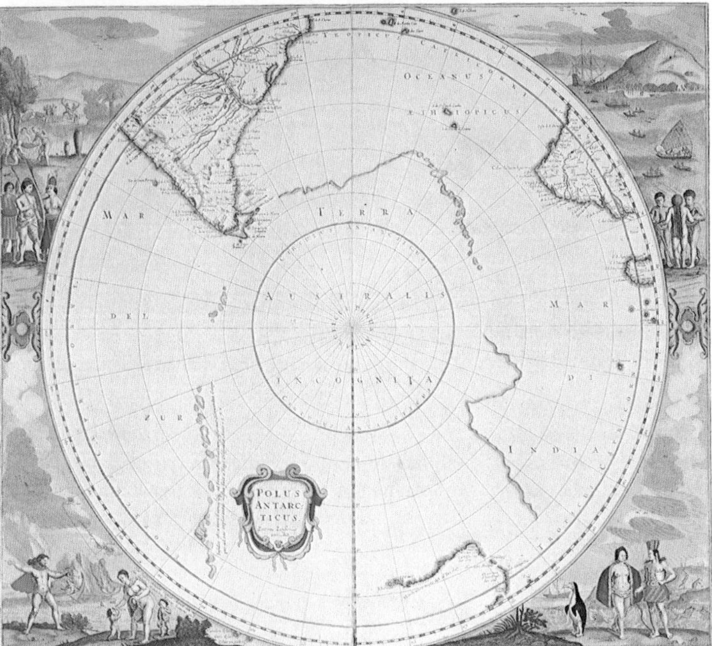

By 1620 (left) Dutch explorers had started to outline the south coast of Australia. There were also some tentative lines around Antarctica — the results of hazy reports from ships straying south.

Pacific via the Straits of Magellan and explore the coastline of the continent beyond 'not in the possession of any Christian Prince'. This last instruction showed that they could not have meant Drake to explore the Peruvian coastline, but that of the great unknown southern continent. It can therefore be fairly said that Drake led the first Antarctic expedition.

Drake reached the Straits of Magellan on 17 August 1578 and a week later they encountered their first penguins. 'Wee found great store of strange birds', wrote Drake's chaplain, Francis Fletcher in his book, *The World Encompassed*, published in 1628, 'which could not flie at all, nor yet runne so fast as that they could escape us with their liues; in body they are less than a goose, and bigger than a mallard, short and thicke sett together, having no feathers, but insteed thereof a certaine hard and matted downe; their beakes are not much unlike the bills of crowes, they lodge and breed upon the land, where making earthes, as the conies doe, in the ground, they lay their egges and bring up their young; their feeding and provision to live on is in the sea, where they swimm in such sort, as nature may seeme to have granted them no small prerogative in swiftnesse.'

On 6 September the small fleet cleared the strait, but the next day it was struck by a severe storm which drove Drake and the *Golden Hind* as far south as 57° where they reached a place where the Atlantic and Pacific Oceans 'meete in a most large a free scope'.

This turbulent place, probably off Cape Horn, proved that Tierra del Fuego was not part of *Terra Australis Incognita,* though map makers refused to accept this for many years.

The great southern continent continued to elude explorers and though interest in it waned, other important discoveries were made towards the end of the sixteenth century.

In 1592, John Davis, the Master of the *Desire*, was driven off the coast of Patagonia, and on 18 August came upon the Falkland Islands. Seven years later the Shetland Islands were sighted, possibly for the first time, when a ship under the command of a Dutch pilot called Dirck Gerritsz was forced to seek shelter amongst them. A book called *Description des Indes Occidentales,* published in 1622, reported: 'The ship of Dirck Gerritsz, which had parted company on the 15th of September with the others, namely Wert and Cordes, was carried by the tempest down to 64° south of the Strait; where they discovered a high land with mountains covered with snow, resembling the land of Norway.'

Although this has been interpreted by some authorities as being too accurately descriptive to be a figment of the author's imagination, a declaration made by one of Gerritsz' crew four years later stated that the ship went only as far south as 56°. However, another statement, made at the same time by a boatswain on another ship, stated that in March 1603 his vessel was blown to 64°S where a lot of snow was encountered. It is possible that the author amalgamated the two accounts. Anyway, from the evidence available, modern commentators believe that the South Shetlands were probably sighted during those early years.

There was one more intrepid early navigator who added a vital discovery to the increasing fund of knowledge about these stormy southern regions. In 1675 a British merchant, Anthony de la Roche, was returning from a trade voyage to the Pacific when a storm prevented him from entering the Straits of Magellan or the Strait le Maire. Instead, it blew him far to the east and south, to a latitude of 55° where he sought shelter in the bay of an unknown coast. He stayed there 14 days before moving on, as a translation of the incident, described by a Spanish captain and published in Madrid in 1690, recounts: 'They found that they were at the end of that Land, near which they anchored, and looking to the SE and South, they saw another High Land covered with snow, leaving which, and the Wind setting in gently at SW, and sailed out in sight of the said coast of the Island which they left to the Westward, seeing the said Southern land in the said Quarters, it appearing that from one to the other was about 10 leagues.'

The island to which la Roche ran for shelter was South Georgia and the 'Southern Land' to which he referred was almost certainly the Clerke Rocks which lie about 48 kilometres (30 miles) to the southeast of the island. They are positioned in almost the exact spot where *Terra Australis Incognita* was placed on a map in the possession of the Dutch East India Company. La Roche had studied the map in Amsterdam, so it is not surprising he thought that he had found the great southern continent.

But it was well over a century more before *Terra Australis Incognita* was sighted at last, and the era of Antarctic discovery began.

AN ELUSIVE PARADISE

Bouvet searches in vain for Gonneville's Eden

In the early sixteenth century, a French navigator named Paulmyer de Gonneville sailed south from Honfleur on a voyage of exploration. Whatever records he kept are now lost, though the account he gave of his discoveries was to influence French thinking for more than 200 years. Tempest-driven in the southern latitudes, Gonneville claimed to have reached a tropical paradise, inhabited by people 'asking nothing but to lead a life of contentment, without work'. He stayed there six months, returning with a cargo of skins, dyes and feathered decorations.

Fact — if it *was* fact — gave way to legend. Subsequent theories placed Gonneville Land in Brazil; south of the Moluccas; southwest of the Cape of Good Hope. No one was sure, only that it lay somewhere in the unexplored regions of the southern hemisphere. Yet the legend persisted and was embellished, firing the imagination of other, would-be explorers. One of these was Jean-Baptiste Charles Bouvet de Lozier, born into a naval family of distinction in 1705.

Orphaned at the age of seven, he was educated in Paris, then sent to work in the shipyards of St Malo. There he studied navigation and, in 1731, gained the rank of lieutenant in the *Compagnie des Indes*. He was already fascinated by the story of Gonneville, and was later to write: 'During my first year as a student I had occasion to study a map of the world. I was immediately struck by the emptiness that surrounded the Southern Pole, simply marked as *Terres Inconnues*, and was seized with the desire to go and explore them. I thought only of going to sea.'

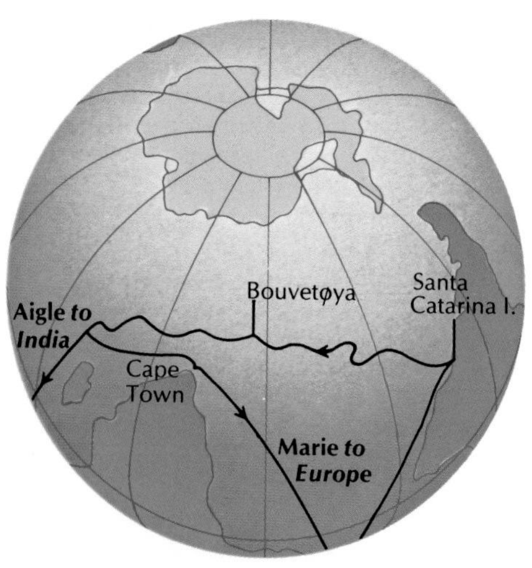

Bouvet submitted a plan of exploration to his employers in 1733. He asked for two seaworthy ships; the larger to be a trading vessel, the other a middle-sized frigate. In return, he promised to seek out staging posts for the French trading vessels *en route* to the Far East and, if possible, to rediscover Gonneville Land. With a young man's arrogance he added: 'If the Company accepts my plans, I insist on being given complete authority and made Governor of whatever I discover. A New Europe offers itself to whomsoever dares to discover it and acquire it in the name of France. All I require are two ships and your wholehearted support.'

The *Compagnie des Indes* hesitated for three years. It was not until Bouvet wrote to the Director General of the *Compagnie*, about the advantages of a French presence in the south, that his plan was finally accepted.

On 4 March 1738, a formal set of instructions was issued. Bouvet was to be given the two ships he had asked for — a 280-tonne trader, the *Aigle* (the *Eagle*), and a companion vessel of less than 200 tonnes, the *Marie*. Bouvet's ship would carry a complement of 92 officers and men, his first lieutenant being an expatriate Irishman, Edmund Hay. The *Marie* was to carry 68 officers and men, under Captain Duclos. The ships were equipped with three, 8.5-metre (28-ft) survey boats, an 18-month supply of food, and a variety of gifts and geegaws to be traded with the natives of Gonneville's southern paradise.

Anticipating the discovery of a tropical Eden, peopled by indolent natives, there was much talk of finding precious stones and varieties of exotic fruits. The 33-year-old Jean-Baptiste Charles Bouvet de Lozier would, he was certain, discover Gonneville Land.

The *Aigle* and the *Marie* left the Breton port of Lorient on 19 July 1738. They set course for the island of Santa Catarina off the coast of Brazil, arriving there in early October. One month later, refitted and reprovisioned, the vessels left port and headed southeast.

In the first week of December the lookouts spotted floating kelp and sea birds wheeling above. Vegetation and birdlife had long been accepted as indications of land. Yet Bouvet and his men were surprised to find the temperature dropping, banks of fog concealing the position of the ships. Those aboard the *Aigle* could hear muffled shouts from the *Marie* though the vessels lost visible contact.

Advancing slowly, they managed to stay together. Regular soundings were taken, though they failed to find bottom at 180 fathoms (329 metres; 1080 ft). The crews, ill equipped for the ever-increasing cold, were wrapped in every garment they could find.

On 8 December the weather cleared and the explorers took the opportunity to dry their weather-rotted clothes. Two days later they crossed the 44th parallel. Bouvet remarked: 'It is here that many cartographers place the *Terres Inconnues*. The fog [turned] as thick as could be . . . We waited in vain for fair weather . . .'

They waited for five days, until 15 December, when the ships were at 48°50'S — as far south of the equator as Paris was to the north. But here there was no equivalent continent, no mirrored capital of France. All Bouvet found was a large iceberg surrounded by floes.

On the 16th he saw penguins, describing them as 'amphibious creatures that look like large ducks, but have fins instead of wings'. More icebergs were encountered, the *Aigle* and the *Marie* tacking cautiously among them. Still following an erratic course southeast, Bouvet became concerned by the ever-present icebergs. 'In effect [they] are floating rocks which are more to be feared than land. If we hit one we will be lost . . .' In another sense they were already lost, not knowing their reckoning of longitude was in error. By the end of December, they were — unwittingly — almost 1600 kilometres (1000 miles) from inhabited land.

One of the few portraits known to exist of the French navigator Jean-Baptiste Charles Bouvet de Lozier.

Christmas was passed amid fog, floes and the frigid winds of the south Atlantic. And then, on 1 January 1739, the lookouts aboard the flagship sighted land. Bouvet cheered his discovery, recording: 'At about 3 pm we saw a very high land, covered with snow, which appeared through the mist. It seemed to us like a large promontory . . . This land lay to the east-north-east at ten to twelve leagues [44-58 km; 30-36 miles].'

By accident — more, perhaps, a miracle of chance — the Frenchman had come directly upon the only speck of land within 20° west and 90° east. A shift of the wind, a coursing of the current, and the vessels might have missed it entirely. But they did not and, on 2 January, the crews were summoned on deck to sing the *Te Deum* and celebrate the discovery of what Bouvet called the Cape of Circumcision.

Unhappily, he was wrong, both in his claim and fixed position. It was true that he had sighted land, but what he believed to be a promontory of the Antarctic mainland was in fact a tiny, isolated island.

For the next 12 days Bouvet attempted to approach the icebound rock. Fog dissuaded him from launching the survey boats, Bouvet fearing they would be unable to find their way back to the mother ships. Food ran short and the crews fell sick with scurvy. In his log of 11

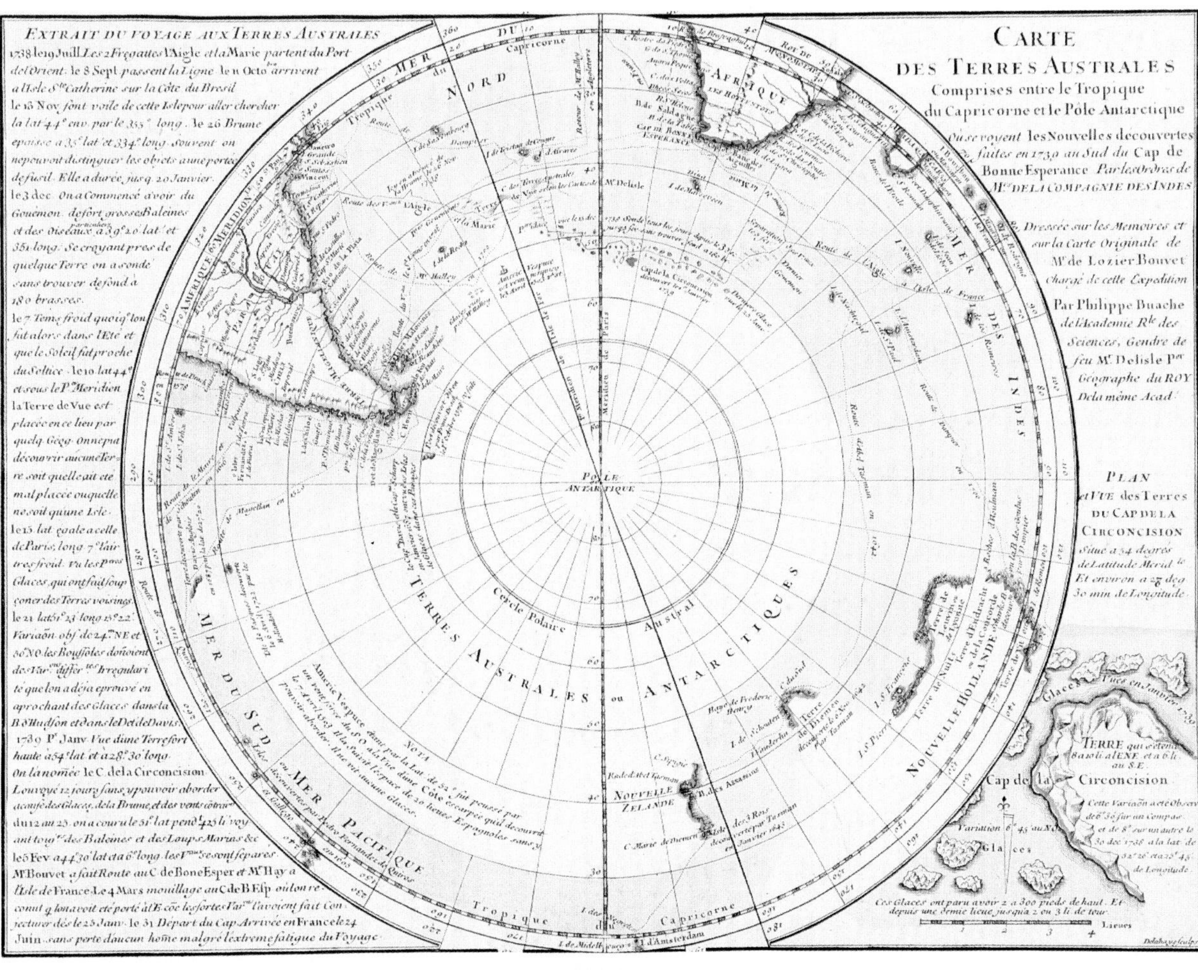

A French map showing Bouvet's discoveries, drawn by the king's first geographer, Phillipe Buache in 1739. Cap de la Circoncision appears almost directly south of Africa at 28°30′E. In fact Bouvet's navigation was at fault and the island was really at 3°24′E. This error led to doubts about the existence of the island, as both Cook and Ross searched for it in vain. Printed around the map are extracts from Bouvet's narrative of the voyage.

Bouvetøya has the distinction of being the most isolated island on earth — the nearest land is over 1600 km (1000 miles) away. Snow and ice-covered, it rises 935 metres (3068 ft) out of the Southern Ocean.

and 12 January he wrote: 'The season advances without improving. Almost everyone is ill ... The only ones [standing watch] are a few of the officers and those young sailors who are still reasonably fit ... [even so] they have all lost their voices ...'

Time and again he fought to draw closer to what he was convinced was a headland. He forced his ships towards it, turning away within 24 kilometres (15 miles) as the ice floes lurched into his path.

Eventually he surrendered to the weather and the illness of his crews. Keeping close to the 52nd parallel, he sailed eastward, skirting the ice for a distance of 2410 kilometres (1500 miles). The presence of seals and penguins confirmed his opinion that the *Terres Australes* lay to the south, beyond the ice. On 25 January, with a number of men seriously ill aboard the vessels, he turned north for the Cape of Good Hope, anchoring there on 24 February.

During the three-month return voyage to France, Bouvet drafted his report to the *Compagnie des Indes*. He reached Lorient on 24 June, and five days later dispatched his letter to the directors. His opening sentence reveals his deep disappointment in the venture. 'I am sorry to inform you that the *Terres Australes* are much further from the Pole than hitherto believed, and completely unsuitable as a staging post for vessels *en route* to the Indies ...

'We have sailed 1200-1500 leagues [5800-7240 km; 3600-4500 miles] in unknown waters, and for seventy days encountered almost continuous fog. We were forty days among the icebergs and we had hail and snow almost every day. The cold was severe for men accustomed to a warmer climate. They were badly clothed and had no means of drying their bedding. Many suffered from chilblains but they had to keep working. I saw sailors crying with cold as they hauled in the sounding line.

'To alleviate the men's discomfort I distributed blankets, hats, shoes, old clothes ... and I opened two kegs of brandy to issue to the crew. The dangers were as great as the discomforts. For more than two months we had been in uncharted waters. We had very little daylight and there were few times when we weren't encountering some kind or risk ... It was not the officers and crew who failed in their mission, but rather the mission that failed them.'

However much the *Compagnie* may have shared in Bouvet's disappointment, they saw fit to add his name to their roll of honour. They expressed their admiration for the explorer in the following glowing terms: 'He is perhaps the greatest sailor and the most experienced seaman who had ever served with the *Compagnie*. He enjoys the finest reputation among his peers.'

The navigational errors committed by Bouvet during his voyage of exploration cast doubt upon the very existence of his Cape of Circumcision. Cook and Ross were both to seek it in vain, since it lay several degrees of longitude west of Bouvet's charted position.

It remained unsighted until 1808, when two English whalers, James Lindsay of the *Snow Swan* and Thomas Hopper of the brig, *Otter*, came upon the island. Like Bouvet, they were unable to penetrate the surrounding ice pack, though their nautical observations fixed the island at 54°22′S and 40°15′E.

The first landing was made in 1822 by the American Morrell. In honour of its discoverer, he renamed it Bouvet's Island. Three years later an Englishman, Norris, chose to rechristen it Liverpool Island. Other whalers and sealers were to follow, and on 1 December 1929, a Norwegian expedition claimed the 57 sq kilometre (22 sq mile) island for Norway, once again crediting its original discoverer by naming it Bouvetøya.

IN SEARCH OF EDEN

Reality falls short of Kerguélen's fantastic claims

Some 30 years after Bouvet's return, France again showed interest in the rediscovery of Gonneville Land (see p70) and the finding of the great southern continent. Various explorers had led expeditions to the Pacific and now King Louis XV and his Minister of Marine were eager to extend their country's influence in the high latitudes of the Indian Ocean.

In 1770, aware perhaps that King and Navy were in a receptive mood, a 36-year-old Breton, Yves-Joseph de Kerguélen-Trémarec, submitted a plan of exploration. Kerguélen's credentials were good. He had entered the Navy at the age of 16, since when he had sailed to Canada and the West Indies. He had twice commanded an armed frigate, protecting French fishing vessels in Icelandic waters.

In September his plan was approved. 'Captain Kerguélen is instructed that all appearances indicate the existence of a very large continent to the south of Amsterdam Island [in the Indian Ocean], which must occupy that part of the globe between 45°S, and the neighbourhood of the Pole in an immense space where no one has yet entered.' With little basis in fact, the instructions added: 'It seems fairly established that Gonneville landed there around the year 1504 and . . . was very well treated by the natives.'

Kerguélen was, if possible, to find this land,

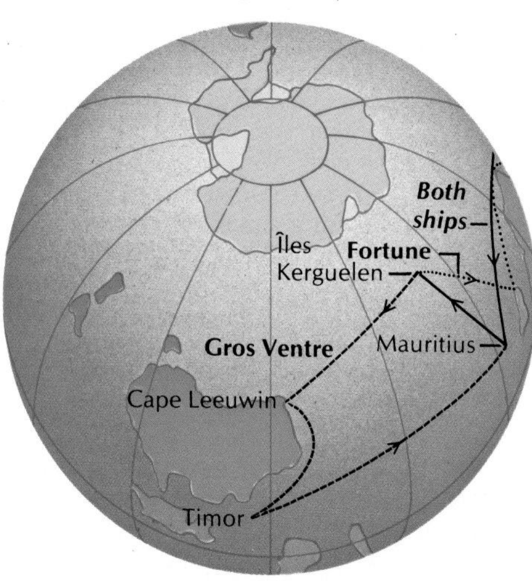

locate a safe harbour for French merchant ships and 'establish bonds of trade and friendship with the inhabitants'. He was given command of a single vessel, the *Berryer*, food and supplies for 14 months, and 300 officers and men.

On 1 May 1771, the *Berryer* left Brest. Aboard ship was an astronomer, Alexis Marie de Rochon. Critical of Kerguélen's navigational abilities, the two men soon fell out. Rochon thought the captain stubborn and autocratic. Kerguélen accused the astronomer of undermining his authority. Ill feeling lasted until the *Berryer* reached Mauritius, and Rochon was later to prove an implacable enemy.

The governor of the island did his best to patch up the quarrel. Impressed by Kerguélen's instructions, he offered to exchange the lumbering *Berryer* for two, more manageable vessels. One of these was a 24-gun corvette, the *Fortune*, the other, a smaller store ship, the *Gros Ventre*. Kerguélen welcomed the offer, though refused a berth for Alexis Marie de Rochon.

The captain of the *Gros Ventre* was a conscientious officer, Francois Alesno Comte de St Allouarn. He was to acquit himself with honour during the months that followed, though ill health forced him to share command of the ship with another Breton sailor, Boisguehenneuc.

After a survey of the Indian Ocean, and a short while spent refitting and reprovisioning the ships, they sailed south on 16 January 1772.

On 3 February, Kerguélen fixed his position as 41°S, 56°20′E. Seaweed was sighted, along with numerous sea birds and penguins. The *Fortune* and the *Gros Ventre* continued to heave southwards, altering course on the 12th to east-southeast. This was in response to birds heading, the explorers believed, towards a nearby coast.

By that same evening land was seen four leagues (18 km; 11 miles) from the ships. It was too late in the day to approach, so the vessels shortened sail and waited for dawn.

At 4 am on 13 February they saw an island and, two hours later, a large headland, its cliffs sheer to the sea. Other islands were sighted, extending from northeast to south for an estimated distance of 25 leagues (111 km; 69 miles).

It was now that Rochon's doubts about Kerguélen's navigation showed themselves well-founded. Without the astronomer's assistance, the explorer fixed his position at 49°40′S and 63°30′E. He was in fact at between 68° and 70°E; 7 degrees out in his reckoning of longitude.

The *Gros Ventre* led the way towards the islands. Ice lay around the bleak, rocky shores. The sea was running high, the air bitterly cold, the form of the land concealed by swirling fog.

Kerguélen, who like so many others believed in the existence of Gonneville's tropic paradise, must have been shocked by his discovery. He decided to stand off from the islands, blaming the *Fortune's* battered rigging. But he knew landfall must be made, and sent one of his officers in a longboat, ordering him to seek an anchorage for the store ship. The boat was almost immediately caught by the current. The *Gros Ventre* was also being driven towards the rocks and, a few moments later, the two craft collided. The longboat's mainmast snapped and the crew were forced to cut away the mizzen mast for fear of being crushed by the store ship.

St Allouarn had meanwhile launched a boat from the *Gros Ventre*. Under the command of the Breton, Boisguehenneuc, this second craft reached a shallow bay, now known as *Anse du Gros Ventre*. Boisguehenneuc claimed the newly discovered land in the name of France.

None of this was witnessed by Kerguélen. The next day the weather worsened, the *Gros Ventre* still lost from view. The *Fortune* remained some distance from the islands. Whatever the problems with her rigging, there is no record of her searching for either the longboat or her consort. Kerguélen rode out one more day aboard the *Fortune*, failed to see land or the store ship, and turned away, his course set for Mauritius.

Reaching the island on 16 March 1772, he contacted his friends, among them the governor, regaling them with a tale of the purest imagination. Fired by Kerguélen's inventive account, the governor wrote immediately to the Minister of Marine. 'If one considers the latitude of the land

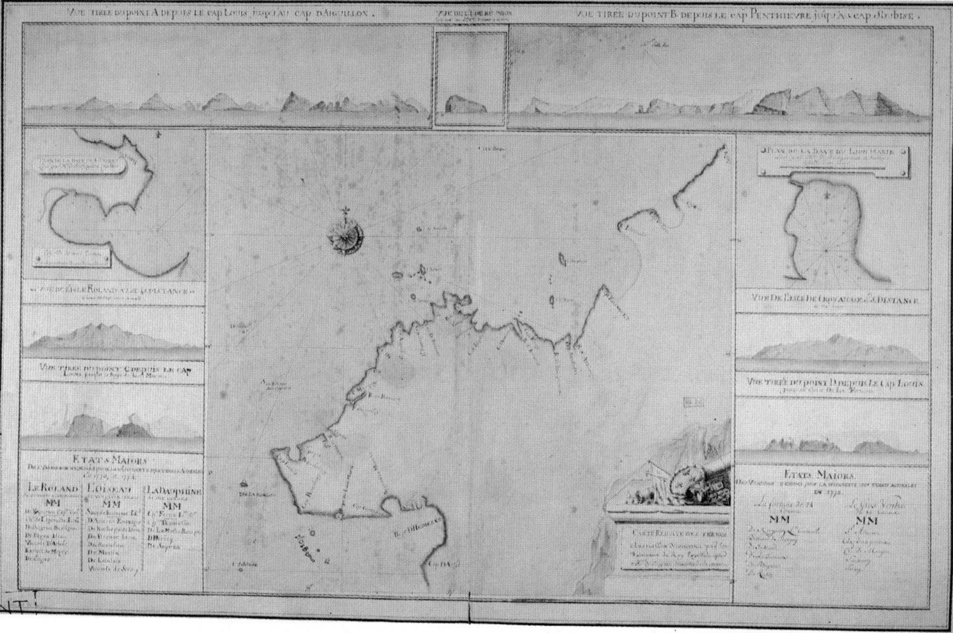

A youthful Yves-Joseph de Kerguélen-Trémarec and (below), a map and views of the northern part of his discovery, Îles Kerguelen, drawn after the voyage of the Rolland, Oiseau *and* Dauphine *in 1773-74.*

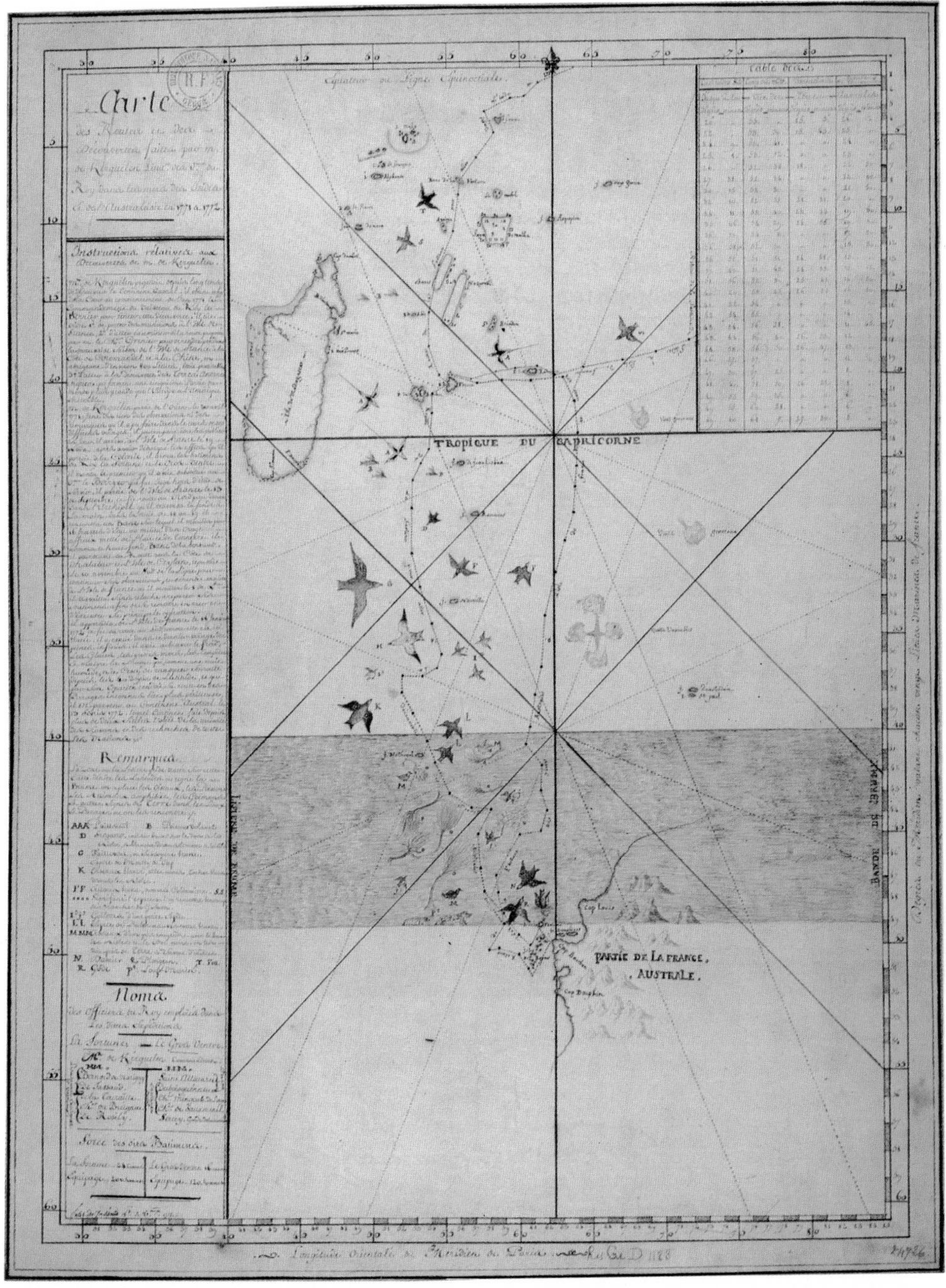

A fanciful map showing the route taken by the Fortune *from the Equator to La France Australe (Îles Kerguelen). The cartographer has imaginatively drawn in at least 1600 km (1000 miles) of non-existent coastline.*

which has been discovered, one cannot fail to attribute to it the mildest and most felicitous climate ... All that [the explorers'] eyes have been able to see is intersected by woods and greenery, which seems to indicate a country that is inhabited and carefully cultivated.'

The Administrator of Mauritius wrote in similar vein. 'Captain Kerguélen has discovered for France, in the space of two months, a new world.'

Kerguélen was now calling his discovery *La France Australe* — South France. During his return he went further, claiming he had found the fifth part of the world. 'It extends to the east by north-east, offering [the chance] of settlements ... This land holds out the promise of all vegetable products ... South France will provide grain crops ... masting timber ... salt works ... [It contains] the very soil of Southern France ...'

Incredibly, Kerguélen's claims were never questioned. France was learning of Captain Cook's achievements in the Pacific. The old king, Louis XV, was anxious to beat the British at their game. True or false, what Kerguélen told his countrymen was what they wanted to hear. A productive southern continent, well away from the Englishman's own backyard. As for the *Gros Ventre*, she would return to France and support Kerguélen's claims. She might even bring back a token of what she had found there — diamonds and rubies, marble and alabaster, foodstuffs and timber, livestock and tropical plants.

Kerguélen was received at Court, promoted over the heads of 86 senior colleagues, and awarded the Cross of St Louis.

Among those who doubted his story was his foremost critic, Rochon. But the astronomer's voice was lost amid the cheers of encouragement. In 1773 a second voyage of exploration was approved and financed, its main object being to colonise Kerguélen's fertile South France. He would be issued with three seagoing vessels, the 64-gun frigate, *Rolland*, a somewhat smaller ship, the *Oiseau*, and a store ship, the *Dauphine*.

The *Gros Ventre* had meanwhile struggled to fulfil the expedition's Articles of Instruction. When the *Fortune* failed to reappear off the Îles Kerguelen in February 1772, St Allouarn assumed she had continued on to Australia. The *Gros Ventre* followed suit. Arriving there in March, the store ship went on to explore the coastline of Timor and Java, returning to Mauritius in September.

The courageous St Allouarn died a few days later, though Boisguehenneuc and the other officers must have been astonished to hear of Kerguélen's version of events. But by then Kerguélen was in France, his story unchallenged.

Surprisingly, no word of the *Gros Ventre* had reached France by the time Kerguélen set sail. Vastly overmanned, he took with him a complement of 700 men, including a number of colonists for his imagined *France Australe*. He also smuggled aboard an extra passenger: a young woman from the then-notorious Rue de Siam in Brest. Her name was Marie-Louise Seguin, more commonly known as Louison. Records reveal that Louison was to accompany Kerguélen throughout his voyage, and that her presence on the *Rolland* was an open secret.

Insanitary conditions soon prevailed aboard the overcrowded vessels. Fever broke out and it was discovered that the hold of the flagship contained 'a prodigious quantity of white worms'. A stopover was made at the Cape of Good Hope, where 80 men were put ashore.

Kerguélen now learned that both the former governor and administrator had been replaced, and that the officers of the *Gros Ventre* had given a very different account of his new-found islands. The authorities received him coolly and, when he asked for men to replace the sick, he was offered the dregs from a punishment battalion.

On 16 October 1773, the *Rolland*, *Oiseau* and *Dauphine* sailed south to rediscover the islands. Two months later they saw land, though the vessels were again beset by adverse weather.

For the next 33 days the ships manoeuvred among the islands. Kerguélen displayed extraordinary indecision, as if once again shocked by the bleak reality of his find. It was left to the captain of the *Oiseau*, Charles de Rosnevet, to send a boat ashore. This time two sealed bottles were placed there, one of which James Cook would find in 1776.

On several occasions the *Oiseau* attempted to guide the *Rolland* inshore. But the flagship stood off, veered away, even set course for the open sea. On 18 January 1774 — blaming the poor state of the crews, the condition of the ships, lack of provisions, the incompetence of his officers — Kerguélen ordered the fleet to set course for Madagascar.

It was the end of his dream, the beginning of his downfall. On 7 September, Kerguélen stepped ashore at Brest. On 13 October a Court of Inquiry was held to investigate various charges laid against him. Less than two months later he was arrested and court-martialled.

Kerguélen stood accused of abandoning both the *Fortune*'s longboat and the *Gros Ventre*, back in February 1772; of conduct unbecoming an officer; of responsibility for the insanitary state of the *Rolland* by filling the gangways with goods he intended to trade for personal profit. The list of accusations included the presence of Louison, smuggled aboard ship 'for his pleasure'.

No doubt embarrassed by their own naive acceptance of his claims, the Navy came down hard on the man who had so successfully misled them. Kerguélen was dismissed from the service and sentenced to 20 years imprisonment in the fortress of Saumur. Cooler heads were later to prevail, and the sentence reduced by two-thirds. Even so, Kerguélen was to serve nearly four years in Saumur, released in 1778 to take part in the war against England.

THE GREATEST NAVIGATOR OF HIS AGE

James Cook plans an expedition in search of the southern continent

Captain James Cook was once described as being 'the most moderate, humane and gentle circumnavigator who ever went upon discoveries', but he was even more remarkable than that. As a naval officer he took no part in great battles, yet his achievements were considerably greater than those who did. For, as an expert seaman, navigator and explorer, he put names on areas of the globe which until then had been empty.

Resolution *and* Adventure *in the Downs, June 1772, after the alterations ordered by Banks had been removed and the* Resolution *had been returned to its original condition. Both were barques, built in Whitby as colliers.*

James Cook was born in the small Yorkshire village of Marton on 27 October 1728 and at the age of 17 he was apprenticed to a shopkeeper in the nearby fishing village of Staithes. He worked there for 18 months before leaving, in 1746, to go to sea as a deckhand on a Whitby collier carrying coal to London.

He spent much of his spare time teaching himself mathematics and astronomy and nine years later he was so accomplished that he was offered the command of a ship of his own. He refused it and instead decided to join the Royal Navy as a seaman. It was inexplicable: the living conditions were dreadful, the food abominable and the pay derisory. And if that was not bad enough there was the added risk of being flogged, hanged or killed in action.

But Cook's ability was soon recognised and two years later he was made Master of the *Pembroke* and given the job of charting the difficult waters of the St Lawrence River in Canada. His work was outstanding and the Admiralty soon realised that he was capable of much bigger things. This was reinforced when, having observed an eclipse of the sun in Newfoundland, he calculated the location of a headland with a precision that was almost unheard of at that time. As a result of this highly original work the Admiralty recalled him to England and put him in command of the *Endeavour*, which was to take Joseph Banks and a group of scientists to the Pacific Ocean to observe the transit of Venus.

The *Endeavour* left England in 1768 and after visiting Tahiti the following year Cook discovered New Zealand and claimed it for Britain. He then sailed west and in 1770 sighted the east coast of Australia. He turned north and on 22 August, on an island off Cape York, he claimed the whole of eastern Australia as a British possession.

By the time the *Endeavour* returned to England in 1771 Cook had not only added significantly to Britain's potential empire in the Pacific, but had also added greatly to the knowledge of that huge ocean. But valuable as that was, one important question remained unanswered: was there or was there not a great southern continent as yet undiscovered?

The possibility had intrigued people for centuries and some had even tried to find it. Cook, although doubtful, was as intrigued as anybody. 'Whether the unexplored part of the southern hemisphere can be only an immense mass of water, or contain another continent, as speculative geography seemed to suggest, was a question which had engaged the attention, not only of learned men, but of most of the maritime powers of Europe.' The British Admiralty, impressed with Cook's success in the Pacific, now decided that it was time to find out once and for all.

Cook was promoted Commander and told to prepare for a second major voyage. His instructions were to travel south to locate Bouvet's Cape Circumcision and to determine if it was part of a great continent. If so, he was to 'take possession of convenient situations in the country in the name of the King of Great Britain'. If it were not part of a continent, he was to go as far south as he could, 'prosecuting your discoveries as near to the South Pole as possible'. He was to circumnavigate the globe in these high latitudes, retreating to the north whenever the weather and the ice made exploration impossible.

The expedition was to be lavishly equipped and during its preparation Cook was denied nothing. From his experience of the last voyage, Cook decided that he should use two ships instead of one and that they should be able to carry a good stock of provisions, have a fairly shallow draught, and be capable of being beached for repairs. The Navy had no ships of that description, but Cook knew where they were to be found. For what he described was nothing more than the Yorkshire colliers he knew so well.

The Admiralty immediately bought two of these colliers and renamed them *Resolution* and *Adventure*. The *Resolution*, which was to be Cook's flagship, was only 33.7 metres (110 ft) long and 10.8 metres (35 ft) across the beam, whilst the *Adventure*, which was to be commanded by another fine seaman, Tobias Furneaux, was even smaller.

Cook's reputation, and the exciting nature of the voyage, meant that he had little difficulty finding good crewmen even though at that time the Navy frequently had to resort to brutal tactics to man its ships. Five officers and thirteen seamen joined him from the *Endea-*

vour, even though they had been back in England for only a few months, whilst the rest were chosen from the many who applied.

One man who was very keen to go was Joseph Banks. After the voyage of the *Endeavour*, Banks had been lionised by science and society and he had enjoyed it enormously. This new voyage would set the seal on his reputation and he immediately took such a leading role that he soon had to be consulted on every detail. If not, he said, he simply would not go.

Banks objected to his accommodation on the *Resolution* and even though Cook gave up his own quarters there was still not enough room for Banks' entourage. This consisted of 13 people and included, incredibly, two French horn players who were to entertain the scientist in a seemly manner. Banks insisted that a large part of the ship be rebuilt to provide spacious quarters and his influence was such that the Admiralty agreed. But the new structures were unwieldy and a sea trial proved what many suspected: the *Resolution* was now so top heavy as to be quite unseaworthy.

The Admiralty ordered the ship to be restored to its original design whilst Banks roared in anger and said, not for the first time, that he would not go. The Admiralty had now had enough of him and said that it would indeed be better if he didn't. But perhaps the most intriguing part of the whole episode was that Banks had arranged for somebody, everybody suspected a woman, to join the ship when it reached Madeira. Nobody knew of it until the ship arrived there, but by then Banks had taken himself off to Iceland!

Cook described the incident in a letter from Madeira in August 1772. 'Three days before we arrived a person left the Island who went by the name of Burnett. He had been waiting for Mr Banks arrival about three months ... [he] said his intention was to go out with Mr Banks ... at last when he heard that Mr Banks did not go, he took the very first opportunity to get off the Island, he was about 30 years of age and rather ordinary than otherwise ... Every part of Mr Burnett's behaviour and every action tended to prove that he was a woman, I have not met with a person that entertains a doubt of a contrary nature ...'

In spite of these distractions, Cook worked tirelessly to prepare the expedition and in the process developed a commendable technique for handling bureaucrats. When he wanted supplies he simply went to the source, explained what he needed, and then wrote his formal application on the spot.

And he needed a great deal. The *Resolution* alone took on 27 tonnes of biscuits and over 14 000 pieces of salt pork. Even so, the daily allowance seems frugal now. On Mondays, for example, each man was given 500 g (18 oz) of biscuits, 225 g (8 oz) of butter, 300 g (11 oz) of cheese, and as much boiled oatmeal as he could possibly eat. Preserved meat was served only four days a week.

Cook was, in fact, always deeply concerned about the welfare of his men and went to considerable trouble on their behalf. At that time all seamen knew the danger of scurvy, a disease that probably killed more men than enemy canons ever did. Suspecting that certain foods made scurvy less likely, Cook loaded many items that had not previously been carried by ships of the Royal Navy. These included nine tonnes of sauerkraut, three tonnes of salted cabbage, and over 100 litres (22 gallons) of 'Mermalade of Carrots'. The men had little enthusiasm for such fare, but they remained remarkably free of scurvy.

Finally, and with little ceremony, the two tiny ships sailed out of Plymouth Sound at 6 am on 13 July 1772 and one of the officers wrote 'Farewell Old England' in large letters in his diary. It was a sentiment echoed in different ways by everybody on board who now faced the three-year voyage.

A MATTER OF SCALE

It is difficult, today, to appreciate just how small Cook's ships really were. The length of the *Resolution's* lower deck was 33.7 metres (110 ft 8 in), her extreme breadth 10.8 metres (35 ft 5.5 in) and the depth in her hold 4 metres (13 ft 1.5 in). By way of comparison, the liner *Queen Elizabeth 2* is 293 metres (963 ft) long, 32 metres (105 ft) broad with a maximum draught of 9.9 metres (32 ft 6 in).

The Resolution *and* Queen Elizabeth 2 *compared.*

James Cook (above) in a portrait that he commissioned for his wife. He was 43 years old when he returned from his great voyage in 1771. Banks, who shared the honours for the voyage, was only 28.

Joseph Banks (right) as a young man. He was originally going to accompany Cook on the Resolution, *but withdrew over a dispute about elaborate alterations he had ordered to the ship.*

ANTARCTICA ENCIRCLED

Cook crosses the Antarctic Circle for the first time but fails to sight the continent

After leaving England at the start of his second major voyage Cook made a leisurely run south and had the benefit of good weather nearly all the way to the Cape of Good Hope. In the course of the next two and a half years* Resolution *and* Adventure *were to circumnavigate Antarctica for the first time, and to prove that no great undiscovered, habitable land mass existed in the southern hemisphere.

The two ships reached Cape Town 109 days after leaving Plymouth and there Cook heard of a voyage in the Indian Ocean made by a Frenchman called Yves-Joseph de Kerguélen-Trémarec and his discovery of land there which he had called *La France Australe*. It was significant news because, like Bouvet's Cape Circumcision, it might prove to be part of the great southern continent.

On 23 November 1772 *Resolution* and *Adventure* sailed out of Cape Town and Cook headed into the unknown waters of the south. Two weeks later he started to look for Cape Circumcision and on 11 December it seemed that *Adventure* had found it. But what they thought was land proved instead to be an iceberg and by the following day the ships were at the edge of a consolidated ice pack which seemed to stretch forever. Unable to go south, Cook turned east, skirting the ice along the southern edge of the Indian Ocean.

On 17 January 1773 they crossed the Antarctic Circle, almost certainly the first ships to do so, but again the ice blocked their way.

For the next two months Cook edged along the ice, probing for a gap that would take him further south. He knew now that Cape Circumcision was not to be found in its reported location and, having passed south of the land seen by Kerguélen, he knew that it too could not be part of a southern continent.

As winter approached Cook retreated from the ice and made for the South Island of New Zealand. He reached Dusky Sound on 25 March having sailed 17 000 kilometres (10 600 miles) through unknown seas.

He spent the winter exploring the islands of the South Pacific and on 27 November, after having been parted from *Adventure* in a storm, he took *Resolution* out of Dusky Bay and once more sailed south towards the ice.

He reached it in the middle of December but, unable to find a way through, he again turned to sail along it.

It is quite incredible that the *Resolution* survived. The rigging and masts were heavy with ice and the sails were like plates of steel, but men still had to go aloft to work the ship. Dangerous though that was, the ice in the sea was an even greater danger. The ship was frequently surrounded by huge icebergs or vast areas of pack ice where a collision could have sent her to the bottom. There can be no finer tribute to Cook's skill as a seaman and navigator than that he was able to survive for weeks on end in a tiny Yorkshire collier without the loss of a single man.

But on 30 January, at his most southerly position, it was clear he could go no further. The ice 'extended east and west far beyond the reach of our sight, while the southern half of the horizon was illuminated by rays of light which were reflected from the ice to a considerable height ... It was indeed my opinion

Whenever necessary the ships took on ice from small bergs and floes that they passed to replenish their supply of fresh drinking water.

A watercolour sketch of the South Sandwich Islands by John Gilbert, master of the Resolution*. He wrote in his log on 31 January 1775: 'This country has the most dreary starved appearance that can be imagined.'*

William Hodges painted this dramatic scene (below) of the two ships in an iceberg-strewn sea.

that this ice extends quite to the Pole, or perhaps joins to some land to which it has been fixed since creation'.

After wintering again in the Pacific, Cook left New Zealand in November 1774 at the start of his third ice cruise. This time he sailed right across the southern Pacific and some five weeks later reached Tierra del Fuego.

After staying there for two weeks he headed northeast into the Atlantic. And then, when everybody least expected it, they saw land. At first even Cook thought they had at last found the southern continent, but instead it was merely an island, covered in ice and desolate beyond belief. He called it South Georgia and was happy to leave it behind.

Although he had hoped for a quick voyage to England, he could not resist sailing a little further to the southeast in the hope of seeing the mainland which he now felt sure existed to the south. But he found no sign of it and towards the end of January he called off the search. Then, almost immediately, he saw a group of islands that were even more desolate than South Georgia. These he named the South Sandwich Islands, and after exploring them for a week Cook at last turned away from the ice for the voyage home.

The *Resolution* reached England on 30 July 1775 having travelled more than 97 000 kilometres (60 000 miles) in a voyage which had lasted three years and eight days. Cook had proved that there was no southern continent, unless it was at the pole itself, in which case it was unlikely to be of much use to anybody.

Cook's reputation was such that this conclusion might well have deterred further exploration for generations had he not recorded in his journal, with typical thoroughness, the large numbers of seals and whales that they had seen in those southern waters. Whilst governments and explorers turned their attentions elsewhere, the owners of the whaling fleets of Europe and America could see advantages where others thought there were none. And it was they, not explorers, who were now prepared to venture into the vast ice-covered waters of the Antarctic.

RUSHING INTO PRINT

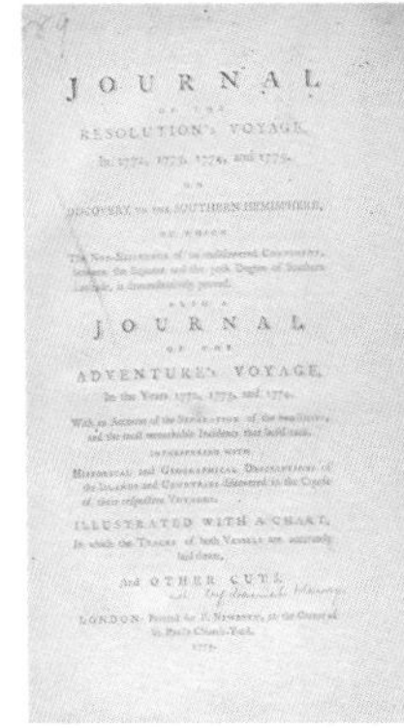

JOURNAL

RESOLUTION's VOYAGE

JOURNAL

ADVENTURE's VOYAGE

ILLUSTRATED WITH A CHART,

And OTHER CUTS

LONDON

Title page of John Marra's account of the voyage. Marra had attempted to desert in Tahiti where he had been 'promis'd a House, Land and a Pretty Wife'. Cook wrote: 'After much difficulty we got him on board again (for he would have been a great loss to us).'

After every major voyage of exploration an excited public waited eagerly to read accounts of it, and Cook's second voyage was certainly no exception. Whilst Cook's own account would be the one in greatest demand, others knew they could make a small fortune by publishing their own versions first.

Although the official account of Cook's first voyage had been written by Dr John Hawkesworth, Cook decided to write the account of the second voyage himself.

He had barely started work, however, when he heard in September 1775 that an account supposedly written by him was about to go to press. He suspected the author to be a gunner called Robert Anderson but when he confronted him Anderson denied it. In which case, Cook told him, he had better find out who it was.

Anderson soon found that the account had been written by a gunner's mate called John Marra and when Marra confessed Anderson made him go to Cook to establish the truth.

Extracts of Marra's account were published under his own name between December 1775 and the following March and this was almost certainly the first account of the voyage.

Meanwhile, John Forster, who had joined the expedition with his son George, planned to publish his own account, but the Admiralty forbade him to publish anything until after Cook's account had appeared. If John Forster could not publish, George could. What was essentially his father's account appeared in 1777.

Cook's own account was published six weeks later. But by then Cook was already on his third and final voyage and thus never saw the result of all his labour.

COOK'S LAST VOYAGE

Tragic end to an extraordinary career

After returning from his second voyage in 1775 Cook was promoted again and then appointed Fourth Captain at Greenwich Hospital. This was a very comfortable form of retirement, but at 46 Cook was not sure that he was ready to retire. Eventually he accepted it, but only on the condition that he could 'quit it when either the call of my country for more active service, or [when] my endeavours in any shape can be essential to the public . . .'

The call was soon to come. The *Resolution,* under the command of Captain Clerke, was to return to the Pacific to take back to Tahiti a native who had been brought to England by Tobias Furneaux after he and Cook had lost contact with each other near New Zealand in 1773. As the *Adventure* was now unseaworthy, Cook was asked early in 1776 to advise on a replacement to accompany *Resolution* on the voyage. Once again he recommended a Yorkshire collier and again the Admiralty followed his advice, naming this one *Discovery.* A few weeks later Cook decided to take command of the expedition.

If the circumstances are a little vague, there is no doubt that the Admiralty greeted the news with enthusiasm. The need to return the native to Tahiti was hardly sufficient justification for sending two ships halfway round the world and, once in the Pacific, the ships could do far more than that. In which case, there was nobody better qualified to command them than Captain James Cook.

With Clerke in command of *Discovery,* Cook was to take the two ships on yet another voyage of exploration in the Pacific. Except that this time he was to sail north to find a sea

The bleak hills of Îles Kerguelen, named by Cook the islands of Desolation. He wrote: 'The first discoveries [sic] with some reason imagined it to be the Cape of a Southern Continent, the English have sence [sic] proved that no such continent exists and that the land in question is an island of no great extent, which from its stirility [sic] I shall call the Islands of Desolation.'

Resolution *and* Discovery *anchored in Christmas Harbour on Îles Kerguelen. Despite French claims, Cook took possession of the island for Britain.*

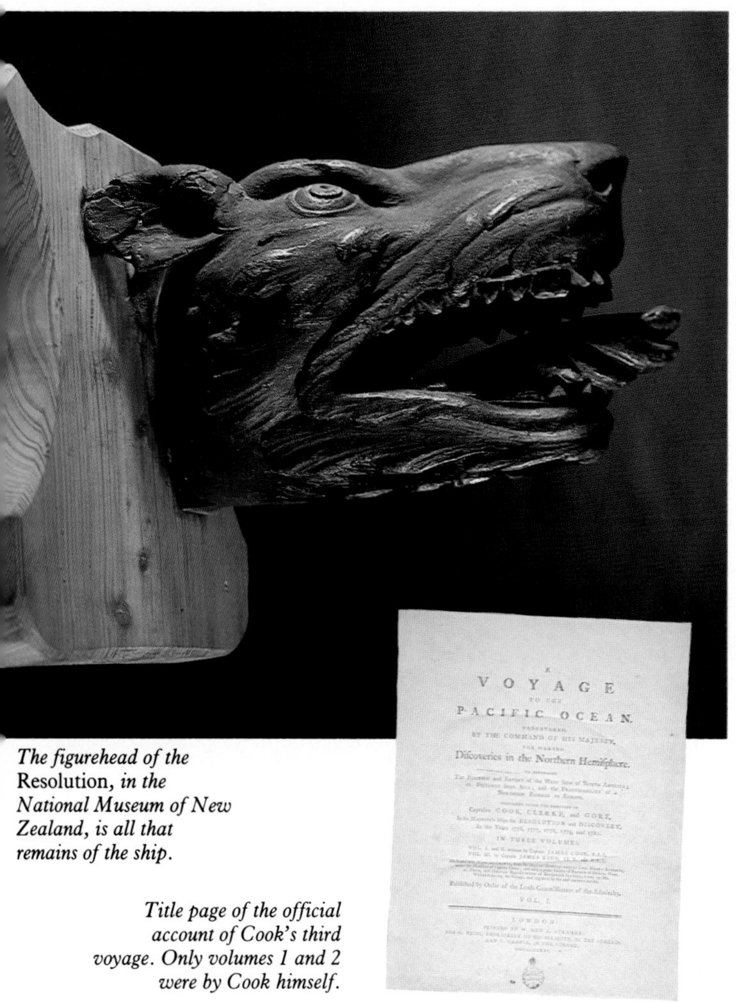

A

VOYAGE

PACIFIC OCEAN.

BY THE COMMAND OF HIS MAJESTY,

Discoveries in the Northern Hemisphere.

Captains COOK, CLERKE, and GORE,

IN THREE VOLUMES.

Published by Order of the Lords Commissioners of the Admiralty.

VOL. I.

LONDON:

The figurehead of the Resolution, *in the National Museum of New Zealand, is all that remains of the ship.*

Title page of the official account of Cook's third voyage. Only volumes 1 and 2 were by Cook himself.

SOLVING THE PROBLEM OF LONGITUDE

Larcum Kendall's first timepiece, K1, is now preserved in the National Maritime Museum in London. It was this same watch that Cook took with him on the Resolution *from 1772-75, and from 1776-79. The instrument, designed by John Harrison and built by Kendall, was purchased by the Admiralty for £450.*

One of the most difficult problems facing the early navigators was to accurately fix their position at sea. The simplest way to determine longitude is to find the difference between local time and that at some fixed point, such as Greenwich. In 1714 the British Government offered a reward to any person who could manufacture a chronometer that would go at a uniform rate, whatever the climate and conditions, and therefore always give Greenwich time accurately. The reward was on a sliding scale: if, after a six-week voyage, the chronometer gave the longitude within 97 kilometres (60 miles) it was £10 000; within 64 kilometres (40 miles), £15 000; and within 48 kilometres (30 miles), the grand total of £20 000.

The first person to produce such an instrument was John Harrison, and it was tested successfully on voyages in 1762 and 1764. A copy of one of Harrison's watches was made by another watchmaker, Larcum Kendall, and it was this very accurate timepiece that Cook took with him on the *Resolution* from 1772-75, and again from 1776-79.

route from the Pacific to the Atlantic. Known in England as the Northwest Passage, its existence had long been suspected but some 50 attempts had so far failed to locate it. If a route could be found, and if it were navigable, it would provide a far quicker voyage from Europe to Asia than the hazardous route around Cape Horn.

Because of the need to call at Tahiti, Cook decided to approach the Pacific from the Indian Ocean. This would also give him an opportunity to investigate the land discovered by Yves-Joseph de Kerguélen-Trémarec, which was to the north of the route Cook had followed during his second voyage.

Resolution was overhauled and was ready to take on her crew in January 1776, although it was March before she finally came out of dock. This time, however, Cook was unable to give the same attention to detail as he had when preparing for the second voyage.

Cook and the *Resolution* left Plymouth on 12 July 1776, leaving *Discovery* to follow later. Clerke was in prison, having rashly stood as guarantor for his brother's debts, but he was able to join *Discovery* a few weeks later.

In spite of her refit, *Resolution* started to take in water before she had left the English Channel and it was a wet and uncomfortable ship that sailed into Cape Town on 18 October. Repairs were made there but they were not successful and *Resolution* continued to leak for the rest of the voyage.

Discovery arrived at the Cape on 10 November and by the end of the month both ships were ready for sea again. They left on the 30th and Cook steered southeast to locate a group of islands which had been discovered some years earlier by Marion du Fresne. The ships crashed through heavy seas pursued by what seemed to be an endless gale until, on 12 December, they saw the first of the islands. Cook named them Prince Edward Islands before sailing further south to look for Kerguélen's discovery.

The weather soon became even worse and, with the added complication of dense fog, the ships had to fire their guns in order to stay in touch with each other. It cleared as they ran east along latitude 48°S and on 24 December they saw land to the south-south-east, exactly where they expected it to be.

The land was an islet off the northwest point of Kerguélen's *La France Australe* which they saw later in the afternoon, and the following day the two ships worked carefully into a large bay and came to anchor near a sandy beach.

When the men were given a day's holiday on Boxing Day, one of them returned with a bottle he had found near a rock on the north side of the bay. In it was a parchment containing an inscription in Latin recording the French visits in 1772 and 1773. Cook used the other side of the parchment to record his own visit and put it back in the bottle together with a silver coin before burying it again.

Cook spent four days exploring the island, making meticulous notes of the coastline and going ashore for a better view of the land. It was unimpressive. Although there was a good supply of fresh water, which they welcomed, there were no trees or shrubs and little grass. Cook called them Islands of Desolation, although they are now known as Îles Kerguelen.

On 30 December 1776 Cook sailed his two ships away from the island to start the long voyage to New Zealand. It was his last contact with the Antarctic.

DEATH IN HAWAII

Cook had been told to wait until the summer of 1778 before starting his search for the Northwest Passage. So he now spent some time leisurely exploring the Pacific islands.

On 18 January 1778 he made his last important discovery — the Hawaiian Islands — and the following month the two ships sailed north up the west coast of America. After probing the coasts of Canada and Alaska in an unsuccessful attempt to find a passage, they sailed through the Bering Strait and crossed the Arctic Circle. Then Cook turned the ships south and headed back to Hawaii.

He reached there towards the end of November and in the middle of January 1779, after exploring the islands, Cook moved the ships to a good anchorage at Kealakekua Bay where he was given an overwhelming reception by thousands of natives.

But when the ships returned to the bay on 10 February the welcome had changed to hostility and when a native stole one of their boats, Cook went ashore on 14 February with a squad of marines to take the king back to the ship as a hostage.

The old man was willing enough, but as they made their way to the water's edge a large group of natives stopped them and urged the king not to go. Further along the shore a chief was killed when he tried to leave the beach and now the mood became warlike. A native approached Cook threateningly, Cook fired at him, and suddenly there was a battle as the natives charged and the marines attacked with gunfire and bayonets.

The action lasted only a few minutes, but when it was over Captain James Cook lay dead on the beach.

A Blank On The Map

Lifting the veil from the hidden continent

It was not until the 1940s and 50s that the last blanks on the Antarctic map were finally filled in. By then only 170 years had elapsed since James Cook's epic voyages, and the first hazy notions about the possible shape of the elusive southern continent. Credit for this feat belongs to a tiny handful of men who were willing to risk all in a battle against the ice.

Scientific mapping of Antarctica started with the great voyages of Captain James Cook after the problem of longitude had been solved by the new Harrison chronometers. Although Cook never claimed to have seen the southern continent, despite crossing the Antarctic Circle three times at widely separated points, he did indirectly solve the major outstanding geographical problem of his time, limiting the mythical continent of *Terra Australis* to a frozen land south of the Antarctic Circle. His charts of the subantarctic islands opened the way for a rush of sealers.

The sealers, ruthless in their exploitation of the seal colonies, constantly searched for new sealing grounds. But discoveries were kept secret and few charts were published. Later, the sealers Smith, Palmer and Bransfield left records of their discoveries, and in 1819 the systematic Russian expedition under Bellingshausen set out. Meticulously planned to complement Cook's voyages, Bellingshausen waited a month in England to purchase three English chronometers and a sextant from the famous firm of Troughton. But his excellent charts were not published for eight years after his return to Moscow in 1821, and they were not available outside Russia until 1836.

Meanwhile, following William Smith's sightings of the South Shetland Islands from the brig *Williams* and his subsequent landing there in 1819, the British Admiralty placed Edward Bransfield in charge of the *Williams*, with Smith as master and pilot, on a properly equipped expedition to survey the islands. Following their charting, the expedition sailed south to sight the mainland of the Antarctic Peninsula on 30 January 1820. A landing was made by Bransfield on Trinity Island, the northern extremity of the Antarctic Peninsula.

In 1821 the British sealer William Powell met Nathaniel Palmer, an American sealer from Connecticut, at the South Shetland Islands. Both men kept detailed accounts of their discoveries and together they explored the South Orkney Islands. Powell published a chart of the South Shetland and the South Orkney Islands soon afterwards.

Unlike most of the sealers, the British mercantile firm of S. Enderby & Sons (later Enderby Brothers) tried to combine trade with geographical discovery. Charles Enderby instructed his captains to search for new lands and published their discoveries. The names of four of his captains, Weddell, Biscoe, Kemp and Balleny loom large on maps.

Following the publication by Karl Friedrich Gauss of his magnetic theories in 1833, three national expeditions set out between 1837 and 1842 to penetrate the Weddell Sea and make magnetic observations. Dumont d'Urville in 1837-40 sighted and named Terre Adélie and Clarie Coast. His magnetic observations indicated that he was close to the South Magnetic Pole, but it was beyond his reach. Wilkes, on his voyage from 1838-42, sighted the Balleny Islands in 1840, then headed westwards towards Peter Kemp's new Enderby Land. He made extensive claims to have seen land, some of which were subsequently disproved; but his chart of the Antarctic continent indicated its general limits for some 1000 kilometres (620 miles). James Clark Ross in 1839-43 wished to follow his own successful observations at the North Magnetic Pole by observations at the South Magnetic Pole. Although he did not succeed in reaching it, he discovered the Ross Sea, Ross Ice Shelf, and Victoria Land.

After these expeditions, exploration shifted to the Arctic for nearly 50 years.

In 1886 the British scientist John Murray published a map in the Scottish Geographical Magazine showing the results of the *Challenger* expedition. Eventually his hypothetical coastline was found to be very close to the truth.

Murray's map, and a growing interest in whaling, stimulated renewed interest in Norway, Australia and Britain, but government and private sponsors were slow to back proposed expeditions. However the Sixth International Geographical Conference in 1895 saw a worldwide appeal for Antarctic exploration.

The renewed interest in the Antarctic ushered in the heroic age of Antarctic exploration. Enthusiasts sought and found support from individual benefactors, societies, firms and governments. The expeditions of Bruce, Gerlache, Filchner, Nordenskjöld and Charcot charted the Antarctic Peninsula. The heroic journeys of Shackleton, Scott, Mawson and Amundsen made a start on mapping the mountains and glaciers in the interior of the continent. Sketch maps of variable quality were published with the reports of the expeditions, and a new map of Antarctica was published by J.G. Bartholomew at a scale of 1:14 million in 1905. Both Scott and Drygalski in 1902 tried the use of captive balloons to extend their observations of the surrounding terrain. In 1911 Douglas Mawson contemplated the use of an aeroplane for investigation of the terrain and mapping purposes, but the aircraft crashed before the expedition started. Mawson and Davis in the *Aurora* linked up the explorations of Scott, Dumont d'Urville, Ross and Wilkes to that of Drygalski, tracing the coastline between Gaussberg in Kaiser Wilhelm Land and King George V Land near the Ross Sea. A controversy arose after the expeditions of Bruce and Filchner about whether there was a channel connecting the Weddell and Ross Seas.

After the loss of Shackleton's *Endurance* and the outbreak of World War 1, there was again a lull in Antarctic mapping.

In 1928 the aeroplane started to provide a wealth of information, but at the same time demonstrated the impossibility of making maps from air photographs without surveys on the ground. In 1928 Sir Hubert Wilkins flew south from Deception Island down the 61°W meridian to 71°S. In a few hours he saw more than earlier expeditions had seen in several seasons. The result was dramatic. Wilkins immediately reported and named a number of east-west channels which he claimed separated the Antarctic Peninsula from the continent and cut it into a number of islands. This corroborated reports from some Norwegian sealers in 1920, and in 1935 was supported by Lincoln Ellsworth who made two flights down the east coast of the peninsula. But all these flights were of little value for mapping; navigation was by dead reckoning in unknown winds, over ground without a network of surveyed points. Ground surveys later proved that the channels did not exist. Sir Raymond Priestley commented that Wilkins' first flights in the Antarctic were 'notable reconnaissance flights, providing through his maps the classic example of the unreliability of air surveys without ground control'. But they did revolutionise Antarctic mapping, and the American Geographical Society published a new map of Antarctica in 1929 at a scale of 1:12.5 million, setting out the new discoveries, including the non-existent channels. Wilkins had mistaken transverse glaciers which flow east and west from low divides on the spine of the Antarctic Peninsula for straits of sea ice.

Wilkins made another unsuccessful attempt to fly across to the Ross Sea in 1929-30, and his flight showed that Charcot Land, discovered by Charcot in 1909-10, was an island.

The British Graham Land Expedition of 1934-37 led by John Rymill surveyed much of the western coast of the Atlantic Peninsula. The combination of ground surveys from sledge journeys and air photographs produced accurate maps, and proved Wilkins' straits to be glaciers; his Hearst Land to be an island.

There were still three great unmapped stretches of coastline: between the Weddell Sea and Enderby Land; Enderby Land and Kaiser Wilhelm Land; and between the Ross Sea and the Antarctic Peninsula.

These major stretches of coastline were explored from 1928 to 1938 by a series of privately sponsored expeditions from America, Norway and the British Commonwealth, organised respectively by the American Richard Byrd; the Norwegian Lars Christensen; and the Australian Sir Douglas Mawson. In each case the enthusiasm of the leader was the key factor in organising the expedition. Each used aeroplanes to search for, and sometimes photograph, new areas of land.

Byrd's expedition of 1928-29 went to the area between the Antarctic Peninsula and the Ross Sea. It was the first from America since that of Wilkes 90 years before, and was the forerunner of a great series of American expeditions. Although Byrd made extensive aircraft flights on this expedition from his base at the Bay of Whales in the Ross Sea, his chief interest was the unknown sector between the Bellingshausen and Ross Seas. He mapped the western coast and hinterland of this region naming it Marie Byrd Land. He was the first to use a fixed aerial survey camera, and his surveyor Ashley McKinley took runs of photos over the Rockefeller Mountains and along the coastline east of the Bay of Whales. In 1929 he made the first flights over the South Pole and disproved the existence of Amundsen's Carmen Land, south of the Queen Maud Mountains. In 1933-35, Byrd again wintered at the Bay of Whales, and proved beyond doubt that Marie Byrd Land was part of the continent, and there was no sea channel between the Weddell and Ross Seas.

The Norwegian exploration and mapping expedition to the Weddell Sea and Enderby Land was organised by Lars Christensen, a whaling magnate, who, in the tradition of the British sealing firm of Enderby Brothers, instructed his whaling captains to combine whaling with exploration. In 1927-28 and 1928-29, his ship *Norvegia* studied whaling possibilities in the waters off Enderby Land and the non-existent Dougherty Island. In 1929-30, the *Norvegia* carried two aircraft in which the captain Riiser-Larsen made many flights. A fine series of charts were published of the coast from the Weddell Sea to Enderby Land and further east, overlapping and supplementing the charting of the third major Antarctic exploration of the time, led by Sir Douglas Mawson. Following a meeting in Antarctic waters, Riiser-Larsen and Mawson agreed that 45°E should be the dividing line between British and Norwegian activities.

Mawson charted the coast between 45°E and 160°E from Kaiser Wilhelm Land to Enderby and Kemp Lands, which had been sighted by British whalers a century earlier. He named Mac.Robertson and Princess Elizabeth Land.

In 1939 two national expeditions set out, the first from Germany under Captain Alfred Ritscher and the second from America under Rear Admiral Byrd.

The German expedition on board the *Schwabenland* sailed for three weeks along the Princess Astrid Coast. Flying boats from the ship took photographs of coastal and inland mountains between longitudes 4°W and 14°E. As the maps published from these photographs were not based on any ground surveys they contained substantial errors of position.

Byrd's third expedition in 1939-41, the United States Antarctic Service Expedition, was sponsored by the United States Government. It was the largest so far organised, with two bases, one in the Bay of Whales and the other at Stonington Island off the Antarctic Peninsula. More of the coast of Marie Byrd Land along the Amundsen Sea was mapped, and the map of several inland mountain ranges were enlarged. Ground surveys were made in the Flood Range, Fosdick Mountains and Rockefeller Mountains. The eastern party extended the work of Rymill. Bellingshausen's Alexander Land was proved to be an island. The east and west coasts of the Antarctic Peninsula as far as 74°S were photographed. Much ground survey work was done.

By the time World War II broke out most of the Antarctic coastline was charted, if not all in accurate detail. Much of the interior still remained to be explored, although the broad shape of the continent was known. Generally, the war also saw the end of private mapping expeditions. The work was now taken over by large well-equipped government organisations going south and wintering in permanent bases.

In 1946, the US Navy organised Operation Highjump — a massive onslaught on the mapping of Antarctica, again under Rear Admiral Byrd. Over 4700 men, 13 ships — including two icebreakers, an aircraft carrier and two seaplane tenders, six aircraft equipped for trimetrogon photography, four helicopters and three light aircraft were employed. Photographs were obtained around the whole continent, except the Weddell Sea sector.

Gradually the gaps were filled in, in more and more detail. Modern techniques and equipment, especially artificial satellites, have led to the production of very accurate maps.

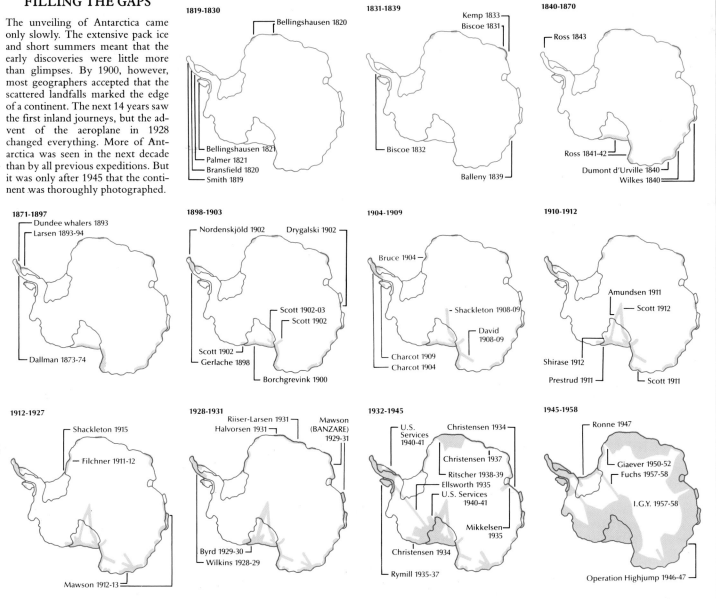

FILLING THE GAPS

The unveiling of Antarctica came only slowly. The extensive pack ice and short summers meant that the early discoveries were little more than glimpses. By 1900, however, most geographers accepted that the scattered landfalls marked the edge of a continent. The next 14 years saw the first inland journeys, but the advent of the aeroplane in 1928 changed everything. More of Antarctica was seen in the next decade than by all previous expeditions. But it was only after 1945 that the continent was thoroughly photographed.

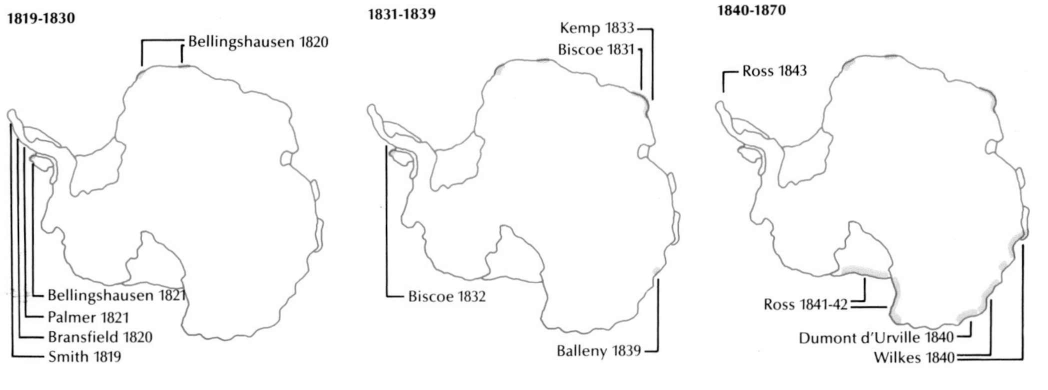

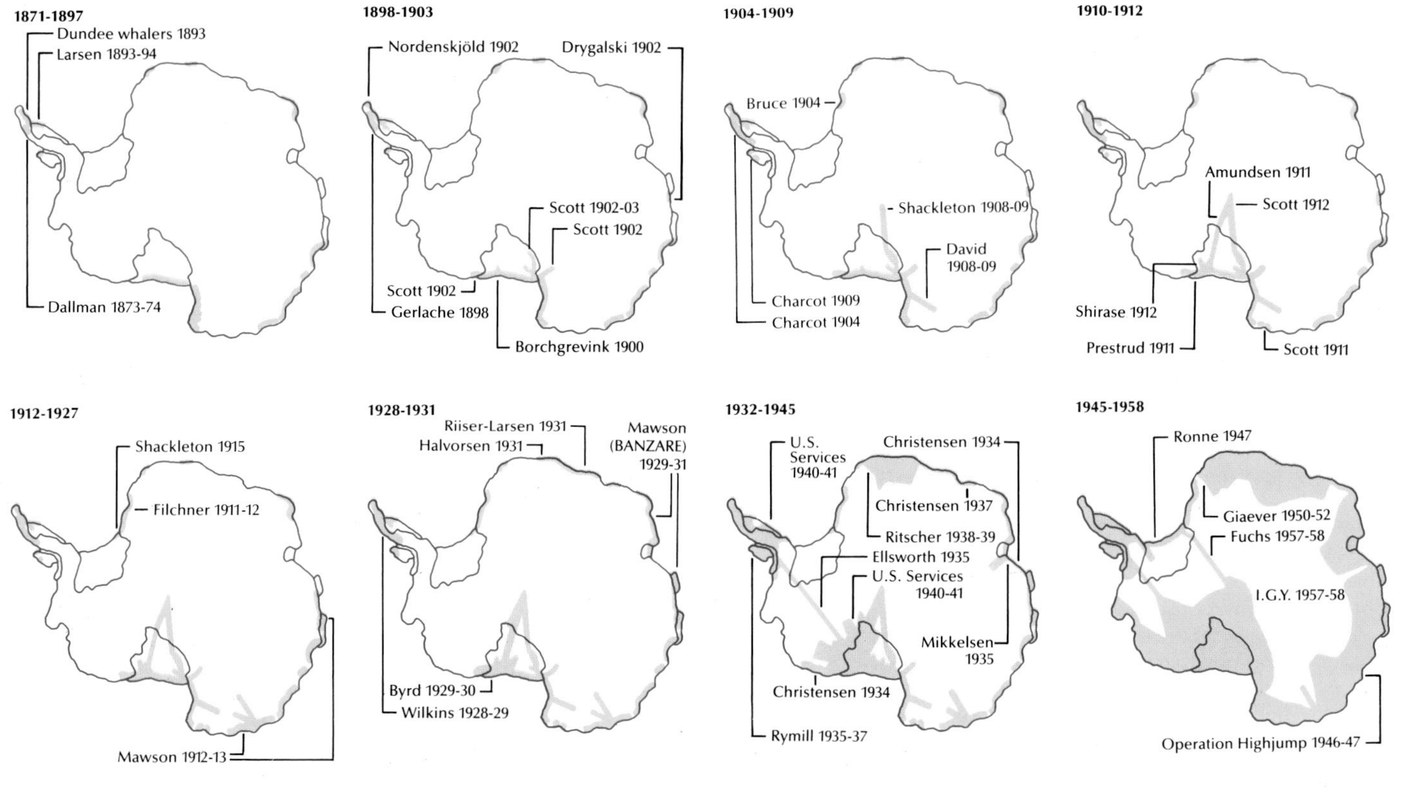

Admiral Faddei Faddeevich Bellingshausen was leader of Russia's first Antarctic expedition.

Admiral Michail Michailovich Lazarev, in command of the Mirnyi, *had once served in Britain's Royal Navy.*

RUSSIA LOOKS SOUTH

Bellingshausen's voyage rivals those of Cook

With the death of James Cook in 1779, the nations of Europe seemed to falter in their search for* Terra Australis, *the great southern continent. Russia, which had hitherto shown no interest in Pacific or Antarctic exploration, continued to concentrate her efforts in Siberian waters, and it was not until 1819 that Tsar Alexander I authorised a scheme whereby ships would be sent to both the north and south polar regions.

The man selected to command the southern expedition was a cautious, patriotic captain of the Imperial Navy, Thaddeus von Bellingshausen. Born in 1779, Bellingshausen had enrolled as a cadet at the age of 10, graduating from the Naval Academy at Kronstadt when he was 18.

Now 40 years old, he was in the Crimean port of Sebastapol when, on 5 May 1819, he was summoned north to St Petersburg. The journey took him more than a month, and he was no doubt surprised to learn that the expedition was expected to leave within six weeks.

The aims of the voyage were twofold. Bellingshausen was to expand on the work done by Cook in the southern latitudes. Also, taking advantage of the Antarctic summer, he was to sail as far south as possible towards the pole.

Tsar Alexander could not have chosen a better man. Bellingshausen hero-worshipped the English explorer and had made a lifelong study of Cook's remarkable achievements.

But the Russian yards failed to supply ships of equal merit. Bellingshausen's flagship, the *Vostok* (*East*), was a recently launched corvette of some 600 tonnes, of pinewood sheathed with copper. Constructed as a 28-gun man-of-war, she was not designed for polar exploration. Yet Bellingshausen had to accept her.

The second vessel, the *Mirnyi* (*Peaceful*), was older, a transport also built of pinewood. The interior of her hull was sealed with sheets of tar-soaked canvas. Seventy tonnes lighter than the *Vostok*, and slower, the *Mirnyi* would time and again hinder the progress of the voyage.

Bellingshausen's strength lay in his officers and crews. The captain of the *Vostok*, Lieutenant Zavadovski, was a proven sailor, while the captain of the *Mirnyi*, Lieutenant Lazarev, had served four years as a volunteer officer with the British Navy. As for the sailors, the Instructions of the Voyage stipulated that none were to be taken 'unless under 35, extremely fit, more than able to endure hard work at sea, and possessing a knowledge of at least one trade other than his own'. There were in all 117 officers and men aboard the *Vostok*, 72 aboard the *Mirnyi*.

In the third week of July the *Vostok* and *Mirnyi* set sail intending to take aboard in Copenhagen two German naturalists. But the naturalists took fright and refused to join the expedition. Bellingshausen sailed on to Portsmouth, England.

From Portsmouth he travelled by coach to London, where he met the President of the Royal Society, Sir Joseph Banks, who had sailed with Cook 50 years earlier. With a vast private income, he had sponsored many an eager explorer, and he now supplied the courteous Russian with books, charts and navigational aids. Bellingshausen also requested naturalists to replace the unwilling Germans. But not even Sir Joseph could produce any volunteers for the voyage.

On 5 September, the *Vostok* and *Mirnyi* left Portsmouth for the south. Bellingshausen noted with regret that the lack of naturalists would leave a gap in the expedition's findings.

Towards the end of the year the Russian vessels were within sight of South Georgia. Acknowledging the presence of nearby sealing ships, the Russians made a careful survey of the coast. Then they headed southeast for the South Sandwich Islands, crossed the 56th parallel and came in sight of their first icebergs. One of these reared 55 metres (180 ft) from the sea, and the sailors stared in amazement at the penguins that crowded the floe. Whales sounded all around the ships as Bellingshausen began a circumnavigation of the scattered South Sandwich group.

On 3 January 1820 he discovered three small islands to the north of the group and named

On 8 January 1820 a party from the Vostok *landed on an iceberg, captured 38 penguins and filled 16 barrels with ice. The penguins were kept in chicken runs and bathtubs placed on the poop deck. Both officers and crew grew to like penguin meat, especially after it had been in vinegar for a few days.*

Vostok *and* Mirnyi *off the Antarctic coast. Claims that this expedition was the first to sight the continent are disputed by supporters of Palmer and Bransfield.*

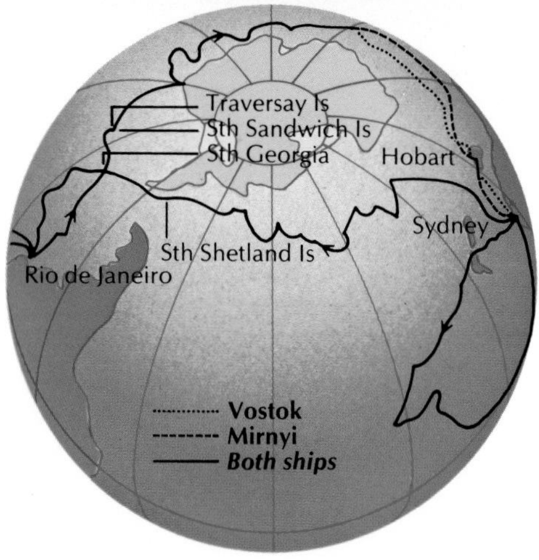

them after his supporter, Baron Traversey. One of these islands was an active and sulphurous volcano. The captain of the *Mirnyi* took his vessel close inshore, then recoiled from the smell — unfairly blaming the penguins clustered on the warm volcanic rocks!

Stocks of fresh water were now running low aboard the corvettes. Bellingshausen sent men off in one of the boats and they filled a number of canvas sacks with chippings from an ice floe. A handful of this was used to make tea, the resulting brew tasted, and the experiment acclaimed a success. Henceforth, the icebergs would supply their fresh water needs.

Careful not to duplicate the work of Cook, Thaddeus von Bellingshausen led his ships along the eastern coast of Candlemas Island, Saunders Island and Montague Island, then southwards through fog and snow.

On 12 January (1 January, and thus New Year's Day in the Russian Calendar) preparations were made for a celebration feast. The officers and men donned parade dress for the occasion, and the day was marked with a breakfast of tea and rum; a dinner of cabbage soup, sauerkraut and pork; rice gruel in the evening, and a generous tot of spicy, hot punch.

At 5 pm, Bellingshausen made one of his rare observations on the marine life around the ship. 'We saw whales playing about in the water, rising perpendicularly about one-third of their whole length, and then diving again, showing their horizontal tails', he wrote. These were probably killer whales.

Five days later, Lieutenants Simonov and Demidov were sent to one of the nearby floes to catch penguins. 'Our booty consisted of thirty penguins. I ordered a few to be sent to the mess ... and the remainder were kept on board and fed on pork....... this appeared to be injurious to them, as they sickened and died after three weeks. The crew skinned them and made caps of the skins, and used the fat for greasing their boots. The penguins ... are good for food, especially if kept for several days in vinegar.'

On 20 January the wind freshened, the sea rose, and the ships found themselves confronted with a mass of drifting icebergs. The *Vostok* took evasive action, turning to the northeast. Out of sight of the *Mirnyi*, Bellingshausen was not to know that at 2.30 that morning, the smaller vessel had collided head-on with an ice floe. All those aboard the *Mirnyi* rushed on deck. The damage was checked, the vessel reported intact. (Yet, three months later, when the *Mirnyi* was inspected in Sydney harbour, Lieutenant Lazarev discovered that a 0.9-metre (3-ft) length of pinewood had been torn from the hull, and that only the tarred canvas lining had prevented the sea from rushing in to the hold.)

When the storm abated, the vessels again made contact, running south-south-east to cross the Antarctic Circle on 26 January. This was the first time ships had penetrated the circle since Cook in 1773 — yet Bellingshausen made no mention of it in his log.

The following day he reached 69°21'S, 2°14'W. Ahead of him lay continuous hillocks of ice, and it now seems clear that Bellingshausen was within 32 kilometres (20 miles) — *and* within sight — of the Antarctic mainland. Yet all he recorded was his position and the weather conditions.

It is possible that Bellingshausen simply mistook the continent for a wall of ice. Or that, like so many of his fellow explorers, he expected land to *look* like land — the earth dark, trees visible, even perhaps signs of habitation. Whatever his reasons, Bellingshausen turned his ships east along the icebound coast.

The dispute as to who first saw Antarctica continues even today. England lays fair claim to it having been seen by the naval captain, Edward Bransfield. The United States prefers to believe it was sighted by the sealer, Nathaniel Brown Palmer. Russia would have it that not only once, but twice, did Thaddeus von Bellingshausen view the mainland of *Terra Australis*. Whether or not he had come within sight of land in January 1820, he would set the question to rest 12 months later.

On 22 February, still venturing east, the *Vostok* and the *Mirnyi* were hit by the worst storm of the voyage. For three days the ships were pounded by heavy seas, their ropes and spars encrusted with ice. Driving snow added to the hazards, concealing the icebergs from the weary lookouts.

Bellingshausen reasoned that the vessels' only escape lay to the north. He managed to signal his intentions to the *Mirnyi*, and the ships retreated towards the 63rd parallel.

By mid-March the Russian corvettes were about 100 days out from Rio de Janeiro. Bellingshausen noted with relief that his crews were fit, though supplies were running low. It was agreed that the two ships would now separate. The *Vostok*, being faster, would go ahead to explore South Australian waters, the *Mirnyi* making her slower way to Sydney.

On 11 April 1820, the *Vostok* anchored in Sydney harbour. Governor Macquarie welcomed the explorer, though Bellingshausen was concerned that the *Mirnyi* had not yet arrived. Then, eight days later, while the officers of the *Vostok* were visiting a recently built lighthouse on South Head, they were cheered to see the *Mirnyi* enter the harbour.

The first southern voyage was over.

A Disappointing Reception

Indifference greets Bellingshausen's discoveries

After a month's respite in Sydney, Bellingshausen took his ships on a four-month exploratory cruise of the Pacific. Back in Sydney in September 1820, Bellingshausen was told by the Russian consul there that an English sealing captain named William Smith had discovered a group of islands on the 67th parallel. These he had called the South Shetlands, claiming them to be part of the Antarctic continent. Bellingshausen immediately decided to go there, partly to verify the claim, but mainly to use them as an entry to the south.

Preparations were made aboard the *Vostok* and *Mirnyi*. Major repairs had been carried out before the Pacific cruise. The rigging had been reset, parts of the copper sheathing replaced on the *Vostok*'s hull, a new section of pine had been inserted in the stem of the *Mirnyi*, and the vessels were again ready to brave the rigours of the polar seas.

A firm believer in hygiene, Bellingshausen insisted that his men and their clothing be thoroughly washed and cleansed. A large tent was erected around a specially constructed stove, and steam was created by means of heated cannonballs. Then clothes and sailors alike were subjected to the purifying vapours of this 'sauna'.

Captain Zavadovski undertook the purchase of provisions. A number of pens were built, and the day before the ships set sail, 46 pigs, along with hens, ducks and sheep were taken aboard. To these were added Australian songbirds, among them parrots and cockatoos.

On the morning of 11 November 1820, the *Vostok* and the *Mirnyi* left Sydney Harbour for the last time. The explorers had been treated with every courtesy by the Governor, and Lieutenant Simonov wrote that 'our visit to that interesting country has remained, and will remain throughout our lives, among our warmest memories'.

In the final week of November the ships were off Macquarie Island, where they exchanged greetings with a number of English and American sealers. Bellingshausen learned that the fur seal population had been wiped out by the hunters, who now resorted to the slaughter of the ponderous elephant seals.

On 8 December, the Russian vessels crossed the 60th parallel south at 163°E. The officers drank a toast to their friends in Kronstadt and St Petersburg, the city ports that lay on the 60th parallel north.

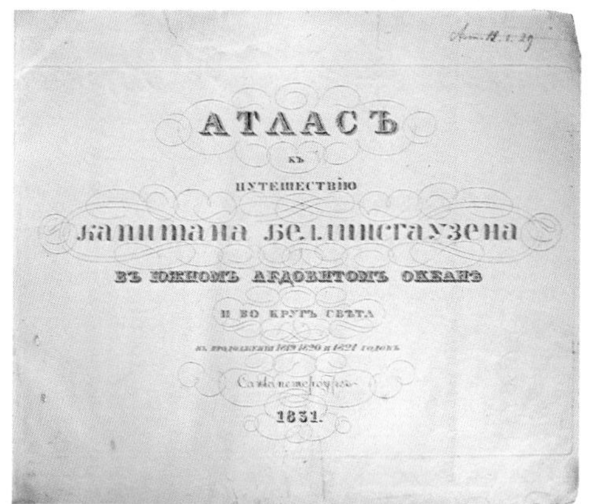

АТЛАСЪ
КЪ
ПУТЕШЕСТВІЮ
КАПИТАНА БЕЛЛИНСГАУЗЕНА
ВЪ ЮЖНОМЪ ЛЕДОВИТОМЪ ОКЕАНѢ
И ВО КРУГЪ СВѢТА
1831.

The title page from the atlas that accompanied the published results of Bellingshausen's voyage. Only 600 copies of the work were ever printed in Russian, and then not until 1831.

A few isolated peaks jut through the ice and snow of Alexander Island. Bellingshausen named the land for Tsar Alexander I of Russia, although he was unable to tell that it was an island.

A drawing of a macaroni penguin from Bellingshausen's narrative.

The following day, sailing almost due south, they saw their first iceberg, their first drifting floes. Ahead lay a solid wall of ice, and the vessels turned southeast. Their hopes were raised when they encountered what they took to be a land mass, dashed when it was revealed as a massive iceberg, eight kilometres (five miles) in circumference. The ships swung eastwards, edging along the pack.

One month out from Sydney, the *Vostok* and the *Mirnyi* were within reach of the 65th parallel, at 169°E. It was now that the weather deteriorated, the ships working their way among pack ice and icebergs, more than 100 of which were in sight at any one time.

By 12 December the corvettes had skirted 610 kilometres (380 miles) of the icebound coast, the weather worsening by the hour. During the night they were hit by a violent gale. Snow and ice were shaken from the rigging, making the decks treacherous underfoot as the vessels rolled wildly. All available hands were on the lookout for the great drifting bergs. The bright tropical birds began to die. Yet as the storm slowly abated, flocks of gulls and petrels appeared, a tantalising indication that land was somewhere nearby.

On 24 December 1820, Bellingshausen's ships crossed the Antarctic Circle at 164°W. They had not penetrated this far south since their first exploratory voyage, 11 months before. But it was a short-lived achievement, for the vessels were soon forced northwards again, battling on through fog and freezing snow.

On the fifth day of the new year, the lookouts reported no less than 144 icebergs in view. On the tenth, the corvettes crossed the circle again, but were once again repulsed by the ice. By 16 January 1821, they had penetrated the circle on six separate occasions — proof, if it were needed, of Thaddeus von Bellingshausen's determination.

For another five days the ships continued their clockwise circumnavigation, probing, always probing to the south. On 21 January they reached the southernmost point of the voyage: 69°53'S, 92°19'W. The weather had cleared and, at three o'clock in the afternoon, a dark speck showed up against the whiteness of the ice. All telescopes aboard the *Vostok* were trained on it. The onlookers waited anxiously for a break in the clouds. Then, as they watched, sunlight sharpened the scene, revealing a series of steep cliffs and rocks, black and free of snow. There was no doubt in Bellingshausen's mind. *He had discovered land within the Antarctic Circle.*

The next day showed the land to be an island, 15 kilometres (9.5 miles) in length and seven kilometres (four miles) across, rising at its highest point to some 1200 metres (4000 ft). It was then the most southerly known land in the world, and Bellingshausen named it *Ostrov Petra I*, Peter I Island, in honour of Peter the Great, founder of the Russian Navy. Fog and ice prevented a boat being lowered, however, and the ships continued eastwards, still bound for the South Shetlands.

On 28 January the explorers enjoyed the finest weather of the voyage. They were within the 68th parallel, birds circling the ships. This encouraging sign was underscored by an-

other: they noted that the sea water was discoloured, as if by earth washed from the land. Soundings were taken, though at 145 fathoms (265 metres; 870 ft) no bottom was reached.

Then came a cry from one of the lookouts, and the shouted report of a mountain peak 64 kilometres (40 miles) away to the east-southeast. Between the ships and the mountain lay an impenetrable field of ice. Nevertheless, the position of the peak could be accurately gauged: 68°43′S, 73°10′W. Other mountains were sighted, free of snow and further away than the first. The evidence was overwhelming: the Russians were gazing in all probability at the Antarctic continent itself.

Thaddeus von Bellingshausen named this second discovery *Bereg Aleksandra I*, Alexander Coast, now known as Alexander Island. Although not strictly part of the mainland, the 320-kilometre (200-mile) long island is joined to it by a deep, 32-kilometre (20-mile) wide shelf of ice. Could the Russians have put a boat ashore and ventured inland over the ice, they would have reached the Antarctic mainland.

Satisfied with his claim, Bellingshausen led his vessels onwards to the South Shetlands.

One week later, while exploring the island group, they came upon eight English and American sealing ships. Their crews were grimly competing for what was left of the fur seal population.

It was here that Bellingshausen met a young American, Captain Nathaniel Brown Palmer, the skipper of a tiny 45-tonne sloop, the *Hero* (see p88). The Russian invited Palmer aboard the *Vostok* where the American — on doubtful evidence — is supposed to have claimed extensive knowledge of the coast that lay to the south. In 1833, 12 years after the event, another American, Captain Edmund Fanning, quoted Palmer's reminiscences. In this account, Bellingshausen tells Palmer: 'What do I see and what do I hear from a boy . . . that he is commander of a tiny boat the size of a launch of my vessel . . . has sought the point I . . . have for long, weary, anxious years searched day and night for?

'. . . What shall I say to my master; what will he think of me?'

On this plaintive note of surrender, Bellingshausen reportedly added, 'I name the coast you have discovered in honour of yourself, noble boy, Palmer's Land'. Debatable generosity from this captain of the Imperial Russian Navy.

Bellingshausen's own account of the meeting makes it sound rather less dramatic: 'At 10 o'clock we entered the strait and encountered a small American sealing boat. I lay to, despatched a boat, and waited for the Captain . . . Soon after Mr Palmer arrived in our boat and informed us that he had been here for four month's sealing . . .' There followed a polite conversation about the weather and sealing before Palmer returned to his boat.

Content with his own discoveries, Bellingshausen set a course northeast, crossing the 60th parallel on 11 February 1821. One month later the *Vostok* and the *Mirnyi* reached Rio de Janeiro, where they remained to overhaul the ships until early May.

It was not until 4 August 1821 that the corvettes dropped anchor at Kronstadt. The voyage had lasted two years and 21 days. Of the 200 officers and men aboard the vessels, only three had died, and there was not one single reported desertion.

But if Bellingshausen, Zavodovski, Lazarev, Simonov and the others were proud of their achievements, Russia accorded them scant recognition. The comprehensive charts and reports were studied — then shelved. Ten years were to elapse before the explorer's findings were even published, and the bulk of his account remains untranslated.

Unimpressed by Bellingshausen's circumnavigation of the Antarctic continent, and by the lack of any spectacular discovery, Russia lost all interest in *Terra Australis*. It was not until 1946 that the USSR sent whaling fleets to the south, and not until the International Geophysical Year (1957-58) that a Russian scientific base was established on the mainland.

As for Thaddeus von Bellingshausen, this dedicated officer continued to serve his country for another 30 years. He attained the rank of Admiral, and was later made Governor of Kronstadt. The Soviet Union now contends that Bellingshausen was the true discoverer of the Antarctic mainland; a claim his nation left dormant for 100 years.

At Macquarie Island Bellingshausen watched the sealers at work. He returned to the ship with two albatrosses, two dead and one live parrot, 'sold to me by one of the sealers for three bottles of rum'.

FIRST SIGHTING?

Smith and Bransfield catch a glimpse of the elusive continent

Towards the end of the eighteenth century, sealing in the southern hemisphere took on all the appearances of a gold rush. The insatiable demands from China and Europe for skins soon cleared all the known sealing grounds leaving sealers desperate to find new land with unplundered rookeries. In their search they made many discoveries.

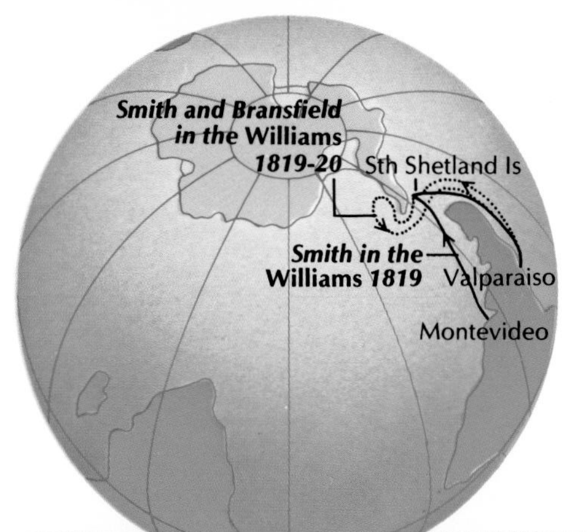

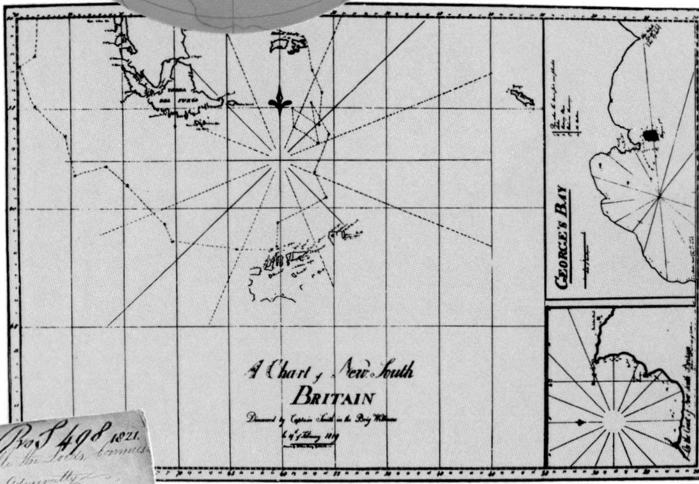

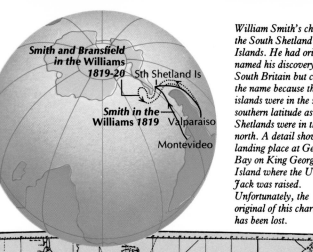

William Smith's chart of the South Shetland Islands. He had originally named his discovery New South Britain but changed the name because the islands were in the same southern latitude as the Shetlands were in the north. A detail shows the landing place at George's Bay on King George Island where the Union Jack was raised. Unfortunately, the original of this chart has been lost.

Sealing voyages to the southern hemisphere occurred regularly during the seventeenth century, and by the latter half of the eighteenth the industry was well established. Between 1793 and 1807 as many as three and a half million seal skins were obtained from places like South Georgia, the coast of Chile, and the Cape Horn region. The profits from some voyages were huge. An early American sealing expedition made a net profit of £52 000.

The boom, however, did not last long, for the sealers literally killed off their livelihood by butchering entire seal rookeries without any thought for the future. So the number of sealers declined. A fall in the Chinese market and the difficulty of finding seals in sufficient quantity, combined with the war between America and Britain, inhibited all but the most enterprising hunters.

The South Shetlands may have been first discovered by a Dutchman, Dirck Gherritz, in 1599. It is also possible that American sealers had known about them for a number of years, but had kept them secret.

In February 1819 contrary winds prevented an English merchant captain, William Smith, from making a normal passage around Cape Horn from Buenos Aires to Valparaíso. Instead, he was forced to the south and west, and on 19 February, between heavy showers of snow, he spotted land.

'Land or ice was discovered bearing south-east by south two or three leagues [14.5 km; 9 miles]', he wrote later in a Memorial addressed to the Admiralty about his discovery. 'Strong gales from the south-west accompanied by snow or sleet — wore ship to the northward at 10 am more moderate and clear, wore ship to the southward and made sail for the land — at 11 rounded a large iceberg; at noon, fine and pleasant weather — latitude by observation 62°01' West — steering in a south-south-east direction — at 4 pm made the land bearing from SSE to SE by E distance about 10 miles [16 km], hove to, and having satisfied ourselves of land hauled to the westward and made sail on our voyage to Valparaiso.'

On reaching port Smith reported his discovery to Captain William Shirreff, the senior British naval officer on the Pacific coast of South America. But Smith had not taken any soundings and Shirreff doubted his claim.

Undeterred by this scepticism, or perhaps stung by it, Smith tried to return to the scene of his find later that year. But on 15 June, after taking nearly a month to reach a latitude of 61°12'S, he was beset by ice. Realising he could not possibly reach the new land during the winter months, Smith turned north and delivered his cargo at Montevideo.

Smith's news that during his earlier voyage he had seen a great many whales and seals around and on his newly discovered land prompted a group of American merchants to offer him large sums of money to reveal its exact position. But Smith had not been able to take possession of what he had seen, and so he refused the offers. Instead, he decided to find another cargo to take round Cape Horn.

In 1821 Smith, then living in London, wrote to the Admiralty in a neat copperplate hand (below) to record his part in the discovery of the South Shetlands and to try to get some reward. He finished with the words: '. . . that your Lordships will be pleased in consequence to grant to your Memorialist such remuneration as in your judgement may seem meet.' The effort was in vain. He never received any money and died, a poor man, in London in the late 1840s.

He eventually set sail towards the end of September 1819, and again deviated to the south to look for the land he had seen the previous February.

At 6 pm on 15 October he was in roughly the same position he had been on his first visit (62°40'S, 60°W), and despite hazy weather he saw land bearing south by east at about three leagues (14.5 km; 9 miles). He sailed towards it and when about seven kilometres (four miles) off he saw that it was a large brown rock (probably Desolation Island). This time

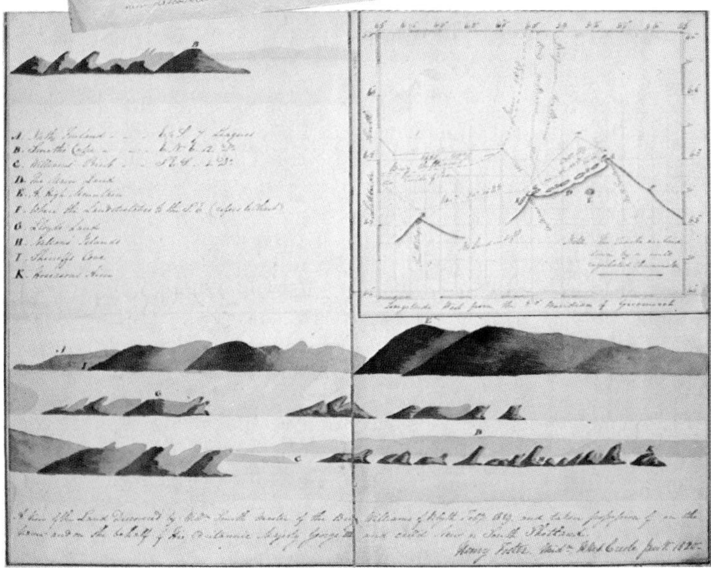

Drawings of the South Shetlands from the sea made by Henry Foster in January 1820. Poor visibility made it difficult to see the true extent of the islands, hence their curious appearance. Cloud, snow and ice merge together. When an icecap is added to these drawings the actual rounded shapes of the islands emerge.

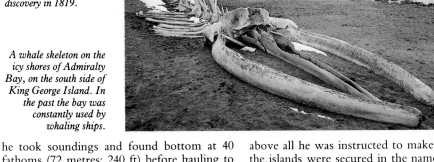

By 1829, when this painting of sealers at work on Deception Island in the South Shetlands was made, the islands were hardly worth a visit from sealers. Almost all the animals had been exterminated in the four years following their discovery in 1819.

A whale skeleton on the icy shores of Admiralty Bay, on the south side of King George Island. In the past the bay was constantly used by whaling ships.

he took soundings and found bottom at 40 fathoms (72 metres; 240 ft) before hauling to the north for the night. The next morning he sailed along the northern coasts of Greenwich, Robert, Nelson and King George islands. Near North Foreland at the eastern end of King George Island a boatload of men was landed, the Union Jack planted and possession taken in the name of the king. Although he had originally named his discovery New South Britain, Smith now changed its name to New South Shetland.

This time Smith reported his discovery to Captain Thomas Searle of the *Hyperion*, who immediately recognised its importance. When Shirreff returned from a diplomatic trip to Santiago it was arranged that Smith's brig *Williams* be chartered by the Admiralty for further exploration. Smith was retained as pilot, but the brig was put under the command of Edward Bransfield, the master of Shirreff's ship, HMS *Andromache*.

Bransfield's instructions were comprehensive and required him to do more than he could possibly carry out in one voyage, but above all he was instructed to make sure that the islands were secured in the name of King George III and that their harbours and anchorages were carefully surveyed.

The *Williams* set sail from Valparaíso on 20 December 1819 and on 18 January 1820 land was sighted at what became known as Cape Shirreff on Livingston Island. They followed the land to the northeast, until they rounded North Foreland on King George Island and came to anchor in George Bay where the Union Jack was planted ashore. The southern coastline of the islands was then charted as far as Barnard Point on Livingston Island. On 29 January Deception Island was sighted, but not investigated. The next afternoon Tower Island was approached and rounded, with a bigger mass of land being seen beyond it.

'At three o'clock in the afternoon', said the *Literary Gazette and Journal of Belle Lettres*, which published three articles based on information supplied by a midshipman aboard... 'they very unexpectedly saw land to the SW; and at four o'clock were encompased by islands, spreading from NE to E. The whole of these formed a prospect the most gloomy that can be imagined, and the only cheer the sight afforded was in the idea that this might be the long-sought southern continent, as land was undoubtedly seen in latitude 64°.'

The ship was then turned eastwards, and later the Trinity Peninsula — they named it Trinity Land — was again sighted, and then Hope Island and Mt Bransfield. After skirting the north coast of D'Urville Island, nearly all of which appeared on Bransfield's chart, the ship passed between Gibbs and O'Brien islets before reaching Elephant and Clarence Islands on 4 February 1820.

A landing was made at Cape Bowles, Clarence Island that same day, and possession taken in the king's name. For the next nine days Bransfield surveyed as much of the coastline as was accessible. Then, just before they departed, Smith went ashore and took a boatload of sealskins from a tiny islet near Elephant Island. For another 10 days Bransfield sailed to the east and south hoping to find more land until he was finally stopped by pack ice in the Weddell Sea. He gave his position at that time as 64°50'S, 52°30'W, though modern commentators have calculated that Smith's single chronometer gave an error of between 3' and 40'. Reluctantly, Bransfield now turned back to Valparaíso.

On reaching port the *Williams* was paid off and Smith immediately fitted her out for a sealing expedition the following summer. This proved entirely successful, despite the number of other sealers in the area. Smith arrived at London Docks on 17 September 1821 with his holds full of skins, only to find that his partners in the business had run into financial difficulties. The brig and her cargo were seized and Smith bankrupted. Like so many of the early Antarctic explorers he died, in the late 1840s, a poor man. The seals on the South Shetlands fared no better, for they were soon hunted to the verge of extinction.

UNCONFIRMED LANDING

Claims and counter-claims from the pioneers

Smith refused to divulge the whereabouts of the South Shetlands to American merchants, but he probably did let some of his friends in on the secret, knowing that while they would take advantage of the knowledge it was in their interest not to tell it to others.

The first known ship to arrive at the South Shetlands after Smith's initial sighting was the *San Juan Nepomuceno* of Buenos Aires, commanded by Carlos Timblon and chartered by Mr Adam Guy who was probably a friend of Smith's. According to contemporary newspaper reports she took 14 000 skins in five weeks before returning to her home port on 22 February 1820.

Another ship to be sent south immediately her owners heard about the new land was the *Espirito Santo*, a sealer with a British crew. Whilst at the Falkland Islands the captain met 20-year-old Nathaniel Palmer, the second mate of an American sealer from Stonington called the *Hersilia*. Palmer had been left on the islands to catch fresh meat while his captain, James Sheffield, searched for the mythical Aurora Islands. The captain of the *Espirito Santo* told the young American that he was on his way to new land which had plenty of rookeries, but declined to give its position.

It so happened that the owner of the *Hersilia*, Captain Edmund Fanning, had for some time believed there was land south of Cape Horn, and had given Sheffield orders to try to find it. So when Sheffield heard about the English sealer he immediately followed it south.

The *Hersilia*'s log, unearthed in 1956, recorded that land was first sighted on 18 January, probably Smith Island. Five days later the ship anchored in what became known as Hersilia Cove on the northeast side of Rugged Island, where she met up with the *Espirito Santo*. The crew of the latter welcomed the Americans, saying there were enough seals for all, which indeed there were, for when the *Hersilia* left on 6 February she had 8868 sealskins on board.

Confirmation of Smith's discoveries and the success of the *Hersilia*'s voyage created enormous interest in New England ports and four sealers, including the *Hersilia*, were fitted out by Edmund Fanning and sent south to make their fortunes. At the Falklands they were joined by a fifth, commanded by Benjamin Pendleton who took charge of what now was known as the Fanning-Pendleton fleet.

By 12 November they had all found the agreed anchorage, between Rugged and Livingston islands. Palmer, now in command of the fleet's tender, the 45-tonne sloop *Hero*, had stopped at the Falklands and told Pendleton that other sealers were on the way. This news, plus the need for a more secure anchorage, prompted Pendleton to send Palmer on an exploratory cruise.

Captain Nathanial Palmer, photographed late in life, after he had become a wealthy businessman and shipowner. He was only 21 when he commanded the Hero *on her voyages in 1820. Most experts dispute Edmund Fanning's claim that Palmer discovered Antarctica, although the controversy continues today. The entry from Palmer's log (left) for 17 November 1820 certainly shows that he sighted the coast of the Antarctica Peninsula.*

Palmer's track took him to Deception Island, and from there he headed southwards. The weather was fine and clear so he must have been able to see Trinity Island ahead and the Antarctic continent beyond.

'These 24 hours', Palmer wrote in his log on 17 November 1820, 'commences with fresh Breeses [sic] from SWest and pleasant at 8P.M. got over under the Land found the sea filled with imense [sic] Ice Bergs — at 12 hove Too under the Jib Laid off & on until morning — at 4A.M. made sail in shore and Discovered — a strait — Tending SSW & NNE — it was Literally filled with Ice and the shore inaccessible we thought it not Prudent to Venture in ice — Bore away to the Northerd & saw 2 small islands and the shore every where Perpendicular we stood across toward friesland Course NNW the Latitude of the mouth of the strait was 63-45S.'

The strait to which Palmer refers is undoubtedly Orléans Strait while 'friesland' was the name given to Livingston Island. Once back across Bransfield Strait he followed the land to the northeast until he found the entrance to McFarlane Strait. Here were found plenty of excellent seal beaches as well as a sheltered inlet to which the fleet soon moved.

Once safely in the more sheltered waters of what became known as Yankee Harbour the task began of hunting seals. Camps were set up ashore and the *Hero* made three separate circumnavigations of Livingston Island. Palmer also undertook a more extensive cruise in January 1821. There is a possibility that he

A reconstruction, from *Fanning's* Voyage around the World . . ., *of the meeting between Palmer and Bellingshausen. Although the two captains certainly met off the coast of Antarctica in 1821, nobody is sure exactly what they said to each other.*

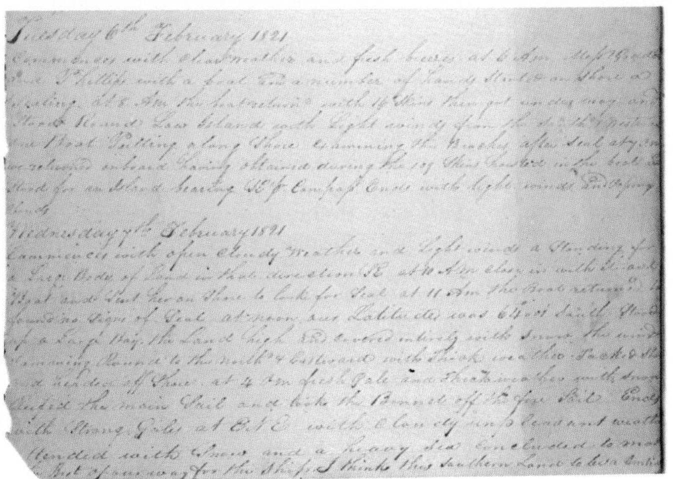

Tuesday 6th February 1821

Wednesday 7th February 1821

This entry from John Davis' log for 7 February 1821 may record a momentous event in the history of Antarctica — the first landing on the mainland. Some claim that the landing place was Hughes Bay on the Danco Coast, but this is by no means certain. The first confirmed landing was not until 1895.

went southwestwards as far as 66°S, but the *Hero*'s log does not confirm this. Many years later Palmer claimed that it was during this voyage that he saw the Antarctic continent, and that, on his return, he came across Bellingshausen's two ships, which were just finishing their circumnavigation of the Antarctic. Palmer went aboard and told the Russian of his discovery, and he later said that it was Bellingshausen who suggested the new land be called Palmer Land. But Bellingshausen, though a scrupulous reporter, makes no mention of Palmer's claim in his journal (see p84). However, it is still known as Palmer Land by Americans, some of whom have long disputed Bransfield's claim (see p86).

Thirty American and 24 British sealers, along with one Australian, were also hunting for skins amongst the islands that summer. In the early 1950s the logbooks of two of them, the *Huron* from New Haven and the *Huntress* from Nantucket Island, were discovered.

The masters of these two vessels, Captains John Davis and Christopher Burdick, arrived at Yankee Harbour on 8 December 1820. The following day the *Huron*'s tender, the *Cecilia*, went in search of rookeries. By 28 December she had made three cruises, including a circumnavigation of the islands, but had procured only 2527 skins, whereas the Fanning-Pendleton fleet had loaded 21 000 skins. The competition had become so stiff that several logbooks record angry encounters between the crews of American and British sealers, so Davis took the *Cecilia* southwards, and after stopping at Smith and Low islands made for Hoseason Island. However, he did not stop there but kept sailing south and on 7 February 1821 his log records a momentous event in Antarctic history.

'Commences with open Cloudy Weather and Light winds a standing for a Large Body of Land in that Direction SE at 10A.M. close in with it our Boat and Sent her on Shore to look for Seal at 11A.M. the Boat returned but found no sign of Seal at noon our Latitude was 64°01′ South. Stood up a Large Bay, the Land high and covered intirely [sic] with snow the wind coming Round to the North & Eastward with Thick weather Tacked ship and headed off Shore. At 4P.M. fresh Gale and Thick weather with snow . . . Ends with Strong Gales at ENE Concluded to make the Best of our way for the Ship I think this Southern Land to be a Continent.'

It would appear that Davis had landed at Hughes Bay and this entry in his log is the first known reference to Antarctica as a continent written by someone who had actually seen the mainland. If this landing really did take place — and there seems little reason to doubt its authenticity — it predates Bull's landing at Cape Adare (see p128) by 74 years.

Davis was back in Yankee Harbour on 10 February and he had aboard 1670 skins. Most of these had come from Low Island and two days later the *Cecilia*, now under the command of Captain Burdick, again headed for the island, and from there he was able to see the Antarctic continent. However, bad weather soon drove him back to Yankee Harbour, and the following month both he and Davis sailed for home. Davis did return the following summer, but left on 17 February 1822.

The Fanning-Pendleton fleet also returned the following summer, with Nathaniel Palmer commanding the sloop *James Monroe*, in which he made several exploratory cruises.

On 30 November, possibly after he had already skirted the Antarctic Peninsula, Palmer was at Elephant Island where he met a young British Captain, George Powell, the master of a sealer called the *Dove*. The two struck up a friendship and it was agreed they should sail together to try to find land to the northeast.

On 7 December the two ships reached a large island belonging to the then unknown South Orkney Islands. Palmer expressed little interest in the new land once he found there were no seals, but Powell landed and took possession of it in the name of the king, and named it Coronation Island. Both ships spent a week in the area before Palmer returned to the fleet's base at Deception Island and left for home on 30 January 1822.

Weddell's ships Jane *and* Beaufoy *at their furthest south — 74°15' — on 20 February 1823. It was to be 1911 before another ship reached this point.*

James Weddell (below), born in 1787, was brought up in a poor family. He was described by contemporaries as being easy and animated.

AN UNUSUAL SUMMER

Weddell sets a new southern record

The writings of Antarctic explorers are full of the bitter cold they endured. James Weddell's account is no exception, but ironically his fame derives from his good fortune in being in the region during exceptionally warm weather. This freak occurrence enabled him in February 1823 to sail further south than any man before him and to discover the sea that now bears his name. No other explorer managed to better this record until Wilhelm Filchner in 1911.

James Weddell joined the Navy in 1796 and by 1815 had risen from ordinary seaman to Master and had earned high praise from his superiors. In 1819 he rejoined the Merchant Service when he was introduced to a shipwright called James Strachan who, with several partners, owned a 160-tonne brig. Weddell persuaded Strachan to give him command of her for a sealing expedition to the South Shetlands, recently discovered. He had never been sealing, but Strachan agreed, for Weddell knew the Antarctic area well from his days in the Navy. Very little is known about this first voyage except that Weddell did visit the South Shetlands, and then independently discovered the South Orkneys, which had only just been found by Powell and Palmer. He returned safely in January 1821 but with insufficient cargo to have made the venture profitable.

The following year a second voyage was arranged. Again, its main purpose was for sealing but if no seals were found it was agreed Weddell would 'prosecute a search beyond the track of former navigators'. The brig, the *Jane*, manned by 22 officers and men, was this time to be accompanied by a 65-tonne cutter, the *Beaufoy*, crewed by 13 men under the command of Matthew Brisbane. On 17 September 1822 they set sail from England.

It is doubtful if the ships, or the provisions they carried, were really adequate for the task ahead. Between 1820 and 1822 no less than seven sealing vessels had been wrecked on the South Shetlands. Both vessels were small, and the damage wreaked on the *Jane*, in particular, shows they were also frail. Time and again the decks of both ships were swept clean by mountainous seas. The brig sprang a leak more than once, and sustained severe damage to her planking and stem.

The rum ration for the crew seems, now, more than sufficient — three wine-glasses a day — but the food ration was scanty and there was the ever-present threat of scurvy. In winter in the Falklands the rations were halved, yet only one man died during this time.

The navigational instruments Weddell took were more than adequate for his task as a sealer — he relates that he spent £240 on three chronometers alone, a good deal of money in those days. However, he was an explorer by nature and fully understood the importance of what he might be doing, and he bitterly regretted not having aboard the array of instruments with which a scientific expedition could expect to be equipped. The accuracy of his observations and the meticulousness with which he charted the South Orkneys and other places, shows him to have been a man who admired accuracy and who, from his own comments, particularly disliked the wild and unsubstantiated claims of some earlier explorers.

Whatever the deficiencies of the ships and their stores the crews enjoyed one incalculable asset, for Weddell, like Cook, was a magnificent leader of men. He knew how to inspire them, and he kept them cheerful and willing during many months in hostile, uncharted seas.

After stopping at Madeira and Bona Vista, Weddell crossed the equator on 7 November and eventually dropped anchor at the Falkland Islands on 19 December for repairs. On 30 December both ships, keeping close company, sailed southwards and on 12 January 1823 the eastern end of the South Orkneys was sighted. By early morning on 13 January they were close enough to Saddle Island to send a boat from each ship to explore it. Later, Weddell also landed and returned with the skins of six seals of an unknown species. Weddell later sent one of the skins to the Edinburgh Museum for scientific examination.

A thorough search around the islands produced only a handful of fur seals and Weddell was forced to conclude they had migrated elsewhere. In the hope of finding some on land to the south he started to sail in that direction, and slowly the two vessels made their way into higher latitudes, groping between icebergs and through dense fogbanks. It was a dangerous business and often Weddell was obliged to heave to and allow his ships to drift, itself a risky undertaking.

By noon on 27 January Weddell had reached the latitude of 64°58'S. The water temperature was 1°C (34°F) and the air temperature 2.8°C (37°F) in the shade, although when the thermometer was moved into the clouded-over rays of the sun it rose to 9°C (48°F). The weather remained settled, and perhaps Weddell could have penetrated even further south, but his mind was still on seals and he turned north

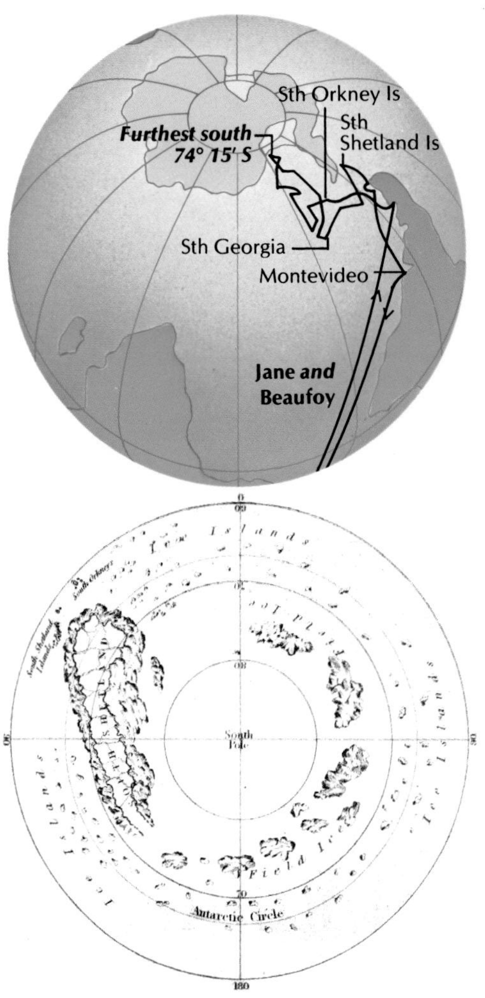

Weddell thought it probable that an ocean existed at the South Pole. He also suggested that constant summer sunlight falling on a polar ocean would melt the ice each year and leave it clear for navigation. He included a diagram (left) and a detailed argument in his book about the voyage.

Jane *and* Beaufoy *passed through a field of icebergs before they entered the relatively ice-free Weddell Sea. One berg was mistaken for a rock because the ice was thickly impregnated with black soil. Weddell hoped that this was an indication that they might shortly sight land to the south.*

in the hope of finding land between the South Orkneys and the South Shetlands. He sailed to within 160 kilometres (100 miles) of Sandwich Land and came close enough to Cook's tracks to know he would not find *terra firma* where he had hoped to. By now any chance of obtaining a good cargo of sealskins had vanished and on 4 February Weddell decided to sail south once more. Brisbane bravely agreed to the plan and in dark and foggy weather, under close-reefed topsails only, the two ships began their historic journey.

Both crews were suffering from the perpetual cold and fog, and were plagued by agues and rheumatism. Weddell did what he could for them, but the constant gales kept the ships permanently wet. However, by 16 February, when the 70°S latitude was reached, the weather improved remarkably. The wind blew moderately from the west, and the icebergs had all but disappeared. Then the breeze veered and gave the ships a fine run to the southwest. Unfortunately, both thermometers had by then been broken but on 18 February Weddell judged the weather no colder than it had been in midsummer in 61°S latitude.

'In the evening we had many whales about the ship, and the sea was literally covered with birds of the blue peterel [sic] kind', wrote Weddell. 'NOT A PARTICLE OF ICE OF ANY DESCRIPTION WAS TO BE SEEN [Weddell's capitals]. The evening was mild and serene, and had it not been for the reflection that probably we should have obstacles to contend with in our passage northward, through the ice, our situation might have been envied.'

At noon on 20 February Weddell's position by observation was 74°15′S, 34°16′W, some 345 kilometres (214 miles) further south than Cook had achieved. The weather was now quite extraordinarily clear and mild, with a gentle breeze blowing from the south. Four icebergs were sighted, but there was no sign of land, a fact that later led Weddell to the theory that there was, after all, no landmass at the pole. Perhaps this doubt, combined with the lateness of the season, convinced Weddell to take advantage of the favourable wind to return to lower latitudes.

The crews were naturally disappointed at this decision, but Weddell made a speech praising their exemplary behaviour and informing them they had penetrated further south than any previous explorer. The colours were then hoisted and a gun fired in celebration. Both crews gave three cheers and an extra ration of rum was distributed. Weddell named the water in which they sailed King George IV's Sea after his sovereign, and then turned north.

The Antarctic part of the voyage was now all but over. After sheltering at South Georgia and then wintering at the Falklands the two ships sailed for the South Shetlands in October 1823. They survived a ferocious hurricane but were prevented from approaching the islands by thick pack ice, and on 18 November Weddell turned west to search for seals around Cape Horn. Both ships eventually returned to England in July 1824.

It is a sad fact that, because no ship has yet managed to sail as far south on the same longitude as Weddell, doubts have been cast on his claim, though there seems to be no other reason to disbelieve him.

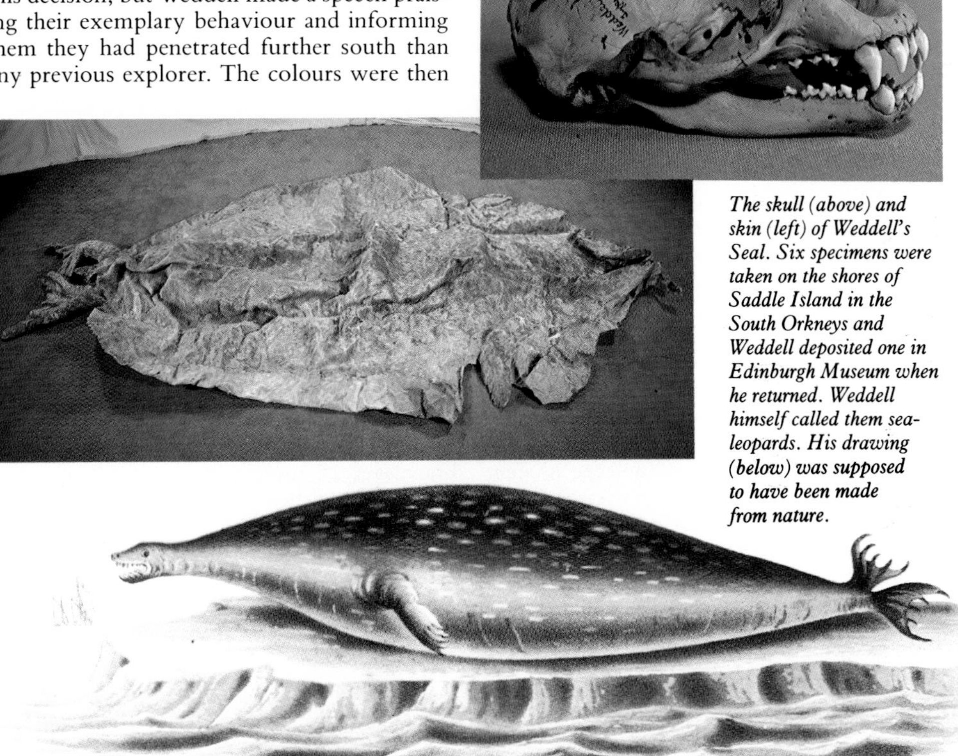

The skull (above) and skin (left) of Weddell's Seal. Six specimens were taken on the shores of Saddle Island in the South Orkneys and Weddell deposited one in Edinburgh Museum when he returned. Weddell himself called them sea-leopards. His drawing (below) was supposed to have been made from nature.

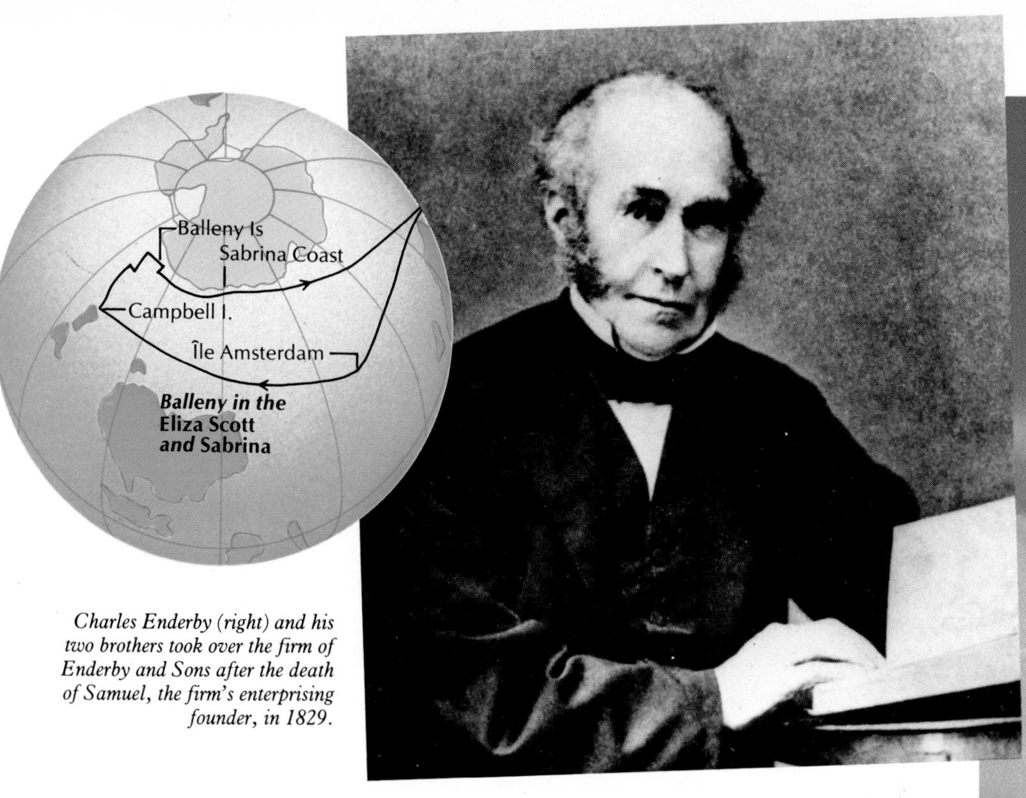

Charles Enderby (right) and his two brothers took over the firm of Enderby and Sons after the death of Samuel, the firm's enterprising founder, in 1829.

ENDERBY BROTHERS

A firm remembered for its enterprise rather than its business acumen

Enderby Brothers of London, the whaling and sealing firm, was much more than a purely commercial enterprise. Encouraged by the firm's owners, Enderby captains were at the forefront of Antarctic exploration for almost 40 years. Although many of their voyages were rich in geographical discoveries, they yielded little profit.

In its time the firm must have been known to all seafaring men. In his classic novel about whaling, *Moby Dick*, Herman Melville wrote that a certain English whaler 'was named after the late Samuel Enderby, Merchant of that city, the original of the famous whaling house of Enderby and Sons'.

It was an Enderby ship that brought tea into Boston Harbour one day in 1773. The subsequent American War of Independence cut Enderby off from his normal trade, so he decided to start sealing and whaling on his own account, and from 1785 the firm began sending ships into the southern oceans.

These voyages were not usually profitable, although one Enderby ship, *Emilia*, had a spectacular success when, in 1790, she arrived in London with a full cargo of sperm oil. She was the first whaler ever to harpoon a whale in the Pacific and return with her cargo by rounding Cape Horn. Another successful voyage occurred in 1819 when the *Syren* found the whaling grounds around Japan.

But what set the Enderby Brothers apart from similar commercial firms of the time was Samuel Enderby's interest in discovering more about the unknown areas his captains visited, an inquisitiveness motivated as much by patriotism as by scientific curiosity. Enderby encouraged his captains to look for new lands. Captain Abraham Bristow, in the Enderby ship *Ocean*, discovered the Auckland Islands, south of New Zealand, in 1805. He was unable to land, but in 1807 he returned and took possession of the islands for Britain. Later, the British Government ceded them to the company as a base for a whaling station (see p58).

In 1829 Samuel Enderby died, and the firm was run by his sons Charles, Henry and George. Charles had inherited his father's interest in the areas Enderby ships visited, and when the Royal Geographical Society was founded in 1830 Charles was one of its original fellows. His interest in the Antarctic had been fostered by reading about Weddell's voyages and by the reports of other captains.

Among the earliest recorded was that of the *Swan*, commanded by Captain James Lindsay, who was engaged in a sealing trip with another Enderby ship, *Otter*. On 7 October 1808, while in latitude 54°24′S, longitude 3°15′E, Lindsay reported sighting an island which he could not approach because of ice. In December 1825 another Enderby master, Captain Norris, in command of the sealer *Sprightly*, rediscovered Bouvetøya. He noted in his log that 'the *Lively* [the consort of the *Sprightly*], by order, hoisted out her boat, and we manned her out of both vessels and sent her on shore, to endeavour to find a landing at the west end of the island. We sounded in its south side, and found from thirty-five to twenty fathoms [64 to 36 m; 210 to 120 ft], black sandy bottom, at a mile [1.6 km] from the shore. Caught a number of small fish, resembling codfish. At 8 p.m. the boat returned, having hoisted the union jack on the shore, etc.' In 1830 Charles Enderby, intrigued by a report that postulated land in the high southern latitudes between the Greenwich meridian and 20°E, sent two sealing ships south under the command of John Biscoe (see p94). When Biscoe returned in January 1833, Charles Enderby was so delighted by his discoveries that he decided to send further ships south again almost immediately. Alterations were made to an Enderby yawl, the *Rose*, and the firm bought a brig, the *Hopefull* [sic].

When the two ships arrived at the Falkland Islands *Hopefull*'s captain, Prior, resigned, probably because he clashed with Lieutenant Rea, a naval representative the Admiralty had insisted join the ships as a condition for the Admiralty guaranteeing a proportion of any losses the firm incurred. Rea did not get on well with his shipmates, referring to them as the most mutinous set of dogs he'd ever encountered. He took command of the expedition and at the end of November 1833 both ships set sail to the south. But the *Rose* was beset by ice about 80 kilometres (50 miles) north of Clarence Island and crushed. Her crew was rescued by the *Hopefull,* but Rea abandoned the voyage.

Through the Treasury guarantee the firm recouped £2539 14s 8d, a substantial proportion of their losses; but they offered to sell the *Hopefull* to the Treasury for a government Antarctic expedition, as they said they would not be undertaking any more Antarctic voyages themselves. The offer was declined.

In the same month that the *Hopefull* and the *Rose* set sail, Peter Kemp, master of the 148-

Heard Island was first sighted in 1833 by Peter Kemp, who may have been working for the Enderbys. It was named for Captain Heard who sighted it in 1853.

tonne *Magnet*, set sail for Îles Kerguelen and from there steered southwards in search of seals. It is by no means certain that the *Magnet* was an Enderby ship. Kemp's journal was probably in the possession of the Royal Geographical Society during its early years but disappeared. He did, however, deposit a chart of his tracks in Antarctic waters with the Admiralty on his return to England, and this shows that while on his way south Kemp sighted Heard Island, though Captain John Heard has always been credited with its discovery. Kemp had almost reached the Antarctic Circle at a longitude of about 60°E when he sighted land on 26 December 1833 and named it Kemp Land on his chart.

Although it is impossible now to prove that the *Magnet* was an Enderby ship, the Enderby Brothers, despite their remarks to the Treasury, did organise several more voyages south in search of land. The first of these took place in 1838-39. Two vessels, the 47-tonne Cowes cutter *Sabrina* and the 134-tonne schooner *Eliza Scott*, were purchased by Charles Enderby. John Balleny, an experienced seaman, was given command of the *Eliza Scott* while Captain Freeman was master of the *Sabrina*. After visiting New Zealand, Balleny and Freeman headed south. On 1 February 1839 Balleny reached the furthest south ever achieved by anyone in these longitudes: latitude 69°02′S, longitude 174°E. But pack ice made any further progress impossible, so he stood off to the northwest, and at 11.30 am on 9 February he first sighted what are now known as the Balleny Islands. A few days later Balleny and Freeman attempted to land on the island with the highest mountain.

'Captain Freeman jumped out and got a few stones', Balleny wrote later, 'but was up to the middle in water. There is no landing or beach on this land; in fact, but for the bare rocks where the icebergs had broken from, we should scarce have known it for land at first, but, as we stood in for it, we plainly perceived smoke arising from the mountain tops. It is evidently volcanic, as the specimens of stones, or cinders, will prove. The cliffs are perpendicular, and what would in all probability have been valleys and beaches are occupied by solid blocks of ice.'

On 2 March, when in latitude 65°15′S, longitude 119°42′E, land was apparently sighted to the south not more than a couple of kilometres to windward. Next day they tried to sail nearer, but the pack ice proved too heavy to penetrate. Neither Balleny's log nor that of the *Eliza Scott*'s chief mate, William Moore, give any further particulars, and although they gave it the name of Sabrina Land they obviously had doubts that it was a real sighting.

On 24 March a gale blew up and the *Sabrina* signalled she was in distress by burning blue lights. At dawn the next day there was no sign of her, and the *Eliza Scott* returned alone to London. She arrived there on 17 September 1839 and unloaded only 178 sealskins, nothing like enough to cover costs. But the tragic voyage did prove that land existed within the Antarctic Circle south of New Zealand.

Enderby Brothers wrote to the Admiralty suggesting another voyage, but received the reply that it would not be in the public interest. Undeterred, Charles Enderby sent the *Eliza Scott*, under the command of Henry Mapleton, Master RN, south again. She set sail on 12 July 1840, but in a severe gale Mapleton lost his rudder and the voyage had to be abandoned.

Reference to one last Enderby voyage is made in *Siege of the South Pole* by Hugh Robert Mill. In February 1850 the *Brisk*, commanded by Captain Tapsell, sighted the Balleny Islands and then steered to the west as far as 143°E, sailing in a considerably higher latitude than that managed by Charles Wilkes. But nothing more is known about the voyage, as all the documents were lost.

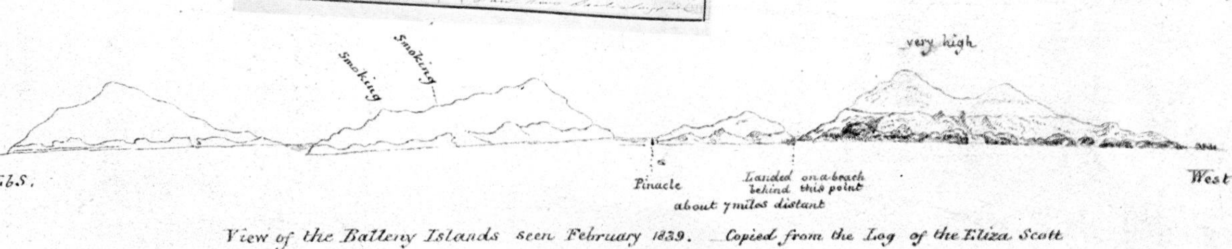

On 9 February 1839 John Balleny on the Eliza Scott, *and Captain Freeman on the* Sabrina, *discovered the Balleny Islands. The* Eliza Scott's *second mate wrote (above right): 'at 4 PM saw the land distinctly bearing about SW. Two large islands and several smaller ones.'*

NIGHTMARE JOURNEY

A remarkable voyage brings fame, but not fortune, to John Biscoe

Of all the voyages recorded by Enderby captains, the two undertaken by John Biscoe in the southern summers of 1831 and 1832 made the most valuable contribution to Antarctic exploration. He was the first man to confirm that a great mass of land did exist in the Antarctic, and one of the first to circumnavigate the continent.

Hobart
Mt Biscoe
Enderby Land
Adelaide I.
Falkland Is
Biscoe in the Tula and Lively

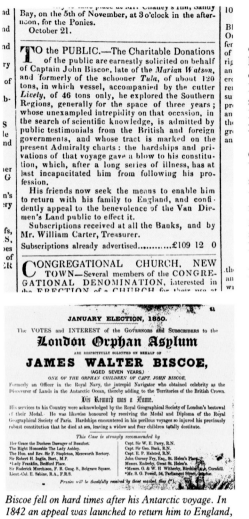

Bay, on the 5th of November, at 3 o'clock in the afternoon, for the Ponies.
October 21.

TO the PUBLIC.—The Charitable Donations of the public are earnestly solicited on behalf of Captain John Biscoe, late of the *Marian Watson*, and formerly of the schooner *Tula*, of about 120 tons, in which vessel, accompanied by the cutter *Lively*, of 46 tons only, he explored the Southern Regions, generally for the space of three years; whose unexampled intrepidity on that occasion, in the search of scientific knowledge, is admitted by public testimonials from the British and foreign governments, and whose tract is marked on the present Admiralty charts: the hardships and privations of that voyage gave a blow to his constitution, which, after a long series of illness, has at last incapacitated him from following his profession.

His friends now seek the means to enable him to return with his family to England, and confidently appeal to the benevolence of the Van Diemen's Land public to effect it.

Subscriptions received at all the Banks, and by Mr. William Carter, Treasurer.

Subscriptions already advertised..........£109 12 0

CONGREGATIONAL CHURCH, NEW TOWN—Several members of the CONGREGATIONAL DENOMINATION, interested in

JANUARY ELECTION, 1850.

The VOTES and INTEREST of the GOVERNORS and SUBSCRIBERS to the

London Orphan Asylum

ARE RESPECTFULLY SOLICITED ON BEHALF OF

JAMES WALTER BISCOE,

(AGED SEVEN YEARS,)

ONE OF THE ORPHAN CHILDREN OF CAPT. JOHN BISCOE,

Formerly an Officer in the Royal Navy, the intrepid Navigator who obtained celebrity as the Discoverer of Lands in the Antarctic Ocean, thereby adding to the Territories of the British Crown.

His Reward was a Name.

His services to his Country were acknowledged by the Royal Geographical Society of London's bestowal of their Medal. He was likewise honoured by receiving the Medal and Diploma of the Royal Geographical Society of Paris. Hardships encountered in his perilous voyages so injured his previously robust constitution that he died at sea, leaving a widow and four children totally destitute.

This Case is strongly recommended by

Her Grace the Duchess Dowager of Beaufort.
The Right Honorable The Lady Ashley.
The Hon. and Rev. Sir F. Stapleton, Mereworth Rectory.
Sir Robert H. Inglis, Bart., M.P.
*Lady Franklin, Bedford Place.
Sir Roderick Murchison, F. R. Geog. S., Belgrave Square.
Lieut.-Col. E. Sabine, R.A., F.R.S.
Capt. Sir W. E. Parry, R.N.
Capt. Sir Geo. Back, R.N.
Capt. E. P. Halsted, R.N.
John Gurney Fry, Esq., St. Helen's Place.
Messrs. Enderby, Great St. Helen's.
*Messrs. G. & W. H Witherby, Birchin Lane, Cornhill.
*Mr. S. G. Powell, 54, Parliament Street, London.

Proxies will be thankfully received by those marked thus (*).

Biscoe fell on hard times after his Antarctic voyage. In 1842 an appeal was launched to return him to England, and after his death on the voyage money was sought to aid his destitute widow and four fatherless children.

The entry from John Biscoe's log recording his sighting of what he took to be the Antarctic mainland on 27 February 1831.

Biscoe's command was a two-masted, square-sterned brig of 150 tonnes called the *Tula*. With her went the 50-tonne cutter *Lively*, commanded first by Smith and later by Avery. The two ships left Gravesend on 14 July 1830 and arrived at the Falkland Islands in early November. After a fruitless search for seals there and around Sandwich Land, Biscoe crossed the Antarctic Circle on 22 January 1831.

By 29 January he had arrived at a latitude of 69°3′S, the farthest south he was able to reach because of ice. For the next three weeks he sailed east through the pack ice, noting the variety of wildlife and the vastness of the icebergs. Then on 24 February he had his first glimpse of land to the south between snow squalls, but it quickly vanished. Biscoe gave his position as being 66°8′S, 43°54′15″E, but modern commentators suspect the accuracy of his chronometers. His true position was probably 46°20′E, making the land he saw the continental ice slope to the west of Casey Bay.

Biscoe tried to close with the land but was prevented from doing so by ice. The next day he had a boat lowered and attempted to obtain a better view of what looked like land beyond a great ice shelf. But after pulling for half an hour he returned to the brig. There is no certainty as to which part of Antarctica he saw on this occasion, but it is likely that he had approached a very large iceberg which either blended with, or partly covered, White Island, Dingle Dome and the continental ice slopes in the vicinity of Casey Bay.

Biscoe's next sighting was much clearer and left him in no doubt at all that he had discovered new land, which he called Enderby Land.

He wrote in his log: '4 pm saw several hummocks to the southward, which much resembled tops of mountains, and at 6 pm clearly distinguished it to be land, and to considerably extent; to my great satisfaction what we had first seen being the black tops of mountains showing themselves through the snow on the lower land, which, however appeared to be a great distance off, and completely beset with snow, field-ice and icebergs. The body of the land bearing SE.'

As the two ships worked laboriously along the edge of the pack ice Biscoe next saw a cape to the southeast which he named Cape Ann, now Mt Biscoe.

On 3 March a severe gale blew up and the *Tula* lost sight of the *Lively*. The wind rose to hurricane force and continued to rage for five days, blowing the brig 193 kilometres (120 miles) to the north-north-west. Gales kept the *Tula* from turning south until 16 March. The next morning Cape Ann was sighted and later that day high land to the south. Biscoe continued eastwards in search of more land but by 3 April neither his ship nor his crew were in any condition to carry on, and reluctantly he headed for New Zealand.

On 21 February 1832 Biscoe rowed ashore on a stretch of mountainous coast that he thought was the mainland of Antarctica. It was, in fact, probably the coast of Anvers Island (right). Biscoe took possession of the land in the name of William IV and named many of its major mountains.

The voyage north must have been a nightmare. On 23 April the carpenter died of scurvy and by 26 April only Biscoe, three men and a boy were still on their feet. In an attempt to save the lives of the rest Biscoe altered course for the nearest port, Hobart, but the next day another crew member died. Biscoe noted in his log that the rest were dangerously ill, but he arrived at Hobart on 10 May without any further casualties.

While the *Tula* struggled back to civilisation, the men on *Lively* were having even greater suffering inflicted on them. After the two ships became separated the cutter's crew of 10 were so much reduced by scurvy and disease that Captain Avery — who must have taken over command at the Falklands — was obliged to turn and make for Hobart. However, they ended up at Port Phillip near what is now Melbourne, arriving there about a month before Biscoe sailed into Hobart. By this time death had reduced the crew to three.

'So dreadful was the situation of these unfortunate men', commented the *Hobart Town Courier* on 17 September 1831, 'that the bodies of two of the number who died below deck could not be got up for several days to be thrown overboard, the survivors being so re-

A painting attributed to Biscoe, entitled 'Terrel di Hugo', presumably Tierra del Fuego. Many ship's captains sketched their landfalls — with varying degrees of skill.

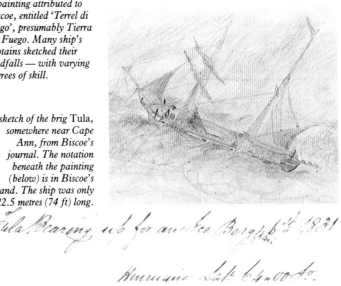

A sketch of the brig Tula, *somewhere near Cape Ann, from Biscoe's journal. The notation beneath the painting (below) is in Biscoe's hand. The ship was only 22.5 metres (74 ft) long.*

Tula Bearing up for an Ice Berg 6th Jan 1831

Hurricane Lat 64.00 S.

duced by sickness and infirmity as to be totally unable to perform the painful and distressing task. At last the master, partially recovering his strength, contrived to make a rope fast round their bodies, and by the help of the tackle succeeded in hauling up first one and then the other and launching them into the deep.'

While the three survivors were ashore recovering from their ordeal the cutter dragged her anchor and was blown up an inlet out of sight. It took the men some weeks to find her. Eventually they summoned up the strength and will to refloat the cutter and sail for Hobart, where they arrived exhausted and starving on 3 September. Here an amazed and delighted Biscoe happened to alight on them just as he was setting off on a second voyage to the Antarctic. It took Biscoe until 10 October to get the cutter and her crew into some kind of shape for another voyage south.

When at last they were able to sail the two ships hunted for seals and whales around the New Zealand coast for three months to try to obtain a profitable cargo, and then a course was set for the Nimrod Islands which Biscoe had great hopes of finding. However, on arriving at the spot where they were marked on the chart he found nothing and he could find no bottom when a sounding was taken.

After continuing for some days Biscoe decided to head southeast once more and to cross James Cook's tracks in the hope of finding land to the west-south-west of the South Shetlands. By 3 February he had reached a latitude of 65°32′S.

Then on 15 February his tenacity was rewarded, for land was sighted late in the afternoon bearing east-south-east. The ships altered course and by noon the next day they were within five kilometres (three miles) of it. Biscoe recognised it as an island and named it after Queen Adelaide. It is now known simply as Adelaide Island.

Although he later saw more mountains to the south — presumably Alexander Island — Biscoe altered course to the north before resuming an easterly direction which took him past the group of islands which now bear his name. On 19 February he landed on an island — he named it Pitt's Island — in search of seals but found none, nor anything of interest. Then on 21 February the ships stood in towards the mainland and a boat with Biscoe aboard was lowered and pulled into a large inlet.

'This being the mainland', Biscoe wrote in his log about what may have been Graham Land but was probably Anvers Island, 'I took possession of it in the name of His Majesty King William IV, the highest mountain I named Mount William'.

The weather was comparatively warm and sunny but there was no sign of seals, so Biscoe headed for the South Shetlands in the hope of finding some there before tne season ended.

Biscoe had now completed one of the first circumnavigations of the Antarctic continent. But though he had achieved the most significant discoveries of land in Antarctica yet made by any man, from his log it is apparent that he was more concerned to find seals before being forced to return home. He did find a few, but then the *Tula* damaged her rudder and Biscoe was obliged to sail her to the Falkland Islands for repairs, and the *Lively* was wrecked there.

Even with these setbacks Biscoe was still intent on taking home a cargo by trying another season in the Cape Horn area. But by now his crew had had enough and one by one they deserted. By 29 September only four men and three boys remained out of both crews.

Conclusive evidence that Antarctica was a continent had to wait until the 20th century, but Biscoe knew what he had achieved.

'I am firmly of the opinion that this is a large continent', he wrote to the hydrographer of the Navy on 10 April 1832, 'as I saw to an extent of 300 miles [482 km]'.

Biscoe's courage and endurance in completing two such memorable voyages were properly acknowledged for he received what was then the equivalent of the Gold Medal of the newly founded Royal Geographical Society.

Climax To A Varied Career

Dumont d'Urville proposes a Pacific voyage and is sent to Antarctica instead

Jules-Sébastien-César Dumont d'Urville

In 1836, it seemed that the 46-year-old naval officer and explorer Jules-Sébastien-César Dumont d'Urville was a man without a future. This was the man who had twice circumnavigated the globe; who was the discoverer, not only of distant lands and islands, but of one of the world's greatest artistic treasures, the statue Venus de Milo, which he also had the foresight to acquire for France.

A number of d'Urville's critics cast doubt on the scientific accuracy of his recently published 20-volume work *Voyages of Discovery Around the World*. As a result, the prestigious Academy of Sciences in Paris had denied him the recognition he felt he deserved. Promoted to the rank of *capitaine de vaisseau* in August 1829, he had since then been offered no seagoing command. Ignored and impoverished, painfully afflicted by gout and reduced to administrative office work in the Toulon naval base, Dumont d'Urville at 46 was a sad and frustrated man; a has-been.

Personal tragedy had also struck the d'Urville household, for in 1835 an epidemic of cholera had swept through Toulon. Dumont and Adèle d'Urville, who had already lost their firstborn son some 10 years earlier, now mourned the death of their only daughter.

Born in 1790 in the fruit-growing region of Calvados, d'Urville was accepted into the Navy at the age of 17. Gifted with a keen intellect — though he was later described as cold, aloof, unlikeable — he headed his class of 1811, and three years later attained the rank of ensign. His interests were extraordinarily wide-ranging. A noted linguist, he mastered English, German, Spanish, Greek, Italian and Hebrew. He studied astronomy, geology, entomology and — as his first love — botany.

In the latter months of 1819, d'Urville sailed from Toulon aboard a hydrographic survey vessel, the *Chevrette*. The object of the voyage was to chart areas of the Black Sea and the Eastern Mediterranean, and it was during a survey of the Mirtoan Sea that the vessel anchored off the island of Mílos.

The captain and officers were greeted by a French consular official. While in conversation with him, d'Urville learned of a statue recently unearthed on the island. The ensign's interest was aroused. He visited the site and, overwhelmed by the beauty of the statue, wrote in person to the French Government, pleading with them to buy it. With commendable speed the authorities instructed d'Urville to buy it 'for whatever it might cost'. It stands now in the Louvre Museum in Paris. King Charles X saw fit to reward d'Urville with the Cross of St Louis, and promote him to *lieutenant de vaisseau*. D'Urville's star was rising.

In August 1822, he was assigned to the 380-tonne corvette the *Coquille* serving under an old friend and senior classmate, Louis-Isidore Duperrey. Captain Duperrey was instructed to undertake hydrographic and botanical research in the Gilbert and Caroline Islands, Tahiti, the Falkland Islands and the stretch of coastline known as New Holland (part of Western Australia). The *Coquille* was no more than a converted lighter, manned by 11 officers and 59 men. Yet Duperrey and d'Urville managed to fulfil their instructions to the letter, returning after 31 months and 13 days, laden down with charts, maps, sketches, specimens and samples.

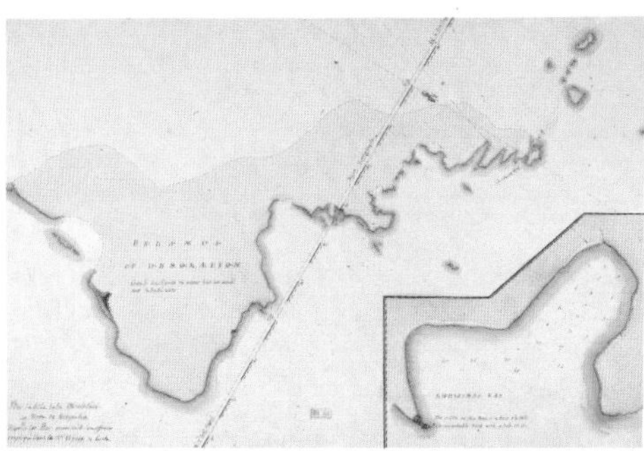

French copies of maps made during James Cook's voyage were carried aboard Dumont d'Urville's ships. This one shows a section of Îles Kerguelen, although neither of the ships called in there.

Rhodymania ornata

The *Coquille* returned to Toulon on 22 May 1825, to be warmly welcomed by representatives of the Government and the Navy. Honours and commendations were heaped upon Duperrey for his amazing voyage.

D'Urville submitted a number of illustrated articles to *Natural Science* magazine, and published a book on the flora and fauna of the Falkland Islands, *Flore des Îles Malouines*. He also sought an appointment with the Minister of the Navy, to whom he presented a plan for further research in the southern oceans. He promised to enrich France with his discoveries, improve hydrographic methods and vowed that, through his findings, merchant vessels would sail more safely in foreign waters.

His plan was approved in December 1825. Not only was he given command of a vessel, but *carte blanche* to choose his officers and crew.

Once again he sailed in the *Coquille*, though the vessel had now been renamed the *Astrolabe*, in memory of an earlier French expedition to the Pacific. His second-in-command was Charles Hector Jacquinot.

On 22 April 1826, the *Astrolabe* left Toulon on what was to be a second successful voyage around the world. The Fijian islands of Matuku and Totoya were discovered, the Loyalty Islands charted, the coastline of New Zealand surveyed, the island groups of the

Illustrations from the 32-volume Voyage au Pole Sud et dans L'Oceanie *published between 1842 and 1851, in which the scientific results of the voyage were recorded in painstaking detail. The names given are those chosen by the French scientist.*

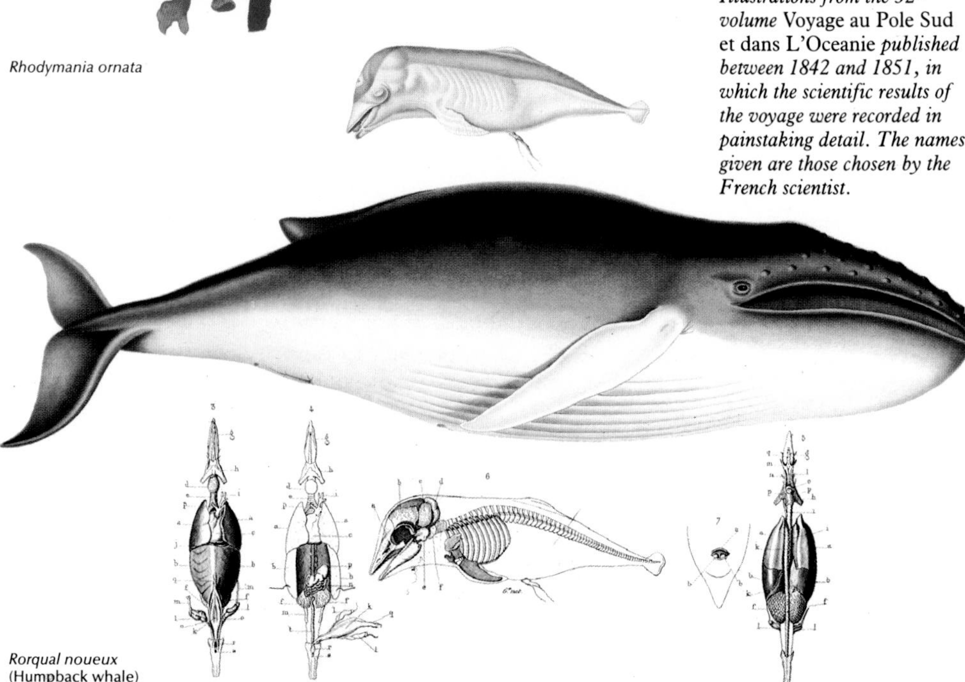

Rorqual noueux (Humpback whale)

During the southern winter the ships explored the Pacific, where in May 1840 they were stranded in Torres Strait.

Tongas and Moluccas mapped and explored. So detailed were the hydrographic records that for the first time these scattered islands could be divided into three major groups: Melanesia, Polynesia and Micronesia. When the *Astrolabe* returned to France on 25 March 1829, she had once again circumnavigated the globe.

Yet there were those who accused d'Urville of arrogance and self-seeking, of treating his crew harshly, and a willingness to exaggerate his findings. For example, in mid-August 1826, he had recorded the *Astrolabe* as being buffeted by a series of 27-metre (90-ft) waves south of the Cape of Good Hope. True or not, it was too much for his critics to accept.

So the rewards and recognition he had expected were denied him. Five months passed before he was promoted to captain, and then he was offered no ship to command. Stationed in Toulon, he remained desk-bound there for the next seven years. Then, early in 1837, d'Urville submitted a modest plan to the Navy Minister, de Rosamel. In it he suggested a further exploratory voyage to the Pacific islands, approaching them via the Straits of Magellan. Although d'Urville's proposals contained little that was new, they were forwarded to King Louis-Philippe, who saw in them the basis for an altogether more ambitious undertaking. The king was interested in extending the influence of France in the southern seas. He was also aware that in 1823 the English explorer James Weddell had penetrated as far south as 74°15′, and that Britain and America were keen to probe the secrets of Antarctica. Why then should France not be represented?

Where d'Urville had requested a single ship, the king granted him two. He was to take them through the Straits of Magellan, across to Pitcairn, the Fijis, the Solomons. From there he was to sail along the northern coast of New Guinea, then to Western Australia, Tasmania and New Zealand. But before this he must sail to the South Shetlands and then south 'as far as the ice permits'.

Captain d'Urville would get his chance to explore the Pacific. But first, obeying his monarch, he must search for the great Antarctic.

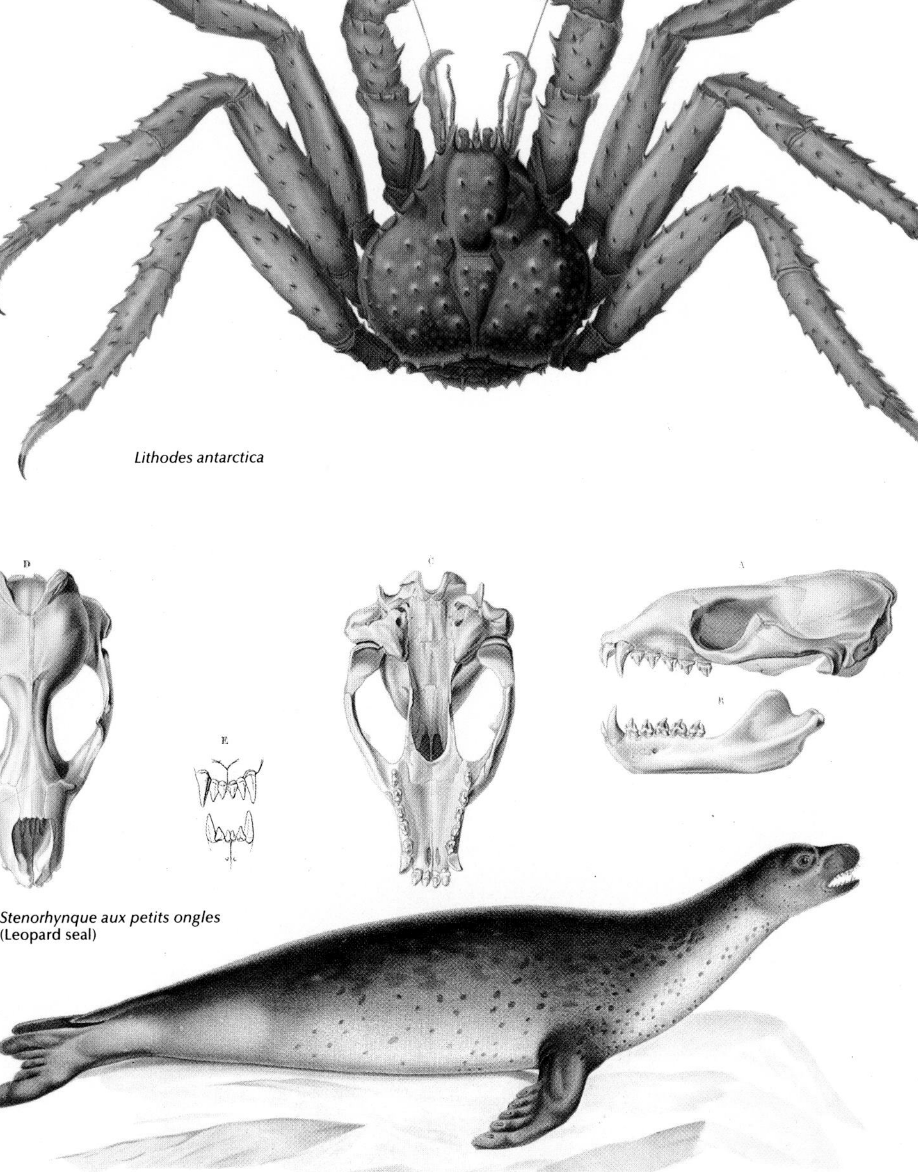

IN WEDDELL'S TRACK

Astrolabe *and* Zélée *fail in their attempts to penetrate the ice*

The two ships — the* Astrolabe *and the smaller* Zélée *— were fitted-out in Toulon for Dumont d'Urville's voyage to the south. The Frenchman intended to follow the tracks of James Weddell and then 'try to go beyond them so as to get as close as possible to the South Pole'.

By June 1837 d'Urville was worried at the time it was taking to prepare his ships. He knew he must reach the Antarctic before December if he was to benefit from the southern summer.

Meanwhile, he selected his officers and crews. As captain of the *Zélée*, he chose his old friend Charles Hector Jacquinot. The *Zélée* would carry 81 officers and men, the *Astrolabe* 17 officers and 85 men.

The men were promised a bonus of 100 gold francs if they reached the 75th parallel — Weddell had reached 74°15'S — and an extra 20 francs for each degree further south. D'Urville was confident, though he later wrote: 'When the expedition was being fitted-out and the men saw me walking slowly and heavily, because of an attack of gout, they seemed quite surprised that I was their commander and some of them exclaimed: "Oh, that old fellow won't lead us very far!"'

By August the *Astrolabe* and the *Zélée* were back in the water, their hulls sheathed with copper. D'Urville received his final instructions and on 7 September, later than he had intended, the two ships sailed from Toulon.

At the end of September they anchored in Tenerife and shore leave was granted. Increasingly anxious and irritated by his men's drunkenness, d'Urville quit Tenerife on 7 October. But the journey southwards was delayed by adverse winds and heavy Atlantic fog, and on 10 December they were still north of the Straits of Magellan. It was imperative to press on, yet essential to carry out repairs to both the *Astrolabe* and the *Zélée*. There was no choice but to enter the straits, where the expedition spent Christmas fishing, hunting wild geese and preparing the vessels for the rigours of the southern oceans.

On 8 January 1838, d'Urville led the corvettes out of the straits and south along the coast of Tierra del Fuego. Four days later they were out of sight of land, running east-southeast into a wilderness of freezing fog and rain.

They were still north of 60°S when they saw

Desolate Joinville Land (now Island) off the tip of the Antarctic Peninsula, was named by d'Urville in 1838.

The crew of the Astrolabe *work frantically to free their ship from the grip of the pack ice (below).*

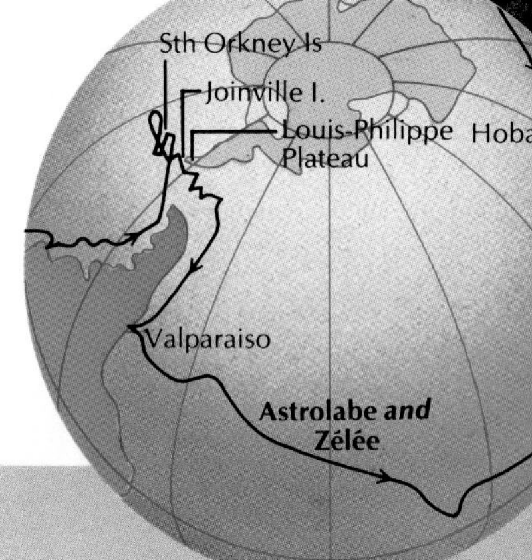

ice — low, irregular floes. It was nevertheless an indication of things to come, 'the advance guard of the formidable enemy the men were going to fight'. D'Urville continued east-south-east and was encouraged to find that on 31 January he was following Weddell's route.

But the weather that had greeted James Weddell in 1823 was not the weather that lay in wait for Dumont d'Urville. The southern summer of 1823 had been extraordinarily mild. The summer of 1838 was not.

On the night of 21-22 January d'Urville was awakened by shouts of alarm from the lookouts. He hurried on deck to see a low wall of ice stretching across the horizon. There was no alternative but to alter course to the north.

The next day they reached the northernmost point of the icefield but neither d'Urville nor Jacquinot could find a way in, and gradually they were forced away from the goal. On 24 January they marked their position as 63°23′S. The following day it was 62°42′S.

Suffering from gout and the onset of migraine, d'Urville accepted the inevitable. Whatever Weddell had achieved, the ice was not going to open for the *Astrolabe* and the *Zélée*.

The corvettes turned to seek respite in the South Orkneys. A few days' rest, d'Urville decided, and they would be ready for another attempt on 'the formidable enemy'.

Weakened by illness, depressed by this setback to his expedition, and deeply suspicious of Weddell's claimed incursion so far south, d'Urville wrote bitterly of his time in the South Orkneys: 'Nothing anywhere in the world could be more gloomy and more repulsive than the aspect of these desolate regions'.

On 2 February 1838, the *Astrolabe* and the *Zélée* were once again sailing south-south-east in search of the great Antarctic. Within 48 hours the lookouts were calling 'Land sighted! Land ahead! Land to the forrard!' It was another icefield, just south of 62°S. His spirits raised, d'Urville followed it westwards and manoeuvred the *Astrolabe* through an inlet in the ice, turning to see the faithful Jacquinot follow with the *Zélée*.

It was a brave attempt by Dumont d'Urville; but foolhardy. During the night he heard the crack and crunch of ice, and by morning the channel had closed behind the ships.

'We then had to use every means at our disposal. Men climbed down onto the ice to tie ropes to the floes ... those who remained on board hauled on them to move painfully forward, while others tried to push the ice aside with picks, pincers and pickaxes...Seeing our two ships, one thought of two crayfish stranded by the tide on a beach full of stones ... and struggling to regain the open sea.'

Five chilling days were spent in the floe-filled lake, and it was not until 9 February that they broke through the drifting ice into open water. Fear and bitter cold had taken their toll. A number of the crew were down with frostbite, as were all three surgeons.

The *Astrolabe* and the *Zélée* eventually succeeded in landing on Weddell Island where the sailors, starved of fresh meat, killed and ate a number of rock-dwelling penguins. In no mood to be critical, they found the oily flesh compared favourably with chicken.

For the next seven days the vessels continued westwards, their progress hampered by fog. On 27 February the South Shetland Islands appeared to the northwest and, a short while later, a sinuous coastline to the south. The Frenchman felt justified in claiming this territory for his king and country, naming it Louis-Philippe Land; the coastline which extended eastwards was called Joinville Land.

The ships remained in the area until early March, charting and mapping the northern extremity of what is now known as Graham Land. D'Urville took his vessels as far south as 63°27′, determined to record every detail of his discovery. Then the surgeon on board the *Astrolabe* informed him that a number of the sailors were showing signs of scurvy. This fact was concealed to avoid alarming the rest of the crew, but d'Urville accepted that it was time to leave these inhospitable waters.

So began a long, slow journey west-north-west towards Chile. By 27 March there were 21 confirmed cases of scurvy aboard the *Astrolabe*, while the *Zélée* resembled a floating hospital. On 1 April a seaman named Lepreux died of the disease. The hydrographer, Dumoulin, was taken ill, as was the *Astrolabe*'s second officer, Demas. The ships crawled north along the coast of Chile, reaching the port of Talcahuano on 6 April. Although the epidemic had been contained on board the *Astrolabe*, there were now 38 cases of scurvy on the *Zélée*.

Dumont d'Urville, 'the old fellow who wouldn't take them very far', had demanded too much of his men. Nine deserted in Talcahuano, and others, desperately ill, were left behind when the vessels limped on to Valparaiso. Here, d'Urville was shocked to learn that his expedition had already been prejudged, and considered an out-and-out failure. Angrily, he confronted his critics, showed them the ships' records, the charts, the geological specimens he had obtained. Opinion swung in his favour, though he had not yet attained his self-appointed goal. Come what may, he *would* reach the Antarctic continent.

On 9 February 1838 the two corvettes finally managed to break out of the pack ice that had imprisoned them for five nerve-racking days. The scale of the vessels can be gauged by the size of the men standing beside them on the ice.

The men hunted seals on the pack ice while they waited for it to break up and free the ships.

LANDING ON AN ISLAND

French explorers celebrate their success with a glass of wine

Between May 1838 and October 1839, Dumont d'Urville led the* Astrolabe *and the* Zélée *across the entire breadth of the Pacific Ocean, exploring the island groups. He reached Sumatra on 7 October 1839 and set sail for Hobart, Tasmania, which was to be his springboard for a third attempt at reaching the great Antarctic.

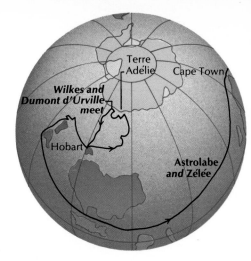

The scurvy which had so afflicted his officers and crews in southern waters was now replaced by an outbreak of fever and dysentery which claimed the lives of 14 men and three officers during the voyage. Another six died in Hobart. With the ships undermanned the two captains, d'Urville and Jacquinot, had to seek recruits.

On 2 January 1840 the *Astrolabe* and the *Zélée* were headed out to sea. Almost immediately they were forced to combat a strong easterly current. The vessels pitched and rolled, adding to the discomfort of the sick. One week out of Hobart, the surgeons reported seven men ill on the *Zélée*, nine aboard the *Astrolabe*.

By 14 January the ships had reached the 58th parallel, ploughing onward through squalls of snow. Ice floes were sighted, and d'Urville was worried that he would once again be confronted by pack ice. On the evening of 18 January they crossed the 64th parallel. At 6 o'clock the following morning, the lookouts counted half a dozen huge icebergs nearby.

By 6 pm the vessels were surrounded by no less than 59 great icebergs, the corvettes inching their way ever southwards. The hydrographer, Dumoulin — fully recovered from the scurvy — climbed the rigging of the *Astrolabe* and reported 'an appearance of land'.

During the evening the wind dropped, the sea now as calm and smooth as a lake. The belief that land was near raised the spirits of all those aboard, and d'Urville wisely chose this moment to allow his crews to relax.

Becalmed for the moment on the edge of the Antarctic Circle, the *Astrolabe* witnessed a sequence of strange events as the austere Dumont d'Urville joined his crews in inviting Father Antarctic aboard the ship.

The celebration over, d'Urville wrote: '... at 9 pm the sun was still above the horizon ... At 10.50 this luminary disappeared, *and showed up the raised contour of land in all its sharpness*. Everyone had come together on to the deck to enjoy the magnificent spectacle.'

The lack of wind forced them to wait, but it was there. Land was there. They had seen it.

On 20 January, d'Urville wrote: '... before us rose the land; one could distinguish the details of it ... Unfortunately an unbroken calm prevented us from approaching it to make the matter certain. Nevertheless, joy reigned on board; henceforth the success of our enterprise was assured.'

The next day, at 3 o'clock in the morning, a faint breeze allowed the ships to make slow progress along a series of ice-walled channels. D'Urville feared his ships would be crushed by the heaving icebergs: 'Their perpendicular walls towered above our masts; they overhung our ships, whose dimensions seemed ridiculously diminutive compared with these enormous masses ... One could imagine oneself in the narrow streets of a city of giants.'

By midday they were within seven kilometres (four miles) of land. It stretched from southeast to northwest, entirely covered with snow and sloping steeply to a height of 1000 metres (3300 ft). There was no sign of soil, no point at which they could safely go ashore.

They turned west, following the coast until 6 pm, when a boat was lowered so that Dumoulin could take sightings from one of the

A bizarre procession (below, top) wends its way around the decks of the Astrolabe *as the crew commemorate the crossing of the Antarctic Circle. Dumont d'Urville, after being showered with rice and beans thrown from the top mast, was presented with a message from Father Antarctic by an emissary mounted on a seal. Later that day, 19 January 1840, they sighted the Antarctic continent for the first time. The next day (below, bottom) was calm, and although land was constantly in sight, they were unable to approach it.*

icebergs. D'Urville gave permission for a second boat to be launched, and Captain Jacquinot lowered a boat from the *Zélée*.

It was nearly 9 pm when the two boats reached an islet that lay a few hundred metres off the coast. Officers and men clambered ashore, carelessly hurling aside a group of unfortunate penguins. As the birds dived away, the tricolour was unfurled and the land claimed in the name of France.

With the flag flying, the men set about exploring the offshore islet. They searched for plants, shells, even lichen, but in vain. All they found were a few chippings of granite — though granite was enough to prove that they had reached not just an iceberg, but land.

Joseph-Fidèle-Eugène Dubouzet, the officer commanding the party from the *Zélée*, recorded the details of the landing and the final departure from the islet. 'We saluted our discovery with a general hurrah', he wrote. 'The echoes of these silent regions, for the first time disturbed by human voices, repeated our cries and then returned to their habitual silence.'

The boats were rowed back in triumph to the waiting corvettes. Dumont d'Urville named the mainland Terre Adélie — Adèle's Land — his wife's land. The wide stretch of water which laps at its shore is now known as the Dumont d'Urville Sea.

One of the meticulous maps prepared by the hydrographer Vincendon Dumoulin, showing the coast of Terre Adélie. The point where the landing parties went ashore was named Pte. Geologie.

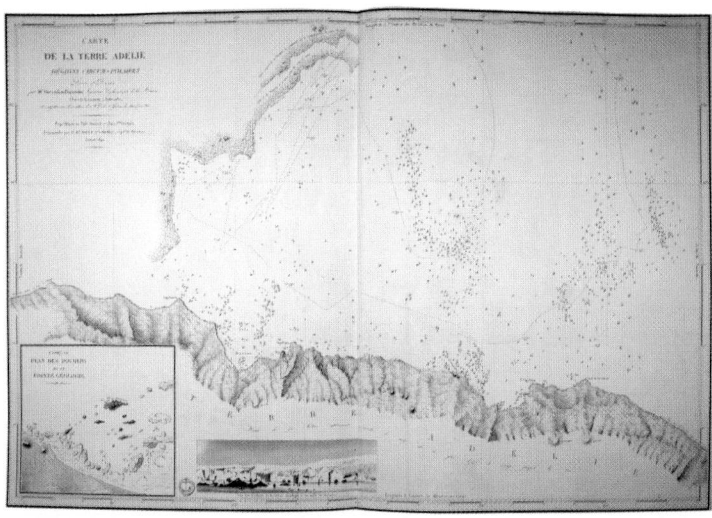

At 9 o'clock in the evening on 21 January 1840 parties from the Astrolabe *and* Zélée *scrambled ashore on the Antarctic mainland. In fact they had to land on a tiny rocky islet a few hundred metres from the coast, which ended in a cliff and was impossible to approach. The tricolour was raised (below, top) and an officer who had the foresight to bring a bottle of Bordeaux toasted the success of the enterprise (below, bottom).*

Almost immediately the weather began to deteriorate. The temperature dropped to below freezing, whirlwinds of snow enveloped the vessels, and the *Astrolabe* lost contact with the *Zélée*. As the violence of the storm increased, d'Urville and Jacquinot feared their ships would be driven on to one of the icebergs, or on to the ice pack itself.

'The *Astrolabe*, floundering in the midst of waves which came over her on all sides, presented a terrifying spectacle; she heeled over to such an extent that her leeward battery was almost entirely covered by the sea. If at that moment she had run against any obstacle, she would have been engulfed.'

On 29 January the vessels were moving rapidly southwest at about 64°48′S, with only a few small icebergs in view. A high sea was running, and the weather was foggy. A little after 4 pm, an astonished lookout aboard the *Astrolabe* sighted a ship approaching from the east closing fast.

The westbound vessel was the brig *Porpoise*, part of an American exploratory expedition led by an aggressive 41-year-old New Yorker named Charles Wilkes. The reasons for what happened next remain unclear, d'Urville claiming that the *Astrolabe* manoeuvred to allow the *Porpoise* to come alongside, the American captain, Cadwalader Ringgold, convinced that the Frenchman hoisted sail and ran. At any rate, it is certain that no signals were exchanged, no greetings shouted, no communication attempted. The *Porpoise* bore off quickly to the west, the *Astrolabe* to the north.

Dumont d'Urville spent a further eight months exploring the southern waters. He returned to Hobart, sailed on to New Zealand, turned north to New Guinea and Timor, north again to the island of St Helena. It was not until 6 November 1840 that the two battered corvettes entered the harbour at Toulon. They had been away three years and two months.

There was no question now of d'Urville being forgotten. Within a matter of weeks he was promoted to the rank of rear-admiral. The Geographical Society awarded him its highest accolade, the Gold Medallion. Jacquinot, Dumoulin and others were also promoted. And, on a final happy note for the officers and crews, the French Government saw fit to share some 15 000 gold francs among the 130 surviving members of the expedition.

A watercolour sketch of Rossbank magnetic observatory, built in Hobart for James Clark Ross during his great voyage of 1839-43.

ANOTHER SOUTH POLE

Source of the earth's magnetic field

Title page of William Gilbert's great work De Magnete, published in 1600. Gilbert was at one time physician to Queen Elizabeth I.

Men have always striven to reach some arbitrary goal, especially when the journey is difficult. The earth's magnetic poles are just such goals. The North Magnetic Pole was reached by James Clark Ross in 1831 and the South Magnetic Pole by Mawson, David and Mackay in 1909.

The magnetic compass had been in use in Europe since at least the middle of the eleventh century. The first person to measure the direction of the earth's magnetic field was Robert Norman, a hydrographer of London, in 1576. He made a compass that could turn in a vertical circle instead of the usual horizontal circle. Such a compass is known as a dip needle. It remained the common way of measuring the angle of the magnetic field below the horizontal (or inclination as it is now called) until early in the twentieth century. Polar explorers used compass and dip needle in their search for the north and south magnetic poles. As a result of measurements with the dip needle Norman realised that the earth's magnetic field is similar to the field of a uniformly spherical magnet.

The situation was clarified by William Gilbert in *De Magnete* published in 1600. Many people consider this to be the first scientific textbook in the modern sense. Gilbert explained very clearly that the magnetisation is distributed throughout the magnetised body and does not reside just at the poles, as had been thought. He also noticed that the shape of the earth's magnetic field is very closely that of a uniformly magnetised sphere, and came to the reasonable conclusion that the earth is uniformly magnetised.

Gilbert's assumption of a uniformly magnetised earth was not questioned until well into the nineteenth century. It had been known for some time that all magnetic materials lose their magnetisation with increasing temperature. Since only the top 48 kilometres (30 miles) of the earth's crust are cool enough for any material to be magnetic, it was clear that permanent magnetisation could not explain the earth's magnetic field.

The source of the earth's magnetic field thus became one of the most baffling problems in earth science — one that has been resolved only quite recently. As far as is known, a magnetic field can only be caused by either magnetised matter or an electric current. The idea that there were large-scale electric currents flowing deep inside the earth struck many difficulties, because it did not fit in with the ideas of the internal structure of the earth as known at the beginning of the twentieth century. In 1912 Sir Arthur Schuster, a British physicist, said: '. . . . the difficulties which stand in the way of basing terrestrial magnetism on electric currents inside the earth are insurmountable'. Many people agreed, even up to the middle of the twentieth century. On the other hand Louis A. Bauer, an American physicist, stated in 1902 that the earth's magnetic field was due 'doubtless to a system of electric currents embedded deep within the interior of the earth and connected in some manner with the earth's rotation'.

Several ways out of this impasse were explored. The possibility that magnetic materials could maintain their magnetisation at high temperatures, if the pressure was also high, was examined but discarded. Several ingenious ideas, such as a modification to the fundamental laws of electromagnetism, and the idea that all rotating bodies have associated with them an inherent magnetic field were discussed and abandoned. It was not until more was known about the interior of the earth, and the development of magnetohydrodynamics, that interest was stimulated in Bauer's idea.

Magnetohydrodynamics is the study of conducting fluids moving in a magnetic field.

A MAGNET AT THE CENTRE OF THE EARTH

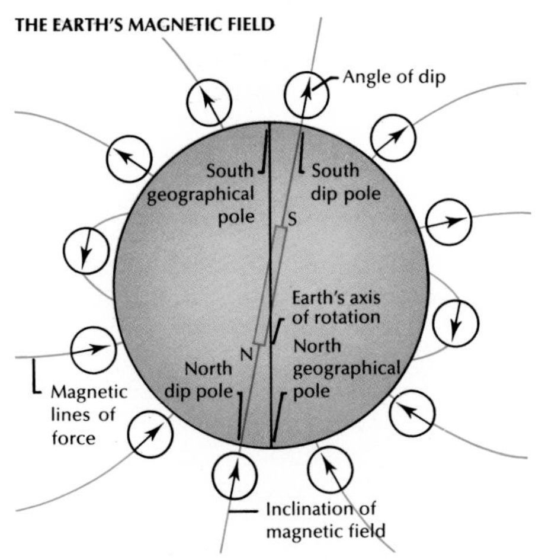

The earth's magnetic field is approximately that of a dipole (two magnetic poles of the same strength but opposite sign) at the centre of the earth inclined to the axis of rotation by an angle of 11°. This dipole can be considered to be a short very powerful magnet at the centre of the earth. The field due to such a dipole is called the dipole field and the points where its axis meet the surface of the earth are called the geomagnetic poles. The earth's magnetic field is nothing like that caused by a long magnet running from the south to the north magnetic pole. If it were, the field would be many times stronger at the poles.

If the earth's magnetic field were simply that of a dipole, it would be vertical — down in the north and up in the south — at the geomagnetic poles. But the magnetic field is only approximately that of a dipole. There is also a non-dipole field, which averages about 10 per cent of the dipole field, and in extreme cases (in the south Atlantic for example) reaches 50 per cent. Because of this the magnetic field is not vertical at the geomagnetic poles. There are, however, two points where the field is vertical. These are the north and south magnetic poles (or dip poles).

Karl Gauss's own dip needle which is now in a museum in Göttingen in Germany where he was director of the observatory. The needle pivots at its centre and is free to move in a vertical plane. It is here concealed by the oblique arm which carries small magnifying glasses used to read the dip measurement on the circular scale.

After much difficult calculation it became clear that certain types of fluid-flow in the earth's core can produce a magnetic field. Bauer's prediction that the rotation of the earth would have a controlling influence has recently been confirmed. Although there are several details to be clarified, there is little doubt now that the main part of the earth's magnetic field is caused by fluid motions in the liquid core at a depth of between 2900 and 5150 kilometres (1800 and 3200 miles).

During the age of discovery in the sixteenth and seventeenth centuries the compass was all-important to mariners. By the beginning of the sixteenth century it was realised that the fact that a compass does not point to the north geographic pole (true north) had nothing to do with inaccuracies in the instrument, but was a characteristic of the place at which the compass was used. An accurate knowledge of the difference between magnetic north and true north became essential, and a great deal of effort was put into determining by how much the compass declines to point north (what is now called declination) at various places, especially over the oceans. The first contour map of declination was made by Edmund Halley, who later became Astronomer Royal. After Robert Norman's invention of the dip needle in 1576 the inclination of the magnetic field was also measured on a world-wide basis.

Mariners needed this information, not simply to navigate during cloudy weather, but also because contours of equal declination run roughly north-south and those of inclination roughly east-west. By being able to measure these two features of the magnetic field they hoped to be able to determine their position, especially longitude, which was very difficult to fix accurately in the days before reliable chronometers were available.

It has been known since early in the seventeenth century that the earth's magnetic field changes slowly with time. At present the dipole field (see box) is getting weaker and the non-dipole field stronger. This has the effect of moving the South Magnetic Pole northwards away from the south geographic pole. Although the movement is slow in terms of human history, it is alarmingly fast on a geological time scale. This is one of the strongest arguments for the liquid core being the place where the earth's magnetic field originates.

One of the major turning points in the history of the earth's magnetism was the work of Karl Friedrich Gauss at Göttingen in Germany. Gauss perfected a method of determining the intensity of the magnetic field but, more importantly, his work led to a way of expressing the observed field in a mathematical form. This resulted in a method of finding the position of the magnetic poles without actually visiting them.

The magnetic field that has been described so far is often called the main geomagnetic field. Although it accounts for practically all of the measured field, there are other magnetic fields originating in various parts of the earth, and two of these play a part in the location of the magnetic poles. One is the local or crustal field. This exists because of magnetic minerals in the crust of the earth, where it is cool enough for material to be magnetic. The other is a field due to electric currents that flow in the space around the earth, and this depends very much on the sun's activity.

The link between the sun and the geomagnetic field is the solar wind that blows outwards from the sun. This is unlike any wind on earth, and consists of electrons and protons.

The effects of these two additional magnetic fields can vary the position of the magnetic poles. The crustal field can displace the pole by about three kilometres (two miles) and can also affect a compass, thus making it difficult to fix the position of the pole from a distance. The magnetic field caused by currents around the earth has a greater effect. Even on a day when the sun is quiet, the pole can move as much as 10 kilometres (6 miles), while during solar storms it can temporarily wander several times this distance.

The first attempts to reach the South Magnetic Pole were made by Dumont d'Urville and Charles Wilkes in 1840. They based their search on Gauss' analysis, which suggested a position of 66°S by 146°E, off the coast of Terre Adélie. However, d'Urville and Wilkes found that they were far from the pole at this position. James Clark Ross had the advantage of this information when he attempted to reach the pole in the following year. In a remarkable voyage he sailed into the Ross Sea and was able to determine that the South Magnetic Pole must be at approximately 75°30'S and 154°E in south Victoria Land. He was unable to find a suitable site on which to land on the coast so was not able to reach the site of the pole itself. But his was the first reasonably accurate estimate of its position.

The South Magnetic Pole was finally reached by Douglas Mawson, Edgeworth David and Alistair Mackay in 1909 after an arduous journey by sledge. The position they found was 72°24'S, 155°18'E, about 370 kilometres (230 miles) north of the site indicated by Ross. This does not mean that Ross' estimate was inaccurate, as the South Magnetic Pole is drifting steadily northwards.

Since the time of Mawson, increasingly accurate analysis of the earth's magnetic field has enabled a continuous drift path to be plotted. Two other expeditions have actually reached the vicinity of the pole, and in each case the position turned out to be close to that indicated by mathematical calculations.

THE WANDERING POLE

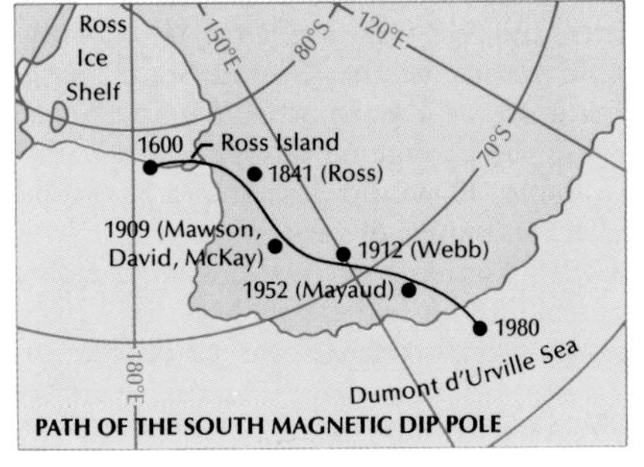

The earth's magnetic poles (dip poles) are the points where a compass needle will stand vertically. Both move quite rapidly across the surface of the globe, travelling, at present, about 10-15 kilometres (6-9 miles) a year in a north to northwesterly direction. First to stand at the South Magnetic Pole were Douglas Mawson, Edgeworth David and Alistair Mackay in 1909 (see p178). The site of the pole was also visited in 1912 by Eric Webb and in 1952 by Mayaud. Positions before 1909 can be estimated from measurements.

STORMY PETREL

Charles Wilkes and the great United States Exploring Expedition

During the first decades of the 1800s, American sealing and whaling ships were plying a profitable trade in the waters off Chile and Peru. There was an ever-growing demand for furs and whale bone, oil for lamps, ambergris for use in perfumes. One by one the fishing grounds were exhausted, and the New England sailors ventured further to the south. By the 1820s they were hunting among the islands of the uncharted Antarctic Ocean, the captains careful not to reveal where they had made their catch. As a result, a number of ships were wrecked on unreported islets, or foundered on unmarked reefs.

Charles Wilkes had a controversial naval career, being court-martialled twice. He was, however, a very competent officer and accomplished much during the US Exploring Expedition, despite the appalling condition of the ships he was given to carry out the voyage.

Demands were made to the United States Government, that an expedition be sent to chart and survey the dangerous southern waters. One of the chief promoters of an exploratory expedition was Jeremiah N. Reynolds, a man who nursed the private theory that Antarctica was an ocean, enclosed within a thick ring of ice.

The Secretary of the Navy, Dickerson, opposed the use of naval vessels and the squandering of government funds. But Reynolds, supported by shipowners and scientists, continued to badger the President, Congress, and the Navy. Eventually, in 1836, an appropriation of $30 000 was granted to fund The United States Exploring Expedition.

Several navy ships were selected for the task, and a veteran officer, Thomas Ap Catesby Jones, placed in command. But Secretary Dickerson barred the way again. He claimed the ships were required for urgent naval duty, that the appropriation had been spent, that not enough men were willing to accompany the expedition. And anyway it was too late in the season for Antarctic exploration.

In 1837, Catesby Jones resigned in disgust. The command was offered to Commodore Shubrick, who declined. Captains Kearney and Gregory were nominated, then thought it politically wise to step aside. There were others, the list growing longer, the officers less prestigious. The next man chosen was Lieutenant Charles Wilkes, a quick-tempered New Yorker. A firm believer in getting the job done, he promptly accepted command.

Granted command on 20 March 1838, he set his date of departure for 10 August. His squadron comprised six motley vessels, all that Secretary Dickerson would allow. The flagship was a 780-tonne sloop-of-war, the *Vincennes*, its consort a smaller sloop, the 650-tonne *Peacock*. An extra deck was constructed aboard the *Vincennes*, though little could be done to improve the condition of the *Peacock*. Captain William H. Hudson said scathingly of his ship, 'The *Peacock* has been fitted out with less regard to safety and convenience, than any vessel I have had anything to do with'.

The third ship was a 230-tonne brig, the *Porpoise*, commanded by another quick-tempered officer, Lieutenant Cadwalader Ringgold. The next two vessels were one-time New York pilot boats. The first, of 110 tonnes, had been schooner-rigged and renamed the *Sea Gull*. Her sister ship, also re-rigged and renamed, was the 96-tonne *Flying Fish*. The final vessel was a store ship, the *Relief*.

At a final count, Wilkes would take with

Sea Gull *and* Porpoise *in a gale off the tip of the Antarctic Peninsula. The severe weather gave Wilkes cause to be critical of the expedition's clothing: 'The men were suffering . . . from the inadequacy of the clothing with which they had been supplied. Although purchased by the Government at a great expense, it was found to be entirely unworthy in the service, and inferior in every way to the samples exhibited.'*

him 82 officers, nine naturalists, scientists and artists, and 342 sailors. Of the latter, only 223 would return to the United States with the expedition, or aboard other American vessels. During the voyage 62 would be discharged as unsuitable, 42 would desert, and 15 would die of disease, injury, or be drowned.

On 18 August 1838 (just one week later than the deadline he had set in March) Wilkes led his squadron on what was to be one of the most important voyages of discovery along the Antarctic mainland.

They went first to Madeira, and from there they managed their way down the coast of South America, clustering in Orange Harbour, near the southern tip of Tierra del Fuego.

By now the 40-year-old Wilkes had taken stock of the situation. He knew that a number of his officers were the protégées of Jeremiah Reynolds. Aware that Reynolds had switched his attention to the Pacific, his followers were unimpressed by the thought of exploring Antarctic waters. It would suit them if Wilkes' expedition failed.

Anchored in Orange Harbour, Wilkes moved fast. He replaced the captain of the *Sea Gull* with his own trusted officer, Lieutenant Johnson. Likewise, the captain of the *Flying Fish* was replaced by Lieutenant Walker. In all, 11 suspect officers were transferred or suspended from duty, the majority of them sent on board the *Relief*. Wilkes then divided the squadron into three. He moved his quarters from the *Vincennes* to the *Porpoise* and, with the *Sea Gull* as tender, prepared to push as far southwards as he could.

A second exploratory group, comprising the *Peacock* and the *Flying Fish*, would be sent south-westwards. Their object was to find — and if possible better — James Cook's most southerly penetration of 71°10'S, the point he had reached in 1774. The remaining two vessels, the *Vincennes* and the *Relief*, were to carry out survey work in the region of Tierra del Fuego and the Straits of Magellan.

Of the nine scientists who accompanied the expedition, only one volunteered to sail on the first exploratory voyage. This was the naturalist, Titian Ramsay Peale. He was offered a berth on Captain Hudson's sloop the *Peacock*,

At the helm of the tiny 96-tonne Flying Fish. *This one-time New York pilot boat forced its way into the ice to reach latitude 70°4′S on 22 March 1839. On that voyage she narrowly escaped being frozen into a field of pack ice, which would have been very serious for she was not equipped to survive such an eventuality.*

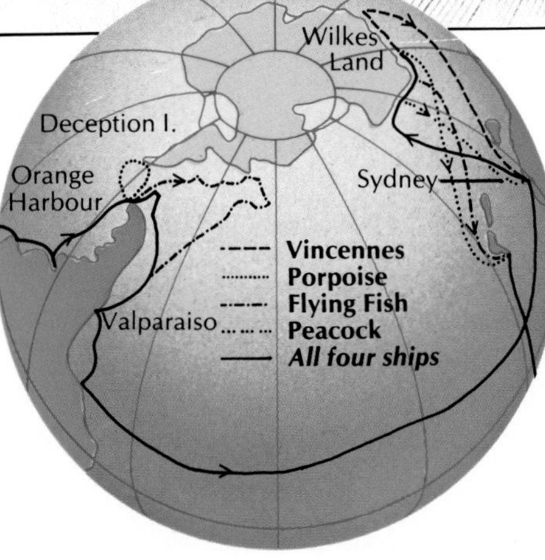

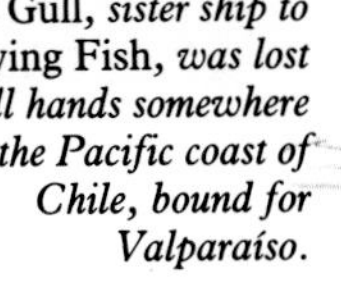

'A mere skiff in the moat of a giant's castle', a sketch of the Flying Fish *from J.C. Palmer's book* Thulia, A Tale of the Antarctic. *In April 1839 the* Sea Gull, *sister ship to the* Flying Fish, *was lost with all hands somewhere off the Pacific coast of Chile, bound for Valparaíso.*

and his diaries offer a civilian's view of the bitter southward passage.

The four departing vessels had taken aboard 10 months' supply of foodstuffs from the *Relief,* anticipating a winter spent trapped in the ice. During the last week of February 1839 they set sail, Wilkes to head south, Hudson to swing southwest. It was dangerously late in the season for such a venture.

One of Wilkes' first tasks was to measure the height and speed of the seas to the south of Cape Horn. He estimated the average waves to be 10 metres (33 ft) high, the seas running at more than 42 km/h (26 mph).

For a few days the *Porpoise* and the *Sea Gull* made good progress, though by early March they were shrouded in fog, the ships coated with ice. The converted pilot boat suffered badly and, on 5 March, scarcely 10 days after leaving Orange Harbour, Wilkes abandoned the expedition. The *Sea Gull* was sent to Deception Island, and her captain was ordered to make landfall there and collect a self-registering thermometer left on the island in 1829. A futile search was made for the instrument, and the *Sea Gull* was battered by a storm.

The *Porpoise* too, had run into trouble on her way back to Tierra del Fuego. Fog-bound near Elephant Island, the sloop was sailing directly towards it when, by sheer good luck, wind parted the grey drifting curtain. Frantic manoeuvring took the vessel clear.

Meanwhile, the *Peacock* and the *Flying Fish* faced hazards of their own. A number of rendezvous points had been agreed, should the vessels lose contact in the fog. Two days out from Orange Harbour the *Flying Fish* disappeared. The *Peacock* waited at the rendezvous, but the tender was not seen again for a month. During this time the *Flying Fish* was hit by a gale which ripped away some of her sails, crushed her boats, and injured the helmsman and lookout. Even so, she managed to fight her way south and, on 22 March, reached 70°4′S, within one degree of Cook's furthest penetration. The ship's surgeon wrote: 'The vessel was beset with ice, whose pale masses just came in sight through the dim haze, like tombs in some vast cemetery; and, as the hoarfrost covered the men with its sheet, they looked like spectres fit for such a haunt ... The waves began to be stilled by the large snowflakes that fell unmelted on their surface; and, as the breeze died away into a murmur, a low crepitation, like the clicking of a death-watch, announced that the sea was freezing.'

Despite the severity of the weather, Captain Hudson insisted on conducting Sunday Service. The officers and men were forced to lay on the deck or cling to the bulwarks as the captain delivered his sermon.

The naturalist, Titian Peale, described conditions aboard the sloop. 'The gun deck has been constantly afloat since we left Orange Harbour ... even my room and the Purser's opposite to it ... the floor being all the time covered and swashing ... I suffered several losses in drawing paper and books.'

Then, on 25 March 1839, the *Flying Fish* was sighted among the floes. Captain Hudson congratulated his colleagues on having crossed the 70th parallel. But the officers agreed that, with the days growing shorter and their ships in poor condition, it was time to sail north. The *Flying Fish* would return to Orange Harbour, while the *Peacock* sailed on to the expedition's next port of call, Valparaíso.

When the schooner-rigged pilot boat reached the shelter of Orange Harbour, she found the *Porpoise* and the *Sea Gull* already at anchor. The *Vincennes* was there, but the *Relief* was away, having taken the scientists to survey the Straits of Magellan. Irked by his own unsuccessful venture to the south, Charles Wilkes was waiting for the store ship to return.

He was not to know that the *Relief* had been almost wrecked near the entrance to the Straits, and that she, like the *Peacock,* had decided to sail directly to Valparaíso. As a result, Wilkes kicked his heels until 20 April, then he took the *Porpoise* and the *Vincennes* north. The lightweight pilot boats were to wait for the *Relief* to arrive then sail with her in the wake of the other vessels.

A confusion of movement — then tragedy.

Alone in Orange Harbour, the *Flying Fish* and the *Sea Gull* awaited the store ship. On 28 April, with no sign of the *Relief,* the two smallest members of the squadron set sail for Valparaíso. At midnight they lost contact, the *Flying Fish* struggling to ride out a nine-day gale. As for the *Sea Gull,* she was never seen again, lost with all hands somewhere off the long Chilean coast.

The Vincennes *in Disappointment Bay (now Fisher Bay) near the Mertz Glacier tongue. Impenetrable ice prevented Wilkes from approaching the land.*

A Disputed Sighting

Confusion over the accuracy of Wilkes' landfalls

By November 1839, 15 months after the expedition's departure from Hampton Roads, the* Vincennes, *the* Porpoise, *the* Peacock *and the* Flying Fish *were at anchor in Sydney harbour. Seven months had elapsed since the loss of the* Sea Gull. *During this time the squadron had sailed north from Valparaíso to the Peruvian port of Callao, then westwards across the Pacific.

As with other exploratory expeditions, the Americans made use of the Antarctic winter to extend their knowledge of the Pacific island groups. Wilkes led his vessels to the Paumoto Islands, Tahiti, Samoa, the Marshalls and Hawaii. Their waters and coastlines were charted, botanical and geological specimens collected by the scientists. Meteorological observations were made and, by the time the squadron set sail from Fiji, southwest bound for Sydney, they had amassed an unrivalled collection of scientific data.

But if their charts, sketches and specimens were in good condition, the ships themselves were not. The *Relief* had already been sent back to the United States as being too unwieldy for Antarctic waters, and the port authorities in Sydney were appalled by the state of Wilkes' fleet.

The aim of the second voyage was to sail as far south as possible from Sydney, then work westward. Yet, with only two months of the Antarctic summer left, the American vessels were no better prepared than on their earlier venture to the ice.

Wilkes admitted, '[The Australians] inquired whether we had compartments in our ships to prevent us from sinking? How we intended to keep ourselves warm? What kind of antiscorbutic we were to use? Where were our ice-saws? To all of these questions I was obliged to answer, to their great apparent surprise, that we had none.'

But Charles Wilkes was still the man who believed in getting things done. Rough wooden housings were built to protect the hatches. Weights and pulleys were attached to the doors, to make sure they swung closed in the bitter Antarctic weather. Charcoal stoves were hung in metal cradles, the portholes covered with tarred canvas, the fabric further strengthened with strips of lead.

Wilkes was once again in command of the *Vincennes*, the *Porpoise* now under Lieutenant Cadwalader Ringgold. The well-respected Hudson was on the *Peacock*; the *Flying Fish* commanded by Lieutenant Pinkney. The ships sailed from Sydney on 26 December.

With the *Vincennes* so laden that stocks of bread were stored in the flagship's launch, Wilkes nevertheless permitted himself the indulgence of a passenger — a dog he fondly, if unimaginatively, called Sydney.

The first agreed rendezvous was Macquarie Island, 1300 kilometres (800 miles) southeast of Tasmania. Seven days of fine weather ushered the vessels southwards. But, in the night of 1 January 1840, the one-time pilot boat, the *Flying Fish,* lost sight of the others. She made obediently to the rendezvous.

Two days later, amid worsening weather, the *Peacock* also became separated from the squadron. She too reached Macquarie Island, but anchored out of sight of the *Flying Fish*.

Blown off-course in a storm, the *Vincennes* and the *Porpoise* passed to the eastward of the island, Wilkes deciding that too much time would be lost if he was to beat his way back. The flagship and brig would go on to the second rendezvous point, and wait there for Hudson and Pinkney.

But Lieutenant Pinkney had other problems to contend with. The *Flying Fish* was leaking badly, waves breaking over her, the schooner's pumps battling the sea. Determined to rejoin the others, he took his ship southwards.

On 9 January the *Vincennes* and the *Porpoise* reached the position marked as the second rendezvous, Emerald Island. But there was no island in view: Wilkes and Ringgold were the victims of inaccurate charts. With no time to spare, they continued south, still hoping to meet up with the strays.

Two days later the leading vessels reached what Wilkes was to refer to as 'the icy barrier'. The *Vincennes* and the *Porpoise* were now at 64°11′S, 164°30′E, and confronted by floes, drifting icebergs and a white frozen cliff to the south. They had, for the moment, sailed as far as they could in the direction of the pole. They must now turn westwards, searching for a passage through the pack ice.

Although the Antarctic summer season was growing short, the explorers were not yet hampered by the dark. Wilkes recorded that on 13 January, 'There was no occasion to light the binnacle-lamps, as newspaper print could be read with ease at midnight'.

On 24 January 1840 the Peacock *was driven stern first into the side of an immense iceberg.*

On 16 January the *Peacock* hove into view — a masterly performance by the stalwart Captain Hudson. Concern was voiced for the *Flying Fish*. The crews feared the 96-tonne schooner had met the same fate as her sister ship, the *Sea Gull*.

The *Flying Fish* finally reached 'the icy barrier' on 21 January, struggled westwards in an attempt to rejoin the fleet, then admitted defeat on 6 February. Still leaking, her crew 'wet day and night', she turned north and arrived at New Zealand five weeks later.

Reunited, the *Vincennes*, the *Porpoise* and the *Peacock* sailed west among the floes and icebergs guarding the approaches to the south.

On the very day that Hudson had come up with Wilkes and Ringgold, a view of land had been shouted by the lookouts. Sightings were made from all three vessels, and Wilkes himself sketched what he took to be a distant range of mountains. He named one of the heights Ringgold's Knoll, though both Ringgold and Hudson regarded the sightings with caution. It was not until the 19th — the ships now sailing some way apart to avoid the risk of collision — that Wilkes felt confident land was visible, both to the south-southeast and southwest. He wrote later, in his five-volume Narrative of the voyage: 'It was between eight and nine in the evening when I was fully satisfied that it was certainly land, and my own opinion was confirmed by some of the oldest and most experienced seamen on board.' He named an aspect of the land Cape Hudson, and noted the *Vincennes*'s position as 66°20′S, 154°30′E.

Two days later, an officer aboard the *Peacock* captured a fine emperor penguin. The bird was found to contain more than 30 large pebbles in its craw — regarded as further evidence of land, as was the comparative shallowness of water, the sounding line touching bottom at 320 fathoms (585 m; 1920 ft).

The *Peacock* was now on her own, out of sight of both the *Vincennes* and the *Porpoise*. An air of optimism prevailed aboard the sloop as she tacked westwards alongside the ice.

Passed Midshipman Eld, one of the two men aboard the Peacock *who claimed to have sighted land from the masthead on 16 January 1840. A controversy continues to this day over that and subsequent sightings. Did Eld and others see the Belleny Islands on the 16th? Did Wilkes purposely falsify the record so that his sighting of land pre-dated that made by Dumont d'Urville on 19 January? Both Eld and his fellow Passed Midshipman had to give evidence on oath before a court martial on their return.*

But on 24 January all this changed. Attempting to get closer to land, Captain Hudson took his vessel into a bay crowded with floes. Whilst manoeuvring to avoid a large block of ice, the *Peacock* went astern and crashed into a second solid floe. The force of the collision threw the sailors to the deck. A hurried inspection revealed that the starboard wheelrope had been carried away, the ship's rudder torn from its fixings. The only way it could be repaired was by lifting it aboard. Meanwhile, the ship was drifting deeper among the floes, towards an immense, wall-sided iceberg. All efforts to alter tack proved fruitless.

For day after day the Vincennes *sailed westwards along the edge of Antarctica, seeking some way of approaching the coast. Every effort was frustrated by the interminable ice barrier, and great numbers of bergs — at one time Wilkes could count 100 without his telescope.*

Further impacts were felt, the stern of the *Peacock* once again shunted against the ice. 'This blow gave it the finishing stroke, by nearly wringing off the head, breaking two of the pintles, and the upper and lower brace.' The ice closed in, grinding against the hull. Anchors were hooked on to the floes, only to be torn loose by the shouldering of the sea. Time and again the *Peacock* was rammed by great masses of ice. The stern boat was crushed, the vessel canting to starboard. Later, with the rudder hauled inboard, carpenters worked throughout the night to repair it.

By eight in the morning of 25 January, the 650-tonne sloop had worked her way free of the bay. The rudder was in position again, though 'hanging by the eyelids'.

There were some aboard who wanted to press on. But Hudson decided the *Peacock* had served her term. She turned north, reaching Sydney in the last week of February 1840.

On 14 February 1840 Wilkes let some of his crew land on the large iceberg to collect water. The men spent several hours sliding down hummocks on the berg.

WILKES' UNHAPPY HOMECOMING

Unedifying squabbles mar the expedition's return

Charles Wilkes was unaware of the* Peacock's *departure. Separated from Ringgold's* Porpoise *on 25 January, the flagship and the other remaining member of the squadron sailed independently westwards, recording each new sighting of what Wilkes was the first to call 'the Antarctic Continent'.

On 30 January, in foggy weather, a look-out aboard the *Porpoise* spied a vessel that was assuredly not the *Vincennes*. Reading her pennants, Ringgold guessed correctly that she was the corvette *Astrolabe*, under the French explorer, Dumont d'Urville.

Acknowledging the Frenchman's seniority, Ringgold manoeuvred to go astern of the *Astrolabe*, then draw alongside. But his tactic gave way to a foolish misunderstanding, d'Urville appearing to crowd on sail and make a run to the north.

Lieutenant Ringgold was not a man to be slighted. In his later report to Wilkes he said, 'I closed with the strangers, desiring to pass within hail under their stern. [But] so far from any reciprocity being given, I saw with surprise sail making by boarding the main tack on board [the *Astrolabe*]. Without a moment's delay, I hauled down my colours and bore up on my course before the wind.'

Dumont d'Urville and Cadwalader Ringgold would both claim they were insulted by the other. They had met, but failed to make their intentions clear, and are now seen as fine explorers, who chose to behave like a pair of touchy prima-donnas.

The *Porpoise* continued westwards, reaching 100°E on 14 February 1840. This was five degrees further than instructions required, and it satisfied Lieutenant Ringgold. His duty done, he returned the sloop eastwards, then north to reach the Bay of Islands, New Zealand, on 26 March.

Again unaware that his flagship was the last of the squadron to continue pressing west, Charles Wilkes had other things on his mind. He still suspected his officers of undermining the voyage, and wrote in his journal, 'I cannot help feeling how disgusting it is to be with such a number of officers . . . who are endeavouring to do all in their power to make my exertions go for nothing'. Nevertheless, he continued to drive the *Vincennes* onward, sighting and naming land beyond the ice. On 12 February he claimed sight of a mountain range within 32 kilometres (20 miles) of the ship. He celebrated with champagne, spent three hours taking observations, then once again sent the *Vincennes* tacking west.

Then, at 6.30 pm on 21 February, Wilkes was faced with a low wall of ice, curling away as far as the eye could see. He named it Termination Land, later changed to Termination Ice Tongue and later still to the Shackleton Ice Shelf. It extends 290 kilometres (180 miles) out from the shore, and was forbidding enough for Wilkes to call a halt to his expedition.

With a number of sightings logged, a list of mountains and headlands named, the tough-minded commander of The United States Exploring Expedition took his flagship back to Sydney. He was convinced beyond doubt that he had won a glorious victory for his country.

Happy to find Captain Hudson and the *Peacock* safe in port, Wilkes announced the discovery of the Antarctic mainland. He dated it as 19 January 1840, sent word of it to the Secretary of the Navy and saw it published in the Sydney *Herald*.

Some weeks later the *Vincennes* and the *Peacock* sailed for New Zealand, where Wilkes made a serious, if well-intentioned, mistake.

Learning that the English explorer James Clark Ross was due to arrive at Hobart, the American dispatched a precis of his own Antarctic voyage, enclosing with it a tracing of his discoveries. Ross received the package in August, queried the information in it, and did not bother to acknowledge receipt of the descriptive letter and chart.

Between spring 1840 and the summer of

1842, Wilkes again traversed the Pacific, undertook a lengthy survey of the North American coast, then sailed to the Philippines and around the Cape of Good Hope. His original squadron had been further reduced by the sale of the *Flying Fish* in Singapore.

By the time Charles Wilkes returned to his homeland in June 1842, his discoveries had been challenged, the outcome of his voyage questioned, and his conduct as commander picked apart by his officers.

Wilkes learned that the English explorer Ross had not only reached the same southern latitudes, *but had sailed across some of the land the American claimed to have seen.*

The inaccuracies contained in the tracing Wilkes had given him led Ross to doubt the reliability of Wilkes' sightings. Ross was correct of course — but so was Wilkes. The American *had* seen the mountains he had noted in his logbook and sketched on his pad. But what he had seen was the phenomenon now known as looming or polar refraction — a desert-like mirage that projects a perfect image relayed by the upper atmosphere, convincing the observer it is far closer than it really is.

Wilkes' case was not helped by his own reassessment of his sightings. Partly perhaps to reinforce his position as the true discoverer of the Antarctic continent, he was now convinced that he had first seen land, not on 19 January as recorded in his log, but three days earlier. January 19 was, after all, the day on which the Frenchman Dumont d'Urville had claimed *his* first view of the mainland.

Brushing aside his critics, Wilkes was nevertheless unable to ignore charges levelled against him by his officers. A Naval Court of Inquiry was convened, culminating in July 1842 in a sad and sordid court martial (see box).

The verdict left him fuming, but he concentrated his efforts on writing the five-volume Narrative of his voyage. It was published in 1845, Congress allowing no more than 100 printed copies. Two of these were offered to

An illustration of a snow petrel from volume eight of the expedition's reports. Altogether 24 volumes were prepared over a period of about 30 years, before work was suspended in 1874. Congress ordered that only 100 copies of each volume should be printed. It has been estimated that the work cost about $300 000.

France, two to Great Britain, two to Imperial Russia, two lodged in the Library of Congress. One each was given to the States of the Union, one to 25 designated countries, one to the Naval Lyceum, Brooklyn. Captain Hudson was given one, as was Captain Ringgold. The commander of The United States Exploring Expedition, the author of the Narrative, was allowed but a single copy.

However bitter the taste of the court martial, Charles Wilkes chose to continue his career in the navy. In 1932, 55 years after his death in Washington DC, the American Geographical Society reprinted the original chart of Wilkes' major Antarctic voyage. Superimposed on this were the tracks made by subsequent explorers. This composite chart shows that although Wilkes was in error between 165°E and 148°E, he was thereafter almost wholly accurate for over 1600 kilometres (1000 miles).

It is still debatable as to who first sighted the mainland. But to Charles Wilkes belongs the honour of having named it with certitude as The Antarctic Continent.

The* Porpoise*, under the command of Cadwalader Ringgold, sighted one of Dumont d'Urville's ships on 30 January, although a ridiculous misunderstanding prevented any contact.

CHARGE AND COUNTER-CHARGE

'We understand that there is to be a nice mess dished up in a short time in the shape of court martials . . . in the eating of which nearly all the officers of the Exploring Expedition are to participate . . . It is said that there are at least a bushel and a half of charges already preferred against Lieut. Wilkes, the commander-in-chief, and that several officers of the squadron have come home under arrest.' New York Morning Herald, 13 June 1842.

This eagerly worded piece appeared three days after the *Vincennes* entered harbour. But by then Wilkes was already the object of gossip and rumour. Various reports had preceded the flagship to New York, newsworthy tidbits concerning the commander's excessive brutality towards members of the crews.

But the rumour that angered him most was that he had 'solicited' command of the expedition. He immediately set about disproving the story, going so far as to procure written denials from the former Secretary of the Navy, Dickerson; former Secretary, Paulding, and the ex-President of the United States, Martin Van Buren, who had left office in March 1841.

Yet accusation and counter-accusation reached the ears of the navy chiefs. Wilkes appealed in person to President Tyler, writing of their meeting, 'I have very great doubts if the President knew who I was, and am inclined to believe he did not, or was determined to ignore all that had anything to do with the Expedition'.

The Navy viewed things differently and convened a Court of Inquiry. It was decided there were charges to be answered, and Charles Wilkes was summoned to appear before a court martial. It was held aboard the man-of-war *North Carolina* at the Brooklyn Navy Yard, starting on 25 July 1842.

Wilkes was not the only one to be charged, though interest would naturally centre upon him. The first of the expedition's officers to stand accused was Passed Midshipman May. Two vague charges were levelled against him — 'Insubordination and mutinous conduct' and 'Disrespect to a superior officer in the execution of his office'. The first charge was quashed, though May was found guilty of the second and publicly reprimanded.

Assistant Surgeon Guillon faced six charges, among these disrespect, neglect of duty, and disobedience to orders. Sentenced to dismissal from the service, this was later commuted to 12 months suspension without pay.

The accusations became ever more trivial. Jealousy and personal ill-feeling tainted the proceedings. Eight officers testified that Wilkes was harsh, overbearing, easily offended, and that, when excited, his manner became violent.

Hudson and Ringgold both spoke up in his defence. They testified that yes, he was of an excitable character, yet prompt and energetic, decided in his manner. Hudson said: 'His manner is like that of every other active officer — he wishes things to be done when he orders them to be done.'

Wilkes met charge with counter-charge. His officers were all volunteers, were they not? He had not spared himself and he did not spare others in the execution of their duties. The United States Exploring Expedition had been financed from public funds. They had all of them, therefore, performed a public service for their nation.

All but one of the charges levelled against him fell apart. How could he be guilty of 'scandalous conduct unbecoming an officer and gentleman' by using the term (which he denied) 'Goddam it'? Was it worth the court's time to accuse him of wearing the uniform of a captain when he was only a lieutenant, yet also commander of the Expedition?

But on the final charge, Charles Wilkes came unstuck. The Court found him guilty of the illegal punishment of seamen, based on an incident that had occurred in Callao, aboard the *Relief.* Six of the crew had stolen liquor from the stores, and Wilkes had ordered them to be punished with more than the legal 12 lashes. There had been similar incidents during the four-year voyage.

The unhappy trial dragged on until September 1842. He was then reprimanded by the Secretary of the Navy, Upshur, a man he had already grown to dislike. Having braved every hazard of the Antarctic Ocean, Wilkes learned that, even if he had been acquitted of all charges, Upshur would not forward him for promotion.

Commander Francis Rawdon Moira Crozier, born in 1796 and an old and close friend of Ross, captained *Terror*.

When James Clark Ross led the expedition to Antarctica in 1839, he was already an accomplished polar explorer.

JAMES CLARK ROSS' GREAT VOYAGE

Unravelling the mysteries of the earth's magnetism

The Antarctic expedition of James Clark Ross between 1839 and 1843 was the most important of its kind in the nineteenth century. Rich in geographical discoveries, the expedition also gathered a mass of information from magnetic surveys and observations. The voyage made a significant contribution to the knowledge of polar navigation and signposted the way to the South Pole.

In the summer of 1838, the British Association for the Advancement of Science held a meeting at Newcastle, England. Attention was drawn to deficiencies existing in the knowledge of terrestrial magnetism. One of the resolutions, therefore, was to fill this scientific gap by calling upon the government to send a naval expedition to the Antarctic. Its purpose would be to determine the position of the magnetic pole and to make magnetic observations 'between the meridians of New Holland [Australia] and Cape Horn'.

The Royal Society was supportive and encouraged the government, led by Prime Minister Lord Melbourne, to give its consent. The following year Parliament voted the necessary funds, and Captain James Clark Ross was appointed to lead the expedition. Few argued with the wisdom of this selection. Ross was not only an expert on the subject of terrestrial magnetism, but was the Navy's most experienced officer in Arctic navigation.

Born in London in 1800, Ross joined the Navy at the tender age of 11 in accordance with family tradition, and was watched over during early years in the service by his illustrious uncle, Sir John Ross.

In 1818, Ross accompanied his uncle on the controversial 'Croker Mountain' voyage in search of the Northwest Passage, and made four further expeditions to the Arctic between 1819 and 1827 with Edward Parry.

Ross consolidated this experience with another four and a half years in the Arctic between 1829 and 1833 when, with the rank of commander, he sailed again with his uncle, this time as his second-in-command. Sir John, anxious to try once more for the ever-elusive Northwest Passage, also wished to demonstrate the advantage of steam-power in polar seas. However, it was to be a voyage of greater significance to his nephew, for on 31 May 1831 James Clark Ross located the position of the North Magnetic Pole on Boothia Peninsula, Northern Canada.

Now, Antartica beckoned. On 8 April 1839, Ross took command of the 370-tonne *Erebus*, with his trusty friend and messmate Commander Francis Crozier as second-in-command of the expedition, and captain of the 340-tonne *Terror*.

The two vessels were three-masted bombs — small, ruggedly constructed warships used for carrying mortars — with shallow draughts and capacious holds. The *Terror* had already proved her worth in Arctic seas during 1836. Each vessel had a double deck, and a double-coppered hull, and was fitted with watertight bulkheads. Both hulls were strengthened from bow to stern with stout timberwork.

Previous voyages in the Arctic had convinced Ross of the need to take precaution against scurvy — the scourge of the mariner. He also intended that 'every improvement that former experience could suggest in preparing the ships for service, and contributing to the health, comfort and safety of their crews should be included'. The Admiralty endorsed this view, and a substantial supply of provisions was taken on board — much more than was usual for such a voyage. These included large amounts of tinned preserved meats, soups and vegetables, as well as cranberries, mixed pickles, mustard and pepper. Throughout the ships' interiors, everything was done to maximise warmth and comfort. Ross knew that a happy and healthy crew was more likely to be an efficient one.

Senior representatives of the Admiralty visited the ships on 2 September to approve the refitting work, and during the next three weeks preparations were finalised. Both ships were degaussed — demagnetised — while moored in the River Medway at Gillingham, and the ships' crews paid three months money in advance, in addition to the wages then due to them. And, as was normal for expeditions of this kind, all received double pay.

On the morning of 5 October 1839, the Lizard, 'the last point of the coast of England', sank from view. The voyage had begun.

The Admiralty's instructions to Ross were specific about many of the expedition's tasks, and outlined a route and timetable for the duration of the voyage. But it was also acknowledged that 'much must be left to the discretion, temper and judgement of the commanding officer'.

By contrast, the Royal Society's instructions occupied a 'small volume of one hundred pages' and 'contained a detailed account of every object of inquiry which the diligence and science of the several committees of that learned body could devise'.

For the first leg of the voyage, *Erebus* and *Terror* were to proceed to Van Diemen's Land (Tasmania), there to set up a permanent station for making magnetic observations. Similar observatories were to be set up at intermediate stations at St Helena and the Cape of Good Hope. These stations were to be ready for use on 29 and 30 May, in order to facilitate simultaneous observations in 'all the foreign and British observatories that constitute the great magnetic co-operation'.

The first iceberg seen on the expedition was on 3 May, '... being not more than twenty feet [six metres] high and evidently fast dissolving ...' as *Erebus* and *Terror* made for Îles Kerguelen in the South Atlantic. Here, the ships' sheep were put ashore to graze and fatten on green grass.

For two months *Erebus* and *Terror* stayed at Îles Kerguelen in the South Atlantic, anchored in Christmas Harbour. Crozier and a team of officers made hourly magnetometric observations, day and night, while Ross occupied himself with 'astronomical, tidal and pendulum observations exclusively'.

Two days after leaving Îles Kerguelen, the ships lost contact with each other as the result of a hurricane. Then the expedition suffered its first fatality. *Erebus's* boatswain, working aloft, fell overboard and was drowned.

Icebergs started to be a problem, making the voyage to Tasmania particularly hazardous. Gales accompanied *Erebus* for most of the way until she finally reached Hobart on 16 August. There, Ross learned that *Terror* and her crew had arrived safely the day before. Captains Crozier and Ross rendezvoused on *Erebus*, then Ross went ashore to Government House to call on the Lieutenant Governor and his wife, Sir John and Lady Franklin.

Ross was delighted to hear that materials for the construction of a permanent observatory had been prepared several months beforehand. The next morning, a suitable site was selected and a party of 200 convicts brought in to start digging a foundation and preparing the blocks of freestone. Within nine days the observatory was virtually finished, a few hours before the observations of 27 August were to begin.

In his narrative Ross records, with some surprise, the unexpected attitude of the convicts to their work. 'I should be doing injustice to my own feelings were I to neglect to express my admiration of the cheerful enthusiasm which the convicts employed in the building displayed throughout the work; as an instance of this, I may mention that after they had been labouring from six o'clock on Saturday morning until ten at night, seeing that a few more hours of work would complete the roofing in, they entreated permission to finish it before they left off; but as it would have broken in upon the Sabbath morning, their request was very properly refused...'

In Hobart Ross read newspaper accounts of the exploits of Frenchman Dumont d'Urville (see p96) and American Charles Wilkes (see p104). Both men had been searching for the South Magnetic Pole in regions of the Antarctic that Ross seemed to consider his own preserve. He was sufficiently piqued by the news to fail to acknowledge the generous gesture made by Wilkes, who had left for Ross at Hobart useful data and a tracing of a chart showing his course and discoveries.

Ross went a stage further and decided to exercise his right to make independent judgements — as outlined in his instructions from the Admiralty — and changed his plans. He would 'avoid following in the footsteps of any other nation' by selecting a more easterly meridian to reach the magnetic pole.

Erebus and Terror manoeuvred through thick ice in an attempt to get as close to the shores of Victoria Land as possible.

THE EXPEDITION'S SCIENTISTS

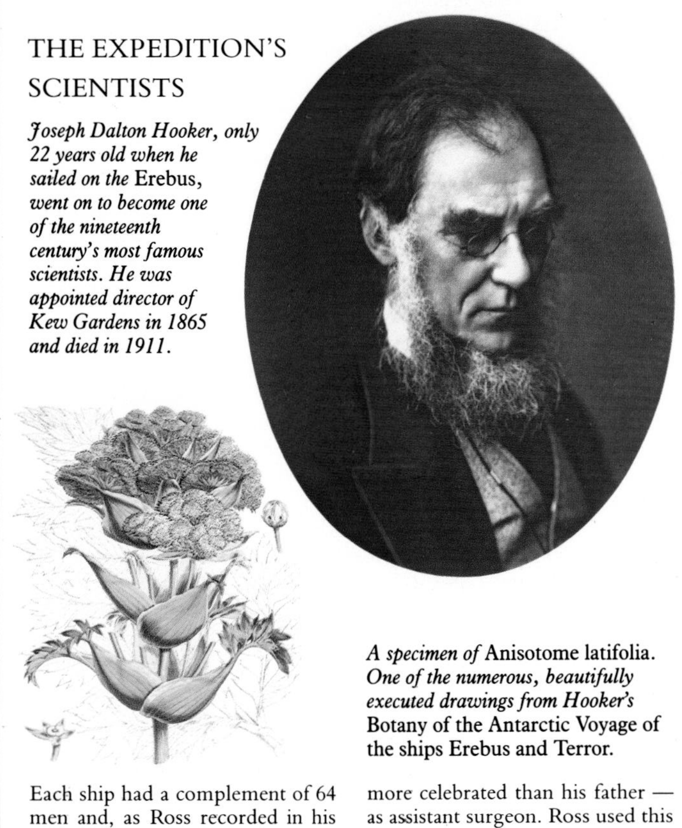

Joseph Dalton Hooker, only 22 years old when he sailed on the Erebus, went on to become one of the nineteenth century's most famous scientists. He was appointed director of Kew Gardens in 1865 and died in 1911.

A specimen of Anisotome latifolia. *One of the numerous, beautifully executed drawings from Hooker's* Botany of the Antarctic Voyage of the ships Erebus and Terror.

Each ship had a complement of 64 men and, as Ross recorded in his account of the voyage, he had numerous applicants wishing to volunteer. Sir William Jackson Hooker, an eminent botanist, asked Ross to take his young son, Joseph Dalton Hooker, on the expedition. Ross had no official right to carry civilians, but enlisted Hooker — a naturalist destined to become even more celebrated than his father — as assistant surgeon. Ross used this nominal title to conceal three other scientists — Robert McCormick as surgeon of *Erebus*, and John Robertson as surgeon, with David Lyall as his assistant, on *Terror*. The second master of *Terror*, John E. Davis, was also a skilled cartographer and artist. His paintings appear on these pages.

A New Southern Record

Both ships halted by a massive wall of ice

James Clark Ross's first season in the Antarctic — from November 1840 to April 1841 — was unpredictably successful. He failed to locate the magnetic pole, but he did make several geographical discoveries, the most intriguing of which was the great ice barrier later named the Ross Ice Shelf.

At daybreak on 12 November 1840, *Erebus* and *Terror* weighed anchor and moved down the Derwent River. Captain James Clark Ross said goodbye to Sir John Franklin and friends, and watched as his host returned to the shores of Hobart.

Nearly 1450 kilometres (900 miles) and one week later, the ships arrived at the Auckland Islands. Immediately visible were two boards, erected on tall poles in a conspicuous spot. Close examination revealed messages painted on them. One stated that Charles Wilkes' American expedition had visited the islands earlier that same year, on 10 March; the other message recorded Dumont d'Urville's visit the following day, 11 March.

After carrying out survey work and magnetic observations, the ships moved on to Campbell Island, a day's sailing away.

At 9 am on 17 December — 15 months after the expedition had left England — *Erebus* and *Terror* weighed anchor and set their courses for the south. Christmas Day arrived and was celebrated in a strong gale, which did not prevent the expedition members from enjoying the usual festivities. Two days later the first icebergs were seen, as well as a great many whales. On 30 December they crossed Thaddeus von Bellingshausen's track, and on New Year's Day crossed the Antarctic Circle. To mark the occasion, all on board were issued with warm clothing, as well as extra food and grog. And, this day, too, was 'kept, as in old England, in conviviality and rejoicing'. Even Billy, the ship's goat on *Erebus*, was given a strong drink, providing some unintentional fun as he staggered about, 'paying the usual penance for his debauchery' next day.

Icebergs and loose ice began to multiply as the ships moved closer to the Antarctic pack — an encircling belt of ice that had yet to be penetrated by man. It stretched before them, 'motionless and menacing'. Bad weather was imminent and Ross waited, hoping it would clear. On 5 January, with the weather still unsettled and conditions poor, Ross decided to 'make the attempt on the ice, and push the ships as far into it as we could get them'.

The blunt-nosed vessels forced their way slowly through a network of cracks and narrow inlets in the outer edge of the pack, where the ice was thickest. After 'about an hour's hard thumping' they came to lighter and more scattered ice.

The ships slowly continued their way through the ice, 'at times sustaining violent shocks, which nothing but ships so strengthened could have withstood'.

At 5 am on 9 January they were once more in the open sea. 'We had accomplished the object of our exertions', wrote Ross. He had discovered the Ross Sea. Now for the South Magnetic Pole.

But the hopes and expectations of Ross and his companions were shattered by the unexpected. On 11 January, land was reported dead ahead. It was impossible . . . unthinkable. But true. At first it was thought to be an 'ice-blink' — a whiteness in the sky caused by the reflection of ice ahead. But soon it was seen to be a paler colour — a mountainous, snow-covered land which, according to Ross's estimation, was about 160 kilometres (100 miles) distant.

Disappointed though he was by the presence of land between his expedition and the magnetic pole, Ross swiftly saw it in positive terms as a 'way of restoring to England the honour of the discovery of the southernmost land, which had been nobly won by the intrepid Bellingshausen, and for more than twenty years retained by Russia'.

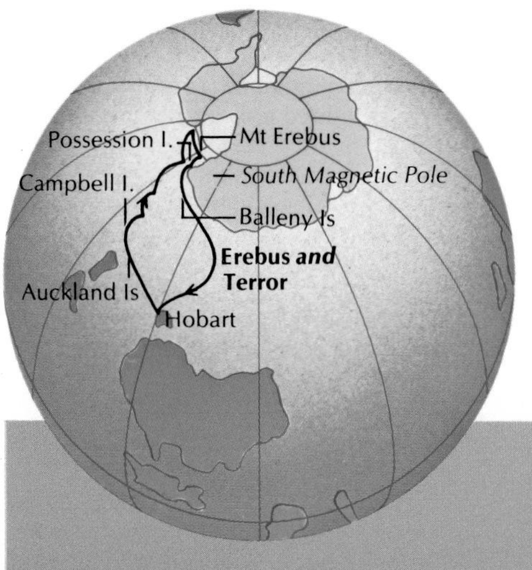

They next saw a magnificent range of mountains, rising to 2440 metres (8000 ft). Ross called that which extended to the north-west Admiralty Range, and christened many of the prominent peaks that he could see.

The frenetic behaviour of the compass needle suggested to Ross that the magnetic pole was a mere 800 kilometres (500 miles) away. He was faced with two options: 'to trace the coast to the north-west, with the hope of turning the western extreme [sic] of the land, and thence proceed to the south; or follow the southerly coast line round Cape Downshire, and thence take a more westerly course'. He chose the second, following the new coast and sailing through the Ross Sea.

On 12 January, the ceremony of taking possession of newly discovered lands was celebrated by Ross and Crozier on the larger of two offshore islands. The mainland was impenetrably surrounded by ice and a heavy surf. A flag was planted on Possession Island and a toast was drunk to 'Her Majesty and His Royal Highness Prince Albert', with the region claimed as Victoria Land.

On 22 January, Ross calculated that they had reached a higher southern latitude than James Weddell had in 1823, and 'spliced the main brace' — a double tot of rum was issued to all on board. On the 27th, Franklin Island was formally possessed. A heavy swell, a rocky coastline and ice combined to make the landing hazardous.

The next day brought another surprise —

what Robert McCormick, *Erebus's* surgeon, described as 'a stupendous volcanic mountain in a high state of activity'. The peak was 3780 metres (12 400 ft) above sea level, and belched flame and smoke. Ross named it Mount Erebus, and another smaller extinct volcano to the east of it, Mount Terror.

As the ships sailed south, Ross saw a low white line 'extending from its eastern extreme point as far as the eye could discern to the eastward. It presented an extraordinary appearance, gradually increasing in height, as we got nearer to it, and proving at length to be a perpendicular cliff of ice, between one hundred and fifty feet and two hundred feet [45-60 metres] above the level of the sea, perfectly flat and level at the top, and without any fissures or promontories on its even seaward face'.

It was higher than the ships' mastheads, and Ross was unable to see beyond it. He realised that the Victoria Barrier, as he called it — it was later named the Ross Ice Shelf — was impenetrable. Said Ross, 'we might with equal chance of success try to sail through the cliffs of Dover, as to penetrate such a mass'.

By the middle of February, after sailing eastwards along the ice shelf for 320 kilometres (200 miles), dredging and sounding in the vain hope of finding some hidden point of entry, Ross had decided to abandon the exploration until the next season.

The expedition arrived at the Derwent River on 6 April 1841. Ross had concluded his first season, gratified that their exploits had been 'unattended by casualty, calamity, or sickness of any kind, and that every individual on both ships had been permitted to return in perfect health and safety to this southern home'.

Ross, Crozier and a small party of officers made a risky landing on Franklin Island in the Ross Sea. Hooker was nearly crushed by a boat when he slipped from icy rocks.

The ships approach the eastern point of Ross Island, named Cape Crozier by Ross.

The great mass of Mount Erebus dominates the skyline when seen from Franklin Island. Ross was surprised to discover that the mountain was an active volcano.

In a brief ceremony on the shores of Possession Island, Ross claimed the lands he had discovered for Britain.

In giant seas and raked by furious winds, Erebus, *barely under control, is swept through a narrow gap between two giant icebergs. The ships had shortly before collided, and* Erebus *had lost rigging and spars after being driven into the face of a huge berg.*

ENCOUNTER WITH AN ICEBERG

Erebus *crippled after the two ships collide*

During the six months before the start of the second season, Ross kept his expedition team fully occupied.* Erebus *and* Terror *were repaired and refitted, and sufficient stores and provisions to last three years were taken on board. Portable observatories were set up and manned near the Rossbank Observatory — built by Ross the previous year.

The expedition finally sailed for the south again on 23 November. In three weeks they were back among the icebergs, and on 17 December they re-entered the pack ice. Christmas Day was spent shrouded in fog, hemmed in by pack ice and threatened by a chain of icebergs.

New Year's Eve was little better, with *Erebus* and *Terror* trapped in a water hole, surrounded by impenetrable ice. Since further progress was impossible, the ships moored opposite each other alongside a massive slab of floating ice as white and as hard as 'Carrara marble'. A central space between the ships was excavated in the ice to make a dance floor — 'the crystal ballroom' — with two elevated chairs for the ships' captains. A refreshment bar was cut in ice nearby. Thus, in the lonely vastness of the Antarctic, the crews welcomed 1842 with wine, 'sculptured Grecian women', song and dance.

Reality swiftly returned as the days passed, with foul weather making progress slow and tedious. On 19 January *Erebus* and *Terror* were in 'an ocean of rolling fragments of ice, hard as floating rocks of granite, which were dashed against them by the waves with such violence that their masts quivered'.

Inevitably, the sea exacted its toll. *Terror's* rudder was smashed by ice; that of *Erebus* was badly damaged. With characteristic understatement, Ross wrote that 'there seemed to be but little probability of our ships holding together much longer, so frequent and violent were the shocks they sustained'.

Somehow, miraculously, they did, and on 4 February, when the storm had subsided, and repairs made, the ships continued southwards.

Towards the end of February, the Ross Ice Shelf was once more in sight. Conditions were grim. So intense was the cold that while crewmen were chipping ice from the bows of *Terror*, a small fish was found frozen in place where it had been thrown against the ship's side. *Terror's* surgeon/naturalist, Dr Robertson, retrieved the fish for subsequent analysis; but the ship's cat moved quicker.

The weather continued to frustrate the expedition's progress. The time and effort involved in 'penetrating a mass of more than a thousand miles [1600 km] in thickness' had left Ross with only a few days in which to pursue his explorations before winter set in. He traced the ice shelf a little more to the east, and sailed a little further south than he had the previous season, and then called it a day. Ross signalled Crozier that the ships were to head for the north to winter in the Falkland Islands.

They recrossed the Antarctic Circle and set a course for Cape Horn. The expedition progressed uneventfully for several hundred kilometres, seeing only four or five icebergs. Then, on 12 March, as darkness and thick snow were falling, the icebergs became more numerous, clustering around them. As visibility deteriorated, topsails were being reefed when a massive berg loomed up ahead.

'The ship was immediately hauled to the wind on the port tack', Ross wrote, 'with the expectation of being able to weather it [the berg]. But just at this moment the *Terror* was observed running down upon us, under her top-sails and foresail; and as it was impossible for her to clear both the berg and the *Erebus*, collision was inevitable. We instantly hove all aback to diminish the violence of the shock, but the concussion when she struck us was such as to throw almost everyone off his feet. Our bowsprit, foretopmast, and other smaller spars, were carried away, and the ships hanging together, entangled by their rigging, and dashing against each other with fearful violence, were falling down upon the weather face of the lofty berg under our lee, against which the waves were breaking and foaming to near the summit of its perpendicular cliffs. Sometimes she rose high above us, almost exposing her keel to view, and again descended as we in our turn rose to the top of the wave, threatening to bury her beneath us, whilst the crashing of the breaking upperworks and boats increased the horror of the scene.'

Providentially, the ships separated safely. But *Erebus*, now completely disabled, was drifting on to the berg 'so close that the waves, when they struck against it, threw back their sprays into the ship'. It was the gravest moment of the expedition, and it revealed the true nature of the commander. Robert McCormick, *Erebus's* surgeon, observed that 'Captain Ross was quite equal to the emergency, and, folding his arms across his breast, as he stood like a statue on the afterpart of the quarter-deck, calmly gave the order to loose the sail'.

Ross then ordered the use of a stern-board (the equivalent, for a sailing ship, of a three-

The formidable cliffs of the great ice barrier towered over the masts of Ross' ships and blocked any hope of progress.

With both ships trapped in the pack, the men set about gathering ice to replenish their dwindling water supply.

New Year's Eve 1841 was celebrated on an ice floe, with games and a grand fancy ball. Both captains watched the bizarre spectacle from thrones carved out of ice.

point-turn) — a measure he regarded as a hazardous expedient that 'perhaps had never before been resorted to by seamen in such weather'. Amid 'the roar of the wind and the sea, it was difficult both to hear and to execute the orders that were given'. It took three quarters of an hour before the ship gathered stern way and finally responded. 'In a few minutes, after getting before the wind, she dashed through the narrow channel between two perpendicular walls of ice, and the foaming breakers which stretched across it, and the next moment we were in smooth water under its lee.'

Considering the extent of the damage — *Erebus* was completely crippled — the repairs were made in a surprisingly short time, and both ships had resumed course by 15 March.

The expedition finally arrived at the Falkland Islands where they stayed, but for a brief spell at Cape Horn, for nearly five months.

Ross sailed for the third and final season in the south on 17 December 1842. His intention this time was to penetrate the Weddell Sea, and add to the discoverer's researches in 1822. Ross crossed his tracks on 14 February, expecting to find the clear sea Weddell had described. Instead, he met with 'dense, impenetrable, pack ice'. Again Ross was foiled by the elements.

On 5 March 1843, having crossed the Antarctic Circle for the third time, Ross reached 71°30′S, 14°51′W. It was the point at which he decided the season was too far advanced to attempt further exploration. He signalled *Terror* to start the long run home.

Ross wrote, in the closing pages of his account: 'The shores of Old England came into view at 5h 20m A.M. on the 2nd of September, and we anchored off Folkestone at midnight of the 4th.' They had been away for just over four years and five months.

A group of steam catchers and their prey. The whale carcases were inflated to stop them from sinking.

The flensing plan (platform) at a whaling station on South Georgia in the 1920s. It was here that whales were cut up and blubber removed to be converted into oil, which was mainly used for lighting.

AN ANCIENT INDUSTRY

Assessing the effects of 1000 years of whaling

Large-scale commercial whaling probably began in the 15th century and by the middle of the 19th century had had a disastrous effect on most of the easily caught species of whales. The introduction of the harpoon gun in 1870 extended the catastrophe to the remaining species.

Commercial whaling is believed to have started with the Basques in the Bay of Biscay about the eleventh century. It spread north along the European coast to Spitzbergen (1611) and westwards to Greenland (1570). Until about 1700 whalers were mainly Dutch and British, but American whalers from New England ports gradually became more active. Up to this time whalers had concentrated on right whales in temperate waters, and on bowhead whales along the edge of the Arctic. About 1712, American whalers found that by going further from the coast they could catch sperm whales in large numbers.

For the next 150 years the Americans dominated the industry, moving south in the Atlantic Ocean, then turning east and west into the Indian and Pacific oceans. When they reached the cooler waters south of the tropics, they again found large numbers of right whales, and these became the mainstay of the industry in the early nineteenth century. Subsequently the whalers turned north in the Pacific Ocean, still hunting sperm whales, until they reached cooler waters and again encountered right whales. Finally, about 1850, they reached the Bering Sea and later pushed through into the Arctic, where they found more bowheads.

Until late in the nineteenth century the whalers worked from quite small sailing ships and made voyages of several years. The actual pursuit and capture of the whales was accomplished from rowing boats carrying about six men. Once the boat had managed to approach within a few metres of a whale a hand harpoon was thrown into its body, and when the whale was finally exhausted it was killed with hand lances. Right and bowhead whales were towed back to camp, on shore or on the ice, where the oil and baleen (whalebone) were extracted. Sperm whales, being taken in the open sea, were cut up in the water alongside the ships, and the blubber (the thick layer of fat under the skin) and the other useful parts were hauled on board.

The oil was extracted, on board or on shore, by boiling down the blubber in large open iron pots (try-pots) on open fires. It was used at that time mainly for lighting. The other valuable product, from right whales only, was the baleen, used to make, for example, 'bones' for women's corsets, umbrella ribs and whip handles.

About 1870 the whole technique of whaling underwent a fundamental change. A Norwegian, Svend Foyn, devised a heavy iron harpoon which could be fired from a cannon. It carried a charge which exploded inside the whale, killing it relatively quickly. He mounted the cannon on small, fast, steamers. These new whalers were able to capture whales more efficiently, and they were now able to catch the fast-swimming rorquals.

By about 1900 the whalers had entered the Southern Ocean and discovered the great herds of blue and fin whales there. Whaling in this region built up steadily, but at first the area covered was greatly limited by the need to tow the catches back to shore stations. However, in 1926, the first 'factory ship' went south. This was a vessel equipped to haul several whales on board at once and process them there, and was accompanied by a group of catchers. Whaling was now independent of shore bases and spread rapidly through the whole Antarctic. In the peak year, 1937-38, 33 expeditions went south and killed 46000 whales.

Argentina was the first country to engage seriously in whaling in southern waters in this century, and it continued until about 1929. The real founder of Antarctic whaling was Norway. Norwegians began working from land stations in 1906 and introduced the factory ships in 1926. The United Kingdom soon became involved and up to 1935 these two countries shared over 90 per cent of the catch. Both ceased whaling in the Antarctic when fin whales became scarce, the United Kingdom in 1963 and Norway in 1968. Since then southern whaling has been dominated by Japan, which began in 1937, and the USSR, which started in 1951. Since 1969 these countries have taken the entire Southern Ocean catch.

Good records have been kept of whale catches during this century. For the eighteenth and nineteenth centuries surviving ships' logbooks and customs records provide fairly accurate figures of the numbers of whales taken in the southern hemisphere. Scientists of many countries, working together through the Scientific Committee of the International Whaling Commission (IWC), have been able to make estimates of the original numbers in the southern seas of most of the principal whales, and of the numbers surviving today.

The right, blue and humpback whales have all been reduced to a very small proportion — perhaps only about one per cent of their original numbers, and the fin and sei whales have also been badly depleted, to about 10-20 per cent. Only the minke whale population remains virtually unchanged.

The slow breeding rate of the whales (one calf every two or three years), combined with the natural death rate of about 4-8 per cent a year, means that the depleted populations can recover only very slowly.

There is now some evidence that the right and humpbacks may be recovering in the southern seas (perhaps up to 7 per cent a year), but it will be years before any changes can be detected in the numbers for blue and fin whales. Until this happens the ultimate survival of the blue whale must give serious cause for concern.

The status of the sperm whale is less easily assessed because, except at a few coastal stations, the catch has been predominantly of males. While these have been reduced, female numbers are relatively little affected. The total southern hemisphere catch has been about

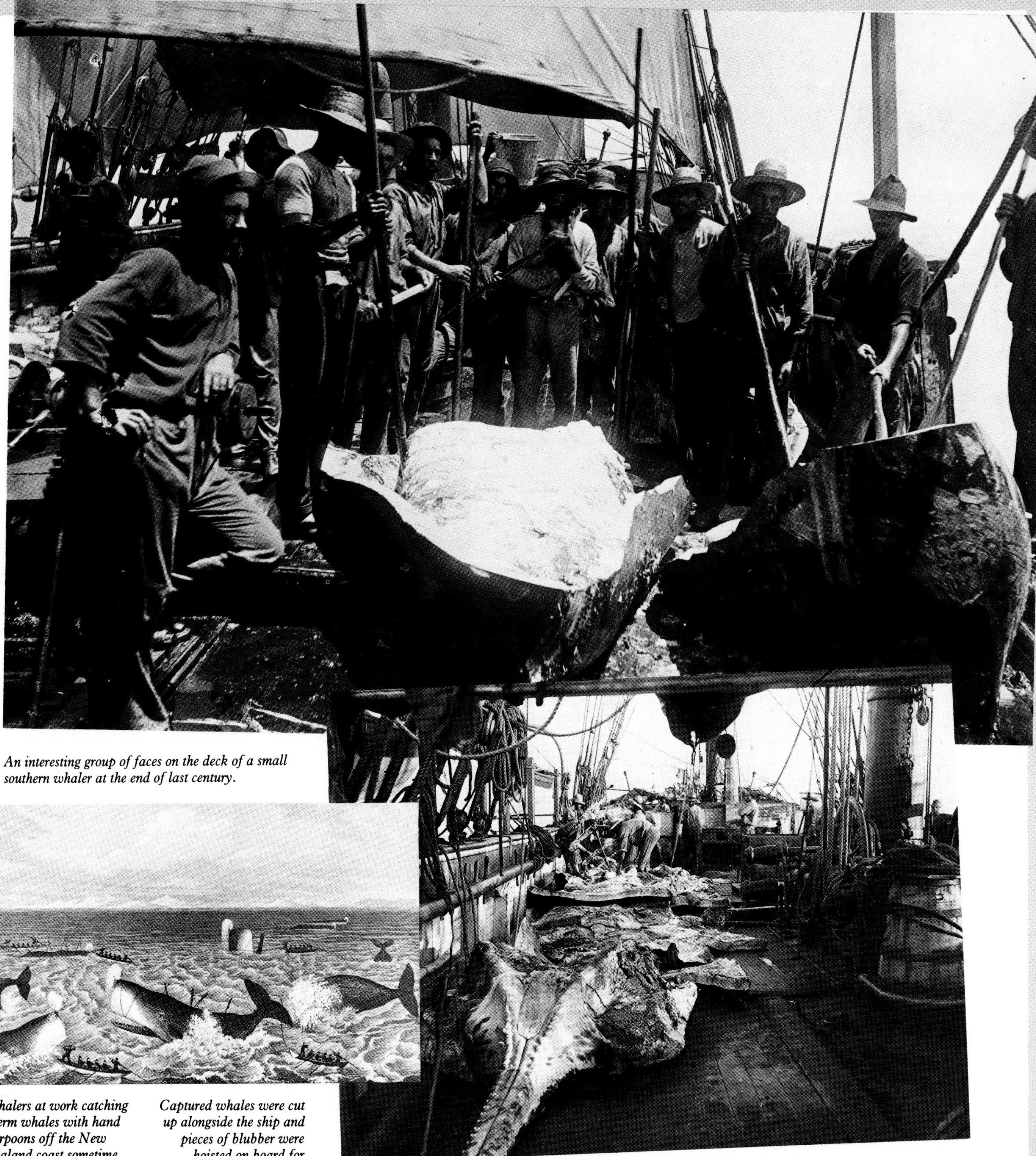

An interesting group of faces on the deck of a small southern whaler at the end of last century.

Whalers at work catching sperm whales with hand harpoons off the New Zealand coast sometime in the late 1830s.

Captured whales were cut up alongside the ship and pieces of blubber were hoisted on board for boiling down.

220000 animals. The number of males has been reduced from about 600000 to 450000, but the females only from 600000 to 500000. The main reduction has been in mature males capable of being harem masters, and this may have had adverse effects on the breeding rate. For this reason the IWC prohibited pelagic (open sea) hunting of sperm whales from 1980.

Three different methods are used to estimate the number of whales in any particular population. The first is by a direct count, either as they pass by on migration, or while they are concentrated in a limited area. Counts on migration have been done successfully from the shore or by flying over them. Minke whales have been counted successfully in this way since 1978 by scientists on Japanese and Russian ships diverted for this work.

The second method is to calculate the relative change in the numbers in the population produced by a known catch, assuming that the average number of whales caught in a day is proportional to the number in the area. Thus, between 1955-56 and 1963-64 the average daily catch of fin whales fell from 3.3 to 1.0, a reduction of 70 per cent. Since the reduction was produced by a catch of 206000, it can be deduced that this number was approximately 70 per cent of the 1955-56 population, which was therefore about 295 000. The original population can then be calculated by adjusting for the catch taken prior to 1955-56 (433000) and the animals born during that time.

The third, less reliable, method is called mark and recapture. The marks used are numbered metal darts, which are shot into the whale with a shoulder gun and lie harmlessly in the muscles under the blubber. Since 1932 about 20000 baleen whales and 6000 sperm whales have been marked. From the proportion of the catch which carries these marks it is possible to calculate the total population.

UNCERTAIN FUTURE

International politics will dictate the fate of whales

International efforts to conserve whales have now led to a total ban on all commercial catching, due to come into force in 1986. Only Japan, Norway and the USSR still have whaling industries, and it remains to be seen if they will observe the ban. Even if hunting stops, the future of some species is in doubt.

Baleen has been of little importance during the twentieth century, and until the last 20 years the most important product, from both sperm and baleen whaling, has been the oil. The oils obtained from baleen and sperm whales are used in quite distinct ways.

Sperm oil is not edible but has a variety of industrial uses, mainly as a lubricant to be used under conditions of high temperature and pressure, and in the tanning of very high grade leathers. Spermaceti, found in the head of sperm whales, is used to make cosmetics.

Baleen whale oil is edible and is now mainly used to make margarine and other foodstuffs. Since about 1955 meat has become the main product from baleen whales. It is eaten by humans, particularly in Japan and Scandinavia.

In present Antarctic whaling, which takes only minke whales, all possible meat is taken from each whale, and amounts to about 4 tonnes per whale from an average body weight of 7.5 tonnes. An average of 0.8 tonnes of oil is extracted from the rest of the carcase.

Until the 1930s whaling operations were virtually unregulated, but in 1931 and the following years there were several agreements between some of the principal countries involved. The main aim was to rationalise the supply of whale oil to the market, but the 1931 agreement did ban the taking of right whales.

In 1946 the International Whaling Commission was established to provide a broad and continuing authority to regulate whaling operations. By the time of its second meeting in 1951 its members were Australia, Brazil, Canada, Denmark, France, Iceland, Japan, Mexico, the Netherlands, New Zealand, Norway, Panama, South Africa, Sweden, the United Kingdom, the United States of America and the Union of Soviet Socialist Republics. This was nearly all the principal whaling countries at that time, and the membership underwent little change until the mid-1970s.

The Commission had power to regulate the numbers and kinds of whales taken, and to set size limits, closed seasons, and protected areas. Although it set limits for the Antarctic which prevented catches rising again to the 1937-38 level of 46 000 — the maximum catch in any one year after 1940 was 41 000 in the 1960-61 season — it did not prevent the gross depletion of the blue and humpback whales, and subsequently the serious reduction of fin, sei and sperm whales. During the 1960's several of the countries ceased whaling, generally because it was no longer economically rewarding. As scientific evidence of the depletion of the whale stocks built up, and public concern about the fate of the whales began to grow, the Commission began to place more effective restrictions on the catching of whales. Blue and humpback whales were fully protected in the Antarctic in 1963. Catch limits for other

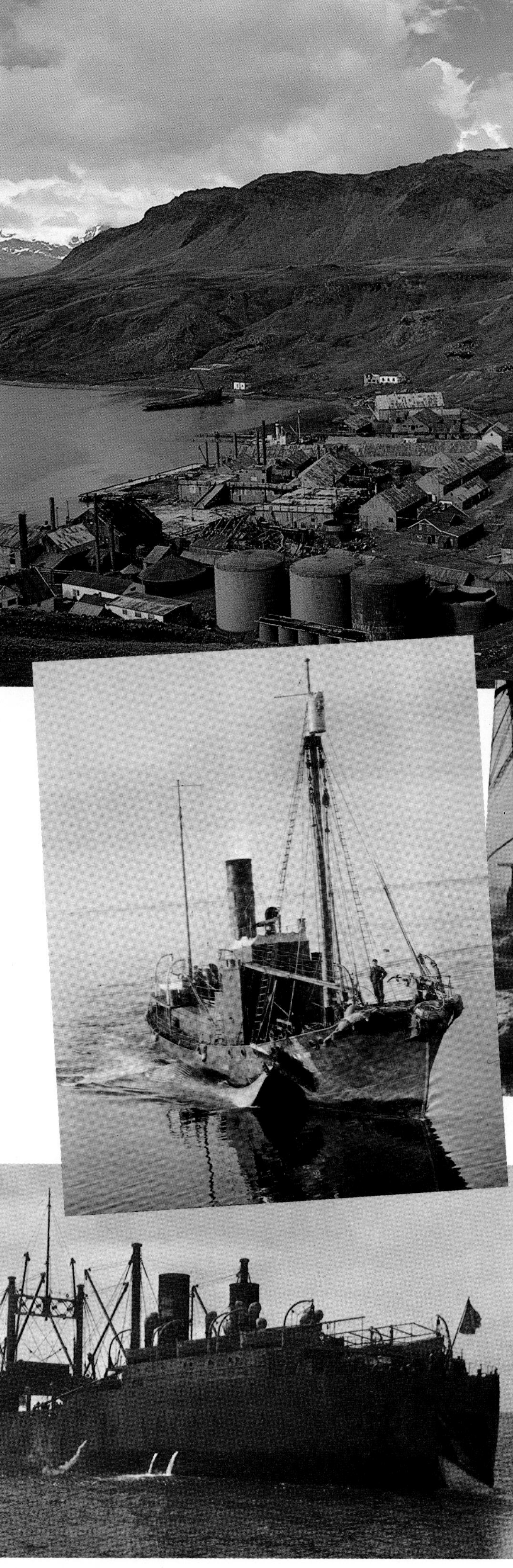

The deserted whaling station at Grytviken on South Georgia is gradually falling into disrepair. This station, opened by an Argentinean company in 1904 and operated by Norwegians, was the first on the island. It changed hands several times after 1959, and finally closed down in 1965. The last station operating on South Georgia was at Leith Harbour. This was operated by a Japanese company until it closed.

A small steam whale catcher towing its prize to the factory ship. The harpoon gun with its explosive head and neatly coiled rope is situated on the bow. The rope from the harpoon ran to a winch on the foredeck, and from there down into the hold.

The factory ship Kosmos *photographed by a member of Sir Douglas Mawson's expedition in about 1930. The first of these vessels appeared in the Southern Ocean in 1926, and by 1937 there were 33 of them, and their attendant catchers, working in the south.*

species were progressively reduced; fin whales being fully protected in the Antarctic in 1976, and sei whales in 1978.

The effectiveness of the Commission's decisions has been limited, both because they apply only to the countries which are members of the Commission, and because they can be ignored even by member countries. In practice they are now almost completely effective although this was not always true in the past. Portugal, with a small operation in Madeira and the Azores, was, in 1984, the only country outside the Commission taking whales. The so-called pirate whalers of a few years ago have ceased operating. Whaling by member countries is scrutinised both by government inspectors and, for the larger operations, by official observers from other countries. Breaches of the regulations, which used sometimes to occur, have virtually ceased.

Changes in the regulations are made difficult by the requirement, in the Whaling Convention, that they must be carried by a three-quarters majority. Since about 1975, however, support for protective measures has been steadily increasing as more countries committed to the protection of whales, and not themselves engaged in whaling, have become members. At the 1982 meeting of the Commission, which 39 member countries attended, this trend culminated in a decision to suspend all commercial whaling from 1986.

But under the rules of the Commission, a country which makes a formal objection to a decision within due time is not bound by that decision. Japan, Norway and the USSR have made such objections and therefore can legally continue whaling. In the 1987-88 season Japan caught 317 Brydes', 188 sperm and 577 minke whales, while Norway caught 375 minke whales, Iceland 100 fin and sei whales, and the USSR 158 gray and 85 minke whales. Many of these activities took place under the guise of 'scientific research', and many observers think that the figures for catches are grossly underestimated. It is certain that the meat from Japan's 'scientific research' ended up on supermarket shelves.

Those who continue whaling run a risk of commercial pressure from countries opposed to the practice. In the United States, for example, existing acts of Congress can be invoked which call for the imposition of sanctions on countries failing to observe the decisions of international bodies responsible for the conservation of fishery resources. These sanctions include restriction of access to fisheries within the USA 200-mile (320-km) zone, and limitations on export of fishery products to the lucrative United States' domestic market.

An interesting fact is that, since the decision to cease whaling in 1986 does not apply to the catching of whales by aboriginal people for their own sustenance, the controversial catch of bowheads by Alaskan Eskimos in the United States could legally continue. Only about 3800 of these whales remain out of an original population of about 20 000, and the Scientific Committee of the International Whaling Commission has advised strongly against any animals being killed.

In early 1990 the future of whaling remains unclear. The International Whaling Commission decision of 1982 was not that whaling should cease permanently in 1986, but that there should be a pause during which the whole question could be further examined. The Commission also decided that, not later than 1990 (the meeting is to take place in April of that year), it would undertake a comprehensive assessment of the effects of the decision to cease whaling, and consider possible changes, including restoration of some catching. Nearly all members of the Commission accept, at least in theory, that whales constitute a resource which can be utilised, provided that the populations are not reduced to an extent which upsets the balance of the marine ecosystem. Several countries are keen for the ban on whaling to be lifted as soon as possible, and will lobby vigorously for that to happen, whatever others think.

There is, however, a contrary view of whaling which has gained considerable popular support around the world in recent years. This view questions the desirability of killing any whales at all. The products obtained from whale carcasses can either be foregone, or manufactured from other sources. Proponents of this view argue that whales should be regarded as a resource of great aesthetic and scientific interest, a vital component of the marine ecosystem, and one better left alone. They also point out that whales face a number of other serious problems, apart from whaling. The oceans are becoming increasingly polluted, and this is having a serious effect on many marine species. There is also a danger that krill – the major food of the great baleen whales – will eventually be harvested on a commercial basis. Russian and Japanese fishermen currently take around 400 000 tonnes annually, although there is no real demand or use for it at present. There has also been a increase in the populations of several krill-eating species around Antarctica, such as crabeater seals, and this may be due to the fact that there is now more krill available because there are fewer whales to eat it. Some experts feel that there is a danger that whale numbers will never recover now that the food once available for them is being consumed by larger populations of other species.

There are clearly many uncertainties about the future of most, if not all, whale species. Numbers of some have been seriously depleted to the extent that may never recover. It would be tragic if just one were allowed to become extinct. Ultimately, the fate of all whales rests with those concerned enough to take whatever action is necessary to ensure their survival.

A whale being dismembered on the deck of a factory ship. The large steam-driven saw (behind the man on the left) helped in the process. Once cut up, sections of the whale were thrown into a boiler that extracted the clear, white whale oil. Visitors to these ships always commented on the powerful stench that pervaded everything.

Whales were hauled through the opening at the back of the ship and up the slipway to the flensing deck. Thirty-three of these ships processed a record 46 000 whales in one season from 1937 to 1938.

A group of Challenger's *civilian staff. Seated at centre is J. J. Wild, the expedition's artist with Rudolph von Willemoës-Suhm on the extreme right and Lieutenant Pelham Aldrich on the extreme left.*

Challenger *at anchor at St Thomas in the Danish West Indies.*

GENESIS OF AN EXPEDITION

The birth of the science of oceanography

On 21 December 1872, HMS* Challenger *put to sea from Portsmouth and began a voyage of exploration that, in the words of Sir John Murray, represented 'the greatest advance in the knowledge of our planet since the celebrated geographical discoveries of the fifteenth and sixteenth centuries'.

Throughout the latter part of the eighteenth century, the Royal Society had been gathering information about the nature of the sea whenever and wherever it could, chiefly through the efforts of scientists carried on naval ships. But their findings had yielded only fragmentary knowledge.

Edwards Forbes, Professor of Natural History at Edinburgh University, unwittingly sowed the seeds of the *Challenger* expedition. Forbes was a pioneer in marine biology who had come to the conclusion that animal life did not exist below 300 fathoms [548 metres; 1800 ft] — the Azoic zone.

Forbes' controversial assertion aroused the interest of many naturalists, including Charles Wyville Thomson, a marine biologist who had met Forbes as a student. In 1868 and 1869 Thomson, with friend and fellow naturalist Dr William Carpenter went dredging in waters off the northwest coast of Scotland.

Both cruises, brief though they were, proved scientifically fruitful and, among other things, revealed the existence of animal life at 2000 fathoms [3657 metres; 12 000 ft], disproving Forbes' earlier claim. They also gave Thomson the appetite for further exploration.

In 1870 Thomson, now himself Professor of Natural History at Edinburgh University, persuaded the Royal Society to finance a global expedition to discover 'everything about the sea'. Gladstone's Liberal Government responded favourably and offered to subsidise the expedition. The Admiralty put HMS *Challenger* at the Royal Society's disposal.

HMS *Challenger* had been built for the Royal Navy in 1858 at Woolwich, near London. She was a three-masted, square-rigged corvette, equipped with auxiliary steam power, and a twin-bladed screw that could be disconnected and lifted clear of the water when the vessel was under sail. Just over 60 metres (200 ft) long, and with a displacement of 2343 tonnes (2306 tons), the warship had served several commissions abroad.

But her service days were over. In the summer of 1872, *Challenger* was converted at Sheerness from a fully armed man-of-war to an ocean-going survey vessel. Captain G. S. Nares — later to achieve distinction as an Arctic explorer — was appointed to command *Challenger*, and Dr Thomson was nominated by the Royal Society to be the scientific leader of the expedition.

The ship's spars were reduced, and the ammunition lockers and all but two of its 30 kg (66 lb) guns were taken out to provide space for a fully equipped chemical laboratory. Existing internal accommodation was reorganised to provide a naturalists' workroom, a well-stocked library, a photographer's studio, and an aquarium for keeping specimens alive.

A 13 kW (18 hp) engine for hoisting the dredging and sounding gear was fitted on the upper deck and, to the rear of this, compass equipment for making magnetic observations. Many tonnes of iron sinkers were carried on board for taking sounding lines to the seabed.

When *Challenger* finally put to sea from Portsmouth on 21 December 1872, with her scientists and a crew of about 240 on board, she was a highly efficient floating laboratory — an extension of the Royal Society.

Among Captain Nares' fine team of deck officers and engineers were sub-lieutenants Lord George Campbell and Herbert Swire, two junior officers who took a keen interest in the work of the expedition and kept private journals of enduring interest. Dr Thomson's team consisted of three naturalists, Rudolph von Willemoës-Suhm, John Murray, and H. N. Moseley. The others in Thomson's team were Y. Buchanan, the chemist, and J. J. Wild, Thomson's secretary and the official artist.

During the first 10 days of the voyage, heavy seas made living conditions uncomfortable and survey work impossible. But once

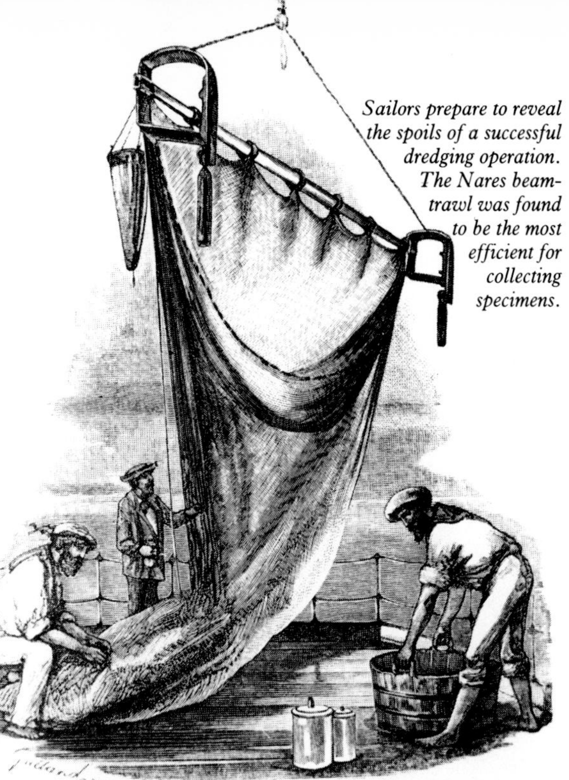

Sailors prepare to reveal the spoils of a successful dredging operation. The Nares beam-trawl was found to be the most efficient for collecting specimens.

The ship's scientists lived in relative comfort. This roomy cabin, complete with bathtub, belonged to Henry Moseley, one of the expedition's naturalists.

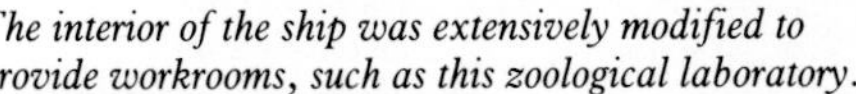

The interior of the ship was extensively modified to provide workrooms, such as this zoological laboratory.

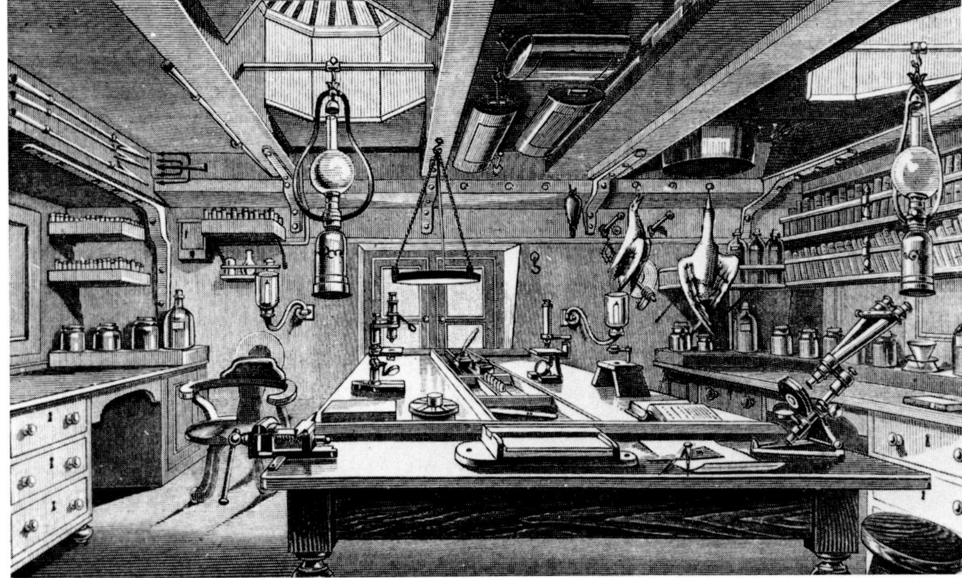

Challenger had crossed the notorious Bay of Biscay, the weather eased and the scientific work of the voyage began. This included regular sounding, dredging, and taking temperatures and samples of the water.

At first, a mixture of inexperience and bad luck created problems: ropes parted, equipment was damaged, and gear was lost overboard. But by the time *Challenger* left her first port of call at Lisbon, a routine approach to the work had been established. It was to continue this way, more or less unbroken, for the next three and a half years.

In the early days, dredging the seabed caught everyone's imagination, and many of the ship's crew would gather round to watch when the trawl and its samples were hauled inboard. William Spry, an engineering sub-lieutenant, who also kept a journal of the expedition, recorded that when the dredge 'appears above the surface, there is usually great excitement among the "Philos" [scientists were dubbed "philosophers" by the ship's officers] who are ever on the alert with forceps, bottles and jars, to secure the unwary creatures, who may by chance have found their way into the net'.

But in 4560 metres (15 000 ft) of water it could take up to three hours to lower the dredge to the bottom, and as many hours again for the ship to drift during the actual dredging process. So the novelty soon wore off, until the whole process was referred to as 'drudging'. For some officers the only pleasure to be derived from the work was betting gin and bitters on whether or not the contents of a haul would contain something interesting.

The largest dredge was similar to a 1.5-metre (5-ft) square net-bag of closely woven rope fixed around an iron framework, its open end braced to a rectangular shape 400 mm (16 in) wide. An iron bar was fixed to the bottom of the bag, and to this were attached a number of 'swabs' — lengths of uncoiled and combed hemp. These 'swept' the seabed behind the dredge and sometimes caught specimens that the bag had failed to trap.

Sounding involved keeping the ship stationary, directly above the place where the sinkers struck the seabed. Steam was raised the night before and when work started the sails were furled, the screws connected and lowered, and the ship turned head to wind. The sounding line was made from 25 mm (1 in) hemp, which had a sinker, two or three thermometers and a water-sample bottle attached to it.

'For every estimated 1000 fathoms [1828 metres, 6000 ft] of depth a weight of one cwt [50 kg] was allowed, so in deep-sea sounding three cwt [150 kg] of iron was usually left at the bottom of the sea to mark our track round the world, and puzzle posterity', wrote Moseley. As an example of the work involved, it took a 150 kg (3 cwt) sinker just under an hour to reach 5486 metres (18 000 ft).

The greatest depth the expedition sounded was 8182 metres (26 850 ft) in the North Pacific, between Admiralty Island and Japan.

'Excepting in a prolonged calm', records Lord Campbell, 'when, if we had coal to spare, we steamed slowly on our way, our voyages were done entirely under sail ... it was the combination of dull sailing, together with stopping at some every 200 miles [320 km] for a whole day, that made our cruises at sea very long and wearisome'.

When *Challenger* finally anchored in the waters off Portsmouth on the evening of 24 May 1876, she had logged 127 634 kilometres

(68 890 nautical miles), spent 719 days at sea, sailed the Atlantic, Pacific and Southern oceans, and entered the Antarctic Circle — the first steam-driven ship to do so.

The *Challenger* expedition had also founded the modern science of oceanography. A daily chain of magnetic observations had been made round the world, and 362 observation stations established. At most of these, the depth was sounded, the sea dredged, and samples of the seabed, as well as water samples and temperatures at intermediate levels, were taken. Atmospheric and meteorological observations were made, and the rate and direction of the current measured. Thousands of new species of marine life were discovered.

Gathering elephant seal specimens on Îles Kerguelen.

J. J. Wild, expedition artist and Dr Wyville Thomson's secretary, sketching Royal Sound on Îles Kerguelen. The expedition spent a month at the islands (seen from a distance, below) establishing an observatory and gathering scientific data.

SUBANTARCTIC EXPLORATION

In the Roaring Forties

During the course of the* Challenger *expedition, a great many uncharted harbours and stretches of coastline were surveyed. In the many foreign ports and places visited, expeditions to the inland were mounted, adding to the scientists' knowledge of local plants and animals.

HMS *Challenger's* crew and scientists enjoyed a welcome break from their survey work at Bahia de Todos os Santos, Brazil. The local inhabitants had entertained them, and there had been trips inland and cricket matches. And to honour the expedition, Bahian officials and English residents were arranging a ball.

Then a member of the crew fell ill with yellow fever. The sick man was swiftly put ashore and the ship sailed. An epidemic was the last thing Captain Nares wanted.

Three weeks later, on 15 October 1873, *Challenger* anchored off Tristan da Cunha, largest of three volcanic islands midway between Argentina and the Cape of Good Hope. The other two islands in the group are Inaccessible and Nightingale.

Almost circular and 41 square kilometres (16 sq miles) in area, Tristan presented a long range of steep black cliffs, surmounted by a plateau of rock, rising at the centre to a snow-capped peak 2440 metres (8000 ft) high. The island had been garrisoned briefly by the British Army in 1816, but evacuated the following year, with the exception of three men. People had migrated to Tristan from the Cape and St Helena until at one period there were as many as 200 settlers. By the time of *Challenger's* visit, the population was down to 84.

In the words of naturalist Moseley, Tristan had a 'peculiar cold barren uninhabitable appearance ... [and a] terrible climate'. It was a bleak place. For three months of the year, the island's weather was fine — but for the remaining nine months it was rain, storms and snow. Nevertheless, the islanders thrived. They had beef cattle, pigs, sheep, ducks and other fowl, and grew plenty of vegetables, and sometimes the men went sealing.

While provisions were bought — at a high price — and taken on board *Challenger*, the islanders mentioned two Germans who lived on Inaccessible but had not been seen for some time. It was assumed they were ill or dead.

In the meantime, Moseley — always among the first to get ashore — was busily collecting specimens with companions. In the afternoon, as they made their way to a higher level 'suddenly a dark squall came scudding over the sea, and rapidly reaching us, and climbing the hill-side, chilled us to the bone. My guide, a small boy, born and bred on the island, crouched down instantly under the tall grass and fern, lying on his side, drawing up his legs, tucking in his head, and screwing himself down into the grass like a hare into her form. We followed his example, and found that the perfection of the shelter to be thus obtained from such scanty herbage was astonishing.'

That same night, *Challenger* moved to a new anchorage off Inaccessible. Half the size of Tristan and 37 kilometres (23 miles) away, the island had 13 varieties of birds and 'several hundred thousand penguins [which] were to be heard screaming on shore and about the ship' throughout the night.

Early next morning, the two Germans mentioned by the Tristan islanders were seen staring at the ship. Captain Nares went ashore and brought the men — overjoyed at being rescued — back on board (see box).

Among the other islands explored by *Challenger* were the Îles Kerguelen in the southern reaches of the Indian Ocean, about 4800 kilometres (3000 miles) southeast of Cape Town, and a little more to the southwest of Australia. Discovered in 1772 by a Breton sailor, Yves-Joseph de Kerguélen-Trémarec, the main island was later known as Desolation Island due to its perpetually rainy weather and its exposure to the winds of the Roaring Forties.

The primary purpose of *Challenger's* visit was to establish an observation station from which the transit of Venus could be tracked later that year. For nearly a month, *Challenger* circumnavigated its coast. Shore parties surveyed the island and collected zoological and botanical specimens.

One distinguishing feature of the island's vegetation was an abundance of Kerguelen cabbage, *Pringlea antiscorbutica*, growing on the cliff slopes in thick clumps. Similar in appearance to a small garden cabbage, it had flowering stalks projecting laterally from the main stalks between the leaves. The cabbage was boiled and eaten with salt pork and salt beef, and although it was soon dropped from the officers' menu it was, according to Lord Campbell, popular with the men.

Shore parties also encountered fur seals and elephant seals. Moseley killed two fur seals, in the interests of his studies, and recorded how two whaling schooners slaughtered 70 of the creatures in one day.

NATURALISTS AMONG THE PENGUINS

The rockhopper penguin, *Eudyptes chrysocome*, was the only species of penguin on the Tristan group of islands. It is 460 mm (18 in) tall, with a black head and back and a snowy-white front. Flaring out from the side of its head, above its eyes, are tufted 'wings' of yellow plumes. The bird's bill is red, strong and deadly sharp.

To explore the islands and collect specimens, it was necessary to cross the rookeries — a hazardous and unforgettable experience. Lord Campbell declared: 'I would rather do many horrible things in preference to walking through a penguin rookery.'

The birds' manure saturated the soil and stimulated the growth of coarse tussock grass until it was as high as a man. The following extract is from the official *Challenger Reports*.

'Immediately on entering the main street of the rookery the explorer is as if in a maze, and cannot see in the least where he is going . . . A plunge is made into one of the lanes in the tall grass, which at once shuts out the surroundings from view. You tread on a slimy black damp soil composed of the birds' dung. The stench is overpowering, the yelling of the birds most annoying and discordant . . . The instant you leave the road you are on the actual breeding ground. The nests are placed so thickly that you cannot help treading on eggs and young birds at almost every step. A parent bird sits on each nest with its sharp beak erect and open, ready to bite, yelling savagely "caa, caa, urr, urr", its red eyes gleaming and its plumes at half-cock, quivering with rage. No sooner are your legs within reach than they are furiously bitten, often by two or three birds at once; that is if you have not got on strong leather gaiters, as on the first occasion of visiting a rookery you probably have not. At first you try to avoid the nests, but soon find that impossible; then maddened almost, by the pain, stench, and noise, you have recourse to brute force. Thump, thump, goes your stick, and at each blow down goes a bird. Thud, thud is heard from the men behind as they kick the birds right and left off the nests, and so you go on for a bit, thump, smash, whack, and thud, "caa, caa, urr, urr", and the path behind you is strewed with the dead and dying and bleeding. But you make miserably slow progress, and worried to death, at last resort to the expedient of stampeding as far as your breath will carry you. You put down your head and make a rush through the grass, treading on old and young hap-hazard, and rushing on before they have time to bite. The air is close in the rookery and the sun hot above, and out of breath, and perspiring with running you come across a mass of rock fallen from the cliff above . . . this you hail as a "city of refuge". You hammer off it hurriedly half a dozen penguins who are sunning themselves there . . . then mounting on the top take out your handkerchief to wipe away the perspiration and rest a while, to see in what direction you have been going, how far you have got, and in what direction you are to make the next plunge. Then when you are refreshed, you make another rush, and so on.'

Visits to the rockhopper penguin rookeries on Inaccessible Island proved to be a painful and frustrating experience.

The two Stoltenhoff brothers pose outside their hut on Inaccessible Island. Frederick, pipe in hand, is third from the right, and Gustav is standing fifth from left. One of the scientists sketched the interior of the hut in which they lived.

CASTAWAYS ON INACCESSIBLE ISLAND

The dream of making easy money brought the Stoltenhoff brothers to Inaccessible Island.

In 1871, Gustav Stoltenhoff was shipwrecked on Tristan da Cunha. During his stay on the island, he heard how 1700 seals had been caught by visiting sealers the previous season. When he got back home, he persuaded his brother Frederick to go with him to the islands with the idea of making a small fortune from the sale of sealskins back in Germany.

Within three months they were on board a whaling vessel bound for the South Atlantic. During the passage, the captain told them they would be better off on Inaccessible Island, 37 kilometres (23 miles) from Tristan. It was fertile, and there were plenty of pigs, goats and birds.

It seemed good advice. On 27 November 1871, the brothers landed on the west side of Inaccessible. They had with them four dogs, an old sailing boat and a huge stock of provisions. During the first two days they built a hut and shot a pig. A few days later, 16 men from Tristan visited them and suggested that the brothers move round to the north side of the island, where they were. This they did. But after 10 days, the Tristan men suddenly packed up and returned home. It was the last time the Germans saw their strange neighbours for almost a year.

The brothers set to and built a hut and planted seeds. The weather was good, and soon they had killed 19 seals. All augured well.

But gradually things changed. Their boat was damaged, so they were unable to reach other parts of the island to supplement their provisions. Fishing during bad weather proved impossible — the heavy surf and a broad swathe of kelp were insuperable obstacles — and the only edible birds they could reach were thrushes.

By cutting the boat in two and making one smaller craft, they managed to reach the west side of the island to kill game. But the following May a gale smashed their boat irreparably. By August they were in a desperate plight, and kept themselves alive only by eating penguins' eggs. When a schooner appeared in October, they were ready to leave. The schooner's captain gave them biscuits and salt pork, and promised to return in six weeks. The schooner never reappeared.

The brothers had been on the island for two years when *Challenger* arrived. In that time they had flirted with death on several occasions, but neither had experienced a single day's sickness. The two men burned their hut, reluctant to leave anything that might be remotely of value to their inhospitable neighbours, and helped *Challenger's* crew in their survey work.

ACROSS THE ANTARCTIC CIRCLE

Searching for clues to the nature of the hidden continent

When HMS* Challenger *left Îles Kerguelen to sail for the Antarctic in February 1874, nobody knew whether the Antarctic was a continent or a group of islands. The* Challenger *expedition aimed to find out in a program that was to survey 'as far as the neighbourhood of the Great Ice Barrier'.

HMS Challenger *in a snowstorm.*

During the early part of the 19th century several whalers, operating in the southern reaches of the Atlantic and Pacific, had reported seeing icebergs with rocks embedded in them drifting northwards. Charles Darwin had inferred from such a report that if one rock-carrying iceberg in a thousand 'transports its fragment [from the south], the bottom of the Antarctic Sea, and the Shores of its islands, must already be scattered with masses of foreign rock'.

If *Challenger* dredged the seabed in this region of the oceans, the quantity and character of geological samples found might provide valuable clues to the existence of the southernmost continent.

Five days after leaving Îles Kerguelen, on the morning of 11 February, the first iceberg was sighted. By 14 February, icebergs were becoming numerous, with 'large blocks of loose ice, grinding against the ship's side' startling some of the crew who were 'turned in'.

Two days later, *Challenger* made history when she crossed the Antarctic Circle — the first steamship to do so. She was using her 1480 square metres (16 000 sq ft) of sail whenever possible, resorting to steam only for dredging, sounding and in emergencies.

One such emergency was not far off. But for the moment, the beauty of the icebergs continued to enchant and fascinate, and those keeping journals sometimes despaired of finding adequate words to describe the sight.

Within 24 hours the sudden arrival of foul weather, and an accident, turned a scene of beauty into a place of wild turbulence.

At 4 am on 24 February the dredge was in place when a gale and snowstorm suddenly blew up. The dredge was hurriedly hauled inboard and *Challenger*, now using steam, sheltered under the lee of a huge berg.

During this task the ship was thrown against the iceberg, carrying away the jib-boom, and 'leaving all the head-gear in a state of wreck, while the men aloft, thinking they would have the top-gallant mast about their heads, scurried down with extraordinary activity'.

The ship sheered off, got steam up ready in all four boilers, and while the wreckage of the jib-boom was hauled in, the gale increased in its intensity, with 'weather thick as pea soup, and small, very hard snow pinging into one's face like a shower of peas blown through a steam-blast'.

At three o'clock in the afternoon, during a thick snow squall, a call came from the fo'c'sle: 'Iceberg close to under the lee bow, Sir!'

Lord Campbell's account vividly describes what came next: 'There is no room to steam ahead, so "full steam astern!" Rattle, rattle, goes the screw, sixty revolutions a minute; "Clear lower deck, make sail!" shriek the boatswain's mates; on deck flies everybody; "Maintopmen aloft, loose the maintopsail!" "Fore part, take in the fore-trysail!" The captain and commander howling out orders from the bridge, hardly heard in the roaring of the wind; officers repeating the howls. The weather-clew of the maintopsail is set aback, the headsails taken in, slowly she gathers stern way, keeping her head turning slightly towards the berg, a towering, dim white mass looming grimly through the driving snow, and then she clears it — a narrow shave!'

Three days later, her survey work complete, *Challenger* made sail, using every square centimetre of her canvas to head for the northeast, an open sea, and Melbourne.

In November 1893 John Murray addressed a meeting of the Royal Geographical Society in London, to present his assessment of *Challenger's* work in Antarctica. He had never seen the continent — nor had anyone else on the expedition — but he painted a convincing word picture of it to his audience.

Part of Murray's evidence was based on analyses of dredging work in the southern waters of the Atlantic and Pacific. Seabed samples had revealed a scattering of continental rock, such as granite, quartz, limestone and sandstone. The further south *Challenger* sailed, the more these rocks proliferated until, at the southernmost point of the voyage, the rocks formed the major substance of each bottom sample. Gauconite — a mineral present in many of the muds surrounding continental coastlines — was also found. It could only mean one thing, claimed Murray: that icebergs had carried these fragments of coastal rock to the north, dropping them on the seabed as the ice melted; fragments that had originated in a southern continent — Antarctica.

The ship had a narrow escape while seeking shelter in the lee of a large berg, when an eddy current carried her headlong into the ice, damaging the rigging.

Challenger *spent only one day at Corinthian Harbour, Heard Island (left). Forty sealers lived on this bleak island.*

On 16 February 1874 Challenger *became the first steamship to cross the Antarctic Circle.*

LASTING TESTAMENT TO A UNIQUE VOYAGE

One of the many splendid illustrations from the Challenger Reports *— a rockhopper penguin,* Eudyptes chrysocome.

HMS *Challenger*, stripped of her mast, fittings and former glory, ended her days as a coal hulk in 1921. The last of the expedition's survivors was Captain Herbert Swire. But the findings of the expeditions live on, in 50 thick volumes published in 1895 as the *Challenger Reports*.

The man responsible for giving the world *Challenger's* 'great scientific cargo' was John Murray. Born of Scottish parents in 1841 in Canada, Murray completed his education at Edinburgh University where he studied subjects as diverse as anatomy, literature and chemistry. But his obsession was natural history.

Acquiring a grounding in medicine, he went to sea in 1868 as the surgeon of a whaler in the Arctic. It was invaluable experience for his appointment as one of *Challenger's* naturalists.

When the *Challenger* expedition was over, Sir Charles Wyville Thomson was appointed to edit the collected material for publication, with Murray working under his direction. When Thomson died in 1882, Murray succeeded him as editor, throwing himself into the mammoth project with characteristic vigour. He wrote seven of the volumes himself, and organised the work of nearly 100 scholars.

When the Treasury started to get anxious about the cost, Murray's strength of character and impatience with petty officialdom won the day. Having acquired some modest riches in his life, Murray finished the project at his own expense.

The Jason *made two voyages to the Antarctic Peninsula between the years 1892 and 1894.*

Carl Anton Larsen, captain of the Jason, *was involved in Antarctic whaling most of his life.*

Captain Larsen (right) with Roald Amundsen (centre) and an unidentified figure in the USA in 1923. Amundsen had a great interest in pioneer whaling in the Ross Sea.

THE WHALERS

A quest for profits leads to important geographical discoveries

During the first 40 years of the nineteenth century British and American sealers and whalers played a pioneering role in mapping the coastal geography of Antarctica and exploring its adjacent seas. In mid-century, however, commercial interest in the region declined and it was another 30 years before whaling expeditions again set out for the southern polar seas. During the 1890s, the work of whalers like C.A. Larsen of Norway was instrumental in the renewal of scientific interest in Antarctica on an international scale.

The years between 1819 and 1845 had seen national expeditions to the Antarctic from Russia, France, America and Britain, but their completion saw what has been termed 'the age of averted interest' in Antarctica. Governments saw little of interest in a region with no scope for colonial expansion.

This period of 'averted interest' in Antarctica coincided with the worldwide decay of the old whaling industry, brought about by a combination of rapidly diminishing stocks of right and sperm whales and competition from petroleum oil, resulting in increasingly unattractive returns from the hazardous business of whaling. Between 1850 and 1872, the number of ships involved in whaling fell from 400 to 72.

But one thing encouraged attempts to keep the whaling industry alive: the fashion industry's insatiable demand for baleen (whalebone) for use in corsets. Only the right whale could supply this substance in commercial quantities. New whaling techniques were evolved in Norway whereby gun harpoons fitted with explosive heads were mounted first on ships' bows, then on small, speedy steam catchers or chasers. But the result of this improved efficiency was that northern waters were soon fished out, and whaling entrepreneurs turned their thoughts to the old reports by Captain James Clark Ross and others of southern right whales in Antarctic waters.

The first reconnaissance expedition took place in 1873 when the German Polar Navigation Company sent Captain E. Dallmann in the steam whaler *Grönland* to look for right whales in the far south. This was the first steam-powered vessel to operate there, but only rorqual whales were sighted, which the ship was not capable of hunting. However, a full cargo of seal oil and skins provided some financial return. The expedition also discovered the Bismarck Strait, separating Graham Land from the Palmer Archipelago, and gave the first report of the existence of the Neumayer Channel. Commercially, however, it was a failure, and nearly 20 years went by before another European whaler ventured south.

This was the Dundee whaling expedition of 1892-93. Inspired by a proposal made by the Arctic whaler Captain D. Gray of Peterhead that the north part of the Weddell Sea should be searched for the whales reported long before by Captain James Clark Ross, the expedition was carried in four ships: the *Balaena* of 400 tonnes; the *Diana*, 340 tonnes; the *Active*, 340 tonnes; and the *Polar Star*, 216 tonnes. The ships were fitted with auxiliary engines, and equipped with muzzle-loading guns to fire harpoons, large-bore rifles firing mushroom bullets, rockets to attack the whale once it had been harpooned, and small chaser boats. The prime objective was to find right whales.

Three medical men who were trained naturalists and scientific observers went on the Dundee expedition, and also a young artist, W.G. Burn Murdoch. The medical men were Dr W. Bruce, oceanographer and explorer, who travelled on the *Balaena*; Dr C. W. Donald on the *Active*; and Dr Campbell on the *Diana*.

Commercially the venture was a failure. Rorqual whales were seen in abundance, but the ships were not equipped to hunt them, and no right whales were seen. However, they did get a full cargo of seal oil and skins. But the unfortunate naturalists were not given the time or facilities they needed to observe natural

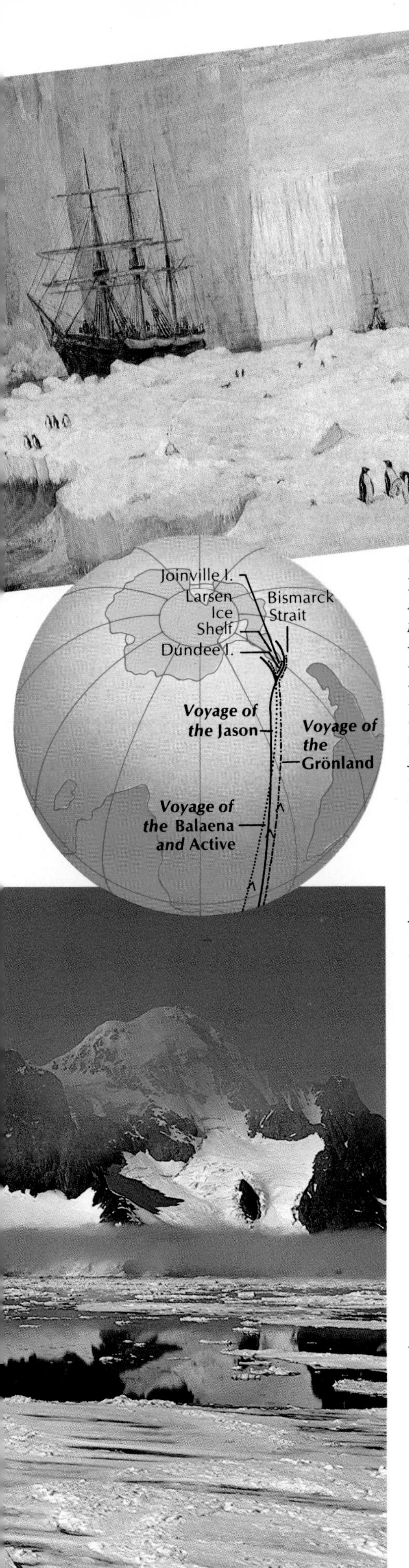

The whalers Active, Balaena *and* Diana *in the Antarctic (above) — a painting by W. G. Burn Murdoch made during the Dundee Whaling Expedition of 1892-93. A sketch (above right) by one of the crewmen shows seals being killed on an ice floe. Three scientists went on this expedition — including William Bruce who was later to sail on the* Scotia.

Lemaire Channel was frequently used by whalers working along the Antarctic Peninsula.

IMPROVING THE KILL

Whaling entrepreneur Svend Foyn.

By 1864 the invention of the gun harpoon with an explosive head had started to revolutionise whaling. Until then rorqual whales were too large or too fast for whalers operating with hand-thrown harpoons. Now species such as the blue, fin and sei whales could all be hunted.

The man responsible for this revolution was a Norwegian called Svend Foyn. Born in 1809, he was already a rich man by the 1860s as a result of his sealing activities. Foyn spent five years and £20000 developing the harpoon and perfecting a method of mounting it on small, fast steam catchers.

phenomena and carry out scientific investigations. This was especially so in the case of Dr Bruce, who was forced to spend most of his time with the crew of the *Balaena* hunting and killing seals. He wrote: 'The scientific work of the expedition was not done in very favourable circumstances; commerce was the dominating note. A great deal more might have been done for the geology and the biology of the Antarctic Regions if some opportunities for landing had been afforded me.'

The other two naturalists were more fortunate, their captains showing more interest in exploration, and the expedition did make some valuable geographical findings. Dundee Island was discovered, and the southern coast of Joinville Island explored. The strait between the islands was named the Firth of Tay.

Although the commercial motive prevented the three naturalists from doing their job to the full, their published reports were of great interest to their peers. But the young artist, Murdoch, expressed their frustration when he wrote: 'And so we turned from the mystery of the Antarctic, with all its white-bound secrets still unread, as if we had stood before ancient volumes that told of the past and the beginning of all things, and had not opened them to read. Now we must go home to the world that is worn down with the feet of many people, to gnaw in our discontent the memory of what we could have done, but did not do.'

While the Dundee expedition was at work, it met with a Norwegian expedition with a similar purpose. Led by Captain C. A. Larsen in the *Jason*, it combined whaling reconnaissance, sealing, and careful exploration of the coasts of Graham Land. Sent by the whaling entrepreneur Christen Christensen, it left Norway on 3 September 1892. It returned in 1893 with no whales, only seal oil and skins. But the information gathered on conditions in the south was such that Christensen decided to send out another expedition. Three steamers — the *Jason*, *Hertha* and *Castor* — worked in the Bellingshausen and Weddell seas from late 1893 to March 1894. Again no right whales were taken, only seal oil and skins, but important observations were made of ice conditions. Coasts were explored on both sides of Graham Land; Foyn Land (now known to be an island) was discovered, as was King Oscar II Land, both on the east coast of Graham Land; and the *Jason* sailed beyond the Antarctic Circle to latitude 68°10'S before being turned back by an ice field. But perhaps the greatest immediate impact on scientific circles was made by the discovery of the first fossils ever located in the Antarctic region. Landing at Cape Seymour on the east coast of Graham Land, Larsen found petrified wood among the hills.

But Larsen, a born explorer, suffered the same sense of frustration as did Dr Bruce and his colleagues: he had been sent out for whale and seal hunting, not to waste his time on scientific exploration.

ON THE MAINLAND

Scramble to be first ashore

Henryk Johan Bull, a Norwegian businessman, was the leading light behind the voyage of the* Antarctic. *The primary aim of the expedition was to seek out right whales in the Ross Sea area. Although it failed to do this, the expedition did result in the first confirmed landing on the Antarctic mainland, 74 years after John Davis' disputed visit.

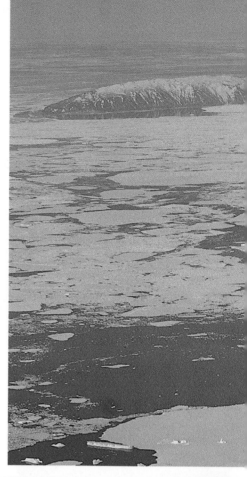

An aerial view of Cape Adare, far left, and ice-filled Robertson Bay in the foreground. The first confirmed landing on the Antarctic mainland was made on the cape, and Borchgrevink returned to winter there in 1899.

Bull, who had emigrated to Melbourne in 1885, tried first of all to get Australian backing for his proposed voyage to the Antarctic, mainly through the Australian Antarctic Committee and the Tasmanian Government. When these efforts failed, he returned to Norway in 1893 and sought the co-operation of the great whaling master Svend Foyn, with whom he was acquainted. To Bull's delight, Foyn offered to finance the expedition.

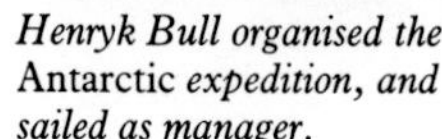

Henryk Bull organised the Antarctic *expedition, and sailed as manager.*

Both Foyn and Bull were motivated by the idea of reviving the once-flourishing Antarctic whaling industry. Foyn was aware of the operations being pursued in the seas adjacent to Graham Land, and so the prospect of success in the untried Ross Sea area appealed to him.

An old steam whaler, the *Kap Nor*, of 226 tonnes, was bought, renamed *Antarctic* and fitted out, the total outlay being £5000, a large sum for those days. It carried eight whaleboats, 11 harpoon guns, and a crew of 31. The master was Captain L. Kristensen, while Bull was appointed 'manager'. But his powers and authority were ill-defined, a situation that led to friction between the two men.

The expedition was planned in three stages: the first, from Norway to Melbourne, when right whales and seals would be sought in the south Atlantic and on subantarctic islands; the second, with a similar purpose, from Melbourne to the islands south of New Zealand; while the final stage would be a voyage from those islands south to the Ross Sea.

Ashore at Cape Adare, Borchgrevink continued to act as if he was in charge. He wrote: 'I had painted a Norwegian flag on a large box, which we fastened to a strong pole near the place where we landed; and leaving the rest of the crew to be entertained by the penguins, I proceeded alone to investigate the peninsula and to make collections.'

The expedition left Tønsberg in Norway on 20 September 1893, by which time the results of the recently completed Dundee and Norwegian whaling expeditions (see p126) were known. Their lack of success was bad enough, but Bull also realised that his late start prejudiced any chance of success in whaling, and in penetrating the pack ice in the Ross Sea area.

On the first stage of the voyage the ship developed a leak, coal supplies dwindled and the only whales sighted in the south Atlantic were fin whales. The *Antarctic* reached the Îles Kerguelen on 19 December 1893 and was nearly wrecked there by wind squalls. Some 1600 elephant seals were taken for oil and skins, valued at the time at £3000. On 23 February the expedition arrived in Melbourne and was enthusiastically welcomed by some of the Australian Antarctic Committee. Bull read a paper to the local Royal Society on whaling and sealing prospects in Antarctic waters, and a local syndicate offered to buy out Svend Foyn, but balked at his price — £10 000.

On 12 April 1894 the ship left Australia to try whaling around Campbell and adjacent islands. Bull remained in Melbourne to prepare for the main voyage to the Ross Sea. Then disaster struck. On 19 May the ship ran aground on Terror Shoal in Perseverance Harbour, Campbell Island, and suffered severe damage. The cost of repairs and of provisioning the ship for the voyage south totalled some £2000, which absorbed the profits made at the Îles Kerguelen.

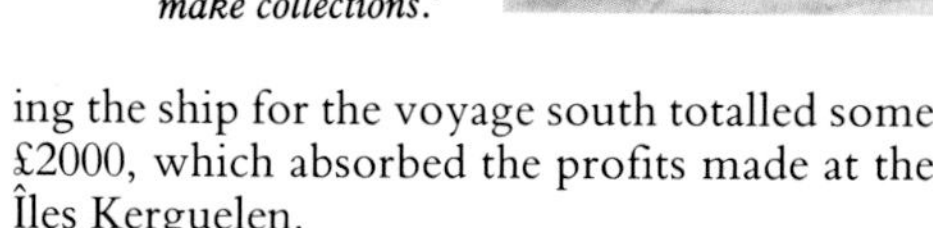

Dr W. S. Bruce, who had gone with the Dundee expedition, and E. Astrup, the Arctic explorer, had been given permission by Svend Foyn to go on the *Antarctic* to the Ross Sea as scientific observers. Unfortunately, they could not reach Melbourne in time for the planned early start. Instead, a young Norwegian settler in Australia, Carsten Egeberg Borchgrevink, was taken on as a 'generally useful hand' with his berth in the forecastle with the crew. For Borchgrevink it was the beginning of an interesting, if chequered, career as an Antarctic explorer and pioneer.

The ship left Melbourne on 26 September 1894 and sailed to Campbell Island where, to Bull's dismay, they found that the sealing season was nearly over. Sailing further south they failed to locate the legendary Emerald Island, but on 6 November they sighted what was at first thought to be an island, naming it Svend Foyn Island, after their sponsor. But it turned

Borchgrevink, sketched by himself, scaling the highest peak on the Possession Islands.

The first confirmed landing on the Antarctic mainland — on 24 January 1895 — led to a squabble over who was first ashore. Borchgrevink depicts himself as making the landing, to the apparent dismay of others in the boat.

out to be an immense mass of grounded icebergs up to 180 metres (600 ft) high. Then another disaster struck: it was found that the ship's propeller was loose on its shaft. Course was made for Port Chalmers in New Zealand where repairs were effected. There two crew members deserted, while seven others refused to go south and were discharged. Four new crew members were recruited at Stewart Island.

By 10 December they were surrounded by pack ice and icebergs. Attempts were made to capture some blue whales, but they lost the tackle, including harpoons. It took the *Antarctic* 36 days to travel through some 800 kilometres (500 miles) of pack ice. On Christmas Day they crossed the Antarctic Circle and the pack ice increased in density. It took eight dangerous days to break through into open water. Morale then rose immediately and a course was set for Cape Adare, with seals being picked up off ice floes on the way.

The cape was sighted on 16 January 1895, but the adjacent Robertson Bay was filled with ice, barring the way. On 18 January a party of seven, including Borchgrevink, made a landing on the Possession Islands. Borchgrevink discovered lichen growing on sheltered rocks — the first time vegetation had been found growing in the Antarctic region proper. The captain erected a pole on the landing place, to which was nailed a box containing his card.

Course was again set for Cape Adare and, the ice not being as dense as previously, a landing was made on 24 January 1895. This was the first confirmed landing made on the Antarctic continental mainland, and resulted in an amusing, if slightly unedifying, squabble as to who actually got on shore first! The captain, in his journal, said: 'I was sitting foremost in the boat, and jumped ashore as the boat struck, saying, "I have then the honour of being the first man who has ever put foot on South Victoria Land".' But Borchgrevink, in a magazine article, claimed: 'I do not know whether it was the desire to catch the jelly-fish (seen in the shallows), or from a strong desire to be the first man to put foot on this *terra incognita*, but as soon as the order was given to stop pulling the oars, I jumped over the side of the boat. I thus killed two birds with one stone, being the first man on shore, and relieving the boat of my weight, thus enabling her to approach land near enough to allow the captain to jump ashore dry-shod.'

To further confuse the issue, one of the four New Zealanders recruited from Stewart Island, A. H. F. von Tunzelman, claimed, and maintained all his life, that he was in the bow and jumped ashore to steady the boat. Bull himself did not enter the competition, merely reporting that 'the sensation of being the first men who set foot on the real Antarctic mainland was both strange and pleasurable'.

A pole, with a box showing the Norwegian colours, was erected. Borchgrevink discovered patches of the same lichen already found on the Possession Islands. Seaweed, jellyfish, rock specimens, seals and penguins were collected.

The ship sailed on to the Balleny Islands, but ice barred a landing. Many fin whales were seen, but no right whales. On 8 February the ship sailed northwards towards civilisation. Many sperm whales were sighted on 4 March, but only one was caught. The *Antarctic* reached Melbourne on 12 March.

Commercially, the expedition was a failure. But the Australian Antarctic Committee and local scientists such as Professor T. W. Edgeworth David were most impressed with its geographical findings, and with the geological and botanical specimens collected. And, as Bull wrote, the expedition had 'proved that landing on Antarctica proper is not so difficult as it was hitherto considered, and that a wintering-party have every chance of spending a safe and pleasant twelvemonth at Cape Adare, with a fair chance of penetrating to, or nearly to, the magnetic pole'.

Further, Bull considered that the expedition had given 'a fresh and strong impulse to Antarctic exploration in general'. In some respects a visionary, Bull outlined his ideas for future whaling expeditions to the Ross Sea area where islands suitable for whaling stations did not exist: '[It] must therefore consist of at least two vessels — the one a small steamer, to do the actual hunting, and the other, a store ship of fair tonnage.' This was a fair forecast of the future oceanic whaling industry.

Bull and Borchgrevink each gave lectures in Melbourne and Sydney in favour of another expedition but, despite much interest, no financial backing was forthcoming.

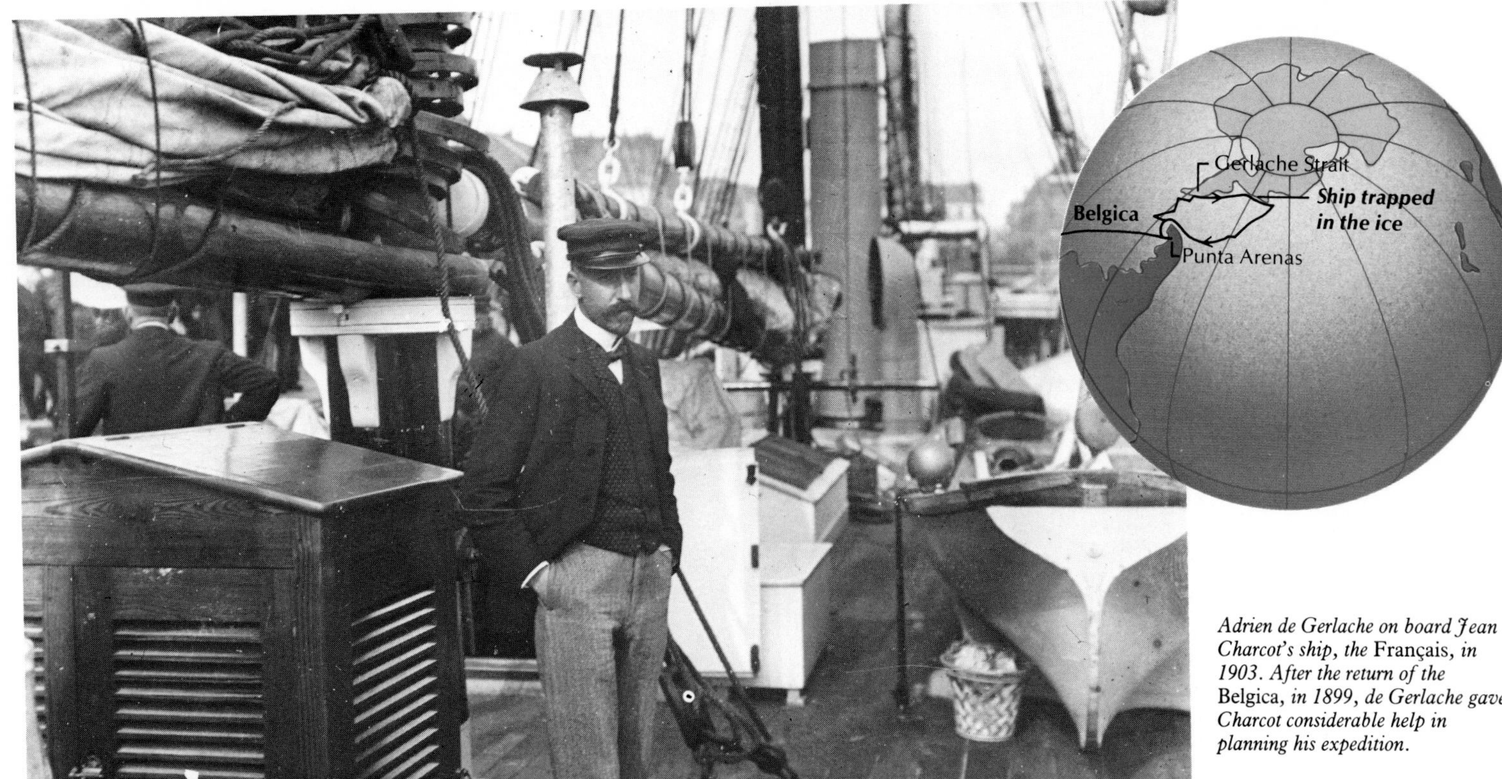

Adrien de Gerlache on board Jean Charcot's ship, the Français, *in 1903. After the return of the* Belgica, *in 1899, de Gerlache gave Charcot considerable help in planning his expedition.*

VOYAGE OF THE *BELGICA*

Controversy over Gerlache's intentions

In July 1895, the Sixth International Geographical Congress was held in London. Its major objective was to rekindle interest in Antarctic exploration. Little of consequence had been achieved in the past 50 years, and the Congress passed a resolution, stating that 'further exploration of the Antarctic regions should be undertaken before the close of the century'.

Those who attended the Congress were probably unaware that preparations for just such an expedition were already under way. The man who intended to lead this voyage of discovery was a 29-year-old lieutenant in the Royal Belgian Navy, Adrien Victor Joseph de Gerlache. Three years earlier, hearing that a Swedish expedition was being formed, he had volunteered to join. But the expedition was abandoned before it set sail.

Fired by his desire to explore the southern latitudes, this idealistic young officer decided he himself would set up an expedition. His timing was faulty, for Belgium was more interested in her newly acquired colony of the Congo. National resources were earmarked for Africa, not the Antarctic.

However, de Gerlache managed to interest the Brussels Geographical Society, who organised a national subscription. The government, having rejected his request for 800000 francs, now offered a mere 100000 francs.

Slowly, fund-raising produced 233000 francs — much of it from the proceeds of village fairs — at which point the Belgian Parliament chipped in a further 60000. When the subscription lists closed, de Gerlache had nearly 300000 francs.

In Norway de Gerlache bought, for 70000 francs, a three-masted whaler, the 30-metre (98-ft) *Patric.* This sturdy, 250-tonne barque had been built for the icy waters of the north.

The 112 kW (150 hp) engine was overhauled. Cabins were built on the afterdeck for the officers and scientific staff. A laboratory was fitted under the bridge. The crew's quarters were crammed in below decks. Finally the ship was rechristened, as the *Belgica.*

On 29 July 1896, Adrien de Gerlache received a letter from a 25-year-old Norwegian who offered to sail, unpaid, aboard the *Belgica.* De Gerlache showed the request to the ship's agent, asking what he knew of the man. The agent's comment was: 'Take him, my friend.' And so Roald Amundsen was added to the ship's crew.

The request for scientists had brought a polyglot reply. The zoologist, Emile Racovitza, was Rumanian. The geologist, Henryk Arctowski, was Polish. The second-in-command, also to be navigating officer and astronomer, was a young Belgian, Lieutenant George Lecointe as was another young officer, Lieutenant Emile Danco. The mate, Amundsen, and a number of the crew were Norwegian. The laboratory assistant was Russian.

And then, failing to find a suitable ship's surgeon, de Gerlache sent a telegraphed cable to the United States of America. The man he wanted was a certain Dr Frederick A. Cook, a 32-year-old native of Sullivan County, New York. Cook had gained polar exploring ex-

Dr Frederick Cook almost took command of the expedition as the men's spirits fell drastically during the polar night spent trapped in the pack ice.

perience in north Greenland, accompanying the man who would one day reach the North Pole, Robert Edwin Peary. He agreed to join the *Belgica* in Rio de Janeiro.

With every *sou* of their pittance spent, the Belgian Antarctic Expedition left Antwerp on 16 August 1897. Overloaded, the converted whaler could make no more than about 9 km/h (6 mph) under steam, her decks scarcely 61 cm (2 ft) clear of the water.

In Rio, de Gerlache welcomed the American aboard. Cook wrote of this later: 'To consent by cable to cast my lot in a battle against the supposed unsurmountable barriers of the south, with total strangers, with men from

The distant mountains of Anvers Island mark part of the western side of Gerlache Strait. The Belgica *was the first ship to penetrate this part of the Antarctic Peninsula. The strait is deep and wide — narrowing at its southwest end to a minimum of 4 km (2.5 miles). It was much used by whalers in the years after its discovery*

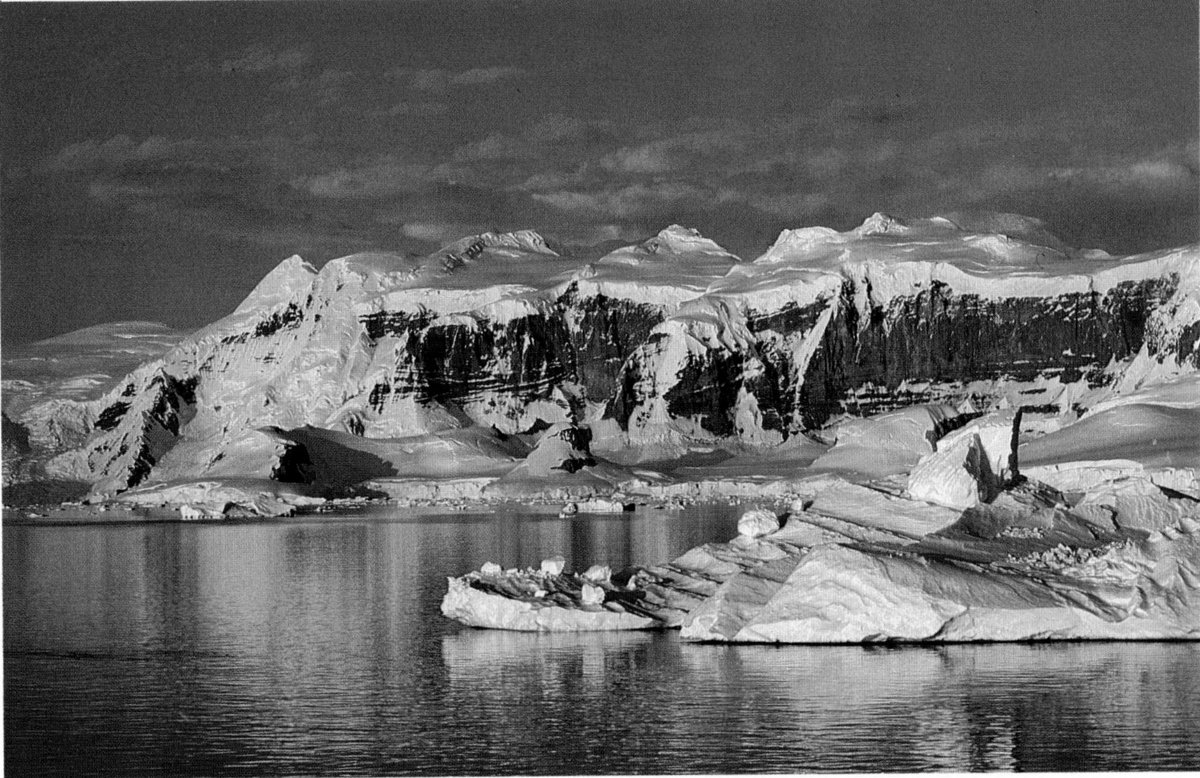

The damaged bow of the Belgica *after an encounter with an iceberg. Time and again the ship was pressed into the ice as they attempted to make headway through the pack. Paint and pieces of timber sheathing littered the wake of the ship.*

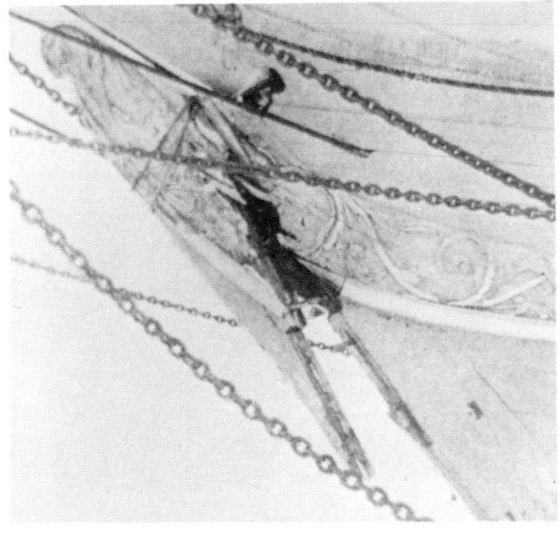

another continent, speaking languages strange to me, does now seem rash.'

But rash or not, Frederick A. Cook was time and again to prove himself the most ingenious and valuable member of the party. He, better than anyone, would understand the grim mental hardships that closed in with the polar winter.

On 1 December 1897, the vessel reached Punta Arenas. There is no recorded reason, but a number of the crew deserted, reducing the complement to 19. Scientific studies were carried out in the region of Tierra del Fuego, and the *Belgica* did not leave until the 14th.

Critics of de Gerlache point to this as the first indication that what happened later was no mere accident. The research work could have been carried out *after* the Antarctic voyage. He was 'wasting time', allowing the southern summer weeks to slip by. However true the accusations, the *Belgica* did not heave into Antarctic waters until 20 January, late in the exploring season.

On 22 January, without warning, a northeasterly gale hit the *Belgica*. Her stores of coal broke free from their containers, pouring across the deck to choke the scuppers. With waves flooding the deck, and the channels blocked, the sailors scrambled to clear them.

In an article Cook wrote for *Century*, he described what then happened. 'At about 3 o'clock in the afternoon Amundsen and I were on the bridge, straining our eyes and levelling our glasses on a mysterious black object ahead, and directly in our course . . . While thus engaged we heard an unearthly cry — a cry which made me shiver because of its force and painful tone. We turned about quickly, but saw nothing to indicate the direction of the noise.

'Amundsen, thinking there'd been an accident in the engine-room, rushed in that direction. I went aft to the quarter-deck, looked astern and saw a man struggling among the white crests. It was [Carl] Wiencke [a sailor]. In trying to free the scuppers he had lost his balance, and in falling he uttered the awful cry.

'With a quick presence of mind he grasped the log-line. I began to draw it in, but he slipped until his hand was stopped by the log. He held on to this with a death-like grasp . . . but there was little to be done.

'With a bravery impossible to appreciate, Lieutenant Lecointe offered to be lowered into the sea to pass a rope around Wiencke. With two men on deck, Lecointe was lowered, but he sank at once with the counter-eddies and nearly lost his life.

'We managed to tow Wiencke to the side of the ship . . . but he gave up his grip on the log-line, and sank.

'Wiencke was a boy with many friends, and his loss was deeply felt . . .'

It was the first tragedy among those who sailed with the *Belgica* . . . but not yet the last. By the following day, Sunday 23 January, the gale had blown itself out. The explorers were now off the west coast of Graham Land, the peninsula unvisited for the past 60 years. Taking advantage of the weather, de Gerlache, Cook, Racovitza and Arctowski took a boat to a nearby island.

The *Belgica* zigzagged slowly between the Graham Land coast and what was now seen to be a long string of islands to the west. De Gerlache named the floe-filled passage Belgica Strait — it would one day be regarded as his greatest geographical discovery, and named in his honour, Gerlache Strait.

Between 23 January and 12 February 1898, the Belgian Antarctic Expedition made 20 separate landings on the islands that fringed the strait. They charted and named the westward islands of Brabant, Liège, Anvers and — in memory of the sailor they had lost — Wiencke. Then they turned the southern end of Anvers Island to fight their way through the pack ice. Heading southwest, they reached 65°10′S, 64°0′W on 13 February. On the 15th the *Belgica* crossed the Antarctic Circle.

The following day, in clear weather, they got to within 32 kilometres (20 miles) of Alexander Island. Beyond was the pack ice.

On the last day of February, with the ship now down to 70°20′S, and 85°W, the explorers entered the pack ice. For a while they found channels, lakes, narrow strips the whaler could cleave her way through. They reached another degree south, a few more minutes west — and then the vessel shuddered and became embedded in the pack ice.

Through the next few days disagreement reigned in the cabins, in the mess-room, on the bridge. Had Commandant de Gerlache come this far south by accident, or was it his intention to let the ship be trapped in the ice?

Efforts were made to free the *Belgica*. But they were not sufficient for his critics, nor to get the undermanned, overloaded vessel out to the open sea. A week was spent bludgeoning at the ice field, but by 2 March the Belgian Antarctic Expedition was imprisoned.

Fixed in the ice, they were now at the mercy of the south. Whether or not de Gerlache had intended to winter below the Antarctic Circle, the multinational party would be the first to undergo the rigours of the long Antarctic night. Two months of unbroken darkness, more than a year of snow and hail, deafening winds, illness and insanity and, for one of the explorers, death.

A LONG NIGHT

Madness stalks the men of the Belgica

Stuck fast in the wastes of the Bellingshausen Sea, the* Belgica *drifted with the ice. The ship's surgeon wrote: 'It is a strange sensation to know that you are moving rapidly over an unknown sea, yet with nothing to indicate movement. We pass no fixed point, and can see no piece of ice stir.'

The ship was in fact drifting 8-16 kilometres (5-10 miles) a day, in a westerly direction. On 2 March, the day the icy key had been turned, locking them in, the explorers were at 71°30′S, 85°16′W.

In an effort to minimise heat loss from the ship, snow was piled up level with the deck. Even so, the Belgian vessel was ill-equipped to face the winter. There was a shortage of lanterns, and not enough stoves to dry out the water that seeped down inside the hull. Research work was attempted, and a small wooden shack erected on the ice.

On 17 May the darkness of the winter night closed in. Within a few days — deprived of all daylight — the men became irritable and morbid. They were perpetually cold, damp, crowded together, struggling to communicate in a Babel of different tongues. The stocks of food were inadequate; all of it soft, much of it tasteless. The endless diet of canned meatballs, canned fish, canned and watery vegetables left them gloomy and listless.

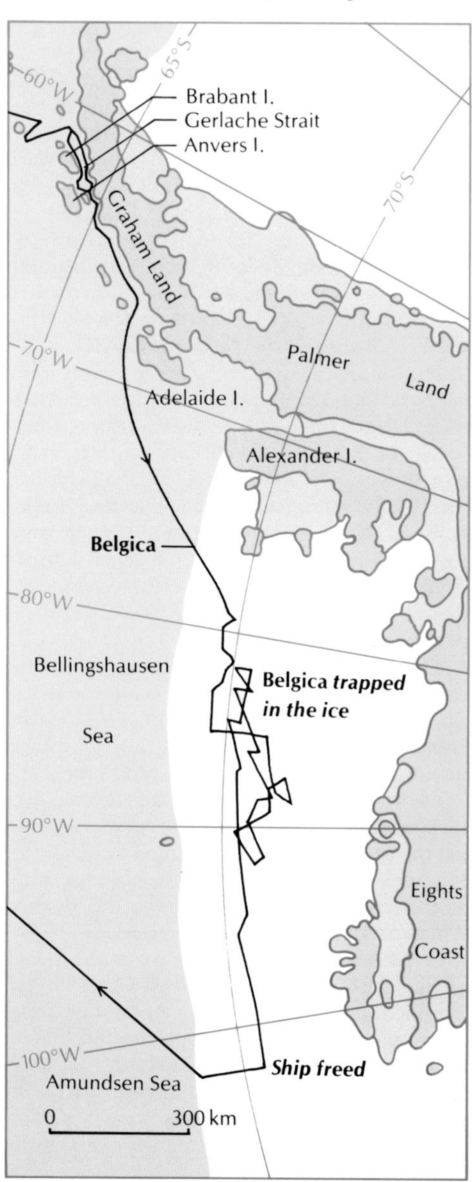

The ghostly Belgica*, photographed by moonlight on 20 May 1898 — three days after the darkness of the long polar night had closed over the ship. Trapped in the pack ice, she was to drift, out of control, for 13 long months.*

Henryk Arctowski, the expedition's Polish geologist (left) and Lieutenant George Lecointe, navigating officer and astronomer, enjoying a cup of afternoon tea.

During May the young Lieutenant Danco fell ill with a weakening heart. Dr Cook had been watching the officer's condition for some time, disturbed to see Danco gasping for breath in the bitter air.

Cook's services were now much in demand. Officers and crew alike were suffering from muscular spasms, lethargy, an angry desire to get away from their shipmates.

On 5 June 1898, the ship's company rallied long enough to salute Lieutenant Danco, whose heart had succumbed to the cold. Henryk Arctowski described the mournful scene. 'In the obscurity of the midday twilight we carried Lieutenant Danco's body to a hole which had been cut in the ice, and committed it to the deep. A bitter wind was blowing as, with bared heads, each of us silent, we left him there . . . And the floe drifted on . . .'

It was now that Frederick A. Cook assumed moral command of the *Belgica*. De Gerlache was doing all he could to make sure the ship was ready to break free from the ice. Amundsen was the perfect mate, an experienced link between the officers and crew. The scientists struggled to continue their researches.

But Cook knew that the men needed sunlight, for the end of the winter would raise their spirits, allow them to leave the confines of the ship. They also needed fresh meat to combat what he recognised as an epidemic of scurvy. But de Gerlache had already tasted seal meat and penguin, and had pronounced them both to be inedible.

Dr Cook himself would later remark with regard to penguin meat: 'If it's possible to imagine a piece of beef, odiferous cod fish and a canvas-backed duck roasted together in a pot, with blood and cod-liver oil for sauce, the illustration would be complete.'

He cleverly presented the problem to de Gerlache, requesting the captain to regard the meat as medicinal and to eat it as an example to the others. Ignore the taste; swallow it down as a duty. De Gerlache unwillingly agreed.

The next thing to do was take the men's minds off their plight. So card schools were organised, bets of 1000 francs accepted, debts (which would never, of course, be honoured) running to a hectic 500 000 francs.

But for all Cook's efforts, the Antarctic night took its toll. One of the crew, who spoke

A distant view of the ice-bound Belgica, *and in the foreground a tent invented by Frederick Cook. The expedition's existing tents were found to be too heavy and complicated for polar use. The design was drawn up and the tent made on board the ship. It held three men and weighed 5.5 kg (12 lb).*

Fresh water on the Belgica *was supplied by the snow melter — a converted condenser from the engine room. The contraption was also adapted to burn seal blubber as fuel, and a quantity can be seen stacked up on the right hand side of the melter.*

The men used saws to cut a 600-metre (2000-ft) channel between the Belgica *and a nearby ice-free lake and freedom.*

no French, assumed that the French word for 'something' really meant 'kill', and attacked whoever used it. Another man climbed on to the ice, announcing his departure for Belgium.

It was not until 23 July 1898 that the first faint glow of sunlight tipped the horizon. The members of the expedition gazed at it in wonderment, and from that moment on their health and spirits improved. They no longer cursed the fishy, greasy seal meat or penguin, but ate it and called it Antarctic beefsteak.

The research work resumed. Soundings were taken through the ice. Astronomical and meteorological observations were intensified. Sledge parties were sent to explore the drift. Wind speeds were measured, the direction of the current gauged, weak men finding the strength to greet the light.

Despite the fact that the winter was over they were still held firm in a massive field of ice, and drifting all the while within the Antarctic Circle. A heated bar was plunged through the ice beside the *Belgica*. Withdrawn, it showed that the field was over two metres (7 ft) thick.

Amundsen, Cook and Lecointe embarked on what was planned as a 15-day expedition. Their intention was to find an exit for the *Belgica*, if possible to skirt the edge of the floe. They were away for a week, huddled at night in a three-man sleeping bag. But all they could tell de Gerlache on return was that the field was too extensive for the *Belgica* to break free.

The expedition was now running short of coal, short of oil for the lamps, all those aboard resigned to a second winter — and with it the likelihood of their deaths in the ice. With the great ice field still drifting to the west, the *Belgica* travelled uncontrolled through August, and on into September.

In October they were cheered to see lakes forming in the ice, their hopes dashed as the ice closed in again, freezing them over. In November snow swept around the vessel, concealing the horizon. De Gerlache and Amundsen were forced to restrain a number of the crew, Cook treating them for the onset of insanity. Attempts were made to celebrate Christmas, though it was drowned beneath a growing flood of panic.

Crowded together, yet separated by the problem of language, the polyglot members of the Belgian expedition sought refuge in their bunks. Nine months had passed since the ice had gripped the *Belgica*.

Yet a watch was still being kept aboard the ship. De Gerlache was there, and Lecointe, and Amundsen, and Cook. Lookouts were posted and, if Christmas passed with lacklustre celebration, 31 December brought a shout from the crow's-nest. A stretch of open water had appeared 640 metres (700 yards) ahead.

It was the American from Sullivan County who suggested sawing and blasting a channel. It would not be easy, with no more than three 1.2-metre (4-ft) saws. But she did have a tonne of the low-powered explosive.

In the second week of January 1899, a party ventured to the edge of the lake, measured the depth of ice at its fringe and began to cut back towards the ship. The explorers battled for a month, working day and night. At the open end of the channel the ice was chopped and sawed into wedges, prised loose, then pushed out into the lake. Further inland, barrels of tonite were buried in the ice and exploded, although to no effect. Even so, by the end of January the men had cut a channel more than 600 metres (2000 ft) in length, and were within 30 metres (98 ft) of the ship. And then the wind changed, the ice field shifted and the sides of the channel squeezed together.

A pall of despondency settled on the explorers. Already low on fuel, the remaining food was now rationed. February would be the final month of the Antarctic summer, after which the days would grow shorter, the weather progressively worse. Cook again feared for the mental state of the men. Even de Gerlache was showing signs of apathy, resignation. There was talk of abandoning the ship and attempting to escape across the ice. But in which direction? And to where?

On 15 February, at 2 o'clock in the morning, a sailor on watch hurried to wake de Gerlache. The ice was moving, the vessel rising and falling on a swell. The channel they had worked so hard to make was once again open!

The engine was started and, for the first time since 2 March 1898, the *Belgica* moved under her own propulsion. Lines were thrown ashore, teams of men struggling to tow the ship forward. A few metres at a time, she nudged her way along the channel, the ice-free lake.

But the battle was not yet won, for 11 kilometres (7 miles) of the field separated the lake from the open sea. Another exhausting month passed before the pack relented.

At midday on 14 March 1899, the Belgian Antarctic Expedition emerged from the pack ice at 70° 30′S, and 103°W. During almost 13 months imprisonment she had drifted across more than 17 degrees of longitude.

Roald Amundsen did not accompany the *Belgica* back home. He preferred to return to Norway aboard a mailboat, taking with him one of his countrymen, a sailor who had lost his reason during that long Antarctic night. The sailor, Tollefsen, eventually recovered, but another man, Knutsen, died shortly after.

For the survivors of this extraordinary voyage it was a time to convalesce. Medals were awarded by King Leopold of Belgium, though the finest accolade came from the men themselves, and was reserved for the American who had joined them as an act of faith, in Rio. They said of him: 'His behaviour won the respect, indeed the admiration of us all . . . He was the most popular man on the expedition . . . Upright, honourable, capable and conscientious in the extreme — such is our recollection of Frederick Cook.'

A LONE-WOLF EXPLORER

Carsten Borchgrevink leads the first expedition to winter on the mainland

Carsten Egeberg Borchgrevink was an amateur adventurer and explorer who, with private backing, achieved a great deal as an Antarctic pioneer. But he had little capacity for leadership, either practical or charismatic. Opportunistic and egotistic, he aroused the active opposition of people and organisations working in the same field. Nevertheless, the value of his work was finally recognised.

Borchgrevink (left) in full polar clothing. Born in Norway in 1864, he migrated to Australia in 1888, where he 'roughed it' for four years before becoming a teacher.

Although the expedition sailed under a British flag and, at the insistence of Sir George Newnes, was called the British Antarctic Expedition, only five of the entire complement were not Norwegians.

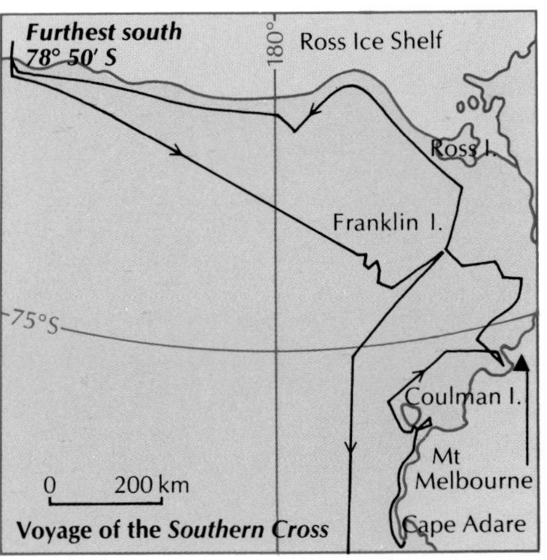

The Southern Cross *took 43 days getting through the pack ice on its way to Cape Adare. Here Borchgrevink takes some sightings with a theodolite to establish their position.*

Borchgrevink's observations and natural science collections made during the *Antarctic* expedition (see p128) convinced him that an Antarctic winter could be safely spent by a scientific party, led by himself, at Cape Adare in Victoria Land.

Returning from that expedition to Australia, Borchgrevink read papers on the scientific results of the voyage to learned societies in Melbourne and Sydney, and later in England. He created a strong impression at the Geographical Congress in London, the eminent historical geographer Dr H. R. Mill declaring: 'His blunt manner and abrupt speech stirred the academic discussions with a fresh breeze of realism. No one liked Borchgrevink very much at that time, but he had a dynamic quality and a set purpose to get out again to the unknown South that struck some of us as boding well for exploration.'

While the British geographical authorities increased their efforts to gain funds and support to send a large scientific expedition to the Antarctic, Borchgrevink offered to lead a small expedition of 12 men in a 200-tonne ship, one aim being to locate the South Magnetic Pole.

In 1897 he returned to Australia to raise funds for his projected expedition, but in vain; local interest now lay with the British plan for a large-scale scientific expedition. In particular the Royal Geographical Society, under the leadership of Sir Clements Markham, was actively concerned to raise the necessary funds, and vigorously opposed schemes such as Borchgrevink's which could conceivably attract much-needed funds from private sources. And this is what actually happened. Borchgrevink was at the time employed by a wealthy British publisher, Sir George Newnes, and persuaded him to provide the sum of £40 000 to fit out a small expedition.

Markham in particular was furious. Dr H. R. Mill, an official of the Royal Geographical Society at the time, reported in his autobiography: 'Markham warned me to have nothing to do with this expedition as the leader was incompetent, the ship rotten, and the money Newnes had given would have sufficed to get the National Expedition on its legs.'

Borchgrevink started to organise his expedition immediately, being determined to get to the Antarctic and spend a winter there before anyone else. The *Pollux*, a ship of 521 tonnes, was bought and re-named *Southern Cross*.

The ship left London on 23 August 1898, arrived at Hobart, Tasmania on 28 November and sailed again on 19 December. Forty-three days were spent getting through the pack ice, the longest period spent to that date in doing so. One of the Balleny Islands was sighted on 12 January. Louis Bernacchi, a young Australian physicist, said: 'One sight in bad weather of that sinister coast is enough to make a landsman dream for weeks of shipwrecks, perils, and death. I can imagine no greater punishment than to be "left alone to live forgotten and die forlorn" on that desolate shore.'

They crossed the Antarctic Circle on 23 January, and on 28 January one of the Russel Islands, first seen by Ross in 1841, was sighted. Then the *Southern Cross* was caught in the pack ice and it was not until 14 February that she broke free. On 17 February the landing place at Cape Adare was visible.

Bernacchi was again impressed — or depressed — by the scene of wilderness and desolation. He wrote: 'Approaching this sinister coast for the first time, on such a boisterous, cold and gloomy day, our decks covered with drift snow and frozen sea water, the rigging encased in ice, the heavens as black as death, was like approaching some unknown land of punishment, and struck into our hearts a feeling preciously akin to fear . . . It was a scene, terrible in its austerity, that can only be witnessed at that extremity of the globe; truly, a land of unsurpassed desolation.'

Landing operations started the next morning and took 10 days to complete. Despite bitter weather and dismal conditions the camp was firmly established, with prefabricated huts, on stony ground beneath the Cape. Borchgrevink named it 'Camp Ridley' after his mother. The wintering party of 10 was chosen and 75 sledge dogs were also landed.

Borchgrevink made particular mention of the way the sleeping quarters were set up. The 10 bunks were fixed to the northern and eastern side walls of the hut and, on the recommendation of the doctor, each was closed after the plan followed by sailors on whaling vessels, with a small opening, 'leaving yourself in an enclosure which can hold its own with our modern coffin', as he put it.

Between 23 and 26 February a furious gale and blizzard nearly wrecked the ship. It survived by steaming at full speed into the wind. A shore party of seven, including Bernacchi and the two Finns, was marooned. Luckily the Finns had brought their Lapp-tent with them, without which the party members would have perished. Bernacchi recounts that all of the dogs came into the tent and, by lying on top of the men, stopped them freezing to death.

On 27 February a group climbed a high ridge between the Sir George Newnes and Sir John Murray glaciers — so named by Borchgrevink — and returned with rock samples and mosses. They also located a quartz outcrop, and Bernacchi remarked on '. . . the striking analogy between the geological formation of the coasts of South Victoria Land and that of the Australian continent'.

The expedition's two prefabricated huts (below) were assembled on a wide beach at the base of Cape Adare — in winter they were joined by a centre section for ease of movement. Borchgrevink named the site Camp Ridley for his mother. For 10 men this was home for nearly a year — from March 1899 to January 1900.

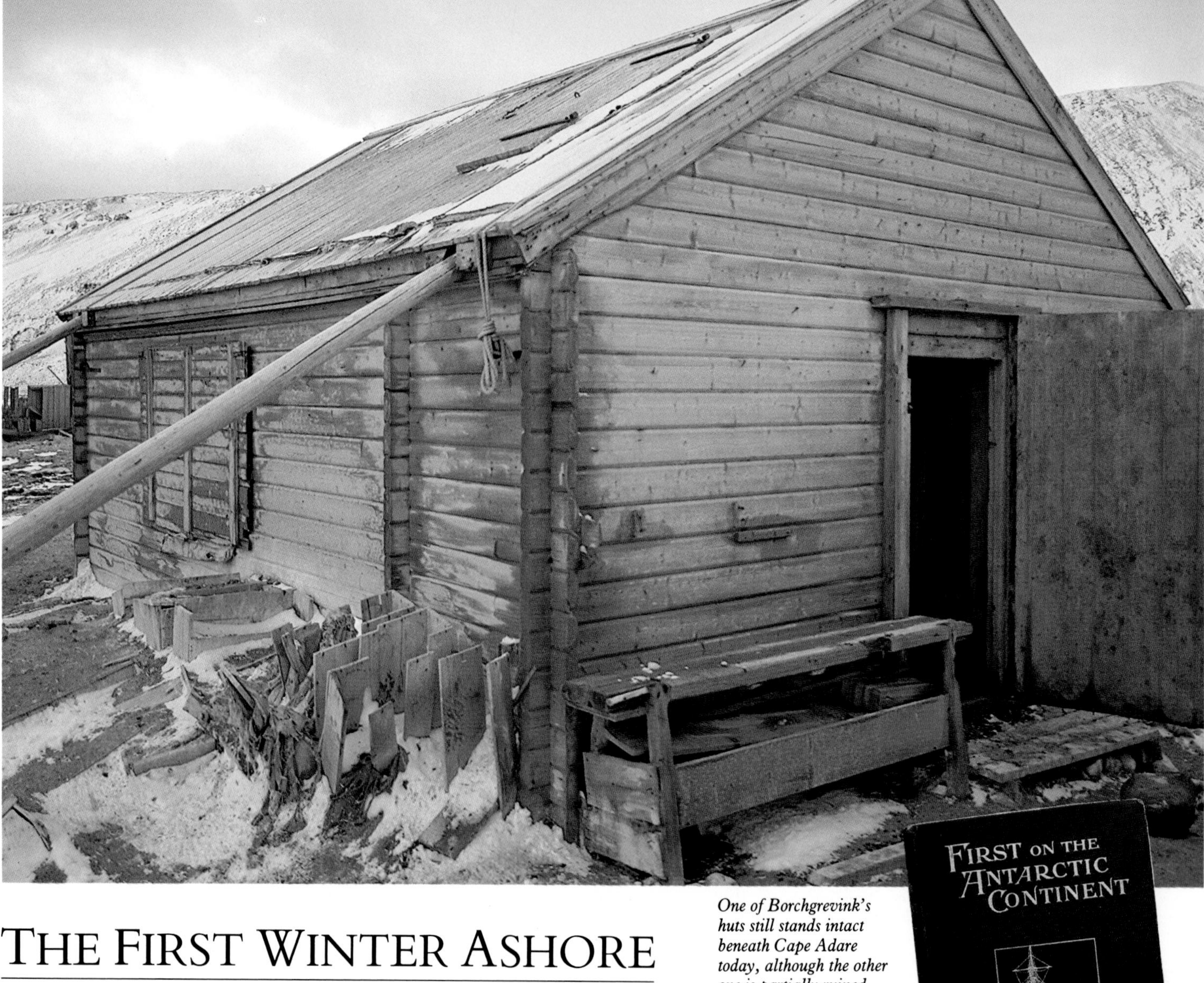

One of Borchgrevink's huts still stands intact beneath Cape Adare today, although the other one is partially ruined.

Borchgrevink's account of the expedition was badly written, and failed to do justice to the value of the scientific work that was actually carried out.

THE FIRST WINTER ASHORE

Britain ignores a pioneering effort

The* Southern Cross *left Cape Adare on 2 March, just in time to avoid being trapped by ice in Robertson Bay. The land party of the 'British Antarctic Expedition 1898-1900' — ten carefully selected men — settled down to the first winter ever spent by humans on the Antarctic mainland. Borchgrevink had to wait for many years before his pioneering work was recognised.

The mean age of the whole party was 27 years, and tests and measurements made at the start covering height, weight, chest measurement, strength and lung capacity showed that the three English members were on average stronger, taller, and heavier than the Norwegians. The two Finns, although small in build, were exceedingly sinewy and capable of withstanding any amount of cold and hardship.

Until the onset of winter on 15 May, members of the party carried out a number of survey trips inland and along the coasts of Robertson Bay, while the zoologists collected specimens of birds, fish, seals and penguins. Then, with the coming of darkness, fierce gales and blizzards hammered the huts.

During the night of 24 July the huts narrowly escaped being destroyed by fire — a candle left burning in a bunk set it alight. Much damage was done before the flames were put out. Then Hanson, the expedition's zoologist, became ill, showing some of the symptoms of scurvy.

The sun returned on 27 July, to the relief of all, but was accompanied by the greatest period of cold. Sledge journeys were begun to survey the coasts of the bay and to collect geological and other specimens.

On the night of 31 August, Hanson, Ellifsen and Bernacchi, asleep in the hut, were nearly asphyxiated by fumes from coals left burning in the stove. Luckily, Bernacchi, awakened by Hanson, managed to throw open the hut door.

There were many other narrow escapes from disaster, especially on badly crevassed ice surfaces covered with snow. One of the Finns actually fell to the bottom of a crevasse. Fortunately he had a knife and, by cutting toeholds in the walls of the crevasse, managed to climb to the top and safety.

Hanson died on 14 October. The cause of death was, and still is, a mystery. He was greatly loved, and was buried at the top of Cape Adare in a grave blasted by dynamite out of rock covering old glacier ice. Bernacchi wrote about the scene: 'There amidst profound silence and peace, there is nothing to disturb that eternal sleep except the flight of sea-birds. In the long dark winter night, the brilliant and mysterious *Aurora Polaris* sweeps across the sky and forms a glorious arc of light over the Cape and the grave. In the summer the dazzling sunlight shines perpetually upon it.'

On 28 January 1900 the *Southern Cross* arrived back at Camp Ridley. Early in the morning when all the party members were asleep, Captain Jensen knocked on the door of the hut, calling 'Post'. Their long ordeal was over, and on 2 February the ship sailed with the party on the next stage of the expedition — to sail around the coast into the Ross Sea and towards the Ross Ice Shelf.

A landing was made on Possession Island, where the pole and tin box set up on the shore in 1895 was found intact. A landing was also made on Coulman Island, followed by one at the foot of Mount Melbourne where a good site for a winter camp was located in Wood Bay. Geological and botanical specimens were collected, and magnetic observations carried out. Later a landing was made at the foot of Mount Terror where Borchgrevink and the captain narrowly escaped drowning when a tidal wave set up by the fall of a vast mass of glacier ice almost swept them out to sea. Colbeck and Bernacchi later climbed to the top of the Ross Ice Shelf, the latter reporting: 'Noth-

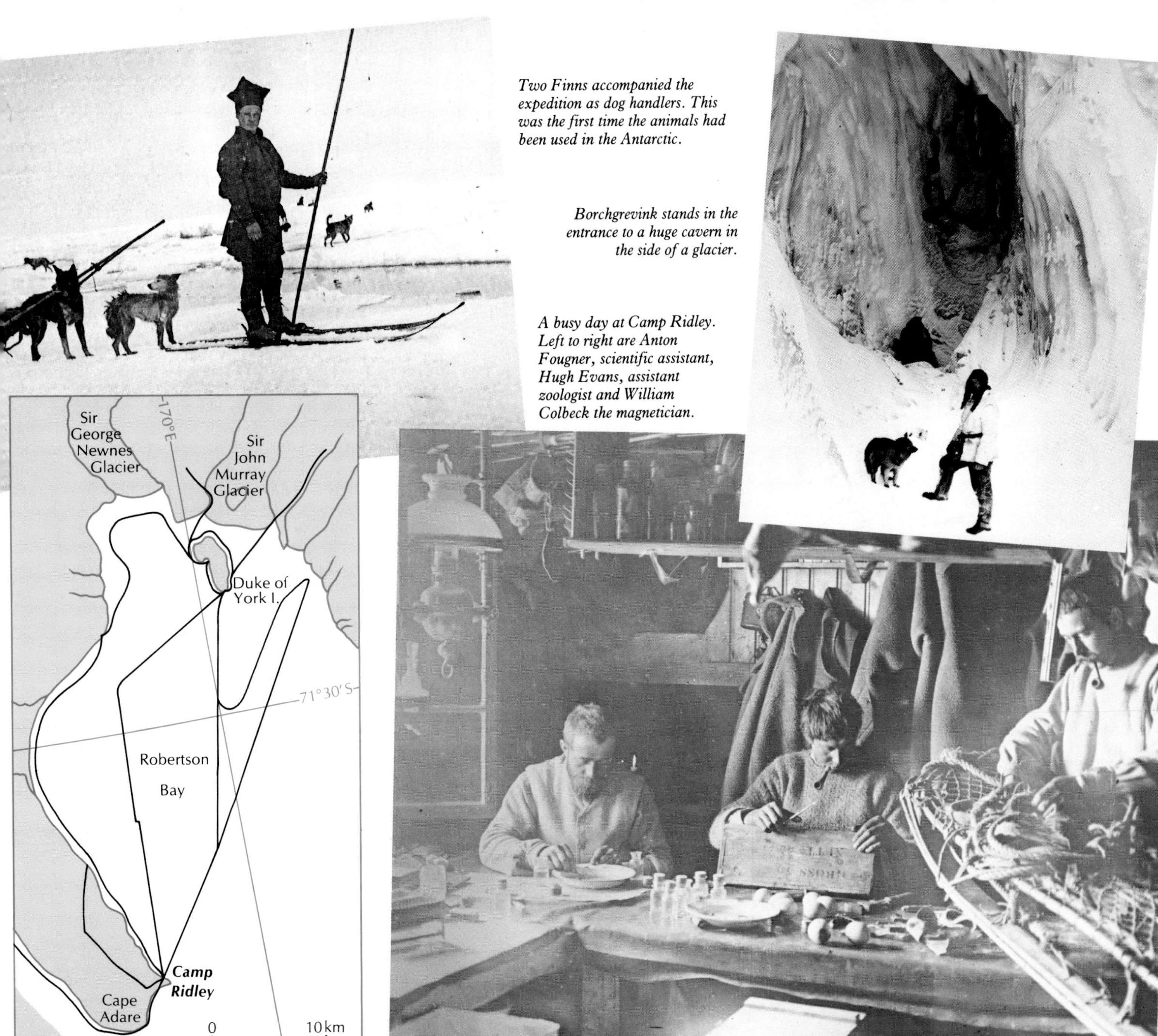

Two Finns accompanied the expedition as dog handlers. This was the first time the animals had been used in the Antarctic.

Borchgrevink stands in the entrance to a huge cavern in the side of a glacier.

A busy day at Camp Ridley. Left to right are Anton Fougner, scientific assistant, Hugh Evans, assistant zoologist and William Colbeck the magnetician.

ing was visible but the great ice-cap stretching away for hundreds of miles to the south and west. Unless one has actually seen it, it is impossible to conceive the stupendous extent of this ice-cap, its consistency, utter barrenness, and stillness, which sends an indefinable sense of dread to the heart.'

The ice shelf was found to have receded 48 kilometres (30 miles) since Ross's day. On 16 February Borchgrevink, Colbeck and one of the Finns set out by sledge over the ice shelf. After travelling 16 kilometres (10 miles) over a featureless landscape they reached an estimated position of latitude 78°50′S — the farthest south reached to that date by anyone. Then on 19 February Bernacchi, Evans, Fougner and Johansen travelled for eight hours over the ice to reach a point between 78°45′S and 78°50′S, where Johansen photographed the other three.

Leaving the ice shelf and any prospect for an extended inland journey because of the lateness of the season and the danger that the ship could be trapped in the ice, they sailed back along their course to Franklin Island. Magnetic observations indicated that the South Magnetic Pole was much farther north and west than previously supposed. Then the ship sailed northwards out of the Ross Sea. They crossed the Antarctic Circle on 28 February, and after that it was homeward bound. They had been away for nearly two years.

The expedition, despite its limited resources, achieved a lot. The scientific observations and collections, though not extensive, comprised a useful addition to detailed knowledge of Antarctica. The expedition's true role was that of a reconnaissance team for the large, well-equipped national expeditions then being planned. It proved that a party could winter ashore with comparative safety and carry out routine scientific work.

But the reception given Borchgrevink in England was rather poor. Interest was focussed on preparations for Scott's expedition. Also, the geographical authorities there had never taken Borchgrevink's venture very seriously, apart from resenting the fact that he had obtained funds they considered should have been made available for their project.

In England and Scotland, Borchgrevink gave numerous lectures to learned societies. He was made a Fellow of the Royal Geographical Society. He visited the USA in 1902, where the American Geographical Society gave a dinner in his honour. His own sovereign created him first a Knight of St Olaf, and later a Knight Daneborg.

But he had to wait until 1930 for English recognition. Then he was awarded the Patron's Medal of the Royal Geographical Society in belated recognition of the value of his pioneering work. In the citation delivered by the President of the Society, it was said: 'When the *Southern Cross* returned, this Society was engaged in fitting out Captain Scott to the same region, from which expedition much was expected, and the magnitude of the difficulties overcome by Borchgrevink were under-estimated. It was only after the work of Scott's Northern Party on the second expedition of 1912 . . . that we were able to realise the improbability that any explorer could do more in the Cape Adare district than Mr Borchgrevink had accomplished. It appeared, then, that justice had not been done at the time to the pioneer work of the *Southern Cross* expedition, which was carried out under the British flag and at the expense of a British benefactor.'

Keeping Warm

An endless battle against the cold

Great ingenuity has gone into designing light, but warm, clothing to protect men working in the most severe climate in the world. In Antarctica a temperature of −30°C (−22°F) is not unusual, and sledging journeys have been made during which the temperature has dropped below −60°C (−76°F). Winds can reach hurricane force.

Of all the Antarctic explorers, Roald Amundsen was probably the most experienced and professional. His upbringing in Norway and 14 years of polar exploration had taught him a lot about cold-weather clothing which was to be of enormous benefit when planning his successful assault on the South Pole in 1911. He insisted on buying or designing almost all the expedition's clothing himself. Where existing articles were not satisfactory he had alternatives specially made — in one case even supervising the manufacture of the cloth for underclothes, to ensure that it contained only pure wool.

Amundsen was particularly proud of one purchase of 200 ex-navy blankets, which were made into suits for all members of the expedition. 'The reader must not imagine', he wrote, 'white blankets, so delicate that in spite of their thickness they look as if they might float away of their own accord. No, they would keep on the ground right enough; they were felted and pressed together into a thick hard mass.' Dyed blue, the suits were warm and strong and very popular. Apart from these each man had three sets of linen underclothes; two sets of thick woollen underclothes; two thick, hand-knitted woollen jerseys; six pairs of knitted stockings; a light jacket; a sealskin suit from Greenland; oilskins and seaboots.

Those who were to work in very low temperatures had additional special clothing. Two hundred and fifty reindeer skins, dressed by Lapps, were sent to Oslo where they were made into clothes like those worn by the Netchelli Eskimos. Each man had a thick and thin reindeer skin anorak, trousers and stockings.

Two windproof gabardine suits each — one light and one heavy — provided loose, easy garments to wear on sledging journeys. Amundsen wrote: 'In these regions one soon finds out that everything that is roomy is warm and comfortable, while everything that is tight — foot gear, of course, excepted — is warm and uncomfortable. One quickly gets into a perspiration and spoils the clothes.' Each windproof suit consisted of trousers and an anorak with stockings of the same material. The heavier anoraks also had a hood. Frequently, when sledging, the men wore only underclothes and one light windproof suit.

The ever-present threat of frostbitten feet is a problem for polar explorers. Soft footwear, such as finneskoe (see opposite) reduce the risk

Richard Byrd's splendid reindeer skin suit, trimmed with wolverine, was based on a traditional Eskimo design. The entire outfit weighed only about 3 kg (6.6 lb), half the weight of its equivalent in wool, and yet gave protection when the temperature dropped below −60°C (−76°F). During the coldest weather Byrd said he rarely wore more than 5.5 kg (12 lb) of clothing.

because the foot can move easily and keep warm. Amundsen, however, planned to travel on skis and for this they needed stiff boots. An Oslo bootmaker prepared a special pair to Amundsen's specifications with thick, stiff soles and a combination of thin canvas and leather for the uppers. Even Amundsen was surprised at the results, and wrote: 'I well remember seeing the boots in civilised Christiana [Oslo]. They were exhibited in the bootmaker's window — I used to go a long way round to avoid coming face to face with these monsters in public. . . . If ever I cherished any illusions on the subject of "a dainty little foot", I am sure the last trace of such vanity died out on the day I passed the shoemaker's window and beheld my own boots.' Despite their prodigious size, Amundsen still found them to be too small and had to have them altered by a member of the expedition. Eventually he was able to fit a wooden inner-sole, seven pairs of stockings and a foot into each of them.

Hands were less of a problem because they could easily be inspected and any trace of frostbite quickly treated. Hide mitts, with a waterproof outer covering, were all that was necessary. Some members of the expedition took woollen gloves, but Amundsen found that they were inadequate against the cold.

During the winter the men went over their clothes, refining and improving them wherever possible. Every member of the expedition became skilled with a needle and thread. 'If we had stayed there', Amundsen wryly observed, 'I am sure we should be sitting and sewing away at our outfit'.

A WELL-DRESSED EXPLORER FROM THE HEROIC AGE

The clothing worn by Charles Royds (below), first lieutenant on the Discovery *during Robert Scott's 1903-05 expedition, represented the best then available to polar explorers. Up until then only two expeditions had wintered on the fringes of Antarctica, and no long trip had been made into the interior of the continent. They could only guess at the severity of the weather they would have to face.*

Furs were only worn on hands and feet. Scott disapproved of them for other garments and wrote: 'We find not only that furs are unnecessary for winter wear, but cannot imagine that they would be otherwise than positively objectionable.'

A fleecy helmet woven from camel hair protected all but the wearer's face. Considerable effort was put into inventing a detachable cover for the nose and cheeks in windy weather. The main problem with any face mask was that the moisture from the wearer's breath froze around the mask and eventually covered his face with a mass of ice. A light peak of gaberdine and canvas eventually proved to be the best protection as it created a layer of relatively undisturbed air in front of the face. In summer, when the glare from the snow was great, a broad-brimmed felt hat was worn.

The outer windproof suit was made from thin, waterproofed gaberdine and consisted of a top, trousers and leggings. The suit had to be easy to put on and to take off, and at the same time completely impervious to blown snow. This last requirement was not easy to meet, and great effort was expended in finding methods of closing sleeves, neck and other openings so that they were completely sealed. Creases also had to be eliminated so that as little snow as possible was brought into the tent.

Officers and men were all clothed in much the same way. Each wore a thick suit of underclothing, one or two flannel shirts, a jersey, a pair of pilot cloth trousers and a pyjama jacket. Any sort of jacket or stiff garment for the upper half of the body was not popular. Some wore a woollen scarf, while others relied on a collar to keep their necks warm.

Hands were protected by woollen halfmitts which extended from the knuckles almost to the elbows. Over these were worn lined fur mitts. In addition, for outdoor work, there were felt and woollen mitts. These could be windproofed by simply wetting them so that they froze — the ice forming an impenetrable covering.

Finneskoe soon became the favoured footwear because they proved to be much warmer than leather, which tended to crack in extreme cold. These fur boots, which originated in Norway, were made from reindeer skin sewn with gut. The sole was made from the forehead of the animal because the fur is thickest there and the pattern of the hair gave a better grip on ice. Socks were worn inside the boots with a padding of a dried grass called *sennegrass*. Sweat absorbed by the grass became frozen and the ice crystals could then easily be shaken out.

Curiously little has changed in the seventy years that separate an explorer from the heroic age (above) and the modern expedition member (left), who demonstrates the clothing issued to all United States personnel working in Antarctica. From left to right he dons: thermal underwear over normal underwear and socks; a heavy woollen shirt, windproof trousers, braces, woollen gloves and quilted inner boot-liners for his feet; a woollen balaclava, a heavy woollen sweater (not standard issue); close-weave cotton field trousers and woollen mittens; a hood, sunglasses, a parka, leather mittens — with bear mitts in his hand for very cold conditions — and mukluks (soft boots) on his feet.

GERMANY ENTERS THE RACE

Imprisoned ship saved by an ingenious scheme

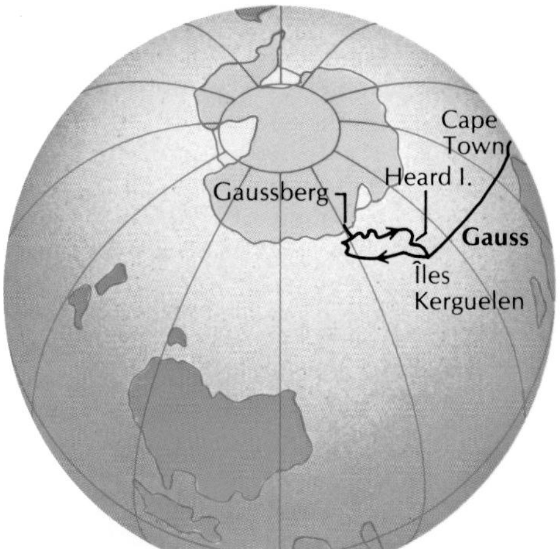

Gaussberg
Heard I.
Cape Town
Gauss
Îles Kerguelen

In the spring of 1902, at the edge of Antarctica, the crew of a German ship, the* Gauss*, laboured to complete a strange task. Under the direction of the geographer, Erich von Drygalski, they carefully spread a carpet of rotting garbage across the pristine white snow that surrounded their ship. It took them a month to lay a trail, which was made up of coal ash, penguin blood, rotten peas, spoiled dried fish and any other rubbish that the men could find on board their vessel.

The purpose of this experiment was not to become the first to pollute the previously unblemished face of Antarctica, but a desperate attempt to free the *Gauss* from the ice that had imprisoned her for eight months. Spring was now almost upon them, and although the ice had started to break up, the nearest stretch of open water was still 600 metres (2000 ft) away. Many attempts were made to cut and blast the ship free. The men drilled holes through the ice by hand — it was from five to six metres (16-20 ft) thick — and these were filled with explosives. Huge steel saws, up to six metres (20 ft) long, were used to make cuts through the ice beside the ship's hull. But progress was frustratingly slow.

The crew began to speculate on whether a second ship would be sent from Germany to look for them. Hans Ruser, captain of the

The design of the Gauss *was based on Nansen's (later Amundsen's) famous ship the* Fram. *The three-masted, auxiliary-engined schooner was 46 metres (150 ft) long, 11 metres (37 ft) wide, with a displacement of 1442 tonnes.*

Crew members show off the wingspan of a small wandering albatross — the wings of a large specimen can stretch for 3.3 metres (11 ft).

On a fine Sunday afternoon stoker Leonhard Müller entertains the crew with a tune on his piano accordion.

A fashionably dressed Dr Gazert, in two-tone shoes and boater, weighs Professor Drygalski on the deck of the Gauss, bound for Antarctica. Detailed physical records were kept of all the officers and crew during the course of the expedition.

Backbreaking work (below, right) by the small crew using six-metre-long (20 ft) saws and explosives created a small pond around the trapped ship and prevented surrounding ice floes from crushing her hull.

Gauss, suggested throwing scores of bottles into the open water, each containing a message with a description of their position and fate. He even suggested that 100 more bottles be launched by balloon with the next northerly wind. Things looked bleak indeed. Then Drygalski, during one of his daily strolls around the *Gauss*, noticed that the ice was particularly mushy and soft where soot from the ship's funnel had settled. The dark ash seemed to absorb sunlight, making the ice underneath melt. It was this observation that gave him the idea for the trail of garbage. When completed, it stretched from the ship's bow towards the open water in the distance.

'Success came almost immediately', Drygalski noted. 'The ice under the dirt started to melt. Within a month we had a long water channel almost two metres [7 ft] deep. Although there were still four to five metres [13-16 ft] of ice underneath, the channel widened constantly', growing into a small pond. By the end of December 1902 rain fell, further widening the artificial channel.

Christmas passed, then New Year's Day. It was not until 8 February 1903, while Drygalski was having an afternoon cup of cocoa in his cabin, that 'we suddenly felt two sharp jolts in rapid succession ... it was like a revelation, and with a cry "the ice is breaking", I jumped out on to the deck'. All the men were already there, watching jubilantly as the ice started to move. The man-made channel was now widening rapidly, its bottom cracking in the direction of the open water. Some members of the crew were still out on the ice so flags were raised aboard the *Gauss*, guns were fired and the foghorn blown. The men made it back safely as the ship eased out of her prison.

Erich von Drygalski, born on 9 February 1865 in Köningsberg, East Prussia, had already successfully completed a four-year expedition to Greenland when 'Antarctic fever' broke out among western nations towards the end of the nineteenth century. In 1898, the German South Polar Commission suggested that there should be a national expedition to Antarctica and that Drygalski, with his background and position as Professor of Geography and Geophysics at the University of Berlin, should be its leader.

Although financing was generous, Drygalski was only allowed to use one ship instead of two, as he had proposed. Permission was granted, however, to have the vessel specially built, rather than to modify an existing ship.

Drygalski took special pride in the fact that his entire expedition consisted of only five naval officers, five scientists (including himself) and 22 crew members. He firmly believed that it would be much more difficult to keep a large crew busy, healthy and well fed.

On 11 August 1901, the *Gauss* left Kiel and headed through the Kaiser Wilhelm Canal into the North Sea on her way to Cape Town. On 2 January she reached Îles Kerguelen. There, an observatory had already been established by the astronomer Dr Enzensperger.

On 31 January 1902 the *Gauss* left Kerguelen, her complement enlarged by 40 Kamchatka dogs. Seven days later the first iceberg was sighted, and from then on they were seen in increasing numbers every day. Navigation became more and more difficult, as the *Gauss* moved slowly between big, drifting floes and huge icebergs on a southeasterly course. It was not until 21 February that land was finally sighted. Drygalski recorded the 'coherent, uniform white contours, and in one place in the north-east darker spots which, when coming closer, also turned out to be ice. But there was no question about it: all the ice was on solid land ... everywhere it ended abruptly at the water's edge, forming cliffs 40 to 50 metres [130-160 ft] high ... the area behind them rose gently to about 300 metres [1000 ft] ...' It was this area, about longitude 90°E, that Drygalski named Kaiser Wilhelm II Land and where he wanted to winter.

Towards the evening of 21 February the ship tried to enter a wide opening between two ice ridges, and it was here that the *Gauss* was finally trapped. 'Later, nobody recalled exactly what happened during the next hours but we all felt that we had become a toy of the elements. A snowstorm blew up, floes and 'bergs closed in ...' During the next days, bad weather alternated with relative calm, but it became clearer every moment that there was no way out. Drygalski ordered the men to try to blast the ship free, but to no avail. By 2 March, 'our fate had been sealed: the trap we had entered had closed'.

A Cosy Winter Hamlet

Impenetrable ice frustrates Drygalski's plans

Although Drygalski had planned to spend the winter in the Antarctic, it was to have been closer to land. Now, magnetic observations posts had to be erected on the ice about 400 metres (1300 ft) away from the* Gauss. *In spring, attempts were to be made to reach the mainland by dog sledge. The expedition made few significant geographical discoveries — their only glimpse of the Antarctic land was a small hill — but then the area they had chosen to explore was particularly difficult to approach.

Members of one of the spring sledging parties in their tent. Drygalski is at the top right.

Officers and scientists aboard the Gauss *celebrate the solstice — 22 June 1902 — in the ship's drawing room. Drygalski is at the head of the table, under the portrait on the wall. Tracks on the right of the photograph are made by burning magnesium from the photographic flash.*

To help his men survive the hardships of the Antarctic winter, not only physically but also mentally, Drygalski had taken special care to make sure that all the things necessary for a normal life were aboard the ship. There were adequate provisions — enough for 30 men for 1000 days — and the cabins and mess-rooms were comfortable.

One of the expedition members, F. Bidlingmaier, described off-duty hours aboard the *Gauss*: 'Sundays were beer-nights, Wednesdays were lecture-nights, but Saturday nights were best of all: on them we sat together behind a glass of grog, united in games or conversation. Clubs sprouted like mushrooms. There were several card-clubs, a gentleman's cigar-smoking-club, glee-clubs, a band composed of a harmonica, flute, triangle and two pot-lids for a cymbal.' Another writer, Hans Harlin, thought that the *Gauss* resembled a cosy German hamlet in winter.

Such an atmosphere enabled every man to give his best. But life during the winter was not all pleasant. Snowstorms raged outside, piling huge drifts over the *Gauss* so she almost disappeared, except for her masts. Temperatures dropped to −28°C (−18°F), cracking instruments, turning petrol into an oily liquid and, worse, cracking dozens of bottles of German beer in the storerooms.

But fortunately there were fine days when work could be done outside. Meteorological kites were flown, and holes up to 30 metres (98 ft) were drilled by hand into icebergs to check on temperature and ice conditions. The men built a windmill to generate electricity, and even recorded the voices of penguins on an Edison phonograph. Hunting expeditions went out for seal and penguin: 'Their hearts and livers made a most delicious ragout . . . we loved it better than our tinned food.'

'By March the situation had stabilized so much that I thought it was time to start the sledging expeditions', Drygalski wrote in his log. The first left the *Gauss* on the 18th and lasted eight days, and led to another great discovery. Three men — second officer R. Vahsel was one of them — travelled with two sledges and 18 dogs. On the third day they reached solid ground, bringing back physical proof — pieces of volcanic rock they had picked up on the slopes and summit of an

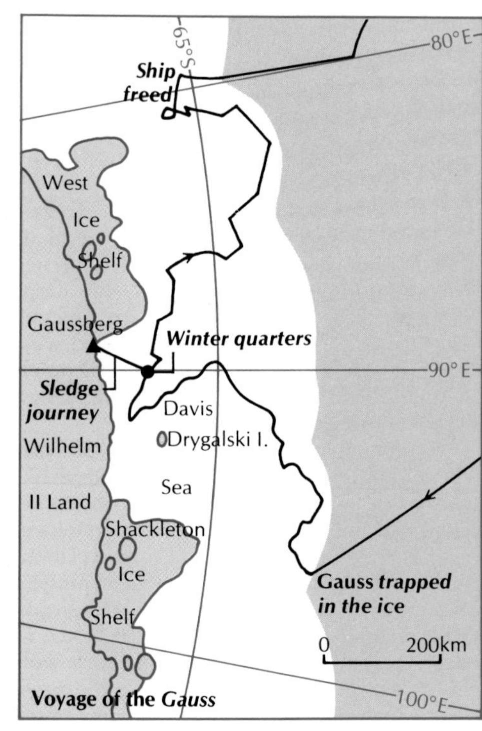

Erich von Drygalski poses in front of the expedition's major geographical discovery — the 400-metre (1300-ft) high hill they named Gaussberg. Drygalski is flanked by Professor Vanhöffen on his right, and Dr Bidlingmaier.

The expedition's balloon was used to survey the surrounding terrain. Drygalski got his first glimpse of Gaussberg from a height of 500 metres (1600 ft).

Dr Gazert instructs four assistants in the use of one of the meteorological instruments.

ice-free hill about 300-400 metres (1000-1300 ft) high. 'We always knew that there was solid land somewhere under the ice. But here, for the first time, we had visual proof!' The discovery, about 80 kilometres (50 miles) from the ship, was named Gaussberg.

Drygalski himself took a look at the discovery under more comfortable circumstances — he climbed aboard the balloon the *Gauss* was carrying and rose to an altitude of 500 metres (1600 ft). 'It was so warm up there I could even take off my gloves . . . the sight from this altitude was grandiose. I could see newly discovered Gaussberg and . . . gave my description via telephone to the deck of the ship. It was the only ice-free landmark in the surrounding area.'

In early April — with the temperature at night plunging to −32°C (−26°F) — a second sledging expedition returned from a 13-day trip to Gaussberg, where the four men had erected a temporary shelter for further expeditions. Drygalski himself decided to take part in the next one — and it was almost his last.

Weather conditions were extremely bad almost from the start, with night-time temperatures hovering around −39°C (−38°F). When he and his companions finally reached Gaussberg on 27 April, six days after leaving the ship, they found the shelter almost in ruins, wrecked by the storms. Hours were spent repairing it. The next days were devoted to geological and magnetic surveys. On the way back to the ship another storm struck. Food ran out, and just when the men were about to kill some of the dogs so they could be fed to the other weakening animals, they discovered a dead seal that had been killed by the previous team. Although men and dogs now had enough food, they had lost their bearings because of the constant bad weather. It was more by luck than good judgment that they finally found the snow-covered *Gauss* again.

Gaussberg, located at 66°40'S, represented the limit of the expedition's progress to the south, and Drygalski asked himself: 'Would it have been honourable to strive even harder, merely so we could report later that we had progressed further, perhaps to 72° or 73°S? This might well have been possible with the utmost effort . . .' Instead, he decided to break off as soon as spring arrived and search for another spot at which to establish new winter quarters. It was then that the garbage trail was started that finally led to freedom (see p140).

In February 1903, with the *Gauss* freed from her icy prison, the expedition started a slow voyage along the Antarctic coast. Although the ship could move now, she had not finally escaped from the ice. Everywhere great floes hindered progress, so the next weeks were spent with the ship travelling on a constantly changing course. Some progress was made to the south, but on 31 March, with new floes threatening to enclose the ship once again, Drygalski ordered retreat. 'It was a most difficult decision, certainly the most difficult one I had to make, but it was necessary. There was no safe place to spend the winter here . . .'

They reached the tip of South Africa on 9 June and immediately Drygalski sent a request to Berlin, suggesting another season in the Antarctic. A few weeks later, on 2 July, the answer arrived — the official order to return.

In retrospect, Drygalski noted with mild criticism that the decision was probably based on the fact that the planners in Berlin had different ideas about the conduct of an expedition and its goals. The Kaiser seemed disappointed that no new territory of importance had been discovered. On 24 November 1903, the *Gauss* reached Kiel again.

Of his achievements, Drygalski wrote: '. . . we found new territory in the Antarctic itself . . . something we can look back to in full satisfaction'. The discovery of this stretch of new land, roughly 1000 kilometres (620 miles) long, just south of the Antarctic Circle, confirmed the theory that there was a coastline at about 66°S, stretching between Knox, Kemp and Enderby Lands.

The expedition brought back so much new material that Drygalski spent years evaluating it. His work resulted in 20 volumes, published between 1905 and 1931.

ROBERT FALCON SCOTT

The opening chapter in the creation of a polar legend

He has been dubbed Scott of the Antarctic — as though they belonged to each other. In 1900, he was an obscure naval lieutenant. By 1904, he was a household name. Eight years later, after his death, he was elevated to the status of English Folk Hero to rank with Nelson. Since then, critics have sought to cut him down to size. But Robert Falcon Scott remains one of the giants of polar exploration.

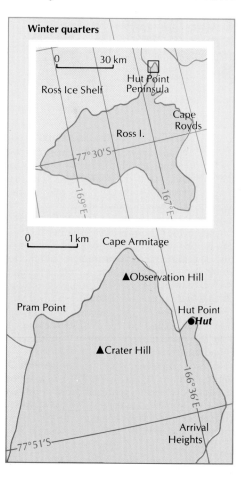

Sir Clements Markham, formidable President of the Royal Geographical Society, and driving force behind the National Antarctic Expedition of 1901-04.

Lieutenant Robert Scott aboard the Discovery *in New Zealand before the final leg of the voyage.*

Scott's hut at Hut Point, Ross Island still contains many of the things that the expedition left behind them in 1904. In the background is the US McMurdo base.

Scott's Antarctic adventures owe their beginnings to Sir Clements Markham, President of the Royal Geographical Society. He was a larger-than-life Victorian who usually got what he wanted. And what he wanted more than anything was to see another British naval expedition to the Antarctic. The last had been under Sir James Ross in 1840. But the international situation in 1896 was considered too fraught for the Admiralty to become involved in bids for glory.

Markham, undeterred, set out to raise funds for a private expedition. He persuaded the august Royal Society to join forces with the Royal Geographical Society, an impressive combination which should make the public pay up. By the end of 1898, however, only £12 000 had been donated. The £50 000 target seemed hopelessly ambitious.

Then, in March 1899, London businessman Llewellyn Longstaff contributed £25 000. That turned the tide. Soon, Queen Victoria was wishing the expedition success, the Prince of Wales became its patron, and a £45 000 parliamentary grant was promised.

On 5 June 1899 Lieutenant Robert Falcon

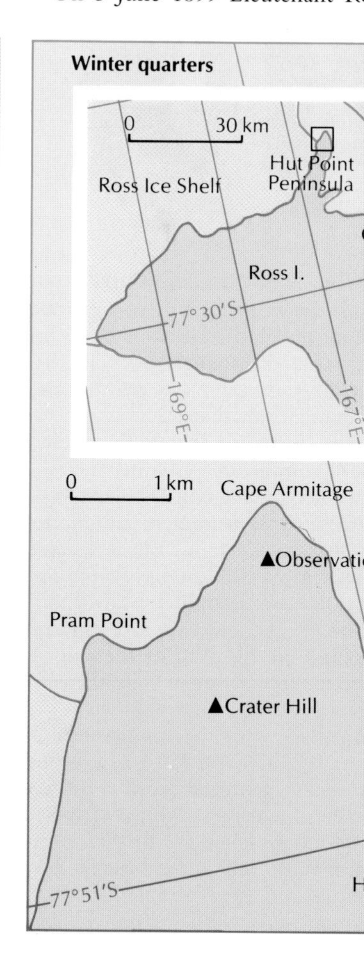

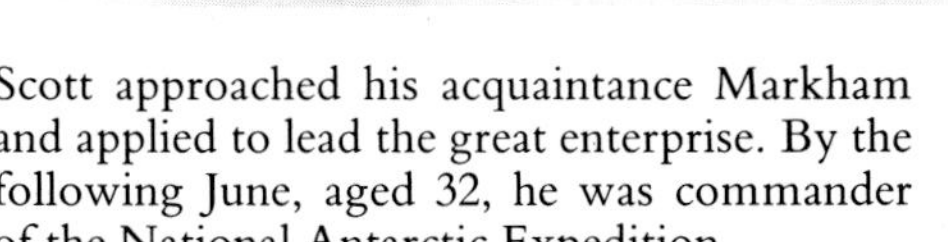

On 4 February 1902 Scott became one of the first 'aeronauts' in Antarctica when he ascended in the expedition's hydrogen balloon to inspect the ice shelf. It took 19 gas cylinders to inflate the balloon, and the ship could only carry enough for three fills.

Scott approached his acquaintance Markham and applied to lead the great enterprise. By the following June, aged 32, he was commander of the National Antarctic Expedition.

Meanwhile, the two Societies found themselves at odds. How should the expedition be organised? What should its objectives be? Who should go on it? Who should be in charge? Arguments raged in the 32-member Joint Committee and in various sub-committees.

All along, Markham was determined that this should be a naval operation, led by a naval officer. The Royal Society had assumed that a scientist would command the polar land party, nominating Professor J. W. Gregory. Markham ensured that he was ousted in favour of Scott.

Markham even managed to get Scott three naval officers and 20 men picked from the fleet. To these were added merchant crew, officers and scientists. So it would be a mixed party that eventually sailed in the brave little wooden ship being built in Dundee. Costing £50 000, *Discovery* was the first British vessel constructed for scientific exploration. She was just 52.4 metres (172 ft) long, but her sides were 660 mm (26 in) thick with a formidable steel-plated bow.

Markham's appeal had raised £90 000 — plenty to pay for ship, provisions, wages and other expenses. Months of preparation and training by Scott and his company followed. On 6 August 1901, *Discovery* left the Isle of Wight and embarked on her long voyage. The day before, King Edward VII had come on board to bid the adventurers Godspeed.

Ahead of the expedition lay a comprehensive program. Besides exploration, research would cover magnetism, meteorology, oceanography, geology and biology.

As *Discovery* bucked through the Bay of Biscay, Scott began to learn the limitations of his ship. Her top speed was 15 km/h (9 mph) and a strong headwind could reduce this to a snail's pace. She also proved greedy for coal, and performed poorly under sail.

Soon after crossing the Line, on 31 August, *Discovery* was found to be leaking. Some of the ship's provisions were damaged, and would have to be replaced in New Zealand. The 'Dundee Leek', as it was subsequently christened, resisted all attempts to stop it and meant pumping throughout the voyage.

On 15 November they reached pack ice. Supervised by zoologist Dr Edward Wilson, the men captured passing bird specimens.

By 30 November, the ship had berthed in New Zealand. Here, the explorers were treated like royalty. Harbour charges were waived, trains laid on to transport stores, officers and men granted free travel. *Discovery* was refitted, and the expedition's magnetic instruments checked at Christchurch. At this time, physicist Louis Bernacchi joined the ship.

Two men o'war and five steamers accompanied *Discovery's* triumphal send-off on 21 December. But the occasion was marred when a seaman, Charles Bonner, fell to his death.

On 2 January 1902, at latitude 65°30′S, the first icebergs loomed. Next day, nosing through pack ice, *Discovery* penetrated the Antarctic Circle.

'Land in sight!' The cry went up at 10.30 pm on 8 January. Rushing from below, officers and ratings stared at the distant Antarctic peaks outlined by the sun. Landing next day at Cape Adare, one party found itself in the middle of a vast penguin rookery.

On the beach stood the hut in which an expedition led by Carsten Borchgrevink had wintered from 1899-1900 (see p136). Bernacchi, a member of that expedition, pointed out the grave of a naturalist, Hanson — then the only human being buried in Antarctica. A tin cylinder detailing *Discovery's* progress was left in the hut, the first of a chain of 'records' to guide the relief ship *Morning* to Scott's group.

Leaving Victoria Land on 10 January, *Discovery* headed south, bound for the Ross Ice Shelf and in search of winter quarters. Gales and a glancing blow from an iceberg were just two hazards that the little ship weathered in following weeks. But all the time, the polar travellers were gaining invaluable experience. Scott learned to question what he saw. For example, tricks of the light caused by snow and clouds made distant objects seem close — a fact that had confused former explorers.

Discovery steamed across McMurdo Sound, site of the eventual winter base, and arrived at Cape Crozier. Here, amidst another extensive penguin colony, the final record was planted — a cylinder attached to a post.

By 23 January, *Discovery* was cruising beside the Ross Ice Shelf. Sixty years earlier, Sir James Ross claimed to have sighted land behind the barrier. But Scott's party could find no supporting evidence. Then, gradually, the signs appeared — layers of sand and dirt in icebergs, black rock patches on ice islands.

At last, the explorers were rewarded with a glimpse of mountains. They had discovered the region afterwards named King Edward VII Land. But fear of being trapped in ice drove Scott to head *Discovery* to her winter home. Tantalising views of the new land beckoned.

However, there was one more stop before the ship returned to McMurdo Sound. On 3 February she anchored in an inlet in the Bay of Whales. The next day Bernacchi, Lieutenant Armitage and four men set off on a sledging trip, and Scott prepared to make perhaps the first-ever balloon ascent over Antarctica—Drygalski was making his flight at about this time.

'Eva', one of the balloons supplied by the Army, was inflated with 240 cu metres (8500 cu ft) of gas from 19 cylinders. Stepping into a 'very inadequate' basket, Scott rose queasily to 244 metres (800 ft), where Eva's progress was halted by a wire rope. From his unsteady perch, he scanned the undulating white plain and could see a black dot that was the sledge party. Sub-Lieutenant Ernest Shackleton ascended next, to take photographs. Then the sledging group returned, having reached 79°3′S — bettering Borchgrevink's record by 29 kilometres (18 miles).

But not every such venture triumphed. Exactly a month later, several weeks after *Discovery* was safely installed in McMurdo Sound, a 12-man team with two sledges and eight dogs set off to update the message at Cape Crozier. On 11 March, four exhausted men arrived back at the ship and broke news of a tragedy. In a blinding snowstorm, a young sailor called George Vince had lost his footing on a slippery slope and plunged over a precipice. His body was never recovered.

Discovery *after the first winter gale. The storm badly damaged the windmill, which supplied the ship with electric light, and although it was repaired on this occasion another storm a few weeks later damaged it irreparably.*

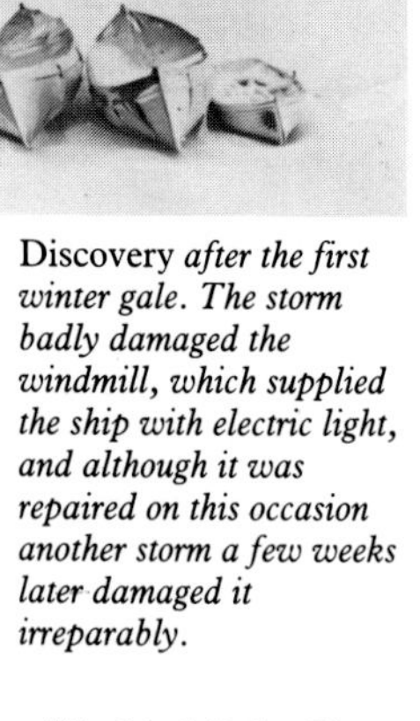

ASSAULT ON THE POLE

Pioneering attempt on the South Pole ends in near tragedy

After George Vince's death, no member of Scott's expedition doubted that this was a hostile continent. On 23 April 1902 the sun vanished. Four months of darkness had begun.* Discovery *was firmly frozen in at McMurdo Sound, and her crew must face winter 800 kilometres (500 miles) beyond the known.

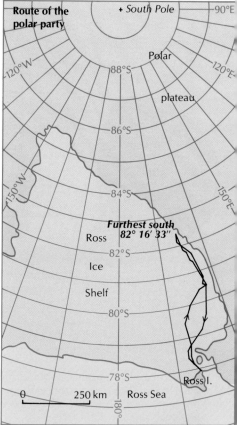

The South Polar Times *was put out monthly by Shackleton and contained articles by both officers and men.*

Sledge teams had already learned some hard lessons: do not march in blizzards; do not be fooled by the apparent nearness of landmarks; beware of frostbite. Men watched for telltale white patches on the faces of their companions, the first sign of frostbite.

Three huts, the two smaller ones full of magnetic instruments, now stood on shore. Below them, the dogs were kennelled. Aboard *Discovery* the winter routine ran smoothly. During the day, officers kept at least as busy as other ranks. Edward Wilson was the most industrious. He saw to the ventilation of living quarters, took meteorological observations, supervised bird-skinning in the main hut — some men had become expert taxidermists — and finished drawings and zoological notes.

But nobody was idle. Hartley Ferrar graded or polished geological specimens in his little laboratory near *Discovery's* bow; Louis Bernacchi tended the magnetic instruments in the huts; Thomas Hodgson hauled exotic fauna from the sea floor.

The days passed pleasantly and productively. Helping to dispel winter's gloom was the *South Polar Times*, a monthly journal printed and edited by Ernest Shackleton. This contained summaries of events, instructive articles, humorous pieces, full-page caricatures and puzzles. Anyone could submit contributions. 'Some of the best', Scott claimed, 'are written by occupants of the mess-deck'.

As winter wore on, Scott's team stepped up preparations for the next season of sledging. A major aim was to conquer the South Pole.

At last, the sun showed its face again. On 22 August, the temperature rose to −15°C (5°F). Within three weeks, sledge parties were setting off on various missions. Scott got ready for the pole. He would lead the attack himself, taking two officers and the dogs. But first, he must reconnoitre the route.

On 17 September, Scott, Michael Barne and Shackleton started out with two dog teams and a fortnight's food, plus stores for a depot. But, only two days later, they were back at the ship — having endured blizzards, an accident to their tent, frostbite and a temperature of −46°C (−51°F).

A second start was made on 27 September. Boatswain Thomas Feather replaced Barne, whose hand had been damaged by frostbite the year before. This time, the reconnaissance party fared better. It set up Depot A, marked by a black flag, with six weeks' provisions and 68 kg (150 lb) of dog food.

Now for the pole! Scott, Wilson and Shackleton set off at 10 am on 2 November 1902 as the men cheered. Next day they caught up to the support party which had gone ahead, manhauling its sledges with supplies for the polar assault group. The two teams continued together. On 13 November, all celebrated their approach to the 79th parallel — a new 'farthest south' record. Half the support party then headed home, the rest turning two days later.

Scott's optimism surged. 'Confident in ourselves, confident in our equipment, and confident in our dog team, we feel elated with the prospect before us', he wrote.

His mood did not last. Progress was pathetically slow. The dogs hardly pulled and the

A watercolour sketch by Wilson of mountains visible to the south from the furthest point reached on the polar journey — 82°16′33″S.

The stresses of polar exploration are etched in the faces of these three men. Shackleton, Scott and Wilson (left to right) before they set out, and after they returned from their southern journey. Three months of hard travelling and scurvy took an awful toll.

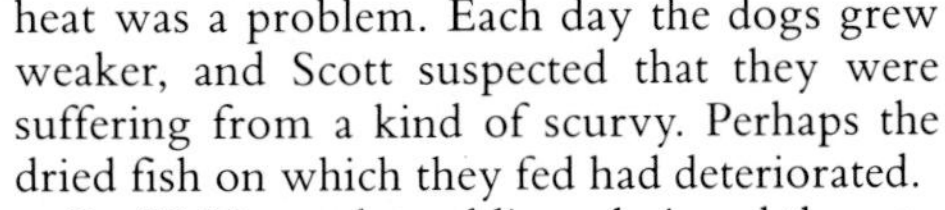

Discovery *in winter quarters, Hut Point. It was originally intended that the ship should return to New Zealand, and the men spend the winter in their hut, but a safe anchorage meant that she could stay.*

heat was a problem. Each day the dogs grew weaker, and Scott suspected that they were suffering from a kind of scurvy. Perhaps the dried fish on which they fed had deteriorated.

On 26 November a blizzard pinned them to camp. Wilson's rheumatism always 'played up' before a snowstorm, and came to serve as a barometer. On 9 December the first dog died. 'The others had no hesitation in eating their comrade. This change of diet may save the better animals', wrote Scott.

At latitude 80°30′S, Scott's party laid down Depot B. Hunger haunted the three men and they tightened their belts. Wilson and Shackleton envied Scott his pipe, which helped dull the appetite. All endured painful snowblindness, despite wearing goggles.

By 20 December, only 14 of the 19-strong dog team were alive. 'How many would survive?' Scott wondered sadly. His tobacco supply had gone, and he was reduced to smoking tea leaves — 'horrid'.

Then Wilson noticed scurvy symptoms in Shackleton and informed Scott. Neither told him. Food obsessed them. Wilson and Shackleton had nightmares, full of untouchable feasts. On Christmas Day they treated themselves to extra food, but Wilson spent the afternoon of Boxing Day in 'horrible agony' from snowblindness.

On 27 December, the trio came upon an inlet overlooked by a majestic twin-peaked mountain. It was christened Mount Markham, in honour of the expedition's founder.

Three days later, Scott and his companions reached 82°16′S. They had come closer to the pole than any other sledge party, but this was their limit.

The homeward trip was a joyless trek. Soon, just seven dogs traipsed behind the sledges, the weaker animals being killed to feed the stronger. Scott confessed: 'I personally have taken no part in the slaughter; it is a moral cowardice of which I am heartily ashamed.'

To speed sledging, they rigged up a sail from a tent floorcloth and by 13 January, Depot B was in sight. The trio ate well. But Scott was increasingly worried about their health. All now showed scurvy symptoms, Shackleton's chronic. His gums were dark and angry-looking, and he was short of breath. He also spat blood in coughing fits.

Getting back to base had suddenly become urgent. They should lighten the sledge load, which meant jettisoning dog food. Miserably, Scott decided the last two dogs must be killed.

Scott doubled the allowance of seal meat to try to beat the scurvy, but on 16 January Shackleton was very groggy, coughing and spitting blood. Twice, he fell heavily, and his companions waited while he recovered. Two days later, Wilson reported his eyes were failing. Scott could still see, but not very well. He concluded that heat had affected the seal meat.

Then, on 28 January, the party spotted Depot A. Weakness and pain were forgotten in the rush to get there. Greedily, the three men unpacked the treasures inside (which included a packet of tobacco) and gorged themselves. Scott and Wilson felt sick for hours afterwards, but were comforted by the thought that they would soon be back at the ship.

Next day, however, a blizzard struck. No hope of moving. On 30 January they plodded forward again, Shackleton carried by sledge. Another blizzard would finish the invalid, Wilson predicted. Luckily, the weather improved. Shackleton rallied, but Scott and Wilson were 'nearly done'.

On 3 February, lookouts sighted the bedraggled figures from a hilltop, and hurried to meet them. After an easy march to *Discovery*, the battered travellers could enjoy the luxury of a shave, a warm bath, clean clothes — and sleep.

TRAPPED IN THE ICE

Discovery *imprisoned for a second winter at McMurdo Sound*

Scott's polar quest was over — for the time being. But much had happened in his three-month absence. During the summer of 1902-03,* Discovery *became almost as busy as a bus terminus, with sledge parties shuttling back and forth to varied destinations. Discoveries were made, but many intriguing questions were yet to be answered.

Robert Scott and Dr Reginald Koettlitz (right), the expedition's surgeon and botanist.

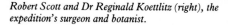

The most important of these exploratory trips was led by Lieutenant Albert Armitage. It aimed to scale the western mountains, find a route to the interior, reach and explore the icecap and investigate any fossil-bearing rocks.

On 29 November 1902, the party set off across frozen McMurdo Sound and headed for the mainland. After days of hard climbing, the men emerged on a plateau 1520 metres (5000 ft) up. Below them lay what was subsequently named Ferrar Glacier — a possible path inland. But how to get down there? And was the glacier itself safe to walk on? The 21-strong team split up, some returning to *Discovery*, others continuing to ascend.

At 1830 metres (6000 ft), the climbers found their way barred by rock and had to turn back. On 16 December, Armitage decided that the party must brave the precipitous slope down to the glacier now called Descent Pass. It was risky, but luck favoured them and they reached the glacier without mishap.

On 18 December the party began its cautious progress up Ferrar Glacier. By New Year's Day, 1903, the climbers had reached 2290 metres (7500 ft). One man, Macfarlane, collapsed. He and half the group remained in

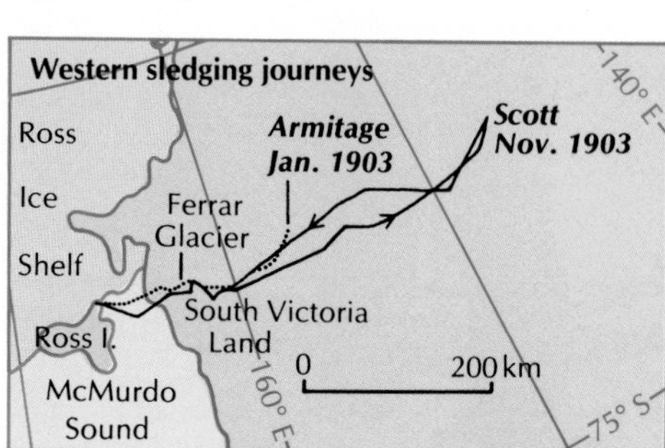

The 'Royal Terror Theatre' opened its doors on 6 August 1902 for a performance by the Dishcover Minstrel Troupe. The venue was the hut, where there was no heating save that provided by the lamps. The outside temperature on the evening was −40°C (−40°F), and inside it was well below freezing.

The mouth of the Ferrar Glacier. Travelling in this area in November 1903, a party led by Scott found themselves in the snow-free Taylor Valley. This was the first of the dry valleys to be discovered, although Scott was not equipped to explore it.

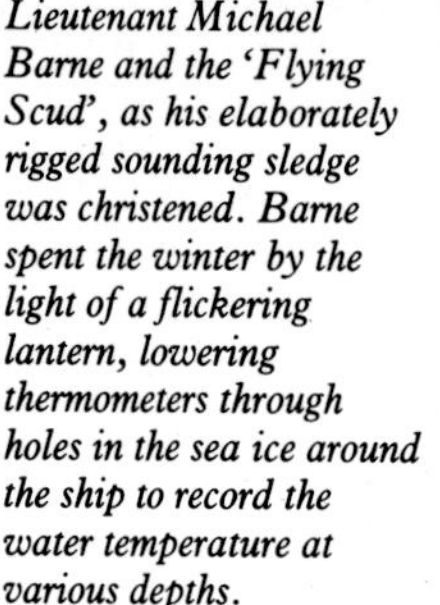

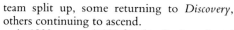

Lieutenant Michael Barne and the 'Flying Scud', as his elaborately rigged sounding sledge was christened. Barne spent the winter by the light of a flickering lantern, lowering thermometers through holes in the sea ice around the ship to record the water temperature at various depths.

camp, while Armitage and the others pressed forward. Four days later, the advance team clambered on to the icecap at 2740 metres (9000 ft). Another historic 'first'.

By 19 January, Armitage's men were back on ship. They brought rock specimens, photographs and enough information to produce a rough map. A successful trip — but frustrating. There had been no time to explore the icecap or the glacial valley.

On the night of 23 January a crewman spotted distant smoke. The relief vessel, *Morning*! Next day, a large group hastened to the ship and learned what had been happening in the wider world. *Discovery* would put to sea the moment her icy prison was unlocked.

Such was the situation when Scott returned on 3 February. *Morning's* master, Captain William Colbeck, chose that evening to make his first visit to *Discovery*, and goggled as Scott and his two companions demolished piles of food. But though their appetites were healthy, the three men were not. Both Wilson and Shackleton had to retire to bed for a long recuperation. Scott's scurvy was less severe, but he experienced an 'extraordinary lassitude'.

The ice was very slow in breaking up. This time the previous year, McMurdo Sound had been clear water. Now 13 kilometres (eight miles) of ice separated *Discovery* and *Morning*.

Scott and Colbeck agreed that *Morning* should not wait for *Discovery's* escape lest the relief ship herself be trapped, so on 13 February the transfer of stores began.

Nine days later, Scott's team tried blasting the ice with explosives. Cracks appeared, but no part of the floe was detached. Scott faced a disconcerting fact: *Discovery* might be frozen in for a second winter. He decided to reduce the ship's company from 45 to 37, also ridding himself of 'one or two undesirables'. But Shackleton had to go too, despite his protests. His health precluded further Antarctic rigours. He was replaced by Sub-Lieutenant George Mulock from *Morning*.

On 2 March, *Morning* departed. By 20 March, several kilometres of ice still stretched between *Discovery* and the open sea. The long polar night began again. *Discovery's* company settled into a now-familiar routine. On 16 May the temperature was −55°C (−68°F), much colder than the previous year, but without the merciless wind. By July, Scott was taking extended walks to get fit for sledging.

The western range, painted by Edward Wilson on 'the day after the sun disappeared', 24 April 1903.

Scott's ship the Discovery *at St Katherine's Dock in London in 1984 where she is being restored by the Maritime Trust as part of a permanent display. She was specially built in Dundee in 1901 for the National Antarctic Expedition, and was the last major square-rigged wooden vessel built in the United Kingdom.*

Mulock, a trained surveyor, made charts of all the survey data gathered by the expedition. This helped Scott plan for the next sledging season. He himself would lead a party to Ferrar Glacier and the icecap. It was agreed that all journeys should be completed by mid-December, so that the whole company could concentrate on trying to free *Discovery* from the ice.

On 7 September, Lieutenant Royds, Edward Wilson and four others set out for Cape Crozier to collect emperor penguin eggs. But the men arrived too late, and found about 100 adults and many chicks. No eggs. But they eventually found a cache of 17 abandoned eggs, weighing 450 g (1 lb) apiece.

Scott now focused on his main target: Ferrar Glacier and the icecap. On 26 October the expedition commander and nine-man party marched briskly away from *Discovery*. The next day the party camped at the glacier tongue. Scott would head for the icecap, while geologist Hartley Ferrar took two men and a sledge to explore the valley.

On 13 November, they reached the summit and struck out across the icecap. A continuous, chill wind blew in their teeth. Scott wrote: 'I could not conceive a more cheerless prospect. Yet before us lay the unknown. What fascination lies in that word! No wonder we were determined to push on, be the outlook ever so comfortless.'

The six-man team divided into two, each hauling a sledge. With Scott were Boatswain Feather and Petty Officer Evans; with Lieutenant Skelton were Handsley and Lashly. They made steady progress for a few days, but eventually Handsley and Feather could take no more and on 22 November they were sent back with Skelton.

The wind plagued them, opening up cuts. At night, the temperature fell to −40°C (−40°F) or below. Scott gave thanks for such sturdy comrades. Evans, a former physical education instructor, displayed 'Herculean strength'. Lashly was a superbly fit man, a teetotaller and non-smoker.

By 30 November, they had completed their outward march. During the homeward journey, Scott, Evans and the sledge plummeted down a crevasse. Lashly hung on to all three until his companions could scramble out.

On Christmas Eve 1903, they boarded *Discovery* to be welcomed by just four men — the rest were feverishly busy at the sawing camp. Scott soon joined them. To his dismay, he found that 32 kilometres (20 miles) of ice stood between *Discovery* and freedom. Attempts to saw a passage through the ice were proving ridiculously inadequate.

But on 5 January, two ships hove in sight — *Morning* and *Terra Nova*. The newcomer, a powerful whaler, had been sent by the government because the Societies could not fund *Morning's* return. Then came news that shook Scott: unless she escaped within six weeks, *Discovery* must be abandoned.

On 15 January, Lieutenant Royds went north to experiment with explosives. Gradually the ice was breaking up. By 1 February, *Morning* and *Terra Nova* were only 13 kilometres (eight miles) off. Four days later, Scott's men began blasting the floe. They made some impact, but on 10 February Scott drew up final plans to abandon ship. 'I don't think I ever had a more depressing evening's work.'

In *Discovery's* wardroom on 14 February, the officers had little appetite for dinner. Suddenly, the meal was interrupted by a cry: 'They're coming, sir!' On deck, the company gaped in wonder as *Morning* and *Terra Nova* raced through ever-widening channels. The floe was fracturing at amazing speed. That night, the relief vessels lay close by *Discovery*.

On 16 February 1904 a 30 kg (66 lb) charge was planted in the ice ahead of the ship. Scott himself pressed the firing key. A thunderous report, creaking timbers, gurgling water . . . and *Discovery* was free.

Man-hauling is probably the slowest and most physically demanding method of travelling in Antarctica. Scott's polar party only exceeded 24 kilometres (15 miles) a day on a few occasions.

ON THE MARCH

Transport that relied on human muscle and endurance

In Antarctica, as in most parts of the world, travel on foot may be the most exacting, and the most rewarding means of progress. A sledging party, with or without the assistance of dogs, fully appreciates the ever constant, ever changing wilderness. A modern explorer, using traditional equipment, may still experience the same conditions and problems that faced the men of the heroic age.

Shackleton's party setting out on their attempt to reach the South Pole in 1908. Using ponies, and later man-hauling, they struggled to within 180 km (97 nautical miles) of their goal.

Before the introduction of tractors in the 1920s, all polar exploration was done on foot, with the help of dogs and horses. Skis, crampons (metal spikes for boots) and snowshoes were all occasionally employed if the conditions called for them.

Modern footwear is much lighter than the traditional 'lauger-kock' of canvas and leather which reached almost to the knee and were worn with a sheepskin inner boot — sometimes stuffed with saennegras or manila fibre for further insulation. Even finneskoe — soft reindeer hide boots, padded with fibre and worn with several pairs of socks — have given way to mukluks. These canvas boots with felt inners are worn with two or three pairs of socks. They have heavy rubber soles and springy inners of nylon mesh which, like saennegras, hold frost formed in the boots. In very cold weather, below −40°C (−40°F), double vapour-barrier boots of rubber or plastic, spaced by nylon 'wool', reduce heat loss to a point where no other insulation is needed. Feet may become damp with perspiration, however, because there is little ventilation. Socks must be changed frequently.

All the footwear mentioned so far is suitable for temperatures well below zero, when the surface of the ice or snow is dry. Because the feet are so well insulated, their heat does not thaw out snow in contact with the boots. For temperatures near zero and above, when boots become wet, and especially on sea ice which may become flooded in early summer, dubbined leather boots are usually worn with several pairs of socks and a nylon mesh sole.

The design of sledges for dog or man-hauling has changed little since the beginning of the 20th century. Fridtjof Nansen standardised the common Norwegian form which he used during his crossing of Greenland in 1888. The Nansen sledge has two runners, bent like skis, 75-100 mm (3-4 in) wide and up to 3.5 metres (11.5 ft) long. Into the runners, which are spaced approximately 460 mm (18 in) apart, are tenoned six pairs of uprights supporting a framework of crossbars and lengthwise slats. The crossbars and uprights are generally rigidly jointed, but all other connections are made with greenhide lashings, allowing the sledge to flex over uneven surfaces such as sastrugi or pressure ice. A 3.5-metre (11.5-ft) sledge will carry loads of up to half a tonne. Traditionally, ash and hickory were almost universally used, and the original Greenland sledges were shod with bone or ivory. Runners now often have steel, or even fibreglass or plastic edges to reduce friction.

Dog and man-hauling harnesses were originally made from canvas, folded several times and stitched. The strain of man-hauling is invariably taken at the waist, while dogs pull from the chest, the strain being taken in front. In more recent times woven lamp-wick has been used for dog harnesses. Any harness must be strong enough to hold its wearer suspended, should he or she fall into a crevasse.

Distances travelled with sledges vary with the surface, weather, temperature, load and the strength of the team. Over difficult surfaces sledging can be utterly exhausting. Frequently jury-rigged sails have been erected on sledges, but with generally indifferent success. No sailing facility has ever become standard equipment. Mawson fitted a light bamboo mast and spar to each of his sledges, but they seldom carried a sail to any worthwhile effect. Scott reported slight assistance from wind for a few hours on his last journey. On Griffith Taylor's geological expedition to Granite Harbour, Forde rigged a sail using six tent poles. With a combination of man and sail power the sledge covered a mile (1.6 km) in 45 minutes. Various ice yachts have been designed for travelling on the sea ice, but exclusively for recreation.

A strong dog team of eight, well driven, will generally cover about twice the distance traversed by four fit men drawing a similar sledge and load. John Rymill, on the British Graham Land Expedition in 1935-37, averaged 21 kilometres (13 miles) a day travelling with dogs over ice and névé. Another party reckoned that they could achieve 35-40 kilometres (22-25 miles) a day over sea ice with dogs, pulling loads of up to 70 kg (154 lb) per dog.

Probably the best sledging journey was made by Amundsen's party on their way to the South Pole and back. They averaged 37 kilometres (23 miles) a day. Under ideal conditions Amundsen and Peary both recorded

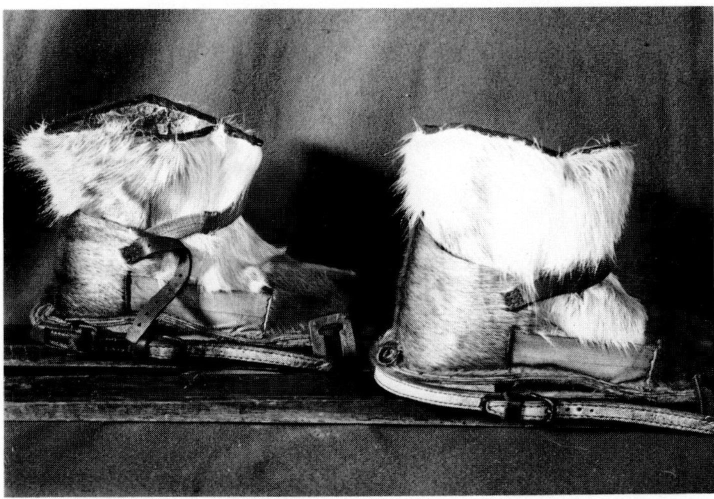

Skis, here adapted to take *finneskoe*, were taken on Scott's 1910-13 expedition. Scott also took a skiing instructor with him — a Norwegian, Lieutenant Tryggve Gran, who was introduced to him by Fridtjof Nansen. Gran gave lessons to the other men, but few took any real advantage of the expert instruction.

A Nansen dog sledge, with a platform at the back for a driver. The basic form of these sledges was settled in 1888 by Fridtjof Nansen during his Arctic travels. Traditionally, no nails or screws are used in their construction. Connections are made using woodworking joints or greenhide lashings. The sledge must be able to flex and twist while travelling over rough terrain.

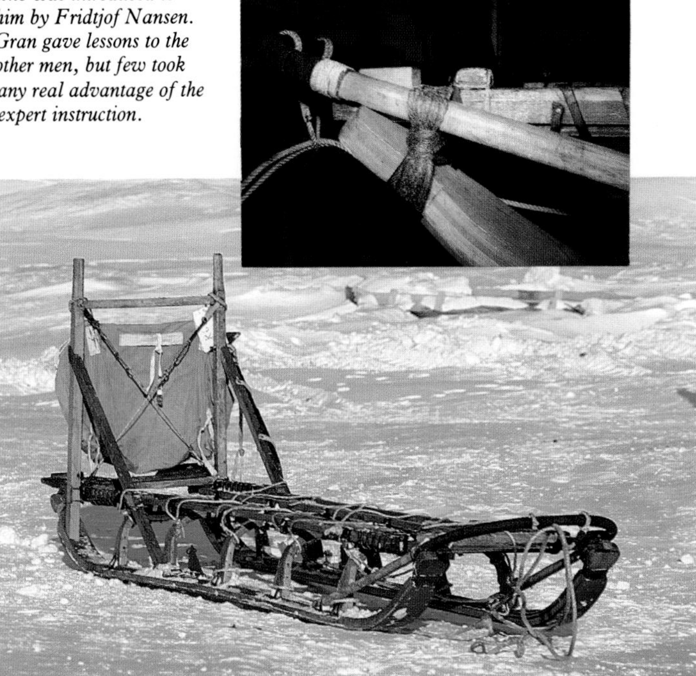

Pony snow shoes at the Cape Evans hut. Without the shoes, the animals floundered helplessly in deep snow. After the first experiments Scott estimated that their use would double the distance they could cover.

A fully laden sledge can weigh half a tonne, and be impossible to right if it capsizes. Loading and unloading is laborious.

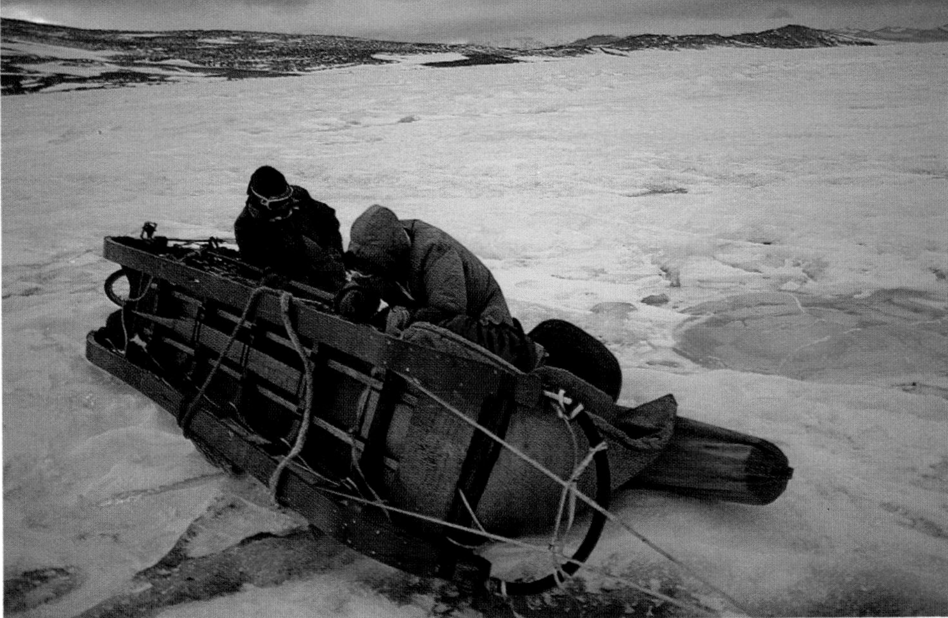

distances exceeding 97 kilometres (60 miles) a day. M'Clintock, an early expert on sledging, cites a dog team travelling 2900 kilometres (1800 miles) in 60 days. Scott's party, man-hauling on their return from the pole, exceeded 24 kilometres (15 miles) a day several times. Scott used both dogs and Manchurian ponies on the outward march, but neither with great efficiency. Floundering in deep, soft snow, and unprotected from the cold, the ponies died in harness, or were destroyed.

Antarctic travel on foot is dominated by the type of surface, ranging from smooth, glassy sea ice to harsh immobile sastrugi — high, sharp troughs and ridges worn in the snow by consistent strong wind and streaming blizzard snow. To these problems must be added the dangers of hidden crevasses, thick blizzards, snow blindness and the occasional white-out.

Most Antarctic travellers began their sledging experiences on the sea ice which extends from the coast for much of the year. The sea ice provided many expeditions with important sledging routes. The surface varies enormously. In places it can be wind-polished and flat, or with a dimpled surface, over which it is difficult to travel, especially in a wind. Some form of spiked footwear is essential.

More commonly, sea ice is overlain with névé or soft snow, often providing an ideal sledging surface, except where metre-high (3-ft) hummocks are forced up by zones of pressure. Well-trained dog teams will always swing round to tackle pressure ridges at right angles, thereby minimising the danger of upsetting a sledge laden with half a tonne of equipment and supplies. Many sledgers have found themselves in a blizzard on heaving pressure ice with an upturned sledge and the dogs, tangled in their traces, fighting furiously.

Wet sea ice may make for heavy haulage, exhausting for men and dogs. The freezing point of brine is lower than that of fresh water so sea ice containing salt crystals will remain damp and clinging in sub-zero air.

In the spring of 1911, Scott's northern party struggled back to Cape Evans in just such conditions. Raymond Priestley graphically described the experience: 'As I have already said, however, we had a strong motive to keep us going, and we pulled equally hard whether up to our ankles or up to our necks in snow. Exaggeration apart, we were frequently floundering for several yards together up to the sockets of our thighs in snow, while the latter was hard and cloggy with a stiff crust, and every step was like drawing a tooth ... The worst of this present type of sledging was that the sledges came along so reluctantly that it was impossible to think of other things. We had to keep our minds on the drudgery in hand or we slackened our effort quite unconsciously, and this meant a standing pull to start the sledges again.'

Skidoos have, inevitably, supplanted muscle power. They have excellent traction, require neither food nor fuel when not in use, and, unlike their living precedents, they have no will of their own. Modern explorers seldom make extensive journeys on foot or with dogs.

Against The Odds

Otto Nordenskjöld's ill-fated expedition

The 1901 Swedish expedition to the Antarctic region south of Cape Horn was one of the most remarkable ever to visit the area. During two years of danger, hardship and suffering the men of the expedition accumulated a mass of invaluable scientific data and only survived at all through a series of extraordinary coincidences that make the story of the expedition read like an intricately plotted novel.

Organised in conjunction with expeditions from Britain and Germany, which were to explore the frozen lands to the south of the Pacific and Indian Oceans, the Swedish expedition was led by a 32-year-old geologist, Dr Otto Nordenskjöld. His party consisted of seven other scientists, and their ship, a stoutly built ex-sealer named the *Antarctic*, was crewed by 16 officers and men under the command of an experienced Antarctic explorer, Captain Carl Anton Larsen. An eighth member, a young geographer-geologist-anthropologist named Dr Gunnar Andersson, was to join the ship at the Falklands as the expedition's leader after Nordenskjöld and his wintering party had been dropped at their wintering station. The plan then was for the *Antarctic* to spend the rest of the summer and the autumn employed in scientific work before returning the following summer to pick up Nordenskjöld. It was a simple plan, but one which went disastrously wrong.

The *Antarctic* left Gothenburg on 16 October 1901 and arrived at Buenos Aires on 15 December. There the party was joined by an American artist, F. W. Stokes, and an Argentinian naval officer, Lieutenant J. M. Sobral. The Argentinian government wanted Sobral to join the wintering party; in return they supplied free fuel, food and help.

The ship left for the South Shetlands on 21 December, arriving there on 11 January. Nordenskjöld landed briefly on one of the islands before going on to explore Orléans Strait.

'We were now sailing a sea across which none had hitherto voyaged', Nordenskjöld recorded in his journal. 'The weather had changed as if by magic; it seemed as though the Antarctic world repented of the inhospitable way in which it had received us the previous day, or, maybe, it merely wished to entice us deeper into its interior in order the more surely to annihilate us. At all events, we pressed onward, seized by that almost feverish eagerness which can only be felt by an explorer who stands upon the threshold of the great unknown.'

Contrary to what had been supposed, they soon saw that Louis-Philippe Land was connected to Danco Land and that the Orléans Strait ran into Gerlache Strait, discoveries that Nordenskjöld later described as being the most important geographical finds of the whole expedition. He wanted to go further, but time was short, so the ship retraced her course until the sound between Louis-Philippe Land and Joinville Island was entered. Although it had been discovered by the French explorer Dumont d'Urville, no ship had ever sailed through, so it was named after the *Antarctic*.

Once through the sound the party landed on Paulet Island then crossed Erebus and Terror Gulf and made a depot on Seymour Island. The ship then continued to steam southwest towards the unknown eastern part of Oscar II Land Coast, but on reaching latitude 66°10'S a great barrier of ice was seen ahead through which there was no path. Nordenskjöld followed the line of ice eastwards in the hope of finding an opening to the Weddell Sea. A position of 63°30'S, 45°7'W was reached on 1 February before the ship had to turn back.

By 9 February land was once more in sight. For his winter campsite, Nordenskjöld chose Snow Hill Island to the southwest of Seymour Island. He and five others were put ashore with all their stores and equipment, including several sledge dogs, and the *Antarctic* steamed back to the Falklands.

The wintering party's first task was to erect the magnetic observatory which would provide shelter until the prefabricated hut they were to live in could be built. A series of severe storms gave them a taste of what was to come, but by the beginning of March the weather had improved sufficiently for Nordenskjöld to make a series of journeys by boat and dog sledge to establish depots. In winter the storms returned with a vengeance. One blew from 15 to 24 July without remission, the thermometer registering −30°C (−22°F) throughout.

It was a great relief when spring came and an attempt could be made to reach the eastern part of Oscar II Coast again, this time on foot. Nordenskjöld, Sobral and a seaman called Ole Jonassen set off, the men towing one sledge and the dogs the other. When the going was good they covered 48 kilometres (30 miles) a day, but it rarely was. And the terrain became difficult and filled with crevasses, down one of which Nordenskjöld very nearly disappeared for good. At last they reached their goal.

'We did not make much ado about choosing our camping-ground', Nordenskjöld noted in his diary on 18 October, 'but pitched our tent

Otto Nordenskjöld working at his desk in the hut on Snow Hill Island. His uncle, Baron A. E. Nordenskjöld, was an Arctic navigator, famous for his discovery of the Northeast Passage around Siberia.

Nordenskjöld, a geologist, chose the site for the Snow Hill Island hut because of the interesting fossils he found in the area.

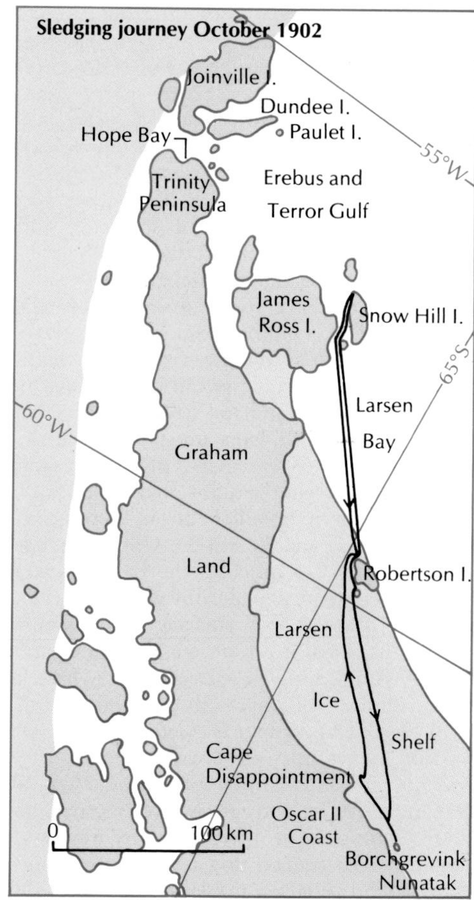

Six men spent two years in the tiny hut which measured 6.4 x 4.1 metres (21 x 13.5 ft).

Nordenskjöld (seated) and Sub-Lieutenant José Sobral, from the Argentinean Navy.

In October 1902 Nordenskjöld, Jonassen and Sobral sledged southwards to Oscar II Coast.

on the ice at the foot of a projecting, brown, weather-worn, rocky headland, torn by the frost into a mass of mighty blocks. The reader can easily imagine with what feelings I hurried forward to these rocks, the first spot trodden by human foot on the whole of the eastern coast of the mainland of West Antarctica.'

But bad weather and bad luck continued to plague them. Jonassen injured his arm, their tent was ripped by a storm, and the dogs found the sack containing their pemmican. They ate it all, along with part of the sack, some harness, and the whip. The time, Nordenskjöld decided, had come to return.

The three men arrived back at the winter camp, exhausted, on 31 October, having covered 611 kilometres (380 miles) in 33 days.

November passed without any sign of a break in the ice. Early in December Nordenskjöld undertook a sledge journey to Seymour Island and made some important fossil finds, including the bones of a giant penguin. But the excitement generated by these finds could not dull the growing uneasiness all felt about the condition of the ice and the whereabouts of their ship. Every day in January and early February the ship was expected, and the weeks passed in increasing tenseness.

On 18 February a storm came in from the south-south-west, bringing with it a mass of snow. The temperature dropped to −10°C (14°F) and by the next evening the sea was completely frozen over. Any hope of being rescued was now crushed and with heavy hearts the men prepared themselves for another long, gruelling winter imprisoned in cramped, damp, bitterly cold surroundings.

When spring arrived again, Nordenskjöld set off with Jonassen on another sledge journey, this time to discover whether the great gulf they had found the previous year behind Cape Foster connected with the bay north of Cape Gordon. Fine weather enabled them to prove that it did after only five days on the sea ice, and they called this stretch of water the Crown Prince Gustav Channel.

Nordenskjöld now made for a promontory on Vega Island in order to obtain a better view of the ice conditions in Erebus and Terror Gulf, as he wanted to cross to Paulet Island. As the two men drew nearer the land Jonassen spotted something strange. At first Nordenskjöld thought that the three moving objects were penguins, but on using his fieldglass he was astonished to discover that they were men.

When they came face to face, Nordenskjöld's bewilderment at the appearance of the trio was total. 'Black as soot from top to toe; men with black clothes, black faces and high black caps, and with their eyes hidden by peculiar wooden frames ... my powers of guessing fail me when I endeavour to imagine to what race of men these creatures belong.'

Even when the men said they were from the *Antarctic* Nordenskjöld did not recognise them. They were in fact Gunnar Andersson, Lieutenant Duse, the expedition's cartographer, and Toralf Grunden, one of the ship's crew. And their story was truly astonishing.

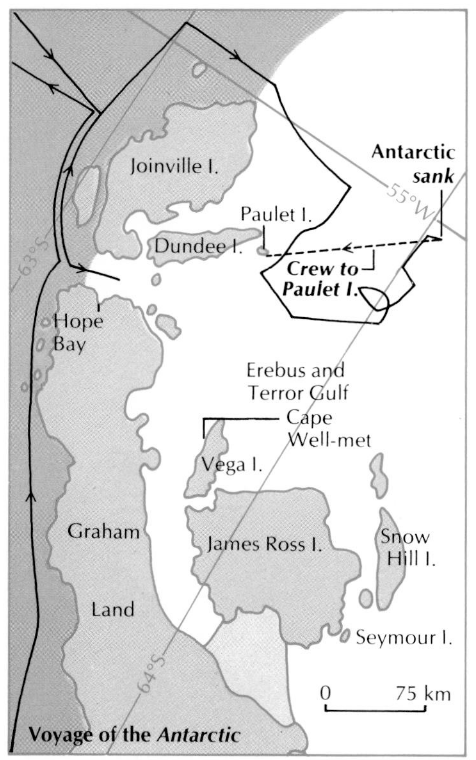

A fierce storm on 21 November almost forced the Antarctic *into an iceberg. It took the combined power of the sails and the engines to avoid a disastrous collision.*

THE SINKING OF THE *ANTARCTIC*

Frantic efforts to save the ship fail as the relentless pack ice closes in

After dropping Nordenskjöld and his wintering party at Snow Hill Island, the* Antarctic *headed back for the Falklands, where she spent the winter of 1902 and picked up Gunnar Andersson. The return journey to the south began on 5 November 1902. Luckily, the men on board had no inkling of the disaster that lay ahead of them.

The first sign of problems ahead appeared in the form of some floating pack ice sighted on 9 November. As the ship's latitude at the time was only 59°30'S, this caused a good deal of consternation. Within two days, the ship was held fast.

The weather was calm and sunny at first, and Carl Larsen was able to ram his way forward for a short distance before again being stopped. Then, on 17 November, a four-day storm began to rage; it broke up the ice slightly, but also put the *Antarctic* in peril.

'At 2.30 am on 21 November', wrote Andersson, 'I was awakened by loud orders from the captain's bridge, and I dressed myself hurriedly and hastened on deck. Three or four ship's lengths on our larboard lay an iceberg which was considerably higher than our mainmast and about three times as long as the vessel... We were in evident danger of being carried by the pack which lay close around the *Antarctic*, right on to the ice-mountain. To add to our difficulties we were in the midst of a blinding snowstorm. The engines were going full speed, and we had the jib and fore-sail set. For a long time the vessel moved slowly forward a few yards, only to be pressed back by the floes, but after a while the pieces of ice gave way before the united pressure of steam and sail, and the *Antarctic* glided past the iceberg into the lead which had been formed in its lee.'

When the storm at last subsided the ship manoeuvred into more open waters around the South Shetlands. After stopping at Deception Island for a short time the party steamed along Bransfield Strait and Andersson and his companions were able to establish that Middle Island did not in fact exist.

The next task of the party was to map the Orléans and Gerlache Straits, which had been incorrectly charted by the Belgian expedition under Adrien de Gerlache in 1898. Every opportunity was seized to enlarge the expedition's botanical and geological collections during the numerous landings Lieutenant Duse made in order to finally solve the mystery of how the two channels were connected.

The charting of the area was completed on 5 December and the *Antarctic* then steamed towards Antarctic Sound which would lead to Nordenskjöld's wintering camp. As the ship approached the sound, however, the passage between the ice became narrower and narrower, and by the time the ship was under the shadow of Mount Bransfield the way ahead was completely blocked.

Andersson spent a day ashore on Louis-Philippe Land to reconnoitre the ice in the sound. Despite his report that Erebus and Terror Gulf was one dazzling sheet of ice, Larsen decided to try and ram his way through the sound. He was an expert at manoeuvring his vessel through pack ice and he managed to force the ship into the gulf before it was once again brought to a halt. After many days spent fruitlessly trying to find a way through the ice, it was decided to try to reach the wintering party by sledge.

The ship was shaken free from the pack ice and Larsen again headed for Antarctic Sound. On 29 December Andersson, Duse and Toralf Grunden were landed in Hope Bay. The three men immediately established a depot for the wintering party in case the ship was unable to reach the camp, and then set off on the 320-kilometre (200-mile) trek to Snow Hill Island.

Larsen and the rest of the men left on the *Antarctic* now tried once more to force a passage southeast. Some progress was made as a severe storm blew the ship willy-nilly southwards while she was still enclosed in the pack ice. Occasionally she was able to manoeuvre, but most of the time she drifted, first bow first, then sideways, then stern first. In this manner Paulet Island and more open water was reached before the ship was again imprisoned. For several days the party sat there waiting for the ice to break. Instead, the reverse happened.

'During the forenoon', wrote one of the scientists, Carl Skottsberg, in his diary on 10 January 1903, 'the pressure on the sides of the vessel — which had begun yesterday — could scarcely be marked, but after dinner, just as we sat down to a hand at cards, the ship began to tremble like an aspen leaf, and a violent crash sent us all up on deck to see what the matter was. The pressure was tremendous; the vessel rose higher and higher, while the ice was crushed to powder along her sides.'

As long as the ship rose above the pressure

of the ice she was safe, but later that night there was another tremendous crash and the *Antarctic* began to list to starboard. Everyone prepared to abandon ship, but luckily the pumps kept pace with the leak. For nearly two weeks the ship drifted southeastwards in the ice, the leak contained by a single pump.

On 16 January a fissure in the ice opened up and allowed her to come upright, then on 3 February pressure from a floe at her bows shook the *Antarctic's* stern loose and for the first time in weeks she was afloat. But this worsened the leak and all the pumps had to be started. Larsen decided to try to beach the ship on Paulet Island.

By 12 February the *Antarctic* had drifted into a large lead that had opened in the direction of Paulet Island. The sails were hoisted and the engine started, but soon the ice closed in again and brought her to a halt. This last effort had made the leak unmanageable and, as the water rose, the order was given to abandon ship.

By 8 am everything was ready. The crew took a last look at what was once their home, and with the water rising rapidly between decks, left the ship.

'We stand in a long row on the edge of the ice', wrote Skottsberg, 'and cannot take our eyes off her . . . The pumps are still going, but the sound grows fainter and fainter — she is breathing her last. She sinks slowly deeper and deeper . . . Now the name disappears from sight. Now the water is up to the rail, and, with a rattle, the sea and bits of ice rush in over her deck. That sound I can never forget, however long I may live.

'Now the blue and yellow colours are drawn down into the deep. The mizzen-mast strikes against the edge of our floe and is snapped off; the main-mast strikes and breaks; the crow's nest rattles against the ice-edge, and the streamer, with the name *Antarctic*, disappears in the waves. The bowsprit — the last mast-top — She is gone!'

The *Antarctic* sank 40 kilometres (25 miles) from Paulet Island and the shipwrecked party now began a nightmare journey to it across the shifting sea ice. The stores had to be ferried from floe to floe by whale boat and often the ice was so rough they had to hack a path with axes. Icebergs constantly threatened to break up the floes on which they camped. After 14 days and a six-hour row, they struggled ashore on Paulet Island on 28 February 1903.

The only glimmer of hope the party had was that Andersson had made arrangements for a rescue operation to be mounted if the *Antarctic* had not returned by the autumn. But everyone knew that no ship could reach the area until the following spring — a lifetime away.

Crew members inspect the ship's broken rudder and damaged planking as the ice presses in relentlessly on the trapped Antarctic.

The final moments of the Antarctic *as the masts disappeared beneath the waters of the Weddell Sea. Desperate work at the pumps had failed to keep the badly damaged ship afloat long enough to beach her on nearby Paulet Island.*

The marooned crew of the Antarctic *spent their first night on the ice in a makeshift tent. Strangely, the loss of the ship came as a relief. The suspense was over, and they knew that they would not see Sweden again that year. All slept sounder that night that they had for several months before.*

Andersson, Duse and Grunden celebrate midwinter day in their makeshift hut at Hope Bay with a banquet of fried meat and fruit soup.

Bleak Winter At Hope Bay

Three men eke out a precarious existence

While the* Antarctic *had been trying to find another route to pick up the wintering party on Snow Hill Island, the attempt being made by Gunnar Andersson, Lieutenant Duse and Toralf Grunden to reach Nordenskjöld's base on foot was also being frustrated by their inadequate knowledge of the area.

They struck off in a south-south-westerly direction which would, according to James Clark Ross's chart of the area, bring them to the inner part of Sidney Herbert Sound. However, instead of finding a continuation of the land after their trek across the eastern end of Louis-Philippe Land the three men found themselves at the frozen entrance of the Crown Prince Gustav Channel.

'We stand silent and perplexed', wrote Andersson, 'and gaze at the new and wonderful scene. Mile upon mile of snowy plain, such as we have never seen before, meets our eyes. One can actually imagine that a gigantic snow-clad city lies before us, with houses, and palaces in thousands, and in hundreds of changing, irregular forms — towers and spires, and all the wonders of the world. At first sight it appears incomprehensible, but it must be, after all, a bay covered with a frozen-in mass of numberless icebergs.'

The three men descended to the bay and set off on skis in the direction of Vega Island. After 15 hours marching, wet and exhausted, they reached the island and set up camp.

They were now convinced they were on James Ross Island and that therefore they would soon be able to reach Admiralty Sound, so after ascending a peak they were dismayed to find their way blocked by a stretch of open water they immediately recognised as Sidney Herbert Sound. But they could also see open water to the south, which meant that the *Antarctic* would, after all, be able to reach Snow Hill Island that summer. They turned northwards with lighter hearts.

Andersson had agreed with Carl Larsen that if the land party had not reached Snow Hill Island by 25 January, but the ship had, then Larsen was to assume the way had been blocked for the three men and that they were to be picked up from Hope Bay between 25 February and 10 March. If, on the other hand, the ship had not reached the wintering party by 10 February, but Andersson and his companions had, then Andersson was to lead both parties back to Hope Bay where they would wait to be picked up by the ship between the same two dates. In fact, the trio were back at their depot on 13 January. They settled down to await the arrival of the ship without a thought that anything could be amiss.

But the days became weeks and the weeks turned into months, and as summer gave way to autumn, the unthinkable occurred to them with increasing persistency. Something had gone wrong.

On 11 February they had taken the precaution of starting to build a winter hut with stone walls up to the full height of a man. The sledge was turned upside down on top of the walls as the basis of a roof, which was then covered with planks and an old tarpaulin. Inside, the tent was pitched to give them double protection from the bitter cold.

The first winter storm came early. It raged for days, delaying completion of the stone hut, but by 11 March, after the floor had been covered with penguin skins and the tent had been pitched, it was ready for occupation.

Once the tiny living space was completely snowed in, the temperature remained at a few degrees below freezing. This they became accustomed to, and indeed dreaded a thaw for it melted the rime on the walls and ceiling.

The three men began to hunt penguins to supplement their meagre supplies and eventu-

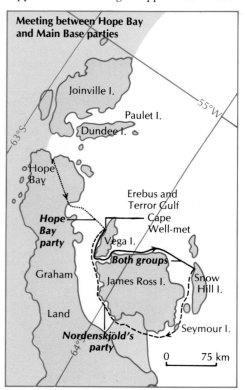

Meeting between Hope Bay and Main Base parties

Joinville I.
Paulet I.
Dundee I.
55°W
63°S
Hope Bay
Erebus and Terror Gulf
Hope Bay party
Cape Well-met
Vega I.
Both groups
Graham Land
James Ross I.
Snow Hill I.
Seymour I.
Nordenskjöld's party
64°S
0 75 km

Nordenskjöld walks forward to greet two men from the Hope Bay Party at Cape Well-met. Both men were filthy, covered in soot and blubber grease, and completely unrecognisable after surviving a desperate winter in their tiny hut.

ally killed 700 of them. Occasionally they caught a seal, and another welcome variation was the few fish they caught with an improvised fish hook and line through the ice holes.

The three took it in turns to cook and they established a ritual of thanking the man on duty with the utmost courtesy. They also took it in turns to entertain one another in the evenings. Thus organised, and with the constant work needed just to stay alive, the winter, at least according to Andersson, passed quickly and amicably.

At long last spring arrived, and after Andersson had reconnoitred their route to see that the channel was frozen up to Vega Island the three men thankfully left their winter quarters on 29 September.

By now all of them were in a filthy condition. Besides their tattered boots, which continually needed repairs, their clothes were ragged and dirty and their faces and beards blackened with soot from the cooking fires and the blubber fat they had burnt to give some light and warmth.

No sooner had they begun their journey, however, than they were caught in a storm which trapped them in their tiny tent.

'The storm grew more and more violent', wrote Andersson, 'while the cold increased in intensity, and during the following night the tent-wall fell on my head and the snow packed itself over me, so that I lay fast as though in a vice. I was not released from my position until the storm had subsided, some 30 hours later.'

When the wind subsided sufficiently the three men struggled on. By 6 October they reached the shoreline and began their trek across the sea ice to Vega Island. On the second day they deviated slightly from their route and to their delight were able to see that already the ice in Erebus and Terror Gulf was breaking up. Conditions for a ship were more favourable now than they had been during the previous January.

Heartened by what they had seen, the three men ploughed on towards Vega Island. Then occurred one of those dramatic changes in temperature that make the Antarctic climate so treacherous. The wind, which had been blowing from the north, died away, and after a few minutes of calm began to blow from the south in ferocious gusts which lowered the temperature to far below freezing. The men's boots became like concrete and their wet clothes froze on them so that they creaked with every step they took.

They reached Vega Island on 9 October and after an anxious search found the depot left the previous summer. The next two days were spent nursing Grunden's frostbite, which Duse was also beginning to suffer from in his little toes. But this did not stop them exploring the island, and Duse was soon able to confirm that Sidney Herbert Sound did indeed connect with the Crown Prince Gustav Channel, but that any descent to it from the island would prove to be very difficult.

They therefore decided to retrace their steps and to begin the last lap of their journey to meet up with their colleagues at the wintering camp via the sea ice around the island. They reached Cape Dreyfus — which, with good reason, they were soon to rename Cape Wellmet — on 12 October.

'At 1 pm', wrote Andersson, 'we had halted at the cape in order to prepare dinner. Groups of seals lay here and there upon the ice; we had just passed by a couple of the animals, and a large family lay some distance further out.

'"What the deuce can those seals be, standing up there bolt upright?" says one of us, pointing to some small, dark objects far away on the ice, in towards the channel.

'"They are moving", cries another.

'A delirious eagerness seizes us. A field-glass is pulled out. "*It's men! It's men!*" we shout.'

At long last the Hope Bay party were back in touch with their leader. But what had happened to the *Antarctic* and her crew?

The Hope Bay hut before the outside passage was complete. The walls were made from stone and the roof from an old tarpaulin. A tent was erected inside and the walls were plastered with a mixture of snow and sea water to seal them.

Icebergs, penguins and pack ice — the bleak scenery in Hope Bay in summer.

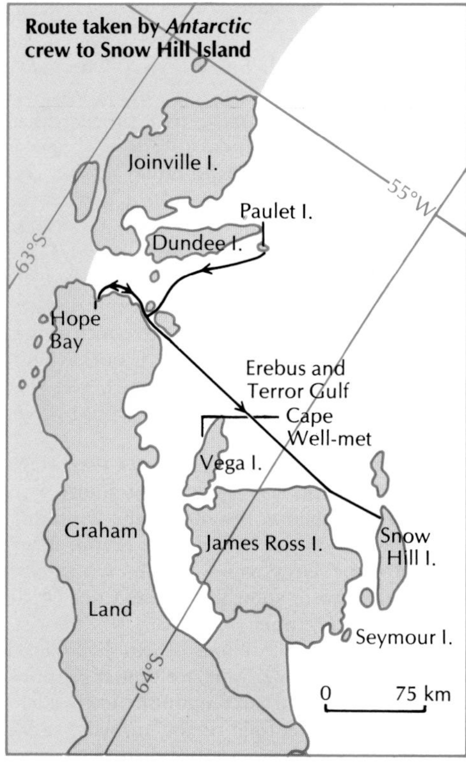

A REMARKABLE REUNION

Rescue ends separation

What in fact had happened to the stranded men from the* Antarctic *– how they had existed through the terrible winter months of 1903 in a makeshift hut on Paulet Island, and had then sent out a second party to contact Nordenskjöld – is another epic story of survival against all the odds.

A few ruined stone walls are all that remain today of the Paulet Island hut in which the crew of the Antarctic *spent the winter of 1903. Except for some tourists in summer, few people visit the island.*

The hut on Paulet Island, and beyond in the bay the Uruguay *which had been sent by the Argentinean Government to search for Nordenskjöld.*

Paulet Island consisted entirely of volcanic rock and basalt. In its middle was a circular lake into which the sides of the hills fell abruptly. Their outside slopes were also very steep but there was some flat ground near the shore which looked ideal for building the marooned party's winter quarters. However, it was soon found exposed to winds so a less level but more sheltered spot was chosen nearby.

The marooned men spent their first full day ashore on Paulet Island, 1 March, hunting penguins and seals, for though they had managed to salvage a quantity of stores it was quite insufficient to sustain all of them for long. It was calculated that at least 3000 to 4000 penguins would be needed to build up an adequate stock of food, but the colony on the island diminished daily as it was the moulting season and once a bird acquired new feathers it left. In the end, only 1100 had been killed, which in fact proved sufficient.

Work was also started on a stone hut. It was an exhausting and arduous task finding and carrying rocks to the chosen site for the double-walled building, which, when finished, measured ten by seven metres (34 x 22 ft). Most of its length was taken up with the dwelling room with the last 3.6 metres (12 ft) being used as the kitchen. Two low stone beds, two metres (seven feet) wide, were constructed along the sides of the living room which took the men's sleeping bags, 10 on each.

By the middle of March winter storms were constant, one of them blowing away the kitchen roof, and often it was not possible to leave the confines of the stone hut for days. Easter Eve was celebrated with helpings of rice porridge, but otherwise the diet was a monotonous round of penguin dishes occasionally relieved with seal meat and fish. Another shortage acutely felt was tobacco and the Second Mate concocted a vile mixture of snuff and dried tea leaves for his pipe.

The winter days dragged on in a wearisome cycle of sleeping, cooking, eating and hunting, with the evenings spent in talking or reading out loud from one of the few books they had brought with them. Sometimes they had a sing-song, but their outward humour at their predicament – their hang-gallows wit as Carl Skottsberg called it – hid a deep-seated fear of what would become of them.

'Many hundred dreams have been dreamed in our island', wrote Skottsberg, 'but I do not know if they helped to brighten our existence. They grouped themselves around two objects – food and rescue. Why, we could dream through a whole dinner, from the soup to the dessert, and waken to be cruelly disappointed. How many times did one not see the relief vessel in our visions – sometimes as a large ship, sometimes as nothing but a little sloop? And we knew the persons on board; they spoke about our journey; took us in their arms; patted us on the back . . .'

But reality was never far away in the terrible storms that raged outside, in the dwindling supply of food they had brought from the ship, and in the haggard faces of their companions. On 7 June Ole Wennersgaard, who had been sick for some weeks, died. Sorrowfully, they buried him deep in a snowdrift until he could be properly interred in the spring.

The months dragged on until at the end of October it could be seen from the top of the crater hill that the ice in the gulf had broken up and the way was clear for a boat to try to reach the three men they had left at Hope Bay at the beginning of the year. Carl Larsen was to be in charge of this perilous trip. He took with him five of the *Antarctic's* crew and the fervent prayer of those he left behind that he would be able to contact a rescue ship.

Larsen set off at dawn on 31 October, but by afternoon he had been forced to pull his boat on to a small ice floe to escape the rising wind and sea. The storm increased in violence during the night and the floe tipped, nearly sending them all to their deaths. Twice they were forced to scramble to a safer position.

Then the weather improved and although progress was agonisingly slow they eventually reached Hope Bay on 4 November. There they found the depot and the stone hut. Attached to the hut Larsen found a board on which had been written that Gunnar Andersson, Lieutenant Duse and Toralf Grunden had wintered there. A sketch map in a flask showed Larsen the route by which at that very time the three men were again trying to reach Snow Hill Island, a journey Larsen now saw he and his party would have to make, too, by water.

Bad weather delayed their departure for three days before they were once more able to launch their boat into the ice-cold waters of Antarctic Sound.

'We broke up at 4 am', wrote Larsen, 'and then rowed the whole day in the direction of Sidney Herbert Bay. Only here and there did we meet with scattered ice. The fine weather continued the whole of the next night, and we were making rapid progress towards our goal when, just as we passed Cape Gage and came into Admiralty Sound we met with a hinder [sic] which could not be forced by the boat. We found the ice extending in a straight line right over the bay towards Cockburn Island and Cape Seymour, and inwards across the whole of the sound. So at 2 am we drew the boat up on the ice and retired to rest.'

As Larsen and his companions struggled across the gulf, not far away a rescue ship was buffeting through the ice around Joinville Island. There had been growing anxiety in Sweden and Argentina about the expedition's safety. The ships belonging to the German and English expeditions had only narrowly escaped the unusually dangerous ice conditions of that summer. The general consensus had grown that the Swedish ship had been trapped in the vicinity of Snow Hill Island, or possibly even lost. Arrangements were therefore made for France, Sweden and Argentina to send ships into the area during the following spring.

Lieutenant Julian Irizar, the Argentinian naval attaché in London, was chosen to lead the Argentinian rescue expedition. An old Argentinian corvette, the *Uruguay*, was extensively refitted and reinforced for the passage south.

While the *Uruguay* was preparing to steam to the winter camp Nordenskjöld returned there with the Hope Bay party. Then, on 26 October, accompanied by Gunnar Andersson and José Sobral, he undertook another sledge journey to Seymour Island where the other two inscribed their names on a boathook and raised it as a signal on a cairn of rocks.

On 7 November, the very same day Larsen began his epic row across Erebus and Terror Gulf, two other members of the wintering party, Gösta Bodman and Gustaf Akerlund, left the camp for Seymour Island.

Also on 7 November, Irizar, having reached the ice shelf off Seymour Island, put ashore a small party to explore. The men returned the same afternoon in great excitement to report the discovery of the boathook planted by Andersson and Sobral on the signal cairn. Irizar inched his ship round the edge of the ice until a tent was seen on the shore. Irizar, accompanied by Lieutenant Yalour, landed, and after waking the tent's occupants – Bodman and Akerlund – the two officers followed the Swedes across the ice to the winter camp.

Nordenskjöld's delight and astonishment at meeting the Argentinians was only dimmed when Irizar told him they had not seen the *Antarctic* nor had any idea of her whereabouts. After agreeing that the winter camp should be disbanded immediately so that the search for the missing ship could start, Nordenskjöld was preparing himself for bed when the dogs started barking. He went outside and there to his amazement he found Bodman greeting Larsen and his party who had just completed a 24-kilometre (15-mile) trek across the ice.

'No pen', wrote Nordenskjöld, 'can describe the boundless joy of this first moment. ... I learned at once that our dear old ship was no more in existence, but for the instant I could feel nothing but joy when I saw amongst us these men, on whom I had only a few minutes before been thinking with feelings of the greatest despondency.'

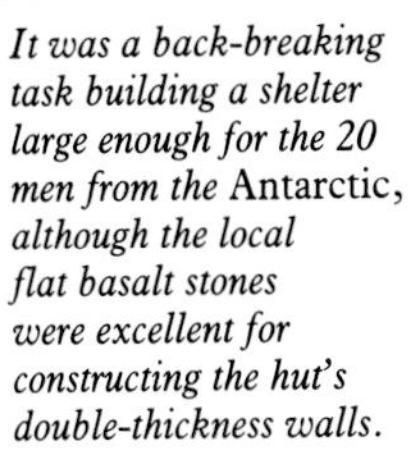

It was a back-breaking task building a shelter large enough for the 20 men from the Antarctic, *although the local flat basalt stones were excellent for constructing the hut's double-thickness walls.*

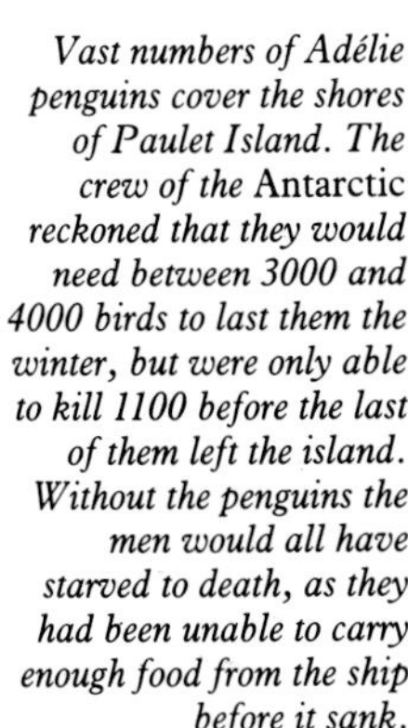

Vast numbers of Adélie penguins cover the shores of Paulet Island. The crew of the Antarctic *reckoned that they would need between 3000 and 4000 birds to last them the winter, but were only able to kill 1100 before the last of them left the island. Without the penguins the men would all have starved to death, as they had been unable to carry enough food from the ship before it sank.*

The crew celebrated Midwinter's Day 1902 with a barrel of porter donated by Messrs Guinness. The celebration almost turned into a riot because the water had frozen and the men were drinking neat spirits.

Scotia *anchored at Port Stanley in the Falkland Islands. The ship returned there after its first winter.*

INDEPENDENT SCOT

William Bruce fulfils his ambition

The 1902-04 Scottish National Antarctic Expedition not only discovered a new part of the Antarctic continent, but a host of oceanographic, geographical and botanical information.

The expedition was planned, organised and led by a young Edinburgh medical student, William S. Bruce, whose consuming passion for oceanography was equalled only by his love for his country. 'While science was the talisman of the expedition', Bruce wrote afterwards, 'Scotland was emblazoned on its flag'.

The spur to Bruce's ambition to lead a Scottish expedition to Antarctica was his visit there in 1893 in a Dundee whaler. In 1900 he was offered the post of naturalist in Robert Scott's expedition; he declined, not just because he was determined to lead his own, but because he refused to be involved in anything as sensational as attempting to reach the South Pole.

The British Government refused to fund Bruce's expedition, and this eventually made its funding a national issue. Two Scottish brothers, the Coats, opened the fund with £11 000, and from this point on Bruce sought only Scottish finance.

In 1901 Bruce was able to buy a sturdy Norwegian whaler which was extensively refitted in a Scottish shipyard and renamed the *Scotia*. She was put under the command of an experienced Arctic navigator, Thomas Robertson, and had a crew of 25.

Bruce took with him a zoologist, a botanist, a meteorologist, a taxidermist, a medical officer who was also a geologist, a bacteriologist, and a bagpipe player who acted as laboratory assistant. Together they made a formidable team. The expedition's main objectives were to undertake extensive hydrographic work in the Weddell Sea during the summer months of 1903 and 1904, and to survey the South Orkneys and study their wildlife.

The *Scotia* sailed from Troon on Sunday 2 November 1902 to the strains of 'Auld Lang Syne'. The local paper later complained the ship had left on the Sabbath with the farewell crowd singing profane songs instead of psalms!

The *Scotia* reached the Falkland Islands on 6 January 1903 and stayed for three weeks. On 3 February the South Orkneys were sighted, and the next day a visit was made to Saddle Island, which had not been landed on since Dumont d'Urville had gone ashore there in 1838.

When they set sail again progress was slow and tedious. It was not until they arrived in the area of South Thule Island in the Sandwich Group that they could entertain hopes of a rapid run south. But the closeness of the pack ice soon began to hamper the *Scotia*'s progress. After forcing her way through the ice she was finally held fast in the position 70°25'S, 17°12'W on 22 February. The temperature fell to −10°C (14°F) and new ice was forming too quickly to contemplate continuing south. When the ship finally shook free of the ice it took her six days to progress half a degree of latitude to the north.

Any thought of finding a more open passage southwards was soon abandoned in favour of finding a suitable wintering place for the ship at the South Orkneys. The chart showed that Spence Harbour looked suitable, but it turned out to be only a small indentation. After another two uncomfortable days at sea a well-protected anchorage was found in a bay on the south side of Laurie Island, a haven they later called Scotia Bay. Within three days the bay was totally filled with pack ice and a week later was completely frozen over.

From the moment they anchored everyone was kept fully occupied. A snowbank had to be built around the ship to keep out the worst of the weather, and on shore construction of a 3.6-metre (12-ft) stone cairn, the starting point for their survey, was begun. On one side of this the carpenter erected the wooden magnetic observatory and painted it a cheerful red,

It took some of the scientists a while to find their sea legs. Harvey Pirie recorded two diary entries: Nov. 9, 'Sick and miserable'; Nov. 10, 'Very sick and very miserable'.

Harvey Pirie (left), geologist, bacteriologist and medical officer, and Alastair Ross, taxidermist.

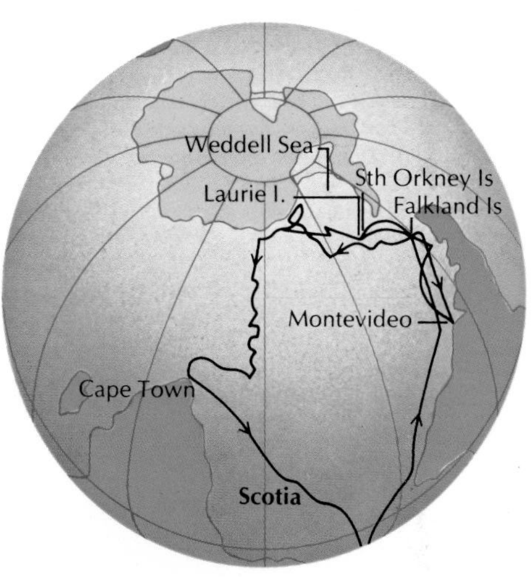

Little was known about the desolate South Orkneys before the Scotia*'s visit in 1903-04. Few expeditions had visited the islands since their discovery in 1821 by Captain Powell.*

David Wilton, a naturalist, practising handstands on the deck of the ship. After leaving Madeira the weather became much warmer and the men slept on deck.

and on the other side work on a stone hut was soon under way. Fish traps had to be laid, skeletons cleaned and bird skinning undertaken, and what wildlife remained during the winter months carefully studied.

All this hard work did not deny the members of the expedition their recreation. They had brought their skis and when weather and time permitted they would climb to the top of a nearby glacier and ski down it.

Although the weather was bitterly cold, small parties were sent out on to the land for short periods from July onwards where they carried out survey work and botanical and meteorological studies. The first one, experimental in nature, travelled with the aid of a dog sledge, to Delta Island at the eastern extremity of Scotia Bay and stayed there eight days taking soundings through the ice, and testing equipment. The ship's medical officer, Dr Pirie, was one of the party and he described a typical day after rising at seven and eating a breakfast of hot porridge, bacon, biscuits and a large mug of cocoa.

'Soon after nine we sallied forth with the sounding apparatus, measuring line, and prismatic compass for surveying . . .

'About thirty soundings we found as much as could be done in a day: each involved cutting a hole through ice at least thirty inches [760 mm] thick, often rather more . . .

'Lunch was taken out on the floe: this consisted of biscuit, butter (which was quite hard and crumbly), cheese, a stick of chocolate, *and* a pipe . . .

'Dusk at six found us once more back in camp. The two lucky ones snugged down in their sacks, while the third cooked dinner. This meal consisted of more biscuit, thawed meat, and a large mug of tea. How the thoughts of that hot tea kept us going all day! The recollection of it is the strongest I have of our camping-out experiences — how both hands having clasped the cup so as not to lose any heat, the warm glow gradually spread and spread, till at last even the toes felt warm ere the cup was drained. Truly it was a cup that cheered.

'The day's work was then plotted out by the light of a guttering candle, and a pipe and chat passed away an hour ere we wooed the drowsy god. The moisture from our breaths and from the cooking stove of course condensed as snow on the walls of the tent, and a considerable amount found its way into our sacks. This gave us a good deal of thawing to do in bed; but notwithstanding that and the howling wind which sometimes threatened to carry the whole tent away, we slept the sleep of the just.'

Winter quarters Laurie Island

Laurie I.
0
1000 km
Scotia
Sea
Weddell
Sea
Antarctic
peninsula

0
5 km
44°40'W
60°46'S
Browns
Bay
Pirie
Peninsula
LAURIE I.
Jessie
Bay
The
beach
Scotia anchorage
Scotia Bay
Uruguay
Cove
Mossman
Peninsula
Cape
Robertson

THE SCOTIA'S SECOND CRUISE

Exploration in the treacherous Weddell Sea

The Scottish National expedition contributed immeasurably to the previous fund of data on the Antarctic. Braving constant bitter cold and frequent blizzards, the scientists of the* Scotia *gathered a wealth of new information and more previously unknown specimens than any expedition that had gone before.

Spring 1903 on Laurie Island brought seals, sea birds and penguins, providing the men of the *Scotia* much-needed fresh meat and eggs as well as subjects for study. But scientific work was still hampered by the extremely cold, foggy weather.

Also, the *Scotia* was still bound in the ice, so the snowbank around the ship was cleared and work began on cutting a canal through the ice to open water. Despite the use of gunpowder, progress was slow as the ice was often five or six metres (16 to 20 ft) thick. By late November the canal was still not completed, but eventually a wind came in from the northeast and the ice began to break up. The *Scotia* was freed on 22 November, and on 27 November set off north, leaving a party of six ashore.

After a short stay at Port Stanley the *Scotia* reached Buenos Aires on Christmas Eve. While she was being thoroughly refitted there, successful negotiations were carried out for the Argentinian Government to take over the running of Omond House — as the stone hut was called — as a meteorological base. So when the *Scotia* set sail again for the south she had aboard three Argentinians.

The shore team had managed to carry on the scientific work in the meantime despite excessively cold weather. They were the first to properly observe colonies of penguins.

With the arrival of the *Scotia* the shore party re-embarked except for the meteorologist R. C. Mossman, and the cook, both of whom had volunteered to remain with the three Argentinians until the following summer.

The *Scotia* now made its second voyage into the Weddell Sea. The Antarctic Circle was crossed at a longitude of about 32°W, but the pack ice did not hinder the ship until the morning of 3 March, when she was brought up short in a latitude of 72°18'S. On taking a sounding it was found that the depth was about half that expected, and Robertson immediately climbed to the crow's nest and in great excitement reported land ahead.

After managing to break out of the ice that

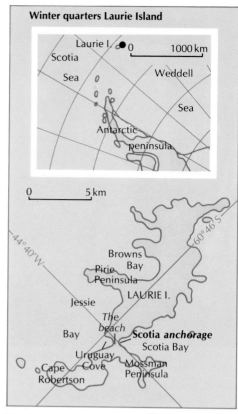

The six-man shore party pose proudly under the Scottish flag outside Omond House. The base was taken over by the Argentinean Government after the last of the Scottish party left in January 1905, and has been constantly manned ever since.

bound her, the *Scotia* was able to force her way further south until a lofty ice shelf stretching in a northeasterly, southwesterly direction, could plainly be seen. Though the ship was unable to approach nearer to it than three kilometres (two miles), during the next 10 days she followed it to the southwest for 240 kilometres (150 miles). Soundings confirmed that the expedition had discovered a stretch of hitherto unknown land. Bruce called it Coats Land after the two brothers who had funded the expedition. They had no means of knowing whether it was an island or part of the Antarctic continent but Bruce guessed, rightly, that it was a continuation of Enderby Land.

The sighting of this new stretch of land overturned Sir John Murray's assumption — based on Ross's soundings, which this expedition was to prove incorrect — that land at this point was 160 kilometres (100 miles) further south.

While skirting the coastline the *Scotia* was once more beset by ice during a blizzard, and she was very nearly crushed. Luckily, the ice went under the ship, lifting her more than a metre (three ft) out of the water. When the storm abated they found they had been driven into a bight in the ice shelf and were now at a latitude of 74°01′S, showing that Weddell had indeed been unlucky not to have discovered the continent just to the west 80 years before.

The party now had to face the possibility of being trapped where they lay throughout the winter months.

'Had not the mental horizon been somewhat cloudy', wrote Pirie afterwards, 'nothing could have been finer than our situation. The air was calm, crisp, and beautifully clear; from the crow's nest one could see to the north only huge bergs — "ice mast high going floating by" — and pack-ice, with every here and there a black dot where a seal or a penguin lay. To the south lay the Great Barrier, sublime and mysterious, inclining one to be in pensive mood brooding over its awful silent loneliness; but the hum of voices from the deck below, or the shouts ascending from the large floe nearby, which served for the nonce [present time] as a football field, soon brought the wandering thoughts back to the worries of our microcosmos, stranded on the edge of the chaos of ice.'

Luckily, on 12 March, some wind came in from the southwest and the ice began to break up. By evening the *Scotia* was free once more, and Robertson was able to make his way into more open water. A course to the northeast was set in order to investigate the veracity of Ross's soundings at 68°32′S, 12°49′W which had so led Sir John Murray astray. As they suspected, with land so near, the bottom was found at 2660 fathoms (4800 m; 16 000 ft) although Ross had reported no bottom at 4000 fathoms (7300 m; 24 000 ft). Ascertaining whether or not the 'Ross Deep' existed was the last of the expedition's objectives, and the *Stotia* now turned for home.

She eventually dropped anchor in Kingstown Harbour, Northern Ireland, on 15 July 1904. The party received a tremendous welcome from the local people, from the press, and from the Coats brothers who were there in their yacht to greet them. The King sent a congratulatory telegram, guns were fired, and the blare of foghorns mingled with the cheers of the crowd.

OMOND HOUSE THREATENED BY A STORM

Mossman, the three Argentinians and the cook, left behind on Laurie Island, carried on the expedition's meteorological and scientific work. As winter approached once more, they built a breakwater in front of Omond House to protect it from storms from the southeast, the bay's unprotected quarter. But on 3 April a southeast gale which rose to hurricane force not only demolished all their work but severely undermined Omond House.

'Every wave we thought would give the finishing stroke', wrote Mossman, 'and to all appearance there was little hope of the southern half of the house standing ... We rapidly collected clothing, bedding, documents, and some other necessary articles, which were placed in the storeroom, and vacated the building. The tents were taken over to the highest point of the north beach as a precautionary measure, but owing to the strong wind could not be pitched. Soon after eight o'clock we gathered together in the magnetic hut, where we awaited the apparently inevitable demolition of the southern half of the house with a composure due doubtless to the numbing effect of the unexpected situation. Everyone was soaked to the skin.'

Fortunately, the wind and sea began to subside and no further damage was done.

The party endured the tedious winter months until the *Uruguay* arrived on New Year's Eve.

The piper and the penguin. Harvey Pirie wrote of the scene: 'To test the effect of music on them [the emperor penguins], Piper Kerr played to one on his pipes ... but neither rousing marches, lively reels, nor melancholy laments seemed to have any effect on these lethargic, phlegmatic birds, there was no excitement, no sign of appreciation or disapproval, only sleepy indifference.'

The Scotia *firmly frozen into the ice of Scotia Bay, Laurie Island, where she remained for eight months from March to November 1903.*

Pirie and Ross with some penguins brought back to the ship so that their calls could be recorded on a phonograph. This expedition made the first thorough study of penguins.

THE INNER MAN

The importance of food in Antarctica's hostile environment

Since the beginning of polar exploration food has been both a problem and a pleasure for expedition personnel. Many early explorers did not have enough to eat and were preoccupied by hunger. Their rations were uninteresting, unappetising and not very nutritious. Although modern rations are excellent, food is still one of the topics most discussed by Antarctic personnel, especially if the food is monotonous or badly prepared.

Seal meat drying in the rigging of Scott's ship Discovery. *Although the dark meat looked unpalatable, the men soon grew to thoroughly enjoy seal steaks. Nobody, however, was ever recorded as having acquired a taste for blubber, which tasted and smelt unpleasant.*

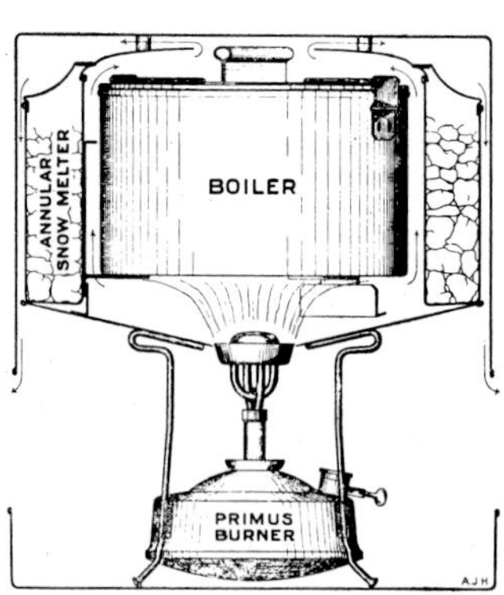

Each member of Scott's ill-fated polar party was expected to live for one day on the rations illustrated (far left) — they are (left to right) cocoa, pemmican, sugar, biscuits, butter and tea. These quantities were reduced as the party became weaker and slower in reaching depots. Hot food was prepared on a Nansen sledging cooker (left).

Problems of size and weight influenced the choice of certain foods for Antarctic expeditions. Sailing ships travelling to Antarctica, and dog sledging or man-hauling groups leaving the coastal bases to work on the plateau, could not carry unlimited supplies of food. Rations had to be light, not too bulky, and easy to prepare on a Primus stove using small amounts of fuel. In addition food had to be standardised for ease of handling into 'man-day' packs. The packaging, too, had to be strong and light. Being concentrated and light with a slow deterioration rate, pemmican became the basic polar ration. Originally a food of the North American Indians, pemmican was made from dried and pummelled lean caribou or buffalo meat mixed to a paste with fat and berries. Adapted from this recipe over the years, pemmican was still in use in the 1960s, together with post-war derivatives. Pemmican was nauseating to many, while others found its gritty consistency hard to take.

Base rations at the turn of the century generally offered good variety and enough to eat. This could not be said of field rations, which were very spartan. Although advice was sought from dietetic specialists, practical experience led to changes in the ration scales. Three different diets were used by Wilson, Bowers and Cherry-Garrard on their midwinter journey to Cape Crozier in 1911. These consisted of tea and butter together with half pemmican and biscuit, mainly pemmican or mainly biscuit. Experiments with these diets caused Scott to change the food he took on his journey to the pole. He took pemmican, biscuits, butter, cocoa, sugar and tea with chocolate and cereals as extras during the early part of the trip, and raisins for special occasions.

Sledging rations eaten by members of Douglas Mawson's 1911-14 expedition were 340 g (12 oz) plasmon biscuit, 230 g (8 oz) pemmican, 57 g (2 oz) butter, 57 g (2 oz) plasmon chocolate, 142 g (5 oz) glaxo (dried milk), 113 g (4 oz) sugar, 28 g (1 oz) cocoa, and 7 g (0.25 oz) tea. About 900 g (2 lb) of food was carried for each man per day, and when reconstituted with water this doubled in weight. A good sledging diet must provide at least one hot, nourishing, and filling meal per day. This was traditionally a 'hoosh' — a porridge-like mixture of pemmican, dried biscuit and water, brought to the boil and served hot. By varying the contents, 'different' meals could be prepared.

Amundsen even calculated on eating his sledging dogs. They were consumed by the men and the surviving dogs, in accordance with a pre-determined schedule.

Depots were generally laid in advance for a major trip, but the weight of food that had to be carried was still considerable. On the Australasian Antarctic Expedition 1911-14, the quantity of food for three men for nine weeks amounted to 215 kg (475 lb). They also had 11.5 kg (25 lb) of special food or 'perks', and 317.5 kg (700 lb) of dried dog food. The Nansen cooker, Primus heater and spares weighed over 11.5 kg (25 lb), while 27 litres (6 gallons) of kerosene in 4.5-litre (1-gallon) tins amounted to 27 kg (60 lb).

In 1902 Scott wrote on the vexed question of food: 'The issue is clear enough: one desires to provide each man each day with just sufficient food to keep up his strength, and not an ounce beyond. It is certainly suggestive of a normally overfed condition in civilised mankind that when it is reduced to this allowance it is conscious of much inconvenience from the pangs of hunger. The great difficulty for the sledge organiser is to arrive at this happy mean... If one really goes into this matter with some thoroughness, as I have had the leisure to do, one is involved in a bewildering array of facts and figures which it would be hopeless to attempt to display with clearness to the reader... In my first year of sledging work I went south with something considerably under the allowance given above [811 grams; 28.6 oz per man per day], when my party suffered much from hunger and grew decidedly weaker; in the second year, with the allowance shown, our strength was fairly well maintained, but there was still no doubt about our hunger. There can be little question, therefore, that polar sledging ranks an easy first as a hunger-producing employment...'

Scott's rations in 1910-13 gave around 17.6-19.3 MJ (4200-4600 kcal) from 200-250 g (7-8.8 oz) of protein, 180-210 g (6.3-7.4 oz) of fat, and 420-460 g (14.8-16.2 oz) of carbohydrate. This did not provide the necessary nutritional and calorific requirements.

Whether a person is physically active or asleep he or she still needs nutritional energy to balance energy expenditure. If the food provides more energy than is being expended, then this is stored as fat. If, on the other hand, activity uses more, then weight will be lost. As well as energy in the form of calories, food must supply essential nutrients such as vitamins, minerals and protein. In one day a 65 kg (143 lb) man expends 2.1 MJ (500 kcal) of energy at rest, between 4.6-8.0 MJ (1100-1900 kcal) of energy depending on the work being done — light to heavy — and between 3.0-6.3 MJ (700-1500 kcal) of energy when not working. This means that a man doing light work will require around 11.3 MJ (2700 kcal) of food energy daily, and a very active man will require 14.6 MJ (3500 kcal). A woman of 55 kg (121 lb) has a daily requirement of 8.4 MJ (2000 kcal)-10.9 MJ (2600 kcal) depending on her level of activity.

Physical activity may increase daily energy requirements by 2.1-4.2 MJ (500-1000 kcal). Hard work such as man-hauling or dog sledging in Antarctica, with its extreme climate and difficult terrain, requires a considerable increase in nutritional energy. Cold-weather clothing and footwear, which may weigh over 10 kg (22 lb) without the addition of frozen sweat, further increases the amount of energy used. Some estimates have suggested that approximately half the food eaten when the temperature is around −40°C (−40°F) is needed to keep the body at its normal temperature and to avoid hypothermia.

There is no agreement, even today, on what constitutes an ideal polar diet, and the ratio of protein, fat and carbohydrate varies between 10-20 per cent protein, 36-45 per cent fat and 42-51 per cent carbohydrate. Some people think that the Antarctic environment increases the appetite for fat, but this is not proven. The ideal balance varies between individuals and also according to the amount of work being done. For sledging in Antarctica the daily requirement is probably 20.9 MJ (5000 kcal) of nutritional energy.

A polar diet, like any diet, is satisfactory if it provides enough energy for a person's needs, plus the essential nutrients such as protein, minerals and vitamins. A lack of vitamin C and depletion of the B group vitamins in all Scott's sledging rations must have contributed to the eventual tragedy. The party's only source of vitamin C was fresh pony meat, and this was not enough to ward off scurvy. Little was known at that time about the role of vitamins. Even today, despite experimental work which has shown that animals in cold regions have an increased need for vitamin C, this has not been shown in humans. Many nations operating in Antarctica, however, give additional vitamin C during winter.

A lack of fuel often prevented field parties from melting sufficient ice to provide the water their bodies needed. Dry air and increased sweating from hard work further reduced body fluid reserves. Some groups would return with large weight losses. Part of this may have been due to lack of calories, but on some occasions over six kilograms (14 lb) were restored in the first 24 hours. The major part of this must have been water.

Wildlife in the form of seals, penguins, birds and fish is common around the coast of Antarctica in spring and summer, but with the onset of winter all leave except the emperor penguins. Many parties, especially those that became marooned, depended on the food they could catch to survive. Scott's Northern Party, for example, survived a winter in an ice cave with only summer clothes and rations for two months. They ate penguins and seals, the blubber of which also gave them heat and light.

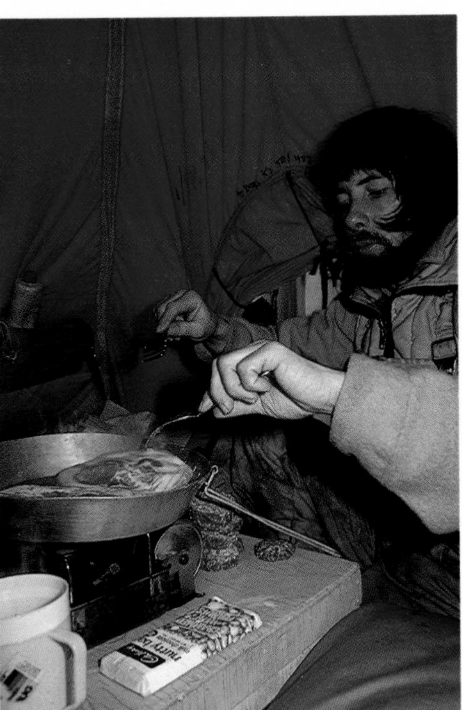

Modern expedition members, even those involved in field work, want for little in the way of food. Frozen foods are easily carried and quickly prepared on a Primus.

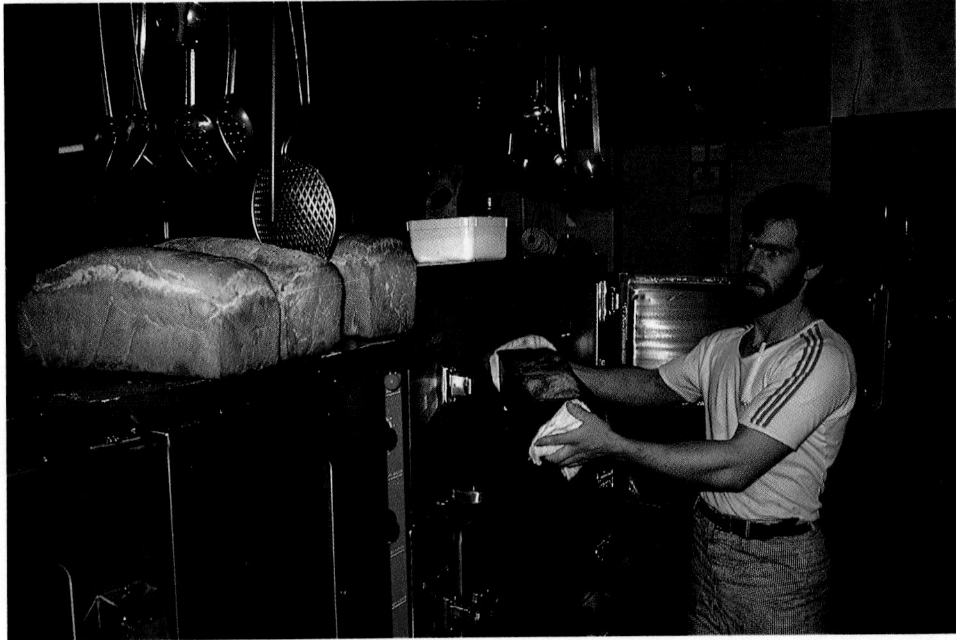

Bread being baked at New Zealand's Scott base. The food available on a modern base rivals that served up in a good hotel or restaurant.

A section through a frozen seal carcase — now used to feed huskies — showing the thickness of blubber. Although few could bring themselves to eat blubber, it was often used to provide heat and light, especially in emergencies.

Penguins' eggs were a regular and very popular item on many early Antarctic menus. These men, with their bags of eggs, were members of Scott's 1901-04 Discovery *expedition.*

Local animals were a regular item on the menus of many post-war national expeditions, but there was always a prejudice against eating them. With present attitudes to conservation most modern expeditions avoid eating any native Antarctic birds or mammals.

Modern techniques of processing and packaging food allow field groups to have a diet similar to that available at a large base station. Fresh frozen meat, vegetables and fruit, and freeze-dried rations, can be easily prepared. Large tractor trains have excellent kitchens and some camps even have dishwashers.

Aircraft and more frequent ships have now guaranteed fresh supplies every year, thus reducing the need for large emergency food dumps and the possibility of having to eat some items more than a year old. Some bases now have greenhouses and with hydroponic techniques are able to produce vegetables.

THE HONOUR OF FRANCE

Jean Charcot invests his fortune in a dream

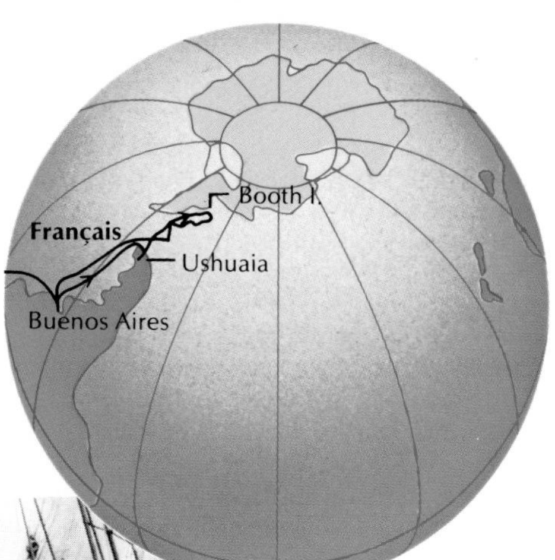

In the early 1900s, a young Frenchman by the name of Jean-Baptiste Charcot followed with interest the progress of three nationally sponsored expeditions to the Antarctic: the Englishman Robert Scott aboard the* Discovery*; the German Erich von Drygalski on the* Gauss*; and the Swede Otto Nordenskjöld on the* Antarctic*. But what part would France play in this quest to the south? None, it seemed — unless Charcot himself set his sights on Antarctica.

Born on 15 July 1867, at Neuilly-sur-Seine, near Paris, Jean-Baptiste Charcot was the son of the distinguished neurologist, Professor Jean Martin Charcot. Obedient to his father's wishes, he had also become a doctor, but he devoted every free moment to his first love — sailing and the sea. In his early twenties, he bought an eight-metre (26-ft) yacht, the *Courlis*. Soon after, he exchanged this for a larger boat, the 15-tonne *Pourquoi-Pas?*, the *Why Not?*.

In 1893, France and family alike mourned the death of Professor Charcot. His son continued to work as a doctor, although the call of the sea became ever more insistent. During the summer months of 1900 he sailed around Ireland, displaying exceptional skill as a navigator. A few months later he made a successful voyage to the Faroes, and thought about leading an expedition to Greenland.

In 1896 he had married the granddaughter

Charcot's ship, the Français *at the quayside in Le Havre. Charcot spent his own personal fortune in having her built and equipped. The staff comprised six unpaid officers and a crew of 14 men, including five sailors, three stokers, a cook and a steward.*

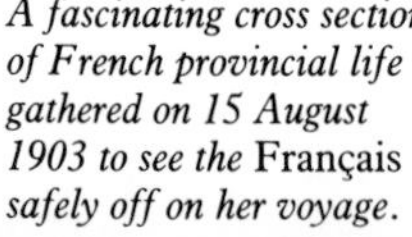

A fascinating cross section of French provincial life gathered on 15 August 1903 to see the Français *safely off on her voyage.*

of the poet and novelist Victor Hugo. But the young couple were incompatible, Charcot's wife being unable to share in his dream. Nevertheless, Jean-Baptiste Charcot felt compelled to follow his new vocation.

On the death of his father he had inherited a considerable fortune: 400 000 gold francs. Along with this he had been left a Fragonard painting — *La Pacha* — and was perhaps the wealthiest general practitioner in France.

But instead of using the money for his own home comforts, he chose to invest it in his dream. His sights set on the north, he financed the construction of a vessel, the *Français,* by the well-known shipwright Gauthier. A three-masted schooner, the *Français* was 46 metres (150 ft) long, 7.6 metres (25 ft) in the beam, with an unladen weight of 245 tonnes.

Charcot and Gauthier agreed that the highest possible standards should be achieved. As a result, the *Français* was built entirely of oak, and the materials used were three times superior to those demanded by the *Bureau Veritas,* the French equivalent of Lloyds of London.

Charcot had already contacted the famous Belgian explorer, Adrien de Gerlache, seeking his advice. On his suggestion, the bow of the ship was reinforced, her keel curving scythe-like up to the bow. The hull was strengthened at the waterline with transverse beams. Watertight partitions were fitted, the propeller shaft fashioned so the screw itself could be drawn up close to the hull.

But the construction of the *Français* drained even Charcot's substantial inheritance. He was reluctant to sell the Fragonard, but sell it he did, to finance the installation of a laboratory on the ship and to buy scientific instruments.

His own fortune spent, Jean-Baptiste Charcot was forced to instal a second-hand engine, a 93 kW (125 hp) motor that would prove to be the gremlin aboard the *Français.*

Then, his vessel designed to brave the waters of Greenland and the north, Charcot changed his plans. In the spring of 1903, news reached Europe that Otto Nordenskjöld and the *Antarctic* were missing. Charcot's mind was made up. Determined to assist in the search for the Swedish explorer, he wrote in buoyant mood to his friend and supporter Paul Pléneau: 'Instead of going North, we should go South! In the South we are certain to succeed, for very little exploration has been done .... We have only to get there to achieve something great and fine.' He asked his friend to let him know if he was willing to participate in such a turn-about expedition.

Paul Pléneau was the director of an engineering company. His reply was worthy of a poet. He sent Charcot a telegram: 'Where you like. When you like. For as long as you like.'

Thus encouraged, the doctor-turned-would-be-explorer addressed himself to the nation and became a salesman for the promised glory of France. Expounding his ideas, he gained the tacit support of the *Academie des Sciences*, the *Societe de Geographie* and the Museum of Natural History. But it was left to the Paris morning newspaper, *Le Matin*, to publicise Charcot's plan. Opening its pages to public subscription, *Le Matin* raised 150 000 francs to underwrite 'The French Antarctic Expedition'. Private contributions poured in, the final sum reaching 450 000 francs.

The elderly President of France, Emile Loubet, approved the planned expedition. Commandant Charcot was to take the *Français* to Antarctic waters, explore the west coast of Graham Land from the north, then venture south to Adelaide Island and, if possible, Alexander Island. They were to chart the coastline and gather botanical, zoological, hydrographic and meteorological data.

Visitors aboard the Français *before her departure. The Belgian explorer Adrien de Gerlache, who had wintered in Antarctica aboard the* Belgica, *gave Charcot considerable help in designing the ship.*

The Français *eventually left two weeks after her intended departure date of 15 August. Two minutes after the first departure a sailor was killed when a tow rope broke loose.*

Charcot's sponsors also required him to confirm whether Antarctica was a single continent or merely several islands, fringed with ice.

In August 1903 the *Français*, equipped and provisioned, was waiting in the Basin du Roi, Le Havre. When Charcot boarded the vessel he was accompanied by his friend Paul Pléneau and the Belgian explorer, Adrien de Gerlache. In all, 21 men climbed aboard the *Français.*

Breasting bad weather, she left the quay on 15 August 1903. A sailor named Maignan was handling the stern rope when a shift of the vessel tore it free from its cleat. Struck by the hawser, he was killed on the spot, and the *Français* made her sad way back to port. On 27 August, this time without mishap, the *Français* left Le Havre. She put in at Madeira, then tracked south-south-west to the port of Pernambuco in Brazil. It was during this two-month voyage that Adrien de Gerlache told Charcot of his wish to return to Belgium. The explorer had recently become engaged, and each day apart from his fiancée increased his unhappiness. Charcot deeply regretted the departure of de Gerlache and had doubts about his own ability to lead the expedition.

The *Francais* reached Buenos Aires on 16 November 1903. Here news arrived to set them cheering. Nordenskjöld and his party had been rescued, though the *Antarctic* herself had been crushed in the ice and sunk. The Swedish and Norwegian explorers arrived in Buenos Aires in December, and the diffident Charcot invited Nordenskjöld to visit the *Francais*. Impressed by the Frenchman's well-planned expedition, Otto Nordenskjöld presented him with five Greenland huskies.

Two scientists, Turquet and Gourdon, came aboard and the *Français* left Buenos Aires on 23 December. It took the schooner a month to reach Orange Harbour, at the southernmost tip of Tierra del Fuego. The expedition set sail again on 27 January 1904, and Charcot wisely called his crew to order. He appealed to their sense of duty, their patriotism, reminding them that the *Français* carried no manacles, no cat-o'-nine-tails. He would allow them their ration of wine, pay their wages, and see to their wellbeing. In return, he placed the honour of France in their hands.

By 1 February they had skirted the South Shetlands and seen their first icebergs. For the next few days they coasted the northwest edge of the Palmer Archipelago.

Then, on 5 February, the engine began to give trouble. Boiler pipes ruptured and the pressure dropped, the ship's propeller jerking as it spun. Charcot nosed the *Français* among a reef of icebergs, seeking shelter in Biscoe Bay, off Cape Errera. On 7 February, taking advantage of fine weather, the vessel continued south to another haven, Flanders Bay, where she remained for 11 days. Open though it was to the northeast gales, it allowed the engineers to seal the pipes and repair the boiler.

On 19 February the *Français* reached an inlet at Wiencke Island Charcot named Port Lockroy, after the Minister of Marine. But when they attempted to go south, they were blocked by the ice and halted by further engine trouble. A violent storm hit the vessel, and Charcot wrote: 'Millions of tiny, hard snow crystals penetrate our skin and eyes like fine needles, causing horrible pain.'

Fighting their way, the explorers reached 65°5′S, 64°W. They found a shallow bay on the north coast of Wandel (now Booth) Island where Charcot decided to see out the winter. He was concerned about the engine problems, but he had nevertheless come as far south as de Gerlache and a degree farther south than Nordenskjöld had reached.

The Français *in winter quarters at Booth Island. A hawser was stretched across the entrance to the small bay that sheltered the ship to prevent ice from pressing in. The men spent the winter aboard the ship, although huts were built ashore to house some of the many scientific instruments.*

THE *FRANÇAIS* AGROUND

Exploration halted after the ship strikes a rock

Jean-Baptiste Charcot and his fellow expedition members aboard the schooner* Français *spent the winter of 1904 in an inlet at Booth Island. Once a chain had been stretched across the mouth of the bay to keep the drifting ice from crushing the ship, the Frenchmen began to prepare for the months ahead.

Various buildings were erected on the island. Stocks of coal and petrol were brought from the *Français*, along with roofing beams, cement pillars and marble slabs, to be used for the magnetic observatory.

Two large, squared-off holes were dug in the ice. Roofed with boards and canvas, they served as freezers for the stocks of meat. A series of smaller holes were dug along the shoreline, ensuring a supply of water for the hoses in case of fire aboard ship. These pools were regularly checked and kept free of ice.

By early April, scientific studies were under way. Lieutenant Matha and a naval apprentice, Rallier du Baty, busied themselves with many astronomical and topographical observations. Turquet collected his zoological samples, the geologist Gourdon classified minerals and rocks. The easy-going Pléneau divided his time between repairs to the engine and a photographic record of the mission.

During those first days of winter, the explorers worked to a steady, productive rhythm. Charcot, aware the men would be crowded together on the *Français*, and that tempers might grow short, had insisted that every man be given as much privacy as possible. Each bunk in the crew's quarters had been equipped with a sliding door. A series of curtained cubicles contained washstands, the lids of which could be lowered to serve as writing desks.

Charcot made sure his hard-worked crew were given a choice of food from the menu, along with their daily ration of wine and rum. It was not for Frenchmen to eat hard-tack, though in fact the cook aboard the *Français* was not French. Known simply as Rozo, he had found his way aboard in Buenos Aires. He wore nothing on his feet but a pair of threadbare slippers. Judged by the critical Frenchmen, he proved to be worthy of his hire. He managed to bake fresh bread every other day, cakes and *croissants* on Sundays.

Lectures were given, concerts relayed through the horn of a wind-up gramophone, old newspaper articles studied and discussed. But, despite Charcot's efforts, the long nights and bitter days began to sap the crew's morale. So he offered them a break in routine by organising a picnic, though a picnic with a difference: an Antarctic picnic.

At 10.30 am on 30 May, all those who could be spared from the *Français* set off for nearby Hovgaard Island. They had no need of boats, for the channel between Booth and Hovgaard was frozen. The ice sometimes subsiding, the men's boots filled with water which crackled as it too froze.

Charcot wrote of the picnic: 'We had to break up the meat and butter with axes . . . An hour and a half later I was able to produce a fine Polar meal, though we had to eat very quickly, dancing about all the time to keep our feet warm.'

Winter fastened its grip. The stove in the messroom gave trouble. Everything was cold, the touch of metal painful. Hands were gloved, faces swathed with scarves. The temperature dropped to −38°C (−36°F) and the *Français* froze at her moorings. All activity was blanketed by fog, howled down by the wind.

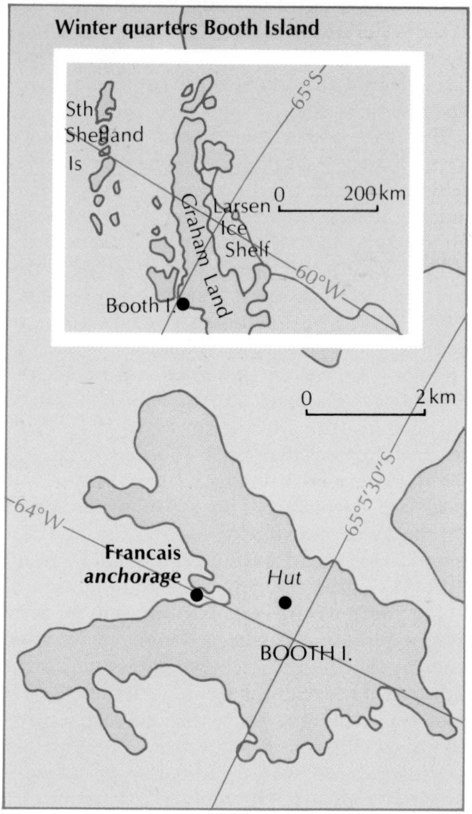

During one of the excursions ashore, Rallier du Baty and three of the sailors lost their way in the fog. A search party was sent out, and the men were eventually found suffering from frostbite and exposure. Aboard ship, Lieutenant Matha fell ill with myocarditis — an inflammation of the heart muscles. Charcot applied a treatment the Belgian de Gerlache had recommended, and by September he was well enough to resume some of his duties.

During a spell of warmer weather, they were able to reach Hovgaard Island by whaleboat, and a few days were spent taking bearings of the nearby coast of Graham Land.

On 24 November the whaleboat was loaded

with camping equipment, 20 days' provisions, scientific instruments and a collapsible sledge — even before Charcot, Pléneau, Gourdon and two sailors had clambered aboard, it weighed 850 kg (1874 lb). Charcot's plan was to go from Petermann Island, 16 kilometres (10 miles) away, to the Graham Land coast.

Petermann Island was reached without mishap, though the ice had to be broken up with axes. But the floes between the island and the mainland were packed too tight to admit the passage of the whaleboat, yet insufficiently solid to support the weight of the men.

So began a superhuman struggle. The men were forced to work *outside* the boat, up to their knees in sub-zero water. Balanced precariously on the shifting ice, they pulled and pushed the heavily laden craft. Inching forward for between 10 and 18 hours a day, it took five agonising days to reach the mainland.

Equipped though they were with dark glasses, they suffered from the effects of snow-blindness, described by Charcot as 'a handful of pepper in the eyes'. Yet they managed to reach the 884-metre (2900-ft) hump of Cape Tuxen, climb to the summit, then spend almost a week surveying the Graham Land coast between Booth Island and the Biscoe Islands to the south.

In the middle of December a southerly wind cleared a large expanse of ice from the entrance to the bay. It was time for the *Français* to break out from her prison.

The explorers had already begun cutting a channel through the ice. The explosive melinite was used to fracture the frozen, floating sheet, the slabs then being attacked with ice-saws, crowbars and picks. The engine was still giving trouble, but it produced sufficient power to drive the vessel.

It was during this escape attempt that the mascot, Toby the pig, died. Greedy as ever, he had stolen fish from a bucket and, by swallowing them, had also swallowed some hooks. Charcot operated, but the animal died and was buried with due solemnity.

With a path clear to the sea, the explorers celebrated Christmas. Charcot took the gramophone ashore and entertained the penguin colony with a concert of popular records. Presents brought from home were opened, including a magnificent cardboard Christmas tree from Charcot's sister Jeanne.

The following day the *Français* raised anchor. Forcing their way through pack ice, they skirted the Biscoe Islands and navigated the channel between Adelaide Island and the Loubet Coast. On 13 January 1905, they sighted Alexander Island 97 kilometres (60 miles) to the south.

Of the events of the 15th, Charcot wrote: 'We were about a mile [1.6 km] from land when, passing approximately a cable's length [185 metres; 608 ft] from a large tabular iceberg more than 150 feet [46 metres] high, the ship received a terrible shock, the bow rearing up almost vertically.'

While travelling at six knots [11 km/h; 7 mph], the *Français* had struck a rock.

Water flooded in. With the engine misfiring, the pumps had to be operated by hand. But these were situated in the stern section of the ship, making it necessary to smash holes in the watertight compartments.

The engineer Libois lowered himself into the icy water in the bows and for several hours attempted to staunch the flood. The commandant and his officers manned the helm, while the others in turn worked the pumps.

Charcot acknowledged that further exploration was impossible. Even now the weather was worsening. All he could help to do was turn the ship north, seek whatever shelter he could find — and pray the pumps kept abreast of the water. The pumps were operated for 45 minutes in every hour, day and night, the men's fingers so cold they froze to the handles.

On 29 January, the vessel reached Port Lockroy, Wiencke Island, where she remained for 10 days while temporary repairs were carried out. On 15 February, the *Français* skirted Smith Island in the South Shetlands, then struggled on towards Tierra del Fuego and the sanctuary of Puerto Madryn. There, Charcot learned that his sister Jeanne had become concerned for the safety of the expedition and had done her best to organise a rescue mission. He also learned that his wife had decided to divorce him on the grounds of desertion.

A happier welcome awaited the explorers in Buenos Aires, where all the ships in port 'dressed' in their honour. The *Français* was put in dry dock, and a careful inspection revealed the extent of the damage: 7.3 metres (24 ft) of the false keel had been ripped away. The Argentinean Government offered to buy her, for use as a supply ship. The terms were generous and Charcot accepted.

On 5 May 1905, Charcot and his companions embarked for France aboard the liner *Algerie*. With them they took 75 packing cases containing the results of their expedition.

It was several months before the details were published, but France already knew she had a hero in Commandant Charcot. Almost 1000 kilometres (620 miles) of new coasts and islands had been sketched and charted, and the expedition had returned with an accurate map of the Graham Land Archipelago.

The explorers had spent a successful, well-organised winter in the Antarctic, survived a near shipwreck and, through their own skill and courage, emerged without loss of life.

The bunks in the crew's quarters had sliding doors for some privacy. The men became irritable and moody during the winter.

Gramophone concerts were a welcome break from the daily monotony of winter life aboard the ship, although the men look far from happy on this occasion. Concerts were held only once a week on Sunday, so that the few records did not become too familiar.

A jumble of old whale bones on the shores of Port Lockroy, Wiencke Island, which was named by Charcot. Factory ships used this inlet, one of the best harbours in the area.

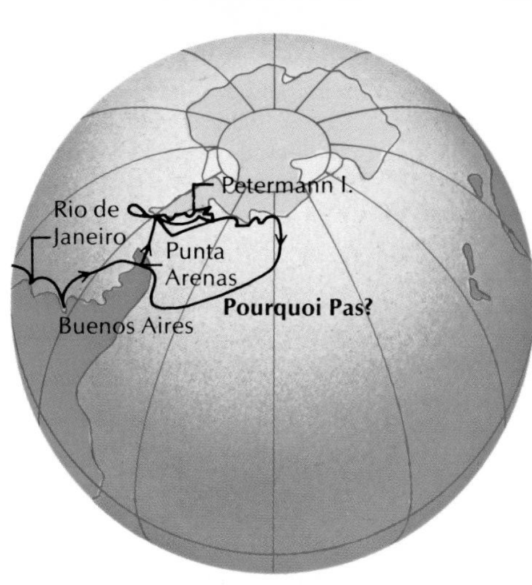

Jean Charcot, centre, and members of the eight-man scientific staff aboard the Pourquoi-Pas? *The men and their specialities are (left to right) H. Bongrain, astronomy, hydrography, seismography and terrestrial gravitation; E. Gourdon, geology and glaciology; E. Godfroy, tides and atmospheric chemistry; L. Gain, zoology and botany; and J. Rouch, meteorology, atmospheric electricity and physical oceanography. Bongrain, Rouch and Godfroy were also naval officers. In addition, the ship carried a crew of 22. Almost all of the crew from the* Français *rejoined for the voyage on the* Pourquoi Pas? *'It would be difficult to discover a better crew than ours', wrote Charcot.*

POURQUOI-PAS?

Charcot returns to complete his unfinished work

***Jean Charcot soon learned the truth of the adage 'nothing succeeds like success'. His plans for a second Antarctic voyage were approved without demur, the government granting him 600 000 francs. He received the official patronage of the* Academie des Sciences, *the Museum of Natural History, the Institute of Oceanography, the* Bureau des Longitudes.**

Charcot and the shipbuilder Gauthier designed another three-masted schooner. Choosing the name he had given to the toy boats of his childhood, Charcot named the schooner the *Pourquoi-Pas?*.

Forty metres (130 ft) long and nine metres (30 ft) in the beam, the *Pourquoi-Pas?* took eight months to build. The same high standards as in the *Français* were set. But where the *Français* had weighed a mere 245 tonnes, the *Pourquoi-Pas?* weighed 800 tonnes. The hull was strengthened with iron sheathing, overlaid with zinc. Three laboratories were installed, two in the stern, one in the mess room. The vessel was equipped with a powerful generator, allowing the expedition a luxury denied those aboard the *Français* — electric light.

With an intended complement of 29 officers and men, Charcot saw to it that the crew's quarters were as extensive as could be managed and included a small sick bay.

On 18 May 1908, the *Pourquoi-Pas?* was launched from the slips at St Malo. Proud of the vessel's performance, Commandant Charcot must have listened with pleasure to the throbbing of the engine. No second-hand 93 kw (125 hp) motor for the *Pourquoi-Pas?*, but a brand new 410 kw (550 hp) machine, custom-built by Labrosse and Fouche of Nantes.

The second French Antarctic Expedition put out from Le Havre on 15 August 1908. Of the 22 crew members, eight had sailed with the *Français*. Of the three officers and four scientists, only the geologist Gourdon was free to keep a further rendezvous with the south. But, Jean Charcot's companions proved to have been well chosen. His second-in-command, Bongrain, later attained the rank of rear admiral, as did the young ensign, Godfroy. The third officer, Ensign Rouch, later became the Director of the Oceanographic Institute of Monaco. The botanist Gain became the Director of the National Meteorological Office, while the zoologist Liouville was to be Director-in-Chief at the Institute of Science.

On *Pourquoi-Pas?* was also the commandant's young wife Meg, whom he had married on 24 January 1907. Meg had insisted on travelling as far south as possible.

On 12 October the schooner dropped anchor at Rio de Janeiro. Charcot described things neatly in a letter to his sister, Jeanne: 'Oppressive heat, torrential rain, visits everywhere, champagne always, gifts and presents showered upon us.'

A similar greeting awaited the French explorers in Buenos Aires, although Jean Charcot was sad to see the remains of the *Français* stranded on a sandbank in the River Plate.

Madame Charcot stayed with the *Pourquoi-Pas?* until the vessel reached Punta Arenas. Then she took her leave of the explorers and began the long, lonely journey back to France.

The schooner left Punta Arenas on 16 December and headed for the South Shetlands. Six days later she reached Smith Island, rounded it and sailed southeast to the harbour at Deception Island. Here, the French expedition found a thriving colony of Norwegian whaling ships, the shore of the bay littered with the skeletons and carcases of their prey. The stench was appalling, but the hunters themselves were cheerful and courteous.

One of the whalers, the *Raun*, put out from the harbour, her captain offering to guide the schooner to a mooring. Employing English as their common language, Charcot and his Norwegian colleagues exchanged visits, information, the tastes of aquavit and cognac.

The Norwegians were happy to welcome the man who had mapped the northern coast of the Graham Land peninsula. They were even now using copies of his maps in their search for new whaling grounds. They were also pleased to have such an experienced doctor in their midst — Charcot saved a sailor from gangrene by amputating his hand.

On 25 December 1908, Charcot chose to leave Deception Island. The Norwegians were surprised — why would he leave the safety of the harbour on Christmas Day? But Charcot regarded it as the perfect omen. The *Pourquoi-Pas?* sailed, aglow with decorations, fog horn sounding, electric searchlight cutting a path through the mist.

On 29 December the *Pourquoi-Pas?* reached Booth Island, anchoring in the bay in which the *Français* had wintered in 1904. Charcot went ashore to discover that almost everything was as the first expedition had left it, and remarked: 'I feel as though I've never been away.' But his intention was to press further south and find a better, ice-free anchorage.

An excellent natural harbour was located at Petermann Island on 1 January 1909, which

The Pourquoi-Pas? *almost ready to sail. The ship was built by the same man who had constructed Charcot's previous vessel, the* Français. *At one stage Charcot planned to buy and refit an existing whaler, but the cost of adapting it would have been almost as much as a brand new ship.*

They had barely begun to explore the islands and channels of the Antarctic Peninsula when disaster struck. The Pourquoi-Pas? *ran aground under the high black cliffs of Cape Tuxen, on the Graham Coast. Despite severe damage to the bow and keel, the crew managed to wrench the ship free as the tide rose about 24 hours later.*

Charcot named Port Circumcision in honour of the explorer Jean-Baptist Bouvet de Lozier.

Three days later, at 5 pm, Commandant Charcot, the geologist Gourdon and Lieutenant Godfroy set out in the ship's launch to reconnoitre the coast near Cape Tuxen. As they intended the journey to be brief, the men dispensed with a change of clothes or emergency rations. Remembering their previous five-day struggle to cross the channel between Petermann Island and the coast, they were pleased to see that the water was free of ice.

They made observations of the coastline and the nearby Bertholet Islands, studying possible passages to the south. Satisfied with their findings, they ate the food they had brought with them and started back for the ship.

By now it was 10 pm and snow was beginning to fall. The channel was no longer open, each narrow fissure blocked by the freezing floes. Time and again the launch butted its way into one of these channels; time and again the pack ice closed around it. The sea was calm, though the snow gave way to sleet. The explorers were soaked, the motor clogged, the launch held in an ever-tightening grip.

Lieutenant Godfroy hacked at the ice with a spade — then gazed in horror as the spade slipped away from his numbed fingers and sank. With no means of propulsion, their only remaining food a handful of biscuits and a bar of chocolate, the men hunched in the boat.

Three days and three nights went by before the men heard the wailing of a siren. Charcot wrote: 'We all shouted together .... We heard shouts of joy and saw the *Pourquoi-Pas?* approaching through the fog and snow. What a wonderful sight it was!'

Less than 24 hours later, Charcot, Gourdon and Godfroy were still wondering at their miraculous deliverance when a dull shock was felt throughout the vessel. History had repeated itself: the *Pourquoi-Pas?* had run hard on to the rocks. Sections of the hull had been torn away, pieces floating to the surface. The stern deck was under water, the bows pinned down with the weight of anchors and chains.

Charcot ordered everything to be moved from the bow section; carried amidships or loaded into the boats. The powerful engine was undamaged, so if the weight could be shifted aft, at the next high tide it might be possible to float the *Purquoi-Pas?* from the reef. But in the event the vessel fought to go astern and failed to pull free. The attempt was repeated, the hull of the schooner torn by the unseen rocks. And then, with a long, slow grinding of stone, metal and wood, the schooner tore herself from the trap.

She retreated to the harbour at Petermann Island where every effort was made to repair her wounds. So well had Charcot and Gauthier designed the ship that she did not immediately take in water. It seeped in later, at the rate of two cu metres (70.6 cu ft) an hour, but the automatic pumps kept pace with the inflow.

If further explorations were to be made, they must be made before winter, and during the latter part of January 1909 the *Pourquoi-Pas?* ventured beyond the Antarctic Circle. She skirted the length of Adelaide Island and proved that it was not, as supposed, a mere 13 kilometres (eight miles) long, but stretched for more than 112 kilometres (70 miles).

The expedition charted every section of coastline that came within view. They entered a vast bay to the south of Adelaide Island, mapped the islands at its mouth and named it for Charcot's beloved Meg: *Marguerite Bay*.

The southern probings of the expedition came to a halt at the end of January. It was time to learn if the second winter would be as productive as the first.

A TANTALISING GLIMPSE

Land beyond the Antarctic Circle

The Second French Antarctic Expedition headed for the harbour of Port Circumcision, Petermann Island, at the end of January 1909. The intention was to spend the winter there before turning south again in the hope of discovering new land. Nearly a year later this aim was realised as the* Pourquoi Pas? *probed the southern ice fields.

The explorers erected four huts on the western shore of the inlet. Each of these was lighted by electricity, the wires strung on bamboo poles between the *Pourquoi-Pas?* and the buildings. The huts were equipped with instruments for magnetic observations, seismographic studies, the measurements of tide and weather. So ambitious was this second expedition that it took a month to off-load the stores, set up and test the scientific equipment.

Charcot and others were now suffering from snowblindness. This had worried him during the earlier voyage, and he had sought to find better protection for the eyes than the smoked glass that was commonly used by explorers. He now issued glasses with a yellow filter, and the results proved encouraging.

To keep the icebergs from the bay, the French perfected the system that had been used to protect the *Français*. Instead of a single chain they used three double-strength iron-wire hawsers, stretched at different places across the inlet. The vessel herself was secured with both hawsers and chains. Charcot saw to it that all the available deck space was roofed and walled with canvas, adding two extra saloons.

Aware that a break in routine was important, he arranged for 23 February — Mardi-Gras — to be celebrated with all the colour and gaiety they could muster. The zoologist, Liouville, shaved off his beard, painted his nose red, and wore an outlandish hat; Gourdon and the botanist Gain disguised themselves as Arabs. In spite of the cold, the explorers paraded ashore, enjoying the chance to show off — if only to the penguins.

March 1909, the end of the Antarctic autumn, was damp and cheerless. Icebergs were already gnawing at the hawsers, the *Pourquoi-Pas?* tossed about by the swell. In April the squalls and storms returned, the temperature dropped and heavy falls of snow buried the provisions stacked ashore.

A day's work in the bitter cold of Petermann Island was enough to sap morale. The explorers returned half-frozen to the ship and the crew looked to Charcot to raise their spirits. Assisted by his officers and the scientists, he used every method he could devise to keep the men's interests alive. Courses were offered in grammar, geography, English and navigation. Liouville gave lectures in first-aid. At Charcot's insistence, the *Pourquoi-Pas?* carried no less than 1500 books. And somehow the commandant had obtained a pile of back copies of *Le Matin*, which he issued day by day.

But perhaps the most popular distraction was supplied by Lieutenant Rouch. In response to a bet, he was writing a romantic novel. It was entitled *L'Amant de la Dactylographe — The Typist's Lover* — and the crew listened keenly as he read each new chapter aloud.

Outside entertainment was offered by the founding of the Antarctic Sporting Club. A track was marked out on one of the lower slopes of the inlet, ski and sledge races held, tin can medals awarded to the winners. Charcot knew that the tough, competitive Frenchmen needed the chance to show their mettle. Better to be physically exhausted than hunched in the gloom of the Antarctic winter, prey to feelings of isolation.

Ironically, it was Charcot himself who fell ill with polar anaemia, his legs badly swollen, his lungs painfully pumping for breath. The weather was against them, and all excursions were halted. He wrote: 'Our life on board goes on, busy yet monotonous. But if the months seem to pass quickly, the hours are long.'

On 18 September 1909, an expedition was sent to Graham Land, though Charcot was too unwell to accompany it. In mid-October he made his first outing from the ship, embarrassed by his weakness, furious that it showed.

On the last day of October the French Antarctic Expedition began loading the mass of data and equipment aboard the schooner. They had once again survived the winter, achieved all they could on the island. Short of coal, they would sail north to the Norwegian colony at Deception Island, re-stock, then thrust their way south again.

They reached Deception on 27 November and were regaled with news of their fellow explorers. They learned that in January 1909, Ernest Shackleton had got within 180 kilometres (97 nautical miles) of the South Pole; and that in April, the North Pole had been reached by the American Robert E. Peary. The French were even more delighted to hear that a compatriot, Louis Blériot, had made the first powered flight over the English Channel.

The good-natured Norwegians offered Charcot the services of a diver, who descended to inspect the damaged hull of the *Pourquoi-Pas?* His advice was ominous and direct: 'Another collision, and your ship will go straight to the bottom.'

The whalers agreed with the verdict. A large chunk of the keel had been torn away. The French could withdraw with honour from the heaving Antarctic waters; *should* withdraw if they hoped to survive the voyage.

But Charcot now suppressed his doubts. Convinced that his companions would share his dream, he swore the Norwegians to silence. The honour of the expedition was at stake. More than that, the honour of his homeland. He was grateful to the Norwegians, but decided to go on.

So on 7 January 1910, the *Pourquoi-Pas?* turned her damaged bows southwards again. Three days later she crossed the 69th parallel, and the explorers saw Alexander I Land (Alexander Island) away to the southeast. Charcot had seen it before — but now he glimpsed something beyond. An iceberg perhaps? Or more than that?

Taking his watch in the crow's nest, Charcot peered beyond the peaks of Alexander Island, his knowledge of the wilderness convincing

The Pourquoi-Pas? *frozen into her winter quarters at Port Circumcision, Petermann Island. Ten hawsers held the ship firmly in place, and more were stretched across the entrance to the bay to keep out ice.*

The wardroom aboard the Pourquoi-Pas?. *The ship was unusually well equipped, with separate cabins for all members of staff, and small but comfortable laboratories. There was also the great luxury of electric lighting throughout the ship. Two of the scientists were even able to grow flowers and vegetables under the wardroom skylight.*

Pack ice in Marguerite Bay. In January 1909 the ship entered this large gulf, south of Adelaide Island, which Charcot named for his wife Marguerite. The expedition explored the bay down to the coast of Alexander Island. Charcot had hoped to winter here, but poor conditions delayed their arrival, and it was not possible to find a suitable harbour before winter.

A series of huts soon sprang up on the small hill overlooking the Pourquoi Pas? *and her winter anchorage. The construction and upkeep of this small village almost turned into a full-time occupation for the men.*

As the snow on the island got deeper a passage was constructed to make trips between the ship and the instrument huts easier.

All expeditions had to be accomplished by man-hauling. Charcot had some motor sledges, but the surfaces were unsuitable for their use.

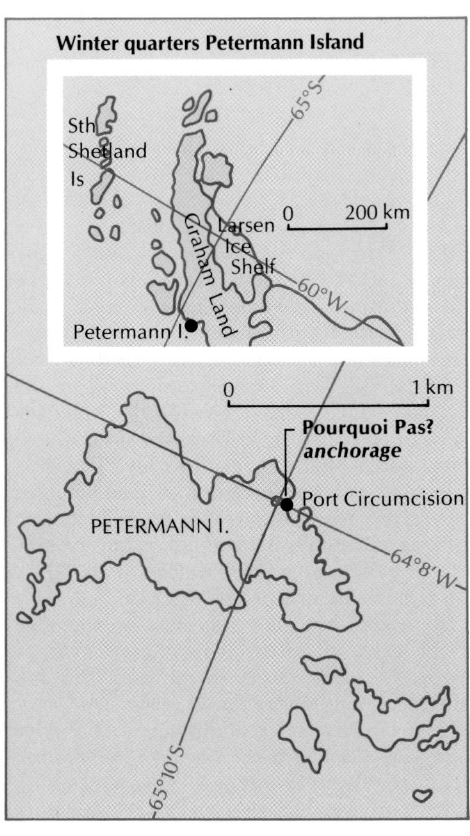

him that *something* lay to the west. 'To everyone's surprise, contradicting my previous orders, I commanded the helmsman to change course. To avoid drawing attention to myself, I descended and ate a quick lunch, then climbed to the crow's nest again, this time taking my binoculars', Charcot wrote.

Another careful study of what lay beyond the island, and: 'There is not the slightest doubt. Those are not mere icebergs that point their peaks toward the sky, but land, new land, clearly visible and a land that is our own!'

He summoned Bongrain to join him in the yards, handed the glasses to his second-in-command and told him to see what he could see. Then added that if Bongrain *did* share his commander's opinion, he was not to yell the discovery aloud. With a fine sense of obedience, the young officer peered through the binoculars, nodded agreement and limited himself to a monosyllabic, 'Oh!'

The *Pourquoi-Pas?* tracked westwards and on 11 January 1910 Jean Charcot claimed the discovery of an unknown headland within the Antarctic Circle. It was situated at 70°S, 76°W, and was named Charcot Land — not for the explorer, but in memory of his father.

Every possible attempt was made to approach it. The sails were hoisted, the engine driving forward. The crew were sent on deck to break the ice with poles. But the *Pourquoi-Pas?* could only make 16 metres (52.5 ft) an hour, all the while risking further damage to her hull. Eventually Charcot withdrew from the dangerous, damaging contest and took the ship on a long sweep to the west.

Exploring the coastline, he followed the pack ice as far as 124°W, then turned away on 22 January. Detailed examination would show how much the explorers had achieved, but they, and the *Pourquoi-Pas?* herself, had reached the limit of their endurance. The ship headed for the welcoming ports in South America.

On 11 February 1910, the *Pourquoi-Pas?* arrived at Punta Arenas. She continued north and by early June had crossed the Atlantic. She sailed up the Seine towards Rouen on 4 June with an escort of naval torpedo-boats. The villages along the riverbank were decorated with flags, the inhabitants cheering these sons of *La Belle France*.

The results of the second Antarctic expedition were impressive. Two thousand kilometres (1250 miles) of coastline and newly discovered territory had been surveyed. Numerous charts and maps had been drawn, so accurate that they were still being used by sealers and whalers 25 years later. There was enough material to fill a 28-volume treatise, illustrated with some of the 3000 photographs taken during the voyage.

The Polar historian, Edwin Swift Balch, wrote that Jean Charcot's explorations 'occupy a place in the front rank of the most important Antarctic expeditions. No one has surpassed him and few have equalled him as a leader and as a scientific observer'.

Robert Falcon Scott remarked that Charcot was, quite simply, 'the gentleman of the Pole'.

Gentleman, explorer, scientist, doctor, philosopher .... And then, during World War I, the commander of a Q-boat in Britain's Royal Navy. For his courageous conduct he was awarded the Distinguished Service Cross.

On the night of 15 September 1936, the *Pourquoi-Pas?* fell victim to a gale off the Icelandic coast. Of the 44 men aboard, there was only one survivor. But the captain, Jean-Baptiste Charcot, went down with his ship.

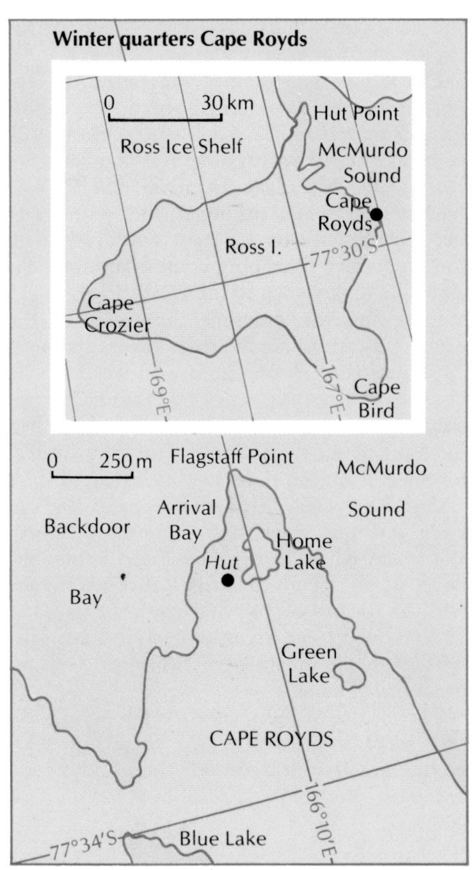

Little appears to have changed at Cape Royds in the 75 years that separate these two views (above) of the tiny hut built by Shackleton's men as a base for their exploration of Antarctica. Inside, food and equipment still lie where they were abandoned in 1909.

HEART OF THE ANTARCTIC

Ernest Shackleton returns to Antarctica in command of his own expedition

Six months before the* Nimrod *left Torquay for Antarctica, Ernest Shackleton stated the object of his adventure: '. . . to reach the southern geographical pole'. The rewards of fame, honour and money for the man who won the international race to the pole would be enormous. But Shackleton, who had the resolution and tenacity of the animal he faintly resembled, the British bulldog, believed in the stern taskmaster – duty.

Shackleton's determination was tested when the expedition was still just a dream: for more than a year he drew up cost-cutting schemes, engineered introductions to rich men in London, told them about the mysteries of the great south land — and went away empty handed. By the end of 1906 he was close to giving up. The Royal Geographical Society, the major sponsor of British explorations, expressed sympathy, though not in the language which counted, that of a large loan. But after several gentlemen agreed to guarantee a bank loan of £20 000, he resumed begging with renewed energy. On 11 February 1907 he was able to tell an RGS dinner that he would spend the next winter in Antarctica.

His limited money hobbled him. While he scoured Norway for ash and hickory sledges, reindeer hide boots, leather sleeping bags and wolfskin mitts, Shackleton tried to buy the *Bjorn*, a ship specially built for polar work, brand new, with powerful engines. He couldn't afford it, and settled on the *Nimrod*, a 40-year-old sealer with decayed masts. As he selected the equipment, Shackleton turned his mind to the men who would accompany him. Four hundred had applied. As he sifted the letters Shackleton pondered his requirements. The men must not only be fit, disciplined and well qualified: they would need the 'marked individuality' common to explorers of the unknown — and they would also have to live together in a cramped hut, completely isolated from the world. Finding a team would not be easy. In the end only two of the shore party of fifteen had previous polar experience.

The *Nimrod* left Torquay on 7 August 1907 and arrived in Lyttelton, New Zealand on 23 November. Shackleton, writing passionate letters to his wife Emily, travelled across France to catch the *India* to Australia — a faster ship which gave him time to recruit scientists and show his gratitude to the Australian Government, which had granted him £5000. He promised Emily he would 'take every care and run no risks', and said their parting was 'the worst heart aching moment in my life'.

To the cheers of 30 000 people, the shriek of steam whistles and the crash of guns, the *Nimrod* steamed out of Lyttleton Harbour on New Year's Day 1908. Beneath the cheers were clouds of anxiety as black as the coal smoke which billowed through the *Nimrod*'s rigging: the barque, jammed to the limit with 255 tonnes of coal, cable, food and equipment, had only 1.04 metres (41 in) of freeboard.

Within an hour the *Nimrod*, towed by the *Koonya* to save precious coal, began to take water through the scupper holes and wash ports. On the fourth morning at sea, Shackleton, with mountainous waves crashing over the deck, asked the *Koonya* to pour oil on the ocean. It helped, but not much. On 14 January they passed their first iceberg; the sea changed from leaden blue to greenish grey. The next morning, with the pack ice visible between light snow squalls, the *Koonya* dropped its tow and headed home, having pulled the *Nimrod* for 2410 kilometres (1500 miles) 'like a reluctant child being dragged to school'.

Shackleton headed for an inlet on the edge of the Ross Ice Shelf, which was 145 kilometres (90 miles) closer to the pole than any other spot the *Nimrod* could reach. But since his last visit to the area kilometres of the ice shelf had crashed into the sea, obliterating what Shackleton hoped would be his landing place. This was bad enough, he thought, but

A makeshift garage of packing cases housed the first car in Antarctica — an 11 kW (15 hp) Arrol-Johnston.

Ernest Shackleton — nicknamed 'The Boss' by his men — was 34 years old when the Nimrod *arrived at Cape Royds.*

what if they had landed there as planned. They would now all be dead. 'The thought of what might have been made me decide then and there that under no circumstances could I winter on the Barrier, and that wherever we did land we would secure a solid rock foundation for our winter home', Shackleton said.

He turned the *Nimrod* east, heading for his second choice for base, King Edward VII Land. Within 36 hours, finding his way blocked by pack ice, and afraid that the drifting icebergs might hold the ship up for weeks, Shackleton turned west and headed for McMurdo Sound.

But the ice frustrated him a third time. The *Nimrod* arrived at McMurdo Sound on 29 January only to discover that 32 kilometres (20 miles) of frozen sea protected Hut Point on Ross Island, where Shackleton had landed with Robert Scott, then his commander, now his rival, on the *Discovery* expedition in 1902. With the white smoke from the volcano Mount Erebus visible against the clear sky, the *Nimrod* waited for nature to break the frozen sea.

The obstinate ice remained, and as his fourth choice Shackleton picked Cape Royds for his winter base, where the bare black rock seemed to offer some protection against storms. On 3 February he, Jameson Adams and Frank Wild ran the whale boat into a natural ice-dock and scrambled ashore.

They finished the shell of the hut in 10 days, though it was not fully sealed, furnished and comfortably insulated against the killing cold for another three weeks.

Within a space 10 x 5.8 x 2.4 metres (33 x 19 x 8 ft) fifteen men had to sleep, eat, work, worry, talk and meet all their social needs for their time in Antarctica. Shackleton had his own cubicle; two men each shared the other seven, and stamped their style on them: Adams' and Marshall's, with their novels by Dickens and bookshelves hung with gauze curtains was 'No. 1 Park Lane'. Professor David and Douglas Mawson, who littered their cubicle with microscopes and tin cans, spectroscopes and straw wrappers, lived in 'The Pawn Shop'. Joyce and Wild inhabited 'Rogues Retreat'.

During the expedition Shackleton penetrated further south than any explorer had done — 580 kilometres (360 miles) further, in fact: he stopped just 180 kilometres (97 nautical miles) short of the pole. He returned in triumph to London in June 1909.

In a Britain uneasy about the threatening rise of Germany, he was living proof of Anglo-Saxon superiority. The press loved him. 'In our age', said a *Daily Telegraph* editorial on 15 June, 'filled with vain babbling about the decadence of the race, he has upheld the old fame of our breed'. Shackleton cheekily advised the secretary of the Royal Geographical Society 'to book the Albert Hall and get the King'. Frowns crossed the gentlemen's foreheads at that. The elder statesman of the Society, Sir Clements Markham, suggested Shackleton had falsified his results, and whispered, incorrectly, that he had never even sat the examination for his master's certificate.

King Edward VII, who liked Shackleton's manner, knighted him. The Government granted him £20 000 to help pay the expedition costs. But, despite the help, Shackleton still had to work hard delivering lectures in Britain, America and Europe to pay off the huge debts he had incurred in putting Britain ahead in the race to the pole.

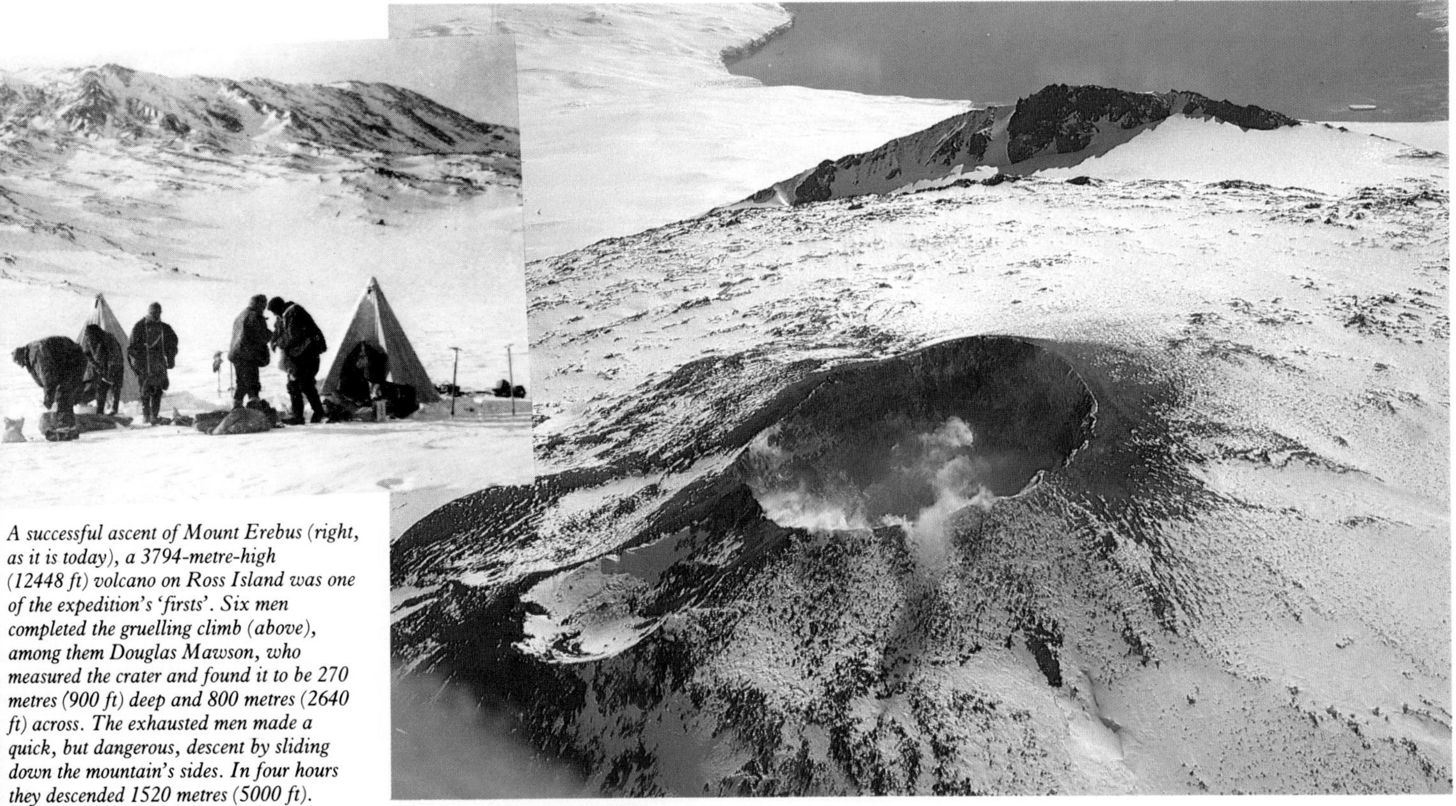

A successful ascent of Mount Erebus (right, as it is today), a 3794-metre-high (12 448 ft) volcano on Ross Island was one of the expedition's 'firsts'. Six men completed the gruelling climb (above), among them Douglas Mawson, who measured the crater and found it to be 270 metres (900 ft) deep and 800 metres (2640 ft) across. The exhausted men made a quick, but dangerous, descent by sliding down the mountain's sides. In four hours they descended 1520 metres (5000 ft).

Winter Routine

Warding off boredom during the five-month polar night

As the Antarctic night closed in, all activity retreated into the hut, except for the few essential jobs that had to be done outside. Shackleton understood that domestic details were the key to morale. If the tiny hut became a pigsty, it would be a symbol that they had left civilisation behind them.

Under the directions of Jameson Adams, the expedition's meteorologist, they built a meteorological screen on a ridge near the hut to measure air temperature, evaporation, wind speed and direction. Adams took the measurements from 8 am to 8 pm; the rostered night watchman made the readings from 10 pm to 6 am.

Douglas Mawson built an anemometer on the highest ridge. It frequently recorded wind squalls of more than 160 km/h (100 mph). In gusts like this, penetrating as a razor, the watchman often had to struggle back to the hut in pitch blackness to relight his hurricane lamp, then lurch back to the exposed ridge praying that the light would hold. But even the simplest measurements are difficult to make in such bitter cold — mercury freezes at −39°C (−39°F) so they had to use a spirit thermometer for the two-hourly checks.

Improvisation governed everything. Professor David made a snowgauge of spare stove chimney parts. To measure evaporation, they hung measured cubes of ice and snow from rods projecting from the hut wall. Sometimes nature improvised for them — the white cloud of steam which hung above the crater of Mount Erebus showed the direction of the upper air currents. 'An excellent high-level

The expedition's small collection of records were played regularly during the winter months.

Bathing in the hut, with the temperature not much above freezing, was a chilly business. Most only bothered with the ritual once a month, or once a fortnight at the most.

Dr Eric Marshall and, above his head, the acetylene gas plant. Four burners, attached to flexible tubes so that they could be moved as necessary, kept the hut well lit.

observatory', Shackleton noted in his journal.

Although there were few land plants to discover — and the Glasgow biologist, James Murray, was thrilled with discoveries of lichen and algae — the water was rich with life. Murray established a dredge, pulled along the bay bottom on a line lowered through a tidal ice crack. The dredge scooped up a variety of 'small fish, crustacea and other marine animals', which Murray dropped into a bucket of water to be carried to the hut. By then the water had frozen and Murray had to thaw the animals out so he could examine them. The astonishing thing was that freezing did not kill the animals. Murray also caught rotifers — microscopic animals — frozen in the lake ice, and while the rest of the party watched in amusement, he would try to kill them, thawing them out then freezing them again, and wondering why they did not die.

As the sun began to set in March, the brilliantly coloured clouds looked like lumpy iridescent rainbows as they hung in luminous contrast over white ice cliffs, pitted with inky black boulders. In April the colours of the aurora merged from deep red to pale green. To Shackleton 'the sunsets were poems'.

Tiny details of the daily routine became major events. Usually the rostered messman would anxiously ask the cook, William Roberts, what the dinner was to be. The cause of his anxiety was whether or not he would have grease-smeared plates to wash up. The weather was another important factor in his life. In a blizzard the chores of emptying dishwater and ashes and getting in fresh ice became small feats of endurance.

Two were exempt from the two-week roster for the night watchman's and messman's jobs — Roberts, who cooked through the day, and Sir Philip Brocklehurst, his toes still black with frostbite after the Mount Erebus climb. The others tended their specialities. Adams wound the chronometers and chronometer watches, checked the instruments and attended to meteorological work. Marshall, the surgeon, attended any wounds — minor cuts healed slowly in the extreme cold — exercised a pony and issued pills. Wild, the storekeeper, issued food to Roberts, opened the cases of tinned food and dug the meat of the day — penguin, seal or mutton — out of snowdrifts. Joyce fed the dogs and trained them at sledge pulling. David geologised. Priestley and Murray worked at floe dredging and checked temperatures in the lake ice shafts. Mawson observed the aurora, studied ice-structures and measured atmospheric electricity.

One job which constantly recurred for all of them was mending socks. Because of their hard boots, socks were invariably showing gaping holes, and they had few spares, so they spent the nights darning or patching with leather, canvas or flannel. Taking a bath was a luxury in the freezing hut. Some bathed once a month, the more fastidious fortnightly.

Some men allowed their subconscious anxieties to surface as they slept, and talked unconsciously to an appreciative audience of one — the night watchman, who would then serve the sleeper stories of his dreams at breakfast time. Some found it a struggle to stay awake for hour after leaden hour, and devised strategies for warding off sleep. Eric Marshall, the surgeon, who had studied cooking in England, baked elaborate cakes and bread to keep his eyes open. The others jeered at this when he put them on the breakfast table, but Shackleton noticed they always went by next day.

The night watchman often boosted the powdery coal with fiercely blazing seal blubber. 'It was a comfort to know that with the large supply of seals ... no expedition need fear the lack of emergency fuel', wrote Shackleton, whose understandable anxiety about fuel pervades his diary. To stay always active surrounded by 14 soundly sleeping fellows was something even the resolute Shackleton found beyond him. 'I often made plans and resolutions as to washing and other necessary jobs [but] when the time came these plans fell through, with the exception of the bath.'

The winter routine, a holiday compared to the exhausting work of building the hut and setting up the base, meant they all stayed up later. By mid-winter, Professor David, more of a night person than the others, had organised an 11 o'clock tea — a cup of tea or hot milk. But by 1 am nearly all were soundly, if not quietly, asleep. The watchman called Roberts and Bertram Armytage at 7.30 am — Roberts to prepare breakfast, Armytage to feed the ponies. At 8.30 he woke all hands. Those who slept in their clothes dressed quickly, 'merely putting on their boots and giving themselves a shake'. The more fastidious tore off their pyjamas then, cursing, pulled on their cold underwear. At 8.45 the table was lowered from the roof, and at 9.00 they all sat down to porridge and hot milk (made, of course, from powdered milk). Sometimes there was a second course of bottled fruit, then tea and a smoke. The breakfast conversation was not scintillating. Lunch was at 1 pm, though the scientific readings and other chores often made this a meal in shifts — the only meal when this informality occurred. Everybody sat down to dinner at 6.30 sharp.

On birthdays and on 21 June, midwinter's day, they broke their teetotal rule and celebrated with what Shackleton described as 'a sort of mild spree'. The leader's optimism shone through the six-month night. 'We were all busy and there was little cause for us to find the time hung heavy on our hands; the winter months sped by.'

George Marston 'trying to revive memories of other days'. Marston was an art teacher who joined the expedition as artist and general handyman.

ANTARCTICA'S FIRST BOOK

One of Marston's drawings from Aurora Australis.

Aurora Australis, *the first book to be written, illustrated, printed and bound in Antarctica.*

The aurora australis — the Latin phrase means 'Goddess of the southern dawn' — is a display of light patterns, streamers and curtains, arcs and rods, filling the heavens in the Antarctic night. The aurora, probably caused by streams of charged particles from the sun passing into the earth's magnetic field, fascinated Shackleton. To ward off boredom, the party wrote, printed, illustrated and bound a 120-page book, *Aurora Australis*, the first published in Antarctica.

Even within the hut, warmed by the constantly burning coal stove, the cold made unusual precautions necessary. Ernest Joyce and Frank Wild, who had taken a quick course in typesetting and printing in England, kept a lamp burning beneath the type-rack to keep the metal warm enough to handle, and a candle beneath the inking plate to stop it setting into a viscous jelly. They learned on the job. After setting pages full of beginners' literals at the start, within three weeks they were setting and printing two clean pages a day.

The artist, George Marston, painted the ghostly lights of the aurora, then etched aluminium printing plates, hoping salt in the hut's water supply would not reduce the prints to an inky smear. Bernard Day cleaned, planed and polished wood from provisions cases for the covers.

The others, in Shackleton's phrase, 'sent in' various literary contributions. At the end of the project, Shackleton was pleased that 'it had at least assisted materially to guard us from the danger of lack of occupation during the polar night'.

JOURNEY TO THE WANDERING POLE

First successful attempt to reach the elusive South Magnetic Pole

The plan was simple. David, Mawson and Mackay were to walk nearly 1600 kilometres (1000 miles) to the point where their compass needle would stand vertically. There they would hoist the Union Jack and take possession of the area for the British Empire.

Some use was made of the motor car. But Shackleton came to the conclusion that it was useless on soft surfaces.

Edgeworth David was 50 years old when he undertook to lead the arduous sledging expedition to locate the South Magnetic Pole. His companions on the 2028-km (1260-mile) march, Alistair Mackay and Douglas Mawson, were 30 and 26 years old respectively. David had only intended to go with the Nimrod *as far as winter quarters, but Shackleton managed to talk him into staying for the duration of the expedition. In March 1908 he also led the expedition that made the first ascent of the 3794-metre-high (12448-ft) volcano, Mt Erebus.*

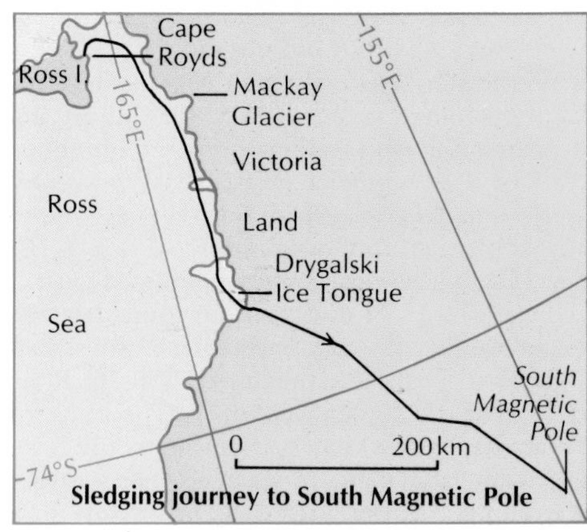

Sledging journey to South Magnetic Pole

Neither the two Australian academics nor the English naval surgeon had previous experience of polar exploration. They were to accomplish their mission, including if possible geological surveys of the Victoria Land coast, the western mountains and dry valleys, without the help of dogs or ponies, pulling sledges and supplies weighing up to 300 kg (670 lb).

At the start, they used a motor car specially adapted for Antarctic conditions to establish two depots 16 and 24 kilometres (10 and 15 miles) from the hut on Cape Royds. The Antarctic mocked them. On 25 September, the car engine overheated and they actually had to wait in the blistering cold for it to cool down.

When the expedition finally left the winter quarters the next day, Mackay had his wrist in a sling after an accident with the car's starter. He told Professor David he was quite ready to go, so long as the other two did not mind the risk of a surgeon with his arm in a sling. They said that they did not.

They lived by improvising. On 1 November, worried by the rate at which their rations were diminishing, they devised an ingenious biscuit tin stove, fuelled by seal blubber, with a biscuit bag wick, which they used to cook seal meat. The next day they travelled at night to avoid the sticky daytime ice.

Food obsessed them. They started reusing previously brewed tea leaves. By 5 November they limited themselves to one plasmon biscuit each for breakfast and dinner, discovering in the process that 'we had never before fully realised how very nice those plasmon biscuits were'. Like hungry children dividing a birthday cake, the three explorers used the traditional technique for dividing food. The duty messman would put three biscuits on the cooker cover, then point to one, asking one of the others with his back turned, 'Whose?' Distribution by blind chance meant there would be no energy-depleting squabbles over the thickest biscuit — and no silently harboured resentments. At the start, they ate the biscuits careless of the crumbs which dropped onto the snow. But by early November they were breaking the biscuits over their pannikins, then tapping the broken chip to make sure they lost no precious crumbs.

Food dominated their conversation. When they stopped to rest 'we could discuss nothing but the different dishes with which we had been regaled in our former lifetime at various famous restaurants and hotels', David noted.

Sudden death was their constant companion. On 11 December, about 1.6 kilometres (one mile) short of the Drygalski Ice Tongue, David plunged through a lid concealing a crevasse six metres (20 ft) from their tent. He threw out his arms, catching the lid on either side, and shouted to Mawson, who crawled from the sleeping bag and rescued him with an ice axe. It was Mackay's turn the following day. While hunting emperor penguins he fell through an ice bridge up to his waist in water.

Death brushed Mawson on 20 December. As they crossed a network of crevasses, David heard a 'slight crash' and Mawson disappeared. David and Mackay discovered him dangling over a deep crevasse, suspended by his harness attached to the sledge rope. As David rushed to get another rope, the harness rope slipped through the crevasse lid and Mawson cried from the abyss that he felt he was going. He only dropped 50 cm (20 in), however. But this heart-stopping experience did not dispel Mawson's scientific curiosity. As he dangled between life and death he grabbed some ice crystals from the crevasse wall and threw them up for examination.

David recorded blandly: 'After this episode we were extra cautious in crossing the crevasses, but the ice was simply seamed with them. Twice when our sledge was being dragged up ice-pressure ridges it rolled over sideways with one runner in a crevasse and once the whole sledge all but disappeared into a crevasse . . . Had it gone down completely it would certainly have dragged the three of us down with it, as it weighed nearly one-third of a ton [340 kg].'

As Christmas approached the Antarctic silence was broken by the roar of mountain torrents around Mount Larsen, and occasionally the menacing crash of an avalanche 'like distant artillery'. On Christmas Day, David and Mawson, having no other gift to offer, gave Mackay, who was suffering from snow-blindness, some *sennegrass* — dried Norwegian grass they used to line their boots — as substitute pipe tobacco.

Both the sun and the cold tormented them — Mawson's right cheek and the tip of David's nose were frostbitten and the sun burned David's exposed hands. The cold stripped skin from their lips and Mawson woke each morning with his mouth glued shut with congealed blood. Their food fantasies grew with their hunger. On 2 January they imagined what they would drink in the real world, now their dream world. Mackay fancied a gallon of buttermilk. Mawson dreamed of the luxury of a basin of cream. David had visions of pots of the best coffee, with plenty of hot milk.

They did not hate the snow. As they neared the magnetic pole, David saw large and beautiful ice crystals formed by the surface snow having thawed and re-frozen, and noted lovingly: 'The heavy runners of the sledge rustled gently as they crushed the crystals by the thousand.' It seemed a sacrilege. The following day, 15 January, Mawson's compass was only 15 minutes off the vertical, and he calculated that if they waited where they were the wandering pole would pass beneath them.

They decided not to wait, but made a last depot of most of the heavy gear and set out on a forced march to the pole. David and Mackay planted a flagpole at the spot. The three then bared their heads, hoisted the Union Jack and posed in front of the camera which David triggered with a string. He said beneath the vast sky: 'I hereby take possession of this area now containing the Magnetic Pole for the British Empire', and they gave three cheers for His Majesty King Edward VII. They were too tired to feel triumphant, but that night, back at the depot after a 39-kilometre (24-mile) forced march, they slept soundly: one of their great fears, that of failure, had gone. Their problem was now to stay alive.

They calculated that to reach the Drygalski depot and signal the *Nimrod* on time, they would have to average nearly 27 kilometres (17 miles) a day from 17 January to 1 February. After two good days, there was an unusual note of discord. Mawson, the messman, added a lump of sugar to their 'hoosh'. Mackay, noticing the change of flavour, cross-examined Mawson about it with the severity of a man who thinks his best friend has betrayed him. When Mawson confessed to the lump of sugar, Mackay said indignantly that this was just the sort of thing that happened when you went sledging with 'two foreigners'.

On 5 February they were within 1.6 kilometres (one mile) of the Drygalski depot. With no sign of the *Nimrod*, they began to talk about how long they should wait before striking out for Ross Island when two sudden explosions galvanised them into action. Mawson screamed, 'A gun from the ship', and dived for the tent opening. Mackay and David followed. As David emerged, Mawson, then 100 metres (330 ft) away, turned and called: 'Bring something to wave.' David grabbed a rucksack, and 'as I ran forward this time, what a sight met my gaze. There was the dear old *Nimrod*, not a quarter of a mile [400 metres] away, steaming straight towards us up the inlet . . .' David was about to thank merciful providence when Mackay shouted: 'Mawson's fallen into a deep crevasse. Look out, it's just in front of you!'

Mackay shouted his two urgent items of news to the *Nimrod* crew: 'Mawson has fallen down a crevasse, and we got to the Magnetic Pole.' A rescue party quickly retrieved Mawson from the six-metre-deep (20-ft) hole and the three exhausted, elated explorers took afternoon tea aboard the *Nimrod*. After their first wash for over four months and dinner then cocoa and gingerbread, they turned in at 10 pm. 'None but those whose bed for months has been on snow and ice can realise the luxury of a real bunk, blankets and pillow, in a snug little cabin', David wrote.

They had travelled 2028 kilometres (1260 miles) with no dogs or ponies in the coldest place on earth. After it was over, David thought they could have done it 'in half the time' with a team of dogs had they known there were abundant seals along the coast. He made no grandiose claims. 'We have pioneered a route to the magnetic pole', he wrote, 'and we hope that the path thus found will prove of use to future observers'.

In a ceremony around a Union Jack planted at the South Magnetic Pole the area was claimed 'for the British Empire'. Left to right are Alistair Mackay, Edgeworth David and Douglas Mawson. Only 20 days from Ross Island, and shortly before they passed the Mackay Glacier (below), David decided they must manage on half rations.

FURTHEST SOUTH

Ultimate success eludes Antarctica's most charismatic hero

Shackleton's attempt to reach the South Pole is really a story of two journeys. The first is the physical struggle from 29 October 1908 to 5 March 1909 — 128 days — through snow so soft the ponies sank up to their bellies, razor-sharp ice, and a climb to 3050 metres (10 000 ft). The second is the psychological struggle, the inner journey each of the four men made as he coped with pain, fear, snowblindness, and the horror which obsessed them all — starvation.

Furthest south. Three weary men beside Queen Alexandra's Union Jack, just 180 km (97 nautical miles) from the pole.

Shackleton's guiding light was duty. As he sat with Jameson Adams, Eric Marshall and Frank Wild at dinner the night before they started from the Cape Royds hut, Shackleton saw sunlight penetrating a ventilator hole and casting a circle of light on the portrait of Queen Alexandra on the hut wall. The circle moved slowly to the portrait of King Edward VII. Since they were about to try to plant the Queen's Union Jack 'on the last spot of the world', Shackleton thought this was a clear good luck omen.

They started at 10 am under a cloudless sky with the wind at their backs, 'everything', Shackleton thought, 'that could conduce to an auspicious beginning'. At lunchtime, however, Grisi, the nervous dapple-grey Manchurian pony, suddenly lashed out and kicked Adams just below the kneecap, exposing the bone. On a journey where a twisted ankle would be a disaster, it was a sharp early reminder of the risks they were taking.

Even the light had the power to change the physical landscape. When clouds and mist diffused the sunlight they could see no shadows. Ledges, mounds and gullies disappeared into a dead flat white plain. When they thought they were on a level surface they would suddenly drop down a metre (3 ft). An invisible mound would stop the sledge dead.

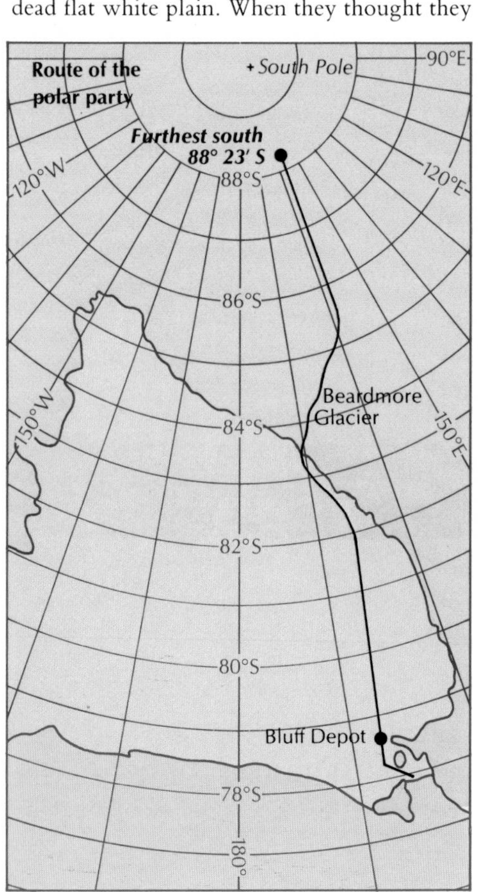

The four members of the polar party safely back aboard the Nimrod, *after their desperate 2736-km (1700-mile) trek. They are (from left to right) Frank Wild, Ernest Shackleton, Eric Marshall and Jameson Adams.*

When the returning polar party reached the Bluff depot their safety was assured. Now, after weeks on starvation rations, they had all the food they could possibly eat.

Crevasses, covered only by a fragile snow-crust, were often so deep they could not see the bottom, nor hear any sound from an object dropped into them. Each was a potential death trap. On 5 November Wild, Adams, Marshall and the pony Grisi were all rescued from crevasses — Marshall twice. Three days later Marshall and Wild pitched their tent right at the edge of an unseen crevasse. The next day another pony slipped into an abyss. They pulled him out, but Shackleton felt the hand of death on his shoulder: 'Three feet [one metre] more and it would have been all up with the southern journey . . . [we would have lost] the horse, all our cooking gear and biscuits and half the oil, and probably Adams as well.'

Almost from the beginning, hunger travelled with them like a spectre. They had food for 91 days. Three weeks out, Shackleton complained to his diary that the daily diet of 960 grams (34 oz) each — mainly wheatmeal biscuits, powdered beef, sugar and cheese or chocolate — seemed very small. He started to wonder what it would be like 'later, when we are really hungry'.

They shot Chinaman, the weakest of the ponies, on 21 November, fed on his flesh and left the rest in a depot for their return. Jameson Adams, who had been unable to sleep for days with the agony of a toothache, submitted to an attempt to pull it, but the tooth broke. The next day the surgeon, Eric Marshall, succeeded in extracting the tooth without the use of tooth-pulling equipment.

Sometimes the Antarctic seemed more like a fantasy than part of the real world. All around was limitless ice, devoid of features, so perfectly silent that the silence itself registered on their ears. Above was a night-time sun, surrounded by rainbow-coloured circles and bows. Once the silence was broken by a deep rumble that made the air and ice vibrate. They thought it must have been a huge chunk of the ice shelf crashing into the Ross Sea 80 kilometres (50 miles) away.

They passed the previous 'furthest south' record, set by Robert Scott in 1902, after 29 days, on 26 November, and celebrated with two tablespoons each of Curaçao. By early December, after nearly a month on half rations, they were thinking constantly of food, fantasising about the feast they would have the next time they went to a good restaurant. After shooting two more ponies, Shackleton, with his soft heart for animals, believed he heard the last pony, Socks, whinnying 'all night for his lost companions'.

Socks, himself scheduled for the revolver in December, met a different end. On 7 December, after a morning sinking to his belly in soft snow, the pony broke through the snow crust on the Beardmore Glacier and disappeared down a crevasse. When they lay on their stomachs to look, they could see no sign of Socks. He had vanished into a 'black, bottomless pit'.

They started eating pony maize. Shackleton maintained his indomitable optimism, saying on 11 December: 'Difficulties are just things to overcome, after all.' But by Christmas, which they celebrated at 2900 metres (9500 ft) with plum pudding, medical brandy, cocoa, a spoonful of créme de menthe and cigars, the Antarctic was pressing them hard. They still had 400 kilometres (250 miles) between themselves and the pole, with only three weeks' biscuits left. 'Tomorrow we will throw away

PRIVATE DOUBTS

Two fears bound the four South Pole explorers together during 128 days of forced, continuous intimacy: the fear of dying, and the fear of falling. Crossing fragile snow-crusts over crevasses, each owed his life to the others several times. They had to share the work, the danger and the food with a relentless equality. Had they all been perfect, they might have come through without friction. But they were not perfect. They were men.

Shackleton, keeping the leader's diary for the benefit of history, was generous to the point of unreality. No note of dissatisfaction or disappointment with Frank Wild, Jameson Adams or Eric Marshall was permitted in his pages. But Wild, who kept a private diary with venomous personal comments written in code, and Marshall, who persuaded himself at Cape Royds that Shackleton was 'vacillating, erratic and a liar, easily scared, moody and surly, a boaster', were much more revealing about the passions concealed beneath the stiff upper lip and about the unique psychic stresses of their journey.

On 23 December Wild, complaining that Marshall did not pull his share of the weight, expostulated: 'I sincerely wish he would fall down a crevasse about a thousand feet deep.' Marshall's comments on Shackleton were poisonous. 'Shackleton moaning over snow blindness, which he has only himself to thank for', he wrote on 5 November. 'Following Shackleton to the Pole is like following an old woman', he said on 14 December, and, a week later, 'Shackleton as cook is hopeless'.

Wild on Christmas Day went as far as to express hatred for the Antarctic itself, the reverse side of the explorer's love that drew him to the icy continent like a magnet. 'May none but my worst enemies ever spend their Christmas in such a dreary God-forgotten spot as this.' In his worst moments, Shackleton, like Professor Edgeworth David, was full of love for the wondrous Antarctic, but Wild was permitted to see the other side of the mysterious hold the continent had on all of them. 'I can now quite sympathise with Scott when he said, "Wherever my destiny may in future lead me, I hope it will not again be to the interior of the Antarctic continent".' Like Scott, Wild was to return.

everything except the most absolute necessities', Shackleton wrote.

In his heart Shackleton knew defeat was looming. Weariness pervaded his diary. 'Everytime we reach the top of a ridge we say "perhaps this is the last", but it never is the last', he wrote on Boxing Day. When they finally reached the immense polar plateau the following day the altitude of 3100 metres (10 200 ft) made breathing hard.

The weather treated them cruelly. A strong head wind, the fear of all polar explorers, cut them to the bone. On 30 December a southerly blizzard restricted them to a mere 6.5 kilometres (four miles) travelling. They were weak from want of food and their hands and feet were always on the verge of frostbite. When they opened a tin of thin over-baked biscuits it seemed a small disaster. By 2 January Shackleton was at breaking point. 'I cannot think of failure yet', he wrote. But he clearly was thinking of it. 'I must look at the matter sensibly and consider the lives of those who are with me . . . man can only do his best . . .' Two days later he capitulated: 'The end is in sight. We can only go for three more days at the most, for we are weakening rapidly.' They struggled through a head-on blizzard on 4, 5 and 6 January. On 7 January, when Shackleton was planning a last desperate dash to reach within 160 kilometres (100 miles) of the pole, a shrieking blizzard kept them in their sleeping bags all day. It was the same on 8 January — 24 hours of miserable confinement.

The last of their journey south began at 4 am on 9 January. They left their sledge, tent and food at the camp and took only the Union Jack, a brass cylinder containing stamps and documents to mark their farthest south, camera, glasses and a compass. At 9 am they reached latitude 88°23′S, longitude 162° — just 180 kilometres (97 nautical miles) from the South Pole. Only the unending white plain showed through their powerful glasses. They quickly planted the flag and the cylinder, stayed only a few minutes, then turned to the one task left to them, survival.

The blizzards which had punished them on the trip south now helped them north. For two weeks they travelled relatively quickly — days of 31 kilometres (19 miles), 32 kilometres (20 miles), 43 kilometres (27 miles) and a wondrous run of 47 kilometres (29 miles) on 19 January, the sledge rushing, under sail, down ice falls and over crevasses. It was too good to last. On the morning of 26 January they had only tea, cocoa and a little pony maize left. That day they travelled 26 kilometres (16 miles) over 'the worst surfaces and most dangerous crevasses we have ever encountered', collapsing exhausted 1.6 kilometres (one mile) short of the food depot.

On 13 February they reached the depot with Chinaman's carcass and ate the liver, which 'tasted splendid'. Three days later they were too weak to lift the sleeping bags through the tent dooorway when breaking camp. At night they had to lift their legs with their hands when getting into the tent. Blisters like golf balls disfigured their skin.

Approaching the Bluff depot, their anxiety over food was pushing them to the point of breakdown. When they discovered three tiny pieces of chocolate and a biscuit fragment at an abandoned camp they 'turned backs' for them. Shackleton drew the biscuit — and experienced 'unreasoning anger' that because he had drawn the biscuit the others would resent him. Good luck was bad luck. Shackleton, ever the detached observer, thought his own anger showed 'how primitive we have become'.

They found the Bluff depot on 23 February. Shackleton described their first sight of it as if deranged: 'It seemed to be quite close and the flags were waving and dancing as though to say "Come, here I am, come and feed".' A biscuit tin which caught the sun was 'like a great cheerful eye twinkling at us'. He climbed to the top of the depot and rolled down three tins of biscuits, then cases of Carlsbad plums, eggs, cakes, plum puddings, gingerbread, crystallised fruit and fresh boiled mutton from the *Nimrod*. 'After months of want and hunger, we suddenly found ourselves able to have meals fit for the gods, and with appetites the gods might have envied.'

They were safe. Or were they? Marshall was suffering badly from dysentery. On 27 February Shackleton decided to leave Marshall and Adams behind on the ice shelf while he and Wild pushed ahead to Hut Point. When they arrived they found a letter saying the *Nimrod* had picked up the magnetic pole party and would shelter under the nearby glacier tongue till 26 February. It was now 28 February. Shackleton, as usual understating the matter, wrote that if the *Nimrod* had gone their plight was 'very serious'.

After a bad night, however, they fired the magnetic hut, and shortly saw the *Nimrod* as if in a mirage. By 11 am they were safely on board. Three hours later, the indomitable Shackleton set out leading the rescue party for Marshall and Adams. At 1 am on 4 March they were all safe on board the *Nimrod*; they had walked 2736 kilometres (1700 miles).

SHELTER

Protection from wind, cold and drift

In Antarctica, shelter is more vital than food. Intense cold may kill more swiftly than any deprivation, save that of air. The fundamental shelter is clothing, which conserves warmth and regulates its escape. It can do no more. To survive, a traveller must have food, rest and some sort of refuge must be found or built.

The entrance to the snow cave in which six members of Scott's 1910-13 expedition spent the winter of 1912. The ice walls of the cave were lined with snow blocks and the floor was a layer of pebbles topped by seaweed.

In still air, even at temperatures well below zero, body heat is undisturbed because a thin layer of warmed air remains close to the skin. A lightly clad person can even sunbathe on a cold day, provided there is no breath of wind. Once even the slightest breeze springs up, however, body temperature drops rapidly. To be caught in a wind without adequate clothing and with no close shelter, is to perish.

Clothing is the first defence against the Antarctic climate. In low temperatures a properly dressed person will be warm while sheltered or active. Sufficiently insulated by a duvet suit and anorak, it is possible to lie buried in snow which, receiving little heat from the body, remains dry and prevents the body's surrounding layer of warm air from being disturbed.

Away from a base, a traveller using a prepared refuge such as a hut, sledge caravan or vehicle, can take off outdoor clothing and relax. Otherwise shelter must be created — a tent, snow cave or igloo. In this it is possible to lay out an insulating mat, get into a sleeping bag and cook a meal in relative comfort.

Apart from the cold, one of the Antarctic traveller's greatest enemies is drift snow. Dry as talc, it lies on the surface of the high polar plateau. Any sustained wind lifts vast quantities into the air to form a dense, all-obscuring blizzard. Drift snow is extraordinarily penetrating. In a major blizzard even a bolt hole in a hut wall may admit literally tonnes of snow, to form great rounded masses. Every fold of outer clothing becomes clogged, and a face mask is plastered with mixed snow and ice.

All buildings in Antarctica are provided with an uninsulated cold porch where snowy outer clothing is removed, brushed and stored before passing through a second door into the warm hut interior.

The Antarctic huts built by the early explorers were not well insulated. They were constructed mainly from wood, made drift-proof with a variety of sealants and tarred or 'Rubberoid' sheets. Inside, a stove burning coal, anthracite and, rarely, oil, provided warmth. Seal blubber gave quick heat, and was often used as an auxiliary fuel. As the snowdrifts piled higher against the walls, the huts became less draughty and the temperature might rise, on occasions, to 10°C (50°F). The men still had to wear heavy clothing indoors. Douglas Mawson wrote of the first weeks in their hut at Cape Denison: 'On one occasion, in the early days, I remember the hut temperature being 19°F [−7.2°C], notwithstanding the heat from the large range. Under these conditions, the writing ink and various solutions all over the place froze . . .'

These early huts were, essentially, only a winter refuge and a starting point for field work during the summer months. They housed the members of the expedition, provided cooking, eating and sleeping space, and

Scott's hut at Cape Evans, under construction. The walls had double boarding inside and outside the frame, with a layer of quilted seaweed insulation between each pair of boardings. Six layers of boards, 'Rubberoid' and seaweed made up the roof, and five layers, including felt and lino, the floor.

most of the facilities needed for photography, the preparations for field excursions, classifying collections and other activities. Some huts were double, occasionally there was a loft. A Stevenson screen placed a short distance from the main hut, for meteorological readings, and a magnetic hut, far enough away to prevent interference, completed the base. Dogs were either tethered on the lee of the hut, beyond the drifts, or given shelter in a lean-to. There was no thought at the time that the huts would last indefinitely. That some still stand today is a tribute to their stalwart construction.

Since World War II bases have become more complex, with multiple scientific functions, each requiring its own building and facilities. Modern buildings are usually made from prefabricated panels, insulated by plastic-foam cores and silvered metal surfaces, or honey comb partitions with reflective foil. These panels are bolted together precisely, with gaskets to make joints proof against wind and drift. Most bases have a central power station to provide electricity for heating, lighting, cooking and much of the scientific instrumentation. The interiors of the buildings are kept at a comfortable living temperature.

A second major change has been consolidation. Since bases are now to be permanent, major rebuilding has had to take place, with widely spaced blocks housing many functions

The cramped interior of a polar tent during a sledging expedition, drawn by Edward Wilson in 1911. Because there was so little space, it was important to establish a routine, and to see that things were put away when not in use. Minor personal quirks soon became major irritations in these circumstances.

instead of separate huts. These save movement, time and labour, especially in a blizzard. They are also fireproof, quieter, vibrate less and are easier to heat than are a lot of smaller self-contained buildings.

A radical experiment in station design was carried out some years ago at one Australian base, Casey. The units were connected in a line, across the prevailing wind, on a raised open iron framework. Men could move through the station in all weathers, and the formation of snowdrifts was prevented by the free movement of air beneath the structure. However, vibration has been a problem, and the new Casey, like most of the major Antarctic settlements, will consist of separate, two- or three-storey buildings.

Before the introduction of motor vehicles, most Antarctic journeys were made on foot, or skis, with all the equipment on a man or dog-drawn sledge. Journeys were usually confined to the summer months when the weather was favourable. In lower latitudes, the noon sun rose high in the sky and softened the snow so it was often better to travel at 'night', when the sun dipped to the south. Major journeys could last for weeks or even months.

The famous polar pyramid tent, derived from the Eskimo skin tent and Indian tepee, was originally made to be thrown over four or five strong bamboo poles spread in position. Mawson's description, written in 1911, could apply to any sledging expedition, virtually to the present day. 'To facilitate their [the tents] erection in the perpetual winds, they were sewn permanently onto the five bamboo poles, instead of being thrown over the latter previously being set in position. Thus the tents opened like large conical umbrellas. A rawhide loop was fixed to the middle one of the three windward legs and, when raising a tent during a high wind, it was the usual thing for a man to be inside gripping the loop to pin down the windward legs and at the same time, kicking out the two leeward legs. On hard surfaces, holes were dug to receive the ends of the poles; at others they were pressed home into the snow by the man inside the tent.

A modern polar pyramid tent pitched in Windless Bight on a journey from Scott base to Cape Crozier. In the background is Mount Erebus. This shape of tent has proved to be the most satisfactory in the strong winds experienced in Antarctica. Properly pitched, a pyramid tent can withstand a gale.

Antarctic expedition personnel receive a lesson in the art of igloo building. All those who go to Antarctica must be trained to survive in any conceivable emergency.

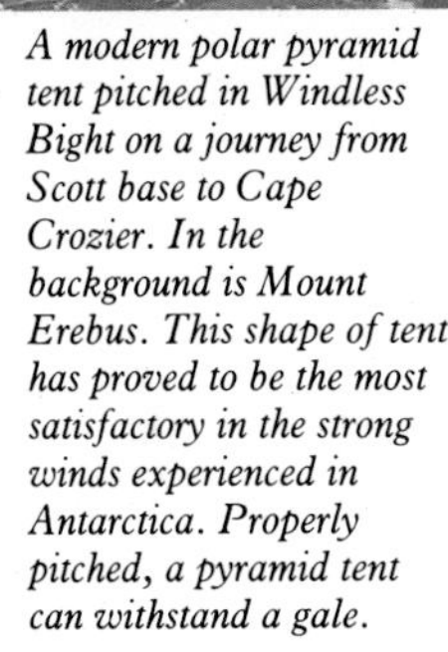

Clothing is the first line of defence against the fierce Antarctic climate. In extreme weather, face masks frequently become coated with ice as moisture from the wearer's breath freezes into a solid sheet. It takes many patient, and sometimes painful, minutes to free the ice from hair and clothing after a return to shelter.

'When pitched, the tent was held down by blocks of snow or ice, helped by spare food-bags which were all piled round a broad flounce. Ventilators, originally supplied with the tents, had to be dispensed with on account of the incessant drift. The door of the tent was an oval funnel . . . just large enough to admit a man, and secured by a draw string.'

On the winter trip to Cape Crozier, made during Scott's 1910-13 expedition, a new type of double tent was tried. It consisted of inner and outer linings spaced a few centimetres apart. Humidified air from the occupants could pass through the porous inner lining and condense as frost on the main tent. As the frost was dislodged by vibration caused by the wind it was directed to the perimeter of the tent instead of falling on the occupants. This has become the standard design for many tents used on expeditions today.

Most modern polar tents have a floor of strong waterproof material sewn into them which extends beyond the outside walls. In windy weather snow can be piled on the flap to anchor the tent, or snow blocks may be built up in a wall for greater shelter. Inside there are usually trap doors — flaps sealed with press studs — in the floor cloth. One provides clean snow for cooking, another, in a blizzard, may be used for waste disposal and as a latrine, or for loose snow. Insulated mats are carried to lay beneath sleeping bags.

Fur sleeping bags always have the disadvantage of holding frost formed from exhaled moisture and sweat. After some weeks of use, it can almost double the weight of a bag, and so clog the fur that insulation is lost. Double eiderdown bags, with silk sheets as inner liners, may be frequently reversed so that the frost will sublimate (evaporate without passing through a liquid state). A person wearing several layers of clothing under a parka will generate frost, not on the inner or outer garments, but in one of the intermediate layers. If a frosted pullover is moved to the outside, the ice crystals will sublimate.

Contrived shelters, using compacted snow as a building material for igloos or snow houses, have much to recommend them. As a base shelter, an igloo may be incomparable. A large coarse-toothed saw and ice axes can be used to quarry and shape the blocks — a job in which expertise is quickly achieved. The igloo provides perfectly calm air, preventing wind chill in the fiercest storm and, surprisingly, warmth from the sun can even be felt inside.

Snow caves have frequently sheltered marooned parties. Spurred by necessity Scott's Northern Party excavated an ice cave on Inexpressible Island, and there spent the winter of 1912. Victor Campbell later described their dwelling: '. . . it will take at least two days' more work to make it big enough for us, but it is shelter from the wind we can hear roaring outside. We spent the day chipping away at the ice walls and floor . . . As snow is a better insulator than ice, we shall line the walls with snow blocks and pack the space between the snow and ice with seaweed. The floor will be a layer of small pebbles on the ice, with seaweed on top of that; then our tent cloths are spread on the seaweed.

A Professional In The Age Of Amateurs

Amundsen makes his plans with meticulous care

It was September 1909. Roald Amundsen waited anxiously at the foot of an imposing staircase. The setting was a vast hallway in a hilltop mansion — the home of Norway's celebrated polar explorer-turned-statesman, Fridtjof Nansen. The first man to have crossed the Greenland Ice Pack in 1888, Nansen had won additional fame by drifting across the north polar ice cap in* Fram *during 1893-6. Now Amundsen had to ask him a question that might affect the rest of his life.

The *Fram* was a unique vessel, specially designed for Nansen to resist the extreme pressures of pack ice in the polar regions. She had admirably proved her worth. Amundsen, fellow-countryman and polar explorer, was eager to 'borrow' her.

Now, hungry to make a similar drift across the pole, Amundsen wanted to do more than Nansen, and get to the pole itself. Would the great man surrender his proprietorial rights over *Fram* and allow Amundsen — 11 years his junior — to use her? For years, Nansen had dreamed of taking *Fram* on an Antarctic expedition; but politics dominated his life, and nowadays, moreover, he had marriage problems. *Fram*, meanwhile, was lying idle.

When Nansen finally appeared at the head of the staircase — an awesome and forbidding figure — his answer was as direct as the setting was theatrical. 'You shall have *Fram*.'

Financing the expedition was more difficult. Not until February 1909 — after Amundsen had done exhaustive fund-raising work in America, and visited London for the Royal Geographical Society's endorsement — did the Norwegian Parliament grudgingly vote him part of the money he needed. Even then, he had to mortgage his house.

The expedition, organised by Leon, Amundsen's brother, was scheduled to start in January 1910. In the previous September, newspapers announced that Amundsen's old friend, Dr Frederick Cook, had already reached the North Pole on 21 April 1908. Less than a week later, the *New York Times* announced that Robert Peary had reached the North Pole on 6 April 1909.

Amundsen was shattered — his leitmotif gone. But his despair was transitory. If the north had gone, then he would try for the south. And he would say nothing to anyone of his intentions. Money had been raised for a northerly expedition — the pretence must be maintained if he were to keep faith with his backers. Particularly Nansen.

Then on 13 September, *The Times* of London announced that Robert Scott intended mounting an Antarctic expedition. Suddenly, Amundsen found himself involved in a race. Secrecy became ever more essential — if Scott heard of his revised plans, he would make a dash for the pole first.

Amundsen's preparations continued. He left nothing to chance. Clothing, equipment, food, dogs and the choice of men to go with him — all were considered with punctilious care.

There were 19 men in all. Lieutenant Thor-

Amundsen, exuding self-confidence, aboard the Fram *in Oslo harbour. Although by now he had made up his mind to try to reach the South Pole — Peary had beaten him to the North Pole — he kept his plans secret from all but a few companions. He was worried that Scott would beat him to his goal.*

The polar party was made up of Amundsen, seated in the centre; Hassel, with a moustache, on his left; Hanssen standing behind and between them; Bjaaland standing behind and to the left of Hanssen; and Wisting standing on the extreme left. Johansen is standing behind, and to the right of Roald Amundsen.

The Fram *and Scott's* Terra Nova *meet in the Bay of Whales. Visits were exchanged, but there was an undercurrent of tension — each side burning to know more of the other's plans and progress. Amundsen remained characteristically reticent, and the final parting was polite but chilly.*

The prefabricated hut was erected in Amundsen's garden in Oslo to test its suitability. It was a sturdy building with 10 bunks and a central kitchen.

THE RACE TO THE NORTH POLE

Robert Edwin Peary, now generally agreed to be the first man to reach the North Pole. He was 53 years old when he achieved his ambition, on 6 April 1909. Peary met Robert Scott in London, when he was there to receive a medal from the Royal Geographical Society, and urged him strenuously, but without success, to take dogs with him to Antarctica.

At the age of 24, Robert Peary wrote to his mother: 'I shall not be satisfied that I have done my best until my name is known from one end of the world to the other.'

No man strove harder to ensure his own success.

Peary was an American naval officer and engineer — with an interest in the polar regions that stemmed from his schooldays — who spent nine winters in the Arctic and 23 years exploring.

Although he had a passionate interest in natural history, fame — rather than science — was the spur that made the North Pole his sole objective. A complex man, tough and self-possessed, he had an imperious nature that alienated him from many, who regarded him as arrogant and conceited.

But he was a brilliant strategist and organiser, and had immense courage. At the advanced age of 53, and with all but two of his toes amputated from earlier attempts to conquer the pole, he finally arrived there on 6 April 1909 with his black assistant, Matthew Henson.

He had kept his word and won a place in history.

However, a debate continues to this day over the question of whether Peary was really the first to reach the pole. The other contender for the title is Dr Frederick Cook, who sailed with Adrien de Gerlache on the *Belgica* (see p 130).

Cook claimed to have reached the pole on 21 April 1908, nearly a year before Peary, but many experts doubt the accuracy of the evidence he was able to produce to back up his story. Other experts also doubt much of Peary's evidence.

vald Nilsen was appointed *Fram*'s captain, and Amundsen's second-in-command. One man Amundsen did not choose was Hjalmar Johansen. He had served with Nansen in the Arctic, and on one occasion had saved his life. A tough and wiry gymnast, he was a champion skier and a good dog driver — a man with much to offer. But post-expedition depression had led him to drink, which in turn had wrecked his army career and his marriage, and left him bankrupt. The expedition, with its enforced abstinence, could give him a new life, argued Nansen. Amundsen felt obliged to agree.

The key to Amundsen's ultimate success was to be his use of dogs. He was both practical and unsentimental about them, and chose those from North Greenland — the hardiest and most able to cope with polar conditions. Ninety-seven dogs were eventually embarked, in the care of Sverre Hassel. Yet another ex-*Fram* man, he was enjoying life in the customs' service, and resisted Amundsen's initial overtures to join the expedition. He would, however, travel as far as San Francisco with the dogs. Amundsen was triumphant: confident in his persuasive powers, he now knew he had another dog driver for the run to the pole.

On the eve of *Fram*'s departure, Amundsen revealed his true intentions to Nilsen, Prestrud and Gjertsen. The remainder still believed that they were to sail round the Americas — the Panama Canal did not exist — through the Bering Strait into the Arctic.

Six months later than originally intended — the change of destination had created inevitable delays — the voyage began. On passage to Madeira, Amundsen addressed himself to a job he had been dreading — writing a letter of apology to Nansen. The final paragraph concluded: 'And so I beg your forgiveness for what I have done. May my coming work help to atone for that in which I have offended.' He wrote a similar letter to the King.

A month later, on 6 September 1910, *Fram* arrived at Madeira. Fresh water and provisions were taken on, minor repairs were made, and those who could, enjoyed a spell ashore. On the evening of the 9th, three hours before their final run to the south, Amundsen ordered everyone on deck. Many of the men were writing last-minute letters home. Disgruntled and puzzled, they assembled to find Amundsen waiting by a map of Antarctica pinned to the mainmast.

He wasted no time in evasive preliminaries. '... it is my intention to sail Southwards, land a party on the Southern continent and try to reach the South Pole', he declared.

Gjertsen, who had long been party to the deception, was amused by the men's reactions. 'Most stood there with mouths agape', he wrote, 'staring at the Chief like so many question marks'. Wily as a fox, Amundsen then asked each man personally, if he would join him on this historic journey. He was free to go home if he wanted — passage paid — but...

The last man to go ashore was Leon Amundsen. He would post the men's letters, and cable Scott — *Beg leave to inform you* Fram *proceeding Antarctic. Amundsen.* But he would do none of these things until the beginning of October — by which time Amundsen knew he would be beyond the point of recall.

It took *Fram* four months and 6440 kilometres (4000 miles) to reach the Ross Ice Shelf. Amundsen chose the Bay of Whales as a mooring for *Fram*, because it would put the expedition 97 kilometres (60 miles) nearer the pole than Scott's, which was at McMurdo Sound.

Unloading started next day, 15 January — Amundsen was wasting no time. A suitable site was found for the base camp three kilometres (two miles) inland, and the first sledge, loaded with supplies, was hitched to a team of eight dogs. Amundsen took the traces and the first of the overland trips started.

For the next three weeks, five sledges shuttled back and forth between *Fram* and the base, with 46 dogs and five men shifting about 10 tonnes of supplies each day. Meanwhile, carpenter Jorgen Stubberud supervised the assembly of a prefabricated hut.

The next day, after a visit from Scott's *Terra Nova*, the base-camp was christened Framheim — 'The home of Fram' — and the depot-laying journeys began. In three weeks, three depots were established at latitudes 80°, 81° and 82°S respectively, with more than 1.5 tonnes of supplies shunted to within 770 kilometres (480 miles) of the pole.

On 21 April 1911, the sun finally sank in a crimson sky ... the long night had arrived.

AN ANXIOUS WINTER

Painstaking preparations for the coming journey

When* Fram *sailed for Buenos Aires she left nine men in the Bay of Whales camp — Amundsen, Lindstrom, Hanssen, Hassel, Johansen, Bjaaland, Prestrud, Wisting and Stubberud. The sun would not rise again over Framheim until the end of August. When it did, men and equipment would have to be ready for the final assault on the pole.

The timetable was inflexible. By an ironic oversight a copy of the 1912 Nautical Almanac — essential for polar navigation — had been forgotten. It meant that the expedition would have to rely upon the 1911 edition . . . and it meant having to reach the pole before the end of the year!

There was much to be done in the four months ahead. Amundsen was also conscious of the problems that could arise from nine men living and working together in such close proximity. The strain of cramped quarters and artificial lighting, of perpetual darkness and the timeless sense of isolation — they could all too easily create friction and tension.

Amundsen introduced a strict routine. For six days a week, all would rise at 7.30 am, breakfast, start work at 9.00 and stop for lunch at noon, sharp. In the afternoon, they would work from 2.00 until 5.15. After that, they were free to do as they pleased.

Domestic chores were to be shared by each man taking his turn as the week's orderly — emptying ashtrays, sweeping up and generally keeping the hut tidy. Each man had two clothes' hooks, so that all superfluous clothing could be kept out of sight in kitbags. And to assist ventilation, nobody was allowed to have anything under the bed, other than his boots.

As well as the hut in which they lived, there were fifteen 16-man tents — most used for storing fuel and provisions; some for the dogs.

Bjaaland and Hassel created a Scandinavian luxury — a steam bath. A bottomless box, large enough to cover a man so that only his head projected from the top, rested on a platform raised about 60 cm (2 ft) off the floor. A tin bath, fitted beneath the platform, was heated by two paraffin stoves. As the water boiled, steam filled the box. The bather had a rope-and-pulley system to lift the box clear when he had finished. Afterwards, a naked trot down the icy passage sealed pores and sharpened senses. It proved a popular Saturday night ritual.

In the months that followed, everyone had specific tasks. Kristian Prestrud was responsible for the scientific observations, assisted by Hjalmar Johansen. Sverre Hassel, dubbed the Managing Director of Framheim's Coal, Oil and Coke Company Limited, kept everyone supplied with fuel for lamps and heaters, assisted by Helmer Hanssen.

Johansen worked in the grocer's and chandler's store, packing sledging provisions of pemmican, chocolate, milk powder and biscuits.

Skilled at woodwork, Olav Bjaaland worked with Jorgen Stubberud, the hut builder and carpenter, in a cavernous workshop, complete with a boarded bench, remodelling and overhauling all the expedition's sledging outfits.

Superfluous weight is a crippling burden for a polar explorer, and every ounce that can be dispensed with is effort saved. By precision planing Bjaaland was able to lighten the equipment without affecting its strength.

As well as preparing two pairs of skis for each man, Bjaaland reduced the sledges by

Fram *moored alongside the Ross Ice Shelf — a photograph taken from the* Terra Nova *by a member of Scott's party.*

Equipment and materials may have changed, but the experience of dog sledging is the same as it was in Amundsen's time.

Hair neatly combed, the men pose for their photograph around the table at Framheim. Amundsen is last on the right.

The newly erected hut and tents were soon almost covered by snowdrifts. Eventually a network of tunnels and caves linked various parts of the camp.

The formidable figure of Fridtjof Nansen. His work in the Arctic had a profound effect on other polar explorers.

A TRUE VIKING

Often referred to as a true Viking, Fridtjof Nansen was tall, blond and blue-eyed — a striking mixture of athlete and hunter, mystic and intellectual, artist and scientist. A legend among polar explorers, and an outstanding Norwegian, Nansen was the consummate planner who — like Amundsen — left little to chance. He even learned the Eskimo language before making his celebrated trip across Greenland on skis in 1888. His three-year drift across the Arctic in *Fram*, that ended with a lonely winter in a crude hut on Franz Josef Land, made him an international figure and led to a career in politics. This was crowned in 1922 with the Nobel Peace Prize for his efforts in alleviating human misery after World War I. His relationship with Amundsen was never close enough for there to have been a real bond of friendship. But Nansen recognised the great qualities in his fellow explorer. Despite Amundsen's deception in using *Fram* to make for the South Pole, Nansen gave him unfailing support, particularly when he was criticised by the British press.

When Amundsen announced his farewell to exploration, Nansen's valedictory oration included the line: 'Your work is a man's work, sprung out of a man's will...'

It could equally have been said of Nansen.

almost a third of their weight. Stubberud achieved similar weight reductions with the sledging cases. As Bjaaland finished a sledge, Hanssen and Oscar Wisting assembled its component parts, using rawhide lashings.

In a tiny, cabin-sized snow cave off the main storeroom, Wisting worked for most of the winter months at a treadle sewing machine. He made valuable weight-saving reductions in their equipment by sewing new tents out of windcloth, complete with integral floors. These new tents were four kilograms (8.8 lb) lighter than the ones they had brought.

Finally, there was the camp cook, Adolf Lindstrom. He was an overweight and good-humoured man whose cakes, according to Amundsen 'slipped down with fabulous rapidity'. Lindstrom was the first up every morning, roused by his alarm clock at 6.00.

Breakfast was hot buckwheat cakes — a speciality Lindstrom learned in America — spread with whortleberry preserve, plus wholemeal bread enriched with wheatgerm, butter and cheese.

Lunch was largely fresh or frozen seal meat, prepared in various ways, supplemented by tinned meats towards the end of winter. For dessert there were tinned Californian fruits, tarts, and tinned puddings or pastries and pies made by Lindstrom. Supper was seal steak, bread, butter, whortleberry jam and cheese.

Coffee was the staple drink. The only alcohol allowed was a hot toddy of brandy on Saturday evenings, and an aquavit — a Scandinavian spirit flavoured with carraway — on Sunday. Birthdays and festive holidays were similarly celebrated.

The food at Framheim was wholesome and nutritious. Amundsen had witnessed first-hand the appalling effects of scurvy while with the *Belgica* in 1897 (see p130). It left him with a healthy respect for a balanced diet, and the need to ensure adequate supplies of vitamin C.

One psychological advantage gained by the men working in different parts of the camp throughout the day, was the pleasure of the evening get-together over dinner. There was always conversation, as well as card games, darts' matches, reading, or sessions of needlework around the main table.

On occasions the gramophone was brought out and their few records played. But this was only done sparingly, in order not to spoil their appreciation.

The dogs also provided a pleasurable diversion for some of the men. Each was responsible for the care and feeding of some dogs.

Despite his shrewd analytical mind, Amundsen was not without his own worries. Johansen's prickly temperament was one concern. Enforced abstinence from alcohol, and a conviction that he was the more experienced polar explorer of the two — he had been to the Arctic with Nansen — made him an uncertain personality to deal with at times.

There was also the worry of Robert Scott. How far had the English advanced? The fact that Scott had motorised sledges was difficult for Amundsen to forget, even though he doubted their efficiency.

By 24 August, when the sun reappeared, the sledges were packed ready to be taken out from their underground stores.

But two more months were to pass before the weather was warm enough for them to start the final journey. They were eight long weeks of extreme frustration for all — dogs included, for they were being harnessed each day without a run. Amundsen's anxieties and vacillations were becoming infectious. Each day he would look at the weather and propose a start, then cancel it. On one occasion he uncharacteristically held a secret ballot — excluding Lindstrom who was to be left behind at Framheim. The result was a split decision for alternative days. Amundsen spun a coin to break the tie. But the winning day had to be cancelled because of a blizzard.

The weather for the run to their first base at 80°S had to offer clear visibility, or there was a real risk of their missing it.

As the days passed the dogs fretted, and tensions increased...

AMUNDSEN WINS THE RACE TO THE POLE

Everything goes according to plan despite some discord

They sped across the snow in exhilaration — eight men with six sledges and 86 dogs. It was Friday, 8 September 1911. After weeks of waiting patiently for suitable weather, Amundsen's party were finally on their way to the first depot at 80°S. Lindstrom was left as caretaker of Framheim.

HOW HE REACHED THE POL

Amundsen Tells the Story of the Final Da

"A PLEASURE TRIP."

(BY CABLE—"SUNDAY TIMES" SPECIAL MESSAGES.)

...DON Saturday Morning. | has reached the Pole as well as Ca
Amundsen."

At the pole, observations were made to make sure they were as close to their goal as possible. Then three men went out in different directions for 20 km (12.5 miles) to make sure they had 'encircled' the actual pole.

Poleheim, 17 December 1911. Inside the tent Amundsen left a note to Scott and a letter for him to deliver to King Haakon. Bjaaland presented his leader with a box of cigars.

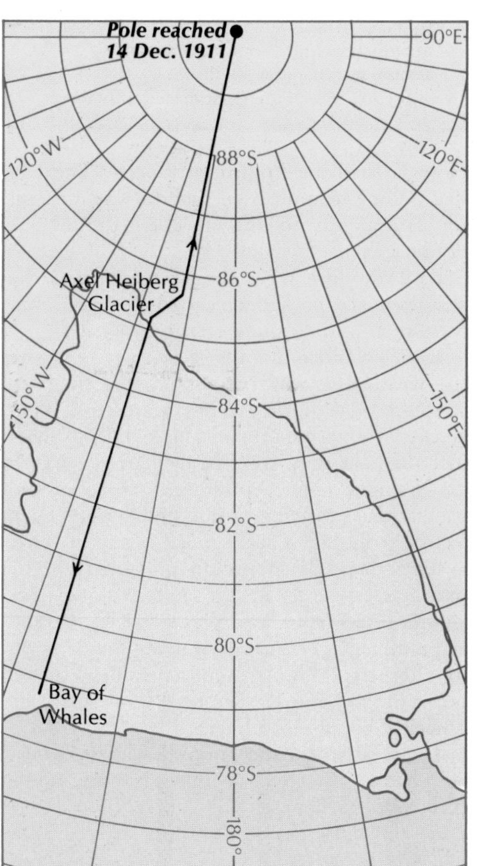

'The going was splendid', wrote Amundsen, and in the next three days they covered 50 kilometres (31 miles). Then their luck changed. On the Monday they woke to find the temperature had plummeted alarmingly, shrouding them in a thick, white fog. It was nearly −56°C (−69°F).

The next day conditions worsened — even the fluid in their compasses froze. Amundsen decided it was too risky to go on. That night it was agreed that if the weather eased they would race on to the depot, unload their sledges, and then dash back to Framheim.

They arrived at the depot on the Thursday. Next evening, Hanssen and Stubberud discovered that their heels were frostbitten. Many of the dogs were also suffering the cold — two of them froze to death as they lay down.

At 7.00 next morning they set off for Framheim. Amundsen, without a sledge of his own, joined Wisting's and, together with Hanssen's, they sped away. Normally they sledged in sight of each other. But on this occasion, the first two sledges moved so fast that they rapidly disappeared from the next sledge driver's sight. This was Stubberud. His dogs immediately slowed down. In great pain with his feet, and with no food or fuel, Stubberud realised he would have to wait for those behind.

It was a long wait. Bjaaland eventually caught up, took the lead, and they both reached Framheim at 6 pm — two hours later than Amundsen's group. Half an hour later, Hassel arrived.

In a neat hand, Amundsen recorded their success in his diary: 'So we arrived and were able to plant our flag at the geographical South Pole. God be thanked!'

Six hours later, at 12.30 am, Johansen and Prestrud finally stumbled into camp. Both were exhausted — Prestrud's frostbitten feet were in a bad way. The two men had come through the last part of the journey in a nightmare of darkness and fog, only able to locate Framheim because of the dogs' barking.

Next morning, at breakfast, Amundsen asked Johansen why they had been so late getting back. It was the spark that fired the explosion. Johansen, bitter at the way the group had been allowed to split up, angrily accused Amundsen of panicking and of bad leadership.

In the shocked silence that followed, Amundsen said nothing. It was what he had

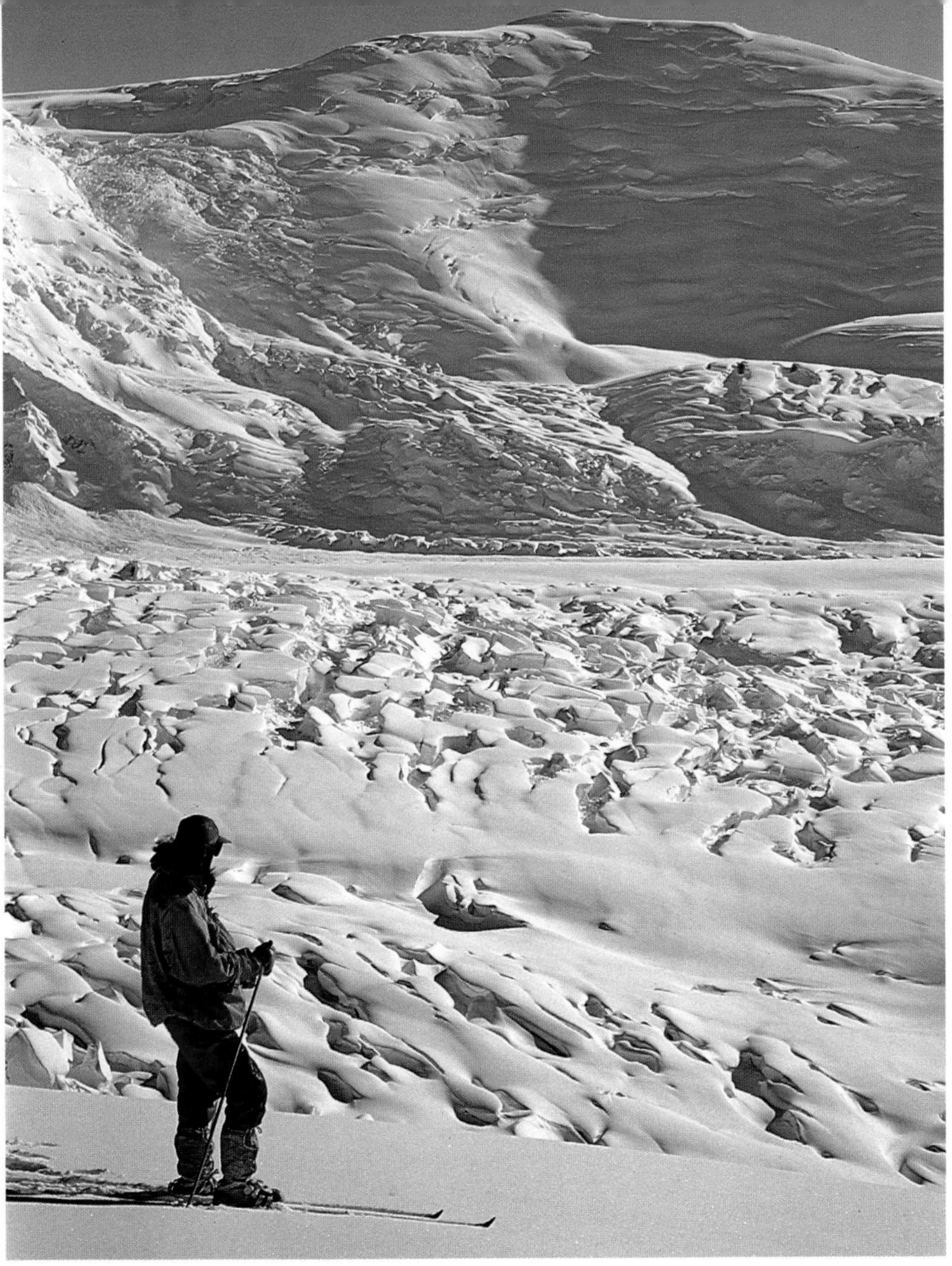

In 1962 a New Zealand party under Wally Herbert repeated Amundsen's route down the Axel Heiberg Glacier and confirmed its difficulty.

always feared — a confrontation with the one man in the expedition with experience to match his own. It was the end of their hitherto splendid unity, for Amundsen never forgave Johansen, or spoke to him without need.

Amundsen explained to the rest why he had gone on ahead so fast — because Hanssen was suffering from frostbite and needed attention urgently. It was not wholly convincing.

At midday Amundsen announced a change of plans. Amundsen would now lead one party to the pole; Prestrud — with Johansen — would lead a second group to explore King Edward VII Land. It was not a totally revengeful decision — Amundsen had decided that if the pole party failed, there might still be a 'first' to be gained for Norway.

Amundsen then spoke to each man on his own — ignoring Johansen — asking for his pledge of loyalty. All gave it — they could hardly do otherwise.

And so on 20 October, the expedition's physical wounds now healed, the party mustered — Amundsen, Bjaaland, Wisting, Hassel and Hanssen. There were four sledges with 13 dogs to each. Amundsen's party made good progress. From time to time they had trouble with crevasses, including one alarming moment when Bjaaland's sledge dropped from sight, suspended by the dogs' traces.

Arriving at the first depot on the 24th, they dug out stores and provisions, and gave the dogs a feast of seal meat and blubber. The next day the party left with all five men on skis.

On the way they saw a snow cairn they had built in April, still standing as they had left it. Its reliability proven, they built 150 similar cairns at intervals on the run to the south. Inside, they left a written record with the distance and bearing to the next one.

Every day they ate their lunch as they built a beacon. Lunch was '. . . nothing very luxurious', wrote Amundsen, 'three or four dry oatmeal biscuits, that was all. If one wanted a drink, one could mix snow with the biscuit.' His experience with Eskimos had led him to regard tea or coffee as undesirable stimulants.

They arrived at their third and last depot, at 82°S, on 4 November. Two days later they left. They were travelling 32 kilometres (20 miles) a day in five hours, building their daily snow cairn in an hour and a half, and then resting for the remainder of the time.

On the 11th, the peaks of a chain of mountains were seen far ahead — which Amundsen later named Queen Maud's Range, after the Queen of Norway. The problem of finding a way past began to preoccupy them. The going also started to get harder, as the flat surface of the ice gave way to a sea of wave-like formations.

At the foot of the range they camped and discussed strategy. They were 550 kilometres (340 miles) from the pole and had 42 dogs left.

Their resultant plan was to take provisions and equipment for 30 days, and make the climb with all the dogs. At the top, 24 of them would be shot — since they would no longer be needed — and the remaining 18 would be retained for the run to the pole. Once there, six more of the dogs would be slaughtered to provide food for the remaining 12 to return.

The next day, 17 November, they started the ascent of the Axel Heiberg Glacier. The sun was warm and they rose 600 metres (2000 ft) in comparative ease, covering 18.5 kilometres (11.5 miles) before making camp. For four more days they continued, climbing laboriously at one point, dropping alarmingly at another. On 21 November they reached the top. They had travelled 71 kilometres (44 miles) and carried a tonne of supplies to a height of 3000 metres (10 000 ft).

Twenty-four of the dogs were now shot and the group stayed at 'The Butcher's Shop' — as they named the spot — for four more days, before setting off in the teeth of a blizzard. They had already waited two days longer than they could afford — they had to press on.

For ten days they struggled, five men and 18 dogs, against appalling weather — 56 km/h (35 mph) winds with sticky, driving snow and thick fog. Blizzard followed blizzard with unrelenting force. At last they reached the plateau, only to be confronted by 'The Devil's Ballroom' — a glacier with a thin crust of snow covering a series of treacherous crevasses. It was the last major obstacle.

On 8 December, with the sun shining in a clear sky, they passed Shackleton's farthest south — 88°23′S. There were 153 kilometres (95 miles) left. Hunger and exhaustion were making the dogs aggressive. The men, too, had their problems, with frostbitten faces, sores and scabs.

As the distance lessened, Amundsen's tensions grew. Would he find that Scott had beaten him to it, after all? The temptation to go flat out was unbearable. Amundsen's obsession got through to them all.

At 3 o'clock on Friday, 14 December 1911, a simultaneous cry of 'Halt' was made by the sledge drivers. The sledge meters had registered their arrival at the South Pole. They had reached their goal; the journey was ended.

THE AFTERMATH

Amundsen and his companions grasped their country's flag pole with 'five weather-beaten, frost-bitten fists' — an action shared by all who had staked their lives in the struggle — and planted it at the geographical South Pole. Amundsen named the plain King Haakon VII's Plateau. They then erected a tent, calling it Poleheim, and Amundsen left a message for Scott, and a letter for King Haakon.

Three days later, with the Norwegian flag flying, they returned to Framheim. The journey was as Amundsen had planned it — comparatively straightforward, with five men and 11 dogs 'all hale and hearty'.

The voyage back to Tasmania was a long and frustrating month for Amundsen — now anxious to be the first with the news. Scott still haunted him. On 7 March 1912, Amundsen finally cabled his brother Leon with the news — his victory was complete.

The hut at Cape Evans still stands today. Volunteers from New Zealand have restored the interior to match, as closely as possible, the way it was in Scott's day.

Winter quarters Cape Evans

SCOTT'S LAST EXPEDITION

Laying the groundwork for a disaster

Scott and the* Discovery *expedition returned from the Antarctic in 1904 to adulation and respect. Men who had prevailed in the icy fastnesses became heroes. Very gratifying, but for a man of Scott's retiring and insecure nature, the social whirl was more a duty than a pleasure.

Scott was promoted to Captain in 1904 and, after an interval, returned to his career. But he found himself glancing over his shoulder as Shackleton prepared the *Nimrod* expedition. There was no love lost between the men; circumstances and temperament made them uncharitable competitors.

In September 1909, Scott declared his hand. He would lead a new expedition. The polar quest and 'securing for the British Empire the honour of that achievement' would be paramount. But a scientific program was also planned. In promoting these twin aims, Scott was appealing to the widest spectrum of interests for funds. A polar assault would fire up the public, he thought, but the Royal Geographical Society needed to be reassured it was supporting more than a vulgar adventure.

Money was harder to find than it had been 10 years earlier, however. Lacking Shackleton's entrepreneurial pugnacity, Scott struggled for money on the lecture circuit until, in March 1910, the Government stumped up £20 000.

Expedition personnel applied in their thousands, though. But there was one man above all others that Scott wanted by him; his companion and confidant from the *Discovery* days, Edward Wilson.

Early in 1910 Scott visited Norway to oversee trials of the motor sledges he planned to take. Transport on the ice was still a vexed question and Scott clung to the British orthodoxy that man-hauling was best. If help were needed, ponies or engines would take precedence over dogs.

Norwegian achievements in the Arctic using dogs were dismissed or patronised by the British, and the fact that ponies and human muscle alone had got Shackleton to within 180 kilometres (97 nautical miles) of the South Pole, impressed Scott.

The *Terra Nova,* a 700-tonne, coal-burning whaler built in 1884, was to be the expedition ship because the *Discovery* was unavailable.

On 1 June 1910, the *Terra Nova* steamed down the Thames, while Scott remained in Britain to prise last-minute funds from reluctant fingers.

A litter of discarded equipment inside the Cape Evans hut (left).

He rejoined the ship at Simonstown, South Africa. At Melbourne, a brief, challenging telegram awaited him: 'Beg leave to inform you, *Fram* proceeding Antarctica. Amundsen.' Scott's reaction was muted, but the team shared his prickly sense of proprietorial right to the pole.

At Lyttelton, all stores were checked, augmented and restowed. The 19 Siberian ponies and 34 dogs arrived, shipped from Russia by Cecil Meares. The photographer, Herbert Ponting, also joined the ship there.

At Port Chalmers 'We filled up with what coal we could squeeze into our already overloaded ship', said Evans, 'and finally left for the Great Unknown on November 29, 1910'. Three days out, a force 10 gale almost sent the shuddering, heaving *Terra Nova* to the bottom. Ten tons of coal were jettisoned and waves deluged the deck-bound animals. The ship was ploughing through pack ice by 9 December. Cape Crozier was the favoured haven for the wintering party because it was close to an emperor penguin breeding ground and to the Ross Ice Shelf which had to be crossed by the polar party. But landfall at Cape Crozier proved to be impossible. So, on 4 January 1911, the *Terra Nova* approached the *Discovery* Hut on the far side of Ross Island, but, Evans noted: 'We found the Strait frozen over . . . I eventually went aloft to the crosstrees and had a look round; we finally decided to land at a place where there appeared to be a very good beach.' That final spot became Cape Evans.

Activity on shore was furious. The weather was fine and morale high. By the end of the first day the hut site had been levelled, and the relieved animals and two motor sledges had been landed. They were all soon working, the sledges towing over a tonne each.

By 17 January the hut was complete. 'Meares has become enamoured of the gramophone', Scott wrote. 'We find we have a splendid collection of records.'

Now, six weeks behind schedule, Scott was anxious to begin his summer program. Three parties prepared themselves: a southern party

Terra Nova (left) moored in McMurdo Sound.

Fuel for the stove being unloaded and stacked beside the hut. Cases of stores were kept close to the walls and provided additional protection from the weather.

to lay supply depots along the proposed polar route; an eastern party to explore King Edward VII Land; and a western party to investigate the glacier region to the west of McMurdo Sound.

Scott's southern plan was 'to go forward with five weeks' food for men and animals; to depot a fortnight's supply after 12 or 13 days and return'. He hoped that this major depot would be established at least as far south as the 80th parallel. On 2 February the party of 13 men, eight ponies and 26 dogs set out with 10 sledges. But the ponies were soon sinking up to their chests in the soft snow, so Scott decided to march at night when the surface would be colder and firmer.

Progress was made but, even so, the length of a night's march, rarely more than 16 kilometres (10 miles), was dictated by the strength of the weakest pony. A depot was laid about 56 kilometres (35 miles) from Hut Point, at Corner Camp, where the party turned south. The weather then deteriorated. A blizzard lasting three days stopped them in their tracks and sapped the strength of the ponies. The dogs, on the other hand, were relatively unaffected by the conditions and temperatures that dropped as low as −29°C (−21°F).

Tending to the ponies became a major chore and at the 79th parallel Scott had Evans and Petty Officers Forde and Keohane return to Safety Camp with the three most exhausted animals. On 17 February Scott decided to push the march no further and the major One Ton Camp was established at 79°28′30″S, over 48 kilometres (30 miles) north of the desired 80°S. It was to be a critical shortfall.

When the party had returned to Safety Camp near the edge of the ice shelf, Scott received further alarming news of Amundsen. The eastern party had sailed to King Edward VII Land in the *Terra Nova* as Scott had trudged south, and, while looking for a suitable landfall, had come across a ship in the Bay of Whales. Surprise changed to a shocked realisation that the ship was Amundsen's *Fram*. Until that moment the *Terra Nova* party, including Scott, had convinced themselves that Amundsen would be making his polar assault from the Weddell Sea coast, on the other side of the continent.

Back at Safety Camp, Scott absorbed the news more stoically than his companions. 'The proper, as well as the wiser, course for us is to proceed exactly as though this had not happened . . .' he wrote. 'There is no doubt that Amundsen's plan is a serious menace to ours. He has a shorter distance to the pole by 60 miles [97 km] — I never thought he could have got so many dogs safely to the ice.'

Scott now waited on the return of the western party. The six-man team, led by Australian geologist Griffith Taylor, was exploring the dry valley and Koettlitz Glacier region.

They returned to Hut Point on 14 March. Scott ordered a final sortie to Corner Camp and, on 13 April, as the sea ice began to refreeze, men and animals were able to make their way to Cape Evans for the long night. By 13 May everyone was accounted for.

A PERMANENT RECORD

Ponting worked long hours trying to get the best possible photographs of the expedition.

Of all the talented specialists Scott took south with him, perhaps the one who produced the most enduring work was Herbert Ponting, the expedition photographer. He was a romantic, as so many attracted to the Antarctic undoubtedly were, but Ponting was also a businessman who had more than an artist's eye for the value of his unique photographs.

By 1910, Ponting had twice travelled around the world, had worked as a war correspondent, a rancher and miner, and had lived in the Orient. His photographic record of his travels was encyclopaedic, and during the long winter nights at Cape Evans his lantern slide lectures were enormously popular. And his Antarctic work was a triumph: elegant, almost formal, studies of the icy beauty and pristine stillness of Antarctica; rare or whimsical wildlife shots; candid snaps of camp life; and, most memorably, portraits of the exhausted men.

Scott noted in his journal: 'Ponting would have been a great asset to our party if only on account of his lectures, but his value as a pictorial recorder of events becomes daily more apparent. No expedition has ever been illustrated so extensively.'

Mt Erebus, the beacon that welcomed sledging parties back to Ross Island, sketched by Edward 'Bill' Wilson.

Thomas Clissold hard at work making bread. To let him know when the dough has risen, Clissold rigged up an alarm, set off when a disc on top of the bread completed a circuit and rang a bell.

WINTER AT CAPE EVANS

Naval discipline rules the lives of Scott's men

During the Antarctic winter of 1911, the Cape Evans hut on Ross Island became more than just the living quarters of a group of dedicated scientists and explorers. It became the southernmost outpost of Empire as well as the wardroom and messdeck of a Royal Navy vessel. And the Edwardian social and naval attitudes, the club-like atmosphere, brought into the hut along with the Nellie Melba records and the volumes of Browning and Tennyson, hint at the reasons Scott's final expedition was such a mixture of real achievement, heroic endurance and eventual tragedy.

The burden of being a British party, of having to adequately represent a great nation and satisfy its expectations, weighed on Scott and his team. Failure was unthinkable. They were also gripped by the romantic Victorian ideals of courage and self-sacrifice; their attitude towards man-hauling is evidence of that. Their flaw was their blinkered insularity, the complacent belief that how England chose to do things was undoubtedly the right way to do things. If, for example, dogs were found to be unruly and inefficient, then that must be the fault of the dogs; that the British could learn doghandling skills from the Norwegians was something they did not wish to concede.

Their hut was tucked in front of the small Wind Vane Hill on the northern side of Cape Evans. It was a well designed 15 x 7.6 metre (50 x 25 ft) structure, 2.4 metres (8 ft) high at the eaves and 4.8 metres (16 ft) at the centre.

Inside, it was divided by a wall of provision boxes into a wardroom for the 16 officers and scientists, and a messdeck for the nine seamen. It was a division of living quarters that seemed natural to everyone, but the familiar naval hierarchy did distance Scott further from his men than Amundsen or Shackleton liked to be from theirs. The tidy formality of a command structure suited Scott's temperament; he pre-

A general view of the sleeping arrangements. The men are (from left to right) Cherry-Garrard, Bowers, Oates, Meares (top) and Atkinson.

Lieutenant Evans observing an occultation of Jupiter. The telephone (on boxes at right), was connected to the hut where observations were timed.

Messrs Heinz & Co were among the many firms that supplied food for the expedition. Presumably this photograph was to be used for advertising when the expedition returned.

ferred to leave riskier rough-and-tumble camaraderie to leaders such as Shackleton.

On the other hand, Scott responded well, if a little stuffily, to people with kind and generous instincts, and he was not unapproachable. The majority of his men did admire him but, by contrast, the leader in the party who was loved as much as admired, and without reserve, was 'Uncle Bill' Wilson.

Within the officers' wardroom, space was allowed for the 1.8 x 2.4 metre (6 x 8 ft) darkroom where Herbert Ponting, the photographer, worked and slept. Next to this room were tiny parasitology and physical laboratories run, respectively, by the surgeon, Dr 'Atch' Atkinson, and meteorologist, Dr 'Sunny Jim' Simpson, one of the team's most brilliant scientists. Scott's personal cubicle, the 'holy of holies' was against the northern wall.

The daily routine throughout the winter, Scott noted on 19 June, 'Possessed a settled regularity . . . Clissold [the cook] is up at 7 am to start the breakfast . . . Between 8 and 8.30 the men are out and about, fetching ice for melting etc. . .There is a stretching of limbs and an interchange of morning greetings, garnished with sleepy humour . . . Soon after 8.30 I manage to drag myself from a very comfortable bed . . . by 9.30 breakfast is finished . . . From 9.30 to 1.30 the men are steadily employed on a programme of preparation for sledging . . . The repair of sleeping-bags and the alteration of tents have already been done, but there are many other tasks uncompleted or not yet begun, such as the manufacture of provision bags, crampons, sealskin soles, pony clothes etc. We meet for our mid-day meal at 1.30 . . . and spend a cheerful half-hour over it. Afterwards the ponies are exercised, weather permitting . . . After this the officers go on steadily with their work, whilst the men do odd jobs . . . The evening meal, our dinner, comes at 6.30 . . . Afterwards people read, write or play games . . . The gramophone is usually started by some kindly disposed person, and on three nights of the week lectures [are given] . . . The majority of candles are extinguished by midnight, and the night-watchman alone remains . . . On Saturday afternoon or Sunday morning some extra bathing takes place; chins are shaven, and perhaps clean garments donned. Such signs, with the regular Service on Sunday, mark the passage of the weeks.'

Scott's last birthday dinner — his 43rd. The 'sumptuous spread' included seal soup, roast mutton and red currant jelly, fruit salad, asparagus and chocolate.

The regular, voluntary, evening lectures, introduced by Scott, were popular with the officers and scientists, less so with the seamen, unless Ponting was giving one of his slide shows, or Scott himself was outlining his plans for the coming summer. The talks and discussions were usually on scientific or expedition subjects and took on the tone of university seminars. Wilson kicked off with a talk about Antarctic flying birds (later, in his role as expedition artist, he also gave a popular talk about painting and sketching). Simpson followed with meteorology, and physicist Charles Wright talked about varying characteristics of ice. Captain 'Titus' Oates, who had charge of the ponies, lectured on their care, and Lieutenant 'Birdie' Bowers discussed sledge rations. Scott made every effort to learn from these sessions, often making notes.

On the midwinter night of 22 June, when the party celebrated Christmas with roast sirloin, plum pudding, champagne and sweetmeats, the new issue of the resurrected *South Polar Times* was read out by Scott to an amused audience. This mainly satirical paper first appeared during Scott's *Discovery* expedition, and was now edited by Apsley Cherry-Garrard.

Birthdays were important personal milestones that assumed more than usual importance so far from civilisation. Within the hut, they became occasions when everyone could claim a glass of champagne, and the birthday boy himself a whole bottle. Far more poignant, of course, were birthday celebrations during arduous sledging trips. Even in extreme conditions it was quite usual for a sledge team to remember a companion's birthday and produce gifts that may have been carried for weeks. If it is the thought that counts, then no gift in the world can have been more valued than those homemade cigars, or few squashed chocolates or sips of liqueur, given by one man to another as they clung, with a weakening grasp, to life itself.

In the Cape Evans hut, as the last candle was dowsed each night, the night watchman, invariably one of the scientists or officers (including Scott), took charge from midnight till 7 am. The galley fire had to be kept stoked up, the acetylene gas plant had to be serviced, the ponies needed checking, and the aurora record had to be updated. Every two hours, Simpson's meteorological and barometric instrument readings also had to be logged.

Throughout the winter, short trips covering the few miles south to Hut Point, or north to Shackleton's hut at Cape Royds, were commonplace. Much briefer excursions, however, were constantly made to three thermometer stations set up within a kilometre or so of the Cape Evans hut. One evening, Atkinson gave the party an unwonted but invaluable lesson by example when, without Scott's knowledge, and against other advice, he ignored deteriorating conditions and set out for one of the thermometer points, confident that he was equal to the quick jaunt. Six hours later he was dragged in, frostbitten and exhausted.

Cecil Meares tries his hand at the pianola, although only Cherry-Garrard and Debenham were very much good at playing. The instrument was used for Sunday service, and was also an important asset in the restricted social life in the hut at Cape Evans.

WORST JOURNEY IN THE WORLD

Privations suffered in the cause of science

During the winter of 1911, three of the Cape Evans party threw down the most defiant challenge to Antarctic conditions the continent had seen. At 11 am on 27 June, Bill Wilson, 'Birdie' Bowers and Apsley Cherry-Garrard set out on a 105-kilometre (65-mile) midwinter trek to Cape Crozier.

On the day they departed, Scott concealed his own anxiety beneath terseness. His brief journal entry ended: 'This winter travel is a new and bold venture, but the right men have gone to attempt it. All good luck go with them!' In reminding himself that 'the right men have gone', Scott seemed to be trying to convince himself that they had not miscalculated, that they were not gambling with the lives of three men.

But Wilson was as experienced in polar conditions as Scott, and he had come to the ice specifically to visit the Cape Crozier rookery in winter when emperor penguins incubate their eggs. It was a project he had been nursing since the *Discovery* days, 10 years earlier. His hope was that the primitive emperor embryo would throw light on the origin of all birds by establishing a conclusive link between reptilian scales and feathers.

The three men travelled south from Cape Evans, pulling six weeks' food and equipment, 343 kilograms (757 lb) on two sledges, a great weight even in favourable conditions.

Once off the sea ice, about 29 kilometres (18 miles) from Cape Evans, the cooler −44°C (−47°F) air from the ice shelf embraced them.

During that second night, 805 metres (880 yds) in from the edge of the ice shelf, the temperature dropped to −49°C (−56°F). Merely breathing became an ordeal, and it was not long before the cycle of sweat and freezing sweat began to leave the three of them either shivering and soaking wet in their sleeping bags at night, or locked into an iron-hard layer of ice during the day's march, as sweat from their exertions froze in their clothing.

On the soft surface of the ice shelf, the sand-like snow dragged at the sledge runners, making it impossible to haul both sledges at once. So began the wearying business of relaying one sledge forward, then the other, so that for every five kilometres (three miles) marched, they advanced only one third of that distance.

Cherry-Garrard found that the worst time of the day was the seven hours spent in their ice-laden sleeping bags, when they were racked with cramp and cold. Wilson insisted on that amount of rest despite the discomfort. Without it they would not have survived the weeks ahead. On the ice shelf the temperature continued to plummet, reaching an absolute low on 5 July of −61°C (−77°F). Often the temperature would not rise above −51°C (−60°F) all day. At such times the merest puff of wind was like a razor, and pauses had to be taken to ensure that feet still had life in them.

Each morning, after breakfast of hot pemmican 'hoosh', biscuits and tea, each man would emerge from the tent and adopt a semi-crouched position or else his clothes would freeze him into an unsuitable attitude for sledge hauling.

All this while, an interesting if unspectacular rations experiment was also being conducted. Each day, 907 grams (32 oz) of food was issued to each man, but the amount of pemmican, biscuit and butter was varied. The ratio was then readjusted until they arrived at the ideal balance. There was also tea, of course.

Over the final 32 kilometres (20 miles) from Cape McKay to The Knoll above Cape Crozier, the three men picked their way painfully in the dark, like blind insects, among the ice pressure-ridges and crevasses. They reached

Remains of the igloo at Cape Crozier where Wilson, Bowers and Cherry-Garrard sheltered during their awful night-time journey to the penguin rookery. Various items, including Wilson's pencils, were found by the first party to revisit the site in 1957.

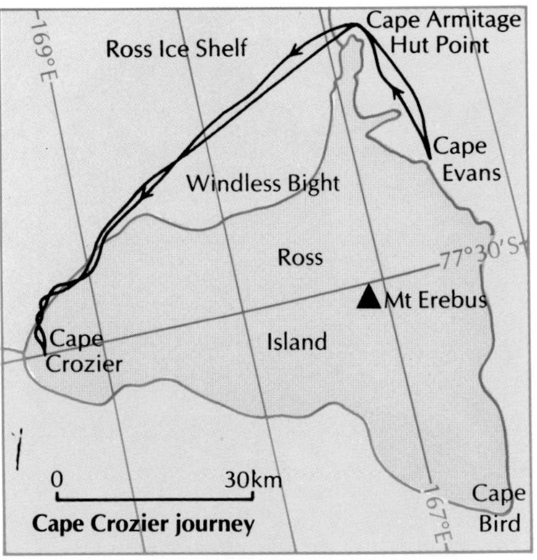

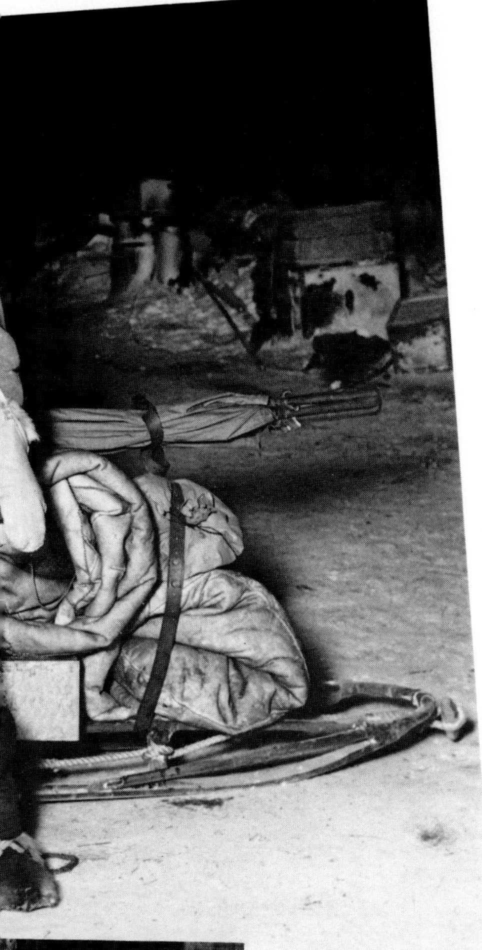

The Cape Crozier party, relaxed and undismayed about the trial ahead. They are (left to right) Bowers, Wilson and Cherry-Garrard.

The exhausted men back in the hut after their ordeal. Ponting saw a look in the men's eyes that haunted him. 'Once before I have seen similar expressions on men's faces — when some half-starved Russian prisoners, after the battle of Mukden, were taken to Japan.'

The Knoll on 15 July and built a solid rock igloo. The 2.4 x 3.6 metre (8 x 12 ft) structure was far from windproof and its roof was an expanse of canvas brought from Cape Evans.

By now, though, the three explorers were forced to turn their attention to the penguin colony for more than scientific reasons. They needed blubber oil to help them eke out their dwindling paraffin supply. On 20 July, after one abortive attempt, they succeeded in clambering down among the thrusting ridges of pressure ice to reach the almost inaccessible rookery. They were surprised to find only about 100 birds. Working quickly in the brief, dim daylight, Bowers and Wilson caught and skinned three birds and took six eggs, three of which were broken during the tortuous climb back to the igloo.

Now, the unrelenting cold was accompanied by a force 4, and worsening, gale, which the party, in its weakened state, felt keenly. 'Such extremity of suffering', wrote Cherry-Garrard later, 'cannot be measured. Madness or death may give relief. But this I know: we on this journey were already beginning to think of death as a friend.'

'Things must improve', said Wilson the next day. That night, however, a strong gust uprooted the tent pitched by the igloo door and, so far as the men in the hut knew, it had been lost for good. As they scrambled into the blizzard to rescue their equipment, the hopelessness of their position sank in. That tent had been the only shelter for the return journey. Without it they would surely die.

Impossible though it would have seemed to them at that moment, there was worse to come. The blizzard that now screamed over the igloo roof sucked at the canvas covering with a power that finally defeated it. The fabric exploded into shreds and, with a violence that left the men almost insensible, the blizzard whirled in upon them, forcing them to retreat into their final, pathetic, refuge — the ice-impregnated sleeping bags. They prayed, they sang hymns, they drew what comfort they could from one another's company and the touching realisation that it was 23 July — Wilson's birthday. Bowers even had sweets on hand with which to celebrate.

Wilson, Bowers and Cherry-Garrard had now been living for four weeks in conditions that, until then, had been endured by men only for a few days at a time. When they slept it was only because exhaustion allowed them to — 'as men sleep on the rack'.

They had not eaten for two days and nights, and now, only by pulling their groundsheet over their heads to protect the primus stove, could they produce a pemmican brew. It was in a mood of despair that they then searched for the tent during the brief gloomy hours of twilight that passed for their day. After some time, Wilson and Cherry-Garrard heard an excited cry from Bowers. Not only had the tent been found 366 metres (400 yards) from the igloo, but it was undamaged.

On 25 July they set out for Hut Point. This time, however, exhaustion was a greater enemy than cold, and they kept banging into one another as they fell asleep on the march. 'Not a meal was passed', wrote Wilson, 'without our having to wake each other up for fear of spilling the pemmican or falling into the cooker'.

But progress was satisfactory. On 31 July they reached Hut Point and, at 10 pm on 1 August, they stumbled into the Cape Evans hut where their frozen clothes were literally cut from their bodies. For 36 days they had endured the harshest conditions men had even suffered, yet survived. At the outset Cherry-Garrard's sleeping bag had weighed 8 kilograms (18 lb). It now weighed 20 kilograms (45 lb), and the balance was ice.

And what of those three hard-won eggs? Eventually, they found their way to Edinburgh University, but they did not provide the evidential breakthrough Wilson had hoped for.

THE MAN WHO EVERYONE ADMIRED

If Scott was the leader of the *Terra Nova* expedition, aloof and wedded to naval etiquette, Bill Wilson was the expedition's father figure — informal, responsive and even-tempered. Wilson's scientific presence was valued in the Antarctic, and his skill as an artist was a useful bonus, but, as Scott knew it would be, Wilson's real contribution was his personal example.

In 1898 Wilson had suffered from tuberculosis, a medical history Scott ignored when he included him in the *Discovery* expedition. And, in 1901, a mere three weeks before the expedition sailed, Wilson married his fiancee of two years, Oriana Souper. On the return of the *Discovery*, Wilson pursued his interest in ornithology and as a close friend of Shackleton's, he was pressed, unsuccessfully, to join the *Nimrod* expedition.

Wilson was deeply religious, but his devoutness was softened by an equally caring interest in his fellow man. As the Cape Evans party were to discover, 'Uncle Bill's' warmth and tact, his ability to listen with understanding, and his clear moral focus, made him an invaluable companion down south. Cherry-Garrard saw him in almost Christ-like terms, and Scott's admiration was scarcely less committed: 'Words must always fail me when I talk of Bill Wilson. I believe he really is the finest character I ever met . . . Whatever the matter, one knows Bill will be sound, shrewdly practical, intensely loyal and quite unselfish.'

Wilson completing a watercolour sketch in the hut. His paintings complement Ponting's photographic coverage of the expedition.

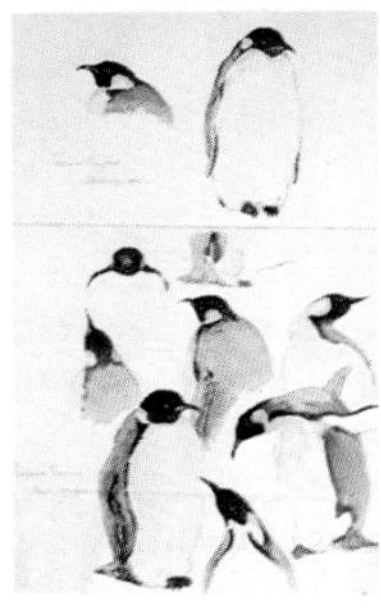

Emperor penguins, object of the Cape Crozier journey, drawn by Wilson.

Entrance to the ice cave where the six men of the northern party, led by Victor Campbell, spent a grindingly miserable winter in 1912. Permanently half-starved, they lived mainly on seals and penguins — eating both flesh and blubber.

When the men emerged after their winter of incarceration they were almost unrecognisable. Unwashed, covered in grease and smoke, and without having changed their clothes for the better part of a year, they were a fearsome sight.

Petty Officer George Abbott — *Commander Victor Campbell* — *Able Seaman Harry Dickason*

THE NORTHERN PARTY

Six men forced to spend the winter in an ice cave

Throughout the two years the* Terra Nova *expedition lived on the ice, the Cape Evans base was the secure haven from which short-term exploratory parties ventured in spring, summer and even autumn. One exceptional departure from that protective Cape Evans hut was made by the six-man northern expedition led by Commander Victor Campbell.

The northern party left Cape Evans on 9 February 1911. Originally, this team had been Scott's eastern party who were directed to explore King Edward VII Land on the eastern flank of the Ross Sea, but that plan was abandoned when they found Amundsen based at the only safe berth in the area. They returned to Cape Evans with news of Amundsen and then sailed to Cape Adare on the northern tip of Victoria Land.

At Cape Adare the winter hut was completed by the beginning of March, and Borchgrevink's two nearby huts, now the worse for wear, were patched up.

Campbell had picked his team carefully, and in the months ahead he would have reason to be thankful that his judgment was sound. Besides Priestley, who was also the meteorologist, and naval surgeon Murray Levick, who doubled as photographer and microbiologist, the team included three seamen: Petty Officer George Abbott, a carpenter; Petty Officer Frank Browning, assistant meteorologist; and Able Seaman Harry Dickason who established himself as the most talented cook in the party. Priestley, the only civilian, was given honorary officer status by Campbell who, if anything, was even more of a stickler for naval protocol than Scott.

After the calm of the early weeks of the Cape Adare sojourn, the hut, held down by wire hawsers, was tested by a hurricane-force blizzard. The anemometer was smashed by a 135 km/h (84 mph) gust and later squalls were even more severe.

Despite the wind, the hut itself was comfortable, and the party's winter program was similar to the Cape Evans routine. But Campbell resented the enforced idleness and, itching to get outdoors, took Priestley and Abbott on a short sledging trial as early in the spring as 29 July. As the season advanced, several exploratory surveys were made of the Victoria Land coastline. But the generally unfavourable sledging conditions frustrated Campbell and it was with some relief that the party greeted the *Terra Nova* when it returned from New Zealand on 3 January 1912.

The northern party then decided to try their luck further down the coast and on 8 January were dropped at Evans Coves in Terra Nova Bay. They had six weeks' sledging rations, a further two weeks' pemmican supply and skeleton rations for four weeks.

In difficult conditions the party attempted to explore and survey the environment of Mt Melbourne to the north. They wrestled with snowblindness and heavily crevassed glaciers, returning to their depot at Evans Coves in time to meet the ship, expected about 18 February. But there was no sign of it (after several attempts to penetrate the pack ice 48 kilometres (30 miles) offshore, the *Terra Nova* had had to abandon its rescue attempt).

As the days dragged by, the six men, at first worried only that the ship might have met with a catastrophe, now began to focus on their own plight. Food was running out, autumn was approaching, and on 21 February the first big gale in the area reached its peak, severely damaging their two tents. Facing the prospect of winter without shelter, heating or enough food, Campbell cast about anxiously for some form of shelter. He was finally forced to settle on cutting an ice cell in a snowdrift on the edge of a granite outcrop they called Inexpressible Island.

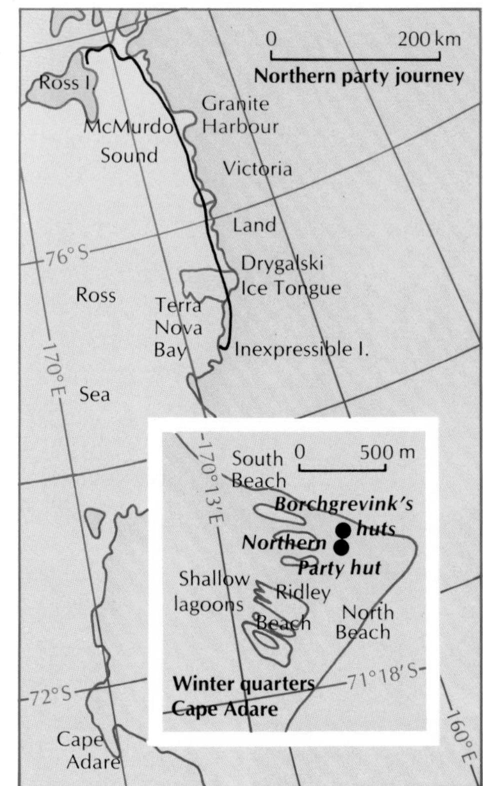

At about this time, Priestley, now in charge of the food, cut the biscuit allowance, the party's only source of carbohydrate, from eight a day to one.

They moved into the ice cave on 17 March. The final dimensions of that dismal cell, at the end of a narrow tunnel, were 3.6 x 2.7 metres

Geologist Raymond Priestley — *Naval Surgeon Murray Levick* — *Petty Officer Frank Browning*

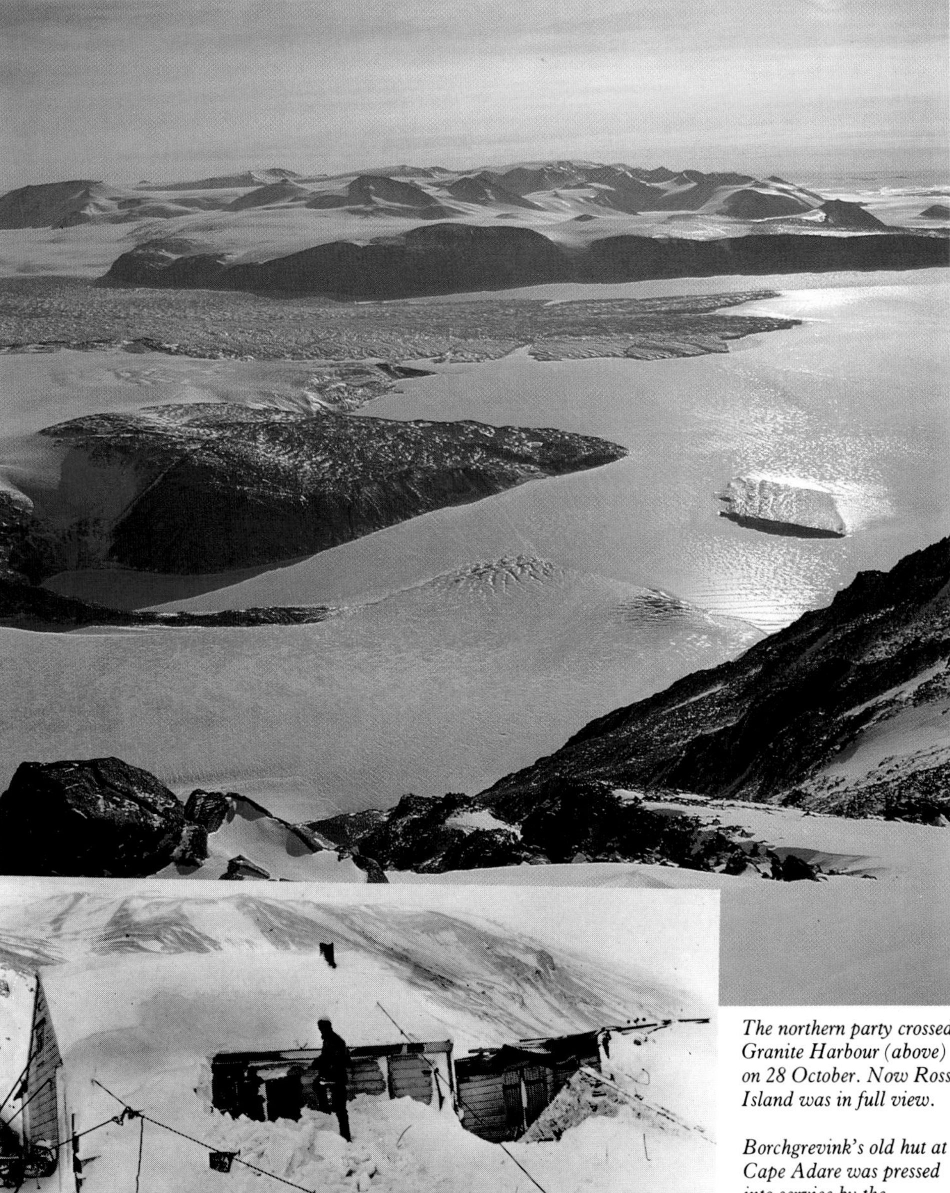

The northern party crossed Granite Harbour (above) on 28 October. Now Ross Island was in full view.

Borchgrevink's old hut at Cape Adare was pressed into service by the northern party during their first winter on the Victoria Land coast in 1911.

(12 x 9 ft), the ceiling being no more than 1.7 metres (5.5 ft) at its highest point, so no member of the party could stand fully upright inside it. The walls were lined with snow blocks and the floor was covered with gravel, pebbles, dried seaweed and the tent floorcloth.

Once established in their cave, Priestley recalculated the food supply. After deducting sledging provisions for the following spring, he had enough to issue each man 12 sugar lumps every Sunday, 43 grams (1.5 oz) of chocolate each Saturday and alternate Wednesday, and 25 raisins on the last day of each month. There were also a few scratchings of tea and cocoa.

Then, on 21 March, one of the few lucky strokes of the winter occurred when Browning killed a badly needed seal and found 36 edible fish in its stomach.

As the winter set in, the unremitting darkness of the cave, relieved only by four tiny blubber oil lamps, each shedding half the light of a match, induced bouts of depression in all the party. Hunger, cold and darkness gnawed at each man, but another particularly unpleasant fact of life was the smell and greasiness of the blubber stove they used as their oil supply ran low. To vary their diet they ate the blubber as well as the flesh of seals and penguins. In the claustrophobic confinement of their poorly ventilated cell, the handling and cooking of blubber and meat on the blubber stove very soon left the cave, the men themselves, and their clothes and sleeping bags saturated with a black, greasy combination of smoke and oil they called 'smitch'. Another, almost surreal, aspect of their ordeal was their nightmares. Each man experienced vivid, tantalising dreams of food, banquets, feasts. They shared their fantasies and for five of them a cruel twist was the fact that Levick invariably managed to consume his imaginary meal, the others always woke up too soon.

Before the winter was even half over, their smitch-laden clothes began to rot off their bodies which meant they risked frostbite every time they emerged from their frigid hovel.

For a while they managed to pass the hours of unending darkness with books. Levick had a talent for reading aloud, and his nightly recitations, from *David Copperfield* for example, by the pin-prick light of blubber lamps, kept them diverted for several months.

Early in September, just three weeks before the weather allowed them to leave their ice cell behind, the party were stricken with enteritis. The debilitating attack, caused mainly by poor hygiene and their inadequate diet, almost killed Browning and Dickason who were therefore a burden rather than a help when the party finally made the break for Cape Evans on 30 September. Indeed, without Levick's constant attention, Browning would undoubtedly have died on the 40-day march. For a long time they had had hardly any carbohydrate to eat and, in the end, the others cut their own biscuit ration to nil so Browning could have more. As it was, he was fading quickly when the party found a food cache at Cape Roberts. Later, at Butter Point, an enormous food supply was uncovered and the six men were able to eat their fill.

Over the final few miles Browning improved, almost as they watched him. On 7 November 1912 they caught sight of Hut Point — a bittersweet moment, as they learned of the polar party's tragic failure.

Exhausted and bitterly disappointed, the five men (left to right) Wilson, Evans, Scott, Oates and Bowers pose for a photograph at the South Pole. Scott wrote: 'We built a cairn, put up our poor slighted Union Jack and photographed ourselves.' All were to die in the bitter struggle to return to their base.

TRIUMPH AND TRAGEDY

'Great God! this is an awful place'

Robert Falcon Scott's final adventure made a faltering start on 24 October 1911 when the two ponderous motor sledges crawled towards the Ross Ice Barrier towing three tonnes of food, fuel and equipment. The tragic story of the next five months has become one of the great tales of Antarctic exploration, ironically eclipsing Amundsen's triumph.

Scott's instruction to the team leader, Lieutenant Teddy Evans, was: 'Proceed at convenient speed to Corner Camp, thence to One Ton Camp and thence due south to latitude 80°30'South.' Privately, he confessed he would be satisfied if they even reached Corner Camp where the ponies would take over sooner rather than later.

Scott's mixed feelings about the motor sledges echoed his vacillations over all forms of transport. His reluctance to trust any completely tempted him into using them all: motor sledges, ponies, dogs and, most important, man-hauling. The contrast with Amundsen's single-minded dependence on dogs could not have been greater. The British were handicapped, too, by their sentimental attachment to dogs. As a result, they were not as disciplined as they should have been, but they could still surprise Scott, even so.

On 1 November, Scott himself left Cape Evans with 10 ponies led by him, Bill Wilson, 'Atch' Atkinson, 'Titus' Oates, 'Birdie' Bowers, Apsley Cherry-Garrard, Charles Wright and Petty Officers Edgar Evans, Thomas Crean and Patrick Keohane. They followed in the tracks of the motor party (Evans, motor engineer Bernard Day, Chief Stoker William Lashly, and Steward F. J. Hooper). Cecil Meares and Dimitri Gerof followed, later still, with 23 dogs hauling two sledges. The entire expedition of 16 men, 10 ponies, 233 dogs and 13 sledges was now spread over 80 kilometres (50 miles) of the ice shelf.

Scott soon had difficulty coaxing the tiring ponies through the thick snow. Sitting out a blizzard, he wrote: 'The weather is steadily sapping the strength of the beasts on which so much depends. In the midst of the drift this forenoon the dog party came up and camped about a quarter of a mile [400 metres] to leeward. Meares has played too much for safety in catching us so soon, but it is satisfactory to find the dogs will pull the loads and can be driven to face such a wind as we have had.' The hint of annoyance betrays Scott's surprise at finding how well-adapted the dogs were as they breezed up in conditions that had halted the pony party.

The dog and pony teams rendezvoused with the motor party, now man-hauling, at 80°30'S on 21 November. Scott's plan was to have the ponies haul their loads to the base of Beardmore Glacier. Along the way a series of depots, supplementing the major One Ton Depot laid during the summer, would be built, each carrying a week's food and fuel for each returning man. But, 97-113 kilometres (60-70 miles) apart, the depots were spread very thinly.

The difficult ice shelf surface continued to be a problem for the exhausted ponies. By the first few days of December, five had been shot, and after the party had been held up by a blizzard for four days, the remaining five were despatched at Shambles Camp near the foot of the Beardmore.

As the party began the 193-kilometre (120-mile) haul up the glacier, from sea level to 3050 metres (10 000 ft), early signs of exhaustion were beginning to appear and they were little over a quarter of the way. Teddy Evans's sledge was making hard going of the soft snow, and Scott showed his anxiety when he wrote with irritation: 'Evans's party could not keep up. It is a very serious business if the men are going to crack up.'

By now the dogs had turned back and three sledges were being hauled by 12 men. Generally the haulers were pleased to be on their own. Before the expedition had started, Bowers had written to Scott's wife: 'Certainly to trust the final dash to such an uncertain element as dogs would be a risky thing, whereas man-haulage though slow, is sure, and I for one am delighted at the decision. After all, it will be a fine thing to do the plateau with man-haulage in these days of the supposed decadence of the British race.' Bowers was not alone in his relief that endless worrying over the animals was now behind them. After the last pony had been shot, Wilson wrote: 'Thank God the horses are now all done with and we can begin the heavier work ourselves.' The British were eagerly embracing the very conditions that all Amundsen's planning had been directed towards avoiding. Both on the polar march, and back in England where Amundsen's achievement would be belittled, the notion died hard that it is only through suffering that a goal is really worth attaining.

Now, on the Beardmore, Scott was also learning the value of other advice he had had before heading south. In Norway, in 1910, he had seen skis being expertly used and was persuaded to take a champion skier, Tryggve Gran, to the Antarctic with him. But during winter preparations, Scott had not insisted that the men learn from Gran. Now, skis were proving invaluable as they struggled with the treacherous glacier. Scott observed: 'The snow around us tonight is terribly soft . . . skis are the thing, and here are my tiresome fellow-countrymen too prejudiced to have prepared themselves for the event.' The men did use skis, but their efforts were pretty amateurish.

At the Upper Glacier Depot, established on 21 December, another support sledge returned to Cape Evans, leaving Scott, Wilson, Oates and P O Evans hauling one sledge, and Teddy Evans, Bowers, Lashly and Crean the other. They were now on the summit plateau but conditions were no more encouraging. There was heavy snow, tiring sastrugi and a vicious southerly wind.

The staleness of Teddy Evans's team continued to frustrate Scott, but on 4 January this final support party turned back. At the last moment, however, Scott asked Bowers to join his polar party which also included Wilson, Oates and P O Evans. Teddy Evans therefore had to haul his sledge back to base with only two other men. It was a dubious plan that left Evans's party undermanned and Scott's with an extra body to feed and accommodate that had not been planned for.

On the support party's seven-week return journey, Teddy Evans collapsed with scurvy, but Lashly and Crean still managed, eventually, to get him to Hut Point, a feat of endurance that earned them the Albert Medal.

On 9 January, Scott recorded with elation that they had finally passed Shackleton's furthest south record of 88°23'. Throughout the march, Scott had made a point of comparing

The broad sweep of the Beardmore Glacier (left to right) — the highway that took Scott and his men through the Transantarctic Mountains.

A cairn of snow was erected over the bodies of Scott, Wilson and Bowers when they were discovered on 12 November 1912, eight months after their tragic death.

his own progress with Shackleton's touch-and-go venture of three years earlier. And he had often been behind Shackleton's schedule.

Now, on the final leg, everyone was feeling colder than they should have, another sign of exhaustion, and on 12 January Scott noted, 'It is going to be a close run thing'. Finally, prophetically, he wrote on 15 January '... the only appalling possibility [would be] the sight of the Norwegian flag forestalling ours'. The next day, 32 kilometres (20 miles) from the pole, Bowers caught sight of a fluttering black speck — a marker flag tied to a sledge bearer. 'The worst has happened. The Norwegians are first at the Pole ... All dreams must go.'

On Wednesday 17 January, at the pole itself, Scott's anguish was unrestrained: 'The Pole. Yes, but under very different circumstances from those expected ... Great God! this is an awful place and terrible enough for us to have laboured to it without the reward of priority.' He then added: 'Now for the run home and a desperate struggle. I wonder if we can do it.'

It was a depressed little party that faced up to the 1290-kilometre (800-mile) trek back to Cape Evans. They set out on 19 January and, exhausting though the man-hauling had become, it was individual reaction to the limited sledge diet and the lack of fresh food that were starting to tell. Worst affected was P O Evans, a powerful man with a normally buoyant temperament who had been the dominant personality of the Cape Evans team. Now, however, the combined effect of incipient scurvy, frostbite and depression took a frighteningly quick toll of the sailor. It fell to Wilson to try to bolster his blighted morale.

Even so, incredibly, valuable time was spent on both 8 and 9 February searching out geological specimens. Altogether 16 kilograms (35 lb) of rock samples were piled onto a sledge being hauled by increasingly weak men for whom mere survival must, by now, have become an over-riding priority. As the food ran low they also lost themselves among the crevasses of the 48-kilometre (30-mile) wide glacier, and managed to reach their next depot after two days on starvation rations.

By now, Evans was almost helpless and Oates, too, was in severe discomfort. As they came off the Beardmore, Evans fell back. When the party returned for him he was floundering on his knees, his hands exposed, his clothes in disarray. He was delirious. That night, 17 February, he died in his sleep.

It was now late in the season and food and fuel quantities at each depot were adequate only if the men covered 16 kilometres (10 miles) a day; but in four days from 17 February, for instance, they managed only 39 kilometres (24 miles). By the beginning of March they were in extremis; Oates's feet were black with frostbite and gangrene had set in. Each step was taken in agony. On about 16 March (the date is uncertain) the exhausted men set up camp in a strong wind and −42°C (−43°F) temperature. In the bitter cold, the laconic Oates, drained of all willingness to continue, walked out into the blizzard. 'I am just going outside, and may be some time.'

By 21 March the three remaining men were within 18 kilometres (11 miles) of One Ton Camp, but the weather had become impenetrable. No further progress could be made and by 22 March their fuel was exhausted. But the whirling drift did not relent. Scott's final journal entry, dated 29 March, ended: 'We shall stick it out to the end, but we are getting weaker, of course, and the end cannot be far. It seems a pity, but I do not think I can write more. For God's sake look after our people.'

The frozen bodies of Scott, Wilson and Bowers were found eight months later by a search party led by Atkinson. On Observation Hill, which overlooks Cape Evans, Hut Point and the Ross Ice Shelf, a memorial cross was erected by the *Terra Nova* party before they returned to New Zealand with their heavy news. On the cross was carved the final line of Tennyson's *Ulysses*: 'To strive, to seek, to find, and not to yield.'

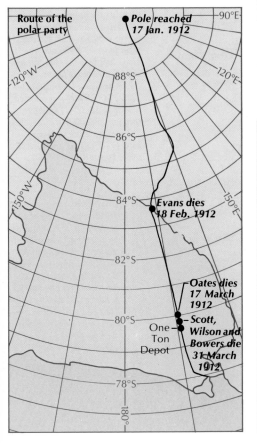

Route of the polar party

Pole reached 17 Jan. 1912

90°E 120°E 120°W 150°W 150°E 180° 88°S 86°S 84°S 82°S 80°S 78°S

Evans dies 18 Feb. 1912

Oates dies 17 March 1912

Scott, Wilson and Bowers die 31 March 1912

One Ton Depot

BRITAIN MOURNS THE DEATH OF A HERO

TRAGEDY OF SOUTH POLE

A THRILLING NARRATIVE.

TOLD BY COMMANDER EVANS.

PARTY OF FIVE PERISHES.

HEROIC FORTITUDE DISPLAYED

CAPTAIN SCOTT'S DYING MESSAGE.

"BOW TO THE WILL OF PROVIDENCE."

The death of Scott and his party made headlines around the world. Amundsen said: 'I cannot read that last message of Scott's without emotion ... And to think that while those brave men were dying out there in the waste of ice, I was lecturing in warmth and comfort in Australia.'

On the Ross Ice Shelf, Scott, Wilson and Bowers wrote their final thoughts to their families as they came to accept the inevitability of death. Scott also addressed the public: 'We are weak, writing is difficult, but for my own sake I do not regret this journey, which has shown that Englishmen can endure hardships, help one another and meet death with as great a fortitude as ever in the past.' It was a ringing affirmation, deeply felt, of the staunchness of the British character, and its sentiments set the tone of a legend that has endured to the present day.

Even before the details of the tragedy were fully known, a memorial service, attended by King George V, was held in St Paul's Cathedral in February 1913. United States President William Taft had sent a message of condolence on behalf of the American people and, indeed, Scott's death had a worldwide impact. The Empire mourned a lost hero at a time when, on the brink of World War I, it was in need of such heroic touchstones.

A memorial fund was opened, raising £74 000, nearly half of which was given to the relatives of the dead men. The remainder was used to settle expedition debts and finance memorials and the publication of expedition data. Amundsen was in the United States when he heard the news. His grief was profound, but it was tempered by some incredulity.

Antarctic Medicine

Isolation and a hostile climate accentuate some common problems

Antarctica is the only continent without any permanent human inhabitants. The handful of people who have wintered and survived there since the turn of the century find it an unusual experience with its complete isolation, extreme cold, long periods of light or darkness, confinement, restricted activity, enforced intimacy and social deprivation. However, they do not have unique medical problems. The same accidents and illnesses occur there as do in temperate regions.

Man's ability to move from the tropical area of his origins to the cold Antarctic has been due to technological advances rather than to biological changes. A naked person at rest can maintain a constant body temperature in still air at 27-29°C (81-84°F), without raising heat production above the resting value. Below an air temperature of 27°C (81°F) heat production has to increase to balance loss. The body's first defence is to raise the metabolism, but there are other natural defences against cold such as increased muscular activity, including shivering.

To understand human temperature regulation the body must be separated into an outer shell (skin, fat and superficial muscle layers), and an inner core of vital organs (brain, spinal cord, heart, liver, kidneys, pancreas and intestinal tract). The vital core is usually at a constant temperature of around 37°C (98.6°F), while the temperature of the outer shell can be varied so that it is cooler towards the surface to act as a buffer against the outside world. Heat loss can be minimised by constricting blood vessels in the skin, which in turn reduces skin temperature, and by actions such as huddling up in a ball to reduce the proportion of the body's surface area exposed to the air.

When the body's core temperature drops it is called hypothermia, and intense shivering usually follows. As the core temperature drops it causes muscular weakness, lack of co-ordination making it difficult to walk, and a dull mental state which prevents the victim from realising that anything is wrong. Unconsciousness may occur when the core temperature reaches 30-32°C (86-90°F), with death below 25°C (77°F), when the heart stops working. Slow hypothermia is insidious and very dangerous. It is treated by preventing further heat loss and slow rewarming. Sudden hypothermia, caused, say, by falling into cold water, is best treated with an immediate hot bath at 42°C (108°F). Hypothermia, or exposure, is not common in Antarctica because those going there are warned about it and instructed on how to prevent it.

A more common cold injury is frostbite, where body tissue actually freezes. Here the injured parts, usually fingers or toes, are frozen solid — white, cold and numb. Rapid thawing in water at 42°C (108°F) is usually the best treatment. If the tissue dies, gangrene can result and can only be treated by amputation. Efficient clothing is obviously very important in preventing both hypothermia and frostbite and improved modern materials have decreased the likelihood of either occurring.

The problems facing explorers of 80 years ago were the same as those facing modern

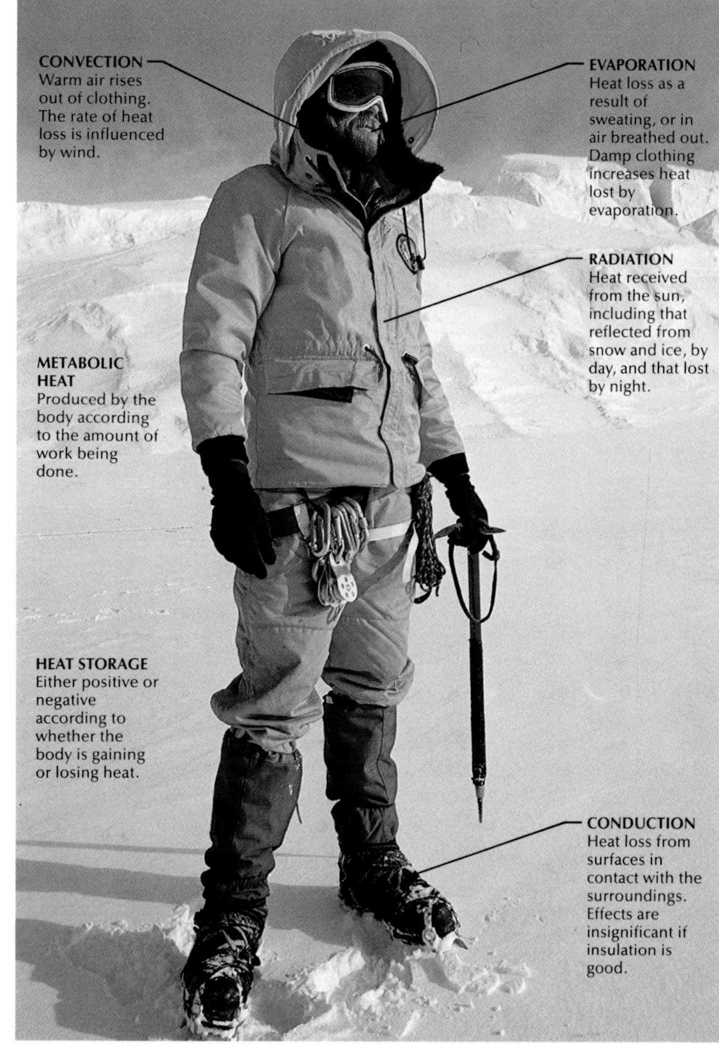

CONVECTION
Warm air rises out of clothing. The rate of heat loss is influenced by wind.
EVAPORATION
Heat loss as a result of sweating, or in air breathed out. Damp clothing increases heat lost by evaporation.
RADIATION
Heat received from the sun, including that reflected from snow and ice, by day, and that lost by night.
METABOLIC HEAT
Produced by the body according to the amount of work being done.
HEAT STORAGE
Either positive or negative according to whether the body is gaining or losing heat.
CONDUCTION
Heat loss from surfaces in contact with the surroundings. Effects are insignificant if insulation is good.

How heat flows to and from a clothed person. Wherever a person lives, a balance must be maintained between the amount of heat produced and the amount lost. This is particularly important in Antarctica where the severe climate can rapidly chill an inadequately protected body. Expedition members must be constantly alert to any changes in their surroundings — particularly increased wind which greatly accelerates heat loss (see wind chill graph, p16).

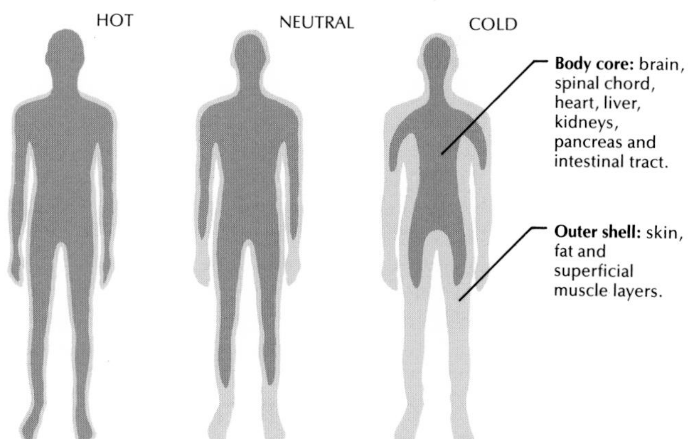

HOT
NEUTRAL
COLD
Body core: brain, spinal chord, heart, liver, kidneys, pancreas and intestinal tract.
Outer shell: skin, fat and superficial muscle layers.

The human body must maintain the temperature of its core of vital organs to prevent death. This is accomplished by allowing the outside surface to cool down gradually so that it acts as a buffer. This cooling takes place by decreasing the blood supply to the skin, fat and superficial muscle layers. The core is kept at a temperature of 37°C (98.6°F). If it is allowed to drop to 30-32°C (86-90°F) then unconsciousness will occur, followed by death at about 25°C (77°F). This condition is called hypothermia.

Scientists of the International Biomedical Expedition to Antarctica testing the effectiveness of various combinations of clothing. Subjects stood outside in extreme weather conditions for two hours while sensors monitored their body's reactions. Men from five countries took part in the experiments during the 1980-81 season.

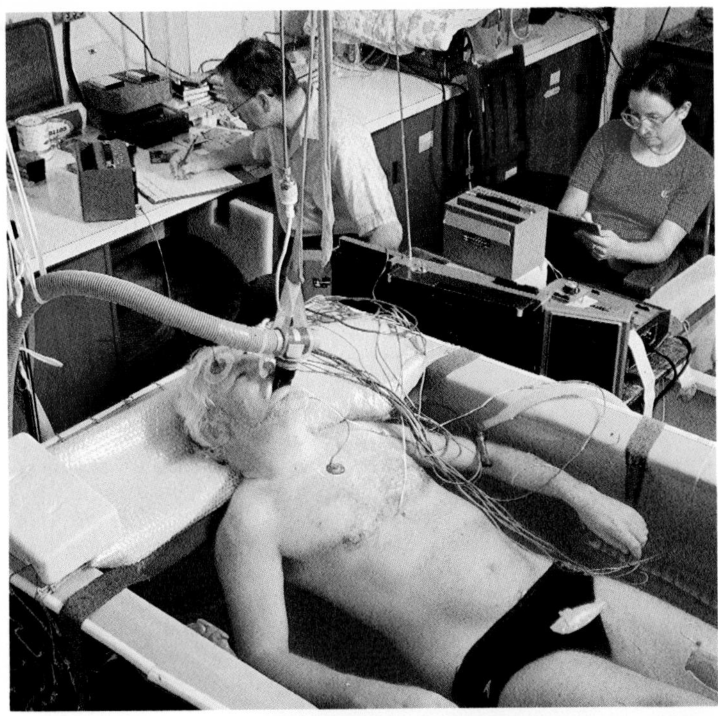

Members of the International Biomedical Expedition in 1980-81 were subjected to periods of extreme cold before they left for Antarctica. The aim of the experiment was to find out whether human beings can become acclimatised to cold. Preliminary results seem to indicate that they can not, although the research is continuing.

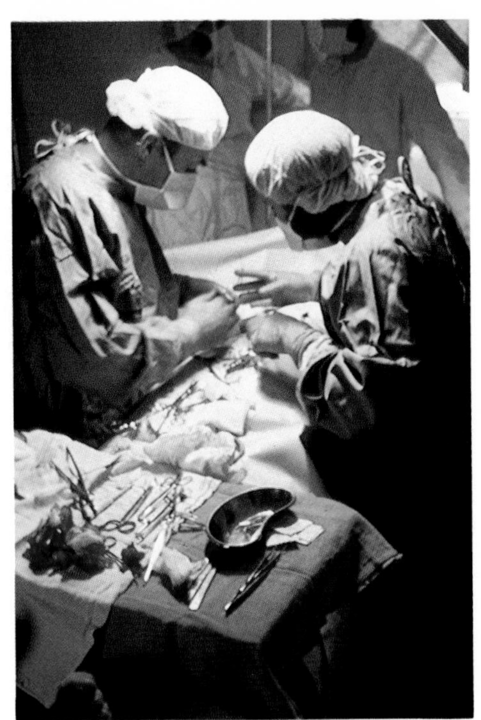

An emergency appendectomy being performed at an Antarctic base. A recent study of appendicitis in polar regions has shown that most national Antarctic expeditions have a higher rate than is found in the country of origin of the expedition members. The reason for this increase is not known at present.

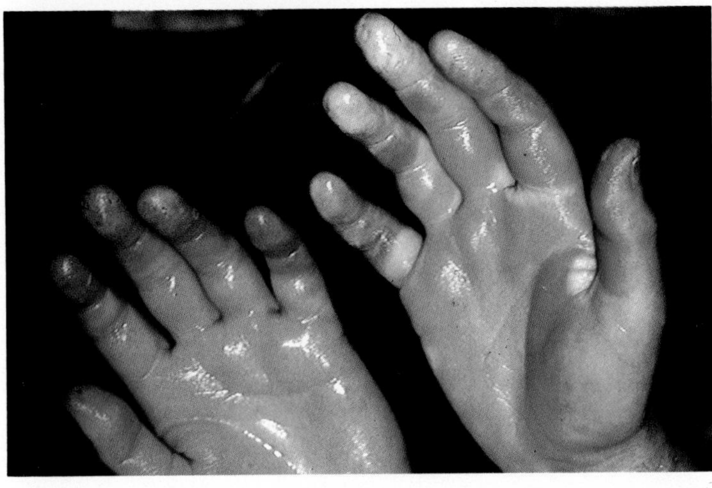

The white, cold, numb fingers of a frostbite victim. Severe frostbite can result in gangrene and amputation, but such cases are rare in Antarctica today.

expedition members, although they were not generally as well equipped to cope with them.

Psychiatric problems were experienced in a number of early groups, but only vague reports were made. McLean, the doctor with Douglas Mawson's Australasian Antarctic Expedition in 1911, made a passing reference to the mental illness of the wireless operator who stayed for a second year in 1913. Mawson included a footnote in his narrative and claimed that the man became normal in summer, but relapsed upon his return to Australia. Many expedition members were said to have mental problems after returning home, and over 10 per cent of the personnel of some expeditions were considered to have become mentally deranged.

Many of the problems encountered by early expeditions can only be explained now, with better medical knowledge. An example of this is the serious illness that affected Douglas Mawson and Xavier Mertz while dog-sledging on the Australasian Antarctic Expedition in 1912. Mertz became delirious and died, and both men were ill and lost large amounts of skin. It was not until more than 45 years later that work by Cleland and Southcott suggested that the illnesses were due to hypervitaminosis A (vitamin A poisoning) caused by eating the livers of their husky dogs. A mere 113 grams (four ounces) of dog liver contains a toxic dose of vitamin A.

Scurvy occurred on many expeditions, and it greatly affected the performance of the men. It is caused by a lack of fresh fruit and vegetables, although it was not until modern times that researchers realised that vitamin C (ascorbic acid) was the ingredient missing from diets of preserved foods.

The complaint was well known to the early navigators and George Anson described the symptoms in his book *A Voyage Round the World in the Years 1740-1744*: 'This disease so frequently attending long voyages . . . is surely the most singular and unaccountable of any that affects the human body. Its symptoms are inconstant and innumerable, and its progress and effects extremely irregular . . . Scarcely any two persons have the same complaints . . . Yet there are some symptoms which are more general than the rest . . . These common appearances are large discoloured spots dispersed over the whole surface of the body, swelled legs, putrid gums, and above all, an extraordinary lassitude of the whole body . . . This lassitude at last degenerates into a proneness to swoon on the least exertion of strength . . .'

Although West Indian lime juice, which had apparently been successful in combating scurvy on James Cook's voyages, was available on Scott's 1901-04 expedition, it was not widely used. Scott, like many naval personnel, was sceptical of its efficacy after reports of scurvy in ships on which juice was issued. The expedition's doctor, Koettlitz, also thought that lime juice was not important in the prevention of scurvy. He followed a course advocated by Nansen of inspecting every tin of meat as it was opened looking for 'ptomaines', which were considered to be the cause of the complaint. The symptoms of scurvy occurred in a number of men on this expedition in the first year, but not in the second. This was probably due to the large number of seals and birds consumed in the second year — fresh meat providing the necessary vitamin C.

Ironically, the issue of lime juice on Scott's expedition would probably not have prevented the complaint. The 'lime juice' used by James Cook was actually lemon juice. This fact was not found out until 1918. On subsequent expeditions, Cook's Spanish lemon juice was changed to Mediterranean lemon juice, and then to West Indian lime juice. True lime juice contains less than a quarter of the vitamin C of lemon juice.

The use of aircraft in Antarctica, and an increase in the size of expeditions, has seen great improvements in the logistic support available, including medical services. Most Antarctic surgeries are now well equipped with all the instruments and drugs available in a modern hospital.

There is a popular belief that Antarctica is germ free, but research has shown that although personnel are often free of infectious diseases while in Antarctica, bacteria and viruses still live in their respiratory tracts.

The most common problems on modern expeditions are wounds or injuries resulting from accidents, and most of these are minor.

In 1961 the physician to the Sixth Soviet Expedition was forced to operate on himself for acute appendicitis. The doctor was the only medical practitioner present, but he was assisted by two co-workers, who held the retractors and a mirror. The operation was a success. Some national Antarctic expeditions now have two doctors at each base.

A Disastrous Start

Filchner's ambitious schemes scrapped as the ice shelf disintegrates

The second German Antarctic Expedition, led by a 34-year-old first lieutenant in the Bavarian army, Wilhelm Filchner, planned to find out whether the southernmost portion of the Atlantic (the Weddell Sea) and the southernmost portion of the Pacific Ocean (the Ross Sea) were separated by a land bridge or whether they were connected by an ice-covered channel. The expedition had barely set foot on the sixth continent when it almost ended in disaster.

Wilhelm Filchner first publicly put forward the idea of another German expedition to the Antarctic in 1908. Despite his youth Filchner was not just an unknown adventurer with a wild dream. At the age of 15 he had joined a military academy and, barely 21, had travelled through Russia for seven weeks. That journey gave him the idea for a one-man expedition into the Pamir, a mountainous region of Central Asia. Taking more leave, Filchner accomplished this feat at the age of 23.

To further his plan for an Antarctic expedition, Filchner managed to gain an audience with the Kaiser. Wilhelm II had not considered expeditions to the polar regions since Erich von Drygalski had returned from his Antarctic voyage in 1903. However, Filchner was finally permitted to raise money by public lottery.

To determine whether or not the Antarctic continent was one piece of land, Filchner's original plan called for two ships, one to enter the Weddell Sea, the other the Ross Sea. Land parties were then to meet in mid-continent. But to save expenses, one ship had to do.

By the northern spring of 1908 Filchner had assembled a scientific team including two doctors, an oceanographer and an astronomer. None of the men had true polar or even far-northern experience, least of all Filchner. So,

Wilhelm Filchner, after his return from Antarctica. He had already established himself as a talented explorer by the time he put forward his scheme for a second German Antarctic expedition. In 1908 he had been granted an honorary doctorate of philosophy by the University of Königsberg.

Filchner's friend Kling took over the ship after the death of Captain Vahsel.

Supplies being unloaded on the ice shelf at Vahsel Bay. The entire area proved to be unstable, and nine days after they started to build camp an enormous stretch of ice broke away.

Filchner's ship, the Deutschland. *Originally named the* Bjorn, *this Norwegian vessel was specially made for polar work, and Filchner was able to acquire it with the help of Ernest Shackleton, Fridtjof Nansen and Otto Nordenskjöld. As a gesture of friendship, Shackleton even supervised the work of strengthening her hull.*

The expedition's 17-metre-long (55-ft) hut was almost complete when the ice started to break up. It took two days to dismantle it as the iceberg it rested on drifted slowly out into the Weddell Sea.

for a trial run, he and six members of his team and one dog crossed parts of Spitsbergen in the Arctic Ocean.

On 4 May 1911 the *Deutschland* left the port of Bremerhaven under the command of Captain Richard Vahsel. Her first destination was Buenos Aires. There the ship loaded new provisions, coal, and 14 tonnes of rock ballast. On 4 October 1911 she eased out of port and fourteen days later reached the island of South Georgia. There, at the southernmost bastion of civilisation, the men spent 48 days at the Norwegian whaling station of Grytviken.

An exploratory trip to the little-known South Sandwich Islands was made, and on 10 December the *Deutschland* finally sailed towards the Weddell Sea.

Her crew realised that for the next year they would be out of touch with the rest of the world. 'None of us knew if we would ever come back alive', Filchner wrote.

Filchner knew that success in the Weddell Sea depended not only on careful planning, but also on weather conditions and luck. Observations over many decades, made mostly by whalers, had shown that ice conditions in the sea were very treacherous, even in the Antarctic summer. Approximately every two years the water appeared relatively free of ice, but that could not be relied upon.

The *Deutschland* had first encountered ice on 15 November. From then on, progress varied. Days on which the crew could work in their shirtsleeves were followed by fog, snow and freezing temperatures. Early in January 1912, the vessel was completely surrounded by icebergs and floes. 'In three days we spotted almost 200 bergs', Filchner wrote. But thanks to the approaching summer, fairly wide channels opened up in the ice and on 27 January bottom samples of blueish clay brought up from 3430 metres (11 250 ft) provided evidence that they were nearing land. Three days later, at 3 pm, the lookout sighted land in the south-east. According to Filchner it presented a magnificent spectacle. An ice cliff, about 30-40 metres (98-130 ft) high, formed its seaward boundary. Behind it, the snow-clad continent gradually rose in gentle slopes to a height of about 600 metres (2000 ft). 'We had reached the cliff of the ice overlaying the Antarctic landmass, land that nobody before had seen or stepped upon, new territory', wrote Filchner. The *Deutschland* had finally reached the southernmost point of her voyage.

Filchner named this land Prince Regent Luitpold Land (now the Luitpold Coast). For several days the *Deutschland* steamed along the ice shelf which Filchner named after Kaiser Wilhelm, but which his emperor later wished to be known as the Filchner Ice Shelf, a name it has retained ever since.

The expedition's goal was now to erect a winter camp (Filchner called it a 'stationhaus') and then cross the inland ice by dog sledge in order to reach the innermost shore of the Ross Sea. The *Deutschland* finally reached an ice-rimmed bay at the foot of a huge ice cliff which looked like a promising landing place. One of its most prominent features was a vast tabular iceberg, a piece of the ice shelf, which had a natural landing ramp. 'There, all the material necessary to erect a "stationhaus" could be easily and quickly unloaded', Filchner later wrote. 'A precondition for the project was, of course, that the berg for the "stationhaus" be resting solidly on the sea floor.'

The unloading of materials and supplies, dogs and ponies started on 9 February. By 17 February the building — 17 metres (55 ft) long and 9 metres (30 ft) wide — was almost complete. But the next morning: catastrophe!

It began at about 4 am with a series of crackling sounds. The noise quickly intensified until two hours later it sounded like the report of cannon shots. Amazingly, most of the men, worn out after working on the building, slept through the noise. 'Then suddenly', Filchner reported, 'a racket erupted as if one hundred pieces of heavy artillery were firing in rapid succession'. Captain Vahsel sounded the alarm: 'All the ice in the bay is moving and the stationhaus-berg has begun to rotate!'

By the time Filchner reached the deck the sea was relatively calm again, but the surroundings had completely changed. Everywhere in the ice new cracks and rifts had opened up. Tonnes of ice had broken loose from the edge of the ice shelf. Worse, the berg carrying the almost completed camp was drifting northwards towards open water. With it, great masses of ice — the biggest piece about 29 kilometres (18 miles) long — were also moving. Clearly, the *Deutschland* was in danger of being crushed while the camp, with some of the men, was being carried away.

The cause of the disaster, Filchner concluded, must have been a spring tide, coupled with a sharp drop in barometric pressure. He later determined that the water level must have surged up by about three metres (10 ft), affecting an area of 600 sq kilometres (230 sq miles) — roughly the size of Paris — and that more than 50 billion cubic metres (17.5 thousand billion cubic ft) of ice had broken loose.

For two days expedition members worked feverishly to dismantle what was to have been their winter home. Winches, then lifeboats, were used to haul the material and the animals back to the *Deutschland* which stayed abreast of the iceberg at a safe distance. The men managed to save enough material to build a new base, and in the end all that was left was a small part of the building and a dog that had refused to be caught. Filchner attached a note to the remains stating the cause of the disaster and the iceberg's original position: 77°45'S, 34°34'W. 'A trail of heavy ice followed it, [so] it was impossible for us to return to Prince Regent Luitpold Land', wrote Filchner.

NINE MONTHS IN THE ICE

The Deutschland's *lonely winter adrift in the Weddell Sea*

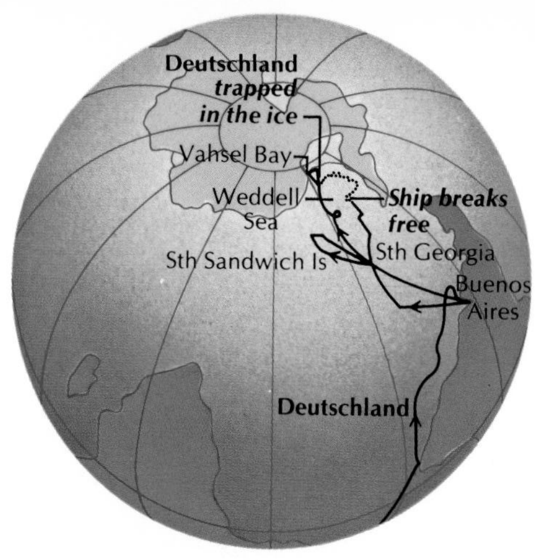

Having failed to establish a base on solid ice, the* Deutschland *drifted for several days, waiting for more favourable weather conditions. Then another attempt was made to land on the continental ice. The men spent several days building two large depots of stores about 100 metres (330 ft) above sea level. Covered by ice, the depots were marked with black flags and poles. Filchner's plan was to retreat to South Georgia, spend the winter there and return the following summer with additional provisions. But it was too late.

It was already early March, and soon fog set in, followed by sub-zero temperatures. At a frightening speed the water froze over. 'The devil himself sealed our fate', Filchner wrote. By 6 March, the *Deutschland* was securely frozen in. Although the ice repeatedly broke up in several areas, the ship remained trapped. Embedded in the pack ice, she was slowly drifting out into the Weddell Sea.

To break the frustration of the long polar night to come, Filchner decided to make the best use of their captivity. Tents and small cabins were erected on the ice and scientific equipment set up. Stables for the ponies and kennels for the dogs were also built. Fortunately, there was enough fuel to keep the boilers and the stoves warm. When refitting the ship in Hamburg, Filchner had insisted on extra boilers that could be fuelled with the carcases of penguins and the blubber of seals to save precious coal. In addition, all the ship's rooms were wired for electric lighting 'to cut down the polar night to a minimum'. For entertainment there were card games, music, sports activities on deck and on the ice, even horse riding.

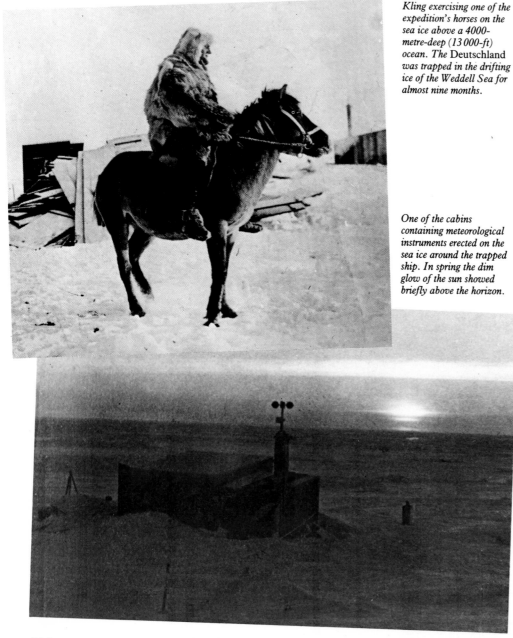

Kling exercising one of the expedition's horses on the sea ice above a 4000-metre-deep (13 000-ft) ocean. The Deutschland *was trapped in the drifting ice of the Weddell Sea for almost nine months.*

One of the cabins containing meteorological instruments erected on the sea ice around the trapped ship. In spring the dim glow of the sun showed briefly above the horizon.

Filchner himself could not take part in most of these activities: he had fallen from a mast and bruised a few ribs. But by mid-June he felt well enough to undertake a short but dangerous trip in search of Morrell's Land, or New South Greenland. Together with officers Kling and Konig, he intended to find out if the land that the American sealer Benjamin Morrell thought he had seen in 1823 really existed. If it did, the *Deutschland* was only some 60 kilometres (37 miles) east of it.

The three men left the ship on 23 June aboard two sledges, each drawn by eight dogs, with provisions for three weeks. Progress was more difficult than anything the men had so far encountered. Daylight never lasted longer than two and a half to three hours a day, with the sun setting around 2 pm, and the pack ice was heaped high. On some days the men only covered six kilometres (under four miles), with a maximum of 24 kilomteres (15 miles) if the ice surface was fairly smooth. The temperature fell to −35°C (−31°F). All men suffered from frostbite, and Filchner wrote in his diary: 'at night we were shivering in competition in our flimsy tent.'

The smallest task took hours because of the cold. Instruments froze over the moment they were taken out of their protective covers and had to be constantly thawed. 'To take a sighting we needed two hours rather than the usual ten minutes', Filchner reported.

When they reached 70°32′S, 43°45′W, they had covered 50 kilometres (31 miles). But still none of the land Morrell — and others — claimed to have seen was in view. A lead weight was lowered through a hole hacked into the ice and, after reaching a depth of 1600 metres (5248 ft), the line broke.

Convinced that Morrell had seen a mirage, the men decided to return to the ship. The journey back proved to be even more dangerous as large cracks had opened in the ice, making detours necessary. Other areas had frozen over with fresh ice so thin that the men were in constant danger of breaking through. But despite the frozen instruments Kling's navigation proved to be phenomenal: on 30 June, eight days after they had left their ship, Filchner and his companions spotted the masts of the *Deutschland* in the distance. During that period the *Deutschland* had drifted about 61 kilometres (38 miles) in a direction southwest by north. Since a wide lead of thin ice separated the men from the ship, they had to be picked up by lifeboats.

During the next two weeks the Antarctic winter slowly came to an end. By 8 August,

The fissured surface of the vast Filchner Ice Shelf. Filchner tried to establish his base on the eastern end of the shelf, but a large section broke away, destroying his partly finished base.

Filchner and Kling scan the horizon in search of New South Greenland — land reported by Benjamin Morrell in 1823. Three men made the dangerous 100-kilometre (62-mile) journey across cracked and shifting ice. They could find no trace of land.

when Captain Vahsel died of an old illness, wide leads had begun to open in the ice. By the end of September the *Deutschland* was surrounded by vast stretches of open water. Steam was raised in the boilers and the ship was ready for any chance of a breakthrough. All the huts, the scientific equipment and the animals were on board. But it was another eight weeks before Filchner was finally able to break free. The *Deutschland's* position was 63°37′S, 36°34′W. 'We had drifted over 10° in latitude', Filchner noted in his log. On 19 December they reached South Georgia.

Filchner's expedition did not realise its main objective — to cross the polar ice from the Weddell to the Ross Sea. But, as Otto Nordenskjöld later pointed out in a preface to Filchner's book, his discoveries on the southern border of the Atlantic Ocean — the Prince Regent Luitpold Land (now Luitpold Coast) and the Filchner Ice Shelf — were important geographical finds. Filchner had also proved that Morrell Land did not exist, at least not where Morrell had claimed it to be.

Filchner himself was more modest. When the *Deutschland* was sold to Austria and he was asked to take part in another expedition, he felt that 'for the time being I had had enough of "Antarctic Doings". Moreover, many experiences had convinced me that truly great successes in the polar ice are granted only to members of those nations where polar research has tradition, namely the Scandinavians, the Russians, the British and the Canadians. I decided to return to my original field of work: Central and East Asia.'

After World War I Filchner made repeated trips to Nepal, where he carried out a survey in 1939, and to Tibet. He was stranded in India when World War II erupted, then spent many years in Poona, also in India. He died in Zurich on 7 May 1957.

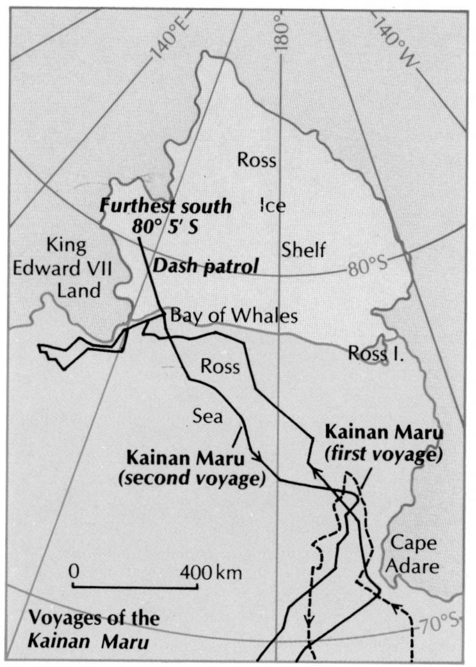

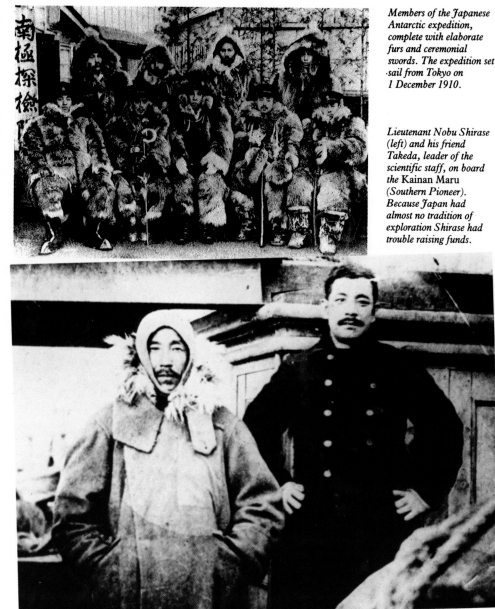

Members of the Japanese Antarctic expedition, complete with elaborate furs and ceremonial swords. The expedition set sail from Tokyo on 1 December 1910.

Lieutenant Nobu Shirase (left) and his friend Takeda, leader of the scientific staff, on board the Kainan Maru *(Southern Pioneer). Because Japan had almost no tradition of exploration Shirase had trouble raising funds.*

ENTER JAPAN

A modest success

When Japan's first expedition to the Antarctic sailed from Tokyo on 1 December 1910 only a handful of students watched it leave. Indeed, it was remarkable that the expedition ever left at all. Its leader, Lieutenant Nobu Shirase, had met with indifference and downright ridicule when he had asked the government for funds, and it was not until he received the support of Count Okuma, a former Premier of Japan, that the public grudgingly gave enough money to meet his modest needs.

The *Kainan Maru*, which was only 30 metres (100 ft) long, reached Wellington in New Zealand on 7 February 1911 and four days later headed south towards the Antarctic. Plagued by bad weather all the way, the men saw their first iceberg on 26 February and, surrounded by hundreds of drifting bergs one of which was 76 metres (250 ft) high, they saw land on 6 March.

They had reached the coast of Victoria Land and from the ship they could see the Admiralty Range in the distance. But conditions made a landing impossible and so they sailed on through the Ross Sea towards Coulman Island. The weather there was even worse. Snow fell continuously, gales buffeted them, and soon they were surrounded by heavy ice. It was impossible to go any further and Shirase ordered his dejected men to turn the ship round and head for Australia.

They reached Sydney Harbour on 1 May 1911 and there they were greeted with suspicion and hostility. A resident in the elegant and leafy suburb of Vaucluse gave them free use of part of his garden, and they were able to erect their prefabricated hut. Captain Nomura and several of the crew returned to Japan in an attempt to raise more funds, while the rest of the party, short of money and food, were forced to live almost as beggars. Shirase was particularly upset by the hostility of the local newspapers and wrote sadly: 'The New Zealand press viewed our attempt with ridicule. The *New Zealand Times* was particularly poignant in its comments upon us. It remarked that we were a crew of gorillas sailing about in a miserable whaler, and that the polar regions were no place for such beasts of the forest as we. The zoological classification of us was perhaps to be taken figuratively, but many islanders interpreted it literally, because crowds of people came to our tents daily to observe the "sporty gorillas" misguided with the crazy notion of conquering the South Pole.'

Fortunately the expedition attracted the attention of Professor Edgeworth David from the University of Sydney, who had been a member of Ernest Shackleton's expedition in 1907, and his enthusiastic involvement did much to reassure the Australian public.

Although Shirase had originally intended to reach the pole, he now realised that he was so far behind Robert Scott and Roald Amundsen as to make his own attempt pointless. So when the expedition sailed out of Sydney Harbour on 19 November 1911 it was with the more modest intention of carrying out scientific exploration on King Edward VII Land.

After celebrating New Year's Day with a traditional banquet (there were, amongst other things, eight different dishes of sea bream), they reached the Ross Ice Shelf on 16 January. A party went ashore at a spot they named Kainan Bay, but found the ice full of crevasses which they could never cross safely.

With the party back on board, the *Kainan Maru* headed west and soon the men were startled to see another ship dead ahead. Thinking at first that it might be a pirate, they were reassured to discover that it was Amundsen's ship the *Fram*, which was waiting for him to return from the pole. Visits were exchanged, but language difficulties made any serious contact impossible.

Shirase was now faced with the task of getting his party to the top of the ice shelf, which was 90 metres (300 ft) high at the place where the *Kainan Maru* was moored. 'We were resolved to scale the so-called insurmountable barrier or die', wrote Shirase. After 60 hours of hard labour by the entire crew a zigzag path had been cut up the almost perpendicular slope, and the first men stood on the summit.

A small party was sent ashore to investigate the ice shelf and when they returned with encouraging reports Shirase decided to make it the starting point of his so-called Dash Patrol. Led by Shirase, it consisted of seven men. Two would remain at the edge of the ice shelf as a base camp whilst the rest would set out

Members of the second expedition on board their ship, *New Year's Day 1912. Lieutenant Shirase is standing fifth from right, and beside him in the white jacket is Captain Nomura, master of the ship.*

The Bulletin

THURSDAY, MAY 18, 1911.

THE JAPS AT VAUCLUSE

The Australian and New Zealand press were particularly hostile towards the Japanese. A Sydney magazine, The Bulletin, *(whose masthead at the time carried the line 'Australia for the white man') published this cartoon. The caption read:* Little Boy at Manly: *'Well! this is about the last place anybody should come expecting to find the South Pole!'*

Three members of the 'Dash Patrol' at their furthest south – 80°5'S — reached on 28 January 1912. They are (left to right) Mitsui, Shirase and Takeda.

with dogs and sledges on a dash to the south.

In the event, it was something less than a dash. On the first day they were forced to camp in a blizzard after covering only 13 kilometres (8 miles). They were able to start again two days later, but as each dog had to pull a load of about 26 kg (57 lb) progress was slow.

They pushed on across difficult country in conditions that were barely tolerable. Then on 28 January, by which time they had covered 257 kilometres (160 miles), Shirase prudently decided to turn back. They flew the Japanese flag from a bamboo pole and saluted the Emperor with a threefold *Banzai* before burying a copper case containing a record of their visit.

Meanwhile, the *Kainan Maru* had left the Bay of Whales to drop a shore party at Biscoe Bay in King Edward VII Land. After climbing a 46-metre (150-ft) ice slope, these men succeeded in reaching the Alexandra Range, which until then had not been seen at close quarters. They were prevented from reaching the top of the mountains by a crevasse and after erecting a memorial board they returned to the ship.

The *Kainan Maru* now made her way back to the Bay of Whales but the wind was against her and it was not until 2 February that she could enter the bay. Even then the sea was still very rough and it was only with considerable difficulty that the Dash Patrol could be taken on board. Its work now completed, the expedition turned for home and after calling again at Wellington, the *Kainan Maru* finally reached Yokohama on 20 June. The expedition had sailed over 48 000 kilometres (30 000 miles) since leaving Japan and although they had not reached the pole, they had achieved everything they had set out to do when they left Australia. In contrast to their silent departure, they were now given a tumultuous welcome.

Antarctic golfers face some unusual problems that more than make up for the monotonous regularity of their surroundings. A coloured ball is an obvious necessity. This course is on the ice at McMurdo Sound near Ross Island.

Members of Robert Scott's 1910-13 expedition were expected to spend a lot of their time gainfully employed. Scott commented: 'It is a delight to contemplate the amount of work which is being done at the station. No one is idle — all hands are full . . .'

Modern bases offer a great variety of pastimes for expedition members. This well-stocked library is at New Zealand's Scott base on Ross Island.

PASSING THE TIME

Simple pursuits help to while away the long winter hours

All the men of the heroic age had one common problem — how to relieve the boredom of the long polar night. Every expedition spent at least one winter, sometimes two or more, in Antarctica. For three months, night closed around their tiny huts and, but for infrequent trips abroad to read meteorological instruments or to tend animals, life was spent indoors.

In an age before television and radio, most knew how to amuse themselves. Their fun was merely an extension of the things that they grew up doing on European winter evenings. Games such as darts, cards, dominoes and chess were, as always, popular. Stories were told, hours were spent in discussing every conceivable topic and for special occasions there were plays and concerts.

The following extracts tell, in the men's own words, how some of the long Antarctic nights were spent:

'I fear the description of one of our Scotia *smokers will seem tame to those accustomed to the luxurious entertainment of a similar feast at home, and yet perhaps no merrier evenings were ever spent than those winter evenings in the South Orkneys. We had little musical talent in the cabin, but we managed very well in the absence of a critical audience. The Captain gave us rollicking songs of the sea, Pirie contributed a few Scottish student songs, Mossman never exhausted his music-hall* repetoire, *and Wilton, we always will gratefully remember, gave us his one Russian song. What it meant he never deigned to explain, but the song was just as sure to come when enthusiasm ran high as it was always welcome . . .'*

R.N. Rudmose Brown on the *Scotia*, 1903.

'In the midst of the revelry Bowers suddenly appeared, followed by some satellites bearing an enormous Christmas Tree whose branches bore flaming candles, gaudy crackers, and little presents for all. The presents I learnt, had been prepared with kindly thought by Mrs Souper (Mrs Wilson's sister) and the tree had been made by Bowers of pieces of stick and string with coloured paper to clothe its branches . . .'

Robert Scott, Midwinter's Day, 1911.

'Hurley's ingenuity at staging jokes often provided much amusement, and he spared no trouble in making them effective. There was one member of the party who was very nervous of fire, as indeed we all were, for a fire would have been disastrous. But he voiced his anxiety too often. Moreover, he had a deep-rooted distrust of the acetylene generator, which he was sure was always on the point of blowing up. One night this member was night-watchman, so Frank took a long length of rubber tubing which always seemed to play a part in his schemes, and immersing one end in the water for the generator, carried the other to his bunk. Here at intervals though the night, and at the expense of his own rest, he blew hard, creating a most satisfactory bubbling. It was too much for the night-watchman. After climbing up several times to investigate and finding nothing to reveal the cause, he at last woke the Doctor [Mawson]. D.I., annoyed at being disturbed, at once spotted the trouble, but did not give the show away. He merely remarked that it certainly was dangerous, but even if it did blow up, nothing could be done before morning, and calmly went back to his bunk again. The night-watchman spent the rest of the night in anxious misery, and it was not until some days later that he came to understand the hilarity which greeted any discussion on the nature and habits of acetylene generators.'

Charles Laseron, with Mawson, 1911.

'We have no books. When we wish to delight the eye with a few printed words, we take out our tins of "Le lait condensé, preparé par Henri Nestlé", or of "Boiled Beef", and read the labels. We endeavour to make up for this want of light reading, by recalling what we have learned under happier circumstances and relating stories — Duse and I, for example, recounting for Grunden all that we remember of "Monte Cristo" and the "Three Musketeers".'

Gunnar Andersson, marooned at Hope Bay, 1902.

'When the day's work was done we would gather round the stove for a quiet smoke and yarn, varied occasionally by lively, if somewhat diffuse, argu-

An informal, if rather posed photograph, of a winter evening in Mawson's main base hut at Cape Denison. The gramophone was always a popular entertainment in the evenings; the same records being played again and again. A continuing topic for conversation throughout the stay concerned a phrase in the chorus from The Mikado. *No one could quite hear it, and on their return to Australia there was a general rush to find the libretto and to discover what the words were.*

Target practice varied the outdoor amusements available to the men of Scott's first expedition in 1901. Energetic games of football and skiing were popular pastimes as they waited for the winter.

One of the main winter chores was the preparation of clothing and equipment for the coming summer. Two of Scott's 1910 party sewing sleeping bags.

ments on such subjects as Evolution, The Irish Question, Idealism in Art, Socialism, etc. At yarning it was the case of one man first and the rest nowhere — for Bill [William Smith, second steward on the Scotia*], when wound up, would relate his salted-down experiences and adventures in every corner of the globe. How they all came to be crowded into one life is still somewhat of a mystery, for on adding up the number of years we ascertained he had spent on different ships and ashore, we found he had lived, at the most modest computation, a hundred and forty-three years! Good old Bill!'*

Dr J. H. Harvey Pirie on Laurie Island, 1903.

'During the evening a singing competition took place: the prize being unanimously awarded to Sir Ernest [Shackleton]. His voice is quaint, vacillating uncertainly between sharps and flats in a unique manner.'

Frank Hurley on the *Endurance*, 1915.

'On the smokey mess deck, divided up by the solid ribs of the ship, the crew, with their energetic faces and their picturesque clothing, patched up according to taste, with knives at their waists, and their hair and beards flowing loose, leapt about and shouted challenges to one another .... These few minutes spent among them with their free but always respectful gaiety, drinking their half-pints with them and smoking the tobacco which they cordially offered us, have done more to raise my spirits than any amount of reasoning could have done.'

Jean Charcot on the *Pourquoi Pas?*, 1909.

'Our stock of conversation had long since been threadbare, and the same old subjects would crop up again and again. As a consequence of this we resorted more and more to chorus songs to pass the time away, and here Browning and I, by reason of good memories and a talent for picking up the words of songs, flourished beyond every one else. As I have already stated, few of us possessed any voice or any idea of a tune, I least of all, but my memory for songs is unimpeachable, and now on the days when Levick and I were messmen, I was expected to sing for at least two hours while the hoosh was being cooked.'

Raymond Priestley, marooned on Inexpressible Island, 1912.

'Then the gramophone made its appearance, and it did me good to see the delight with which it was received. They seemed to like this best after all, and every man had music to suit his taste. All agreed to honour the cook for his pains, and the concert therefore began with "Tarara-boom-de-ay", followed by the "Apache" waltz. His part of the programme was concluded with a humerous recitation. Meanwhile he stood in the doorway with a beatific smile; this did him good. In this way the music went the round, and all had their favourite tunes.'

Roald Amundsen, Framheim, June 1911.

In a howling blizzard, Mawson's men gather ice for the hut's water supply. They had chosen as a site for their base the windiest place on earth. An almost continuous torrent of frigid air swept down from the polar plateau and over their hut. The wind severely limited the expedition's work.

Location of Main and Western bases

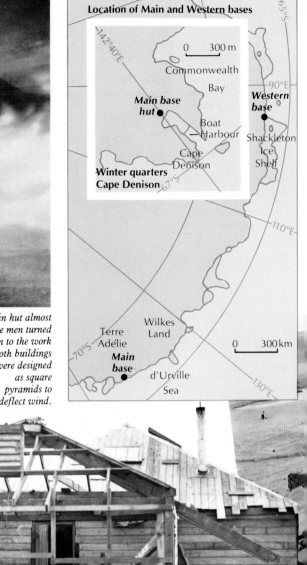

142°40'E
0 300 m
Commonwealth Bay
Main base hut
Boat Harbour
Cape Denison
Winter quarters Cape Denison
67°S
65°S
90°E
Western base
Shackleton Ice Shelf
110°E
Terre Adélie
Wilkes Land
70°S
Main base
d'Urville Sea
0 300 km
130°E

HOME OF THE BLIZZARD

The windiest place on earth

With the main hut almost complete, the men turned their attention to the work room. Both buildings were designed as square pyramids to deflect wind.

After Shackleton's heroic failure to reach the South Pole, the world held its breath as Scott and Amundsen made their own highly public bids for the prize. But even as they were establishing their bases in January 1911, an Australian geologist, Douglas Mawson, was quietly and successfully pleading his case for an Australasian expedition to chart the 3200-kilometre (2000-mile) coast directly south of Australia.

Mawson had first developed the idea during a visit to Europe in February 1910 and had discussed it with Captain Scott, hoping to graft the plan onto the *Terra Nova* Expedition. Scott was unwilling to expand his already ambitious program but was nevertheless anxious to include the experienced and indomitable Australian in his team. Mawson declined, deciding after talking to Shackleton to take the initiative himself.

The Australasian Association for the Advancement of Science liked what Mawson was telling them, but limited their assistance to a £1000 donation and a large slap on the back. Mawson's tenacity, however, so thoroughly tested on Shackleton's *Nimrod* expedition when he and Professor Edgeworth David and Dr Alistair Mackay had slogged their way on an unforgiving route to the South Magnetic Pole, was certainly equal to raising expedition funds and personnel.

In the main, Mawson's team was drawn from Australian and New Zealand universities. His ship was the 600-tonne *Aurora*, a 35-year-old sealing vessel built in Dundee which, refitted and strengthened, was still robust enough to cope with the Antarctic pack ice.

The entire party rendezvoused in Hobart late in 1911, the *Aurora* having been sailed from London by its captain, John King Davis, another *Nimrod* veteran.

Mawson, keen to use modern technology, planned to take an aeroplane and, more impor-

The expedition's elaborate medical kit. Many of the bottles were returned unopened. Most used of all the pills in the kit were the laxatives.

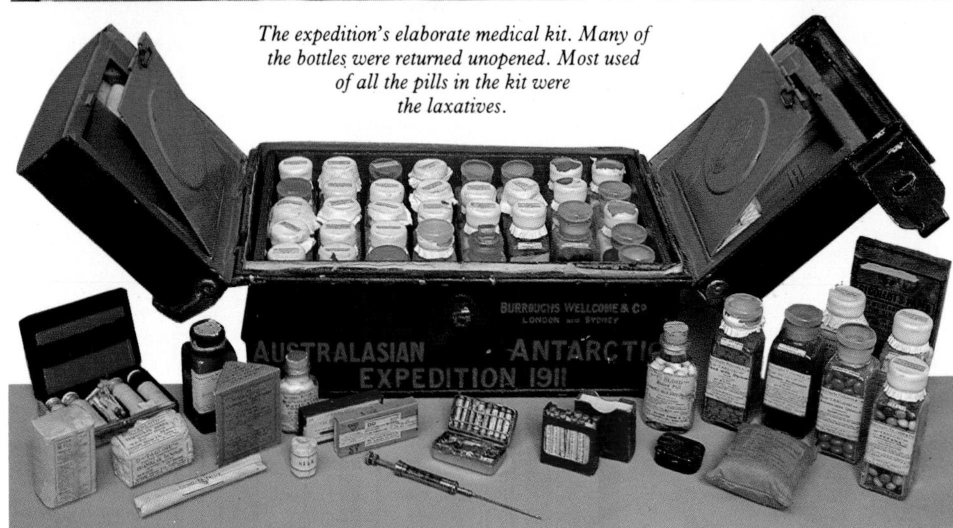

A group of curious penguins inspect the Aurora, *moored at the ice edge.*

A wall of cases helped to shield the hut. Beyond are the waters of Commonwealth Bay.

Stripped of its wings, fittings and covering, the Vickers REP aeroplane was used as a tractor for towing sledges. Even if the machine had not been damaged in a crash in Adelaide before the expedition departed, it is doubtful whether it would have been able to fly in the extreme winds at Cape Denison. The machine cost £900.

FIRST AEROPLANE IN ANTARCTICA

Mawson's air-tractor appears, with hindsight, to have been something of the expensive folly that prototypes often are.

An elaborate public demonstration was arranged at an Adelaide racecourse, aircraft being practically unknown in Australia at the time. But during a trial flight on the morning of the demonstration, the pilot managed to crash.

The machine was equipped with sledge runner, but at Cape Denison the relentless winds kept it in its hanger until the early summer of 1912. The engine, unreliable at the best of times, was a poor operator in extreme cold, but Bickerton, the mechanic, did coax it into life. After cautious trials, he made several runs at up to 32 km/h (20 mph), and towed payloads of up to 363 kg (800 lb) between the main camp and a depot, Aladdin's Cave, about nine kilometres (5.5 miles) south of Cape Denison. Taxed with a 500 kg (1100 lb) load on the western summer sledging journey, however, the engine seized and the tractor was abandoned.

tant, the first radio, to the Antarctic. Obviously it is impossible to overestimate the value of radio in a hostile environment, and for that reason, Mawson's first expedition project was the installation of a wireless relay station on Macquarie Island, 1370 kilometres (850 miles) southeast of Tasmania. The expedition sailed from Hobart on 2 December 1911 and established a five-man party at the northern tip of Macquarie Island.

The party continued south on 23 December, planning to make a landfall west of longitude 158°E, the western limit of the *Terra Nova* survey. Mawson had also wanted to land two further parties along the unexplored coast, but was only able to make two landfalls.

Eventually, the *Aurora* came across a promising 16-kilometre (10-mile) wide bay Mawson named Commonwealth Bay, and there, on 8 January, they spotted a more or less hospitable 1.6-kilometre (one-mile) long rocky outcrop in front of an evenly sloping rise of inland ice that could be used by sledge parties. On either side the glacial ice was heavily crevassed. Time was pressing and Cape Denison, as it was now called, became Mawson's main winter quarters. By 19 January unloading had been completed, the worst difficulty struck by the innocently contented party being two or three gales gusting to 112 km/h (70 mph) which cut up the harbour with 1.2-metre (4-ft) waves.

Now, more than halfway through January, the *Aurora* struggled along the coast to drop the eight-man Western Party, led by Frank Wild, the expedition's third *Nimrod* veteran, on the Shackleton Ice Shelf at Queen Mary Land 2410 kilometres (1500 miles) from Cape Denison. The 36 tonnes of stores were unloaded and, in four days, hauled up a 30-metre (100-foot) ice cliff by means of a flying fox.

Back at Cape Denison, the huts of the other two by now combined parties were erected, the smaller hut being joined to the larger on its leeward side. By 30 January the 18 men were sleeping inside.

The pyramidal roof sloped to within 1.5 metres (5 ft) of the ground where stacked crates continued the sloping line to ground level so that any winter wind would find no vertical resistance. This commonsense precaution was taken because the party expected the area to be windy. The grim reality they had yet to grasp, however, was that they had built their hut in the single most relentless and violent wind corridor on Earth.

But from February onwards, the lessons taught by the worsening wind were quickly learned — anything not tied down would be lost, anyone caught outside without crampons would scarcely be able to claw his way back to the hut, and calm days were so rare that routine outside chores had to be taken on in hurricane-force blizzards. Throughout March and April the wind often blew for days on end at speeds between 96 and 128 km/h (60 and 80 mph), gusting to more than 160 km/h (100 mph), and occasionally peaking above 320 km/h (200 mph). The average wind speed for every hour of every day in May was 98 km/h (60.7 mph), and on 15 May the wind averaged 145 km/h (90 mph) for 24 hours. Over the first year at Cape Denison, the wind averaged nearly 80 km/h (50 mph). In Europe and the USA the average was about 16 km/h (10 mph).

During lulls, the men worked feverishly outside, but were then caught by 'whirlies', freakish miniature whirlwinds that could gather up any object in their path and hurl them through the air. On one occasion the 152-kg (335-lb) lid of the air-tractor case was tossed 40 metres (50 yards) and, an hour later, it was tossed back again. The generally abrasive effect of drift in the grip of a whirlie or hurricane also quickly became apparent — rusty dog chains were polished, ropes were frayed and wood was etched.

As the party settled in for the winter, grateful at least that the drift compacted around the hut had shut out all draughts, the wind dominated their lives.

Winter evenings were whiled away in talk, games and domestic chores.

Mawson's hut still stands, although it has been much worn by the incessant winds of Adélie Land.

SUMMER SLEDGING

A demanding program completed

Mawson's Australasian Expedition, like other pre-World War I parties, planned to make several depot-laying sledge trips before the spring. It was the orthodox routine — the scope of summer sledging depended on thorough winter preparation — and Mawson expected no more than the usual problems.

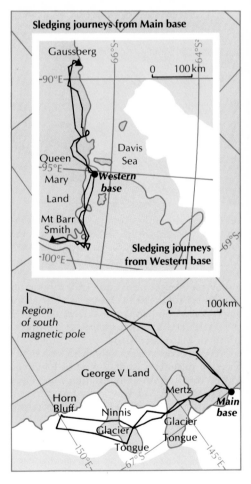

Sledging journeys from Main base

Sledging journeys from Western base

It took the party a few weeks, therefore — until about the middle of February 1912 — to realise that there was almost nothing conventional about the weather being forced upon them. Indeed, the combination of factors — the sloping terrain and general topography that gathered and funnelled vast reservoirs of fast-moving inland air through Cape Denison — was unique. The 'river of wind' was outside the experience of previous explorers.

A New Zealander, 'Azi' Webb, had charge of the magnetographs, instruments that monitored the nearby South Magnetic Pole. He and Frank Stillwell, the geologist, built two sturdy huts for the instruments. The main magnetograph house eventually needed the protection of a 30-tonne stone windbreak.

At the end of February, despite the appalling conditions, Mawson decided to risk a brief reconnaissance trip with Cecil Madigan, the meteorologist, and Lieutenant R. Bage, the expedition's astronomer. They planned to erect flags on the featureless landscape to guide returning sledge parties. They managed to trek about 9 kilometres (5.5 miles) before deteriorating weather forced them back to base.

One important project, the erection of the two radio masts, was begun on 4 April but could not be completed until 1 September. Even so, some of the rigging work had to be tackled in 96 km/h (60 mph) winds. Then, on 13 October, the aerial system was smashed to the ground again. During the few weeks it was serviceable, however, messages transmitted were picked up by the *Aurora* and at Macquarie Island. But their replies were not received.

Communication was not re-established until February 1913, when two-way communication between Adélie Land and Macquarie Island was achieved for the first time.

Confined as they were during the winter of 1912, the men depended on their own inventiveness to relieve the frustration of those largely inactive months. Mawson's relaxed and egalitarian style helped, and so did the mateyness of the predominantly young university graduates in the party. Games, concerts, satirical turns and the tomfoolery of the most successful running joke of the winter — debate over the merits of the 'crook cooks' and the 'unconventional cooks' as each man paraded his domestic skills — kept the party buoyant.

After midwinter celebrations, the expedition prepared for spring sledging and on 9 August Mawson, Madigan and British Army Lieutenant B. E. S. Ninnis headed south into a relatively gentle 64 km/h (40 mph) gale. At 9 kilometres (5.5 miles), they dug an ice shelter, Aladdin's Cave, and set up a supply depot.

In September there was an unprecedented five days of calm weather, an event scarcely to be believed. Several of the men ferried food and equipment to Aladdin's Cave and three sledging parties later set out to get the feel of conditions and test the equipment. Still uncertain about the weather, Mawson limited the parties heading south, west and southeast, to 14 days and 80 kilometres (50 miles). Two groups made little headway against bitter winds of up to 128 km/h (80 mph), one party achieving only 4 kilometres (2.5 miles). The western party did, however, manage an outward march of 80 kilometres (50 miles), but returned frostbitten and exhausted.

During October the weather was so bad that

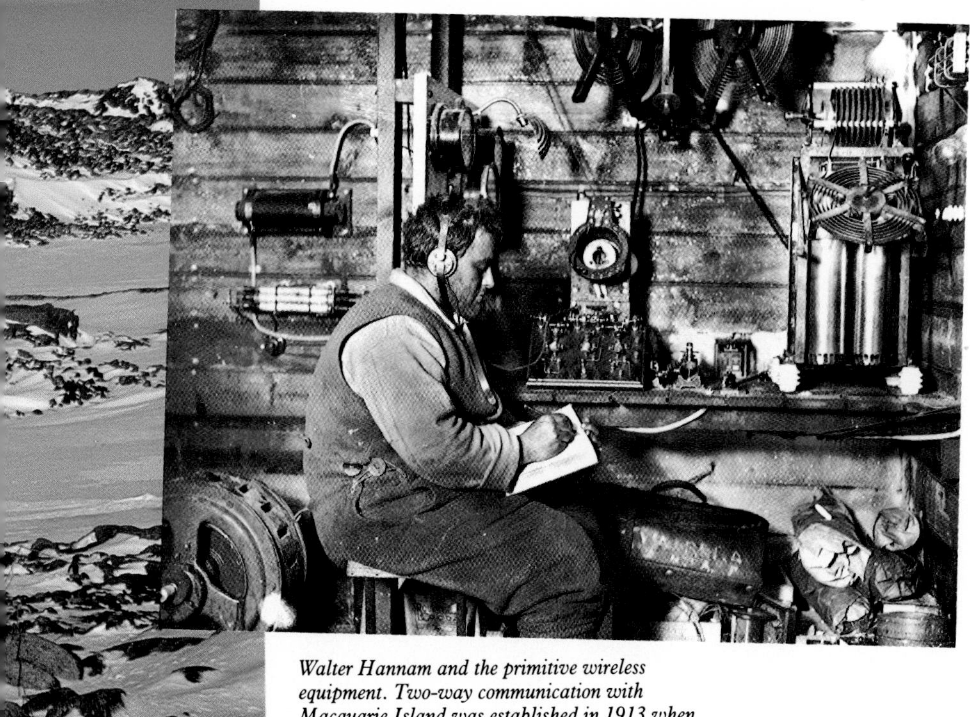

Walter Hannam and the primitive wireless equipment. Two-way communication with Macquarie Island was established in 1913 when news of the death of Ninnis and Mertz was sent, and news of Scott's death received.

Hunter, Murphy and Laseron on one of the summer sledging expeditions. The snow mound behind marks a food depot for the party returning from the South Magnetic Pole.

no sledging was possible, much to Mawson's frustration, but in November five parties took advantage of marginally improved conditions. Three were to head east, one south to the magnetic pole, and one west. Mawson himself planned to lead the potentially most hazardous Far Eastern trek, using the dogs.

A combined Southern and Support Party left Aladdin's Cave on 10 November, heading south in atrocious conditions. Mawson's instructions to all parties had been to observe an absolute deadline for return on 15 January when the *Aurora* would be waiting. With this thought in mind, the Southern Party leader, Bage, pressed forward into gale-force winds while Webb tirelessly took complicated magnetic declination readings to help guide them towards the elusive magnetic pole. On 22 November, after about 105 kilometres (65 miles), the support party returned to the hut. As the three men continued south on their 960-kilometre (600-mile) round trip, the temperatures grew cooler and at night they were regularly below −29°C (−20°F). They reached their farthest south on 21 December when time and food were running short. Webb calculated they were about 80 kilometres (50 miles) short of the exact polar point.

The Near and Eastern Coastal parties had left the main base on 8 November to rendezvous with Mawson's Far Eastern Party 29 kilometres (18 miles) southeast of Aladdin's Cave. Part of the Near Eastern Party's function was to provide support for the other two. They then worked along the coast between Cape Denison and the Mertz Glacier Tongue.

The Eastern Coastal Party, led by Madigan, enjoyed probably the most spectacular scenery of the expedition. By 10 December they had crossed the treacherous and deeply crevassed Mertz Glacier, an achievement in itself, and, with four weeks' rations in hand, tackled the Ninnis Glacier. Once past that barrier, they reached a vast rocky cliff, Horn Bluff. The party's farthest east camp, 434 kilometres (270 miles) from Cape Denison, was pitched in this region on 18 December. On the return journey they struck particular trouble and were delayed by blizzards and deep, soft snow while recrossing the exhausting Mertz Glacier. They finally reached a food cache on Mt Murchison after three days on nothing more than a mug of penguin broth each.

The Western Party, led by Frank Bickerton, planned to traverse the coastal highlands west of Cape Denison and hoped to use the air-tractor. But its temperamental engine was not equal to the punishing conditions and it was abandoned early on. The combination of driving drift and soft snow further impeded progress, the party covering only 50 kilometres (31 miles) in the first week's march. One extraordinary discovery at this time, however, was a tiny meteorite, the first ever discovered in Antarctica. The farthest west camp was pitched on Christmas Day, 254 kilometres (158 miles) from base, 156 kilometres (97 miles) of which had been covered on the only five consecutive days of good weather they had enjoyed.

At Cape Denison everyone, including the *Aurora* crew, now awaited the return of Mawson's overdue Far Eastern Party, unaware that he would eventually stagger in, alone and exhausted, and with a tale to tell that has had few rivals in polar exploration.

The imperturbable Frank Wild was in charge of the Western Base in Queen Mary Land, about 2410 km (1500 miles) away from the Main Base. Five exploratory journeys in the summer of 1912-13 investigated over 480 km (300 miles) of difficult coastline.

WORK OF THE WESTERN PARTY

The eight-man Western Party under Frank Wild, a 38-year-old veteran of both Scott and Shackleton expeditions, settled into their 6-metre (20-foot) square hut, 'The Grottoes', towards the end of the 1912 sledging season. Conditions were difficult but not as hurricane-prone as at Cape Denison. Even so, an early disappointment was the felling of the radio mast by the first blizzard.

Throughout the winter, the party paced themselves, working each day from 10 am to 1 pm. Winds blew at up to 160 km/h (100 mph), all but burying the hut in snow. But depot-laying trips were still made as early as August, and sledge parties later explored and mapped the coastline.

Wild's eastern thrust was brought up short by the severe crevasses and undulations of the Denman Glacier, 193 kilometres (120 miles) from base. The western team crossed the Helen Glacier, discovering vast penguin rookeries and, by Christmas, reached Gaussberg, discovered 10 years earlier by Drygalski. The entire party was relieved by the *Aurora* on 23 February 1913.

Bage prepares a meal in Aladdin's Cave — an ice cave 9 km (5.5 miles) from Main Base. The Southern Party (Bage, Webb and Hurley) shared the cave with Mawson, Mertz and Ninnis on 10 November, and were the last to see all three alive. Mertz is on the extreme right of the photograph.

A selection of expedition rations brought back to Australia in 1914. In the foreground is one of the spoons fashioned by Mertz, after the accident, from timber taken from a broken sledge.

WILL TO SURVIVE

Mawson's lonely trek to safety

After the frustrations of an inactive winter, Mawson was relieved to finally feel the pull of willing dog teams as his three-man party pushed southeastwards on 17 November 1912. The 18 Greenland dogs were hauling three sledges with an eagerness that was barely controllable. But Mawson, Ninnis and Mertz were pleasantly surprised by the vigorous pace.

By the end of November they had negotiated the treacherously crevassed Mertz Glacier and were facing the 'tumultuous and broken' Ninnis Glacier where progress 'amid rolling waves of ice' was slow. Then, for three days from 6 December, the party were trapped by a 113 km/h (70 mph) blizzard. Rations were reduced and, after digging out the dogs and sledges on the 9th, they pressed on through deep snow.

Dr Xavier Mertz, the expedition's skiing expert, was a 28-year-old Swiss law graduate from Basle, an experienced mountaineer and Switzerland's ski-running champion. He and B.E.S. 'Cherub' Ninnis had been in charge of the dogs all winter and were now close friends.

On 13 December one of the sledges was discarded and on the 14th, Mertz, ahead on skis, signalled that he had spotted yet another snow-covered crevasse. Mawson crossed easily enough, but then came a horrified shout from Mertz. Mawson spun round. There was nothing behind him. Not a sign of Ninnis. Rushing back, the two men stared down the gaping crevasse and saw, on a ridge about 46 metres (150 ft) down, a dog, whining, its back apparently broken. Beneath that, there was only the abyss. Mertz and Mawson called into the depths for three hours. Every strand of rope they had would not reach even as far as the crippled dog.

Mawson and Mertz were now faced with a fight for survival. Ninnis's sledge, hauled by the six fittest dogs, had carried the most indispensable supplies, including the tent, most of the food and spare clothing. On the remaining sledge was barely 10 days' food for the two men and nothing for the six dogs. They were 506 kilometres (315 miles) from the hut.

They still had a spare tent cover, the cooker and kerosene. But they had laid no depots on the outward journey, thinking they would be taking an easier route home. Back at the discarded third sledge, they picked up a few useful items and jettisoned everything not essential. A crude tent was made by draping the tent cover over skis and sledge struts. The dogs were fed worn-out finnesko, mitts and raw-hide straps. On 15 December the weakest dog was killed to feed the others and the men. The pattern was repeated for the next 10 days, until the last of the animals collapsed. Although the meat was tough and stringy, without a vestige of fat, every morsel was eaten — even the paws, well stewed.

By Christmas Day they were 257 kilometres (160 miles) from the hut. On most days they covered about 10 kilometres (6 miles). On 30 December, they managed 24 kilometres (15 miles); Mawson was surprised that Mertz did not share his elation. The next day, Mertz asked to come off the dog-meat diet, and try a meagre portion of their remaining sledging rations. On 1 January 1913 he developed stomach pains, and on the 2nd his strength had almost gone. They rested on 5 January and on the 6th they tried again — to delay was to die.

Finally Mertz agreed to be hauled on the sledge by Mawson who even had to help Mertz in and out of his sleeping bag. One hundred and sixty kilometres (100 miles) southeast of the winter quarters, on 7 January,

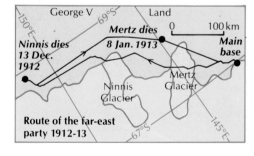

George V Land
150°E
69°S
0 100 km
Mertz dies 8 Jan. 1913
Main base
Ninnis dies 13 Dec. 1912
Mertz Glacier
Ninnis Glacier
Route of the far-east party 1912-13
67°S
145°E

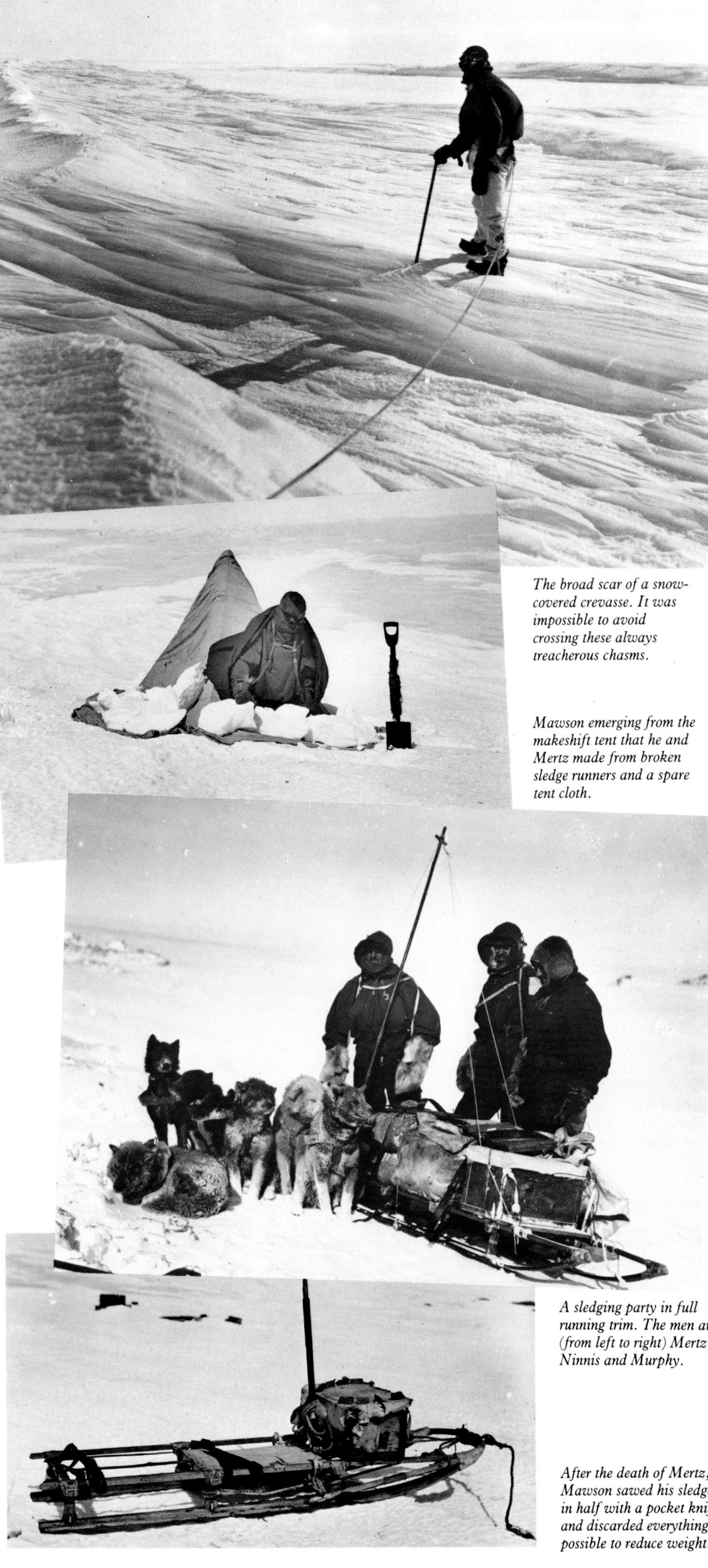

The broad scar of a snow-covered crevasse. It was impossible to avoid crossing these always treacherous chasms.

Mawson emerging from the makeshift tent that he and Mertz made from broken sledge runners and a spare tent cloth.

A sledging party in full running trim. The men are (from left to right) Mertz, Ninnis and Murphy.

After the death of Mertz, Mawson sawed his sledge in half with a pocket knife and discarded everything possible to reduce weight.

Mertz became delirious. Finally, he seemed to rest. A few hours later, Mawson reached over to touch his arm. It was stiff and cold.

'For hours I lay in the bag', wrote Mawson, 'rolling over in my mind all that lay behind and the chance of the future. I seemed to stand alone on the wide shores of the world . . . My physical condition was such that I felt I might collapse at any moment . . . Several of my toes commenced to blacken and fester near the tips and the nails worked loose. There appeared to be little hope . . . It was easy to sleep on in the bag, and the weather was cruel outside.'

In the morning Mawson rallied. He buried Mertz in his sleeping bag, and made a rough cross from sledge runners after sawing the sledge in half to lighten his load. On the 11th, the soles had literally separated from his feet, so he bandaged the thick skin back on. His body was now raw and tender in many places, his hair was falling out and his fingers were festering. On 15 January he covered only 1.6 kilometres (one mile).

Then, on 17 January, Mawson, almost stupefied with exhaustion, found himself dangling in a crevasse at the end of his 4.3-metre (14-foot) harness. The enfeebled explorer began to haul himself out. He reached the lip of the crevasse only to tumble back again.

'My strength was ebbing fast; in a few moments it would be too late. The struggle occupied some time, but by a miracle I rose slowly to the surface. This time I emerged feet first . . . and pushed myself out . . . Then came the reaction, and I could do nothing for quite an hour'.

By now it was taking Mawson two hours to set up camp at the end of each march, his movements laboured and clumsy. On the 27th a blizzard brought him to a standstill, but on the 29th, his food almost exhausted, he spotted a snow cairn. It had been built by McLean, Hodgeman and Hurley who had been searching for the party. They had left a food parcel and a note only hours before. The *Aurora* was waiting. And Aladdin's Cave was only 37 kilometres (23 miles) away.

Mawson arrived at the cave at 7 pm on 1 February, but the weather closed in mercilessly and trapped him for a week. Eventually, he set out in spite of the conditions, arriving at Cape Denison in time to see a departing speck on the horizon — the *Aurora*.

Mawson was welcomed as though back from the dead by the six men who had remained to continue the search, and the *Aurora* was immediately recalled by radio. The ship made a determined attempt to return, but conditions were prohibitive.

At Cape Denison, the seven men reconciled themselves to another winter of blizzards and cocoon-like confinement. But they were well provisioned, the repaired radio aerial survived the spectacular winds which were climaxed by a hurricane that averaged 172 km/h (107 mph) for eight hours. Mawson, Madigan and Hodgeman made a sledge trip in late November and on 12 December the *Aurora* returned.

By 24 December 1913 their two-year sojourn was over and after more than a month cruising the Antarctic coast, Captain John Davis turned the *Aurora* north to Australia on 5 February. The ship entered Gulf St Vincent on the 26th. 'The welcome home', wrote Mawson, 'the voices of innumerable strangers — the hand-grips of many friends — it chokes me — it cannot be uttered!'

All those who try it, value the experience of dog sledging above all other Antarctic memories. Now, however, the pleasure of travelling through the unique Antarctic landscape, away from clanking machines and the institutionalised life of a station, can be experienced by very few. Dogs have all but disappeared from Antarctic bases.

Huskies always sleep outside, curled up and frequently completely covered by drifting snow. Their thick coats provide excellent insulation. Deaths sometimes occur, but only in severe weather and low temperatures.

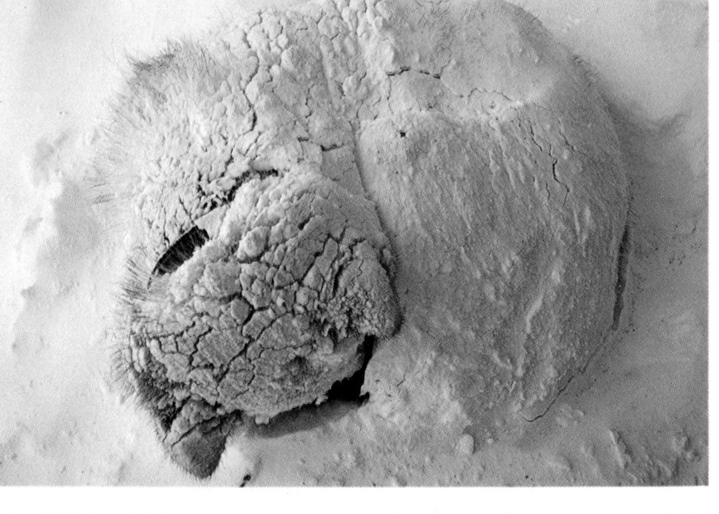

SLEDGE DOGS

A slice of Antarctic history that refuses to die

There is magic in the air when the sledge load is lashed down, yelping huskies are harnessed and clipped in pairs and the anchor plate finally ripped away at precisely the right moment. As one, the dogs are away in a flash, catapulting the creaking wooden sledge across the snow. The whole world is suddenly bound up in the eagerness, strength and teamwork of the straining huskies. Today, dog sledging can be enjoyed by very few who visit Antarctica. This unique form of transport, that took Amundsen to the pole, has all but disappeared from a frontier tamed by the internal combustion engine.

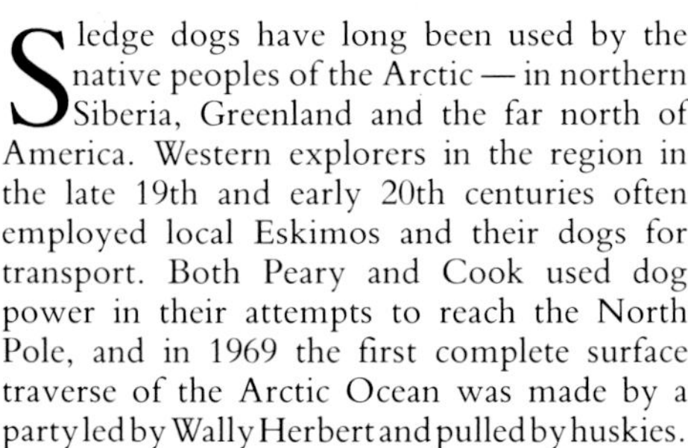

Sledge dogs have long been used by the native peoples of the Arctic — in northern Siberia, Greenland and the far north of America. Western explorers in the region in the late 19th and early 20th centuries often employed local Eskimos and their dogs for transport. Both Peary and Cook used dog power in their attempts to reach the North Pole, and in 1969 the first complete surface traverse of the Arctic Ocean was made by a party led by Wally Herbert and pulled by huskies.

The first Antarctic expedition to use dogs was that led by Carsten Borchgrevink in 1898-1900 (see p134). Although he labelled his 90 dogs as 'savage beasts hungering for fresh meat and blood' and described his control over them as 'marginal', he did think them good companions. His midwinter sledging journey with 29 dogs was a highlight of the expedition.

Dogs were used on almost every other Antarctic expedition until the modern era. They were, of course, critical to Amundsen's successful assault on the South Pole in 1911. Robert Scott used dogs on both the *Discovery* expedition of 1901-03 (23 Samoyeds) and the *Terra Nova* expedition of 1910-13 (54 Siberians). He was not, however, experienced or astute enough to gain a great deal of benefit from them. His inability to properly tame and train them meant that he placed his reliance in Siberian ponies and man-hauling instead.

Even on Richard Byrd's expedition in the 1920s and '30s — better known for their extensive use of aircraft — dogs had a large part to play. There were 100 dogs at Little America in 1928 and 145 at Little America II in 1933.

With the revival of interest in Antarctica after World War II the dogs returned. The British began stocking their peninsula bases with dogs as early as 1945, but it was not until the International Geophysical Year and the Commonwealth Trans-Antarctic Expedition of 1955-58 that dogs were again extensively used for exploration. Over 60 dogs were gathered at New Zealand's Scott base — collected from Australia's Mawson station, Greenland and even Auckland zoo — to find routes up glaciers for Sir Edmund Hillary's tractor party.

By 1959 the dog population at Scott base had dropped to only 26, although some new animals were imported from Greenland in 1961. Expeditions using dog power continued to explore the Transantarctic Mountains until the mid-1960s. One such journey in Northern Victoria Land in 1963 covered a record of 2500 kilometres (1550 miles) in a season.

From the mid-1960s onwards 'tin dogs' — motor toboggans — gradually replaced the real thing. The French and Japanese changed over to machines early on, and the Australians relinquished their dogs at Davis station in 1965 and at Casey in 1970. The British on the Antarctic Peninsula were the last to use dogs extensively. Up until 1975 they were almost solely dependent on dog power. At one time there were 150 dogs at British bases.

Sadly, there are now only about 70 huskies left in Antarctica. There are about 25 at the British Antarctic Survey's Rothera base on the Antarctic Peninsula, 25 at Australia's Mawson base and 20 at the Argentine base Esperanza in Hope Bay. The last 14 dogs from New Zealand's Scott base on Ross Island (pictured here) were exported from the continent in 1987. They were donated to the American Will Steger from Minnesota

A fully grown husky (left) is a large and powerful animal. A base dental check (above) reveals teeth that an angry dog (right) will not hesitate to use on its companions.

who had just returned from driving his own dog teams to the North Pole. Some of the Scott base huskies were used by Steger for his south-north traverse of Greenland, and in turn during the successful 1990 International Trans-Antarctic Expedition (see p 278).

Because most Antarctic work today at government bases is undertaken in vehicles, it has become increasingly difficult to involve a dog team and their driver in each summer's science programme. Use of the dogs has therefore been largely recreational during the 1970s and 1980s. It is, however, still appreciated that dogs are much safer than tractors on heavily-crevassed glaciers and over sea ice, so some field parties still prefer to use a dog team rather than a vehicle.

It now seems certain that the few remaining dogs will leave the bases in the not too-distant future. With ice-free land at a premium, the British dogs at Rothera will probably disappear after the completion of a large permanent runway presently under construction in front of the base. In recent years dogs have been allowed to remain at government bases as long as they did not cost too much in time and money. There have been criticisms from conservationists over the shooting of seals to feed the dogs, but others claim that this is a small price to pay compared with the psychological benefit of having the animals around during the long winter months.

HANDLING A DOG TEAM

The everyday details of training and using dogs varies from base to base according to tradition and experience. The day-to-day details in the following account are based on what was the common practice at New Zealand's Scott base, before their pack was disbanded in 1987.

The dogs at Scott base lived further south than any other husky population. The general conditions, with low temperatures and a lack of sunlight for long periods during the winter, created very tough animals. The original Greenland huskies were supplemented with new animals from time to time. The average weight for males was 36-54 kilograms (80-120 lb) and for females 32-43 kilograms (70-95 lb).

Because of the amount of handling and petting by staff and visitors, most base huskies are very tame and affectionate towards humans. They can, however, still be extremely savage towards each other, and will fight to the death if allowed. A dog handler quickly learns which dogs are compatible on a sledge trace. Good handlers experience few fights. Serious fights occur close to home when the dogs are excited, or near the dog lines when they are eager for a run. During field work they soon settle down into a routine and would rather rest during halts than fight. Usually a dog and a bitch are paired together on a trace, although changes are required when a bitch comes into heat.

A bad fight can involve the whole team of nine or eleven dogs and can be a frightening experience. Often two people are required to pull the tangle of dogs harnesses and traces apart. The only time a dog handler gets bitten is when he attempts to break up a fight in the wrong way. Then he can get nipped on the hand or arm, for in a fight the dogs lose all control. A good handler can let all of his dogs off the chain, especially after a run, and they will mingle quietly until called back.

General sledging practice is to harness four to five pairs of dogs together, with one lead dog out in front. The trace – a single nylon rope nine metres (30 ft long) – has two 61 cm (2 ft) leads clipped in pairs at equal distances along it. Each dog wears a harness made from soft cotton lampwick which is custom-made so that it fits under the dog's 'armpits' without chafing.

The dogs also wear a conventional leather collar which is used for securing it at night. The harness has to be removed otherwise it would soon be chewed to pieces. Leather collars are also chewed, and these are often soaked in kerosene or reinforced with tin plate to foil dogs that persist in gnawing their harness.

There are other systems of linking dogs to a sledge, but tangles are less frequent with a pairs system, and are easier to sort out when they do occur. However, the pairs system does allow a cunning dog to escape from pulling much weight. Such 'freeloaders' keep their trace just tight and no more. With a fan system – each dog on a separate trace – this is not so likely.

Size and sex are no guide to a good sledge dog. Often small scrawny females are tougher than big males, and will keep pulling even in atrocious weather. Both males and females are also used as lead dogs. Handlers have to experiment to select the best animal, and then it is a matter of patience and constant training.

Each handler develops his own commands – their effectiveness is often a matter of voice control and tone, rather than the actual word itself. Stop, go, left and right are all the signals that are necessary, apart from the dog's name.

Dog handlers often come from a farming background, where they have bred and handled a lot of animals. Often they are musterers, hunters or bushmen who can turn their hand to anything practical such as carpentry, sewing and tractor driving. A good handler must have endless patience, a strong, kind, but definite voice and he must never lose his temper with the dogs. Whips are never used. Above all he must be prepared to put in many hours of extra work in the evening when others have gone to bed.

Dogs are checked at the end of each day for cuts and scratches, torn foot pads and to see if the bitches are on heat. At base, teeth are checked every month when the dogs are weighed.

The dogs eat 680 grams (1.5 lb) of fresh seal meat a day, although in summer they are only fed every second day. Thirty-five Weddell seals would feed 20 dogs for a year. This diet is supplemented with kitchen scraps. In the field the dogs receive 680 grams (1.5 lb) of pemmican – a mixture of fat, oatmeal, meat-meals and vitamins – on working days, and 450 grams (1 lb) on the occasional rest days.

GRAND PLANS

Shackleton attempts the first Antarctic crossing

Shackleton's appeal to potential backers in 1913 and 1914 was a 'hard sell' of which a modern advertising agency could be proud. The expedition would undertake 'the greatest Polar journey ever attempted'. The plan was ambitious, yet even some of his admirers wondered if he was attempting too much.

The *Endurance* was to establish the first-ever base on the Weddell Sea, the stormy, ice-jammed foot of the Atlantic Ocean. Six men, led by Shackleton, would walk 2900 kilometres (1800 miles) across the continent, cutting through the South Pole and linking up with a party from the Ross Sea at the top of the Beardmore Glacier. It would be the 'first crossing of the last continent', and the first 1450 kilometres (900 miles) would be across a wilderness never before explored. They would open up 'vast stretches of unknown land'. They would discover whether the immense polar plateau dipped gradually to the Weddell Sea or it fell away in a steep cliff. 'Every step will be an advance in geographical science', Shackleton promised.

Neither he nor the 5000 eager adventurers who applied to join the expedition early in 1914 was to know then that it would be a complete failure, perfect in its futility, and that not one man from the *Endurance* would succeed even in setting foot on the continent. As the war clouds darkened over Europe, the Norwegian-built *Endurance* waited in England, and the *Aurora*, which was to carry the Ross Sea party, in Hobart, Tasmania.

When Shackleton read the order for general mobilisation on Monday 4 August 1914, he immediately told all expedition hands that he wanted to wire the British Admiralty offering the ships, stores and men of the expedition for war service. There was no dissent. Within an hour the Admiralty wired: 'Proceed'. Winston Churchill wired his thanks. But Shackleton, sensitive to the suggestion that there was something unpatriotic about leaving England in her hour of peril, noted that 'the expedition was not going on a peaceful cruise to the South Sea Islands, but to a most dangerous, difficult and strenuous work'. He sailed from Plymouth in the *Endurance* on 8 August. After an uneventful voyage to Buenos Aires, the ship sailed for South Georgia, the southern outpost of the British Empire, on 26 October. Their last news of the war was that many thought it would be over within six months.

After getting advice on the currents and pack ice from South Georgia whalers, they sailed from the island on 5 December. Two days later the ocean suddenly changed colour from green to deep indigo. That evening they encountered a heavy belt of pack ice and began six weeks of dodging between gigantic floes and bergs through ever-narrowing sea lanes.

Protecting the *Endurance's* rudder and propellor, the ship's Achilles heel, was their main concern. Sometimes they were forced to turn the ship into a huge ice chisel, ramming it repeatedly into an ever-enlarging V until at the third or fourth try 'a black, sinuous line, as though pen-drawn on white paper, would appear, broadening as the eye traced it back to the ship. Presently it would be broad enough to receive her and we would forge ahead.'

Shackleton on the bridge of the Endurance *bound for Antarctica.*

The crew played football on the sea ice as they waited for the Endurance *to be freed from the pack.*

Once the ship had been firmly frozen in, the dogs were removed from the deck and housed in 'dogloos' on the ice.

Shackleton thought the pack ice was like a gigantic natural jigsaw puzzle. 'As the pack gets closer the congested areas grow larger and the parts are jammed harder until it becomes "close pack" ... where the parts do not fit closely there is, of course, open water, which freezes over in a few hours after giving off volumes of "frost smoke". In obedience to renewed pressure this young ice "rafts", thus forming double thicknesses of a toffee-like consistency ... the opposing edges of heavy floes rear up in slow and almost silent conflict, till high "hedgerows" are formed round each part of the puzzle ... All through the winter the drifting pack changes — grows by freezing, thickens by rafting and corrugates by pressure.'

By early January they had shifted only a few kilometres further south. With the *Endurance* moored to a floe on 5 January, some crewmen relieved their frustration with a football game on the ice — until the ship's captain, Frank Worsley, dropped through the rotten ice while retrieving the ball and had to be retrieved himself. Another menace presented itself: killer whales. A killer would show a lizard-like head beside a floe, spot a resting seal, dive, then smash through the ice, seizing the seal in its formidable teeth. The creatures were enormously powerful, and the expedition found a hole 7.6 metres (25 ft) in diameter smashed by a killer whale through ice one metre (3.5 ft) thick. When the photographer Frank Hurley was taking a dog team over thin ice, he heard whales blowing behind him and dashed for the

Ghost ship. Frank Hurley's dramatic photograph of the Endurance *during the long winter night. Immense forces in the huge field of drifting ice that imprisoned the ship forced up ridges of tumbled blocks.*

Attempts to cut a passage through the ice proved fruitless. Plumetting temperatures froze the water as fast as the men could break up the ice and clear it from the surface.

solid ice. 'No need to shout "mush" and swing the lash. The whip of terror had cracked over their heads and they flew before it. The whales behind . . . broke through the thin ice as though it were tissue paper, and, I fancy, were so staggered by the strange sight that met their eyes, that for a moment they hesitated. Had they gone ahead and attacked us in front, our chances of escape would have been slim indeed . . . Never in my life have I looked upon more loathsome creatures.'

The *Endurance* was frozen in solidly by 19 January. Mirages made the view from the ship resemble an hallucination. 'Icebergs hang upside down in the sky; the land appears as layers of silvery or golden cloud. Cloud-banks look like land, icebergs masquerade as islands . . .'

They converted the ship into winter quarters, calling it The Ritz, set-to training the dog teams, and sublimated their frustrations in football and hockey games on fields of ice. The *Endurance* was caught between gigantic floes which could crush her as easily as a man squashing a butterfly. Shackleton gave orders to clear the sides of the ship so nothing would prevent her from rising as the ice pressed in. On 15 April there was another wonder: the sun set *twice* — apparently a mirage caused by a band of water heating the air. On 1 May they said goodbye to the sun and the 70-day Antarctic winter night began. 'All hands are cheery and busy', Shackleton recorded, 'and will do their best when the time for action comes. In the meantime we must wait.'

But they could not rely even on the sun's disappearance. On 8 May it rose at 11 am and set 40 minutes later, rose again at 1.10 pm and set 10 minutes later. The navigation officer, who had announced its final disappearance a week earlier, had to explain to his jeering friends that it was not a mistake, it was a refraction of two degrees more than normal.

They celebrated Empire Day, 24 May, singing patriotic songs and telling each other that the might of the Empire would quickly prevail against the Kaiser. Through the coldest winter on earth, tacticians of varying skills calculated the strategies of the British, French, Russian and German armies, fighting in their imagination the bloodiest war in human history. On 15 June Frank Wild, the cool, resourceful second-in-command, started favourite at 6 to 4 in the Antarctic Derby and won the 640-metre (700-yard) dog team race against four others. All 28 men had a bet, and the wagers which counted were not those made in money, but the ones laid in chocolate and cigarettes.

Nearing winter's end, a ferocious blizzard, the worst they had experienced, swept the *Endurance*. The ship was invisible from 46 metres (150 ft) away and Shackleton ordered that no one should venture beyond the kennels beside the ship. The *Endurance* trembled under a 113 km/h (70 mph) wind. By 22 July, with the ice breaking up, the crashing, grinding floes made a sound like the roar of distant surf. Pressure ridges were forming all around the ship. 'Numerous cracks and leads extended in all directions to within 300 yards (270 metres) of the ship', Shackleton wrote. 'Thin wavering black lines close to the northern horizon were probably distant leads refracted into the sky.'

On 26 July the top of the sun appeared for one minute, 79 days after the last sunset. 'All hands are cheered by the indication that the end of the winter darkness is near', Shackleton said. But the hope engendered by the sun was as brief as its appearance.

DEATH OF *ENDURANCE*

Adrift on an ice-covered ocean

The return of the summer sun — 'Old Jamaica' — brought the possibility of escape to the* Endurance. *As the pack ice started to break up, it might open a water channel to the open ocean. But when the pack broke it was a death-trap. The winds and currents ground giant ice floes against each other with relentless force. Blocks of ice as big as city buildings jumped 'like cherry-stones squeezed between thumb and finger'.

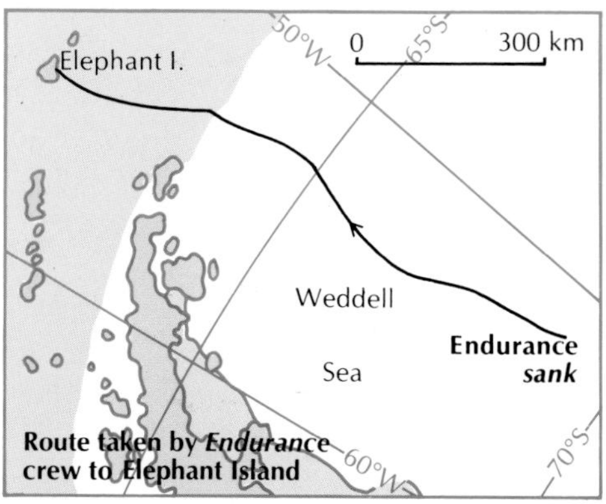

The Endurance *heels over as a pressure wave in the sea ice advances on her. The relentless force of the ice buckled the ship's timbers and soon water was pouring in faster than the pumps could discharge it. The ship was doomed and Shackleton gave the order to unload stores and equipment onto the surrounding ice.*

On 24 October, the *Endurance*, quivering under the immense pressure, started to leak badly. As they desperately tried to caulk the seams with blanket strips, even Frank Worsley, the cheerful, resilient ship's captain, baulked. 'This is not a pleasant job. We have to dig a hole down through the coal while the beams and timbers groan and crack all around us like pistol-shots. The darkness is almost complete and we mess about in the wet with half-frozen hands.'

Shackleton ordered the boats, gear, provisions and sledges lowered to the floe. The *Endurance* had been locked in the ice for 281 days, drifting an estimated 2410 kilometres (1500 miles) and finishing 917 kilometres (570 miles) northwest from where the ice had first embraced her. Shackleton was emotionally overwhelmed. 'It is hard to write what I feel. To a sailor his ship is more than a floating home, and in the *Endurance* I had centred ambitions, hopes and desires . . . It was a sickening sensation to feel the decks breaking up under one's feet . . . Just before leaving I looked down the engine-room skylight as I stood on the quivering deck and saw the engines dropping sideways as the stays and bed-plates gave way. I cannot describe the impression of relentless destruction that was forced upon me as I looked down and around. The floes . . . were simply annihilating the ship.'

Frank Wild surveys the wreck of the Endurance *(below). They abandoned the ship on 27 October, and almost a month later, on 21 November, what was left of the stern rose briefly in the air as she slipped beneath the waters of the Weddell Sea.*

The 28 men pitched five tents 90 metres (300 ft) from the ship, but a pressure ridge started to split the ice beneath them. They moved twice during the day. At night, after supper cooked on the blubber stove, Shackleton, unable to sleep, paced the ice thinking. He planned to walk to Paulet Island 560 kilometres (350 miles) away, where Otto Nordenskjöld's expedition had left a small hut and a cache of food in 1903.

After four days travelling over deep soft snow and rotten ice, they abandoned the attempt and set up Ocean Camp on a thick, heavy old floe about 2.4 kilometres (1.5 miles) from the wrecked ship. As they retrieved food from *Endurance* some men regretted the whimsical amateurism of the expedition, groaning as the boat hook retrieved cases of jelly instead of stomach-filling wheat flour.

Hurley also salvaged volumes of the *Encyclopaedia Brittanica* and several packs of playing cards as protection against one of the worst enemies — boredom. Huge imaginary fortunes changed hands at poker. They consumed hours arguing vigorously about the details of life in ancient Egypt and in Park Avenue, New York. But the encyclopaedia was balm for the body as well as the mind. Its saltpetre-treated pages were fine pipe lighters and also worked well as cigarette papers.

On 21 November 1915 the *Endurance* raised its stern and slipped into the black sea, the ice closing forever over her. The men watching from the camp lookout found the spectacle sickening and a wave of depression swept over them. Shackleton said quietly, 'She's gone, boys' and ordered an extra half sausage each.

With the ice around them rotting and breaking up, Shackleton decided on 20 December to march westward to reduce the distance to Paulet Island. Anxious to move, they advanced Christmas to 22 December, celebrating with their last good meal for eight months — anchovies, baked beans and jugged hare. Wild and Shackleton reconnoitred the route, marking it with pieces of wood, tin and small flags. Then they hauled two boats in relays, about 55 metres (180 ft) at a time. Shackleton was afraid that if the boats got too far apart a

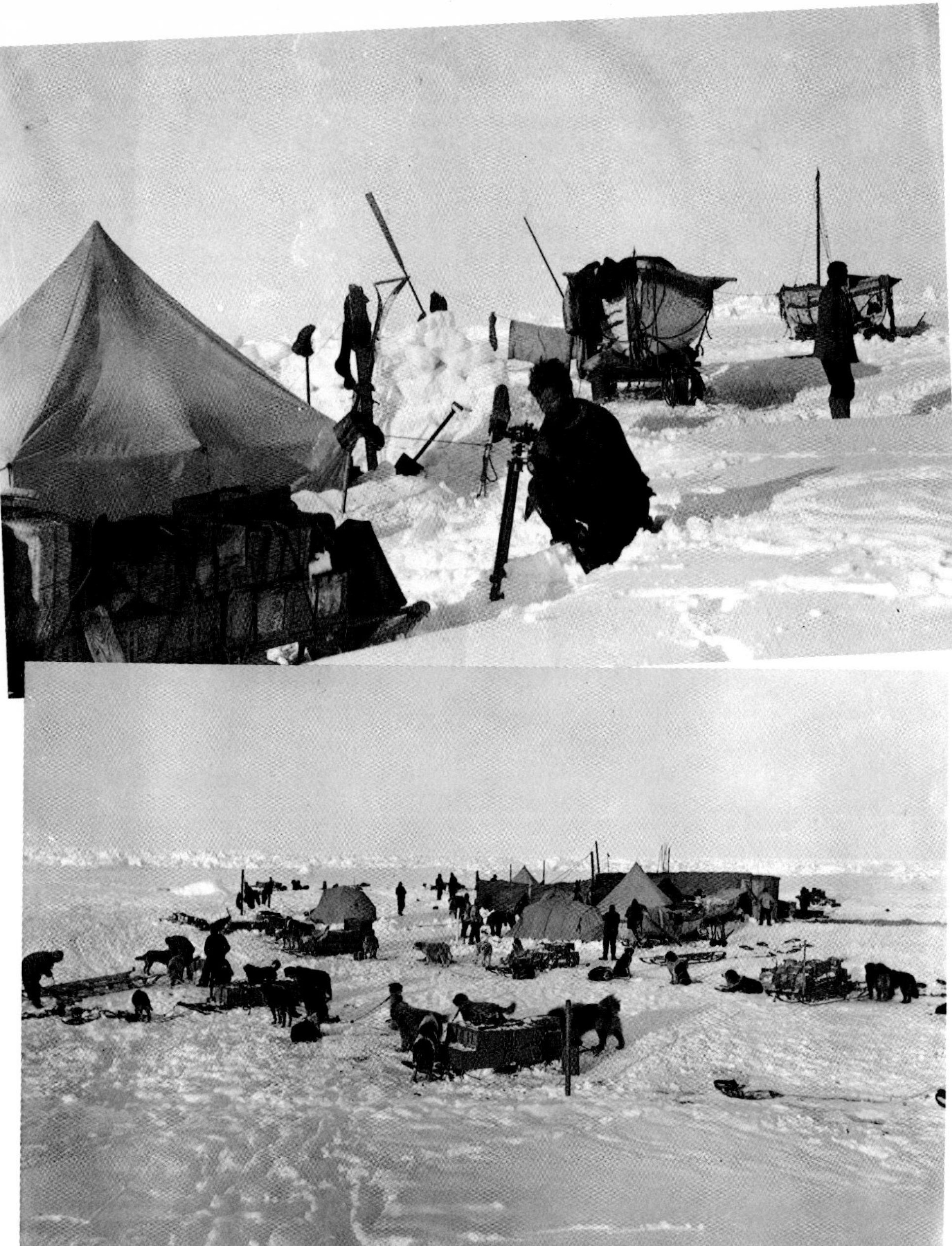

are two in the water'. Shackleton saw a man in a sleeping bag floating in the 1.2-metre (four-ft) wide channel. He flung himself down, grabbed the bag and with a powerful heave pulled the fireman, A. Holness, onto the floe. Seconds later the ice closed. Fortunately Holness was the only one in the water.

They pushed the heavily laden boats into the water lanes at 8.00 the next morning and by 11 am had reached a stretch of open water. Spray, freezing quickly to ice, covered men and gear. Again they retreated to the shelter of the pack ice, found a solid berg and camped.

The men looked pinched and drawn, but Shackleton drew strength from Frank Wild, who sat at the tiller of the *James Caird* unmoved by fatigue, his steel-grey eyes surveying the ice-filled ocean as serenely as if he was on a bench in Hyde Park. On 12 April Shackleton discovered that instead of making a good run west, they had actually drifted 48 kilometres (30 miles) east. After whispering to Wild and Worsley he decided not to break the news to the men, but told them that they had not made as much progress as expected.

As Elephant Island showed to the north-north-west, a gale separated the *Dudley Docker* from the other two boats. She headed for a narrow rocky beach below the high ice cliffs, and to the crew's great relief they sighted the other boats making for the same haven.

Shackleton, in the *Stancomb Wills*, landed first and returned to supervise the landing of the heaviest boat, the *James Caird*. When he landed the second time his eye fell on a bizarre spectacle. Men were reeling about the beach as if they had uncovered a secret supply of rum, laughing uproariously, letting pebbles trickle through their fingers. It was the delirium of men who had not been on land for 16 months.

Ocean Camp (left) was established on the sea ice about 2.4 km (1.5 miles) from the stricken ship. They were floating on an ice-covered ocean 560 km (350 miles) from the nearest land. Two of the ship's boats (above left) were hauled over the ice on sledges.

sudden crack in the ice might mean that the rear one would be lost. They left *Stancomb Wills* behind. Now if their ice floe disintegrated, 28 men jammed into two boats about six metres (20 ft) long would be at the mercy of the Weddell Sea.

Hauling the boats was killing work in snow up to their knees. They stopped every 18 metres (60 ft) panting for breath. On 29 December, with the ice ahead too cracked to carry them, they retreated 800 metres (2600 ft) and camped on a solid floe, but it cracked during the night as well. They quickly shifted to a strong old floe, surrounded by ice too soft to sledge over, but with not enough open water to launch the boats.

They crossed the Antarctic Circle on New Year's Eve, adrift on an ice raft. 'Thus, after a year's incessant battle with the ice, we had returned ... to almost the same latitude we had left with such high hopes and aspirations twelve months previously; but under what different conditions now! Our ship crushed and lost and we ourselves drifting on a piece of ice at the mercy of the winds', Shackleton wrote later. Meanwhile, Wild returned to Ocean Camp for the abandoned *Stancomb Wills*.

Worried that an endless diet of seal meat would damage morale, Shackleton continually rearranged the menu: seal stew, fried blubber, dried vegetables and milk, tea and flour were not much to work with, but he found that 'the slightest variation was of great value'.

On 17 May the rapidly drifting ice had carried them abreast of Paulet Island, but 96 kilometres (60 miles) of decayed ice ruled out any chance of reaching it. Their attention now turned to Elephant and Clarence Islands, and King George Island further to the northwest.

The disintegrating ice forced them into the boats on 9 April. The floe split directly beneath the site of Shackleton's tent and he watched the crack widen with the impression of his head and shoulders on one side and his body and legs on the other. Two hours after the first split, with the channels wide enough to take the boats and a five-kilometre (three-mile) pool of open water only a short distance away, they threw their stores into the boats and cast off. The *Dudley Docker* got caught between two floes, but a line from the *James Caird* pulled her free. By evening they retreated to another floe, hauled up the boats, pitched tents and lit the blubber stove.

Responding to an 'intangible feeling of uneasiness' at 11 pm, Shackleton wandered around the berg and noticed it was end-on to the swell and vulnerable to cracking. As he started to walk to the watchman to warn him, the floe, lifted by a swell, cracked directly beneath a dome-shaped tent. It stretched apart as the crack widened, and a voice cried: 'There

DIFFICULT DECISIONS

Frank Hurley, an Australian photographer, accompanied the expedition and recorded its trials and tribulations in some of his best photographs. The trans-Antarctic expedition was his second trip to Antarctica, as he had been with Douglas Mawson at Commonwealth Bay from 1911 to 1914.

When the ship was abandoned, Shackleton ordered Hurley to leave his hermetically sealed cases of films and negatives behind because only food could be carried on the difficult march to safety. Unbeknown to Shackleton, however, Hurley returned to the wreck and dived into the gloomy, ice- and water-filled interior of the ship to salvage some of his work. This was an extremely risky operation as the ship was poised over a deep ocean, held in place only by tongues of ice projecting through her shattered timbers.

Shackleton was annoyed when he found out, but accepted the situation and together the two men sat down to choose the films and photographs that were to be saved. Hurley smashed over 400 rejected glass plates on the ice so that he could never change his mind. All the photographic equipment had to be abandoned too, although Hurley was allowed to retain one small pocket camera and three spools of film.

A member of the 1971 Joint Services Expedition holds up a copy of Hurley's photograph against the landing site on Elephant Island.

The narrow beach at Cape Valentine (below) provided little protection from high tides and heavy seas. Three days later they moved.

LIFE BENEATH THE BOATS

Castaways on Elephant Island

Frank Wild's indifference to the delirium of the 14 April landing at Cape Valentine on Elephant Island was the mark of experience. Wild, the old Antarctic hand, was not deceived by the sudden comfort of solid land. Perhaps he suspected what an inspection soon confirmed — tides and gales would push the sea to the base of the 610-metre (2000-ft) cliffs.

The cape would not be a refuge for long, and they did not know if the island had any safe camping ground. Shackleton kept the bad news to himself, thinking that at least there was food — the beach and the shallows were full of seals.

Wild, with four of the fittest men, left in the *Stancomb Wills* at 11 the next morning to search for a safe camping ground. On the stark beach, men darned their clothes, cleaning rusty needles on the rocks, overwhelmed by fatigue as the strain of the last days caught up with them. The rising tide forced them to pull the boats closer to the ice cliffs. By nightfall the boat party had not returned. Shackleton, calming his anxiety with his faith in the imperturbable Wild, lit a blubber flare. At 8 pm the men emerged like ghosts from the darkness of the sea into the fire's glare. Wild told Shackleton he had found a sandy spit 11 kilometres (seven miles) to the west.

Labouring through a raging sea which soaked them to the skin, they shifted to the spit, which they then named Cape Wild, on 17 April. As they hauled the boats ashore, the chief engineer, L. Rickenson, turned deathly pale and staggered in the surf. Surgeon A. H. Macklin diagnosed a heart attack.

Shackleton was not dismayed. 'As we clustered round the blubber stove, with the acrid smoke blowing in our faces, we were quite a cheerful company . . . Life was not so bad. We ate our evening meal while the snow drifted down from the surface of the glacier and our chilled bodies grew warm.' At 2 am a wave lapped under Shackleton's tent flap, and they retreated to high rocks at the end of the spit.

Shackleton noticed thousands of ringed penguins mustering in lines at the water's edge at 8 am. At first he thought it was just a big fishing expedition — then he realised the birds were about to migrate, and they would lose a precious reserve of food. The men rushed to club the departing penguins, but they were too late, although they saw with relief that the meaty gentoo penguins were making no sign of following their ringed cousins.

Shackleton, reasoning that the deserted penguin rookery was sure to be safe from the sea, decided to camp there. Wrinkling his nose at the stench, he decided they would have to put up with it for safety's sake.

By next morning some of the men had had enough. They complained about their frozen gloves and headgear, said they wanted dry clothes and were too sick to work. It sounded like the threat of the first strike in the Antarctic. Shackleton acknowledged that frozen gloves and helmets were uncomfortable, but told the men to keep them thawed by sleeping with them under their shirts.

As Shackleton planned the perilous rescue

voyage to South Georgia — 1290 kilometres (800 miles) away — the cook, T. Green, suddenly collapsed. Shackleton replaced him with a man who had reached breaking point — he said he wanted to lie down and die — and was gratified to find that the strenuous job of keeping the galley fire alight revived his spirits. Afterwards Shackleton found him concerned about drying a pair of socks.

The *James Caird,* with Shackleton and five crew, left on Easter Monday, 24 April. The Antarctic celebrated their departure with a two-week blizzard. Wild decided to make a hut from the two remaining boats and scraps of old tents. They erected parallel stone walls to support the bow and stern of the two boats laid side by side, stretched sails and tent floor cloths over the upturned hulls and fastened tent canvas to act as walls.

Rickensen, still weak and shaken from his heart attack, was given the warm berth above the blubber stove. The pungent smoke stung their eyes till A. Kerr, the second engineer, made a tin chimney with biscuit case lining.

They solved the problem of light by sewing celluloid windows — panes from a photograph case — in the walls. Then there was the water. When the temperature rose to just above freezing, the hut became a drainage pool. On one day in May they bailed out 728 litres (160 gallons) with a saucepan.

They celebrated midwinter's day on 22 June with a cocktail comprising a pint of hot water, ginger, sugar and a teaspoon of methylated spirits. Some thought it tasted like Veuve Cliquot. Hussey's banjo, the last thing saved from the *Endurance*, was a tonic. At Saturday night concerts the men, accompanied by the banjo, would sing vulgar, vivid songs about each other's appearance, habits and character. If a man was hurt, he avenged himself with a song about the songwriter the next Saturday.

Food was getting short by the beginning of August. They started digging up discarded seal bones and stewing them in sea water. They found seaweed boiled in sea water 'very tasty' — but it only increased their appetites for solid food. When they dreamed of feasts they were true united Englishmen. Twenty-one said they would have suet pudding. They finished the methylated spirits on 12 August and thereafter toasted their sweethearts, the men aboard the *James Caird*, and the King with hot water and ginger. Surgeons McIlroy and Macklin amputated the toes on one of Blackborrow's feet by the light of a blubber stove.

Each morning as he rolled up his sleeping bag, Wild said, 'Get your things ready boys, the boss may come today'. He knew that hope was as important as the seal steaks if they were to survive the gales, the frostbite, the boils and the demoralisation of their stinking home. On 30 August they were nearing lunch when Marston spotted the Chilean trawler *Yelcho* in an opening in the mist. He screamed 'Ship O!' but the men thought it was the call for lunch. A few moments later the men inside the hut heard him sprinting towards them. He shouted, 'Wild, there's a ship! Hadn't we better light a flare?' As one, they scrambled for the door. Those behind ripped down the canvas walls. Wild put a pick through their last tin of petrol, soaked clothes in it, walked to the end of the spit and set them ablaze.

Blackborrow still could not walk. His friends carried him in his sleeping bag and propped him on a high rock to watch the marvellous scene. As the boat approached Shackleton shouted: 'Are you all well?'

Their first meal aboard the *Yelcho* was a disaster with their hunger-atrophied stomachs. As they lay on cushions and settees that night, many could not sleep despite the wonderful warmth and comfort. 'It was just heavenly to lie and listen to the throb of the engines instead of to the crack of the breaking floe or the howling of the blizzard', one man said. 'We intend to keep August 30 as a festival for the rest of our lives.' They had been 105 days on Elephant Island.

After a couple of days on the narrow beach at Cape Valentine, the men moved 11 km (7 miles) to Point Wild where they set about drying their clothes (below). In the modern photograph (left), the camp site was on the rising ground beyond the narrow part of the spit.

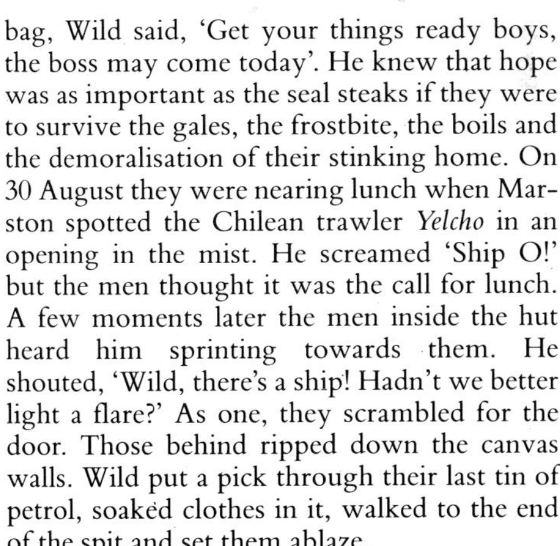

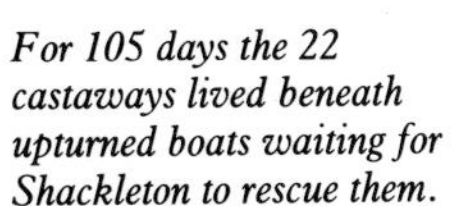

For 105 days the 22 castaways lived beneath upturned boats waiting for Shackleton to rescue them.

THE BOAT JOURNEY

Shackleton risks all in a desperate bid to reach safety

The voyage to South Georgia meant sailing 1300 kilometres (800 miles) in a weather-beaten boat, buffeted by mountainous waves and gales, beneath a cloud cover which made navigation a matter of luck. Shackleton tried it only because the alternative was freezing to death on Elephant Island. He thought there was no chance at all of a rescue ship searching for them on the island. Only one month's food was taken — they would die anyway if the voyage took longer.

Mount Paget, highest point on South Georgia's mountainous spine. Shackleton's party crossed to the northwest of this peak.

Having made the decision, Shackleton inspected the *James Caird,* which in his mind's eye appeared to have shrunk. The cheery, wisecracking Timothy Macarty covered the boat with case lids, sledge runners and canvas. Like most of the 28, he wanted to sail on the *James Caird;* if she was lost then those left behind would die too.

On 24 April, Easter Monday, the *James Caird* set out with a crew of six on her epic voyage, and their first serious accident occurred just as the boat cleared the breakers. One of the two fresh water casks being towed out by the *Stancomb Wills* hit a rock and opened a hole. Half their 164 litres (36 gallons) of drinking water was brackish.

As they made five km/h (three mph) between the icebergs, Worsley, the quick and brilliant navigator, found the scene fantastic. He saw castles, churches and exotic creatures in the bergs. 'Swans of weird shape pecked at our planks, a gondola steered by a giraffe ran foul of us, which much amused a duck sitting on a crocodile's head. Just then a bear, leaning over the top of a mosque, nearly clawed our sail ... All the strange, fantastic shapes rose and fell in stately cadence with a rustling, whispering sound and hollow echoes to the thudding seas...' They were glad to clear the ice, not knowing they would soon crave a lump to relieve a thirst burning their throats.

The six-metre (20-ft) James Caird *being launched on her epic voyage to South Georgia. Six men completed the hazardous 1300-km (800-mile) trip.*

They made good distance — between 97 and 113 kilometres (60 and 70 miles) — in a day. Then a blizzard struck. From deep in troughs between giant waves, the sail flapping idly, they would climb to the crest where the wind struck like a bomb-burst in water that looked like white wool. They had no dry place — the sleeping bags started to smell as if they were fermenting — and no rest. The deck covering was too low for them to sit upright so they ate with their chests pressed against their stomachs, feeling each mouthful squeeze uncomfortably down their throats. The taste of salt water was perpetually in their mouths. The spray froze on the boat till she was 'more like a log than a boat'. They chipped it away, clinging on desperately with one hand as they wielded the axe in the other. Nothing could save a man who fell overboard.

At midnight on the tenth night, Shackleton, at the tiller, saw a pale line on the horizon to the southwest and called that the weather was clearing. Seconds later, he realised that it was not a break in the sky at all, but the white crest of a truly mountainous wave, the biggest he had seen in 26 years' experience of the sea. He screamed: 'For God's sake hold on! It's got us!' The wave smashed over the *James Caird*, flinging her forward like a cork. She lurched and settled in the tortured water. Six men grabbed saucepans, buckets, anything at hand and bailed for their lives. After 10 minutes the *James Caird* lifted as if coming to life from a sodden stupor. The next day Worsley's glimpse of the sun showed they were within 160 kilometres (100 miles) of South Georgia.

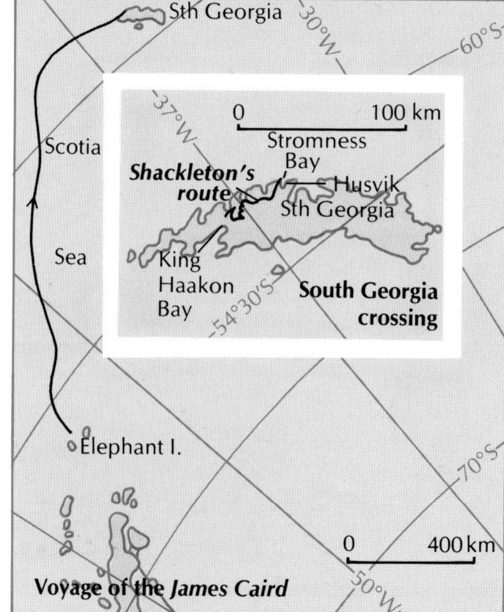

Drinking salty water from the damaged cask — Shackleton limited them to 280 ml (0.5 pint) a day — their tongues swollen, their mouths dry and their throats burning, they sipped their one cup of hot milk at night and dully hoped for the sight of land. They sighted kelp, then two shags, a sure sign land was no more than 24 kilometres (15 miles) away, on the morning of 8 May. Shortly after noon, Macarty spotted the black cliffs of South Georgia through a break in the clouds. But as they neared the shore, blind rollers showed uncharted reefs along the coast. A night landing would be suicidal. They waited for dawn, but at 5 am a shrieking hurricane drove them

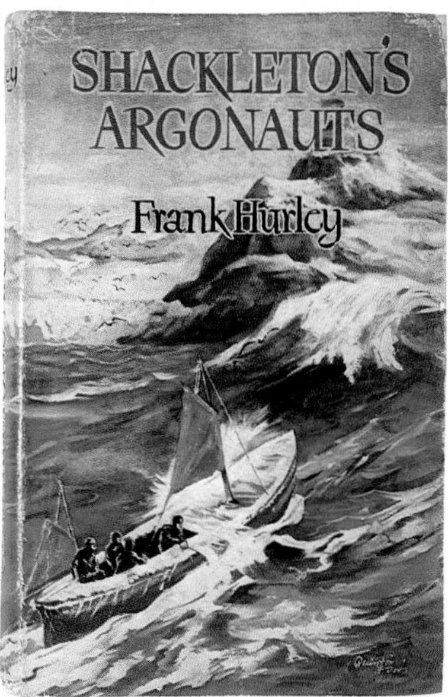

Apart from Shackleton, two members of the expedition — Worsley and Hurley — published accounts of their trip. This painting is based on one by George Marston.

The crew of the Endurance *at Punta Arenas (below). At the centre is Captain Luis Pardo of the* Yelcho, *who is also featured on this Chilean stamp.*

towards the island — and deadly peril. The roar of the breakers against the unseen cliffs warned them their position was desperate. As the *James Caird* bumped the reef, water poured in. Late in the afternoon Shackleton thought their chances of surviving the night were 'small indeed'. Then, as the boat wallowed in the backwash from the iron-bound cliffs, the wind shifted and the gale eased. As it did so, the pin locking the mast to the thwart fell out. Had it done so during the hurricane nothing could have saved them.

They stood offshore for another night, almost beyond caring, their last water gone, longing for the dawn. The next day they headed for King Haakon Bay, found a gap in the jagged reef, and as dusk approached touched the beach and landed.

At 2 am on the first night ashore, Shackleton woke them abruptly, shouting, 'Look out boys, look out! Hold on! It's going to break on us!' His fingers dug into Worsley's shoulder. He was staring at the black snow-crested cliff opposite the cave, seeing it as the giant wave which had nearly killed them.

McNeish and Vincent were too weak to attempt the 27-kilometre (17-mile) journey over South Georgia's mountains and glaciers to Stromness whaling station. No-one had ever penetrated as far as 1.6 kilometres (one mile) from the island coast.

Shackleton decided to leave the sick men in Macarty's care. He set out on 15 May with Tom Crean, second officer on the *Endurance*, and Worsley. Bone-weary from the cramped boat, they had little more than willpower to keep them moving. After 20 hours' climbing over icy slopes, snowfields and glaciers they stopped to rest at a rocky spur. They lay with their arms around each other — the wind from the mountain peaks chilling them. Worsley and Crean were sound asleep in two minutes, but Shackleton, by now a creature of the Antarctic, shook them awake. 'Sleep under such conditions merges into death', he said. They walked on, so stiff that for 270 metres (300 yards) they could not straighten their knees. As they approached Stromness Bay, they heard the steam whistle calling the whalers to work. Shackleton thought it was the sweetest music he had ever heard. But once again the last lap was difficult and dangerous. Faced with a 9-metre (30-ft) waterfall, with impassable ice cliffs on both sides, they were forced to lower themselves through the bitter water. Shivering, evil smelling, their hair matted, their clothes filthy, they started to worry what any women at the whaling station would think of these uncivilised ruffians.

At the wharf, they told the man in charge they had just crossed the island and he looked at them as if they were mad. They followed the man to the manager's house. Shackleton introduced himself then said, 'Tell me, when was the war over?' The manager said, 'The war is not over. Millions are being killed. Europe is mad. The world is mad.'

They washed, shaved, and dined on 'coffee and cakes in the Norwegian fashion', then changed into Norwegian suits. Worsley boarded a whaler bound for King Haakon Bay while Shackleton started to prepare for the rescue voyage to Elephant Island. The next day when Worsley arrived the three men waiting under the upturned *James Caird* were delighted but puzzled. 'We thought the boss or one of the others would have come', Macarty said. 'What's the matter with you?' Worsley asked. Suddenly they realised the clean-shaven neatly dressed stranger was the same man as the hairy, soot-streaked apparition who had left them three days ago.

They returned to Stromness Bay. The next morning Shackleton, Worsley and Crean left on the Norwegian whaler *Southern Sky* for Elephant Island. One hundred kilometres (60 miles) from the island the pack ice forced them to retreat to the Falkland Islands. Then the Uruguayan Government lent Shackleton the trawler *Instituto de Pesca* but again the ice defeated them. They went to Punta Arenas in the Magellan Straits, where British and Chilean residents subscribed £1500 and Shackleton chartered the schooner *Emma*. In the pack ice 160 kilometres (100 miles) north of Elephant Island the auxiliary engine broke down. For the fourth try the Chilean Government lent Shackleton the steamer *Yelcho* under the command of Captain Luis Pardo. As the *Yelcho* manoeuvred through the icebergs and reefs off Elephant Island, Worsley saw Shackleton, tense as a helmsman in a hurricane, peering through his binoculars and counting the black figures spilling from beneath the upturned boats on Cape Wild. When he reached 22 he shouted, 'They're all there, skipper!' As he lowered the binoculars Worsley thought he suddenly looked years younger. He had never lost a man in all his perilous years on the ice

Seven of the 10 men marooned ashore on Ross Island after the disappearance of the Aurora *(above) survived.*

The Aurora's *anchor still lies embedded in the ground near Scott's hut at Cape Evans. For 10 months after she was blown out to sea she drifted helpless in the ice and was carried 1770 km (1100 miles) to the north.*

THE ROSS SEA PARTY

Heroes that history forgot

In September 1914 the second part of Shackleton's trans-Antarctic expedition left London to join the* Aurora *in Sydney. The ship left on 15 December 1914 and arrived near Scott's 1901 base at Hut Point on 7 January. Their job was to lay depots for Shackleton's party as they came across the pole from the Weddell Sea. Dick Richards, a member of the expedition living in Melbourne in 1984, tells of their experiences.

'On 21 January 1915 three parties were put overboard on to the sea ice to journey south in a preliminary effort to gain experience for the newcomers, and to establish two depots, one in the vicinity of latitude 79°S — the Bluff Depot — and the other at 80°S. My own party, consisting of Ninnis, Hooke and I, got back to Hut Point after about three weeks.

'On returning to Hut Point we found open water in the McMurdo Sound and were picked up by the ship which had been searching the shores of the sound for a safe winter anchorage. None could be found so it was decided to winter off Scott's hut at Cape Evans. Accordingly the ship was made ready for wintering with two anchors at the bows and seven steel hawsers from stern to shore, together with a heavy cable from the midships section of the ship. The ship was now iced-in and considered safe for the winter so the boilers were partially dismantled. Four men — Stevens, Gaze, Spencer-Smith, and myself — were put ashore to occupy Scott's hut ... a quite commodious structure measuring 15 x 6 metres (50 x 20 ft).

'We were now split into three parties — six men camped at Hut Point, separated by sea from the four of us at Cape Evans. The rest of the expedition were on the ship which was thought to be secure about 270 metres (300 yards) off-shore. However, on the night of 6 May, a furious blizzard blew up and the *Aurora* broke all moorings and was taken down the sound still embedded in the surrounding ice.

'On 2 June the six men that had been cut off at Hut Point, crossed the ice and arrived out of the darkness, to our great satisfaction. Soon consideration had to be given to the new circumstances and its effect on our planning. Clothing had to be improvised and sledges and tents and primuses were not new.

'We cut up an old canvas tent for windproof garments and used quite a lot of discarded undergarments left by Scott's party. Our sledge and one tent were old and gave trouble. Footgear was made out of old fur sleeping bags and we used Scott's old primuses which gave trouble on the journey. Considerable thought was given to plans for the sledging. We realised it would involve arduous man-hauling and several meetings were held to formulate a plan which involved placing a week's supply of food for six men at every degree south to Mt Hope at 83°40'S. It was proposed that four trips should be made from Hut Point to the Bluff Depot, about 145 kilometres (90 miles) away, then three trips from the Bluff to 80°S, and from there a run through to Mt Hope. On the first trip to the Bluff Depot no dogs were taken. We had only four left and we thought at first that they would not be able to accommodate their pace to the slow trudge of man-hauling. In the event they adapted splendidly and ultimately we owed our lives to those four dogs — Oscar, Gunner, Towser and Con. The first journey to the Bluff proved so arduous that we decided to try them on the 2250 kilometres (1400 miles) remaining, and this decision was vital to our success.

'The sledging started on 1 September and continued for seven months. The task before us should have been simple enough, but because of lack of equipment and hauling power it proved extraordinarily difficult.

'The first break in the planned work occurred at 80°S when three of the party, Cope, Gaze and Jack, were sent back with a defective primus. Another primus became defective at 82°S and it was then resolved that all six of us — Mackintosh, Spencer-Smith, Wild, Joyce, Hayward, and myself — should go on to Mt Hope. However, at 83°S Smith collapsed from scurvy. After discussion we left him in a tent alone while the rest of us went on for about 64 kilometres (40 miles) to complete the final depot at Mt Hope. Here, on 26 January, we left two weeks supply of food, after which we set off on the first stage of our journey home.

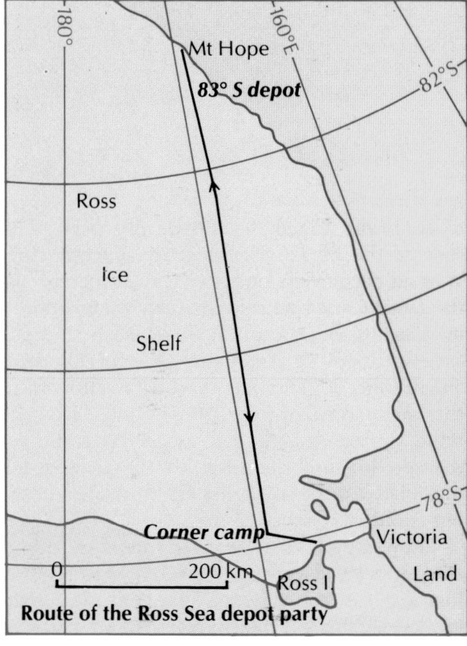

Route of the Ross Sea depot party

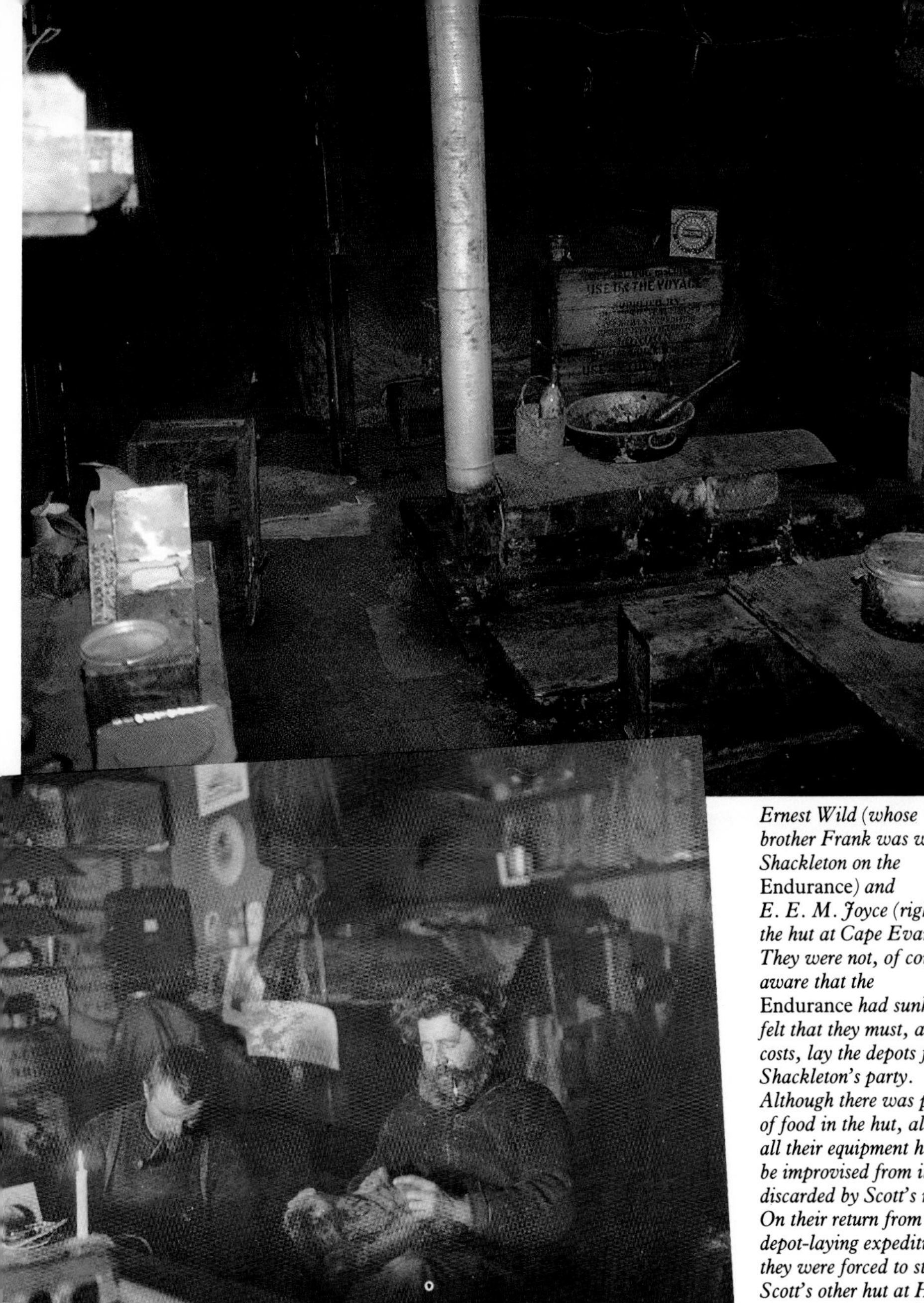

Ernest Wild (whose brother Frank was with Shackleton on the Endurance*) and E. E. M. Joyce (right) in the hut at Cape Evans. They were not, of course, aware that the* Endurance *had sunk so felt that they must, at all costs, lay the depots for Shackleton's party. Although there was plenty of food in the hut, almost all their equipment had to be improvised from items discarded by Scott's men. On their return from the depot-laying expedition they were forced to stay at Scott's other hut at Hut Point for five months. The blubber stove that they built (above) is still there.*

'We sighted Spencer-Smith's camp on 29 January. He had had a lonely vigil and we found him quite incapable of walking, so from there, for 40 days and over 480 kilometres (300 miles), he travelled in his sleeping bag on a sledge, and was never again on his feet. Also by this time it was obvious that Mackintosh could do little in the way of hauling the sledges, and he got progressively worse. In this way we continued until 17 February when we were held up by a severe blizzard some 16 kilometres (10 miles) south of the Bluff Depot.

'We were immobilised there for six days in quite impossible weather. We were now out of food and in normal circumstances we would not have attempted to travel as there was absolutely no improvement in the conditions. But as we were situated it was imperative that we kept moving.

'After about half an hour the weather had not improved and Mackintosh could go no further, so we pitched a tent and left him and Spencer-Smith with Wild to look after them both. Joyce, Hayward, and I, went on to try and reach the depot. How we reached this I do not know. We knew the bearing for our course, but we had nothing to steer by. The only way we could proceed was to put Joyce on course in the lead at the end of a long rope, and to note the blizzard direction in relation to this. We checked the direction about every half hour with a prismatic compass held in the bare hand. We had earlier discarded everything possible to save weight and that included our sledgemeter, so we were reduced to estimating our distance travelled.

'We barely made it. The journey took three days and the dogs and ourselves had been without food for some time and we were weak with scurvy. We stayed some time at the depot gathering strength and mending the tent which was in danger of splitting. As soon as possible we loaded up with food and started back for our companions. Turning our faces south again we trudged on for three days through a heavy blizzard. On the third day we stopped and camped, as we estimated that we were now near the spot where we had left the others. Again we looked from our tent during intervals in the storm, and in one such lull we saw the black speck of their camp among the snow.

'Wild was in good shape but Spencer-Smith was pretty weak and Mackintosh could barely walk. With Smith on the sledge and Mackintosh hobbling, we reached the Bluff again on 1 March. The next six days were a struggle with both Smith and Mackintosh riding on the sledges, a situation that was only possible because of the gale-force following wind. When the wind dropped progress became desperately slow as Hayward could not now contribute much in the way of help. We staggered on till 7 March when we were unable to proceed. After consultation we decided to leave Mackintosh in a tent with food and to try to get Smith to Hut Point, which was now about 64 kilometres (40 miles) away. There we thought we might be able to save Smith's life with the seal meat that would be available. But on 8 March he died.

'On 11 March we reached Hut Point where we at once took steps to provide the fresh seal meat which would give us the vitamin C missing from our diet for the past six months. On 14 March we went back for Mackintosh and returned with him to the hut.

'We found the hut a grim place for the next few months. We five men were separated from the other four at Cape Evans by 21 kilometres (13 miles) of sea, which could not be crossed until it froze over later in the year. The hut was only a shell with one corner partitioned off by canvas to provide some shelter from the draughts. No food had been left there so we had only seal meat to eat. Light came from seal oil in empty tins with an improvised wick.

'All the party were suffering from scurvy and Mackintosh and Hayward were badly affected. However, on our severely restricted diet of seal meat all made a good recovery. So much so that on 8 May Mackintosh and Hayward decided to cross the 21 kilometres (13 miles) of sea ice to Cape Evans. We tried to dissuade them, for there was an 11-kilometre (seven-mile) stretch which went out to sea whenever there was a blizzard, but Mackintosh appeared anxious to see to things at Cape Evans. They set off at 11 am promising to make for the land if there was a blizzard. A blizzard did blow up and it was three days before we could follow their tracks out over the ice. Some five or six kilometres (three or four miles) from the hut we found new ice and no trace of the men. We had to wait until July when we all crossed to Cape Evans to find whether or not they had got across safely. . . . Unfortunately we learned that they had not arrived.

'From July 1916 until 10 January 1917, when the rescue ship arrived, it was a bit of a struggle to get by. We had been marooned ashore away back in April 1915 with largely what we stood up in. One Godsend was the fact that the *Encyclopaedia Britannica* and a 1912 HMV gramophone had somehow found their way into the hut. We had had no anxiety then about the security of the ship's anchorage, so we had not bothered to transfer to the hut any supplies of clothing, fuel, medicines, soap, tobacco and spirits, to name but a few items. Of general stores Scott's party had left plenty.

'The remaining few months until we were rescued were occupied with efforts to obtain fuel and improvise clothing. Many seals were needed to get blubber for heating, and clothing was augmented with items left in the hut.

'We heard nothing whatever from the outside world between December 1914 and 6 January 1917, and during this period the world we knew had changed almost beyond recognition. I suppose we were just about the only people in the world in complete ignorance of the momentous events of those years.'

HISTORIC HUTS

Monuments to the men of the heroic age

In July 1917 the heroic age of Antarctic exploration ended after Ernest Shackleton's ill-fated attempt to cross Antarctica. In the 18 years since Carsten Borchgrevink had first wintered at Cape Adare in 1899, 14 expeditions from eight countries had struggled to unlock the mysteries of the last continent.

Some of the early explorers built their bases on moving ice shelves, since the coast was so steep and inaccessible. Amundsen's *Framheim* at the Bay of Whales has not been seen since he left it in 1912. Like other huts built on the ice shelf it was long ago carried out to sea as the shelf edge broke away.

But most of the huts built on land have survived and they preserve a unique record of the struggles of the early explorers. The huts were the centres of men's lives for anything up to three years. When the ships returned to collect them, much equipment and even personal belongings were left behind.

The cruel Antarctic weather which made the explorers' lives so difficult, has preserved the huts as they left them — literally frozen in time. The damage has been restricted to the effects of wind, while inside ice and snow has drifted in through cracks and broken windows and accumulated. Little normal decay has occurred in the sub-zero temperatures.

When the American explorer Richard Byrd visited McMurdo Sound in 1947 he recorded that Scott's hut at Cape Evans 'appeared somewhat disorderly after the buffeting of thirty-five winters. The frozen carcase of a dog stood on four legs as if it were alive. Seal carcases from which fresh steaks might have been cut lay about. Scattered around the cabin were cartons of provisions still good to eat. A box of matches ignited easily.' On visiting Scott's earlier hut at Hut Point, Byrd wrote: 'The timbers looked as if freshly sawn. Printed directions for putting them together which were found pasted on one wall might just have come off the press.' The visitors also noted boxes of biscuits, mutton carcases and pony snowshoes scattered nearby. A hitching rope was in such good condition it was used to secure a helicopter which had been damaged on landing. This hut, like the one at Cape Evans, was full of ice and snow.

The surviving huts and shelters are in two main areas — around the Ross Sea, and on the Antarctic Peninsula.

Of the three huts at McMurdo Sound in the Ross Sea the oldest is at Hut Point, built by Captain Scott's 1901-04 expedition. The party lived on board ship and used the 11 x 11 metre (37 x 37 ft) prefabricated hut as a base for their sledging journeys. Being the most southerly it was regularly used by later expeditions on their way to and from the interior of Antarctica.

At Cape Evans, 27 kilometres (17 miles) north, is the base of Scott's last expedition of 1910-13 — the point from which he left on his tragic journey to the pole. The 15 x 7.6 metre (50 x 25 ft) hut was also for three years home for the members of the Ross Sea Party from Sir Ernest Shackleton's 1914-17 attempt to cross Antarctica.

The hut at Cape Evans on Ross Island was built by members of Robert Scott's 1910-13 expedition. It was from here that Scott and his party made their tragic attempt on the pole. This was also home for members of Shackleton's trans-Antarctic expedition of 1914-17, marooned when the Aurora *blew out to sea.*

The desiccated remains of one of Scott's huskies still lies chained to the outside of the Cape Evans Hut. The expeditions left large quantities of equipment behind.

Herbert Ponting's darkroom in the Cape Evans hut. It is now rather untidier than it was when the meticulous photographer left Ross Island in 1912.

A further 13 kilometres (8 miles) north is the 7 x 5.8 metre (23 x 19 ft) hut built by Shackleton as living quarters for the members of his 1907-09 *Nimrod* expedition.

These huts are in the New Zealand sector of Antarctica and in 1959 a Huts Restoration Committee was set up by the New Zealand Government. Its main aims were to clear the huts of ice and snow, to restore them as closely as possible to their original appearance, and to recover any historic relics from the huts and surrounding areas.

In December 1960, a six-man New Zealand party led by historian Mr L. Quartermain started to restore Shackleton's hut at Cape Royds. The interior was returned as nearly as possible to its original appearance, while outside, the walls of the garage were reconstructed, and the ice was removed from the adjoining stable. Many relics were found, including parts of the Arrol-Johnston motor car, the first motor vehicle taken to Antarctica. Additional fittings for the car, such as the ski attachments for the front wheels, have been found in recent years. These were previously only known from an artist's impression.

The same summer, Quartermain's party restored the Cape Evans hut. This presented a more formidable task. The stables were collapsing, and the hut was estimated to be more than two-thirds full of ice. Only the galley remained relatively clear, yet even here there was thick ice on the floor in which chair and table legs were firmly embedded. Further in, ice extended almost to the ceiling. Using picks and shovels the ice was gradually removed and blocks containing artefacts were placed outside to thaw in the 24-hour sunlight.

In this way, many items from Scott's last expedition and Shackleton's Ross Sea Party were recovered. Among them were the cue and balls for the game of bagatelle played during Scott's expedition, and the bicycle ridden by the Australian geographer Griffith Taylor on a short excursion across the ice.

From the Ross Sea Party there were improvised canvas trousers, home-made footwear and gloves stitched from sleeping bags, old canvas or seal skins — also an unusual dome-shaped tent, the only tent landed from the *Aurora* in 1915 before it broke its moorings.

The sledging diary of R.W. Richards, one of the seven survivors of the Party, was dug out of the ice at the head of his bunk. It was returned to the owner who later used it as the basis for a book about the expedition.

Now, 20 years since restoration, the hut appears as it was when occupied by the explorers. On the laboratory shelves are the innumerable bottles and jars and pieces of scientific apparatus used by Scott's men. The bottles still contain the original chemicals, but not many of the labels have survived. Captain Oates' bunk has been rebuilt and is again draped with pony harness and pony snowshoes. In Dr Edward Wilson's corner is an emperor penguin, perfectly preserved. And Ponting's darkroom remains much as he must have left it, well stocked with photographic chemicals, a film dryer and a tripod.

The ceiling and walls of the hut are dark with soot from the seal blubber stoves which the Ross Sea Party had to use when marooned without fuel. Two anchors from the *Aurora* lie where they were abandoned when the ship broke its moorings, 70 years ago.

Following restoration of the huts at Cape Royds and Cape Evans, the Antarctic Treaty Consultative Committee, in July 1961, agreed that steps should be taken to preserve the hut at Hut Point. In January 1964 restoration commenced and, as with the hut at Cape Evans, a

Seventy polar winters have gradually eaten away the timber surface of the Cape Evans Hut. All the historic huts are being eroded away and must be protected.

The remains of the hut built by Scott's Northern party on the wide beach beneath Cape Adare. The hut, built in March 1911, is now almost in ruins. The area is subjected to powerful winds that even threatened to demolish the building at the time it was occupied by Commander Victor Campbell (leader of the party) and his five men. This party also used the huts built by Borchgrevink during his stay at Cape Adare.

The oldest hut on Ross Island — erected by Scott's Discovery *expedition in 1901 at Hut Point. No-one from that expedition lived there — a safe winter anchorage was found for their ship. It was, however, used by later expeditions and was home, for a time, for members of Shackleton's trans-Antarctic expedition. This building is near New Zealand's Scott base and the large US McMurdo base, and is therefore probably the most visited of all the historic huts.*

The hut at Cape Denison, built by Douglas Mawson's expedition in 1911, is badly in need of restoration. The ice and snow were cleared from its interior some years ago, but the fierce winds of Adélie Land have badly eroded the outside timber. A team from Australia started work on the difficult job of preserving the isolated building in late 1984.

Shackleton's hut at Cape Royds, built in 1907. Victor Campbell, with some other members of Scott's expedition visited it in 1911, and he later wrote: 'The whole place was very eerie, there is such a feeling of life about it. Not only do I feel it but others do also. Last night after I turned in I could have sworn that I heard people shouting to each other.'

four-man party had to remove large quantities of ice. Again, many interesting items were recovered, recorded and returned to the positions where they were found. Some items, such as an original script for the comedy play *Ticket of Leave*, boxes of dog biscuits and an awning from the *Discovery* were left by Scott's first expedition. Other items such as 10 hand-carved chessmen, a bag containing a tobacco substitute, some seal carcases and blubber lamps made from old provision tins had been left by the Ross Sea Party when they stayed in the hut for various periods during their ordeal.

Since 1969 the huts have been maintained by annual caretaking teams. Windows have to be reglazed, timbers refastened and snow or ice removed. In addition the caretakers have acted as tour guides for the many visitors.

Several more improvised shelters in the Ross Island-McMurdo Sound area have been rediscovered. Perhaps the most famous is the rock shelter at Cape Crozier built by Wilson, Bowers and Cherry-Garrard in July 1911. When found by a party led by Sir Edmund Hillary in 1957 its contents included a sledge and Wilson's sketching pencils.

Later in 1959 a party also located the Granite Hut at Cape Geology on the western side of McMurdo Sound. Griffith Taylor built this in 1911 to serve as a kitchen during his second geological excursion. In January 1963 a party of geologists in North Victoria Land found the famous ice cave on Inexpressible Island. The cave's entrance tunnel was still visible and marked by a seal skin lining supported by a ski pole and length of bamboo. Many discarded items were found nearby.

The geologists also found a fully provisioned depot at Hell's Gate Moraine, adjoining Inexpressible Island.

There are other huts scattered around the Antarctic coast. Urgent restoration work was carried out on Douglas Mawson's hut at Cape Denison by Project Blizzard – an Australian expedition – in 1984-85 and 1985-86. Their work included emergency repairs and limited maintenance. When Mawson revisited his old hut in 1931 he was surprised to find it still standing. 'Remarkable effects of snow-blast erosion were evidenced on the exposed timbers,' he said. 'In many places the planks had thus been reduced in thickness by more than half an inch [13 mm]. Inside the hut, which had been sealed so long, great masses of delicate ice-crystals hung in festoons.'

Excavation of this hut in the past has required the use of an electric percussion hammer, a chain saw and ice axes. Again many relics have been found. As each item was located, it was photographed, recorded and returned to its original position. The oldest hut on the continent, that built by Carsten Borchgrevink at Cape Adare in 1899 to spend man's first winter on the Antarctic mainland, is still standing, although not much work has been done on it. His stores hut nearby has lost its roof, as has the nearby hut built in 1911 by Scott's Northern party.

Little restoration work has been done on the remaining huts. It is important to preserve these structures and the historic artefacts associated with them. Fortunately, under the Antarctic Treaty, it is forbidden to remove any historic artefacts from the continent. Many relics will not, however, survive unless conservation measures are undertaken. The huts may require specialised treatment fairly soon if they are to remain standing.

The bow of the water boat is just discernible in this winter view of the hut. Beyond, across a frozen channel, are the mountains of Lemaire Island, about 1.6 kilometres (one mile) away. The meteorological instruments were housed in the structure on the right.

POLAR MISADVENTURE

A masterpiece of bad planning leaves two men marooned for a year

In spite of its impressive title, this ill-conceived expedition might well have been planned round a convivial bottle of port in much the same way that the characters of Jerome K. Jerome's* Three Men in a Boat *planned their holiday on the Thames.

Three members of the expedition (left to right) Lester, Bagshawe and Cope, outside their makeshift hut.

A view of the hut from the meteorological screen. The men slept inside the boat, which is just visible on the left. The 'lounge' and kitchen were contained in the tall structure which partly covered the centre section of the boat. The entrance was on the right.

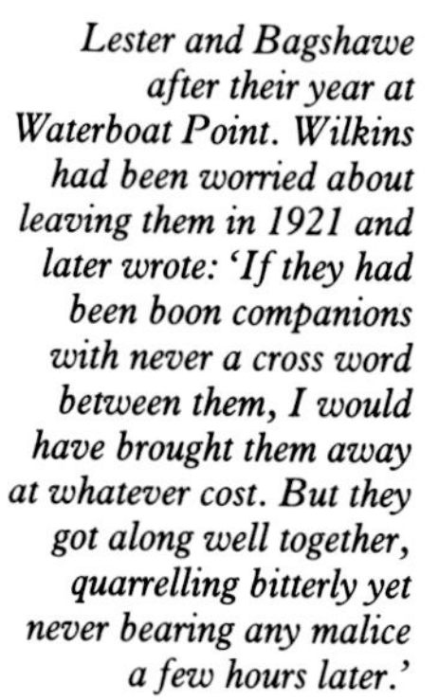

Lester and Bagshawe after their year at Waterboat Point. Wilkins had been worried about leaving them in 1921 and later wrote: 'If they had been boon companions with never a cross word between them, I would have brought them away at whatever cost. But they got along well together, quarrelling bitterly yet never bearing any malice a few hours later.'

The leader, in name at least, of the British Imperial Expedition was John Cope. He had been the surgeon on Shackleton's 1914-17 expedition, and his plan now was so ambitious as to be quite amazing. He intended to take 12 aircraft to Graham Land in the Antarctic Archipelago and from there make the first flight over the South Pole.

The other members of the expedition were to be Hubert Wilkins, a pioneer aviator from Australia; Thomas Bagshawe, geologist; and M. C. Lester, surveyor. Although excited at the prospect of making the first polar flight, Wilkins was not impressed by his colleagues. As far as he was concerned, Cope was a nice fellow but hopeless at organising anything; Bagshawe was only 19 years old and not exactly an expert geologist; and Lester, in his early twenties, was not exactly a surveyor either, having been second mate on a tramp steamer.

When Cope cabled Wilkins in Australia with the news that he could not afford to buy even one aircraft, Wilkins decided to withdraw. But Cope argued that they would still be able to do useful work by extending the survey that Nordenskjöld had carried out in 1901-03 and he eventually persuaded Wilkins to join him in Montevideo for the journey south. Lester and Bagshawe were to leave separately, and the four would all meet at Deception Island.

Deception Island was used as a base each summer by Norwegian whaling ships and these ships would take the members of the expedition to the island and provide sea transport whilst they were there. This was important, for Cope's plan now was to go by whaler to Hope Bay, on the tip of Trinity Peninsula, and to sail from there in a lifeboat to Snow Hill Island, where they would establish their base in Nordenskjöld's hut.

The four men reached Deception Island by Christmas Eve, 1920, but Hope Bay was iced

Paradise Bay is famous for its spectacular scenery. Waterboat Point is at the entrance to the bay, in the distance. On the rocky point in the foreground is the Argentinean base Almirante Brown. The steep mountains and glaciers that fringe the Antarctic Peninsula foiled Cope's plans to cross to the Weddell Sea coast.

in and it was impossible for the ship to take them there. Instead, the captain suggested that he land them on the Danco Coast south of Andvord Bay on the western side of Graham Land. The expedition could then cross to the east coast and start their survey where Nordenskjöld had left off.

Cope agreed and on 12 January the men were landed on a point south of the bay. They called it Waterboat Point after a ruined water boat which had been beached there eight years earlier by a Norwegian factory ship. The boat was nine metres (30 ft) long and it was soon pressed into service to provide sleeping quarters and a living area. Unfortunately there was only a metre (3 ft) of headroom, which made moving about hazardous, so they built their tiny hut alongside the boat and constructed a new 'lounge' on the deck above the cramped sleeping quarters.

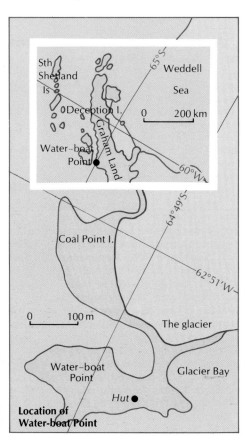

Location of Water-boat Point

After making a few short journeys, by the end of February they knew that they would not be able to cross the mountain ranges to reach the Weddell Sea. With the expedition at a dead end, Cope held a meeting in the hut and announced that he would go to Montevideo and return the following season with a ship to take them round to Hope Bay. Wilkins, now totally exasperated, said he would leave too, although he said nothing about coming back. But Lester and Bagshawe, to the surprise of the others, said that they would stay. They had come to carry out scientific observations, and that was what they intended to do.

On 26 February Cope, Wilkins and Lester left in the lifeboat to find a factory ship, leaving Bagshawe alone at Waterboat Point. They returned a week later in the *Bjerk* and after a flurry of packing Cope and Wilkins sailed out of the bay as Bagshawe and Lester waved farewell from the lifeboat.

'It was strange and a little frightening to be left as we were, two people alone on a vast continent equal in area to Europe and Australia combined, with a year to pass before we were due to see any other human beings again.'

It was not quite true, for a few days later a factory ship called at the point and the captain told them that he would return as early as he could the following season to pick them up.

The first job was to improve the hut and the water boat for the winter. Lester, seaman that he was, spent days sewing canvas to make screens to cover the openings whilst Bagshawe killed penguins for winter meat. 'On the 19th, when I had slaughtered two hundred, I stopped killing the poor little fellows, and very thankful I was.' He then started on the seals.

On 18 April Bagshawe celebrated his twentieth birthday. 'In honour of the occasion I produced a Christmas pudding, brought from England . . . After seal and penguin meat the pudding tasted as good as dinner at the Criterion. We indulged in a cigar each after supper.'

But as winter approached, so the weather deteriorated. 'Everything freezes. Tonight my ink-pot has frozen up and the mince froze as we were eating it. We sit and shiver and try to laugh at our discomforts; it's not much use to moan and groan.' In truth, they had much to moan about. They had only a hammer, a saw and a handful of nails, together with a gramophone, an ample supply of unreliable matches and a few boxes of creme de menthe sweets.

They were determined to collect scientific data and started a program that would have daunted many Antarctic veterans.

By the time they celebrated Lester's birthday on 25 September their clothes were in tatters and they had eaten minced seal almost every night since the beginning of March. Today, at least, they would have a 'proper' meal. It consisted of fried sardines, stewed apple rings, and Christmas pudding with brandy sauce. They got drunk on the brandy sauce and, after a totally dissipated evening, slept non-stop for 10 hours. When the weather improved they erected a calibrated pole to measure the rise and fall of the tide. It took them three hours, after which they were 'exceedingly chilly', and then took hourly readings for 30 days. In early December, when the penguins started to lay their eggs, they maintained a log of their development. They even waited until there were enough to satisfy scientific curiosity before collecting some for the kitchen.

They were still hard at work on Sunday 18 December when suddenly they saw a ship. It was the *Graham*, a whale catcher from the *Svend Foyn*, whose captain had promised to come back for them.

'They arrived with the idea that they could take us away there and then, but they soon understood that we had many things to clear up and that we could not leave immediately.' Anxious to complete their work, Bagshawe and Lester arranged to be picked up a few weeks later so that they could complete their logs and pack their instruments and specimens.

On 13 January 1922, a year and a day after Bagshawe and Lester had first arrived at Waterboat Point, the whaler returned for them.

'We were soon on board and as we sailed bade goodbye and good luck to our former home. Lester seemed quite upset, and we both felt miserable as we watched the hut disappear from sight, left to the mercies of the wind and weather. We had pleasant times there as well as dull ones and it had been our protector against the weather and even against death.'

Shackleton, 47, and looking old and tired, says goodbye to friends as the Quest *prepares to sail from London in September 1921. John Rowett, the man who financed the expedition, is on Shackleton's right.*

DEATH OF A LEGEND

Sir Ernest Shackleton goes home to die

Why did Ernest Shackleton and Frank Wild not only risk everything in the ice at the edge of the world, but return again and again? Shackleton had a short explanation. 'I go exploring because I like it and because it's my job. One goes once and then one gets the fever and can't stop going.' Wild was more mystical: once you had been to the white unknown, he said, you could never escape the call of 'the little voices'.

The voices were calling them north to the Arctic early in 1921, when the Canadian Government promised support for an expedition to the Beaufort Sea to discover whether there was land near the North Pole and to make contact with still unknown Eskimo tribes. Then the Government was voted out and the incoming Government said there would be no money for Shackleton. He quickly switched to a new plan: another Antarctic expedition to map 3200 kilometres (2000 miles) of the continental coastline, to comb the South Atlantic for 'lost' reefs and islands, to improve existing charts, to pioneer aviation in Antarctica and to make extensive meteorological and geological research. His old school friend, John Rowett, backed the scheme.

But Shackleton found the years catching up with him. He was 47 and he suffered pains in his chest and shoulders.

When the *Quest*, a 125-tonne wooden Norwegian sealer, sailed for Rio de Janeiro in September 1921, Hubert Wilkins, the expedition's photographer, thought the agent who bought her must have been 'drunk and seeing double'. Before the *Quest* cleared the River Thames the engine had broken down three times. When she staggered into Rio under sail the tail shaft was out of alignment and the keel was buckled like a snake. While Shackleton buoyed the crew, singing songs and telling stories, the two doctors, Macklin and McIlroy, worried about his health, urging him not to push himself too hard. Shackleton knew the doctors were right. He told his wife in a letter from St Vincent: 'I am not very well, but I think in a couple of days will be my old self.'

In Rio his impatience increased the pressure. 'I am mad to get away', he wrote to a friend, adding that he had not been well, that the years were mounting up, but it was all due to worry. On 17 December he was too ill to work.

The *Quest* left Rio for South Georgia on 18 December. A gale struck on Christmas Day, postponing their celebratory dinner. It blew out on Boxing Day, but another howling westerly bruised them during 28 and 29 December. Then the engineer reported a further catastrophe — that the furnace had sprung a leak, and they must reduce steam till they reached South Georgia. Shackleton, finally forced to look failure in the face, was depressed and irritable. He complained about everything — the macaroni cheese was not crisp enough, the dinner plates had not been heated. At a time when the whole expedition was coming apart. Shackleton tried to regain his sense of control by fussing over trivia. Yet, with neuralgia pains stabbing his broad back, he worked long hours on the bridge, deaf to the doctors' pleas that he get some rest.

His heart lifted as they sighted their first iceberg on 2 January. On 3 January, a clear and beautiful day, he said he had been worrying so much that 'when things are going well I wonder what internal difficulty will be sprung on me'. The next day they sighted the snowy mountains of South Georgia. Shackleton spent the day on the bridge with a pair of binoculars reminiscing about his epic voyage from Elephant Island. His heart was full. 'At last after 16 days of turmoil and anxiety, on a peaceful sunny day we came to anchor at Gritviken [sic].' After a cheerful dinner Shackleton rose and said, 'Tomorrow we'll keep Christmas'.

A little after 2 am, Dr Macklin, on the anchor watch, heard a whistle from Shackleton's cabin. 'I can't sleep tonight', Shackleton said. 'Can you get me a sleeping draught?' Macklin noticed that Shackleton had only one blanket on a freezing night, went to his cabin for a heavy blanket, returned and tucked the boss in. Shackleton was unusually quiet and receptive. Macklin, seizing his opportunity, told him he had been doing too much, he would have to take things more quietly, sleep regularly and eat properly. Shackleton joked: 'You are always wanting me to give up things. What is it I ought to give up now?'

As the horrified Macklin watched, Shackleton suffered a massive heart attack. When he realised the boss was dying, Macklin, aware that the death would cause a sensation and that there might be an inquiry, raced for Dr McIlroy. As soon as he entered Shackleton's cabin McIlroy said, 'Yes, he's gone'.

The doctors dreaded what they had to do next: tell Frank Wild. As they entered Wild's cabin, Macklin lit the oil lamp while McIlroy said, 'We want to wake you up thoroughly. We have some bad news — the worst possible.'

Wild sat bolt upright. 'Go on with it. Let me have it straight out.'

McIlroy: 'The boss is dead.'

Wild, the man who had looked death in the eye as calmly as a stroller looks in a shop window, was stunned. 'Dead, do you mean? He can't be dead.' But he recovered quickly and asked for the details.

At breakfast a few hours later Wild told the crew: 'I want you all on the poop.' They gathered, chattering excitedly about what this meant, whether the expedition had gone broke. Wild came up, broke the news quickly and said, 'The expedition will carry on'.

As Wild prepared to honour Shackleton by completing the expedition, his body sailed for Montevideo on the *Professor Gruvel* on 19 January. Hussey, whose banjo had warded off the menace of the ice on Elephant Island, cabled Lady Shackleton from Montevideo. 'We have lost the best friend we ever had.' Lady Shackleton decided he should be buried in South Georgia, the scene of his greatest triumph.

Wild, anxious to penetrate the Antarctic before the ice jammed the South Atlantic, had no time to wait for instructions from John Rowett. The *Quest* was short of both stores and equipment, the engines were not reliable, the ship leaked, the weatherproof bridge admitted a freezing draught along the floor which caused Wild agony on the night watch. Wilkins thought Wild was mad to go on, and that Shackleton himself would not have persevered. Wild too had doubts, but decided that 'having put my hand to the plough there was to be no turning back'.

When they reached the ice, Wild, who had spent nearly half his life exploring the Antarctic, put his doubts behind him. 'As I stood on the bridge I saw amongst my men nothing but elation ... [Those who] saw the ice for the first time were fascinated by it, and amongst the old hands there was obvious pleasure at again meeting the pack. Old McLeod, veteran of many expeditions, said to McIlroy, "Here we are home again!" ... As I gazed south over the ice with the cold clean air in my nostrils I too felt elated...'

Wild brought the eye of a lover, an artist, to the ice. 'The old floes passed slowly from pale pink to crimson, and as the sun came over the rim, to the most delicate heliotrope', he said one February morning. 'The darker newly frozen ice changed from bronze to light apple green. To the west a large golden moon was poised in a cloudless sky, turning the floes to the palest of gold.' Such scenes entranced Wild, making him feel what he described as 'a sort of wondering lostness', compared to which civilisation was artificial and ugly. During Antarctic twilights he had seen 'the most materialistic and unimpressionable of men strung to an absolute silence... The very sledge dogs stand stock still, gazing intently into the farness, ears cocked, listening — for what.'

They remained in the ice making observations and soundings till 21 March. J. W. S. Marr, the boy scout, made the discovery now familiar to a generation of international jet travellers: that eating is a good way of passing the time. 'It must appear that our watch is very hungry, but this is not so. It is merely our very effective method of passing four long hours on the bridge', he wrote in his diary. On 5 April they returned to South Georgia and prepared the cairn overlooking Grytviken harbour. A plate on the cairn reads: 'Sir Ernest Shackleton, explorer. Died here 5 January 1922. Erected by his comrades.' Shackleton's body had been buried on 5 March while the *Quest* was still away in Antarctic waters.

Back in Cape Town on 18 June the South African Prime Minister, General Smuts, entertained them and Wild received orders from John Rowett to return home.

They entered Plymouth Sound on 16 September. Wild was thrilled when Rowett, the first aboard, told him: 'Old man, you've done splendidly.' He allowed himself to feel satisfied: his work in Antarctica was now done, he said, but he would always be glad that it had been his lot to 'pioneer and guide the groping fingers of knowledge on the white edges of the world'.

Members of the expedition gather around Shackleton's grave on South Georgia. He was buried there — the scene of his greatest triumph — at the special request of his widow.

A British soldier, garrisoned on South Georgia after the conflict with Argentina, stands beside the memorial erected in Shackleton's memory by his friends and comrades on the Quest.

The Quest, *originally a Norwegian sealer, proved to be in disastrously poor condition. She was top heavy and the engine kept breaking down. The best speed she could manage was 8 km/h (5 mph).*

Frank Wild (second from right) took over as leader when Shackleton died. Dr Macklin (extreme right) was with Shackleton when he had his fatal heart attack.

Christmas dinner, 1925, in the dining room of the Discovery Committee's Marine Biological Station at Grytviken on South Georgia. Around the table (from left to right) are Rumbolds of the Government Office; Dr Archie Clowes, hydrologist; Dr Neil Mackintosh, a zoologist who later went on to become Director of Discovery Investigations; Dr Harrison Matthews, zoologist; Dr John Wheeler, zoologist, and Stewart.

SOUTHERN DISCOVERY

Pioneering research into the life of whales

The vital work of conserving the world's largest mammal, the whale, reaches further back than many people realise; for as long ago as 1917 a British Government interdepartmental committee was set up to review the excesses of the whaling industry which then flourished in the Antarctic.

This step was considered necessary as new processes of hydrogenation — which turned whale oil into an edible form — had recently been introduced, and there was increasing awareness that not only were whale products becoming more important to the industrialised nations, but that these mammals were in danger of being hunted to extinction.

After the war this committee produced a fact-finding report and recommendations, but it was not until 1923 that the British Government acted by forming a committee which had the finances and the authority to set up the whaling industry on a scientific basis. In fact, the committee soon realised it was impossible to recommend a sensible policy of conservation because simply not enough was known about whales. It was this lack of knowledge that the committee set about correcting by instigating a scientific program which was to span over a quarter of a century.

The following year, 1924, Scott's old ship, the *Discovery*, was purchased and a brilliant zoologist, Dr Stanley Wells Kemp, was appointed the first expedition's leader. A number of scientists were also selected to carry out the brief of the Discovery Committee — as it now came to be called — to investigate in the Falkland Islands waters the feeding and breeding habits of the whale, and the distribution pattern of krill and plankton, among other things.

At the end of 1924 five scientists left for the South Atlantic taking with them a prefabricated laboratory which was to be erected on South Georgia at Grytviken near the Norwegian whaling station that operated from there each summer. They started work on 5 February 1925 and by 11 May, when the station closed down for the winter, the carcases of 241 whales had been examined. It was, as one of them, F.D. Ommanney, wryly described in his book, *South Latitude*, a very dirty undertaking.

'When the whale was killed he was filled with air to make him float. He has also been decomposing gently since then so that directly the body cavity is opened there is an explosive outrush of gas. The gas stinks. If you cut too deep with your knife, as you often unavoidably do, there is an equally explosive outrush of liquid, yellowish-brown faeces and you become covered in this if you do not dodge it quickly as you often unavoidably do not.'

During the following years a total of over 1600 whales were measured and dissected by the scientists, and from this they were able to discover the breeding times, period of gestation, rate of growth, and age of maturity of the various species of whale caught.

As the *Discovery* needed an extensive refit the main party was not able to sail until 5 October 1925. They arrived at South Georgia on 20 February and during the next two months carried out the first provisional biological and hydrographical survey of the whaling grounds before sailing to South Africa for the winter, where work continued on whales landed at the Saldanha Bay whaling station.

Before returning to the Antarctic in September 1926, the *Discovery* was joined by another research ship, the *William Scoresby*, whose work was to mark whales, take plankton and hydrographic samples, and trawl with a commercial trawl in the waters around the Falkland Islands. The idea of marking the whales was to track their migration routes to polar waters rich in plankton and krill in spring, and to warmer waters for breeding in autumn. They were marked by shooting a numbered silver-plated stainless steel pin into them, on which were instructions for its return by the whaling station eventually bringing the whale ashore.

During her two seasons in the Antarctic the *Discovery* made a number of 'stations' — the ship was stopped to catch specimens of plankton and measure the depth, temperature, and salinity of the water — so that a pattern of plankton distribution was built up. In this second season she sailed south to the whaling grounds around the South Orkneys, the South Shetlands, and the Bransfield Strait, while the *William Scoresby* carried out a trawling survey between the Falkland Islands and the east coast of South America.

It was decided, fortunately before the onset of the 1930s depression, to replace the stout-hearted but elderly *Discovery* with a ship specially constructed for the task, *Discovery II*. The work of the Discovery Committee might otherwise have ended. Originally, the Committee's work had been funded by the Falkland Islands Dependencies who levied a royalty on the whalers that used the islands as their base. However, as the size of the whalers increased, making them independent of any shore station, so this source of income dwindled and by 1931 it had become financially necessary to close the biological station at Grytviken on South Georgia, and to put the *William Scoresby* out of commission.

Just at the time the Discovery Committee was faced with curtailing its activities, Kemp, who had led the first two expeditions, was pressing it to accept that not only must the survey go on, but that it must continue for a further 10 or 15 years if it was to keep pace with the whaling industry which was becoming ever more widespread.

A Committee report delivered in 1932, far from recommending a winding down of the Committee's work, strongly advised that it should be expanded. It also recommended that the *William Scoresby* be recommissioned to concentrate on the vital task of whale marking. The report was accepted by the government, money was found for further research, and the *William Scoresby* put to sea once more.

Though the work of both ships in the succeeding years was almost wholly involved in marine research, some important surveys were undertaken — notably that of the South Sandwich Island during *Discovery II*'s first commission (1929-31) — while valuable assistance was given to the British Graham Land Expedition, and to expeditions led by Sir Hubert Wilkins and Admiral Byrd.

During her second commission (1931-33) the *Discovery II* became the fourth ship to circumnavigate the Antarctic and first to accomplish it in winter. She also completed a survey of the South Shetlands and plotted the approximate position of the Antarctic Convergence. Another circumnavigation, this time in summer, was planned for her fourth commission (1935-37), but this was abandoned until 1937-38 so that a rescue expedition could be mounted to help the American explorer, Lincoln Ellsworth.

Altogether, the *William Scoresby* undertook eight commissions between 1926 and 1951 while the *Discovery II* undertook six, and during this time the rudiments of whale conservation were at last introduced.

In 1929, Norway, the country most actively engaged in catching whales, brought in legislation preventing the hunting of certain species, and all calves and suckling mothers. The following year minimum size limits were imposed, and in 1931, 26 countries agreed to an International Convention to regulate the industry and this came into force in 1936. However, the first really effective whaling regulations were not introduced until 1937 when nine countries agreed to a new minimum size of whale to be caught, and to put an inspector on each factory ship.

Despite the introduction of these regulations a record 46 000 whales were caught in the Antarctic in 1937-38, 9000 of which were immature, and it was not until an International Whaling Convention was set up in Washington in 1946 that the proper principles of whale conservation began to be applied. But it can be truly said that without the detailed research of the Discovery Committee and its group of young scientists — research which by 1963 had filled 34 volumes — no conservation would have been possible. It was without doubt the greatest scientific effort in the history of exploration.

Scott's old ship, the Discovery, *at anchor in Grytviken harbour. After Scott's 1901-04 expedition she had been bought by the Hudson Bay Company for use in the Arctic fur trade. In 1923 she was purchased for the Discovery Committee and extensively refitted to replace badly deteriorated timber. Her masts, spars and rigging were also replaced and at last some of Scott's suggestions for improving her sailing qualities were carried out.*

Lincoln Ellsworth (centre, in dark suit) aboard the Discovery II *after his trans-Antarctic flight. He and his pilot Herbert Hollick Kenyon had been picked up from Richard Byrd's old base Little America after being reported lost. F.D. Ommanney wrote afterwards of the arrival of Kenyon: 'He was shaved, washed and spruce and exuded an air of well-being which . . . . was something of a disappointment to us. We had conjured up in our imaginations thin features, covered by a matted growth of beard . . .'*

Discovery II *sailed for southern waters for the first time in 1929. The old* Discovery *had neither the power nor the speed for the work she was expected to undertake.* Discovery II*'s last Antarctic voyage was in 1950-51.*

The Discovery scientists had to work on the flensing platform — measuring and examining the whales as they were being dismembered for boiling down.

THE WOMEN THEY LEFT BEHIND

Unsung heroines of exploration

Men of the great age of exploration returned from Antarctica as heroes, to bask in the spotlight of public adulation. Scant attention was paid to their wives, often condemned to spend years on their own, holding together home and family with little money. Only when the heroes died were their women paraded as objects of public pity.

When Anne Coulman married James Clark Ross in 1843, it was only after her family had extracted a promise from him not to go on any more long voyages of exploration. He had just returned from an absence in the Antarctic of over four years.

Perhaps Anne's father remembered the affair of Joseph Banks. In the excitement of preparing for his voyage with Captain Cook in 1768, the 25-year-old Banks proposed to Miss Harriet Blosset. For three years Miss Blosset sorrowed and talked of death, but worse was to come when the travellers returned and Banks did not speed to her side. In answer to her eventual letter, Banks declared undying love but said he was not the marrying kind. Confronted, Banks promised immediate marriage, but shortly after wrote again as before — love forever, marriage never.

Elizabeth Betts was more aware of what she was in for when, at 21, she married a naval officer, James Cook. She had five months with her husband before he went to sea, presenting him on return with a six-weeks-old son. For the next four years Cook spent summers in Newfoundland waters and winters at home. In this period his wife had two more sons and a daughter. At home after his first great voyage he found his daughter had died at the age of four, and a boy, born a few days after his departure, had not survived. One year later he delayed leaving on his second great expedition until he received word that his wife had been safely delivered of a son. He came back to find that that child had died as well. Within 10 months Mrs Cook had given birth to another boy, and four weeks later her husband set sail once again. The widow, in her grief four years later, was not comforted by her eldest boys; they were already at sea, following their father's profession.

In the age of Antarctic exploration, patriotism and the spirit of adventure conquered qualms about leaving womenfolk and children. Few of the public writings of the explorers reveal any contrition at condemning loved ones, not only to loneliness, but to gnawing anxiety about the dangers.

True, some expedition journals contain terse references to womenfolk at home, with toasts after dinner, emotions choked back manfully.

Times and consciences gradually changed. In 1907, on his way to the Antarctic, Ernest Shackleton wrote to his wife Emily: 'I shall not run any risk for the sake of trying to get to the "Pole" in the face of hard odds. I have not only myself but you and the children to consider . . . and if inclined to do anything rash I will think of my promise to you and not do it.' And so he did, turning back when within 180 kilometres (97 nautical miles) of the pole.

Commandant Jean Charcot with his wife and daughter before his departure on the Français *in 1903. Their marriage did not survive his eighteen months away in Antarctica.*

Robert Scott and his wife Kathleen on the bridge of the Terra Nova *on 26 November 1910. They were not to meet again. She did not hear of his death until 1913.*

He wrote to Emily that he had found the willpower to retreat because 'I thought you would rather have a live donkey than a dead lion'. He promised then, and in 1917, that 'quietness in all ways [would] be our portion' but each time restlessness overtook him.

Kathleen Bruce married Robert Falcon Scott in 1908. 'Con', as his intimates knew him, and his strong-willed unconventional bride, already a successful sculptress, decided that each should give full freedom to the other's ambitions. Kathleen in fact played a key role in the realisation of her husband's plans to lead an expedition to the pole. In 1910, to be with him as long as possible, she travelled to South Africa, Australia and New Zealand, leaving behind baby Peter, nine months old. Then, she wrote: 'There followed the long enforced separation from Con. I did not mind, my worship continued unabated. Christians do not see their God but they worship and love Him with unabated ardour.' She kept a journal, intended for her husband's eyes only. 'September 1st [1911]. Tomorrow will be our wedding day. We shall have been married three years. I bet anything you won't remember it . . . One hasn't got one's husband in the body, but one has got him so very firmly in the spirit that it spoils everything. One can't think of loving anybody else, and yet one's whole being is crying out, "You are young, you are healthy, go out and love." I think decidedly I had better get back to work.' She set down her intense annoyance that photographs of Peter were used in a publicity stunt without her knowledge; pangs of conscience about spending nine guineas on a dress; and 30-month-old Peter asking, on 11 March 1912, '"Mummy, is Amundsen a good man?" I said, "Yes, I think he is." Then he said "Amundsen and Daddy both got to the Pole. Daddy has stopped working now."' When the awful news came, there was no reproach and no self pity.

The London Daily Mirror was quick to capitalise on the pathos of the deaths of Captain Scott's party. It published photographs of Kathleen and Peter; of Birdie Bowers' white-haired mother; of Oriana Wilson; of Petty Officer Evans' wife and three children. Captain Oates' mother did not appear. Bitter over his death, she would not accept any pension. Payments from a nation overflowing with sentiment included £48 a year to Evans' widow, and a charity sum of £1500. Kathleen received £300 a year, £8500 outright and, as if Captain Scott had returned to be knighted, the title of Lady Scott.

Roald Amundsen seems to have been one of the explorers who did not mind that the only females in Antarctica were penguins, seals and their ship. Thoughtful and thorough as an explorer, he left for the Antarctic hoping that the married woman he loved would divorce her husband and be ready to marry him on his return. She did not. 'For that reason', he wrote, 'I consider I am absolved from my responsibilities in that direction'.

When Douglas Mawson chose his men in 1911, married status may well have weighed in his decisions. Having himself became engaged not long before, he doubtless appreciated the anguish of separation and the harmful effect it might have on the men. Of the 37-man shore party, only two had wives.

In 1910 Dr Charcot treated the wife of a Norwegian whaling captain on Deception Island, but it was 1935 before a woman stepped on to the Antarctic continent. Caroline Mikkelsen accompanied her husband, captain of a whaling factory ship, although they spent only a short time ashore.

The first to live in Antarctica were two American women, who in 1947 spent a year with their husbands on Stonington Island near the Antarctic Peninsula. Finn Ronne had decided that his journalist wife Edith's reports would be useful for his expedition. This caused some consternation, and a few of the crew members even threatened to leave the ship. As a compromise, the crew accepted that two women would be better than one, and the chief pilot's wife Jennie Darlington was taken too. One British expeditioner with Vivian Fuchs, on meeting the women, was reminded of the Marx Brothers story about a plea for help from people imprisoned in a castle: 'Here we are, seven men and two women — send us five more women.'

For many years now, most bases have seen women scientists working on equal terms with men. Marriages have taken place in Antarctica, and babies have been born there. In 1979 Michele Raney became the first woman to over-winter at the US polar station.

For many expeditioners, a term in Antarctica speeds repayment of a mortgage. For others, the lure is adventure. For many, it is an escape. For wives, mothers and lovers, the time passes with no great anxieties about the men's safety. There is frequent contact by telephone, ham radio or telex. The greatest hazards to relationships are said to occur during the period of readjustment on return.

Sir Ernest and Lady Emily Shackleton on the deck of the Endurance *before she sailed in 1914. On this occasion Emily was not to see her husband again for two years. He had already been away in Antarctica for almost four of the previous 13 years.*

One of Wilkins' two Lockheed Vega monoplanes and the baby Austin at the whaling station on Deception Island. The car was fitted with eight wheels bound together by chains, and was used for hauling fuel from the ship to the plane.

Sir Hubert Wilkins was 40 years old when he took on the job of organising the Wilkins-Hearst Expedition. He was a skilled pilot and had been knighted in 1928 for his work in science and exploration.

The plane had to be hastily hoisted back on board the William Scoresby *when the ice of Beascochea Bay started to melt during unusually warm weather.*

FIRST ANTARCTIC FLIGHT

Errors reveal the limitations of aerial exploration

Sir Hubert Wilkins was an adventurer in the classic mould whose two unique expeditions to Antarctica in 1928 and 1929 were the first to use aircraft and aerial photography to survey some of the great tracts of still unknown Antarctic terrain. Wilkins' discoveries from the air were not of the overriding importance that some contemporary commentators gave to them. But he did pioneer the use in Antarctica of modern equipment like aircraft and wireless telegraphy.

Wilkins' first introduction to the Antarctic came in 1920 when he was part of John Cope's ambitious British Imperial Expedition (see p230), and he later joined Ernest Shackleton aboard the *Quest*.

The Wilkins-Hearst Expedition was sponsored by the American Geographical Society and was widely supported. The Vacuum Oil Company of Australasia donated $10 000 and the news rights were sold to William Randolph Hearst's American News Service for $25 000. With such secure financial backing Wilkins was able to purchase two Lockheed Vega monoplanes of the very latest design and to take with him two other pilots, an engineer, and a radio operator. They sailed from New York on 22 September 1928 for Montevideo where they boarded the 15 000 tonne *Hektoria*, arriving at Deception Island on 6 November.

The plan was to take off from either the ice on the harbour, or the snow on the land, so that Wilkins could reconnoitre the Weddell Sea and select a more southerly base.

A short flight was undertaken on 16 November, the first to be made in the Antarctic, and 10 days later both planes took to the air to look for a better place from which to operate. As none could be found it was decided to try to land on the harbour ice which a cold snap had apparently made sufficiently firm. This nearly brought disaster as the aircraft broke through the ice and was nearly lost. In the end the land runway had to be extended, and on 20 December Wilkins and his co-pilot took off with a full payload.

'For the first seventy miles [113 km] we flew a little east of south over the waters of Bransfield Strait', Wilkins later wrote in his autobiography, 'which were studded with icebergs and occasional drifts of pack ice. Dead ahead

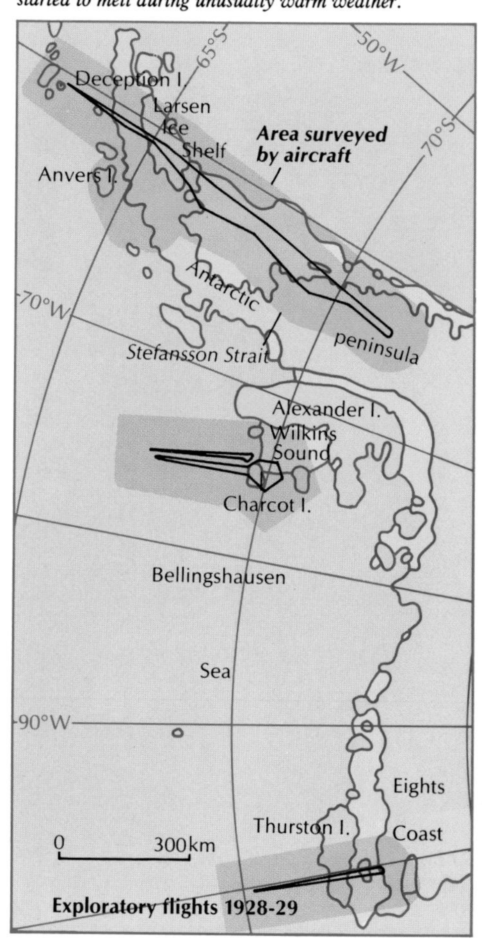

There were few possible sites for a runway on Deception Island and it was a backbreaking task levelling patches of tough lava. The final strip ran for 800 metres (880 yds) over rough surfaces, up over a hill, down across ditches, up another rough slope and down to the harbour. If the plane failed to get into the air it would then crash into the water.

was Trinity Island, with peaks rising to six thousand feet [1830 metres]. We flew around this, making for the big peninsula jutting from the Antarctic continent — Graham Land . . .

'Flying at six thousand feet [1830 metres], we expected to come in over Graham Land. Eight years before, I had tried to reach the top of that plateau on foot, always encountering a sheer cliff at the top of a ten thousand foot [3050-metre] elevation. Now I hoped to discover that the near edge of the plateau itself was much lower.

'This time, I had a tremendous sensation of power and freedom — I felt liberated — when we were approaching Graham Land by air. The contrast was most striking between the speed and ease of flying in by plane and the slow, blind struggles of our work along that coast a few years before. It had taken us three months, on foot, to map forty miles [64 km]; now we were covering forty miles in twenty minutes, and I had scarce time to sketch the principal terrain and shoreline features in my notebook before the scene had entirely changed and I was drawing a crude map of the next section of this area.

'No one had climbed to the Graham Land plateau summit, and I was thrilled to realize that for the first time, human eyes — our eyes — were going to see it . . . for the first time in history new land was being discovered from the air.'

Wilkins continued to fly over Graham Land until they reached 71°20'S, 64°15'W, by which time they had used nearly half their fuel supply. They turned back and landed safely at Deception Island after 11 hours in the air. They had covered nearly 2100 kilometres (1300 miles), almost a thousand of which had been over previously unknown terrain, and returned with many photographs and much new information. Most of this subsequently turned out to be incorrect — Wilkins, for instance, reported that Graham Land was divided into islands by four channels, the southernmost of which he called Stefansson Strait.

A second much shorter journey, totalling about 800 kilometres (500 miles), was made on 10 January over the same territory before both aircraft were stored for the winter while Wilkins returned to New York.

In September 1929 Wilkins returned to Deception Island but was once more held up by bad weather and the poor state of the landing strip. The ice was again much too thin to use and after a few local flights Wilkins decided to fall back on his emergency plan. This entailed accepting the offer of the British Colonial Office to take one of the aircraft aboard their ship, the *William Scoresby*, and to sail south to find a better landing strip.

The *William Scoresby* sailed from Deception Island on 12 December and after passing through the Bismarck Strait into the Pacific Ocean sailed as far as the southern tip of Adelaide Island but without finding a suitable stretch of smooth ice. Reluctantly, Wilkins was forced to return and on 18 December the ship anchored in sheltered water at Port Lockroy on Wiencke Island.

The weather now improved and the next day the plane was lowered overboard and a flight was made across the peninsula to Evans Inlet. But the engine was not running smoothly and Wilkins decided to return to the west coast. During the return journey he spotted what looked like flat ice in Beascochea Bay. As soon as the plane was aboard again the ship sailed for the bay.

By lunchtime the next day both the plane and the specially adapted Austin car had been unloaded on to the ice. However, to Wilkins' dismay both now began to sink through the melting ice, and on looking at the thermometer he saw it was registering 12°C (54°F), possibly the highest temperature ever recorded in that area. Both car and plane were hurriedly hoisted back on to the ship which now moved southwest in the hope of finding a better landing place. It was thought that by following the edge of the pack ice to somewhere north of Charcot Island a suitable spot might be found, but the ship had only travelled 48 kilometres (30 miles) past the southern tip of Adelaide Island when it was stopped by pack ice.

By now the ship had consumed more than half its fuel oil so it was decided to wait on the edge of the ice until the weather improved sufficiently to make another flight. After one abortive attempt Wilkins managed to get into the air on 27 December and he headed towards Charcot Island in appalling visibility. The mountains on the island had been charted at over 610 metres (2000 ft), but the plane was soon forced down to under 150 metres (500 ft) by the poor visibility.

'The compass was running wild', Wilkins wrote in the *Geographical Review* in July 1930. 'There was only the grey blank wall ahead. Beneath us I could faintly see what appeared to be land-fast ice — ice without a crack in it. I asked Cheesman to turn, and as we swung I thought I caught a glimpse of the dark cliffs of Charcot Land looming dimly through the haze. It was heart-breaking to have reached the land we sought with gas enough to take us at least two hundred miles [320 km] farther and then be forced to turn back.'

But forced back he was. However, he was able to make a second flight to Charcot Island two days later and by following the coastline made the discovery that it was an island. After flying over it, he dropped two Union Jacks near Cape Mawson and Cape Byrd with documents claiming the area for Britain.

The return of bad weather precluded any more flights from the area so the ship moved back to Port Lockroy. On 5 January 1930 Wilkins flew to Deception Island via Gerlache Strait and Trinity Island, surveying as he went, while the *William Scoresby* returned to the Falkland Islands to refuel. By the time she arrived back at Deception Island, on 25 January, it was becoming very late in the season, but Wilkins nevertheless decided to sail southwest once more. On 30 January he did manage a short flight over the pack ice but was soon driven back by an approaching storm.

A final flight was undertaken on 1 February when Wilkins and his co-pilot took the plane almost due south in very bumpy conditions. They had flown about 370 kilometres (230 miles) without seeing land when they became enclosed in a grey, misty snowstorm. They were then in a latitude of about 73° and having dropped another Union Jack by parachute they returned to the ship.

Conquest By Air

Byrd flies south to duplicate his Arctic triumph

In the mid-1920s not many people thought it was possible to fly to the South Pole. Reaching the pole at all was a hazardous business. So far only two parties had succeeded and only one had returned. Flying was hardly less hazardous and for most the thought of flying there was the height of folly. But not to Richard Byrd. When he left New York in 1928 he had the best-equipped expedition that had ever gone to Antarctica.

The City of New York *moored alongside the ice in the Bay of Whales.*

Born in America in 1888, Byrd had spent the First World War as a flying instructor with the United States Navy. In 1926 he and Floyd Bennett had made the first flight over the North Pole, and on their triumphant return to New York Amundsen asked Byrd what he was going to do next. 'Fly over the South Pole', he said. Amundsen not only believed him, he even gave him some advice. 'Take a good plane, take plenty of dogs and only the best men.'

Byrd followed Amundsen's advice meticulously. When he left he had with him three aircraft: a Ford monoplane with three engines, a Fokker Universal and a Fairchild monoplane with folding wings — all adapted for high altitude flying in cold conditions — together with 95 dogs and a team of over 50 men.

After taking on stores at Dunedin in New Zealand, the expedition reached the Ross Ice Shelf on Christmas Day 1928. The first task was to find a site for the base. Byrd found it east of the Bay of Whales and a fortnight later a complete village had sprung up. It was called Little America.

On 15 January 1929 Byrd made his first Antarctic flight and on the second flight two weeks later he found a range of mountains that had not been seen before. He named them the Rockefeller Mountains and later a team of geologists led by Laurence Gould left in the Fokker to explore them more closely.

They landed safely and set up camp. The weather was appalling but a week later they were able to radio Little America with the news that they had finished work and would fly back when the weather eased. Instead, the wind increased and they struggled to save their aeroplane from destruction. At times the airspeed indicator registered over 160 km/h (100 mph) and the tethered plane had all the appearances of flight.

In the end, the wind won. One night the plane lifted from its moorings and flew backwards for nearly a kilometre (900 yards) before crashing back to the ice. From the tent Gould thought the damage was slight, but when they reached it they saw it was a total wreck.

The men spent the next few days huddled in their tent listening to the wind and working out when they should start the walk back. Then, in a break in the weather, they heard a plane and knew Byrd had found them.

When the party returned to Little America a few days later it was obvious that the flying season was over. Byrd wrote: 'As the sun went down for the last time, the darkness closed in and the aurora jerked into fantastic patterns across the sky, we burrowed deeper and deeper. The planes were dragged into deep pits and covered with tarpaulins, the tunnels were

Richard Byrd, 40 years old, directs operations at the Bay of Whales. All the equipment had to be sledged 14 km (9 miles) from the ice-edge to Little America.

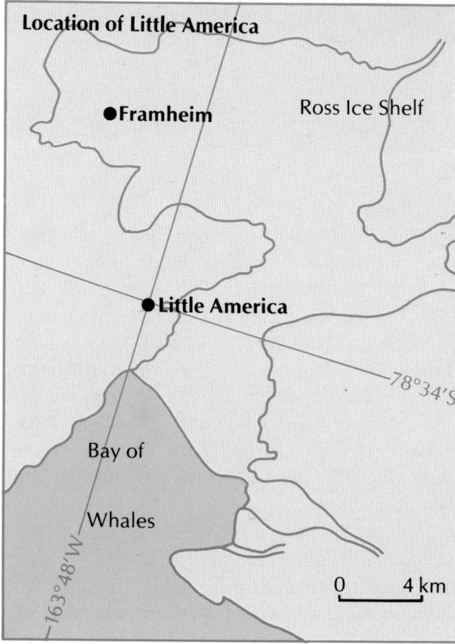

Paul Siple was chosen from among the Boy Scouts of America to accompany Byrd. Then 19, he served only as a dog handler, but went on to a distinguished career in the United States' Antarctic Service.

roofed over, and the buildings became enveloped in snow. As blizzards pounded the surface, and the darkness above us was a never-ending cyclone of sound and drift, we were snug below. Time didn't drag; for we never lacked plenty to do.'

Like a colony of moles, the men spent the winter at Little America making preparations for the polar flight and for an overland trip that the geological party was to make to the Queen Maud Mountains. On 3 July the temperature fell to −53°C (−64°F) and it was not until 24 August that the sun rose once more.

In October a team was able to leave to establish store depots for the geological party. Some 320 kilometres (200 miles) from their base they had to cross a heavily crevassed area which Amundsen had called 'The Trap'. Men and dogs picked their way gingerly over the fragile ground.

The geological party left on 4 November on one of the most important geological missions still left in the world. Travelling was hard and distances deceptive. On the final approach to the mountains, after weeks of travelling, they found themselves surrounded by crevasses. There was no alternative but to push on. To reach safe ground they had to cover more than 64 kilometres (40 miles) of difficult country that day. One man was so tired that he fell asleep with his spoon halfway to his mouth.

Little America during the long polar night, when the camp was completely snowed over. Only the 20-metre (65-ft) radio towers and a few chimneys marked the site of a bustling underground city which was home to the 42 men.

Three members of the geological party — (left to right) Freddy Crockett, Eddie Goodale and Norman Vaughan — at the cairn on Mt Betty built by Amundsen's party during their return from the South Pole in 1912.

But the effort was soon to prove worthwhile. A few days later Gould found samples of sandstone and coal on Mount Fridtjof Nansen and in doing so proved that the mountains were not volcanic, but were part of the earth's crust that had been forced upwards.

After making a lengthy journey along the range to set foot on land which Byrd had claimed for the United States, the party paused at Mount Betty to try to find a cairn that Amundsen had built 18 years earlier on his return from the pole. They had climbed this mountain earlier and had found no trace of the cairn, but now they saw it as a speck of rock on a lower ridge.

Inside the cairn was a tin of kerosene, a waterproof packet containing boxes of matches and a tin can with its lid tightly in place. 'It was the climax', wrote Gould, 'the high spot of the summer for all of us, when I pried off the lid of this tiny can and took out the two little pieces of paper. One was just a piece rudely torn from a book and contained the names and addresses of Wisting and Johanssen who had helped Amundsen build the cairn, and the other was a page carefully torn from the notebook of Amundsen himself. We did not need to be able to read Norwegian to make out the fact that he had on this paper told of his successful achievement of the South Pole.' The note finished: '. . . Passed this place on the return with provisions for 60 days, 2 sledges, 11 dogs. Everybody well.'

They replaced the tin of kerosene and added a note of their own before rebuilding the cairn.

Gould's party returned to Little America on 19 January 1930. None of the men had had any experience with dog teams before this trip but now, 10 weeks and 2000 kilometres (1250 miles) later, they were Antarctic veterans.

Highlight of the winter was the Fourth of July Talent Quest — a curious combination of musical comedy chorus and Negro minstrels. Freddy Crockett, second from left, was unanimously declared to be 'the handsomest woman who had ever been in the Antarctic'.

A pilot's conference in the library at Little America. They are (from left to right) Dean Smith, Alton Parker, Richard Byrd, Bernt Balchen and Harold June.

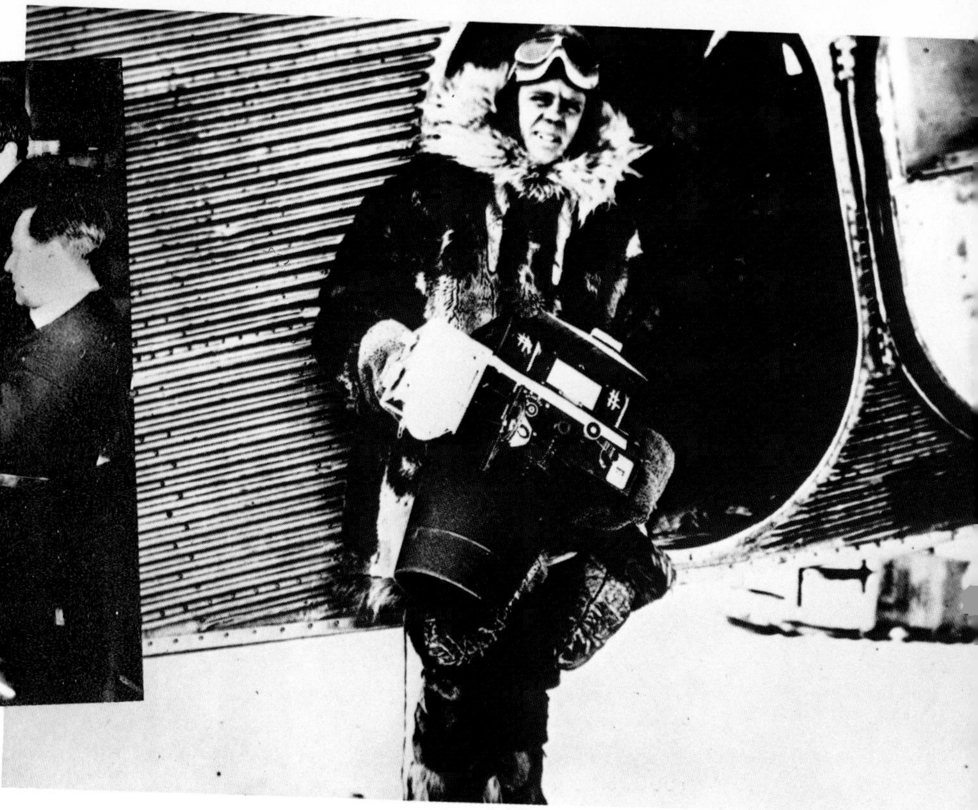

Captain Ashley McKinley, aerial surveyor and third-in-command of the expedition, at the door of the Floyd Bennett *before the polar flight. His aerial survey camera took rolls of film 23 metres (75 ft) long.*

FLIGHT TO THE POLE

Sixteen hours to repeat Amundsen's journey

Richard Byrd's flight to the South Pole, the first ever to be attempted, meant flying for hundreds of kilometres across the rolling, featureless surface of the Ross Ice Shelf, then passing through a mountain range some 4560 metres (15 000 ft) high for the final stage across the polar plateau. The plane could not climb high enough to fly over the mountains. Instead it would have to fly through a pass created by a glacier. Clearing the head of the pass would be the critical part of the flight.

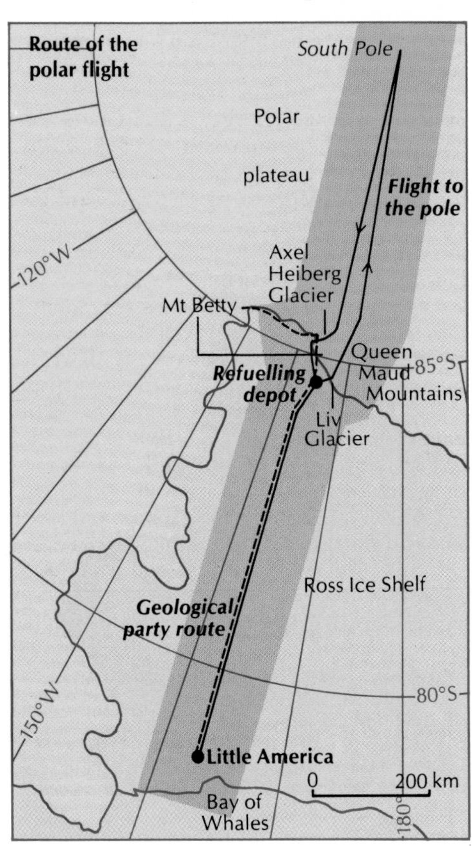

By the time the Antarctic winter set in and the men retreated to the underground quarters of Little America, Byrd had already discovered some of the difficulties of flying in the Antarctic. There were no charts, icing could seriously reduce a plane's ability to fly, and selecting a suitable landing site away from the base was notoriously difficult. Magnetic compasses spun dizzily because they were so near to the South Magnetic Pole and instead Byrd used a sun compass developed for his earlier flight to the North Pole.

Even starting aircraft engines was difficult and hazardous. Each engine had to be heated by a flame contained in a flameproof cover and then filled with warm oil. Once, fuel dripping from the tank had fallen on the cover and ignited. They had managed to douse the flames but it was a nasty moment.

Although Byrd had experienced many of these difficulties in the Arctic, there was an added complication here. Because the Antarctic was completely uninhabited a forced landing far from base was considerably more serious for, with nobody to help them, the survivors would have to rescue themselves. A flight of any distance could only be made safely if dumps of stores had been laid along the route. Even so, the aeroplane had to carry the basic equipment men would need to reach the nearest dump.

Although the Ford tri-motor which was to be used for the polar flight had the capacity to carry this equipment, the weight of it seriously reduced the plane's performance. They would not be able to fly to the pole and return to Little America without stopping. They would have to take on more fuel on the return trip.

Before they could make the flight to the pole, therefore, they would first have to fly across the Ross Ice Shelf and install a fuel dump at the base of the Axel Heiberg Glacier in the Queen Maud Mountains. It was vitally important, for if this flight was not successful they could not make an attempt on the pole.

With the winter finally over, they took off on 19 November on the 700-kilometre (440-mile) flight to the glacier. On the way they saw men of the geological party helping the dogs to pull the sledges across the crevassed ice, and felt embarrassed as they flew above them at 160 km/h (100 mph).

The plane landed safely near the base of the glacier and within half an hour they had established the most southerly fuel dump in the world. They kept the engines running so that they would not have to drain them of oil, but on the return flight they wished they had saved fuel instead. They were about 160 kilometres (100 miles) from Little America when the fuel ran out. All three engines stopped and the plane had to make an emergency landing on the ice. Men and aircraft escaped injury, but they were marooned for three days before another aircraft reached them with extra fuel.

But with fuel safely deposited at the foot of the glacier they were ready for the polar flight. All that mattered now was the weather, for it would have been madness to attempt the flight in anything but clear conditions. And it was at the glacier, and on the plateau, where it mattered most. Then on the morning of 28 November the geological party sent a radio message saying that the weather over the plateau was clear. It was the moment for decision and

The Ford tri-motor Floyd Bennett *coming in to land at Little America on 29 November 1929 after a successful flight of nearly 16 hours to the South Pole and back.*

The South Pole. In 1912 five men had sacrificed their lives to reach this desolate snowplain. Byrd wrote: 'One gets there, and that is about all there is for the telling.'

the meterological officer at Little America made it quickly. 'You had better go now', he told Byrd, 'another chance may not come'.

Four men were to make the flight: Bernt Balchen, pilot; Richard Byrd, navigator; Harold June, radio operator; and Ashley McKinley, photographer. They checked their equipment for the last time and at 3.29 in the afternoon Balchen lifted the heavy plane from the runway.

Visibility over Little America was bad and at first it was like flying in a bowl of milk. But soon they emerged into clear blue sky and far ahead were peaks glittering in the sun.

As they approached the mountains several hours later they grew anxious. Would they be able to clear the 'hump' — the narrow pass at the head of the glacier — or would the flight end in a tragic encounter with the side of a mountain too high for their overloaded plane?

Byrd had intended to fly up the Axel Heiberg Glacier to the plateau, but as they approached he saw the Liv Glacier to the right and thought it looked more inviting. The question was whether to use the Axel Heiberg — altitude known — or the Liv, which was wider but which might be blocked by mountains. Byrd could not spare fuel for exploration. He had to decide now. He chose the Liv, and hoped for the best.

Soon the plane was being tossed about like a leaf in the turbulent air that poured down the glacier. The wings shuddered and the engines roared as they tried to lift the plane above the 'hump'. But it was no good. As the plane hovered at the very limit of its altitude Bernt Balchen felt the controls go slack. Through the noise and turbulence he shouted to Byrd he would have to reduce weight or turn back.

They could reduce weight by jettisoning fuel or food. But they would need the fuel to get back, and the food if they crashed. Byrd decided the fuel was more important and soon a bag of food was on its way to the barren ground beneath them.

The plane climbed, but not enough. 'Quick!' yelled Balchen. 'Dump more!' Another bag was thrown out and again the plane climbed slowly through endless minutes. As they approached the 'hump', and the point of no return, the nose lifted and they flew over the pass with only metres to spare.

Although they were now above the polar plateau there was no time to relax. The way was now clear but they would need very accurate navigation to reach their target. Just after midnight Byrd obtained a successful sunsight with the sextant which showed that they were about 89 kilometres (55.5 miles) from the pole and at 1.14 all calculations showed that they had arrived.

At 1.25 they turned for home, heading first for the fuel dump at the foot of the Axel Heiberg Glacier. There they refuelled and at 10.10 am they landed successfully at Little America. In a flight of 15 hours and 51 minutes they had made a journey that had taken Roald Amundsen three months, and which had killed Robert Scott and his men.

Byrd's triumphant return to New York on 19 June 1930. The United States' Congress promoted him to Rear-Admiral, and President Hoover presented him with a special gold medal struck in his honour.

GOING PLACES

The age of the tin dog

Machines now provide the main form of surface transport in Antarctica. They have taken over from skiing, manhauling and dog sledging in a mechanical revolution that has been slow in coming to Antarctica. The difficult terrain, extreme winds and low temperatures provide many problems for any type of vehicle.

Even in the early days of exploration mechanical vehicles were tried by Ernest Shackleton and Robert Scott, both of whom expressed doubts about the worth of dogs. They could see the possibilities of high-speed travel on the smooth, hard surfaces of sea and shelf ice.

Shackleton's Arrol-Johnston motor car worked well in the early stages of his 1907-09 British Antarctic Expedition, but conditions on the shelf ice were very different from those that he had experienced during his earlier visit with Scott in 1902. The snow was much softer and the wheeled vehicle bogged, despite the use of skis under its front wheels.

Scott benefited from Shackleton's experience and took specially built tracked motor sledges. Unfortunately mechanical failure accounted for two of them, and the third broke through the sea ice while being unloaded.

A petrol-driven air tractor sledge faired no better when taken to Commonwealth Bay by Douglas Mawson in 1911. It was, in fact, a wingless aeroplane fitted with long runners instead of wheels. After several short runs at speeds of up to 32 km/h (20 mph), it set off into the interior towing four sledges. Several kilometres from Commonwealth Bay it developed what Mawson described as an 'internal disorder' before seizing so suddenly that the propeller smashed and it had to be abandoned.

In 1929 Richard Byrd had no greater success with a Ford snowmobile which broke down after 120 kilometres (75 miles).

Although the snowmobile had not been a great success, Byrd did take three modified Citröen cars on his second expedition in 1933. The rear wheels were converted into tracks and the front wheels clamped to short metal skis. This was the first successful over-snow motor vehicle to be used in Antarctica. But despite this, dogs remained the mainstay of Antarctic exploration up until the 1950s.

World War II led to many advances in the construction and engineering of tracked vehicles. The French still use the last of 40 military Weasels acquired by Paul-Emile Victor from United States' forces in France after the war. Operation Deepfreeze in 1955-56 and the International Geophysical Year in 1957-58 saw the establishment of many bases and the start of regular tractor journeys into the interior.

The first major tractor journey to make headlines around the world was the Trans-Antarctic Expedition under the command of Vivian Fuchs in 1957-59 with Tucker Sno-cats specially modified for the trip. They were supported by tracked and winterised domestic Ferguson tractors used by Sir Edmund Hillary's party from New Zealand.

Long journeys are now supported by a va-

This Arrol-Johnston was the first car taken to Antarctica, in 1907. Shackleton hoped that it could be used for towing loads over the Ross Ice Shelf, but soft snow rendered it almost useless and it was quickly bogged. In charge of the car was Bernard Day, who was the only person allowed to drive it.

Despite all the problems that Scott had with his motor sledges in 1911, he still thought that they had great potential. 'Seeing the machines at work today', wrote Scott, 'and remembering that every defect so far shown is purely mechanical, it is impossible not to be convinced of their value'.

Mawson's Vickers REP monoplane crashed before it left Australia in 1911. Stripped of its wings and fabric covering it was taken and used for towing sledges. The engine eventually seized and the vehicle was abandoned.

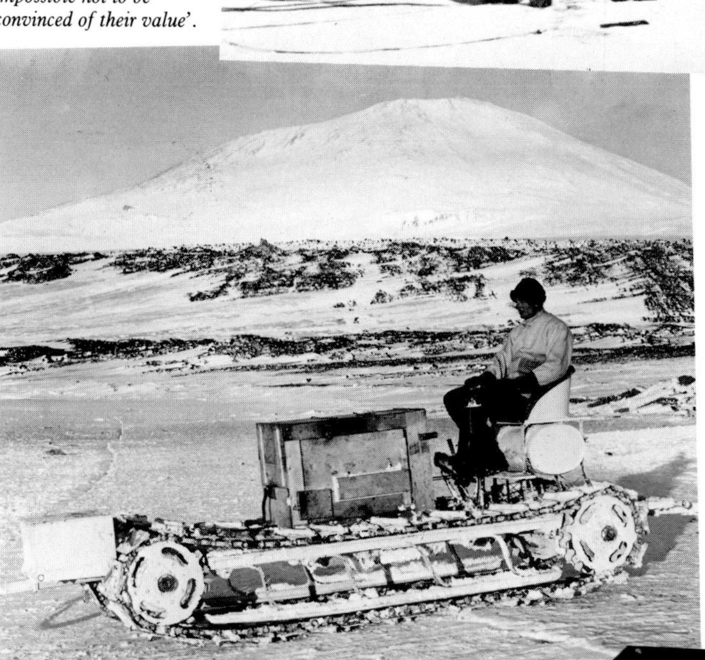

A United States' traverse tractor in use in 1967. Polar travel tests vehicles to the utmost. The constant flexing which results from travelling over very rough surfaces breaks open welds and damages mechanical components.

Giant Russian tractors in 1960. Huge machines like these carry parties of scientists for long trips across the polar plateau. In this way teams can operate independently for several months at a time, often covering 3000 to 4000 km (1800 to 2500 miles) in a season.

Russian vehicles, 1960

A small Australian tractor in use in the 1970s. Each national expedition has its own vehicles, and experiments are always being carried out to find the ideal transport. Even hovercraft have been tried, but without much success so far.

A small field party setting out from Scott base. The plywood caravan is mounted on a sledge and towed by the caterpillar tractor. Four men will live and work in the hut for the eight weeks it will take to complete the scientific research. The skidoo drives in front of the tractor, finding the safest route through any difficult areas.

In 1939, on his third Antarctic Expedition, Richard Byrd took with him two previously untried vehicles. For short-distance hauling there were two light army tanks (below) which proved to be successful. For long distances there was the ambitious Snowmobile (see p249) which was a complete failure.

Swedish motor toboggan

Motor toboggans — tin dogs — have taken the place of real dogs. Grip is provided by rubber tracks with metal claws. On an expedition, and towing sledges weighing up to 500 kg (1100 lb), they usually travel at about 8 km/h (5 mph).

A hot-air blower raises the temperature of a truck so that it can be started. Despite improvements to fuel and lubricants which keep them fluid at low temperatures, and devices for heating engines, cold-weather starting is still a major problem with internal combustion engines in Antarctica.

riety of tractors, some specially built, but the main haulers are often low ground-pressure, wide-track versions of heavy bulldozers which may weigh up to 32 tonnes.

The largest tractors used in Antarctica are the Russian Penguin and Kharkovchanka vehicles which weigh 33.5 tonnes and can haul 73-tonne sledges at speeds of 8 km/h (5 mph) on the polar plateau. They may travel 3000 to 4000 kilometres (1900 to 2500 miles) on a journey and can remain in the field for several months at a time.

The tractor train is still the main form of transport for major trips on the polar plateau, where long stops for such tasks as drilling and ice measurement make aircraft too costly. Each tractor usually hauls a number of sledges, the bulk of the load carried often being drums of fuel which, when empty, can be welded together to make route-marking beacons for the return journey. The remainder of the load consists of living caravans, scientific and mechanical workshop vans and food for those aboard. People travelling in the vehicles can talk to one another by radio. Vehicles always travel in pairs for mutual support — never on their own, except in an emergency.

A tractor train on a journey from the coast may meet a number of hazards. Sea ice may be one to two metres (3.5 to 7 ft) thick overall, but it can be thinned by strong currents near islands, headlands, or narrows, and may also be crossed by cracks that have refrozen and are now weak. Large areas may break up and drift out to sea with no warning at all. The tide crack — the junction between land and the sea ice — is also a hazard, as is a similar zone where glaciers and ice sheets move down to become ice shelves. At the latter there are often formidable crevasses, ice fractured by pressure, and even miniature rift valleys to be crossed.

The initial slopes of the plateau may be steep enough to force parties to work in relays, and it is sometimes necessary to winch vehicles up steep slopes. Often katabatic winds near the coast scour the snow from the surface leaving slippery blue ice on which vehicles have little grip. Ice on the coastal plateau is often thin — compared with high areas towards the pole where it may be 3000 metres (9800 ft) thick — and can be severely crevassed where it moves over the bedrock beneath.

All these problems make the coast probably the most hazardous area for vehicles. Echo location has been used successfully by United States' expeditions to detect crevasses, but most parties rely on men moving ahead of the vehicles to probe the surface. Marker poles or drums, checked and replaced every few years, show safe routes through dangerous sections.

Once on the plateau the problems are different, but no less significant. The extremely low temperatures, often −50° to −60°C (−58° to −76°F) and sometimes lower, make metal brittle and cause it to snap. When powerful tractors attempt to free frozen sledges weighing 20 to 50 tonnes at the start of a journey, great strain is placed on linkages and other components. Sastrugi two to three metres (7 to 10 ft) high — like frozen surf — cause vehicles and caravans to roll like ships at sea, straining and flexing every joint and frequently cracking welds. The workhorse for travel near bases and in mountain areas is the standard motor toboggan — nicknamed the tin dog — and this will probably be the case for a number of years to come, although some new machines have been tried. Japanese expeditions have tested air cushion vehicles, but they have limitations.

Navigation in Antarctica is little different from the techniques used by ships at sea, except that the compass may become unreliable anywhere near the South Magnetic Pole. Celestial navigation has been used since the earliest Antarctic land expeditions, but this is now being replaced by satellite navigation. Australian tractor trains use radar to pick up bamboo poles, allowing vehicles to keep moving in poor conditions on known routes. Various other ways of aligning vehicles, using mirrors and even radio beacons, have also been tried.

Vehicles and aircraft have always been difficult to start in cold climates. In the 1950s and '60s petrol was added to the sump oil to keep it from solidifying. Carburettors sometimes had bowls in which flaming rags or fuel could be burned, and blowlamps were often used to heat frozen engines. It was sometimes even necessary to boil up engine oil over a Primus in the tent to coax a reluctant engine into life.

Some of these problems have been cured with the introduction of fuels and lubricants that remain fluid at temperatures down to −60°C (−76°F), and sump and cabin heaters driven from power vans. However, the problem has not been entirely eliminated, as every Antarctic mechanic knows.

A remarkable photograph by Frank Hurley looking down on the deck of the Discovery *from the top of the mainmast as she steams through the pack ice.*

CONFLICTING CLAIMS

Nations move to divide the Antarctic cake

In 1923 Britain established the Ross Sea Dependency, claiming that territory in addition to the Falkland Islands Dependencies, and levying royalties from whaling companies operating in both areas. Sir Douglas Mawson had long advocated that Australia should do something about her interests in the far south, but, in the pre-Depression years, there seemed little hope of mounting an expedition.

Then, on 29 March 1924, the French took an unexpected interest in Antarctica. Recalling the voyage of Dumont d'Urville in 1840, and perhaps with a desire to collect whaling royalties, a French presidential decree claimed an appropriate slice of Antarctica — Adélie Land. Since this was directly south of Australia it evoked an indignant response.

But the French action was unsupported by ships or settlement, and attention turned to the very active Norwegian whaling interests. Lars Christensen, a Norwegian whaler and ship owner, was projected as a twentieth century Enderby, greedily seizing Antarctic resources. One of his ships, the *Norvegia*, equipped for science as well as whaling, made a first voyage in the summer of 1927-28. Afterwards Christensen claimed land for Norway between longitudes 20°W and 60°E and also Bouvet Island in the South African sector of the Antarctic. Both claims, based on extensive and efficient exploration and whaling, conflicted with British interests, even overlapping Biscoe's Enderby Land which had been claimed for William IV of Britain in 1831.

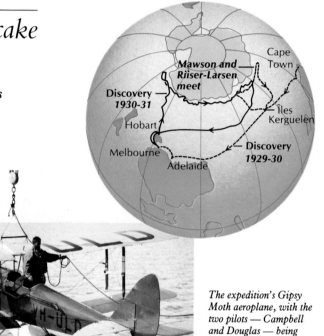

The expedition's Gipsy Moth aeroplane, with the two pilots — Campbell and Douglas — being hoisted on board the Discovery *after a flight near the MacRobertson Land coast.*

As a result of this upsurge in interest, a new expedition was planned, to be led by Sir Douglas Mawson. It was to sail in Scott's old ship, the *Discovery*, which was to be commanded by the veteran master of the *Aurora*, John King Davis. The enterprise received the support of the British, Australian and New Zealand governments, and private donors, foremost amongst them being Sir MacPherson Robertson, a Melbourne businessman.

On 12 March 1929 the Antarctic Committee, in Melbourne, defined the aims of the expedition. It was to attempt to chart the Antarctic coastline from Enderby Land (45°E) to King George V Land (160°E), 'making landings to plant the flag; carrying out inland surveys by plane; making hydrographic surveys; and studying meteorological conditions, geological formations, and the fauna of the region, especially the numbers, species and distribution of whales'. Because of representative interests and support, the expedition was to be called the British, Australian and New Zealand Antarctic Research Expedition — BANZARE for short.

The *Discovery* sailed from Cape Town on 19 October 1929. A Norwegian expedition left in the same month, organised by Lars Christensen, with the object of circumnavigating Antarctica, and making scientific studies, especially of whales. There was much publicity, inevitably including some sensational reports of national rivalries and competitive claims. The Norwegian press indignantly declared that 'Norway had as much right to any "no-man's land" which she might discover, as anybody else'.

After calling at Îles Crozets, Îles Kerguelen and Heard Islands, in the southern Indian Ocean, the *Discovery* headed south to an unknown coastline. Aerial survey, by S. A. C. Campbell and E. Douglas, on the last day of 1929, revealed indistinct icescapes, probably continental, at latitude 66°11'S, and longitude 65°10'E. A flight on 5 January 1930, by Mawson and Campbell, confirmed an extensive new coast of ice cliffs, rocky mountains and nunataks. Mawson named the area Mac.-Robertson Land.

On 13 January 1930, a party landed on Proclamation Island, a steep offshore fragment of Enderby Land, and named it. The British flag was raised, and the claim to full sovereignty of the territory — including Enderby Land, Kemp Land and Mac.Robertson Land — south of latitude 60°S and between latitudes 47° and 73°E was read to a small shore party and a few penguins.

Mawson wanted to spend longer in the area to carry out scientific work as well as mapping, but Captain Davis was worried that the *Dis-*

Discovery *cutting through pack ice on her way south from Cape Town and Îles Kerguelen.*

The final proclamation ceremony at Cape Bruce, turning point of the voyage, 14 Feb. 1931.

covery might run out of coal and become stuck in the pack ice. Essentially a summer expedition, wintering had never been contemplated. Bad weather prevented an attempt to obtain extra coal from a South African factory ship, and the expedition then sailed for Kerguelen and Australia. There was some disagreement between Mawson and Davis, but the functions and attitudes of the commander of a polar expedition, and of the captain of a ship in ice are probably never in complete harmony.

The second half of the BANZARE, again under the command of Sir Douglas Mawson, sailed from Hobart on 22 November 1930, and returned on 19 March 1931. Captain K. N. MacKenzie replaced Captain J. K. Davis as master of the *Discovery*, but again there were problems of divided command and limited coal supplies — although *Discovery* did refuel three times at sea by arrangement with Norwegian whalers and a Swedish collier.

The ship called first at Macquarie Island, and then made a search for the Royal Company and Emerald Islands. These island groups had been reported by old whalers, although it is now known that they do not exist. Steering south and west, they reached Cape Denison on 4 January 1931. Mawson again stepped ashore at Commonwealth Bay, and visited his 1911 base. Here, magnetic measurements revealed that the South Magnetic Pole had moved a long way since 1914.

Then, steadily, the ship sailed along the Adélie and Wilkes Land coasts to the Banzare Land coast, Queen Mary Land, Princess Elizabeth Land and Mac.Robertson Land, to eventually cross its course of the previous year. Flights reinforced surveys made from the *Discovery*, various landings were made, and flag and proclamation ceremonies enacted.

Following BANZARE, a British Order in Council, of February 1933, affirmed the King's sovereignty over Antarctic territory south of latitude 60°S and, apart from Adélie Land, between longitudes 160°E and 45°E. These regions were placed under the control of the Commonwealth of Australia, from the date of her acceptance. The Acceptance Bill was ultimately proclaimed and came into operation on 24 August 1936.

The scientific work of the expedition took many years to prepare and eventually appeared in the BANZARE scientific reports, although some results remain unpublished even now.

Mawson (left) and Captain Riiser-Larsen met on board the Discovery *on 14 January 1930. Both men got on well despite national rivalries.*

AN AMICABLE AGREEMENT

It was inevitable that Captain Hjalmar Riiser-Larsen, in the *Norvegia*, should make contact with Sir Douglas Mawson, in his *Discovery*, and this happened on the day after Mawson's landing on Proclamation Island, 14 January 1930 at about 66°20′S, 47°E, off the coast of Enderby Land. Larsen came on board the *Discovery*, and described his coastal explorations that had started about a month earlier.

Because the explorers' claims overlapped, somehow the words and fluttering flags had to be reconciled. Fortunately, the British claim to Enderby Land had been recognised by the Norwegian government. Lars Christensen instructed Larsen that only land west of longitude 45°E could be claimed for his country. After the meeting Mawson and Larsen kept in their proclaimed sectors, respectively east and west of the 45th eastern meridian.

Both men held each other in mutual respect, but territorial arguments continued for a long time amongst Norwegian historians. Norwegian and British maps showed little compromise, and continued to use their own names for features.

BYRD SETS THE PATTERN

Scientific research becomes the goal

On 17 January 1934 Richard Byrd returned to Little America, the base camp which had been established during his first expedition. Why had he come back? The first expedition had achieved what he had set out to do and the American public had treated him as a hero. But that expedition, whilst certainly successful, had raised as many new questions as it had answered and Byrd was anxious to take the work further.

Byrd modified and enlarged his 1928 base.

This second expedition, then, had been raised specially to carry out scientific research in the Antarctic and there would be no attempt to reach the pole. Consequently it was a much bigger expedition than the first and, because of the Depression, had been much more difficult to organise. There were 56 men in the wintering party, including 18 who had been with Byrd before, 153 sledge dogs and an absolute mountain of scientific equipment. There were also three aeroplanes, an autogiro (which crashed), a Cletrac tractor, two Ford snowmobiles, and three Citroëns that had originally been designed for desert use.

But when Byrd looked at Little America for the first time since his hurried departure four years earlier, it was with emotion as well as with scientific curiosity.

It took him half an hour to clear away the snow and reach his old room. Part of the roof had collapsed, but otherwise it was just as he had left it. On the table lay a copy of a magazine which he had been reading the day he left. In the mess hall the lights still gave off a feeble glow, powered by batteries that had survived four Antarctic winters, and men of this second expedition were able to have their first meal at Little America from food that had been left four years earlier by departing men of the first expedition.

Soon, however, the scientific work was in full swing. Some could be done at Little America and scientists there installed equipment that would provide new information about the Antarctic weather, sky formations and the upper atmosphere. But much of the work would have to be done farther afield, and when conditions improved groups of scientists left

Expedition discipline was relaxed and informal. All the men were specialists, knew their jobs and got on with them. Byrd counted on the men having pride in their work.

The expedition's aircraft — (left to right) a Kellett autogiro, Pilgrim monoplane, Curtiss-Wright Condor and a Fokker monoplane. Both the autogiro and the Fokker were wrecked in crashes.

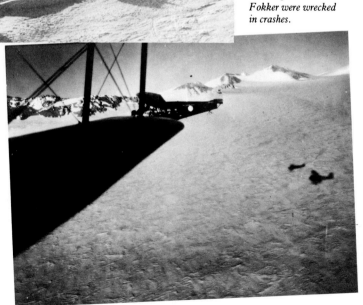

The Pilgrim monoplane, and beyond, the rugged Rockefeller Mountains. The Pilgrim was given to the expedition by an airline, which up to then had been using it in passenger service. Byrd's aviation crew were disappointed when the padded seats and toilet were removed to save weight and fuel.

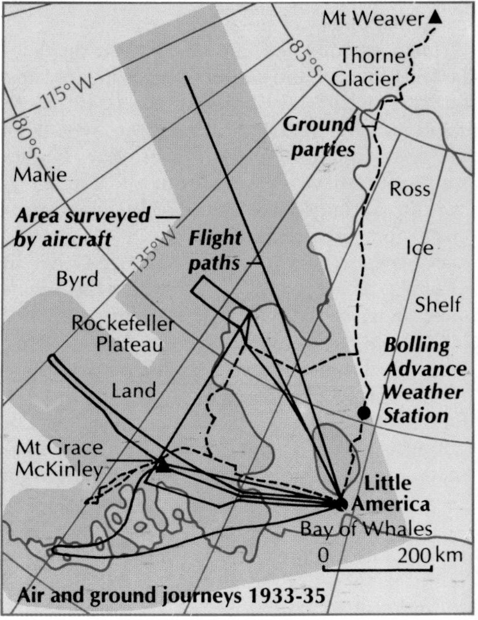

the base camp to study geology, life forms, and a hundred other things.

One of these parties, consisting of four men, set out on 27 September in one of the Citroën tractors. Their main job was to lay dumps of food every 56 kilometres (35 miles) to supply a sledge party that would later travel to Marie Byrd Land, and to lay a depot for them at Mount Grace McKinley nearly 370 kilometres (230 miles) east of Little America.

The weather was still too cold to use dogs and the journey would have been impossible without the tractor. Even so, it was a hazardous undertaking because motor vehicles had so far been a total failure in the Antarctic.

Travelling was not easy. The navigator had to lie with his compass on a metal-free sledge which was pulled by the tractor. He had a number of switches which were connected by cable to a cluster of lights on the tractor's dashboard. With these switches the navigator could give steering directions to the driver.

Another man on the sledge measured the distance travelled and every 400 metres (1300 ft) he jabbed an orange flag into the snow.

A blizzard trapped them for a week on the outward journey and it took a day of hard digging to uncover the tractor, but they reached Mount Grace McKinley, established the depot and headed back to Little America.

When they arrived on 18 October they had only 114 litres (25 gallons) of fuel left and there was barely a cupful of oil in the engine. But they had covered some 845 kilometres (525 miles) of difficult country and in the process had proved that motor vehicles could be used successfully in the Antarctic.

Although it lacked the 'glamour' of an assault on the pole, Byrd's second expedition added a great deal to the scientific knowledge of the Antarctic. For example, they proved that there was not a strait connecting the Ross and Weddell Seas and so established that the Antarctic was a single continent; they measured the depth of the continental icecap; they found and studied considerably more life forms than had been suspected; they accumulated an enormous amount of data about the Antarctic weather; and they discovered hundreds of new mountains and a vast new plateau. They even discovered, through almost continuous observations, that the earth was bombarded by more meteorites than anybody had ever thought likely.

Nor had the expedition been without drama. Not long after they arrived one of the men fell ill with stomach pains. One evening, with the pains becoming worse, the doctor realised it was appendicitis.

The patient was moved to the radio shack whilst the doctor searched through a pile of crates in the hallway of the Administration Building to find his instruments. Suddenly his oil lamp went out and as he refilled it in the darkness the hot mantle sent a stream of burning oil across the hallway. The small room immediately filled with smoke and the burning oil started to flow round the stack of crates.

Two men rushed out of the building for help, but the rest, including the doctor, were soon trapped by smoke and flames.

As Byrd wrote later: 'Fire and an appendectomy are just about the most unhealthy things that can happen in the Antarctic; but when they occur simultaneously, and when the fire threatens to destroy the only tools you have to operate on a poor devil waiting to go on the table, you have a situation needing no description.'

Prompt action soon extinguished the fire and the charred box of surgical instruments was carried across to the radio shack. There, the patient was laid on stretchers across the top of an unfinished table and ether was used to put him to sleep. The stove had to be extinguished because of the ether and as the operation dragged on the room got colder and colder. Finally the doctor removed the appendix, which was twice as long as normal.

The Administration Building had suffered little damage and the operation was a complete success. But, as one man said, it had been one hell of a night.

THE END OF THE AMATEURS AS GOVERNMENTS TAKE OVER

In 1939 the United States Congress established the US Antarctic Service which, under government sponsorship, was to send a new expedition to the Antarctic to consolidate previous American exploration and to examine more closely the land in the Pacific sector.

The expedition, again under the command of Richard Byrd, consisted of 59 men, 130 dogs, 3 aircraft, 2 light army tanks and 2 tractors. The scientists and dog drivers were civilians but most of the technicians came from the US Army, Navy and Marine Corps.

The work was to be carried out from two base stations and when the expedition arrived in November 1939 they established the West Base at the Bay of Whales about 8 km (5 miles) from Little America, which by now had been virtually destroyed by movement of the shelf ice, and the East Base was set up some 3200 km (2000 miles) to the east on Palmer Peninsula.

The sun went down on 21 April and scientific work was carried out at the bases during the winter. Then when the sun finally returned in September, dog and tractor teams left to establish food and fuel dumps for the research parties.

From West Base these consisted of a biological party and a geological survey party which went to the Edsel Ford Mountains; a Pacific Coast survey party, which went to Mount Hal Flood; and a geological party which went to the Rockefeller Mountains.

At the East Base a weather station was set up on the Peninsula; a survey party went to the Eternity Range; sledging parties went to the Weddell coast and to King George VI Sound, and aerial surveys were made from the base.

All these parties had returned to their base by January 1941 and West Base was evacuated by the end of that month. East Base was also closed down but because of bad weather it was the end of March before the expedition was reunited.

This expedition returned with a mass of new scientific information. But it also had a feature that was of interest to the general public: it was the first to return with colour photographs.

The 30-tonne Snow Cruiser was a disappointment. In theory it was to be able to carry an aircraft on its back for distances of up to 8000 km (5000 miles), and to cross 4.5-metre (15-ft) crevasses. In practice the huge tyres provided inadequate traction, and its electric motors were not powerful enough. It was moved only from the ship to West Base where it remained for the rest of the expedition.

Dr Paul Siple, now a veteran on his third Antarctic expedition with Byrd, was in command of West Base.

North Star, *one of the expedition's ships, near the site of East Base in Marguerite Bay (below right), and (below left) unloading the Beechcraft at West Base.*

ALONE

A bold experiment that went badly wrong

Richard Byrd had long been interested in the weather at the Antarctic. As there was almost no information about weather patterns inland, Byrd had decided that his second expedition would establish a temporary inland weather station and man it through the long Antarctic winter. Called the Bolling Advance Weather Station, it was to be established about 198 kilometres (123 miles) from Little America.

Byrd had intended to have three men at the station, but additional work at Little America meant that there was now not enough time to carry supplies for that number before the start of the winter. If not three men, perhaps two? Byrd had doubts: 'Jammed together in a silent, dark, dead, bitter cold environment, staring at each other for six months. Could it possibly work out? Personally I would prefer the grave hazard of being alone.'

Byrd felt unable to ask two men, let alone one, to spend the winter at the station. If there were to be one man, it would have to be him. 'Besides', he wrote, 'I wanted to go, and welcomed the opportunity to go alone'. It was just as well, for no one else wanted the job.

On 25 March 1934, with the temperature at −59°C (−75°F), Byrd and a crew of two left Little America to fly to the advance base. The aircraft then returned and Byrd joined the ground party which had brought the equipment overland.

The hut, which was only four paces by three, was erected in a hole in the ice so that only the roof was above the ground. Inside was a bunk, a radio transmitter, an oil-burning stove, and shelves holding books and a gramophone. Two tunnels, each about 10 metres (30 ft) long and a metre (3 ft) wide, were cut into the snow from the hut to act as storerooms and to house the generator.

On 28 March the ground party left to return to Little America. 'I stood at the trapdoor and watched the two Citroëns move away. Their red hoods and rounded canvas superstructures made a jaunty picture . . . I watched until the noise died out, until the receding specks had dropped for good behind a roll in the Barrier; until only the vanishing exhalations of the vapour remained.'

Byrd soon settled down to a comfortable routine as the winter started, but he also learned something of the dangers of being alone. One day, whilst taking a walk in the darkness, he realised that he had gone far beyond his last route marker and he could no longer see it. Fighting panic, he built a mound of ice and scratched an arrow in the ice to indicate his return direction. His first attempt to retrace his steps failed, but he did manage to return to his mound of ice. The next attempt was successful and, having found the marker on his 29th step, he was able to make his way back to the hut.

In spite of this, Byrd found the first few weeks very rewarding. 'This was one of the greatest and most satisfying periods of my life. I enjoyed the solitude and silence. I enjoyed watching the stars and the aurora in the darkness of the winter night. I really liked everything about it.'

And then things started to go wrong. By the end of May the temperature was −71°C (−96°F), and with the cold came the wind '. . . rising out of nowhere. Then the Barrier unwrenches itself from quietude; and the surface, which just before had seemed as hard and polished as metal, begins to run like a making sea.'

Inside the hut the wind screeched in the ventilators and rained like hammer blows on the roof. But when the wind direction indicator failed he realised he would have to go out to clear it of snow. It was a futile job and he returned to the trapdoor entrance to the hut. He could not open it.

'Panic took me then, I must confess. Reason fled. I clawed at the three-foot [one-metre] square of timber like a madman. I beat on it with my fists, trying to shake the snow loose; and, when that did no good, I lay flat on my

For half of the four and a half months that he spent alone at the advance base weather station Byrd was incapacitated and almost killed by carbon monoxide fumes from the stove and a faulty electrical generator.

The rescue party — (left to right) Pete Demas, Thomas Poulter and Bud Waite — ready to set out from Little America to rescue Byrd marooned at the advance base. The difficult 198-km (123-mile) night-time journey took the Citroën tractor three days to complete.

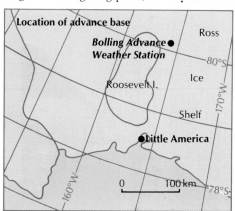

Location of advance base

Bolling Advance Weather Station
Ross
Ice
Shelf
Roosevelt I.
Little America
80°S
78°S
170°W
160°W
0 100 km

belly and pulled until my hands were weak from cold and weariness. Then I crooked my elbow, put my face down, and said over and over again, You damn fool, you damn fool.' Then he remembered that a week earlier he had stabbed a shovel into the ice not far away. Groping in the darkness, he found it with his foot and used the handle as a lever to open the door. 'When I tumbled into the light and warmth of the room I kept thinking, How wonderful, how perfectly wonderful.'

But the real danger, one even more deadly, came much more stealthily than a blizzard. On 31 May Byrd was having a radio session with Little America when the engine driving the generator started to run unevenly. He went to the tunnel to investigate and found the air thick with exhaust fumes. He tried to adjust the engine, then fell unconscious to the ground. When he recovered he struggled back to the radio and signed off without telling them what had happened.

He managed to turn off the engine before collapsing on to his bunk and by the end of the day he barely had strength to light a candle. But he realised that the engine could not have been entirely to blame, for carbon monoxide poisoning does not come that quickly. The stove must also have been slowly poisoning him with its own fumes.

'The sun was nearly three months away. I could not persuade myself that I had the strength to meet it ... That night, as never before, I discovered how alone I was...'

Byrd called the next day Black Friday. Hardly able to move, he contemplated death as rationally as he could. 'Great waves of fear, a fear I had never known before, swept through me and settled deep within. But it wasn't the fear of suffering or even of death itself. It was a terrible anxiety over the consequences to those at home if I failed to return ... The only conscious resolve left was to write a message to my wife — a last grasping touch of the hand.'

Byrd needed to explain to her why he could not call up Little America — that by doing so he would put the lives of his men at risk as they tried to make an impossible midwinter journey. He wrote other letters and thought of the last entry in Robert Scott's diary: 'For God's sake, look after our people.'

Day followed day. Sometimes his mind cleared, but mostly he moved and thought as one close to death. Slowly, painfully slowly, he read the meteorological instruments and even carried out a radio schedule with Little America. It was important that he did, for they would have taken his silence as an SOS. He used the stove only long enough to keep the room from freezing. He slept and occasionally he ate. And over the days he slowly improved. One day he was able to play a record on the gramophone and as the hut throbbed to the Sound of *Adeste fidelis* (Come All Ye Faithful) an inner voice told him: 'You are on the mend, you really have a chance. One in a hundred, perhaps, but still a chance.'

Although his despair started to lift, physically and mentally he was now an old man. He dreaded the radio sessions with Little America because they required a physical and emotional effort that he could ill afford. He knew now that his survival depended on a miserly use of whatever reserves he had left.

Then in the middle of June, Thomas Poulter, one of the scientists at Little America, said over the radio that he wished to take his research party out earlier than planned as the conditions were now becoming more favourable. He wanted to leave in about a month to establish a depot on the Southern Trail.

It was several days before Byrd realised the significance of his request. On the next radio session he said he would probably return to Little America with the base laying party, although he did not say why. What he did say was that they were not to take any risks.

But at least it seemed that Byrd might receive help by the end of August instead of having to wait until October, especially when Poulter later suggested that his party might as well use the advance base instead of setting up one of their own.

Poulter and his tractor party left Little America on 20 July but they ran into bad weather almost immediately and soon reported that they were having difficulty finding the flags that marked the route. Byrd, who was by now surviving as best he could, followed their progress on the radio and once, when there was little news, he even went outside in the hope of seeing them.

Then on 26 July he learned over the radio that Poulter had lost the route when about halfway to the advance base and, following Byrd's instructions, had returned to Little America. Byrd finished his diary entry that day with: 'He did a good job in returning safely to Little America — my relief is boundless. The news is opportune, for I have been very low.'

Poulter left Little America again on 4 August, by which time the men there had at last realised that Byrd was ill. But the clutch failed on the tractor and again Poulter had to return. He started again on 8 August with only two men, knowing that his journey had now become a rescue mission.

Byrd was convinced that they would not be able to reach him. But he was wrong. After averaging less than 3 km/h (2 mph) in almost impossible conditions, Poulter reached the advance base at midnight on 10 August. Byrd, who had been outside watching their lights advancing across the barrier and burning flares, said: 'Hello, fellows. Come on below. I have a bowl of hot soup waiting for you'.

It was more than two months before Richard Byrd was strong enough to leave the advance base and it was not until 14 October that he was able to board an aircraft to fly back to Little America.

'I climbed the hatch and never looked back. Part of me remained forever at latitude 80°08'South: what survived of my youth, my vanity, perhaps, and certainly my skepticism. On the other hand, I did take away something that I had not fully possessed before: an appreciation of the sheer beauty and miracle of being alive...'

It took Byrd two months and four days to recover sufficiently from his ordeal to take the risk of flying back to Little America. He was not able to bring himself to write about his experience for four years.

One of the Citroën tractors that was used for the journey to rescue Byrd. Three of these machines were given to the expedition by André Citroën himself, when Byrd could not find a suitable American vehicle.

HOME FROM HOME

Tiny outposts of humanity in a hostile land

There have been bases in Antarctica since 1899 when Carsten Borchgrevink erected two prefabricated wooden huts on a rocky cape in Victoria Land. Borchgrevink, and the explorers of the heroic age who followed, did carry out scientific research but their huts were never intended to be permanent.

In 1903 W. S. Bruce built a new kind of base, a meteorological station on Laurie Island in the South Orkneys. This was the first station built purely for scientific research. When Bruce's expedition left the following year, the British Government showed no interest in continuing the station so Bruce handed it over to an Argentinean relief party. The Argentinean Government has maintained it since that time, and it remains the oldest permanently inhabited base in the Antarctic region. It is now known as Orcadas scientific station.

By 1908 there was a new reason for building in Antarctica. In that year Britain made the first formal claim to Antarctic territory and by 1943 over 80 per cent of the continent had been notionally divided up. Governments realised that if their claims were to have much weight in any future dispute over Antarctic sovereignty, then they would have to be supported by some form of regular presence and activity.

By the late 1940s permanent bases had been established on subantarctic islands and a number of summer stations built on the continent, but it was only in 1954 that the first large, permanently maintained base was established on the continent itself when Australia built Mawson base.

The burst of national and scientific interest in Antarctica during the International Geophysical Year of 1957-58 led to an increase in the number of bases. By the end of 1958 there were 50 bases, belonging to 12 countries, operating in the region. The United States built the first permanent inland base at the South Pole. The Soviet Union followed with Vostok at the geomagnetic pole, still the coldest and highest of all bases.

All building in Antarctica is difficult. Even bases built on the relatively temperate subantarctic islands, or the two per cent of the continent free of permanent ice, face problems of accessibility and isolation. These buildings tend to be conventional in design and are anchored where possible to a rock platform. But it is the bases built inland on the ice, or on the floating coastal ice shelves, that pose unique construction problems.

All Antarctic ice is moving and unstable, making it difficult to construct foundations. A building will also give off heat and sink slowly into the ice. The British base Halley sank nine metres (30 ft) before it was replaced.

Another problem arises with strong winds which blow large amounts of loose surface snow over the surface of the continent. This snow accumulates in drifts around any object such as a building, and never melts. The weight of the ice and snow starts to distort the walls and roof and eventually covers the whole building, sometimes causing it to collapse. The United States Byrd station was completely covered within five years of being built.

A number of radical building designs were developed in the 1960s to increase the life span of bases. The Australian Casey base was built in 1969 on a long raised platform facing the prevailing winds. Snow blew underneath the platform rather than building up against it.

Another solution was adopted for the new Byrd station in 1961. That base was built in a large trench cut out of the ice and covered by

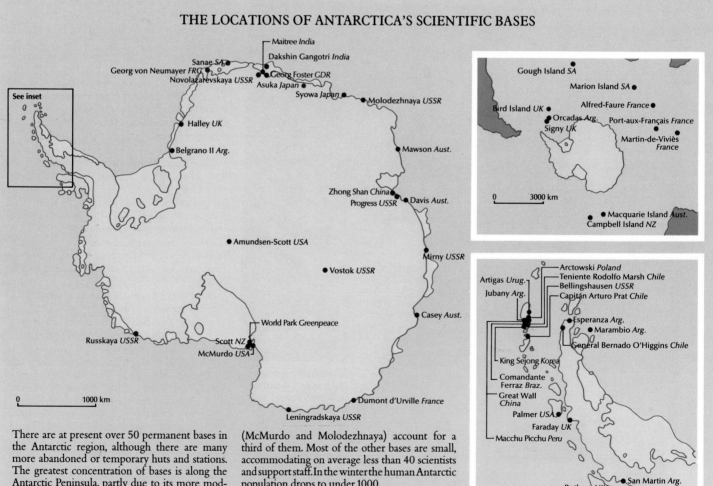

THE LOCATIONS OF ANTARCTICA'S SCIENTIFIC BASES

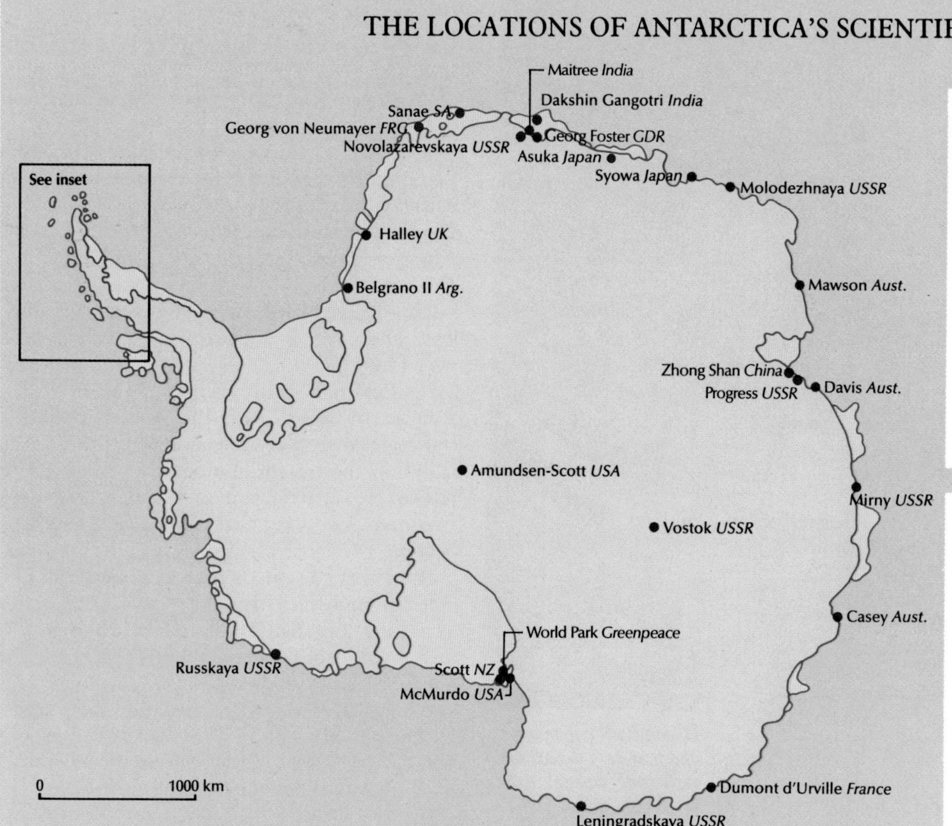

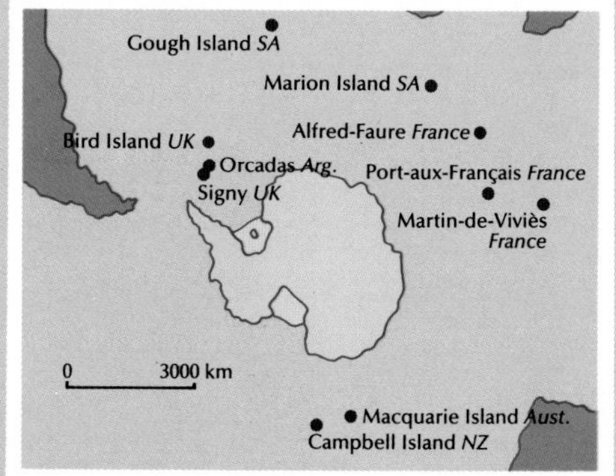

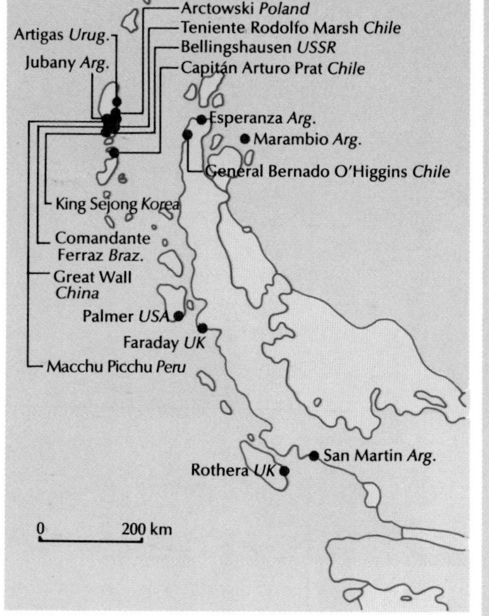

There are at present over 50 permanent bases in the Antarctic region, although there are many more abandoned or temporary huts and stations. The greatest concentration of bases is along the Antarctic Peninsula, partly due to its more moderate climate and partly because Argentina, Chile and the United Kingdom all lay claim to this sector. Over half of the bases here have been set up by these nations.

Each summer over 2000 people live in Antarctica, and the largest American and Soviet bases (McMurdo and Molodezhnaya) account for a third of them. Most of the other bases are small, accommodating on average less than 40 scientists and support staff. In the winter the human Antarctic population drops to under 1000.

The scientific work varies from base to base. Some are purely biological laboratories, some are weather stations and some study upper atmosphere physics. Others still are there mainly to maintain a national political presence, and the scientific research is of poor quality.

a steel arched roof so that the buildings are sheltered from the wind and snow. But this method is expensive, and because the ice is constantly moving, the walls of the trench are gradually shifting inwards.

The South African SANAE base, which needed replacement in 1979, used a cheaper variation of the trench design. The buildings were placed within a galvanised steel tunnel which is better able to withstand the weight of ice building up around it. The buildings can always be removed from the tunnel and used again if the weight of the ice becomes too great. The United States South Pole base, Amundsen-Scott, was protected by a dome built between 1971 and 1975. The original base, built in 1957, had sunk over 10 metres (33 ft) into the ice and had moved with it more than a kilometre (1100 yards) from the pole.

A typical modern base is split into different buildings: living quarters, laboratories, a diesel-powered generator, a radio station, weather station and stores, which often hold a year's supply of food. The buildings might be connected by corridors, sometimes underground to allow easy movement in bad weather. There is often an emergency shelter some distance away in case of a bad fire, a constant worry in the very dry Antarctic air.

Fuel consumption is very high. Not only do the bases need year-round heating, but a lot of fuel is used to melt snow to provide water. The United States experimented with a nuclear power plant at their McMurdo base between 1962 and 1972. However, it performed poorly and had to be removed from the base along with over 11 000 cubic metres (38 800 cu ft) of radioactive rock.

All but one of the Antarctic bases today are run by government polar agencies, often with the support of the armed services. The number of bases has now reached 52, with the United States' McMurdo base on Ross Island being by far the largest on the continent.

The main Soviet research station is Molodezhnaya, built in 1962. The Russians have concentrated their bases in east Antarctica, although one recent base, Russkaya, was built on the Marie Byrd Land coast.

The United Kingdom has five bases, including one on South Georgia that was disrupted in 1982 by the Falkland Islands' war. The only British base on the continent, Halley, is a geophysical laboratory first built in 1956.

Argentina has five bases, one of which is being run as a colonial settlement. Chile has three bases. One, on Deception Island, was destroyed by a volcanic eruption in 1969 and had to be re-sited. Australia also has three bases – all in its own sector, plus one on Macquarie Island – and New Zealand has Scott base on Ross Island plus another on Campbell Island. Brazil, China, East Germany, France, India, Japan, Korea, Peru, Poland, South Africa, Uruguay and West Germany all maintain at least one permanent base. The only non-government base was established by Greenpeace, the environmental organisation, in 1987. Its World Park base at Cape Evans on Ross Island has a staff of four.

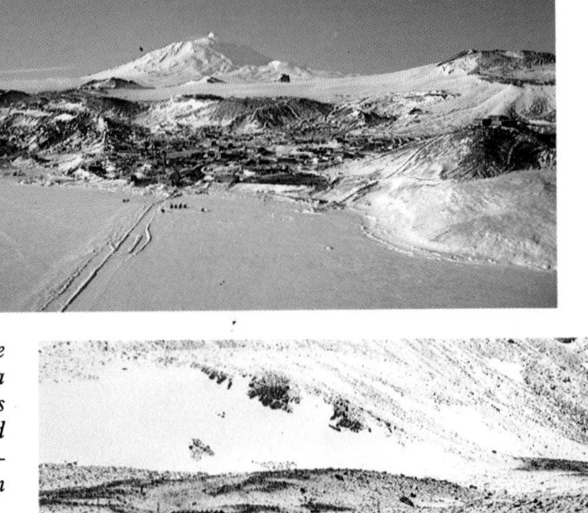

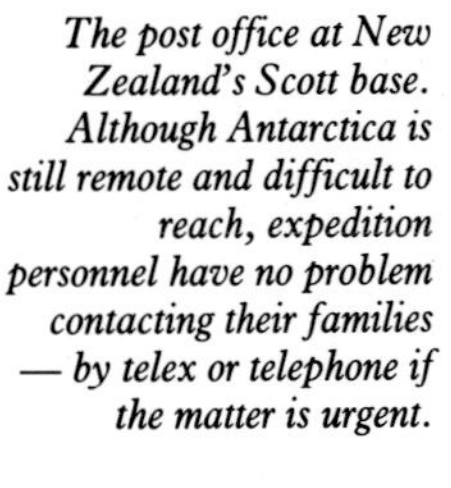

The post office at New Zealand's Scott base. Although Antarctica is still remote and difficult to reach, expedition personnel have no problem contacting their families — by telex or telephone if the matter is urgent.

The giant United States' McMurdo base on Ross Island. Beyond, with vapour rising from its summit, is Mount Erebus. This is the centre of US operations in Antarctica, and site of the continent's biggest airport — Williams Field — built on the ice.

Argentinean families are now living at Esperanza base at Hope Bay. It was here that the first child was born in Antarctica — Emilio de Palma — in January 1978.

Garbage disposal in Antarctica is a problem. The ideal solution would be to return it to where it came from. Instead it lies in great piles, largely unaffected by decay.

A huge geodesic dome, 50 metres (160 ft) in diameter, covers the buildings of the United States' Amundsen-Scott base at the South Pole. The barber's pole, topped by a silvered ball, marks the exact location of the earth's axis or rotation.

Some bases can provide their personnel with occasional fresh vegetables raised in a greenhouse. These tomatoes are being grown at the Polish base, Arctowski, on King George Island.

The Penola *under sail. She was a 130-tonne Brittany fishing schooner with twin auxiliary screws, built in 1905.*

The bleak Argentine Islands were the expedition's first winter base in 1935.

DEDICATED AMATEURS

Enthusiasm matters more than money

John Rymill's British Graham Land Expedition was the first and last of its kind. Its members were amateur explorers who sought to explore the unknown, not so much for science but because it was there, a challenge to the limits of human versatility and endurance. Measured by its achievements it was the least expensive Antarctic expedition ever mounted. Its cost, over three years, was less than £20 000.

The venture was conceived by Gino Watkins, the young explorer of Greenland, talking light-heartedly to Rymill and others in a billowing tent on the Arctic Circle. They would all sail down to the end of the earth and sledge across Antarctica to the Bay of Whales, in the Ross Ice Shelf. On the way, they would make a detour across India, and climb Mount Everest!

Next day, 20 August 1932, Watkins disappeared amidst the ice, on a kayak journey.

Later, it was decided that Rymill should attempt a journey by ship, sledge and aeroplane on the western side of Graham Land, the blizzardly spine that projects northwards from Antarctica to within 965 kilometres (600 miles) of Cape Horn. Then Rymill's party would sledge east to the Weddell Sea. To the west they would explore the southern reaches of Charcot's Marguerite Bay, and the territory east of Alexander and Charcot Islands.

The ship's captain and the chief engineer, both Royal Navy men, were the only professionals. Their crew would be amateurs. Members of the shore party, no matter in what capacity they joined the expedition, would all have to dig, build, carry, sledge and cook.

Rymill found an old Brittany fishing schooner which he bought for £3000 and renamed the *Penola*, after his home in South Australia. A single-engined de Havilland Fox Moth, equally satisfactory as a ski or sea plane, was the one aircraft they could afford. Surface exploration would be by dog sledge.

John Rymill, who organised and led the British Graham Land Expedition, was born in Melbourne, Australia, in 1905. Before travelling south, he had accompanied Gino Watkins to Greenland on the British Arctic Air Route Expedition. Rymill recruited a number of his companions from that expedition to accompany him on the Penola, *including Hampton, Bingham and Riley.*

The Colonial Office and the Royal Geographical Society, in London, made donations, but the entire responsibility for the venture rested on the shoulders of John Rymill.

The *Penola* left England on 10 September 1934. Stores and dogs were relayed by cargo ship over half the world to Port Stanley, in the Falkland Islands. At Port Stanley, working parties from HMS *Exeter* and the research ship *Discovery II* altered *Penola's* rig to one more suited to pack ice. *Discovery II* also transported the aircraft, dogs and heavy stores from the Falklands to Port Lockroy.

Here, on 22 January 1935, came the *Penola*. As her engine mounting was misaligned, she had travelled down from the Falklands under sail. The aircraft was launched and, after an exploratory flight, Rymill selected his proposed winter quarters in the Argentine Islands.

In the calm waters between the islands and Graham Land, two ship journeys were made between Port Lockroy and Winter Island (as

Whiling away the winter hours in the hut. The men are (left to right) Quintin Riley, W. E. Hampton and W. L. S. Fleming.

Penola *and the Fox Moth aeroplane anchored in a bay in the Argentine Islands, March 1935.*

The northern hut, in the Argentine Islands, took three weeks to build. Forty-five pups were born and raised in kennels around the building.

the southern landfall was named). *Penola* made her final winter landfall on 14 February.

Penola had to be unloaded using small boats in an area where the ice had been blasted from the tide cracks along the shoreline. The timbers of the two-storey house had to be sorted, and the building erected. Scores of huskies to be segregated into family groups, suitably housed, and then trained as teams.

An aerial reconnaissance on 28 February made Rymill determined to move his base further south the next summer. But the immediate purpose of the flight was to observe the condition of the sea ice, and plan sledging journeys which might lay depots and reveal suitable landing areas for the plane on the frozen sea around Adelaide Island.

As the sea ice thickened, sledging became more ambitious, until the pattern of islands that lay scattered roughly north and south in clusters parallel to the spine of Graham Land became familiar to the expedition members.

By late August, deteriorating ice barred further penetration to the south, though exploration continued close to the base. A month later, all sledging was halted for the season.

Rymill was greatly encouraged by a wireless message from Lincoln Ellsworth who, in November 1936, had flown from Graham Land to the Bay of Whales. He claimed to have seen Stefansson Strait, which Rymill hoped would lead them to the Weddell Sea.

It was decided that, after the *Penola's* summer movements were accomplished, she would return to the Falkland Islands and winter there. Then an examination of the first year's winter quarters revealed such warping and expansion in the timbers that its demolition and re-erection at a new base appeared impracticable. As soon as the *Penola* was freed, therefore, she would first sail north to Deception Island and obtain a large supply of timbers which were stored, unclaimed, at the deserted whaling station. This was accomplished during January 1936.

Meanwhile, Rymill, Stephenson and Fleming made a short exploratory journey east, in an attempt to reach the main plateau of Graham Land. But they found the icefalls and glaciers too rough and hazardous to cross in the brief time available.

In little more than a fortnight, the base was vacated and all gear, stores and dogs were loaded onto the *Penola*. On 17 February she set out on her voyage of discovery, planning to reach the open sea beyond Pendleton Strait, then coast southwest along the western side of Adelaide Island until she was able to make an easterly crossing of Marguerite Bay.

Hampton and Stephenson remained behind until they were summoned south by Meiklejohn's wireless message, sent on 25 February from *Penola's* anchorage at the Leonie Islands.

A day or two later, a reconnaissance flight revealed majestic mountains — including a vast chain that seemed to connect Alexander Island with the mainland glaciers — and, much closer, the winter fast ice that would limit the *Penola's* southward journey. A few kilometres north of the fast ice edge, Rymill and Hampton found a suitable wintering site in what were subsequently named the Debenham Islands. Hampton and Ryder then flew across, making sketch maps of the rocks and reefs in these uncharted waters. Very early on 29 February, the *Penola* pushed her way through the pack ice to her destination, just south of the 68th parallel, and close to Graham Land.

Work began immediately to establish the new base, erect the house, bring in supplies of seal meat, and arrange stores. It was too late in the season for the *Penola* to linger. On 12 March she left to spend the winter in the distant Falkland Islands.

George VI Sound at Fossil Bluff, halfway down the east coast of Alexander Island. Stephenson's party had travelled a little beyond this point in October 1936. They could see no sign of channels on the west coast of the sound, reported by Wilkins, that might take them across to the Weddell Sea coast.

The last sledging party returning to their base in the Debenham Islands in December 1936. The sea ice was breaking up, and large open leads between the floes made travel slow and difficult.

EXPLORING THE PENINSULA

Wilkins' discoveries proved to be false

The adventure of polar living, to match danger with daring, were the prime considerations of the British Graham Land Expedition. Nevertheless, the expedition did make a significant contribution to the geographical knowledge of Antarctica during the summer of 1936-37, including the discovery of King George VI Sound.

On 12 March 1936 *Penola,* northward-bound, disappeared behind the icebergs. The wintering party began to investigate the three channels, now within aerial range, that supposedly connected the far southern reaches of Marguerite Bay with the Weddell Sea. Also to be inspected and charted were the eastward extensions of Alexander and Charcot Islands.

To the surprise of Rymill, however, a flight south by Hampton and Stephenson could find none of the three passages seen by Hubert Wilkins during the first Antarctic flight in 1928: the Casey and Lurabee Channels, and the Stefansson Strait whose existence Lincoln Ellsworth had so recently confirmed. Another flight revealed, east of Adelaide Island, vast cloudy fjords and highlands.

Where was Stefansson Strait? Rymill decided to concentrate all efforts in the unknown far south. Marguerite Bay did not freeze over sufficiently for extensive sledging until 9 June. From the base there was no satisfactory route leading east onto the upland plateau of Graham Land. However, Wilkins' channels were much farther south. With three sledges, the one tractor they had brought with them, and a strong team comprising Bingham, Stephenson, Riley and Bertram (who had taken Roberts' place), Rymill set out to lay a depot for more extensive movement south.

The expedition nearly ended in tragedy when a blizzard struck and the temperature rose to just below freezing. Ice floes shattered and broadening leads of dark, icy water opened up. Amid rafting pressure ice, the tractor, with most of the depot supplies, had to be abandoned. The party managed to climb up onto a small island, gratefully christened Terra Firma, on 19 June. Here they spent Midwinter's Day, entertained by Bertram's penny whistle. That small island has since been seen countless times.

Eventually, Rymill and his companions all got back to base safely. The tractor and provisions were expendable, although unsuccessful attempts were made to retrieve them later.

During July and August two teams surveyed Laubeuf Fjord, flanking Adelaide Island along its eastern coast. As the sea ice was thick and holding well, there was much hunting for seals. They also spent time repairing sledges.

Then, on 15 August, a flight north and west of Alexander Island revealed the feature by which the British Graham Land Expedition would be remembered: a great white channel stretching beyond the farthest southern horizons. They named it King George VI Sound.

Further flights were made in the same month by Rymill, Hampton and Stephenson, sceptical of the existence of the supposed east-west corridors intersecting Graham Land between the newly discovered sound and the Weddell Sea. Possibly, as was later confirmed, there had been confusion by both Wilkins and Ellsworth between the presumed seaways and

A corner of the southern base hut (below) in the Debenhem Islands. It was completed and occupied on 24 March 1936.

Alfred Stephenson on the float on the expedition's De Havilland Fox Moth. The aeroplane proved invaluable for planning the movement of both sledging expeditions and the Penola.

Rev. W. L. S. Fleming, the expedition's chief scientist and chaplain, preparing a meal on the Aga cooker at the southern base in the Debenham Islands.

glacial valleys falling from the great peninsula. Early Antarctic flights could only surmise, but surface travel was necessary to confirm the validity of aerial observations.

A flight on 4 September revealed a way by which a sledging party might reach the shelf ice of the long southern arm of the sea. The coastal land-based ice, and shelf ice to the east, could become part of a loop that descended to the sound beyond the chaos of floes and rafted ice that blocked a direct approach to its barrier front.

Two sledging parties prepared to set out immediately. It was the beginning of a long season of convoluted journeying. Stephenson, Fleming and Bertram, with three teams, would follow the shelf ice south and, if it existed, find Stefansson Strait and thereby attempt to reach the Weddell Sea. Bingham and Rymill, with two teams, would accompany the others as far as they travelled east, then steer west, south of Alexander Island into an equally unknown desert of ice.

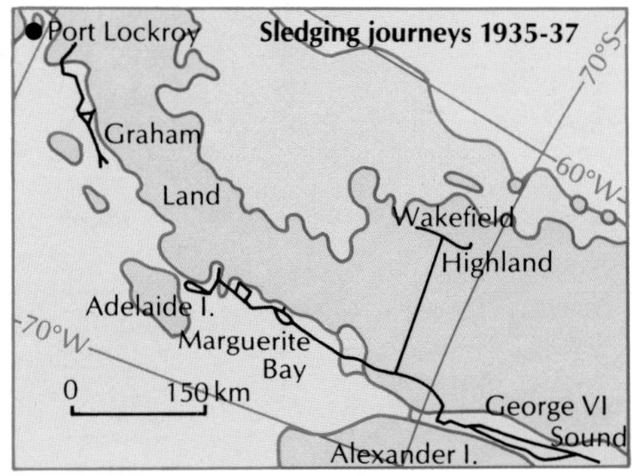

On 5 September all parties left together. Heavy going and bad weather dogged them, but by 20 September they were south of the barrier edge, with the worst crevassing and pressure ice behind them. Then there was a change of plans. For a while Rymill and Bingham reinforced Stephenson, Fleming and Bertram, until their southern route was clear and a suitable landing place for the plane was found. Then on 24 September, 145 kilometres (90 miles) from base, Rymill and Bingham turned back. To this lonely, flat wilderness, they would fly in supplies to establish a depot.

By 10 October, six flights had been made to this depot. A flight on 19 October continued down the great channel for 354 kilometres (220 miles). The channel seemed endless.

Rymill and Bingham now returned to sledging and, leaving supplies at strategic points, again reached the depot. With half loads, they then sledged up to the top of the pass that had given them a route to King George VI Sound. Here they met Stephenson's party returning. They turned and accompanied them to the depot camp 700 metres (2300 ft) below.

Stephenson had travelled southwards for 320 kilometres (200 miles) to a point from which he could see rock exposures. Beyond this the channel broadened and disappeared south-south-west, apparently south of Alexander Island. The discovery in two areas of early Cretaceous fossils and of ferns and other primitive vegetation, which indicated vast changes of climate, had been very exciting.

Stephenson's party continued back to the base in the Debenham Islands. Rymill and Bingham attempted a crossing of Graham Land, branching off from the top of the strategic pass which was by then part of a familiar route. Blizzards were frequent but ultimately, on 22 November, they came within sight of mountains fringing the east coast of Graham Land. In the latitude of Wilkins's reported Casey Channel, they found a glacier descending to the Weddell Sea.

For 30 days, Rymill and Bingham were within sight of the east Graham Land coast. Then they turned for home and reached the base, after 870 kilometres (540 miles) of sledging, on 5 January 1937. Together, Stephenson's and Rymill's sledging totalled almost 2100 kilometres (1300 miles).

Some more flights were made, including one that further delineated Alexander Island. Then *Penola* was summoned. She duly arrived on 13 February 1937, and on 12 March the whole party sailed for home.

Words from Stephenson's diary sum up the explorer's greatest reward: 'Everywhere was complete calm and silence; there was not a sound from the other tent . . . We were further south than anybody else in the world, and, apart from our companions at the base, there was no human being within 1500 miles [2410 kilometres]. It made one feel extremely insignificant to see and think of such vast areas untouched by man, and in which man has had no influence whatsoever.'

First Across The Antarctic

A millionaire's dream fulfilled

Although Lincoln Ellsworth was not the greatest explorer of the Antarctic, he had one feature that was unique amongst such men. He was rich. As the son of an American millionaire, he could have made a very distinguished name for himself by simply financing expeditions and sharing in whatever social prestige they created. But that was not enough for him. Lincoln Ellsworth could afford to be a true adventurer. Unconcerned about social prestige, he wanted to be where the excitement was.

In 1926 he supported one of Roald Amundsen's expeditions and flew over the North Pole with him in an airship. By 1933 he was ready for his next adventure and started to wonder what it might be. Richard Byrd had already flown over the South Pole four years earlier and so Ellsworth decided to tackle what he called the last great adventure in Antarctic exploration: a flight right across the continent.

His intention was to fly from the Bay of Whales on the Ross Sea across to the Weddell Sea, and then fly back — a distance of nearly 5500 kilometres (3400 miles). He would make no attempt to fly to the pole and, because the expedition had no scientific pretensions, it could be small. Small, but not cheap.

Ellsworth bought a 15-year-old wooden fishing boat in Norway. He sheathed it in oak and armour plate to turn it into an icebreaker, and renamed it *Wyatt Earp* after his western hero. He also bought an aeroplane. Made for him by Northrop at a cost of £10 000, it was a low-wing metal monoplane.

Called the *Polar Star*, it had a top speed of 370 km/h (230 mph), which was fast for its day, but a system of flaps brought the landing speed down to little more than 80 km/h (50 mph). Further, by digging trenches in the snow the plane could be lowered until the wings rested on the surface, so making it much more stable when it was parked in high winds.

After spending a month at Dunedin in New Zealand, Ellsworth's expedition reached the Bay of Whales in January 1934. The chief pilot, Bernt Balchen (who had piloted Byrd's successful polar flight) made a trial flight three days later and Ellsworth decided that he and Balchen would leave on the trans-continental flight at 9 am the following day.

It was a beautiful morning as the technicians skied out to the plane to prepare for the flight. Then, at 7.30, disaster struck. 'Suddenly', wrote Magnus Olsen, second mate on the *Wyatt Earp*, 'from within the deep caverns far below the surface of the ice barrier, came ominous sounds like the tuning up of a mighty orchestra. It was as if the whole universe itself had begun to vibrate.

'For the same reason that during a phenomenon like the total eclipse of the sun, when birds and beasts are numbed into silence, this unexpected, demoniac, and mightly stridulation, paralysed us into total immobility. We stood rooted to the spot, so great was the terror which engulfed us. As the ominous sound continued, it was as if a mammoth organ, hidden behind macrocephalic stalactites, began to play accompanied by gigantic "cymbal" crashes.

'Before these terrifying blastings and crashings had subsided, I discovered that I was alone on an ice floe! Beside me was a cluster of oil drums which rolled backwards and forwards as the ice craft rocked violently. I looked in the direction where the plane had sat waiting to take off, but there was no sign of it, and only one of the mechanics stood on an ice floe which had been part of the runway.'

Many square kilometres of the ice shelf, which until then had been a smooth plateau,

Lincoln Ellsworth flanked by pilot Bernt Balchen, on his right, and expedition organiser Hubert Wilkins in Dunedin, 1933.

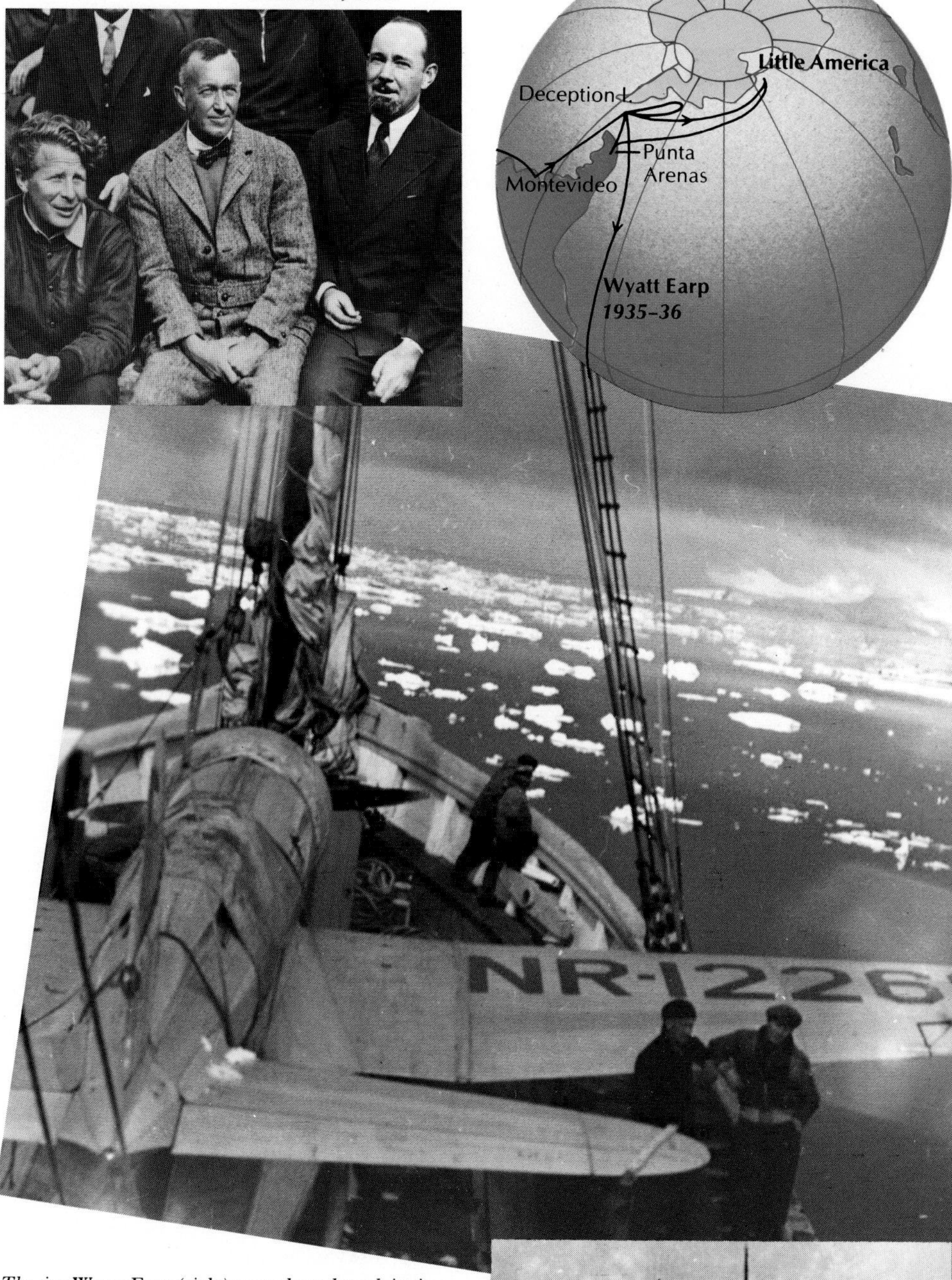

The tiny Wyatt Earp *(right) noses through pack ice in search of a suitable starting point for the trans-Antarctic flight. By the time the plane (above) made its successful flight it had travelled 77 000 km (48 000 miles) backwards and forwards to Antarctica on the ship.*

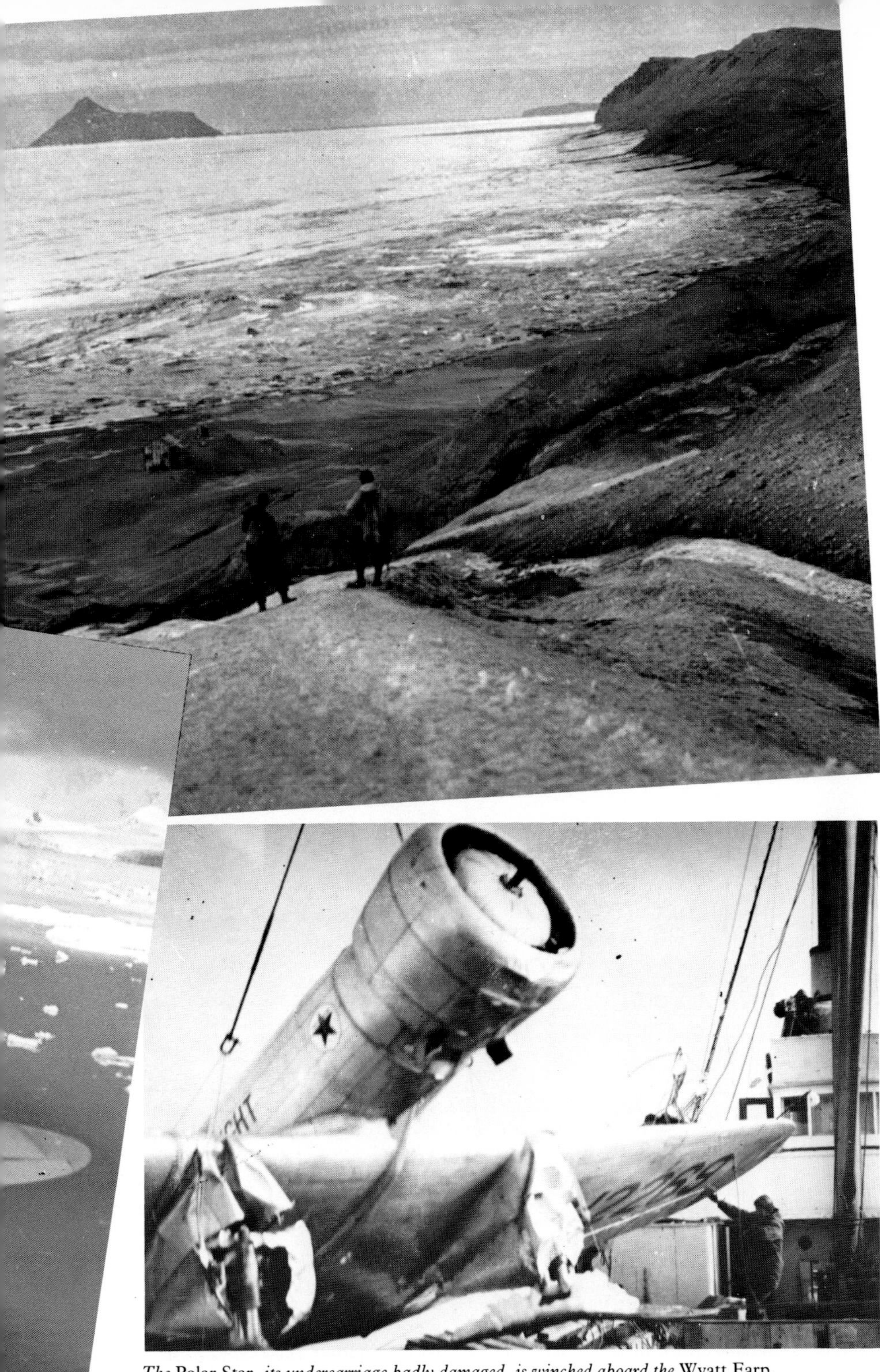

Two members of Ellsworth's expedition survey a scene of icy desolation from the barren heights of Snow Hill Island. Below, on the shores of the bay, is the hut used from 1901 to 1903 by the Swedish expedition led by Otto Nordenskjöld. The inside of the hut was much as it had been left when Nordenskjöld's party rushed to board their rescue ship, 30 years before. Books, clothes, tools and food still lay where they had been dropped.

The Polar Star, *its undercarriage badly damaged, is winched aboard the* Wyatt Earp. *During the expedition's first season in Antarctica the Ross Ice Shelf had been chosen as a base for the flight. Shortly before the aeroplane was due to take off a huge area of ice broke away, leaving men and equipment stranded on a series of icebergs. All the men were rescued, but the plane was so badly damaged that plans for the flight had to be abandoned until the following year.*

had broken up into small floes which were already drifting away, taking men and equipment with them. The ship, which was fortunately still in the Bay of Whales, was able to rescue the men and, with everybody on board, they turned their attention to the aeroplane.

They found it hanging by its wings from two ice floes. It was half submerged but they thought the damage might be quite minor. It took several hours to winch the plane on to the ship, and then they found how wrong they had been. The hydraulic system was badly damaged and the landing gear had been practically demolished. As they realised that the whole purpose of the expedition had been destroyed, the men stood in silent groups as if they were at a funeral.

Ellsworth took his expedition back to the United States and, after Northrop had repaired the plane, they returned to the Antarctic later that year. Meanwhile he had decided that this time he would fly the route in the opposite direction — from the Weddell Sea to the Bay of Whales — because he would be able to start about a month earlier.

They made their base at Deception Island in the South Shetland Islands and started to prepare for the flight once more. But when a mechanic tried to start the engine one morning a block of frozen oil in one of the cylinders resulted in a broken connecting rod. They had spares of almost everything but connecting rods, so Ellsworth sent the ship to South America to pick up a spare which Pan American flew down from New York. The ship returned in the middle of November with its tiny cargo and 10 days later the plane was operational once more.

By this time, however, the snow on Deception Island had started to melt and it was no longer suitable as an airfield. So the expedition moved to Snow Hill Island, about 160 kilometres (100 miles) further south.

The problem now was the weather. Bernt Balchen had tried to convince Ellsworth that three men should make the flight and when he failed, Balchen had insisted that the flight should only be attempted in absolutely clear conditions. As week followed week the sky remained overcast and stormy and finally, on 3 January 1935, Ellsworth ordered his men to pack up for the voyage home.

Then, only a few hours later, the weather cleared and Ellsworth changed his mind: he and Balchen would make the flight after all. After a hurried scramble of loading and final briefings, the two of them climbed on board and, after a hair-raising takeoff, headed south on the first leg of their trans-continental flight.

An hour later Ellsworth looked up from his calculations and was appalled to find that Balchen was flying north, back to Snow Hill Island. When he asked why, Balchen said it was because he had seen bad weather further south and that he was not prepared to commit suicide. Ellsworth, who had seen only a small squall ahead, was furious and realised that the weather would never meet Balchen's exacting requirements.

Nevertheless, when they returned to Snow Hill Island the weather closed in almost immediately. In two months they had seen only 12 hours of continuously clear skies and Ellsworth once more gave instructions to load the ship for the voyage home.

But it was not to be quite that easy. After days spent battling the pack ice, the ship was forced to return to Snow Hill Island to wait for better conditions. This time they anchored on a different part of the coast and realised, to their excitement, that they could see the hut Otto Nordenskjöld and his men had built as their base in February 1902.

When Nordenskjöld's ship was crushed by ice a year later, he and some of his men had been trapped at this base until November 1903, when they had abandoned nearly all they had in their haste to board the rescue ship before it too could be damaged. Ellsworth and his men, who were the first to visit this hut since then, saw all the signs of a hasty getaway. Clothes and personal gear were strewn round the hut, a pair of skates still lay on the ground near the door, and against one wall were boxes of sardines, mustard, pepper and chocolate. The chocolate tasted fine, but nobody cared to experiment with the vintage sardines.

It was the end of March before the ship was able to find a way through the ice to start the voyage home. By then Ellsworth had decided that he could never hope to make his trans-continental flight with Balchen. But he had not for one moment thought of giving up. It was simply a matter of finding another pilot who was willing to take the risk.

Ellsworth (above, right), Hollick-Kenyon and (right) the two Northrop monoplanes.

EPIC FLIGHT COMPLETED ON FOOT

Radio failure raises fears of disaster

In November 1935 Lincoln Ellsworth returned to the Antarctic to make another attempt at the trans-continental flight. By this time the aircraft had travelled more than 77 000 kilometres (48 000 miles) to and from the Antarctic but so far had clocked up only a handful of flying hours. But at least Ellsworth had found a new pilot — a quietly spoken Englishman by the name of Herbert Hollick-Kenyon.

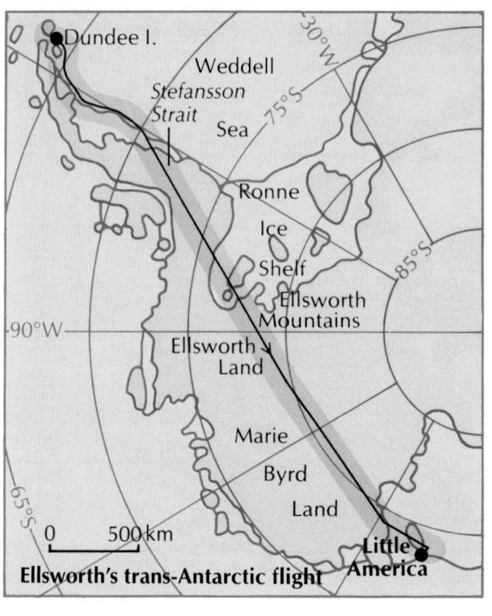

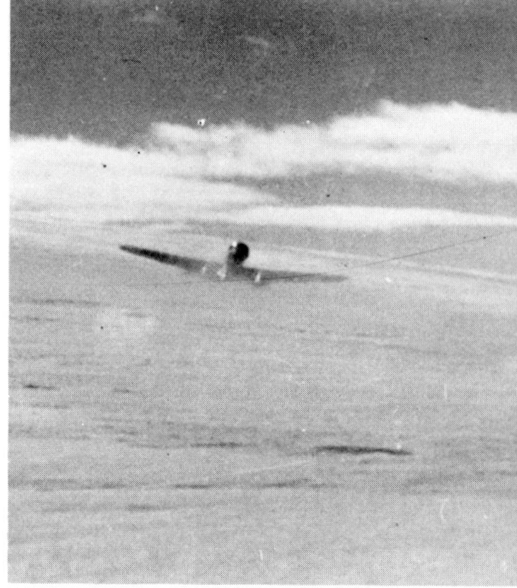

The base camp for the expedition was established at Dundee Island, which Ellsworth had explored after the failure of his second attempt. The flight from there to the Bay of Whales would be 3700 kilometres (2300 miles) long and Ellsworth expected it would take about 14 hours. As the plane would need to land to refuel, it would have to carry additional equipment, such as camping gear, a sledge and an extra radio, to support them on the ground.

On 21 November Ellsworth and Kenyon took off in perfect conditions on what they hoped would be the successful flight to the Bay of Whales. But after flying nearly 970 kilometres (600 miles) the fuel gauge started to swell and Ellsworth, fearing that it might burst and cover Kenyon with fuel, decided to go back. By the time they reached Dundee Island they had been flying for 10 hours, but their goal was as elusive as ever.

It was a simple matter to repair the gauge but two days went by before the weather was clear enough for another attempt. This time, thought Ellsworth, they *must* succeed.

They left at 8.05 in the morning and flew south over the now familiar Antarctic Archipelago. Then, just after midday, they crossed the valley incorrectly identified by Hubert Wilkins as Stefansson Strait and started to fly over the unknown mainland. 'It falls to the lot of few men to view land not previously seen by human eyes. It was with a feeling of keen curiosity and awe that we gazed ahead at the great mountain range which we were to cross . . .' Ellsworth, in a philosophical mood, called the mountains the Eternity Range. Later in the afternoon the radio failed and they lost contact with the *Wyatt Earp*, but there was nothing they could do about it so they went on.

After a few hours they left the mountains behind and started to cross a vast plateau of monotonous ice. But then the clouds started to reduce visibility and they decided it was time to land. They had been flying for 14 hours and were now about 2900 kilometres (1800 miles) from Dundee Island and 800 kilometres (500 miles) from the Bay of Whales. Ellsworth raised the American flag over what he said was the last unclaimed land on earth.

They stayed in the camp for 19 hours before taking off for the next part of the flight. But poor visibility forced them to land after only half an hour and they had to wait three days before conditions improved. Even then they were short-lived. Their next flight lasted barely an hour before bad weather forced them to land once more.

They hardly had time to pitch their tent before a blizzard came screaming across the open plateau. It trapped them for eight days and even after it passed the conditions were not much better. But Ellsworth, bored with the monotony, decided to go on. They dug the plane out of the snow and after warming the engine they were ready to take off into a sky that was far from promising.

Conditions improved as they went and after flying for four hours they landed to refuel for the last time. They were now only 200 kilometres (125 miles) from the Bay of Whales and in an area well explored by Richard Byrd.

They took off again at 6.00 the following morning and four hours later they reached the northern end of Roosevelt Island. But half an hour later the plane lost speed and, with the fuel exhausted, the *Polar Star* sank wearily but safely on to the snow.

Kenyon stood on the wing to look for Little America and thought he saw it about 6 kilometres (3.5 miles) ahead, but after sledging for

25 kilometres (15.5 miles) they found it to be merely an old pressure ridge. Realising they would need their tent and sextant, both of which were on the plane, they went back for them. By the time they got back to the ridge they had covered 75 kilometres (47 miles) of hard travelling in less than a day.

The next day fog reduced visibility to 30 metres (98 ft) and they had to travel entirely by compass. And they started a routine that was to go on for days: 15 minutes of sledging, followed by a four-minute rest. They did this for six hours and were able to cover about 16 kilometres (10 miles) each day.

Late one afternoon they at last reached the edge of the ice shelf and suddenly found themselves looking down at the Ross Sea some 60 metres (200 ft) below. They retreated from the edge and camped for two days before setting off to follow the bay round to Little America.

They reached it on 15 December — 22 days after leaving Dundee Island on what they thought would be a 14-hour flight. Even so, Little America looked far from inviting and Ellsworth, even in those circumstances, thought it was the most desolate remains of inhabitation he had ever seen. On the surface was a jumble of poles and masts and only the tops of stove pipes, sticking through the snow like rigid plants, gave any sign of the living quarters below.

They found a skylight and climbed down into what had been Byrd's radio shack but which, unfortunately, was now empty of radio gear. But it had two rooms and a roof and they were happy to settle there to await the arrival of the *Wyatt Earp*.

On 15 January, whilst Ellsworth was asleep, Kenyon heard an aircraft overhead and rushed out in time to see a parachute hit the ground. It had a parcel of supplies attached to it and a note from the captain of the Royal Research Ship *Discovery II* asking them to go to the shore to meet a party of his men.

Having lost radio contact with the plane, the captain of the *Wyatt Earp* had raised the alarm and the Australian government had sent *Discovery II* on a rescue mission. With two aircraft and Royal Australian Air Force crews, she had left Melbourne exactly a month after Ellsworth and Kenyon left Dundee Island.

Kenyon set off alone, and was shortly afterwards climbing aboard the *Discovery II*. Meanwhile Ellsworth, who was suffering from a frozen foot, struggled on for a kilometre before settling down to wait for his rescuers. 'I saw through the fog, which magnifies frightfully in those regions, what appeared to be a whole army marching towards me; in reality there were six men.'

Three days later the *Wyatt Earp* sailed into the bay after carrying out her own search, and as the *Polar Star* was being loaded on board, Ellsworth left for Melbourne on *Discovery II*.

He had proved that two men could fly freely about the Antarctic and that with care they could land and take off almost anywhere, instead of having to operate from prepared bases. But whilst he was proud of his achievement he was furious to learn that the world thought they had been 'lost', and, having been lost, that they had now been 'rescued'.

'Of course, this was not true. At no time was there the slightest doubt in our minds as to our location.' They had simply made their way to Little America and waited for the *Wyatt Earp*. It might not have been exactly as they had planned, but it was something he had spent three years trying to do.

Ellsworth returned to the Antarctic for the last time in 1938 having said that he intended to fly some 800 kilometres (500 miles) inland from Enderby Land. But during the voyage he said privately that his real intention was to claim land near Wilkes Land, an area which had already been claimed by Australia.

Unconcerned about the legalities, Ellsworth and his new pilot, J. H. Lymburner, took off on 11 January 1939 from the coast near Princess Elizabeth Land. Flying due south as far as latitude 70°S, Ellsworth dropped a canister which contained a document claiming a vast area of land on behalf of the United States of America and, for the last time, turned for home.

Lincoln Ellsworth, then 58 years old, had spent six years travelling nearly a million kilometres (620 000 miles) to make two flights. They had cost a sizeable amount of his considerable fortune, but as far as he was concerned they had been worth every cent.

With its engine at full throttle, the Polar Star *(above) roars down the makeshift ice runway on Dundee Island. The 3540-kg (7800-lb) plane carried 1270 kg (2800 lb) of fuel for the 14-hour flight to the Bay of Whales — 3700 km (2300 miles) away.*

The plane made four landings between Dundee Island and the Bay of Whales. On one occasion the flyers were trapped in their tent for eight days waiting for a violent blizzard to pass.

Just 26 km (16 miles) short of their goal, the Polar Star *ran out of fuel. Ellsworth and Hollick-Kenyon were forced to complete their journey to Richard Byrd's base Little America on foot.*

DAY IN THE LIFE

The daily routine of modern exploration

Probably more is known about the explorers of the heroic age than about the daily routines of the 2000 or so people who live and work in Antarctica each summer. This first-hand account of a day at a small New Zealand base would be familiar to expedition members working at other stations anywhere on the continent.

An evening camp on the shiny ice surface of a glacier. Everything must be securely tied down before going to sleep as the Antarctic weather can change very quickly.

Stores and equipment being loaded onto a Nansen sledge in preparation for a field trip. Fully loaded, the sledges can take half a tonne of equipment.

An early breakfast. The sun streaming through the window is deceptive, because the time is only shortly after midnight.

'It is mid-October, early summer here in Antarctica. The day begins at 6.30 when the fire-watch, who has done the rounds of the base all night, wakes me and the other 55 inhabitants.

'Blearily I rub the double-glazed window to scratch off some of the frosted condensation, squinting against the sunlight to see what the day is like. Yesterday's blizzard, which hammered dry powder-snow into every nook and cranny, drifting up buildings and vehicles, has blown itself out. The base is serenely calm today, and I can see the plume from Mount Erebus wandering into the cloudless sky.

'This is a day I've been planning for 12 months. Four of us — three geologists with me as guide and field assistant — are going to do some detailed geological mapping in the Transantarctic Range, some coastal mountains about 200 kilometres (125 miles) away from Scott base. We will take everything we need for 10 weeks on three wooden Nansen sledges pulled by motorised toboggans. We will use a fuel dump which a helicopter has left high up on a glacier, but our only link with the base will be by the tiny high frequency radio.

'We began preparing months ago in New Zealand, compiling equipment lists and calculating fuel consumption. Our routes were plotted carefully on the few aerial photographs that are available, to lessen the chances of having to cross a major ice-fall or a badly crevassed stretch. Then there was a week-long training course in the Southern Alps of New Zealand, going through the purposes of the expedition and brushing up on the techniques of crevasse rescue, first aid, and the repair and maintenance of the machines and equipment. Those days in the Alps, spent mountaineering or just camping and cooking, meant that our little group, all individualists, could get to know each other. That is vitally important if a team is going to work together effectively. Delays caused by breakdowns or bad weather bring out the worst in everyone. You can get irritated just by the way a tent mate scrapes food from the bottom of a saucepan.

'While I'm dressing, I can hear the yelping

of the huskies tethered down on the two-metre (7-ft) thick sea ice in front of the base. Perhaps a skua is taunting them. I only need to put on woollen underwear for now in the centrally heated base. We will put on all our outer garments, balaclavas and insulated boots at the last minute before we leave. It is important to sweat as little as possible, so your clothes do not lose their insulating properties.

'While washing in the ablution block I am careful not to waste any precious water, although this will be my last decent wash for some time. It takes tedious effort and precious fuel to melt ice for water on a kerosene Primus. Every drop will be used straight away for hot fruit drinks — everyone gets a raging thirst in this cold, dry land. I wander through to breakfast in the communal kitchen, mulling over what I will say in my last letter home for several weeks.

'Over breakfast of bacon and eggs, I cast my mind back over the last busy week spent sorting and checking our stores and equipment in the field store at the far end of the base. With so much to do if we were to meet our deadline for departure, each day's work was long and tiring. When there is constant daylight, you really appreciate how restful it is to have darkness at night. We also had to get used to many unfamiliar sights and smells, let alone complex base routines.

'As I savour a third cup of tea, I mentally tick off the few last-minute chores. We have to carefully chose and tested every single item, from polar tents and skis to fuel cans and Primus prickers, during a two-day 'shake down' journey and survival course. We made minor changes to some of our 20-day ration boxes, allowing for individual likes and dislikes. Last night we lashed everything down firmly under canvas covers on the sledges. All we have to do now is preheat the engines and dig the sledges out of the drifts left by the tail end of the blizzard last night.

'Our face masks, covering nose and cheeks, and goggles, have to be wriggled into position before we pull on our cumbersome driving gauntlets. The sledge runners are frozen to the snow so we have to heave the sledges sideways to free them before the rubber- tracked toboggans can jerk them away. The base photographer records us leaving, but it is too cold for a

Each of us has a number of set jobs to do before we can relax. Vehicles need to be fuelled and checked for loose bolts, then tucked under tarpaulins for the night. The sledges have to be tensioned between ice screws so they cannot blow away if the wind gets up.

'While the other three pitch the two polar tents and fasten them to the concrete-hard sea ice with storm guys and ice screws, I crawl inside to arrange the foam mattresses and double down sleeping bags on either side. A little kitchen is soon organised between the beds in one tent. Being careful not to spill any kerosene on my fingers I fill the Primuses then sort out food for tonight and tomorrow morning. Before long, circles of salami are sizzling in the pan and chips of ice are crackling away in a pot on the other stove, for the first of many brews of tea. The radio aerial that the others

A blizzard mask protects the wearer's face from the worst effects of cold while travelling. Small patches of frostbite were common in the early days of Antarctic exploration, and even modern travellers must always be on the look out for areas of white, frozen skin on their own, and their companions', faces.

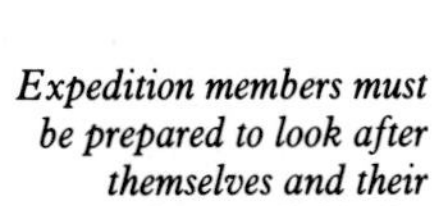

A field party about to set off after a break. The snowmobiles travel across a good surface at about 30 km/h (19 mph).

Expedition members must be prepared to look after themselves and their vehicles on a field trip.

pick up radio batteries from the Post Office technician, and do a final check to see that aerial, radio and batteries are working properly. A box of meteorological instruments has to be collected from the laboratory as we will be keeping records every day. One of us must sign for medical drugs at the tiny first aid room. Then there are stainless steel Thermoses to be heated and filled with hot sweet tea for the journey.

'We all attend a briefing session with the base leader, double checking our radio schedule and the dotted lines on our maps, and then we say goodbye. After adjusting windproofs and double-skin driving goggles in the warmth of the garage, I wander down to our vehicles and sledges parked near the edge of the sea ice — checking before I slam the door behind me to see there is no snow jammed in the hinges.' The carpenter has enough to do without repairing another split door.

'All our basic camping and sledging gear has been meticulously overhauled by the dog handler during the long dark winter months. We flag-waving send-off, and besides, everyone else is busy getting ready for the next science party to arrive.

'How exciting to be sledging again! Riding side-saddle on the front toboggan I nudge its vee-shaped nose ski over fluted ribbons of sastrugi. You have to drive the toboggans with some care so that super-cooled metal springs and bolts do not snap as we jolt over the bone-jarring frozen ocean. We will take it in turns to lie on top of the loaded sledges — that's good fun too because the wooden parts of the sledges are held together by leather and cord lashings, no screws, so although they look flimsy they can twist and turn as the three-metre (10-ft) long plastic-shod runners ride over each piece of broken ice.

'We push west across the ice covering McMurdo Sound towards the Royal Society Range and its majestic 4000-metre (13000-ft) peaks. We are keen to have an easy first day to enable us to settle into sledging and camping routines, so we stop at 5 pm in the lee of a stranded iceberg on the far side of the sound.

have strung out is lowered through the ventilator tube at the apex of the tent, and I plug it into the set perched on top of the kitchen box.

'The others elbow their way inside through the tunnel entrance of the double-skin tent, clicking their heels together fastidiously to make sure that no snow is brought inside. We all clip our goggles, mitts and face masks to the apex of the tent where they will dry quickly in the warm air. Later on we will take them, and our inner boots, into our sleeping bags for the night.

'At precisely 6 pm we switch on the radio and hear: "Event 15, Event 15, this is Scott base. How copy? Over."

'Soon we have steaming mugs of tea warming our fingers and faces, and we snuggle down into our bags to dream of another magical polar summer ahead.'

One of the Dornier Super Wals moored against the ice edge. The expedition concentrated on aerial surveys and few landings were made.

HITLER'S POLAR AMBITIONS

Germany plans to annex an Antarctic territory

In 1938 aerial photography of the Antarctic continent was still in its infancy. Although individual photographs had been taken from balloons and some aeroplanes, the pictures we have today of Mars and Saturn are far more complete and detailed than those of the southernmost reaches of our own planet before World War II.

The simple explanation is that there were no airfields in the Antarctic or close by, from where planes could take off for extended photographic missions. The impetus for an expedition came ostensibly from Germany's growing desire to rebuild and enlarge her whaling fleet of seven whalers (mostly chartered) and 50 hunting boats. But more information about the Antarctic was needed, enlarging the material gathered by Erich von Drygalski and Wilhelm Filchner. All the experts agreed that a conventional expedition using the traditional dog sledging method would last far too long and be too costly. So on 9 May 1938 Reichsfeldmarschall Hermann Göring, chief of the Luftwaffe, was asked to grant the use of a so-called 'aeroplane mothership' to a proposed Antarctic expedition. He readily agreed, appointing 60-year-old Captain Alfred Ritscher head of the venture.

Technical preparation began in September of that year. At the time Germany had no aircraft carriers. Instead, the airline Lufthansa used aeroplane motherships as floating supply bases for their trans-Atlantic traffic. Hydroplanes, carrying mainly mail between Africa and South America, landed near the ships to refuel. Hauled on deck by a crane, they were relaunched by catapult.

Lufthansa agreed to lend the expedition its ship *Schwabenland*, and the ship's two hydroplanes *Boreas* and *Passat*, 10-tonne Dornier Super Wals. They were pusher-propeller aircraft, and each carried a pilot, a navigator, mechanic and photographer. The captains, Rudolf Wahr and Richardheinrich Schirmacher, were also on loan from Lufthansa. The *Schwabenland,* 8488 tonnes, was almost 143 metres (468 ft) long, with a maximum width of 18 metres (59 ft). Her top speed was 11 knots (20 km/h; 12 mph), and her main feature was a powerful catapult, which could accelerate a load of up to 14 tonnes to a take-off speed of 150 km/h (93 mph).

Captain Alfred Ritscher was nearly 60 when Göring chose him to lead the expedition to Antarctica. He had some experience in the Arctic from 1912 to 1913.

Lufthansa — and of course Göring — were especially interested in finding out how aeroplane engines, fuel pumps and oil pumps would operate at Antarctic temperatures. (Such temperatures were encountered only two years later over the battlefields of Russia.)

The expedition aroused the hostility of Norway which regarded the *Schwabenland's* area of operations – Queen Maud Land — as her territory. On 14 January 1939 a formal proclamation was issued by King Haakon of Norway claiming the area between 20°W and 45°E. This Norwegian claim was recognised by Australia, Britain, France and New Zealand, but was ignored by the Germans.

Hitler's Germany never had recognised the 'sector theory' of Antarctica. Under that, the southernmost nations of the world, and those conducting active research in the south polar regions, could lay claim to certain parts of the Antarctic continent. German lawyers had another theory (see box).

On 17 December 1938 the *Schwabenland* left the port of Hamburg, her crew already getting a taste of bitter polar weather as the temperature dropped to −17°C (1°F), something very unusual for that rainy city. A little more than a month later the ship left the island of Bouvetøya and proceeded south along longitude 3°24′E, making contact with the vessels of the German whaling fleet. Finally, on 20 January 1939, near the edge of the Antarctic pack ice, the *Schwabenland* dropped anchor at 69°14′S, 4°30′W. The same day, the first photographic reconnaissance mission was flown.

'On each flight', Ritscher wrote, 'under the most favourable conditions we could probably photograph an area of roughly 200 000 sq km [77 200 sq miles] from an altitude of 3000 metres [10 000 ft]'. The weather was not always favourable, of course. On average, the area of terrain covered daily was considerably smaller but except for a few minor technical problems, the planes' engines and the camera equipment held up splendidly.

'We penetrated southward up to 600 kilometres [370 miles], but then had to turn back because inland altitudes of 400 metres [1300 ft] hindered further progress', Ritscher reported. 'The camera was purring away almost without interruption.' One of the pilots later recalled in an interview with the German press: 'But always we see only ice, ice, ice. Then, suddenly, like needles sticking out of it, mountains and peaks become visible, shining in a strange, rust-brown colour.'

The Lufthansa crews took a great number of colour photographs. After seven long-distance missions the flying period ended on 23 January when they had recorded six reels of film 360 metres (1181 ft) long, containing 1800 - 18 x 18 cm (7 x 7 in) frames. They showed an area of 250 000 sq km (96 500 sq miles). Most of the photographs cover the land between 11°W and 19°E, the borders 'staked out' by aluminium darts thrown from the planes.

Later, in Germany, some detailed maps were produced based on the *Schwabenland* photographs. They showed new mountains, including a circular chain of high peaks extending from 71°S to 73°S. The most prominent peaks were named after German explorers such

The aircraft were launched by catapult from the Schwabenland, *and had to be accelerated to 150 km/h (93 mph) before they could become airborne. A crane on the ship lifted the aircraft back aboard after they landed on the sea.*

An expedition member records their surroundings on film. Few landings were made, and the consequent lack of ground control made the expedition's elaborate maps useless.

as Alexander von Humboldt, Georg von Neumayer, Erich von Drygalski and Wilhelm Filchner. Unfortunately, a lack of ground control made it impossible to fix the latitude and longitude of the photographs accurately, and most of the work was wasted.

Three landings were made on the ice edge. On 29 January a party aboard the *Passat* flew to a small bay at about 69°55′S and 1°9′W. Almost five hours were spent ashore taking photographs and surveying after the pilot, Rudolf Wahr, had planted the swastika. A second landing, from the *Boreas*, was made on 30 January at about 70°18′S and 4°22′E. This time, however, the ice began to move and bergs threatened to obstruct the stretch of water from which they were to take off, so the expedition had to be curtailed. The following day the *Boreas* landed a fishing biology student, Erich Bastlen, about 515 kilometres (320 miles) east of the previous day's landing point. Here they rounded up five emperor penguins and returned them to the ship. A final attempt to land a large party by boat on 5 February almost met with disaster when an approaching storm made navigation in the ice-filled waters very hazardous. The attempt was called off after one man was nearly drowned.

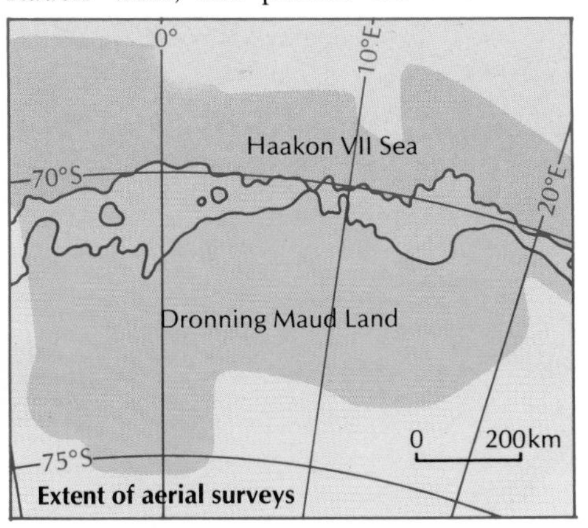

On 1 March the *Schwabenland*, her mission successfully completed, reached Cape Town and arrived back in Hamburg on 10 April 1939. Congratulatory telegrams from Hitler and Göring were the first messages brought aboard, and the surveyed area was named Neuschwabenland.

A second expedition was planned, but World War II prevented it. Ritscher died in 1963, and only in 1981 was another German station — this time West German — erected in the Antarctic.

STAKING A CLAIM

German experts in international law considered that to lay claim to new territory one had to do it physically, by occupation, or at least symbolically, for example by staking it out as gold diggers had done in the old American West.

'So one of the first things', Ritscher wrote in his expedition report, 'was to prepare aluminium darts each one and a half metres [5 ft] long, their tails engraved with the national flag [the swastika]. We intended to drop these darts every 20 to 30 kilometres [12 to 18 miles] along our flight paths.' Tests on alpine glaciers had shown that when thrown from a plane the darts penetrated at least 30 cm (12 in), even into solid ice. The shaft stuck out as a marker.

A drawing of one of the darts dropped from the planes.

Operation Highjump

Bringing the technology of war to the Antarctic

In 1946 the United States Navy mounted the largest Antarctic expedition ever attempted. It involved 13 ships, 23 aircraft and over 4700 men. Planned primarily as a testing and training exercise for the Navy, it was also aimed at establishing a United States presence in Antarctica.

Overall command of the operation was given to Richard Byrd, who was by then the most experienced Antarctic explorer alive. The expedition's 13 ships — known as Task Force 68 — were under the command of Rear Admiral Richard Cruzen.

The expedition was divided into three groups. The Central Group with two ice-breakers, two supply ships, a communications ship and a submarine were to penetrate the pack ice and establish a base at the Bay of Whales in the Ross Sea. From there they were to carry out aerial surveys of the interior of the continent. Two other groups, each consisting of a seaplane tender, a tanker, a destroyer and three Martin Mariner seaplanes, were to sail respectively east and west around the continent carrying out surveys.

Full use was to be made of equipment and techniques developed during World War II such as a radar-equipped fire control director which was to be used as a range finder, and a magnetic submarine detector which was to serve as an airborne magnetometer to study the nature of the rocks beneath the plane.

Ships of the Central Group entered the Ross Sea pack ice on New Year's Eve 1946. Aerial surveys seemed to indicate that the pack was not particularly heavy that year, but this proved not to be the case. For two weeks the expedition wrestled with the worst ice seen since Ross first visited the area in 1841. On one occasion the 6660-tonne icebreaker *Northwind* had to batter its way through a wall of ice nine metres (30 ft) thick. That task took an hour, although the icebreaker could normally push through one-metre (3-ft) thick ice with no difficulty at a speed of 18 km/h (11 mph).

The ice, however, presented far more problems for the four following ships. Their thin 13-mm (0.5-in) steel hulls were soon dented as the ice prised apart by the icebreaker threatened to close in on them. Finally, on 14 January 1947, the ships emerged into clear water and the next day arrived at the Bay of Whales.

For three days *Northwind* worked smashing up an estimated 15 million tonnes of ice in the bay so that the ships could unload. The site of Little America III, abandoned in 1941, was soon located, although it had moved 2.4 kilometres (1.5 miles) with the ice shelf in the intervening six years.

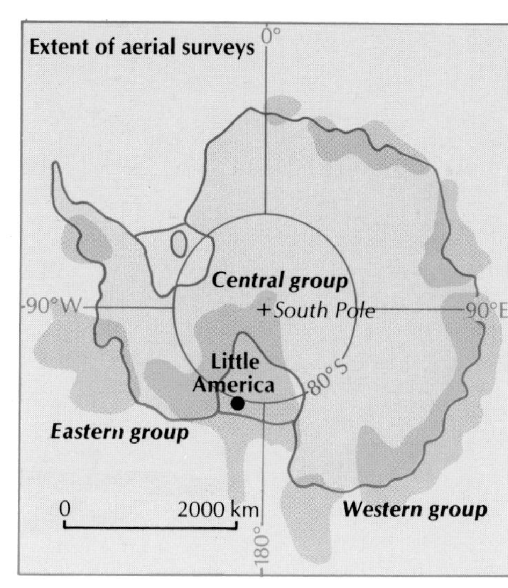

The new base, a temporary camp of tents to house 300 men, was set up about 3.2 kilometres (2 miles) north of Little America III. Nearby a landing strip was built to take the six twin-engined R4D aircraft (Navy versions of the Douglas DC-3).

The aircraft, and Byrd, were aboard the aircraft carrier *Philippine Sea* which reached the edge of the pack ice late in January. From here they were to fly to Little America IV.

There were, however, a number of uncertainties about this phase of the operation.

Rear Admiral Richard Byrd (centre) was Officer-in-Charge of Operation Highjump. He is flanked by (right) his son R.E. Byrd and Rear Admiral Cruzen, who was in command of Task Force 68.

The icebreaker Northwind *leading the Central Group through the Ross Sea. The ships had to pass through 960 km (600 miles) of ice.*

The submarine* Sennet *had to be towed out of the pack. Drifting ice was threatening to damage her, and she could not keep up with the other ships in the Central Group convoy.

A tent city soon sprang up on the shores of the Bay of Whales, about 2.4 km (1.5 miles) from the spot where the ships were moored. Fifty-four pyramid tents, each with a wooden floor, housed the men at the base.

Inside the abandoned base Little America III the men found 'a crystal-walled palace throne room hung with glittering chandeliers'. Remains were found of all Byrd's old bases despite the snow which was accumulating at a rate of about a metre a year. Even the radio towers of Little America I, built in 1929, were still visible. Originally 20 metres (65 ft) high, now only 5.5 metres (18 ft) showed above the surface.

Firstly, these were the largest planes ever to have taken off from an aircraft carrier. Their long wingspan meant that they could only use the runway forward of the superstructure that rises above the carrier's flight deck, cutting the length available for take off from 256 metres (840 ft) to only 122 metres (400 ft). The aeroplanes usually needed a runway 760 metres (2500 ft) long, and there had been no time to make a trial flight from the carrier before the expedition left America. The second problem concerned landing and taking off at Little America. No one was sure if the heavy aeroplanes could land on a snow and ice runway or, once down, if they could take off again.

Byrd himself was aboard the first of the planes to take off on 29 January. JATO bottles (rocket propulsion tubes) had been attached to the side of the aircraft and the carrier was manoeuvred for a 56 km/h (35 mph) run to help the planes get airborne. 'From the vibration of the great carrier', wrote Byrd, 'I knew when the captain had got the ship up to about 30 knots (56 km/h; 35 mph) and it was time to take off. We seemed to creep along the deck at first and it looked as if we would never make it . . . But when our four JATO bottles went off along the sides of the plane with a terrific, deafening noise I could see the deck fall away. I knew we had made it.'

A few hours later all six aeroplanes were safely down at Little America and Byrd was poised to undertake an intensive series of flights. In the next four weeks the planes spent 220 hours in the air, flying a total of 36530 kilometres (22700 miles). Hundreds of thousands of square kilometres were explored, and at least three major mountain ranges discovered. Each plane was equipped with five cameras, three of which photographed a swath of land 113 kilometres (70 miles wide) while the others recorded information on time and altitude. Under ideal conditions about 260000 sq kilometres (100000 sq miles) of land could be photographed in one mission.

On 15 February two aircraft made the expedition's longest flight to a point about 160 kilometres (100 miles) beyond the South Pole. Byrd was aboard the leading aircraft on what was to be his second flight over the pole. On this occasion there was none of the nail-biting anxiety that there had been on his 1929 flight (see p242), when there had been doubts about whether or not the plane could gain enough altitude to reach the polar plateau. There were, however, other problems with altitude and cold. Byrd wrote: 'We had no oxygen equipment. The effects of anoxia soon became apparent in the uncoordinated speech, staggering gait, and happy-go-lucky attitude of some members of the crew.'

While most of the Central Group's operations were concentrated on aerial exploration, a tractor party did visit the Rockefeller Mountains 480 kilometres (300 miles) southeast of the base, to set up a weather outpost and emergency fuel dump.

On 22 February the icebreaker *Burton Island* arrived at the Bay of Whales to evacuate the party. All the planes, stores and equipment were secured for possible future use, and the following day the men sailed from Antarctic waters, bound for New Zealand.

In the meantime, the Eastern and Western Groups had been making their way steadily around the Antarctic coast, the aircraft making flights as the weather permitted. On 11 February a flight from the western group made what became the most widely publicised discovery of Operation Highjump — a snow-free oasis in the Bunger Hills. This barren patch of snow-free rock, dotted with lakes, covers an area of over 260 sq kilometres (100 sq miles). Some of the lakes were large enough for a landing, and a few days later a party visited the area to make a preliminary examination. The discovery caused a minor international sensation after a Navy press release spoke of a 'Shangri-la' and reported, erroneously, that vegetation had been seen.

Finally, with the weather worsening, the Western Group turned for home on 1 March 1947, to be followed three days later by the Eastern Group.

The expedition met all its major objectives. Icebreakers and helicopters had been used for the first time in Antarctica. Nearly 3.9 million sq kilometres (1.5 million sq miles) of Antarctica had been sighted. Over 70000 aerial photographs had been taken covering 60 per cent of the Antarctic coastline — 25 per cent having been seen for the first time.

OPERATION WINDMILL

After the return of Operation Highjump to the United States it was found to be impossible to construct maps from the expedition's 70000 aerial photographs because there were no accurate ground control points. Some 30 prominent features were therefore selected and a new expedition, named Windmill, was planned to take survey parties to these points so that they could pinpoint their exact locations. Helicopters based on icebreakers were to be used as transport.

The icebreakers *Edisto* and *Burton Island* reached the pack ice on Christmas Day 1947 and headed for the Davis Sea and their first target points. In 23 days nine points along a 960-kilometre (600-mile) stretch of coast were surveyed, and a team was landed in the Bunger Hill, which it was hoped might provide a good site for a base.

After their success on the Wilkes Land Coast the ships set sail for Little America and the Ross Sea. However, it was already too late in the year and they were unable to survey any more of their target points.

LAST GREAT JOURNEY

A bold scheme to be first across Antarctica

The Commonwealth Trans-Antarctic expedition of 1955-58 was the first to tackle the crossing of the Antarctic continent since Shackleton had failed in the years between 1914-17, and the first to succeed in this gigantic venture.

The idea for the expedition came to explorer Vivian Fuchs while confined to his sleeping bag by a protracted blizzard on Alexander Island in December 1949. But the hugeness of the task, plus the scepticism of some experts and the vast expense involved, meant his idea lay fallow for some years. However, he had a stout ally in Sir James Wordie, who had been Ernest Shackleton's Chief of Scientific Staff, and in 1953 he asked Fuchs if he was still interested in seeing the project through. Fuchs said he was, and as he was working for the Falkland Islands Dependencies at the time, the Governor, Sir Miles Gifford, who was also involved in backing the expedition, asked him to draw up a plan.

What evolved on paper was a 3200-kilometre (2000-mile) journey from the head of the Weddell Sea to McMurdo Sound in the Ross Sea, via the South Pole. The expedition was to be supported by such modern aids as aircraft and Sno-cats, and would be split into two. Fuchs and his party would establish a base on the Weddell Sea, and the following summer would cross the continent. That same summer a second party would arrive at McMurdo Sound, set up a base and reconnoitre a route from the polar plateau back to the base, establishing depots for Fuchs.

Early in 1955 a general committee was established, Queen Elizabeth II became the expedition's patron, and the British Government announced a £100 000 grant towards its cost. This was soon followed by financial support from New Zealand, South Africa, and Australia, plus industrial companies, trusts, societies, and even schools. Later, the New Zealand Government assumed responsibility for the Ross Sea party which New Zealander Sir Edmund Hillary was appointed to lead.

The Canadian sealer, *Theron*, chartered to carry Fuchs' party to its base by the Weddell Sea, sailed on 14 November 1955. Aboard her, apart from the normal stores and equipment, were two aircraft, a Sno-cat, some specially adapted tractors, and 24 dogs. Even though *Theron* was built for working in Arctic waters she had a difficult time forging her way through the ice to the Weddell Sea.

'It is impossible to describe adequately this forceful butting of the ice', Fuchs recorded in his diary. 'The ship runs up through crowded brash forcing two or three foot [one metre] plates of ice many yards in extent, beneath the keel, or up-ending them alongside the hull. Then with a shuddering bump the bows rise on a floe — up and up we seem to go — when suddenly she subsides and cracks go shooting across the ice. Other times she hangs there with her bows up and we go astern to try once more. Over and over again the process is repeated, gradually breaking away the obstruction, while the ship jars, twists and shudders till one feels she will fall apart.'

Eventually, with the help of air reconnaissance, a way was found through the ice to Vahsel Bay where Shackleton base was to be set up. Initially, Fuchs had planned to stay with the wintering party until 14 February, by which time a start would have been made to laying the foundation of the advance party's main hut. But a fierce blizzard blew in early February, and it soon became obvious that if *Theron* did not sail immediately she would be trapped for the winter.

The eight men who watched her sail away were now surrounded by 300 tonnes of stores which had to be shifted to the base site. They made the huge Sno-cat crate their winter home, and began the laborious task of shifting the stores off the sea ice. They were hindered first by a series of mechanical breakdowns and

Safe in a small dock cut in the sea ice, the Magga Dan *waits while stores are unloaded. This spot in Vahsel Bay was not far from the site of Wilhelm Filchner's ill-fated base* *(see p202)**. The black specks in the distance are the buildings of Shackleton base where the advance party spent the winter of 1956.*

MV Theron *beside the ice at Halley Bay in January 1956. If the Weddell Sea pack ice had been impenetrable, the expedition planned to use this site for their base, although it added 320 km (200 miles) to the trans-Antarctic journey.*

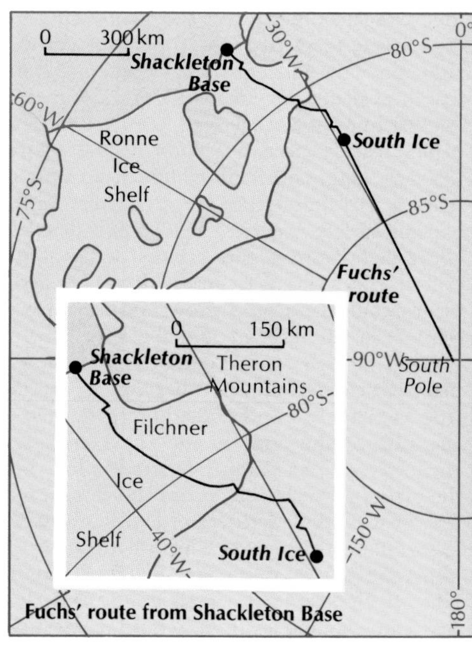

then by a fierce storm which raged for days and kept them confined to their crate. When they were eventually able to emerge they found that the ice on which the remainder of the stores were still stacked had disintegrated. Lost was a Ferguson tractor, all the coal, the timber for a workshop, a boat, and various engineering stores. Luckily all the food had already been moved up to the base site, but 300 drums of fuel had been swept away, which meant strict fuel economy.

Despite blizzards and the extreme cold, work continued on the erection of the permanent hut. On 2 August the lowest temperature, −53°C (−63°F), was recorded, but not long afterwards the first glimmer of daylight was seen on the horizon.

Meanwhile, Fuchs and his party in London were organising the stores and men necessary for the next stage of the expedition. On 15 November 1956 Fuchs sailed on *Magga Dan*, which reached Vahsel Bay on 13 January 1957.

One of Fuchs' priorities was to establish a depot well to the south of Shackleton base for the main transcontinental party. After some extensive aerial reconnaissance a site for South Ice, as the depot came to be called, was chosen.

As equipment and food were airfreighted into South Ice, additional air reconnaissance was undertaken to find the best route to the depot from Shackleton base. By 22 February the hut at the depot was ready and a month later the three members of the wintering party were installed.

Three of the Ross Sea party, including Sir Edmund Hillary, had accompanied Fuchs in *Theron* during the Antarctic summer of 1955-56, and on their return to New Zealand their plans for establishing a base at McMurdo Sound, to be called Scott base, were pushed

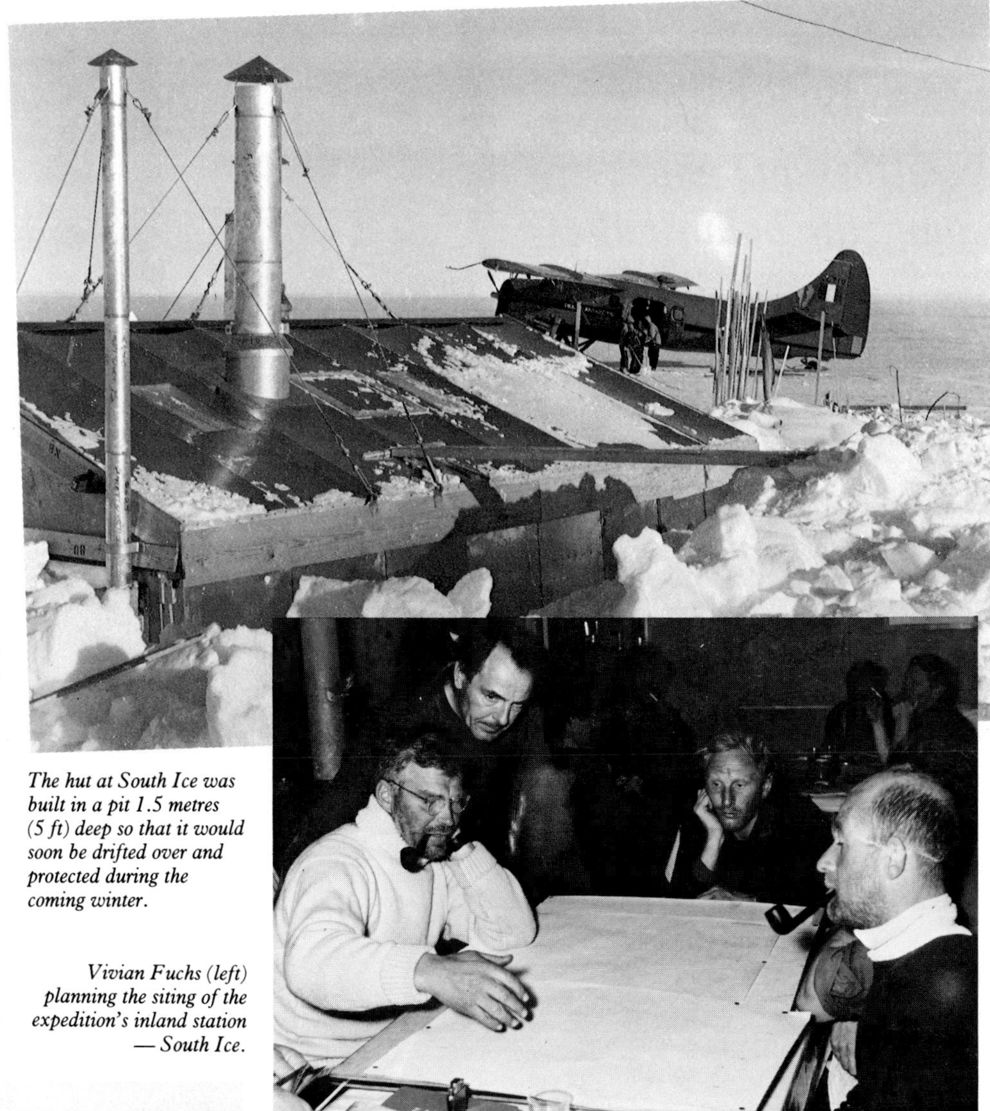

The hut at South Ice was built in a pit 1.5 metres (5 ft) deep so that it would soon be drifted over and protected during the coming winter.

Vivian Fuchs (left) planning the siting of the expedition's inland station — South Ice.

Hillary's tractor train ready to set off on its journey south. The men lived in a small plywood hut — the caboose — which was towed on a sledge behind one of the tractors. Sleeping space for four men and a lot of equipment was crammed into a space just 1.2 x 3.6 metres (4 x 11 ft).

ahead. The party — expanded to include five scientists who would undertake the research program of the International Geophysical Year — had grown from its original concept of being merely a support party for Fuchs into being New Zealand's first major effort to explore its own Ross Dependency.

While Hillary had been aboard *Theron* three of his party had gone to the Ross Sea to reconnoitre a suitable site for the base at McMurdo Sound. A tight budget meant that all field work would have to be undertaken by dog teams supported by two aircraft. However, the expedition was lent five tractors and two Weasels for unloading and transporting stores from the expedition ship, the 900-tonne *Endeavour*, to the base site.

Endeavour left New Zealand on 21 December 1956 and arrived at McMurdo Sound on 3 January 1957. An air reconnaissance convinced Hillary that Pram Point on Ross Island made a better site for Scott base than the one originally chosen. This, plus the fact that a dog team soon found that using the Ferrar Glacier as an outlet to the polar plateau was impractical, meant that some major rethinking had to be done. Then the dog teams sent out to explore the possibility of using the Skelton Glacier as a means of reaching the polar plateau had to return because of illness. With time running short, Hillary decided he must land on the glacier himself with a view to airfreighting the dog teams to the foot of it. This proved to be a tricky undertaking.

'From the air the snow looked excellent and we came down low several times to examine it', Hillary wrote. 'Finally John [Claydon] decided to land and we tightened our safety belts . . . I peered out of the window as the snow came smoothly up towards us. When we were almost touching, our angle of vision changed and I was aghast to realise that the surface, which had appeared so smooth from above, was in fact liberally peppered with sastrugi — some of them several feet high.

'We touched with a tremendous crash — the snow was as hard as iron — and crash followed crash as we lurched from one bump to the next and rocked violently around in our seats. It really seemed as if we were for it! John had seen the danger and reacted immediately. He swept the throttle open and tried to lift the plane off once more. The propeller clawed at the air, there were a couple more resounding crashes, and then, to our immense relief, we floated up to safety.'

Eventually, a better landing place was found and four members of the expedition, along with 18 dogs and all the necessary equipment, were airfreighted to the foot of the Skelton Glacier, and a depot was established. This party then started up the glacier.

At the same time, another team set off from Scott base to pioneer the route from the base to the Skelton depot. Later, a second depot was established by air at the top of the Skelton Glacier on the polar plateau itself. Hillary now had two well-stocked depots 290 kilometres (180 miles) and 466 kilometres (290 miles) from his base. The first successful crossing of Antarctica was poised to begin.

SUCCESSFUL CROSSING

Tractors and Sno-cats tame the polar wastes

On 10 September 1957 Sir Edmund Hillary left Scott base with three of the adapted tractors, one Weasel and four sledges to investigate the Ferrar Glacier. Various other sledge journeys were also undertaken that month and by the end of it both men and dogs were in peak condition for the main trip southwards to pioneer the route for Vivian Fuchs.

Trailing plumes of exhaust smoke, the vehicles of the crossing party inch their way across a seemingly limitless plain of snow and ice on their way to the South Pole. Giant sastrugi drastically slowed their progress.

One of the Sno-cats poised over a huge crevasse. It took five hours and the combined efforts of five vehicles to drag it back to firm ground. A cable had to be attached to the front to prevent it falling vertically.

Convinced now that the Skelton Glacier was the best route, Hillary split up his men into three teams. A northern sledge party would approach the polar plateau via the Mackay Glacier; a party of three with dog sledges were to be flown to the Skelton depot; and Hillary and three others would set off in three tractors and the Weasel from Scott base to cover the route Fuchs would be taking once he reached the South Pole.

The northern party started on 4 October and Hillary's party 10 days later. Skelton depot was reached on 20 October. Two days were spent repairing the Weasel and then Hillary's party, along with the dog team that had been flown in, started up the glacier, and by 28 October they had reached 1520 metres (5000 ft). The next day one of their aircraft dropped them their mail and the pilot informed Hillary that he had just airfreighted in two men and their dogs to the Plateau depot, which was reached by Hillary on 31 October.

Hillary knew they were now in a strong position, for they had with them all the fuel and food necessary to establish the next depot for Fuchs and his men. More fuel and stores were flown in during the next few days, so that both parties found themselves overloaded when they started southwards on 8 November.

The weather was bad, the terrain became increasingly difficult, and Hillary could only cover 56 kilometres (35 miles) the first week. The vehicles were constantly plagued by mechanical problems and consumed large quantities of fuel, but just as Hillary thought the whole journey must come to an ignominious end the going improved. On 25 November they reached an area suitable for aircraft to land on and Hillary decided this was where they would place the next depot, called simply Depot 480. Their position was 79°51′S, 148°E, 338 kilometres (210 miles) from Plateau depot.

Two members of the expedition set off on 1 December with light loads to reconnoitre the route to the likely site of the last depot, while other teams went off to undertake more survey work. On 6 December the last stores for Depot 480 were flown in and Hillary started south once more.

The vehicle party — towing not only sledges but a kind of caravan on skis which they called their 'caboose' — drove for long hours during the first two days and succeeded in covering 150 kilometres (93 miles). Shortly afterwards the Weasel broke down and its load had to be transferred to the three tractors. The next 145 kilometres (90 miles) proved to be extremely difficult, but by 15 December the site for the final depot, Depot 700, was reached, and by 20 December it had been fully stocked from the air.

Hillary's task was now officially over, but he was only 800 kilometres (500 miles) from the South Pole, three of his vehicles were still in working order, and he had sufficient fuel. He had already communicated his thoughts about carrying on to the pole to his committee in New Zealand; and had arranged with Admiral Dufek in charge of the US base on Ross Island to pick him up at the South Pole and fly him and his team back to Scott base if he did decide to reach it.

Both the committee and Fuchs were reluctant for Hillary to continue. But Hillary could see no reason why he should not reconnoitre the rest of the route to the pole for the British team, especially as it seemed doubtful that Fuchs, badly delayed by appalling terrain, would be able to achieve his objective that summer without considerably increasing his average speed. The New Zealander therefore decided to press on.

For several days the going was good and by 30 December the three tractors were less than 320 kilometres (200 miles) from their objective. But the increasing altitude — they were now at 3050 metres (10000 feet) — and then some very bad terrain reduced both their efficiency and their precious stock of fuel.

On 2 January Hillary was 113 kilometres (70 miles) from the pole with only 819 litres (180 gallons) of fuel left, just enough provided he made no navigational error. For 24 hours they drove south without stopping until at 8 pm on 3 January they saw the flags that marked the South Pole. They camped the night there and then drove to the nearby American South Pole station. When they arrived he had exactly 91 litres (20 gallons) of fuel left.

'I was swept into a confusion of congratulations, photographs, and questions, and then led off by friendly hands towards the warmth and fresh food of the Pole Station', he wrote. 'But before I descended underground I took a last glance at our tractor train — the three farm tractors, tilted over like hip-shot horses, looked lonely and neglected like broken toys cast aside after playtime; the caboose . . . now seemed more like a horse-box than ever; and the two sledges had only the meagre load of a half-full drum of fuel. Yes! There was no doubt about it — our tractor train was a bit of a laugh! But despite appearances, our Fergusons had brought us over 1250 miles [2000 km] of snow and ice, crevasse and sastrugi, soft snow and blizzard to be the first vehicles to drive to the South Pole.'

Meanwhile, Fuchs and his party were hav-

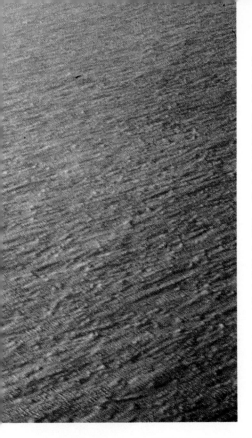

ing a difficult time moving south from their base. Extreme conditions delayed the relief of the men at South Ice. Eventually a relief team was flown in there on 8 October and on the same day a vehicle party left Shackleton base to reconnoitre the route to it. A few days later two dog teams were flown to the Shackleton Range. Their objectives were to find a route up the western ice wall; to survey the eastern end of the range; and to find the best area for geological work to be carried out.

The dog teams had no great difficulties in pursuing their missions, but the vehicle team, led by Fuchs, soon ran into an area full of crevasses. Fuchs decided the only safe way to proceed was with the help of air reconnaissance. This showed that they had to withdraw to the 80-kilometre (50-mile) depot and then strike west for seven kilometres (four miles) before heading south again.

'We had now to strike camp', Fuchs wrote, 'turn the sledges round, rope the vehicles together ... and retire to the depot. Being encompassed on all sides by crevasses made this a long and laborious task, involving endless probing of the surface to establish safe areas where the vehicles had sufficient room to manoeuvre. At last ... we began our first attempt at driving the vehicles roped together like climbers on a mountain.'

The technique of driving roped together and of probing the route ahead proved to be a slow business and South Ice was only reached on 13 November. Two days later Fuchs was flown back to Shackleton base and on 24 November, 10 days later than planned, he set off once more with the main party which was to make the transcontinental crossing. They reached South Ice on 21 December after a second, hardly less hazardous journey.

After a short rest the four Sno-cats, three Weasels, and the Muskeg tractor started for the South Pole on Christmas evening, while ahead of them two dog teams pioneered the route they were to follow.

'It was impossible to go round the high ice-hard ridges, for they formed a great field that extended out of sight in all directions,' wrote Fuchs. 'The best that could be done was for each driver to judge the course for his own particular type of vehicle ... Sometimes, when there was no easier way, vehicles and sledges had very deliberately to be driven at a speed of half a mile an hour [0.8 km/h] or less over vertical drops.'

The appalling conditions caused mechanical problems and three of the vehicles were abandoned. But Fuchs pressed on, and on 18 January he camped for the night at 89°37'S, and then the next day drove triumphantly to the South Pole where he was greeted by Admiral Dufek, Hillary and a crowd of over 30 other people from Amundsen-Scott station.

On 24 January Fuchs and his party started out again in what was now a race to reach Scott base before winter closed in. They reached Depot 700 on 7 February 1958, where Hillary joined the party. The Plateau depot was reached on 23 February, after some difficult ground had been covered without mishap. Then came the long descent of the Skelton Glacier. The Skelton depot was reached in the early hours of 27 February but the party was soon pressing on to finish the last lap of the transcontinental journey.

On 1 March the longest run yet achieved — 120 kilometres (75 miles) — was recorded. Before starting out the next morning the Sno-cats were decorated with all available flags and at 2.03 in the afternoon Fuchs and his men arrived at Scott base. They had covered the 3472 kilometres (2158 miles) in 99 days at an average rate of 35 kilometres (22 miles) per day, and had completed a unique journey.

An historic meeting three kilometres (2 miles) from the South Pole on 19 January 1958. Vivian Fuchs (centre) arrived with the crossing party to be met by Sir Edmund Hillary (left) and Rear Admiral George Dufek, Officer-in-charge of Operation Deepfreeze.

Hillary in one of the three Fergusons. These modified farm tractors were fitted with rubber tracks to improve their grip, but were difficult to steer. The cramped cabins gave scant protection from the weather.

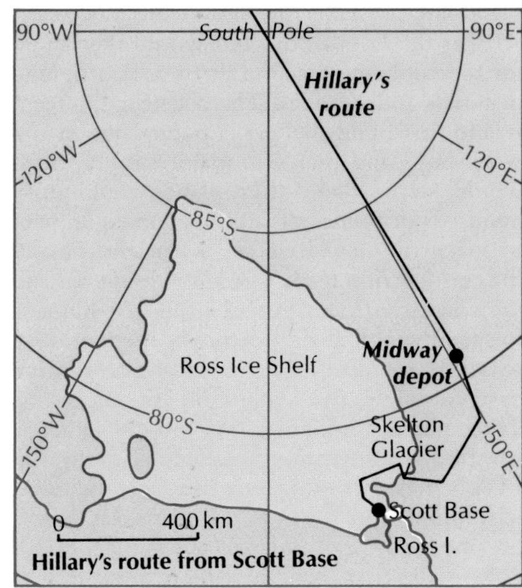

TECHNOLOGY CONQUERS THE POLE

Man returns after 44 years

The International Geophysical Year of 1957-58 closed one chapter of Antarctic history and opened a new one. Although still very much a frontier, the continent had now really been tamed. Men had braved the most inhospitable climate the world could offer, and survived in relative comfort. Technology had defeated the wilderness.

Operation Deepfreeze was planned in two stages. Deepfreeze I in the summer of 1955-56 was to establish an airfield at McMurdo Sound capable of taking the heavy aircraft that would ferry supplies to the South Pole base which was planned for the following year. A base was also to be built near Richard Byrd's old Little America bases in the Bay of Whales, and from there land parties were to try to establish an inland station in Marie Byrd Land, although this was not accomplished. Seven ships and 1800 men were involved in the first year's operation.

Deepfreeze II in 1956-57 was to see a permanent station built at the South Pole and the establishment of three other IGY stations — Byrd station in Marie Byrd Land, Wilkes station in Vincennes Bay and Ellsworth station on the Filchner Ice Shelf.

Although Admiral Richard Byrd was nominally in command of the expedition, effective control was given to Rear Admiral George Dufek. Byrd, then 68 years old, made his last trip to Antarctica in December 1955. He died two years later in 1957.

After the successful completion of phase one of Operation Deepfreeze, preparations were made for the most challenging task — the building of the South Pole station. Twelve ships and 3400 men were involved in the expedition's second year in Antarctica.

The plan was to first establish a support base near the Beardmore Glacier where supply planes returning from the pole could stop and refuel, and also as a base for emergency rescue missions if they were necessary. Once the supply base was established a test landing was to be made at the pole to see if the surface was suitable for the aircraft. If all went according to plan, two Skytrains would each land two teams of men at the pole. They would use a theodolite to make sure they were indeed exactly at the South Pole and would then radio for the Globemaster aircraft to start dropping materials and supplies. The construction team would first build shelters, a power station and workshops and then the major supply drops would start. Plane after plane would drop hundreds of tonnes of supplies and equipment to make the new base self sufficient. Finally the construction team would be flown out and the scientists flown in to be the first humans to spend winter at the bottom of the world.

On 31 October 1956, with the Beardmore base complete, the test flight got underway. Three planes took part: a Skymaster to act as pathfinder, a Skytrain to make the landing and a Globemaster to carry emergency supplies.

Admiral Dufek was aboard the Skytrain and became the eleventh man to stand at the South Pole — the first since the departure of Robert

Admiral Byrd (left) returned to Antarctica for the last time in December 1955. Standing next to him is Paul Siple, who was to be scientific leader at the pole station. Behind the group is the tip of the radio mast of Little America I, built in 1929. Twenty-six years of snowfall had all but buried the 20-metre (65-ft) metal towers.

The ships of Task Force 43 carve their way through the Ross Sea pack in December 1955. The convoy was made up of three icebreakers, three cargo ships and a tanker.

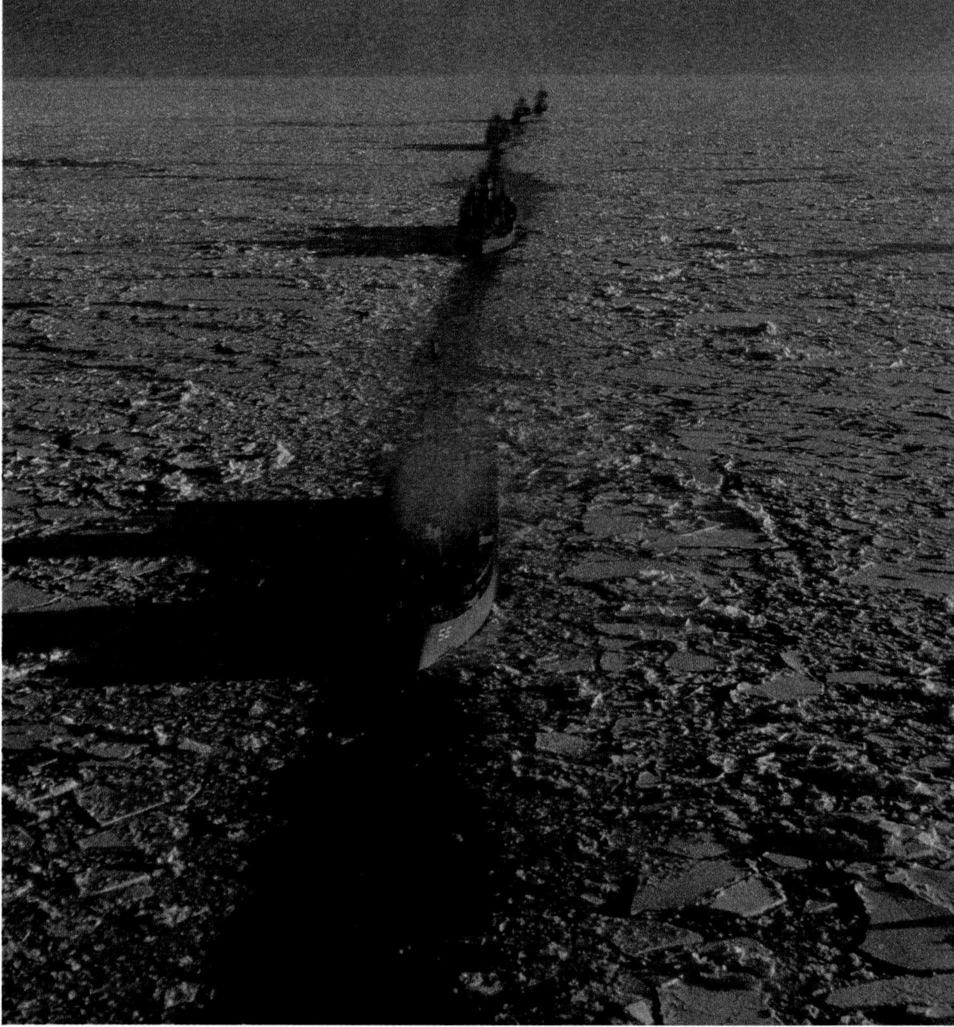

Tractors plough their way across the snow of Marie Byrd Land on their way from Little America V to establish Byrd station at 80°S, 120°W in December 1956. The reconnaissance party that preceded the tractor train took six weeks to complete the hazardous journey and used 2130 kg (4700 lb) of dynamite to expose numerous hidden crevasses.

The South Pole station — named Amundsen-Scott for the two explorers — almost complete. A party of 18 men were the first to winter at the pole in 1957.

The Stars and Stripes was the third flag to fly over the snowy wastes at the South Pole. On 31 October 1956, Admiral Dufek (right) stepped out of a US Navy plane and became the eleventh man to stand at the southern extremity of the earth.

Scott's expedition in January 1912. Dufek wrote of the landing: 'The plane came in smoothly, touched the surface, bumped a little — but I knew she was under control. She slowed to a stop, but Shinn kept his engines turning over. It was 8.34 pm, October 31.

'Strider opened the door and I stepped out onto the South Polar Plateau. It was like stepping out into a new world. We stood in the centre of a sea of snow and ice that extended beyond our vision. How deep the ice that lay beneath our feet was, no one as yet has determined. Bleak and desolate, it was a dead world, devoid of every vestige of life except us. The bitter cold struck me in the face and chest as if I had walked into a heavy swinging door. The temperature was −58° Fahrenheit [−50°C]; 90° below freezing. The wind was just a little under ten knots [18.5 km/h; 11.5 mph]. I looked at the surface. It was hard and rough as Hawkes had predicted. The hard *sastrugi* extended endlessly in a flat surface to the horizon in all directions.'

Over 760 tonnes of building materials, food, fuel and supplies were airdropped for the South Pole base — an immense task that took 84 supply flights. The station was completed and occupied by March 1957 and 18 men settled down for the 186-day polar night.

Chief of the scientific staff at the South Pole was Paul Siple, who, when 19 years old, had been with Richard Byrd on his first Antarctic expedition in 1929. On 18 September 1957, with the temperature at a record −74°C (−102°F) Siple, Bob Tuck, military leader at the South Pole base, and the expedition's dog, Bravo, took a walk around the world:

'Our route lay along a straight row of red flags set at 100-yard [91-metre] intervals. The surface over which we plodded was fantastically beautiful, but so rough that we stumbled as we clambered over the high and low sastrugi, the wind-hardened polar snowdrifts.

'All winter long the wind had blown with hardly a let up, and with gusts as strong as 54 miles per hour [87 km/h]. Sweeping across the featureless plateau, it sculpted the surface into fantastic shapes . . .

'Bravo was first to reach the red trail flag that marked the Pole. In fact, he had already made three trips around the world before we arrived . . . Not to be outdone, Jack and I also strolled around the world, at a 100-ft [30-metre] radius from the flag.'

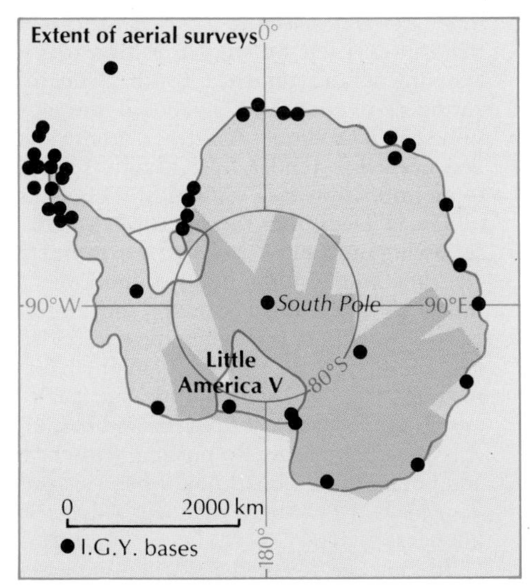

GENESIS OF THE INTERNATIONAL GEOPHYSICAL YEAR

The idea for the International Geophysical Year was originally put forward in 1950 by an American scientist Dr Lloyd Berkner. There had been two previous Polar Years, the first in 1882-83 and the second in 1932-33, although both had been mostly concerned with the Arctic. Berkner felt that a new polar year could take advantage of modern techniques for studying the earth's surface and atmosphere. The years 1957-58 were suggested because sunspot activity would be at a maximum then, and the data gathered would provide an interesting contrast with that gathered in 1932-33 when activity was at a minimum.

The idea was enthusiastically received and there followed a series of meetings at which details of the organisation were worked out. It was agreed that two areas would receive special attention — Antarctica and outer space.

Twelve countries became involved in the IGY Antarctic program — Argentina, Australia, Belgium, Chile, France, Great Britain, Japan, New Zealand, Norway, South Africa, the USA and the USSR. Over 40 stations were established on the Antarctic mainland and peninsula and a further 20 on various Antarctic and subantarctic islands. Scientists carried out a range of research programs that embraced all the geophysical sciences — such as glaciology, meteorology, geomagnetism and upper-air studies.

The most dramatic events of the year were undertaken by the largest participating countries. The United States established a permanent base at the South Pole (Amundsen-Scott); the Soviet Union established a base at the Pole of Inaccessibility — the furthest point from all Antarctic coasts; and Britain, in conjunction with New Zealand, made the first land crossing of the continent via the South Pole.

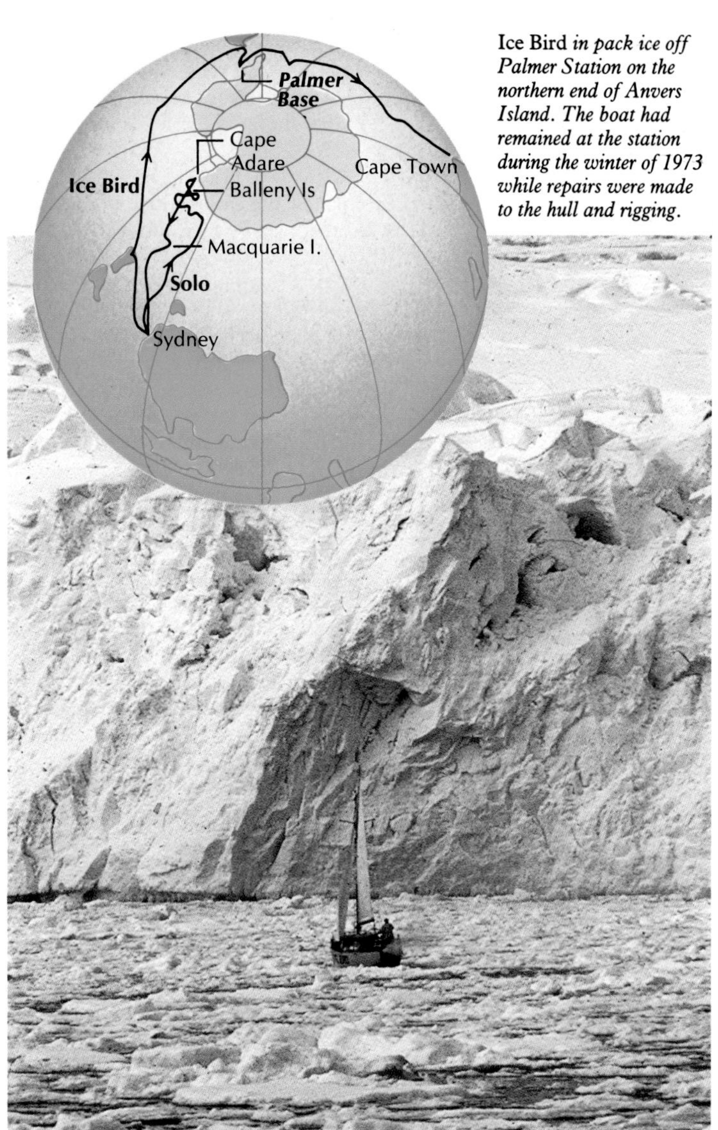

Ice Bird *in pack ice off Palmer Station on the northern end of Anvers Island. The boat had remained at the station during the winter of 1973 while repairs were made to the hull and rigging.*

Ice Bird *beset by pack ice. For four days the yacht was trapped in a swiftly moving field of ice that swept her bodily northwards with its drift.*

Lewis manoeuvres Ice Bird *through narrow leads in the ice as he attempts to free her from the pack. He gradually managed to work his way forward into clear water.*

LONELY ODYSSEY

Single-handed voyage to the wildest seas on earth

'No one had sailed alone to Antarctica. To reach it, relying entirely on my own resources, was to accept the ultimate challenge of the sea. The disadvantage was that the most accessible part lay 9650 kilometres (6000 miles) east of Australia.' Here David Lewis tells his own story.

'On 19 October 1972 I set out alone from Sydney in the 10-metre (33-ft) steel sloop *Ice Bird*. After a call at Stewart Island, New Zealand, I headed south-eastwards to the 60th parallel, where I turned due eastwards and ran before gale after gale, the cockpit and deck snow covered, the main fresh water tank frozen, the mast and spars sheathed in ice. Daylight was continuous.

'Disaster struck on 29 November. The bottom dropped right out of the glass heralding a storm of hurricane intensity — winds in the 167 km/h (104 mph) range and huge breaking white seas some 15 metres (50 ft) high. I cowered in the cabin trying to steer downwind with lines rigged to the tiller. Suddenly my whole world spun round as *Ice Bird* was picked up bodily, hurled upside-down and rolled right over. The 3 mm (0.125 in) steel of the cabin was split and dented, the forehatch torn off, the mast broken at the deck, the radio and self-steering gear destroyed. Water sloshed up to my knees as I extricated myself from the ruined stove and crunched along the cabin over broken instruments, wading among waterlogged charts, sleeping bag and clothing. I closed the forehatch as best I could and bailed for the next six hours, my gloves lost somewhere and forgotten.

'By the second day the wreckage had been cleared away and I belatedly realised that my hands were frostbitten. The situation was not encouraging. Four thousand kilometres (2500 miles) still to go to the Antarctic Peninsula and very close to the spot in my atlas as the furthest point from land in any ocean.

'I attempted to rig the spinnaker pole as a makeshift mast but it was too fragile to be of much use. There was another hurricane force gale and a second capsize a fortnight later. At length, by using the main sheet as a tackle, I succeeded in raising the short but sturdy boom as a jury mast and set sail again in earnest towards Antarctica. The pain in my hands was agonising. Living and sleeping in wet garments and sleeping bag was not very comfortable. Eventually, after two weary months, I sighted the 3050-metre (10 000-ft) peaks of the Antarctic Peninsula through the cloud wrack of a gale and three days later, on 29 January 1973, after many close shaves among bergs and skerries, brought up at the American Antarctic base Palmer. After a month spent on repairs with the help of the hospitable Americans the battered *Ice Bird* was hoisted out of the water and placed in a makeshift cradle for the winter. I left by ship to fulfil a magazine assignment and returned south again in the spring (November 1973) aboard the expedition ship *John Biscoe*. A further month's work was needed to render *Ice Bird* fully seaworthy — an impossible task without my kind hosts.

'On 11 December the pack ice cleared. The following morning I set sail towards the south. *Ice Bird* was within eight kilometres (five miles) of the British base in the Argentine Islands (now Faraday) when the pack closed in and she was beset. So she remained for the next four days. By this time the pack had swept bodily back northwards and had begun at last to open a little. By pushing from behind, and poling with a boathook when this proved dangerous, I gradually manoeuvred the yacht into clear water.

'*Ice Bird* and I visited an Argentine base and later a British one, both fully as hospitable as

Disaster nearly struck when Lewis got off the yacht to push her through the pack. The flow he was standing on split and the boat slid gently away from him. Eventually he managed to push his floe towards the boat and safety.

the Americans had been. I finally left the British base of Signy in the South Orkneys on 8 January 1974, to encounter a concentration of icebergs far beyond my previous experience. So great was the number that I could no longer sail during the nights that were now drawing in. I was forced to lower sail and hope that the bergs' drift and the yacht's would be the same. Fog and blinding snow showers completed the nightmare. To make matters worse, the new self-steering gear was smashed by drift ice.

'After three weeks we won clear of the bergs and the way ahead seemed set fair. On 24 February a hurricane-force gale rolled *Ice Bird* over, destroying the mast constructed at Palmer. Three weeks later she limped into Cape Town under the now familiar jury rig. Here my voyage ended.'

After the voyage of the *Ice Bird* David Lewis returned to Australia and helped to establish the Oceanic Research Foundation — an organisation designed to carry out independent research and exploration. One of the foundation's first ventures was a voyage aboard the yacht *Solo* to the Balleny Islands and Cape Adare. David Lewis takes up his story:

'This expedition grew out of the *Ice Bird* voyage, but was totally different in concept. The former was an adventure, the latter was motivated by our foundation's belief that Antarctica merited commitment by individuals as well as governments; that there was a place for low cost energy conserving expeditions able to update the techniques of the heroic age with modern technology. For the mountaineers, scuba divers, yachtsmen, naturalists and bird watchers who must constitute the next wave of explorers would need such knowledge.

'The 19-metre (62-ft) steel yacht *Solo* was a cramped platform for eight expeditioners. No more than six permanent bunks were available; every cranny was crammed with stores and equipment when we left Sydney on 15 December 1977. Lars Larsen, veteran of North Greenland and the Antarctic was second in command. Doctors Pieter Arriens and Peter Donaldson were geologist and botanist. Jack Pittar cared for our electronics. Fifty-nine-year-old Dorothy Smith and Fritz Schaumberg were the mountaineers. Ted Rayment was movie photographer and I was leader.

'Seventeen days under sail from Sydney found us in the pack. Two days later, due to my carelessness, *Solo* was holed by ice. The leak was small and easily patched with Neoprene and cement, but the blow to our morale and to my prestige as leader was severe. To their great credit the party agreed to continue.

'The steering compass was by now inoperable due to the proximity of the South Magnetic Pole and we were reduced to steering by the angle to the briefly glimpsed sun and by the lines of the swells. The radar, which Jack later mended, had broken down. It was with some relief, as we crossed the Antarctic Circle on 9 January that we heard Peter cry 'Land!' — Buckle Island in the Ballenys.

'A force 11 gale intervened before we saw land again. Fortunately the storm had driven the pack south off Sturge Island, the largest and southernmost of the group, where no seaborne landing had been made. We motored along beneath towering ice cliffs to the southeastern cape, round which we came unexpectedly upon an ice-free haven. Here we anchored, the first ship to do so in the Ballenys, and remained 20 hours in what is now Solo Harbour. Pieter hammered off oriented rock samples that have helped to date the islands and throw light on continental drift in the area. Landing through the surge was not altogether easy. Dorothy had a bad time washing about on a floe until she was able to take a jump.

'We landed the following afternoon on Sabrina Islet. Here it was my turn to get a wetting when I swamped our "rubber duck" in landing. Soil specimens collected included two new species of fungi.

'Heavy pack frustrated further landings and we turned south towards Cape Adare on the mainland. *Solo* hove-to under the headland, stopped by fast moving pack. Two landings were made by "rubber duck", specimens were collected and the two huts (Borchgrevink's and Scott's) were filmed.

'After an unsuccessful attempt to reach the Ballenys again Peter Donaldson conducted rather hair raising measurements of water salinity and temperature in the close vicinity of icebergs. A call was made at the Australian base on Macquarie Island and *Solo* re-entered Sydney Harbour on 3 March 1978.

'The little expedition had covered 11 605 kilometres (6266 nautical miles) using only 1600 litres (352 gallons) of diesel fuel — a reminder of the efficacy of sail. Cost effectiveness was established in that the total cost, including loan repayments, was $21 800. Six scientific papers, a book and a film resulted from the venture.'

Solo *anchored off the Balleny Islands. David Lewis and his crew made the first-ever seaborne landing on the largest island in this remote group.*

ANTARCTICA THE HARD WAY

Three men complete the second land crossing

Between September 1979 and August 1982 three British explorers — Sir Ranulph Fiennes (leader), Charles Burton and Oliver Shepard — completed a circumnavigation of the earth via the poles. During their journey they became only the second party to cross Antarctica — the first was led by Vivian Fuchs and Sir Edmund Hillary in 1958. Sir Ranulph Fiennes takes up their story on 29 October 1980 as the three men set out on skidoos from their base, Ryvingen, near the coast of Dronning Maud Land, on the first leg to the South Pole.

'Charlie and Ollie wear five layers of clothing, topped by Eskimo wolfskin parkas. I too have five underlayers, but my outer one consists of a large duvet jacket of duck down; perhaps not quite as warm as theirs but much easier to move about in and see out of. Despite three-layer footwear, mitts, caps, goggles and facemasks, the cold cuts through as though we were naked.

'I lead, pulling my two heavily laden sledges, making across the Penck Glacier for the high wall of ice called the Kirwan Escarpment. Nearing the escarpment, I notice that it is grey, not white, and realise that this means sheet ice, honed to marble consistency by centuries of wind. I look back once, the others are black specks on the rolling dunes of the Penck. To the east, streamers of blown snow crest the escarpment but right now beside the cliffs visibility is good and I spot the curve of a slight re-entrant. With adrenalin pumping away all feeling of coldness, I tug the hand throttle to full bore and begin the climb.

'Will the rubber tracks grip on this incline of ice? If they don't, we're in trouble. I try to will the skidoo upwards, to force every ounce of power from the little engine. Twelve hundred pounds [544 kg] weigh down my two bouncing, leaping sledges, a hell of a load for a 640 cc engine at 7000 feet [2130 metres] above sea level. Twice I wince inwardly as the tracks fail to grip. Flinging my weight forwards, then rocking to and fro, I pray aloud. An uneven patch saves the situation, allowing renewed grip and another surge of speed which carries the skidoo — just — up the next section.

'The climb seems to go on for ever. Then at last an easing of the gradient, two final rises and, wonderful moment, the ridgeline. Fifteen hundred feet [460 metres] above our winter camp and forty miles [64 km] from it I stop and climb off. Such moments of pure elation are fleeting and rare. I savour the feeling. To the north the peaks of the Borga massif seem now like mere pimples in the vast snow sea.

'The immediate vicinity of the escarpment is no place to linger, so we take a last look at the distant mountains then press on south. By dusk there is nothing to see in any direction but endless fields of snow.

'The thirtieth of October is unpleasant. A thirty-knot [56 km/h; 35 mph] wind stirs the snow and soon sets up pea-souper conditions. We climb gradually: the true plateau is still 4000 feet [1220 metres] above us. Hard ice bumps, not visible in the gloom, upset our skidoos. As they roll over, the riders must jump well clear to ensure their legs are not crushed between the ice and the machines.

'When we packed up our three-man tent Ollie told me he felt very tired. This was unusual from someone who never complains about his sufferings. After four hours' travel he staggered off his skidoo and lurched over un-roped. His speech was slurred.

'"I'm getting exposure. Must stop a bit."

'He was shivering. As medic he knew exactly what symptoms to expect. In these conditions it would take us two hours to make camp so Charlie and I merely unpacked the vehicle tarpaulin and, struggling against the wind, secured it around a sledge in such a way as to provide a small windproof shelter. We boiled water from snow and gave Ollie two mugs of tea and some chocolate. He is physically the toughest of us all, so if he is already shivering on day two, despite full polar gear and a wolfskin, then we will have to be very careful indeed.

'There were of course other problems; largely mechanical. The task of starting the engine at a temperature which engines do not like. Make one wrong move or an out of sequence action and long delays are caused. Try to engage gear too soon and your drive belt will shatter into fragments of brittle rubber. Turn the ignition key a touch too hard and it will break off in the lock. Get the choke setting wrong or out for too long and the plugs will foul up. Changing plugs at −50°C [−58°F] with any sort of wind makes your fingers cold again and the first hour purgatory.

'Sometimes the whole day might pass without a word spoken between us. For ten unspeakably long hours we head south. By 5th November the snow surface is still reasonable so there is little to divert the mind from the nag of feet and hands and face. As you travel you are forever kicking one foot or the other, against the chassis or booting the air hard to keep the blood down in those faraway toes.

'Without your right hand on the throttle grip the skidoo stops just as a car does if you take your foot off the accelerator. So when you want to wing your freezing throttle hand about in windmill motions you have to use your left hand across your chest on the right handlebar where the throttle grip is. To steer like this is not too effective and, on a rough surface, not feasible. When it is rough going therefore your throttle hand goes through a good deal of unpleasantness.

'December . . . now the polar summer was with us and life was positively comfortable in terms of temperature for we were well into the −30°s Fahrenheit [−20° Centigrade]. But the sastrugi did not improve. Day by day they increased in size and number. The sastrugi ridges resembled a ploughed field with the ridges running directly across our line of advance. For 200 miles [320 km] these ridges averaged two to three feet high [600-900mm].

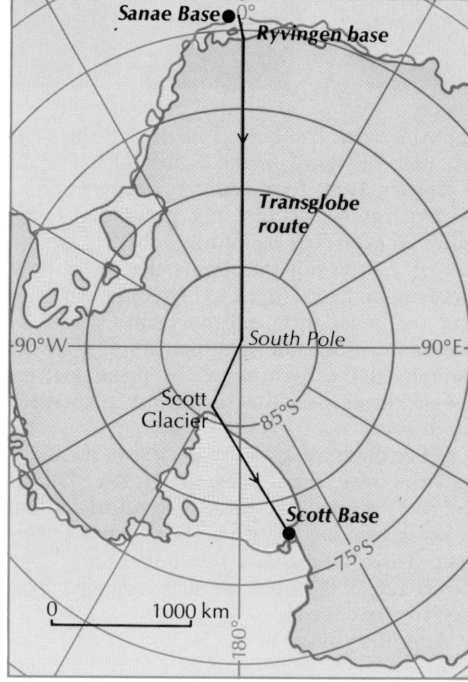

But the four-inch [100-mm] raised blade at the front of our skidoo skis could only mount a sheer-sided obstacle twelve inches [300 mm] high, so we had to hack paths through these ridges with our ice axes. Then we had to manoeuvre the skidoos over each ridge, followed by each of our sledges. If we pulled the sledges on our standard fifty-foot [15-metre] tow ropes, they just became caught up between ice furrows and jammed, so we changed to five-foot [1.5-metre] tow ropes which, in the event of a crevasse fall, would probably have meant the sledges would have quickly followed the skidoo downwards into the abyss.

'With breaks of one or two kilometres [1100 to 2200 yards] between them, these forbidding sastrugi fields carried on for 300 miles [480 km], sometimes almost impassable, sometimes mere serried waves of ice bric-a-brac. With increasing frequency whiteout conditions clamped down. To negotiate even the lesser sastrugi belts without a clear idea of where the bumps were, would be asking for trouble so we always stopped until the light improved.

'At 0435 hours on 15 December 1980, we finally arrived at the bottom of the earth. The American scientists at the cosy South Pole

The winter camp at Ryvingen. The huts were made from two-layer cardboard which could fit easily inside the plane.

Oliver Shepard examines a crevasse on the Borga Massif. These chasms present the greatest danger to travellers.

Over 480 km (300 miles) of bone-jarring sastrugi confronted the crossing party as they made their way towards the South Pole. Exhausting hours were spent hacking a path through the highest ridges.

Charles Burton at a camp above the Scott Glacier before the long descent from the polar plateau to the Ross Ice Shelf.

station were friendly and hospitable. We camped, 100 yards [90 metres] from the metal dome that houses their work-huts but, in exchange for washing up dishes and cleaning the canteen, we ate with them.

'With our base group all at the Pole I wanted to press on. The second half of our journey involved some 180 miles [290 km] to the edge of the high plateau, a 140-mile [225-km] descent down a mountain-girt valley — the Scott Glacier, and 600 miles [960 km] over the Ross Ice Shelf to the sea at McMurdo Sound.

'Early on 28th December, in a whiteout with wind gusting to forty knots [46 mph; 74 km/h], we skirted the east side of Garner Ridge, and followed the Klein Glacier for a dozen miles [19 km] to the mist-blurred outline of the Davis Hills. Here the Scott and Klein Glaciers clash with a silent but ferocious force, creating a jumble of gleaming chaos for some miles.

'The crevasse field ended in a mile or so. Then gradually our route veered north-north-east and the Scott Glacier fell away before us to reveal a breath-taking panorama of mountain and glacier, ice field and sky. The world seemed to start at our feet, dropping 2000 feet [600 metres] to the far horizon where our highway disappeared between the cliffs of Mount Walshe and the Organ Pipe Peaks. Keeping to the centre of the glacier we made good time for thirty miles [48 km] until a rash of rotten snowbridges collapsed beneath us. Everyone suffered shocks. As usual Ollie at the back was worst off.

'We veered to the western flank of the glacier but Charlie's sledge collapsed a wide snow bridge. I saw Ollie struggling to help extricate the dangling load but was not going back over one step of the perilous route unless needed, so I sat and watched until they were again en route. We climbed over 1000 feet [300 metres] to a high wild pass where the wind bit through our clothes and whipped up spirals of snow from the granite fortress of Mount Ruth and its senior twin Mount Gardiner. To the west we could see a ragged company of primordial peaks spearing the sky, mere reminders of the vastness of their ice-buried bulk. Around them curled serpentine rivers of ice bearing names from the "heroic age" of polar exploration; the Amundsen, Axel Heiberg and Devil's Glaciers.

'From the pass we climbed still higher to the north until at the extremity of the detour, we arrived at the crown of a steep valley leading back down to the Scott Glacier. Charlie, careful never to sound excited about anything, described the subsequent downhill journey:

"The descent was a nightmare which I don't care to recall. Some people will think it must have been easy, simply because we descended so quickly. All I can say is let them try. Ran and Ol were as frightened as I was, even if they don't admit it. That's why Ran kept going hour after hour without stopping. He zigzagged in every direction trying to avoid the worst areas. He didn't have much success and on one of the upper ledges we found ourselves right in the middle of a major pressure zone. Great ice bubbles and blue domes reared above us as we slithered along a maze of cracked corridors, totally trapped. My sledge took an eight-foot [2.4-metre] wide fissure diagonally and broke through the bridge. My skidoo's rubber tracks clawed at the blue ice, slipped sideways and the sledge began to disappear. I was lucky. A patch of grainy white ice gave the tracks just enough forward purchase to heave forward again. The sledge wallowed up and over the forward lip of the crevasse . . .

"I could mention a hundred or more such incidents during the descent. Each of us could — but what's the point? Nobody who wasn't there, who hasn't felt the deadly lurch of snow giving way under his seat, hasn't seen the line upon line of white or blue telltale shadows in a major crevasse field and been forced to carry on going over more and more, for hour after hour, can imagine the sweaty apprehension we experienced."

'On the last day of 1980 we moved due north for fifty miles [80 km] and away from the crevasses that shift about the foot of the glaciers. The surface was excellent once on the move but its slushy texture made it hard to tug out the sledges from a standing start. The snow thrown up by our skidoo skis landed on our clothes: the sun then melted it for the temperature was +1°C (34°F).

'There was no longer any need for face-masks or sweaters. Life was comfortable, easy and carefree. Following the northerly push I switched half-left on to a heading which I was confident would miss the great complex of disturbance called the Steershead Crevasses. Gradually the mountains to the left tapered away until as on the plateau there was nothing but ice and us.

'On the fifth day out from the glacier's snout, we completed seventy-nine nautical miles [146 km] in ten hours. The glare was intense and I navigated by storm clouds to the west. On the seventh day we crossed the 180° meridian which, at this point, is also the International Date Line. We increased our mileage for the day to ninety-one nautical miles [168 km] and used only a gallon for each eight miles [35 litres/100 km]. On the ninth day despite a semi-whiteout we drove one hundred nautical miles [185 km] and likewise on the tenth when, at noon a white mushroom cloud first became visible on the horizon ahead and to the right: the steam cloud of Mount Erebus. Beneath this 13000-foot [4000-metre] volcano nestled our goal, Scott Base.

'On 10th January after eighty-one nautical miles [150 km] and some unpleasant crevasses, we camped at the tip of White Island. Two hours out from Scott Base, Charlie's skidoo developed piston trouble. Ollie had carried a spare engine all the way from Ryvingen, now he put it to good use.

'Next day at six p.m. Roger Clark, the New Zealand Commander of Scott Base, came out to meet us with a sledge drawn by huskies. He led us over the sea-ice, scattering docile seals and screaming skuas, to Pram Point where the wooden huts of his base huddle by the edge of the sea. Above on the rocks some sixty New Zealanders looked down as a kilted piper struck up the haunting tune, "Amazing Grace".

'In 67 days we had crossed Antarctica but the circumpolar journey was not yet half complete.'

ANTARCTICA THE LONG WAY

Twin triumphs for the spirit of adventure

After nearly a century of ambitious plans and ill-fated attempts to cross Antarctica with dogs, the journey was finally completed in March 1990. Not only was this the fourth crossing of the continent, but it was also by far the longest. Will Steger and his team covered 6400 km (4000 miles) in their journey, compared with 3472 km (2158 miles) for the first crossing party in 1957-58.

American Will Steger's private dream of crossing Antarctica began in 1986 following a chance encounter with French adventurer Dr Jean Louis Etienne on the north polar icepack. Both were on different expeditions to the North Pole – Steger's team with dogs, Etienne alone on skis. They swapped telephone numbers, agreed that it would be nice to travel together in Antarctica, and then continued on their separate ways.

The chance contact was followed up, and soon became an ambitious plan for the longest ever Antarctic crossing. Over the next three years Steger and Etienne gathered together experienced team mates and support staff; bred and trained huskies at Steger's home base in Ely, Minnesota; raised over $(US)11 million in expedition funds, and had a 120-tonne yacht built as a communications base. The group chosen to make the crossing comprised Steger (45), Etienne (43), Victor Boyarsky (43) from the Soviet Union, Qin Dahe (43) from China, Keizo Funatzu (33) from Japan, and Geoff Somers (40) from Great Britain.

To test themselves in the conditions of cold, wind, altitude and monotony that they knew they would have to face in Antarctica, five team members (without Qin Dahe) set off to make a north-south crossing of Greenland with dogs in the spring of 1988. The 2400-km (1400-mile) journey was completed without the help of prelaid depots or airdrops.

All the planning completed, the expedition finally got underway in July 1989. A Soviet Ilyushin 76 aircraft took off from Minneapolis, USA, bound for a Chilean airfield on King George Island, off the tip of the Antarctic Peninsula. On board were the expedition members, together with 40 huskies and tonnes of sledging equipment. They were met at the airfield by Qin Dahe, who was able to show them around the Chinese Great Wall station which was to be their base during the early part of the expedition.

On 27 July 1989 a ski-equipped Twin Otter aircraft flew men, dogs and equipment from King George Island to Seal Nunatak, on the edge of the Larsen Ice Shelf. Only now did the enormity of the task they had set themselves sink in – ahead lay 6400 km (4000 miles) of some of the toughest country on earth. First they had to complete a mid-winter traverse of the mountainous Antarctic Peninsula, before the long climb to the South Pole at an altitude of 2835 metres (9300 ft). Then followed a trek across the desolate polar plateau to the Soviet Union's Vostok base – the coldest place on earth – before the descent to Mirny, another Soviet base on the coast.

The first part of the journey was supported by Adventure Network International, a Canadian company. During the 1988-89 season Geoff Somers had used Adventure Network aircraft to lay seven depots of food and equipment along the Antarctic Peninsula as far as the Ellsworth Mountains. It was essential that all of these depots were found.

Weather on the Antarctic Peninsula is notoriously bad. One blizzard struck the party with winds of 160 km/h (100 mph) and temperatures as low as –43°C (–45°F). A dog died and 15 others had to be evacuated to South America. Later, recalling 13 precious days confined to a tent, Steger said: 'There were some pretty black moments, and I could see the desperation of other explorers like Scott.'

On 11 December 1989 the expedition reached the South Pole, having taken 137 days to cover 3205 km (1992 miles). This was the first expedition to reach the pole using dog teams since British huskies arrived in January 1958 in support of the Commonwealth Trans-Antarctic Expedition (see p 270). Two of Steger's dogs, Sam and Yeager, became the first huskies to reach both the North and South Poles.

Depots had been placed between Vostok and Mirny by staff from Soviet bases during the previous season, and by providing fuel at the South Pole the Russians had made it possible for the expedition's aircraft to bring in supplies at the crucial mid-point of the crossing. The sledgers left the South Pole on 16 December 1989, racing to reach the coast before the onset of winter.

At first a frozen ocean of sastrugi up to 1.5 metres (5 ft) high made travelling extremely difficult, often tipping the sledges over, sometimes trapping men underneath. During one such capsize Steger injured his back. However, conditions improved and on the latter part of the run to Vostok the expedition averaged 40 km (25 miles) a day.

Russian scientists greeted their arrival at Vostok on 18 January 1990 with fireworks and warm hospitality. Theirs was the first

Dogs and men are dwarfed by the size of the chasm that yawns beneath their feet. Crevasses are perhaps the most serious hazard facing polar explorers. Sometimes snow bridges over them will support the weight of a loaded sledge, and sometimes they will not. A plunge into the depths of a monster like this would certainly be fatal.

Expedition members push on into a strong headwind and blowing snow. When conditions are really bad there can be a white-out, which Keizo Funatzu described as: 'like being inside a ping-pong ball'.

The pole at last, after 137 days and 3205 km (1992 miles). From left to right - displaying their own national flags - are Keizo Funatzu, Victor Boyarsky, Will Steger, Jean Louis Etienne, Qin Dahe and Geoff Somers.

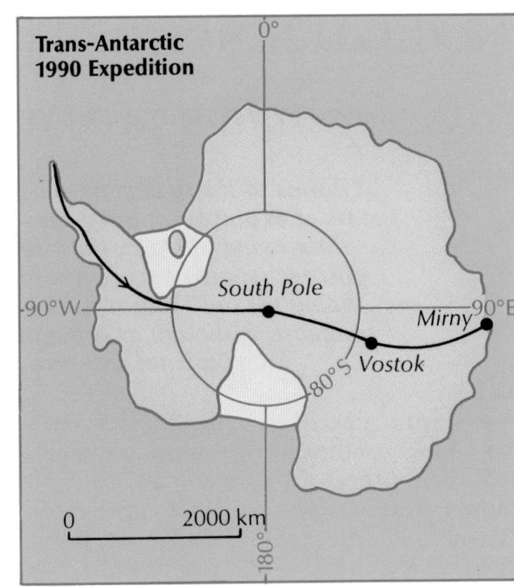

unmechanised crossing of the Zone of Inaccessibility (the area between Vostok and the pole). Only 1370 km (850 miles) now remained, but this last leg involved a descent of 3500 metres (11 500 ft), across an area criss-crossed by treacherous crevasses.

On day 216 – 26 February 1990 – the expedition reported: 'see ocean and first icebergs'. The epic was nearly over – but not quite yet. A sudden fierce blizzard stuck, preventing any movement. Keizo Funatzu was lucky to escape with his life when he became lost in the blizzard while feeding the dogs. After wandering about disoriented he dug a hole in the snow and curled up in it. He was discovered 11 hours later, miraculously without frostbite.

Finally, after 221 days of almost continuous travelling, the expedition sledged into Mirny base on 3 March 1990 to be greeted by Soviet scientists, film crews and journalists. Among many congratulatory messages sent to Mirny was one from Reinhold Messner and Arved Fuchs (see box). It read: 'Congratulations on one of the great polar journeys of all time. Let us now fight for a "World Park Antarctica".'

THIRD CROSSING

While Will Steger's party was making the fourth crossing of Antarctica, another two-man expedition completed the third crossing of the continent.

Italian mountaineer Reinhold Messner, together with Arved Fuchs, a German, (no relation to Sir Vivian Fuchs) manhauled plastic sledges from the Ronne Ice Shelf to Scott base on Ross Island in 92 days.

Their journey started on 13 November 1989 and they reached the pole just 48 days later, having received only one lot of extra supplies by aircraft in the Thiel Mountains. However, the second leg was even more daring. Everything had been pared to the minimum. They carried all the food and equipment for the journey on their sledges - a weight of 132 kg (292 lb) - and they had no radios, and no plans for any resupply stops on the way.

Despite having to cover some difficult ground as they followed the Mill and Beardmore Glaciers through the Transantarctic Mountains, the two men reached Ross Island on 12 February 1990, just 39 days after leaving the pole. Their journey proved, yet again, the effectiveness of properly planned private expeditions to the continent. The age of adventure is far from over.

DECIDING ANTARCTICA'S FATE

Co-operation produces a unique document

Claims to the Antarctic continent in its short history of 250 years of exploration have been based on discovery, occupation, the raising of flags, the issuing of decrees, the printing of postage stamps and geographical continuity. It is unique in being the only major landmass that has not been taken by conquest, although at times warfare has been perilously close as a final solution to conflicting claims.

To gain a perspective on Antarctic territorial conflict it is necessary to examine the history of the important, but little known, Scottish National Antarctic Expedition of 1902-04 led by W.S. Bruce. Bruce, using a converted Norwegian whaler, the *Scotia*, was first to carry out oceanographic exploration in the Weddell Sea. He established a wintering base on Laurie Island in the South Orkney group. At the end of his explorations, Bruce offered his stone-built meteorological station on Laurie Island to the British, who, surprisingly, rejected his offer. Bruce was deeply hurt by this snub. He promptly gave it to the Argentinians who had been so helpful to his expedition. From these beginnings in 1904, Laurie Island still remains an Argentinian base and the longest continuously occupied station in Antarctica. It is an occupancy claim that has provided this South American republic with considerable ammunition in its continued disputes with the United Kingdom over Antarctic territory.

One of the earliest formal claims to Antarctic territory came in 1908 when the British Letters Patent of 21 July consolidated the United Kingdom's territorial claims dating from 1775 to the Dependencies of the Falkland Islands. These territories included Laurie Island in the South Orkney group.

The claim was so carelessly planned that it took in part of South America in error and to the embarrassment of the British they had to reframe it in 1917. However, in so doing, the United Kingdom steadfastly ignored the Argentinian counter claim of 1908 to Antarctic territory. This was the beginning of sovereignty disputes in Antarctica that continued for the next 50 years and even resulted in open conflict in 1982. It ultimately led, by a circuitous route, to the formation of a settlement heralded as one of the most effective and forward-thinking peace treaties yet formulated by man — the Antarctic Treaty.

By the 1940s, Antarctic territory had been claimed by Argentina, Australia, Chile, France, the United Kingdom, New Zealand, Norway and South Africa. South Africa restricted its claim to a few subantarctic islands, while Norway confined its claim to a coastal zone. The remainder took pie-shaped wedges from the Southern Ocean to the South Pole.

Apart from Argentina, Chile and the United Kingdom, whose claims overlapped, each claimant nation had recognised the others' territory. The USA, the USSR, Japan, Germany and Belgium, at different times, and at different levels, have all made discoveries and claims in Antarctica, but for various reasons have not been prepared to assert them. Japan in the 1951 peace treaty agreed to forego any claims it had to the southern continent.

Peru, Brazil and Uruguay have all registered their interest in various sections of the Antarctic Peninsula, and Poland, with a long history of Arctic exploration, became involved in Antarctic affairs in the late 1950s.

The emergence of the Antarctic Treaty in 1959 followed the almost simultaneous thrust of international politics and science into the affairs of the continent.

The British continued a policy of territorial acquisition into the 1920s by handing the Ross Dependency to New Zealand by an Order in Council in 1923. France reinforced its claim to Terre Adélie in 1924, and Australia received 6.5 million sq kilometres (2.5 million sq miles) of the Antarctic continent from Britain in 1933. Norway formalised its claim to Queen Maud Land in 1939 to protect its discoveries and whaling interests from Germany. A year later Chile issued a decree 'to fix with accuracy the limits of a sovereignty that has existed since the sixteenth century'.

These wedge-shaped claims, themselves a contentious issue, derived from the sector theory formulated by Senator Poirier in the Canadian Parliament in 1907. Such a procedure had been applied to disputed territories in the Arctic, where the wedge was formed by a northward projection of the boundaries of the countries concerned.

Thus, sector theory joined discovery and effective occupation to form three bases for claims of sovereignty over Antarctic territory. Only one basis — that of continuous occupation and effective control — is generally accepted in international law.

Both Chile and Argentina have applied geographical proximity, as well as geographical affinity, to support claims over the Antarctic Peninsula. Argentina further invoked a Papal Bull of 1498 in which the Pope decreed that the world should be split equally between Portugal and Spain. Affinities to Spain left no doubt in Argentinian minds as to who owned the Antarctic Peninsula, but unfortunately this same decree was invoked by Chile in 1940.

The United Kingdom maintained a steadfast and resolute attitude to Chilean and Argentinean claims, both of which overlapped with hers. She felt the Antarctic Peninsula belonged to her, and with due ceremony tore down flags and stations of foreign usurpers, arrested and deported illegal immigrants back to their country of origin, and went about her business of research, discovery and annexation.

The USA was one of many countries gravely concerned with the continuous bickering of its allies over this disputed territory. In the late 1940s, it found itself at odds with the USSR and saw the possibility for yet another wedge being driven into the Antarctic pie — only this one would be red.

Although the United States, through its nationals, had made numerous claims to Antarctic territory it did so from the standpoint that it neither recognised the sector principle of sovereignty, not any claim of any form in Antarctica. Thus, although making its own claims from time to time, the USA appreciated that any claim it made to Antarctic territory had no more validity than that of claims made by other countries. The USA has never asserted territorial claims in the Antarctic, but it still reserves the right to do so.

With an extensive history of polar exploration and discovery to its credit, the USA felt that it could be politically neutral but intelligently informed on matters of the Antarctic. In 1948 it took the diplomatic initiative of proposing to Argentina, Australia, Chile, France, New Zealand, Norway and the United Kingdom that the Antarctic be made the subject of some international trust territory. Alternative proposals included an eight-power condominium (to include the USA) and the placing of Antarctica under a United Nations Trusteeship system. But of all claimant nations, only one, New Zealand, was prepared to relinquish its claims.

The American fear of Soviet intervention was realised on 8 June 1950 when the Russians forwarded a diplomatic note to those countries who had attempted to negotiate a condominium. It stated that the Soviet Government did not recognise any claims to Antarctic territory and neither did they make claims on their own behalf. The Russians refused to recognise as lawful any decision on the Antarctic regime taken without its participation.

In view of the long Soviet history of discoveries in the Antarctic (Bellingshausen and Lazerev in 1819-21), coupled with commercial activities in these areas, the Soviet note seemed reasonable. Russia had protested to the Norwegians on 27 January 1939 on the unlawfulness of the separate solution of the question of state ownership of the Antarctic.

Today, international scientific co-operation is taken for granted, but this was not always so. One of the first efforts to unite polar activities was the idea of Karl Weyprecht, a lieutenant in the Austrian Navy. A veteran of Arctic exploration, he had proposed in 1875 that scientific programs in both the Arctic and Antarctic should be co-ordinated. Weyprecht did not live to see his ideas come to fruition, but they were acted on and the first International Polar Year was held in 1882-83. Twelve nations established 14 bases in the polar regions to make co-ordinated observations of the climate and the earth's magnetism.

Such was the success of this venture that it was agreed that International Polar Years be held at 50-year intervals. The second International Polar Year was held in 1932-33, but it was the impatience of one man for a third International Polar Year that ultimately led to the greatest international peacetime scientific co-operative endeavour of all time. That man was Dr Lloyd Berkner, a member of Richard Byrd's expedition of 1928-30. Berkner, together with Dr Sydney Chapman, a British auroral expert who had participated in the second International Polar Year, were guests at the home of Dr James Van Allen (a noted geophysicist after whom the Van Allen radiation belts are named). It was here, in April 1950, that Berkner voiced his frustration at the prospect of a long wait for the third International Polar Year which was not scheduled until 1982-83. He reasoned that the techniques

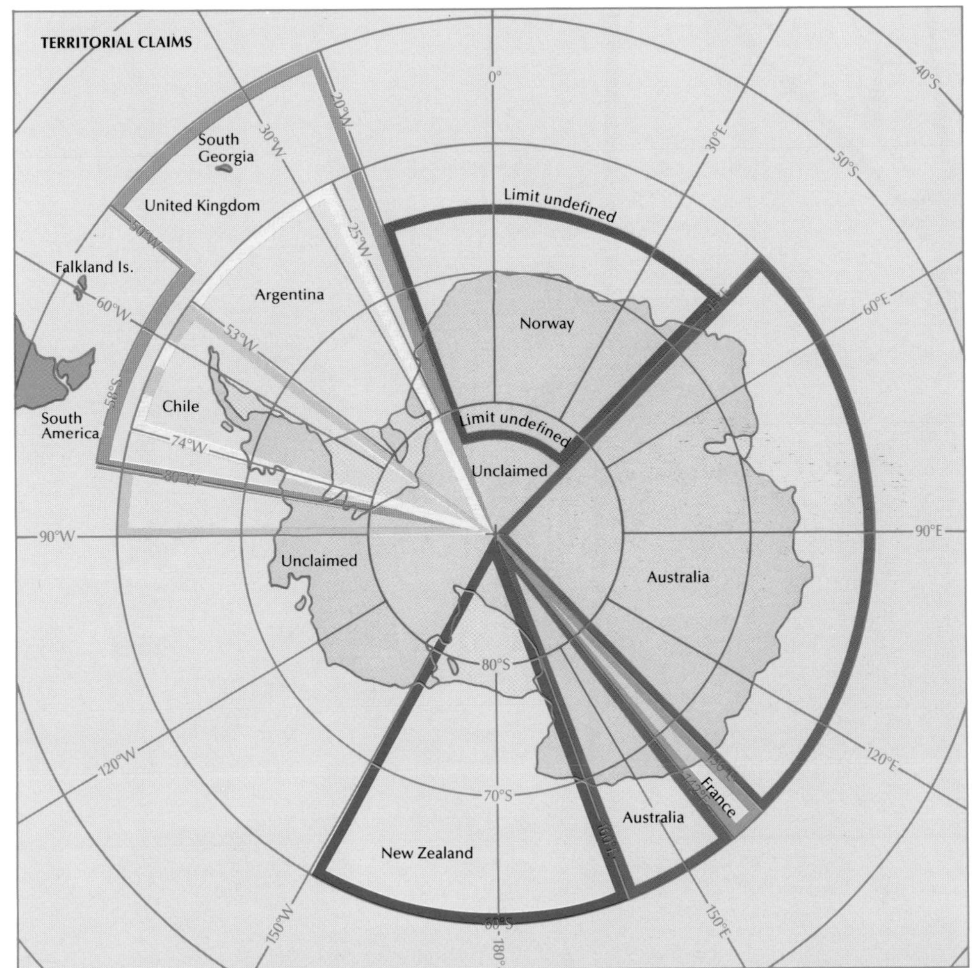

then available for exploring the upper atmosphere and earth's surface had advanced considerably in the past 20 years, and that this new technology should be used as soon as possible.

His suggestion was forwarded to the International Council of Scientific Unions (ICSU) who gave it their blessing by setting up a special committee to initiate planning for the third International Polar Year. At the suggestion of the World Meteorological Organisation (WMO) the concept of a Polar Year was extended to include the entire globe. Thus was born IGY, the International Geophysical Year. It was proposed that it be held for 18 months from June 1957 to December 1958. It was the 'year of the quiet sun', when solar activity was at a minimum. A special committee to handle the scientific co-ordination and logistics for IGY was established in 1953 – the Comité Spéciál de l'Annėe Geophysique Internationale, or CSAGI.

The ICSU's own special committee selected two areas for special attention — outer space and Antarctica. It was this decision that paved the way for the Antarctic Treaty.

The first Antarctic conference was held in Paris from 6-10 July 1955. General G. R. Laclavére, elected chairman of the meeting, emphasised to all those present that this was a conference about science, not politics or national boundaries. The nations present that applauded and endorsed his opening address were later to become the first signatories to the Antarctic Treaty. Given the unanimity of this meeting, there were many who wondered if science could achieve what politics had failed miserably to do – to establish international accord in Antarctic matters.

The ICSU, representing 67 nations, had already given its backing to IGY, and 12 of these nations submitted plans for Antarctic field stations. Between them, they established over 40 stations on the Antarctic continent, and a further 20 on islands.

The Russians moved into Australian Antarctic territory and the USA onto the Antarctic Peninsula and into New Zealand's Ross Dependency. Even before IGY had finished, moves were afoot to continue the unique scientific endeavour on this continent. At the Paris Antarctic Conference of 1957 the USA, the USSR, Belgium and Argentina favoured an extension, while Australia, Chile, South Africa and the United Kingdom were opposed. France, Japan, Norway and New Zealand preferred not to commit themselves. The realisation that both the USSR and the USA intended to stay in Antarctica was sufficient to persuade others that co-operation should continue beyond IGY, and all the IGY participants agreed to a 12-month extension.

The ICSU approved the formation of a Special Committee on Antarctic Research — SCAR (later to become Scientific Committee on Antarctic Research) and it held its first meeting at the Hague in 1958. The committee consisted of delegates from each of the nations actively engaged in Antarctic research. To this committee were added representatives of other specialist scientific committees which would have overlapping interests in Antarctica. SCAR was to become, and still is, one of the most effective international committees ever formed.

In April 1958 the USA took the initiative in convening a conference to discuss the future of Antarctica. President Eisenhower revealed the national plan: 'The United States is dedicated to the principle that the vast uninhabited wastes of Antarctica should be used only for peaceful purposes. We do not want Antarctica to become an object of political conflict . . . We propose that Antarctica shall be open to all nations to conduct scientific or other peaceful activities there. We also propose that joint administrative arrangements be worked out . . .' But there was much hard work before the conference was called and concluded. A preliminary working group met in June 1958 in Washington and over 60 meetings later, by October 1959, the draft treaty had been prepared. The conference was convened in Washington on 14 October 1959, and signed on 1 December of the same year. The signatories were Argentina, Australia, Belgium, Chile, France, Japan, New Zealand, Norway, South Africa, the United Kingdom, the USA and the USSR. The treaty was ratified on 23 June 1961. By early 1990, Poland, Brazil, the Republic of (West) Germany, India, Uruguay, the People's Republic of China, Italy and the German Democratic Republic had all received consultative status. A further 18 countries had acceded to the treaty: Bulgaria, Canada, Czechoslovakia, Denmark, Hungary, the Netherlands, Papua New Guinea, Peru, Spain, Romania, Sweden, Cuba, Greece, Finland, the Republic of (South) Korea, the Democratic People's Republic of (North) Korea, Austria and Ecuador.

ANTARCTICA – A WORLD PARK?

Among the first to propose that Antarctica should be made a world park were members of the Second World Conference on National Parks. At a 1972 meeting in Yellowstone National Park, USA, the conference directed a resolution to the twelve Antarctic Treaty nations to: '. . . negotiate to establish the Antarctic continent and surrounding seas as the first world park, under the auspices of the United Nations . . .'

A similar concept was promoted by the New Zealand Government in 1975, with the qualified support of Chile. However, the proposal received little encouragement.

In June 1988 the text for the Convention on the Regulation of Antarctic Mineral Resource Activities (CRAMRA) was completed. All that was required was the signatures of the claimant states. Everyone thought that its signing, and therefore ratification, was as good as done.

Then, on 22 May 1989, Australia stunned its Antarctic treaty partners by declaring that it would not sign the agreement. Perhaps even more surprising was the support given to the Australian position by French Prime Minister Michel Rocard, who indicated that France would not sign the CRAMRA agreement either. Both countries expressed support for the idea of an Antarctic world park instead. It soon became clear that other countries also had reservations about the agreement.

Thus the concept of an Antarctic world park may come about more from default, rather than reasoned debate among the treaty partners. What Australia's decision has done is to provide an opportunity for, as Prime Minister Hawke stated, '. . . the sheer weight of public opinion to determine the future of Antarctica'.

Indeed, public concern about environmental issues, and the consequent growth of the conservation movement, may prove to be the salvation of Antarctica. Organisations such as Greenpeace (which supports the concept of a world park) and The Cousteau Society (which is calling for a convention for the conservation and protection of the Antarctic) can rally considerable public support – support which can be translated into votes.

THE SPECTRE OF EXPLOITATION

Facing up to future problems

The concept of an exploitation-free Antarctic is an ideal that many have worked for, and will continue to do so. However, to expect that this should be the case is being both unrealistic and impractical. Many believe, rightly or wrongly, that for its survival the world needs the protein and energy locked in the seas and bedrock of Antarctica.

Whether it be food, minerals, precious metals or simply water, man has always justified the exploitation of resources whether they be common or rare. It is too much to hope that an exception would be made for the resources of Antarctica.

Nevertheless a major breakthrough was achieved in December 1980 when all the signatories to the Antarctic Treaty signed the Convention on the Conservation of Antarctic Marine Living Resources. This convention came into force when ratified by a majority of signatories to the treaty on 17 April 1982. It is far from a perfect agreement. There is yet much to be resolved within its articles, but it is a convention that can be built on.

The Scientific Committee on Antarctic Research (SCAR) and its specialist committees, by formulating this document hope to both internationalise and protect the Antarctic marine ecosystem. This convention encompasses not only the marine living resources south of 60° south latitude, but also the marine living resources of the area between that latitude and the Antarctic Convergence. The living resources include everything apart from whales (covered by the International Whaling Commission) and seals (covered by their own convention). Conservation is defined within the convention to mean rational use — more specifically it does not deny harvesting. The resources are considered renewable provided rational use prevails. The convention is open for signature by any nation that is interested in research or harvesting activities in the area. Those that sign it agree to its articles, which include some articles of the Antarctic Treaty, as well as the Agreed Measures for the Conservation of Antarctic Flora and Fauna.

Strangely, the particular resource that generated this unique document is not even named in the convention. This resource is krill, *Euphausia superba*. It is believed to exist in vast quantities. Current estimates suggest a standing stock of up to 5000 million tonnes, of which whales eat 43 million tonnes, fishes 60 million, birds 40 million, seals 80 million and squid 100 million tonnes per year. It is thought that humans could take between 80 and 150 million tonnes annually without significantly altering the balance. But nobody really knows, and this is what BIOMASS is all about.

Yet another creation of SCAR — BIOMASS is an acronym for the Biological Investigation of Marine Antarctic Systems and Stocks. As an experimental investigation of marine resources it has two main phases, FIBEX and SIBEX — respectively First and Second International Biological Experiments.

Years in the planning, FIBEX was launched in December 1980 and January 1981 when the largest multi-ship experiment in biological oceanography got underway. Eighteen ships from 11 countries, Argentina (1 ship), Australia (1), Chile (1), France (1), West Germany (3), Poland (1), Japan (4), South Africa (1), the United Kingdom (1), the USSR (3), and the USA (1), headed for the southern oceans.

The purpose of this experiment was a detailed study of the physical, chemical and biological properties of the southwestern Atlantic and southwestern Indian Ocean sectors of the Southern Ocean during February 1981. Many of the vessels also took part in the krill patch survey — an as near as possible simultaneous krill-sampling program over many different parts of the ocean.

All the data has been fed into a central unit, processed and made available to all who contributed information. It is important that the BIOMASS program and Convention on Marine Resources are not considered as sepa-

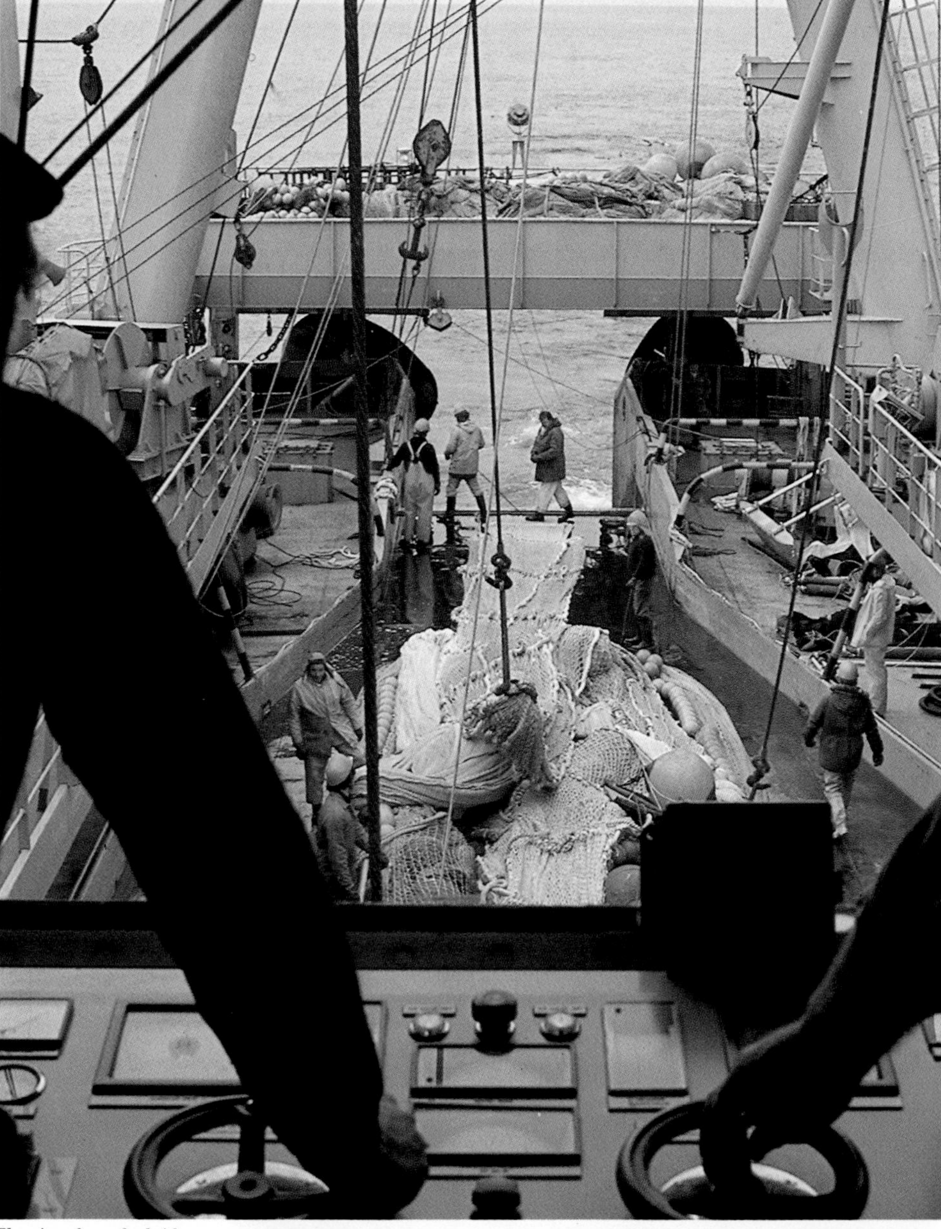

The view from the bridge of a German trawler fishing for krill. Germany and some South American countries gave up krill fishing as uneconomic after a brief trial.

A net full of pink krill – the staple food of baleen whales. In 1990 only the Soviet Union and Japan were fishing for these creatures. The annual catch of around 400 000 tonnes is ground up and used as animal feed.

SAVING THE SEALS

Once in danger of being wiped out, elephant seals, and all other Antarctic seals, are now protected by an international convention.

The early history of Antarctica is the history of the rape of a great continent's biological resources. Nevertheless, the Antarctic Treaty has brought more than a glimmer of hope in this area. While the treaty carefully avoids any reference to whaling activities, or any other form of exploitation in Antarctica, international co-operation has evolved in the conservation of Antarctic wildlife.

In the infant years of the treaty, in 1961, the question of the exploitation of seals arose at a consultative meeting. In contrast to the history of sealing, these moves were concerned not with exploitation, but protection.

Such thinking anticipated potential exploitation some time in the future, although, of the six species of seals found in Antarctic and subantarctic waters, four of them had never suffered the depredation that stocks of fur and elephant seal had. These were Ross, crabeater, Weddell and leopard seals. Even 20 years after IGY, surprisingly little was known about the Antarctic seals. For instance up to 1963 only a dozen or so Ross seals had ever been seen. Yet an experimental sealing expedition in 1964 by Norwegians shot over 100.

SCAR undertook to bring together the scattered knowledge on Antarctic seals and in 1972 formulated a unique document — unique because it gained acceptance for the protection of the fur, elephant and Ross seals south of 60° south latitude and set quotas for catch limits on the crabeater of 175000 (15000000), leopard 12000 (220000) and Weddell seals 5000 (730000), (estimated total population in brackets). The Convention for the Conservation of Antarctic Seals was finally ratified on 11 March 1978, seventeen years after its inception.

rate entities — the convention, for instance, makes no attempt to set catch quotas for krill or any other marine organism — it does not do so because the information is not available. This is largely the responsibility of BIOMASS, which through its investigations will ultimately provide guidelines for harvesting.

The BIOMASS program parallels the famous Discovery Investigations (see p234), but has the advantage that it can report and recommend to an international body that has in principle agreed to the conservation of Antarctic marine living resources. The convention is an achievement second only to the Antarctic Treaty in its scope and farsightedness. Whatever the real potential for the rich harvests of the southern oceans, many important factors remain to be considered. The attraction of krill is not its economy, but the size of the harvest. At present it is an expensive form of protein in comparison to equivalent sources in other oceans. As such it cannot be promoted as fulfilling the protein needs of underdeveloped countries – it is unlikely that they will ever be able to afford it.

The success of the Convention on Marine Living Resources partly rests with the ability of the consultative parties to recognise, amongst other things, that the resources do not belong to any one nation, and that they are for everyone to share who is prepared to accept the recommendations for their protection.

It is difficult for any nation to claim exclusive rights to a marine living resource because the resource can move around easily, although it is acknowledged that a claimant nation could declare a 200-mile (320-kilometre) Exclusive Economic Zone. Such an action would be a futile gesture, for not only would this run counter to the principle of the Antarctic Treaty, but present knowledge about the abundance of krill indicates that the greatest concentrations are found within the overlapping claims of Argentina, Chile and the United Kingdom.

A more likely reason for the declaration of a 200-mile Exclusive Economic Zone will come if major deposits of oil and natural gas are found. If they are found, who do they belong to, and who receives royalties and regulates the industry?

The first meeting of the proposed regulatory body for minerals exploration met in Wellington, New Zealand, in 1978 under the chairmanship of Chris Beeby. His mandate was to bring together the consultative parties to the treaty, and to hammer out an agreed procedure that would permit prospecting and the exploitation of minerals in Antarctica, yet at the same time provide protection for the environment.

It took 10 years of at times tense negotiations before the 67 articles of the Convention on Regulation of Antarctic Mineral Resource Activities (CRAMRA), and an additional 12 articles forming an Annex for an Arbital Tribunal, were agreed upon.

There can be little doubt that, in spirit at least, the convention is concerned to protect the integrity of Antarctic ecosystems. It was even agreed that no nation would undertake preliminary investigations of mineral resources until the document had been signed. Proponents say that, whatever its faults, the convention as it stands is better than no convention at all.

However, such a convention appears to be a contradiction in terms. How can it be possible to prospect and mine for minerals yet – as article IV of the convention states – avoid '. . . significant adverse effects on air and water quality, significant changes in atmospheric, terrestrial and marine environments, significant changes in the distribution, abundance or productivity of populations of species of flora and fauna'?

Also, mining activities would almost certainly lead to a decrease in international cooperation. Inevitably the emphasis of Antarctic endeavour would shift from scientific pursuits to the development of technology to help exploiters cope with the difficult environment.

There is little doubt that old wounds would be reopened between nations with conflicting territorial claims. It is hard to imagine a country permitting others to develop mines in an area that has been bitterly disputed – as some on the peninsula have been – for almost a century.

But above all, the short-term gains to be had from any exploitation of Antarctic minerals can only be just that. The energy locked in Antarctic rocks is non-renewable. It might stave off the need to search for clean alternative energy sources for a short time, but the basic problems would remain unsolved.

The usual consensus principle, which had operated throughout the Antarctic Treaty and its conventions, was dropped for the Mineral Convention in favour of a complex formula for voting. This required that a minimum of 16 of the 20 participating parties must ratify the agreement, and that all seven former claimants to Antarctic territory, together with the USA and the Soviet Union, must be among the signatories.

Politically it was a sensible and necessary requirement, and one that everyone concerned expected to be easily fulfilled. After 10 years of negotiations, all that was required was a series of signatures on the dotted line. It therefore came as a bombshell when Australia, followed by France, declined to ratify the convention, saying that they preferred the idea of an Antarctic world park. Whatever the motives behind their move, the decision won the support of environmentalists, and a brief reprieve for Antarctica. The vital task now is to make sure that an acceptable plan for Antarctica's future is found quickly.

THE NEW EXPLORERS

Thomas Cook of London were the first to propose tourist visits to Antarctica in 1910. But it was the Chileans who took the initiative when they flew tourists over their Antarctic territory in 1956. Not to be outdone, an Argentinean vessel, the *Les Eclaireurs,* landed 100 tourists in the Argentine sector in 1958. Non-nationalistic tourism came of age in 1968 when the *Magga Dan,* chartered by the father of Antarctic tourism, Lars Eric Lindblad, took 24 passengers to the Ross Dependency.

Antarctic flights were slow in gaining popularity. There were only eight flights between 1956 and 1976. However, in 1977 Qantas and Air New Zealand took five flights to Antarctica, 18 in 1977-78, and 17 in 1978-79. Not everyone was happy with this new development. At the tenth Antarctic Consultative Meeting, held in Washington in early September 1979, the treaty nations made their concerns about commercial overflights clear. Flight operators were warned that their activities exceeded existing capabilities for aircraft control, communications and search and rescue. Then, on 28 November 1979, tragedy struck. An Air New Zealand DC 10 crashed into the slopes of Mount Erebus, killing all 257 passengers and crew aboard.

Tourists have never been welcome in Antarctica. They breached the all-male domain of this elite continent, disturbed the work of scientific stations and left litter - directly or indirectly - on and around the continent.

There are, however, positive aspects to Antarctic tourism. The world at large came to know Antarctica largely through the tourists who visited it, and because of the interest these visits created. Scientists and base personnel had to be more careful in matters of conservation and the environment - particularly about rubbish disposal. Most curiously, the presence of female tourists and tour guides played a large part in forcing governments to re-examine the all-male policy for staff at bases. Now female scientists and support staff are an accepted part of the Antarctic scene, and few would argue that life in Antarctica is anything but all the better for it.

PART THREE: ANTARCTIC ATLAS AND CHRONOLOGY

Some of the people, places and events described in this book will be unfamiliar. To assist readers the following pages contain these features: an atlas of all Antarctica showing the most visited places at a large scale; a time chart of events from the earliest times to the present day; and biographies of all the major figures in Antarctic exploration.

A Continent Revealed

Satellites complete the job of mapping Antarctica

By the time of the International Geophysical Year, in 1957-58, most of Antarctica had been photographed from the air and various national expeditions were laboriously filling in details of the land in their spheres of operations. There was, however, much work to be done which had to wait for the era of international co-operation that followed the IGY, and the development of modern satellite technology.

True international co-operation in the task of mapping Antarctica did not start until 1958. Then, in the wake of the International Geophysical Year, the Scientific Committee on Antarctic Research (SCAR) was created to co-ordinate all scientific work in Antarctica. A series of permanent working groups were established by SCAR, including one of geodesy and cartography, which since its inception has had its secretariat in Australia's Division of National Mapping. This working group set as its objective the complete and systematic mapping of the Antarctic continent. It standardised scales, symbols and a datum for mapping. Equally important, it created a group of colleagues in the nations involved in Antarctic research who knew and corresponded with each other, shared their experience and co-operated on joint projects. Each of the twelve nations involved established an Antarctic mapping centre which exchanged maps and survey data with the others. As with so much in Antarctica, mapping benefited from this sense of international co-operation which transcended national frontiers.

In January 1959, British surveyors made the first distance measurements in Antarctica using Tellurometers, which calculate distance by measuring the time that it takes radio waves to travel between two units. These devices were to revolutionise surveying throughout the world, as simple traverses could now replace complicated nets of triangulation. It was even possible to connect the South Shetland Islands to the mainland of Trinity Peninsula by direct measurement — some of the lines were over 100 kilometres (62 miles) long. Other nations soon introduced Tellurometers, and helicopters became commercially available for transporting surveyors to their survey stations.

A pattern of operations began to emerge. Ships brought in light aircraft and helicopters each summer. Large semi-permanent camps were established far inland, the heavy stores being driven in by tractor train in the spring, and the scientists arriving by air. These operations were expensive, but they were extremely productive. Areas selected for their scientific interest were systematically photographed from the air, sometimes in colour, not only for mapping but also to help the geologists. The ice, the mountains and the land beneath the ice were all surveyed. The Russians carried lines of levels inland over the icecap from Mirny to Vostok for 1400 kilometres (870 miles), and then 2200 kilometres (1370 miles) to the coast again at Molodezhnaya. The British criss-crossed Antarctica with a network of flights from which both the height of the ice and its depth to the rock beneath were determined. The surface of the land beneath the ice, never seen by man, was gradually mapped.

In recent years artificial satellites have revolutionised Antarctic mapping. By 1980 it was possible to establish the position of a survey station to within a metre or so using Doppler satellites, while pictures of Antarctica north of 80°S can be obtained from the Landsat satellites. The fine detail on Landsat images still does not equal that of air photographs, but each picture covers an area 185 kilometres (115 miles) square, and the problem of joining them up into accurate maps is much less than of joining together a host of photographs at larger scale, especially over ice, where it is often impossible to identify common points on adjacent photographs.

Landsat photographs lack one great attribute of overlapping air photographs, however; they do not enable surveyors to see the world stereoscopically, and thus to draw contours.

ABOUT THE MAPS

The shape of Antarctica and its relationship to the other continents is unfamiliar to many people. In this case it is no help to use the common mapping convention of always placing north at the top. For an observer at the South Pole, all directions are north. To help readers position themselves, all maps in this book have been drawn with one orientation — as seen on the next page. Detailed maps used to show the tracks of explorers follow the same convention. If a reader wishes to see where a detail fits into the overall map it is an easy matter to find the grid lines, and thereby the relevant section of land or sea on one of the following maps.

Common colours have been used for all the explorer maps — orange for land or permanent ice cover, mauve for more or less permanent ice shelves, blue for open water and white for pack ice — if it is relevant to the story. The extent of pack ice obviously varies from season to season, so it is only shown where it was used as a highway by expeditions, or when it imprisoned a ship. The extent of land seen from aircraft, shown as shaded strips or patches, is only approximate.

Occasionally, land and ice outlines plotted by the explorers have been used to make sense of their stories. Parts of these early outlines were wrong or incomplete. Accurate maps appear on the following pages.

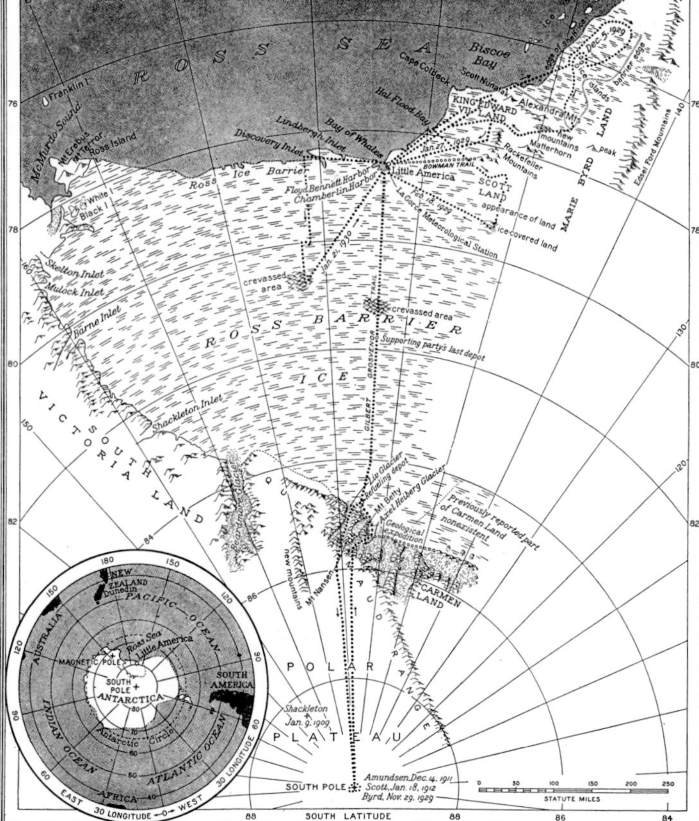

A map of the Ross Sea region prepared after the return of Byrd's first expedition in 1930. It is difficult to appreciate that so little was known about the shape of Antarctica in such recent times.

A satellite position-fixing station set up on a hilltop in west Antarctica. The exact location of features can now be established with great precision.

THE VIEW FROM SPACE

The United States' Landsat satellites circle the earth at an altitude of about 917 kilometres (570 miles) scanning a strip of land 185 kilometres (115 miles) wide beneath them. The satellites do not take photographs of the ground, but analyse the scene with a number of sensor systems. The information from these sensors is transmitted back to earth where it can be rendered into an image. These images can be combined in a number of ways and printed in different colours to emphasise particular details such as vegetation, water or ice. The smallest object that can be seen on the ground is about 64 metres (210 ft) across. The satellites fly over the same spot every 18 days, so if the area is free of cloud, it is even possible to track large individual icebergs.

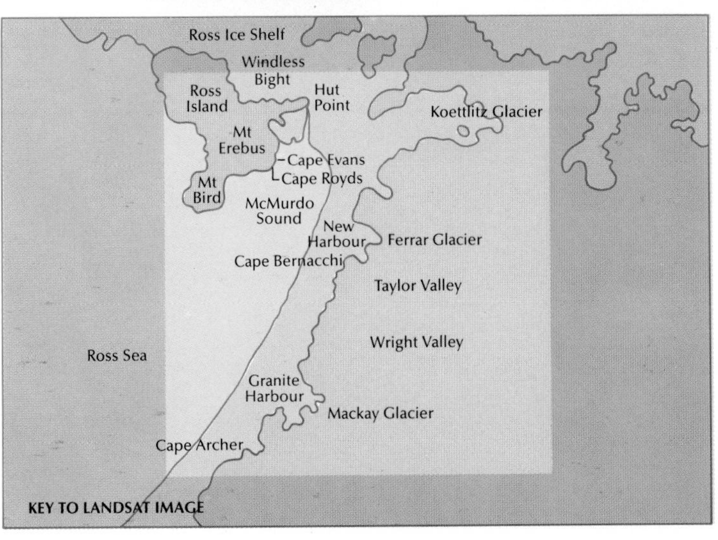

An extraordinary view of Ross Island, McMurdo Sound, the dry valleys and part of Victoria Land taken by Landsat in mid-January 1973. The passage from McMurdo Sound to Hut Point Peninsula is kept open by icebreakers so that supply ships can reach the American McMurdo base. The ice in Erebus Bay, and along the coast of Victoria Land, usually breaks up as the season progresses. The junction between light and dark ice running from Victoria Land to the Hut Point channel marks the edge of the Ross Ice Shelf.

THE ANTARCTIC CONTINENT
0
500
1000 km
0
500 miles
See page 316 for map gazetteer
FOR DETAILED MAP SEE PAGE 290
FALKLAND ISLANDS
TIERRA DEL FUEGO
POWELL I.
LAURIE I.
SIGNY I.
CORONATION I.
SOUTH ORKNEY ISLANDS
CLARENCE I.
ELEPHANT I.
KING GEORGE I.
GREENWICH I.
SOUTH SHETLAND ISLANDS
SMITH I.
DECEPTION I.
BRABANT I.
ANVERS I.
BISCOE ISLANDS
ADELAIDE I.
Drake Passage
Moody Point
Antarctic Sound
Bransfield Strait
Erebus and Terror Gulf
Trinity Pen.
Prince Gustav Channel
Larsen Inlet
PALMER ARCH.
Graham Land
Jason Pen.
FOYN COAST
Cape Alexander
LARSEN ICE SHELF
Cape Agassiz
HEARST I.
LOUBET COAST
BOWMAN COAST
Matha Strait
Marguerite Bay
WORDIE ICE SHELF
ETERNITY RA.
BLACK COAST
STEELE I.
Smith Inlet
Kemp Pen.
Smith Pen.
LASSITER COAST
Palmer Land
BATTERBEE MTNS
Cape Jeremy
Cape Vostok
ALEXANDER ISLAND
George VI Sound
WALTON MTNS
Wilkins Sound
CHARCOT I.
LATADY I.
Ronne Entrance
SMYLEY I.
ENGLISH COAST
Rydberg Pen.
Eltanin Bay
BRYAN COAST
VENABLE ICE SHELF
Pfrogner Point
PETER I ØY
FAREWELL I.
ANTARCTIC PENINSULA
ANTARCTIC CIRCLE
SOUTHERN OCEAN
Weddell Sea
Cape Adams
SWEENEY MTNS
HAUBERG MTNS
ORVILLE COAST
RONNE ICE SHELF
BERKNER ISLAND
Gould Bay
Vahsel Bay
Weldon
Hayes
Stancomb Glacier
Constellation Inlet
HERITAGE RANGE
Rutford Gl.
Mt Bentley
SENTINEL RA.
VINSON MASSIF
ELLSWORTH
MOUNTAINS
Ellsworth Land
HOLLICK-KENYON PLATEAU
WHITMORE MTNS
Bellingshausen Sea
Amundsen Sea
MCNAMARA I.
Seraph Bay
Evans Pen.
Koether Inlet
THURSTON ISLAND
Noville Pen.
Peale Inlet
Cape Flying Fish
Demas Ice Tongue
EIGHTS COAST
ABBOT ICE SHELF
JONES MTNS
HUDSON MTNS
COSGROVE ICE SHELF
WALGREEN COAST
Pine Island Bay
Thwaites Gl.
BURKE I.
Thwaites Iceberg Tongue
Bear Pen.
Marie
Byrd
Land
Mt Takahe
KOHLER RA.
CRARY MTNS
EXECUTIVE COMMITTEE RA.
Mt Sidley
DOTSON ICE SHELF
Martin Pen.
WRIGHT I.
Cape Leahy
CARNEY I.
Cape Gates
BAKUTIS COAST
GETZ ICE SHELF
HOBBS COAST
SIPLE I.
DEAN I.
GRANT I.
FORRESTER I.
AMES RA.
FLOOD RA.
Hull Gl.
Mt Berlin
Land Gl.
FORD RA.
RUPPERT COAST
Cape Burks
CRUZEN ISLAND
NICKERSON ICE SHELF
Block Bay
SOUTHERN
A
B
C
D
E
F
55°S
60°S
65°S
70°S
75°S
80°S
60°W
50°W
40°W
30°W
20°W
70°W
80°W
90°W
100°W
110°W
120°W
130°W
140°W
150°W
160°W
21
22
23
24
25
26
27
28
29
30
31
33
34

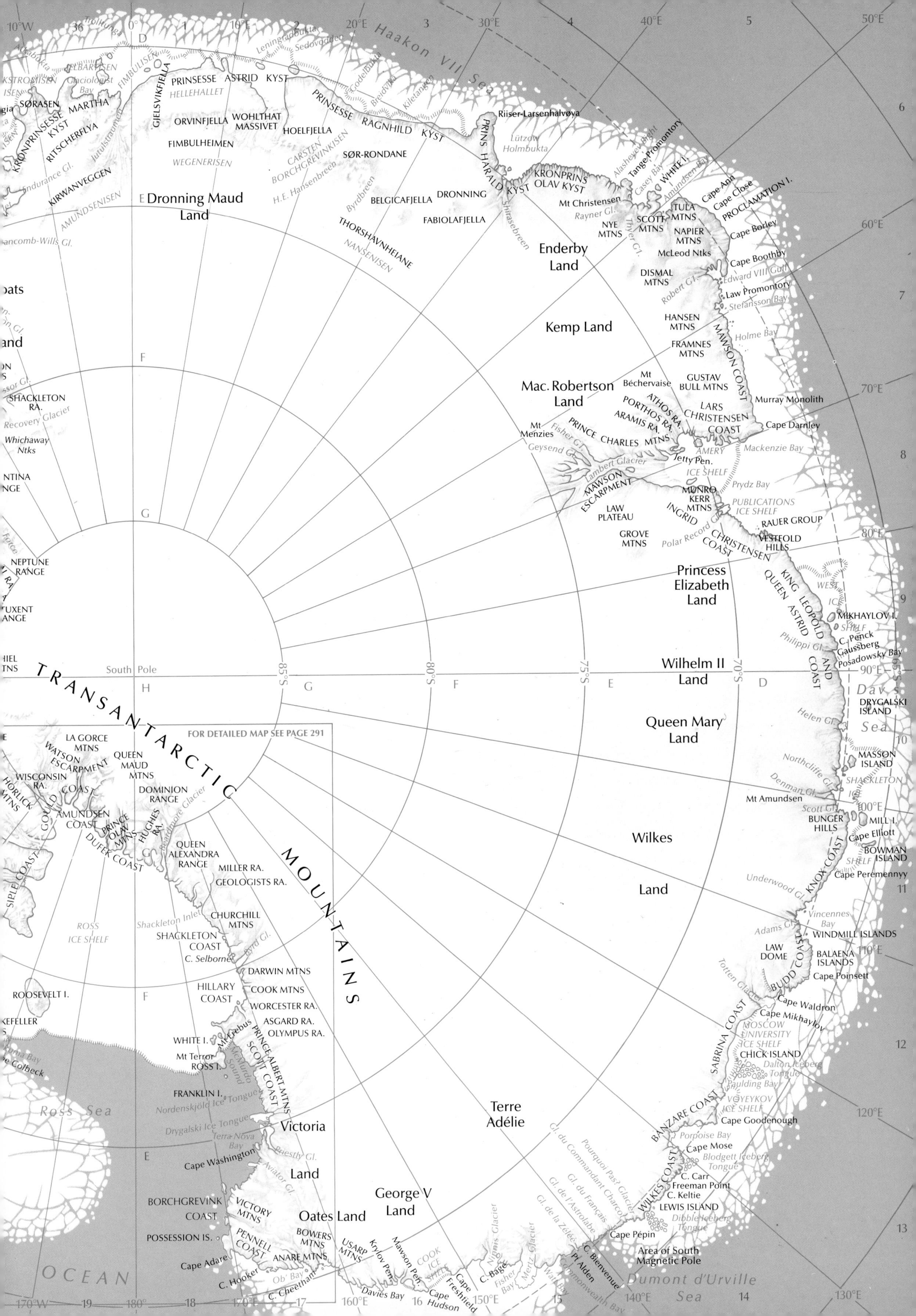

Haakon VII Sea
Dronning Maud Land
PRINSESSE ASTRID KYST
PRINSESSE RAGNHILD KYST
PRINS HARALD KYST
KRONPRINS OLAV KYST
KRONPRINSESSE MARTHA KYST
Riiser-Larsenhalvøya
SØR-RONDANE
BELGICAFJELLA
DRONNING FABIOLAFJELLA
Enderby Land
Kemp Land
Mac. Robertson Land
Princess Elizabeth Land
Wilhelm II Land
Queen Mary Land
Wilkes Land
Terre Adélie
George V Land
Oates Land
Victoria Land
TRANSANTARCTIC MOUNTAINS
South Pole
FOR DETAILED MAP SEE PAGE 291
MAWSON COAST
LARS CHRISTENSEN COAST
INGRID CHRISTENSEN COAST
KING LEOPOLD AND QUEEN ASTRID COAST
KNOX COAST
BUDD COAST
SABRINA COAST
BANZARE COAST
WILKES COAST
AMERY ICE SHELF
PRINCE CHARLES MTNS
Cape Darnley
Mackenzie Bay
Prydz Bay
VESTFOLD HILLS
Davis Sea
DRYGALSKI ISLAND
MASSON ISLAND
SHACKLETON ICE SHELF
BUNGER HILLS
WINDMILL ISLANDS
LAW DOME
MOSCOW UNIVERSITY ICE SHELF
Dumont d'Urville Sea
Area of South Magnetic Pole
Cape Adare
Ross Sea
ROSS ICE SHELF
ROOSEVELT I.
OCEAN
QUEEN MAUD MTNS
DOMINION RANGE
QUEEN ALEXANDRA RANGE
SHACKLETON COAST
HILLARY COAST
SCOTT COAST
BORCHGREVINK COAST
PENNELL COAST
POSSESSION IS.
ROSS I.

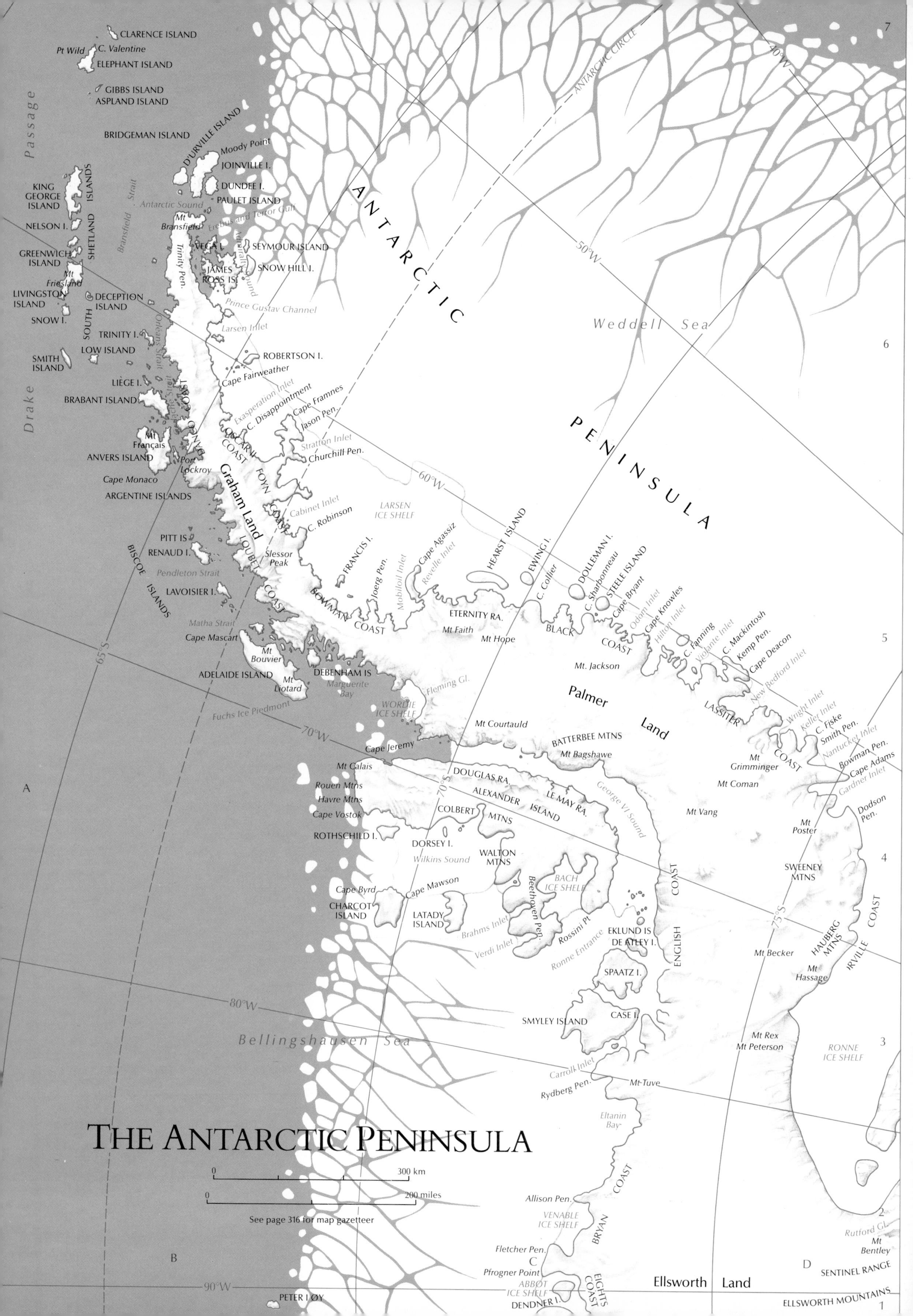

THE ANTARCTIC PENINSULA
0
300 km
0
200 miles
See page 316 for map gazetteer
CLARENCE ISLAND
Pt Wild
C. Valentine
ELEPHANT ISLAND
GIBBS ISLAND
ASPLAND ISLAND
BRIDGEMAN ISLAND
D'URVILLE ISLAND
Moody Point
JOINVILLE I.
DUNDEE I.
PAULET ISLAND
Antarctic Sound
Erebus and Terror Gulf
Mt Bransfield
Bransfield Strait
KING GEORGE ISLAND
NELSON I.
GREENWICH ISLAND
SOUTH SHETLAND ISLANDS
Drake Passage
VEGA I.
SEYMOUR ISLAND
JAMES ROSS IS.
SNOW HILL I.
Trinity Pen.
Mt Friesland
LIVINGSTON ISLAND
DECEPTION ISLAND
SNOW I.
Prince Gustav Channel
Larsen Inlet
TRINITY I.
LOW ISLAND
SMITH ISLAND
Orléans Strait
ROBERTSON I.
Cape Fairweather
LIÈGE I.
BRABANT ISLAND
Exasperation Inlet
C. Disappointment
Cape Framnes
Jason Pen.
Mt Français
ANVERS ISLAND
Port Lockroy
Cape Monaco
ARGENTINE ISLANDS
DANCO COAST
OSCAR II COAST
Stratton Inlet
Churchill Pen.
Graham Land
FOYN COAST
Cabinet Inlet
C. Robinson
LARSEN ICE SHELF
ANTARCTIC
PENINSULA
Weddell Sea
ANTARCTIC CIRCLE
40°W
50°W
60°W
70°W
80°W
90°W
65°S
70°S
75°S
PITT IS
RENAUD I.
BISCOE ISLANDS
Pendleton Strait
LOUBET COAST
Slessor Peak
LAVOISIER I.
Matha Strait
Cape Mascart
Mt Bouvier
ADELAIDE ISLAND
Mt Liotard
DEBENHAM IS
Marguerite Bay
Fuchs Ice Piedmont
WORDIE ICE SHELF
Fleming Gl.
FRANCIS I.
Joerg Pen.
Mobiloil Inlet
Cape Agassiz
Revelle Inlet
HEARST ISLAND
EWING I.
DOLLEMAN I.
C. Collier
C. Sharbonneau
STEELE ISLAND
Cape Bryant
Odom Inlet
Cape Knowles
Hilton Inlet
BOWMAN COAST
ETERNITY RA.
Mt Faith
Mt Hope
BLACK COAST
C. Fanning
Violante Inlet
C. Mackintosh
Kemp Pen.
Cape Deacon
New Bedford Inlet
Mt. Jackson
Palmer Land
LASSITER COAST
Wright Inlet
Keller Inlet
C. Fiske
Smith Pen.
Nantucket Inlet
Bowman Pen.
Cape Adams
Gardner Inlet
Mt Courtauld
BATTERBEE MTNS
Mt Bagshawe
Cape Jeremy
Mt Calais
Rouen Mtns
Havre Mtns
Cape Vostok
DOUGLAS RA.
ALEXANDER ISLAND
LE MAY RA.
George VI Sound
COLBERT MTNS
ROTHSCHILD I.
DORSEY I.
Wilkins Sound
WALTON MTNS
Mt Grimminger
Mt Coman
Mt Vang
Mt Poster
Dodson Pen.
SWEENEY MTNS
BACH ICE SHELF
Beethoven Pen.
Cape Byrd
Cape Mawson
CHARCOT ISLAND
LATADY ISLAND
Brahms Inlet
Verdi Inlet
Rossini Pt
Ronne Entrance
EKLUND IS
DE ATLEY I.
ENGLISH COAST
HAUBERG MTNS
IRVILLE COAST
Mt Becker
Mt Hassage
SPAATZ I.
SMYLEY ISLAND
CASE I.
Bellingshausen Sea
Mt Rex
Mt Peterson
RONNE ICE SHELF
Carroll Inlet
Rydberg Pen.
Mt Tuve
Eltanin Bay
BRYAN COAST
Allison Pen.
VENABLE ICE SHELF
Fletcher Pen.
Pfrogner Point
ABBOT ICE SHELF
EIGHTS COAST
DENDNER I.
PETER I ØY
Ellsworth Land
Rutford Gl.
Mt Bentley
SENTINEL RANGE
ELLSWORTH MOUNTAINS
A
B
C
D
1
2
3
4
5
6
7

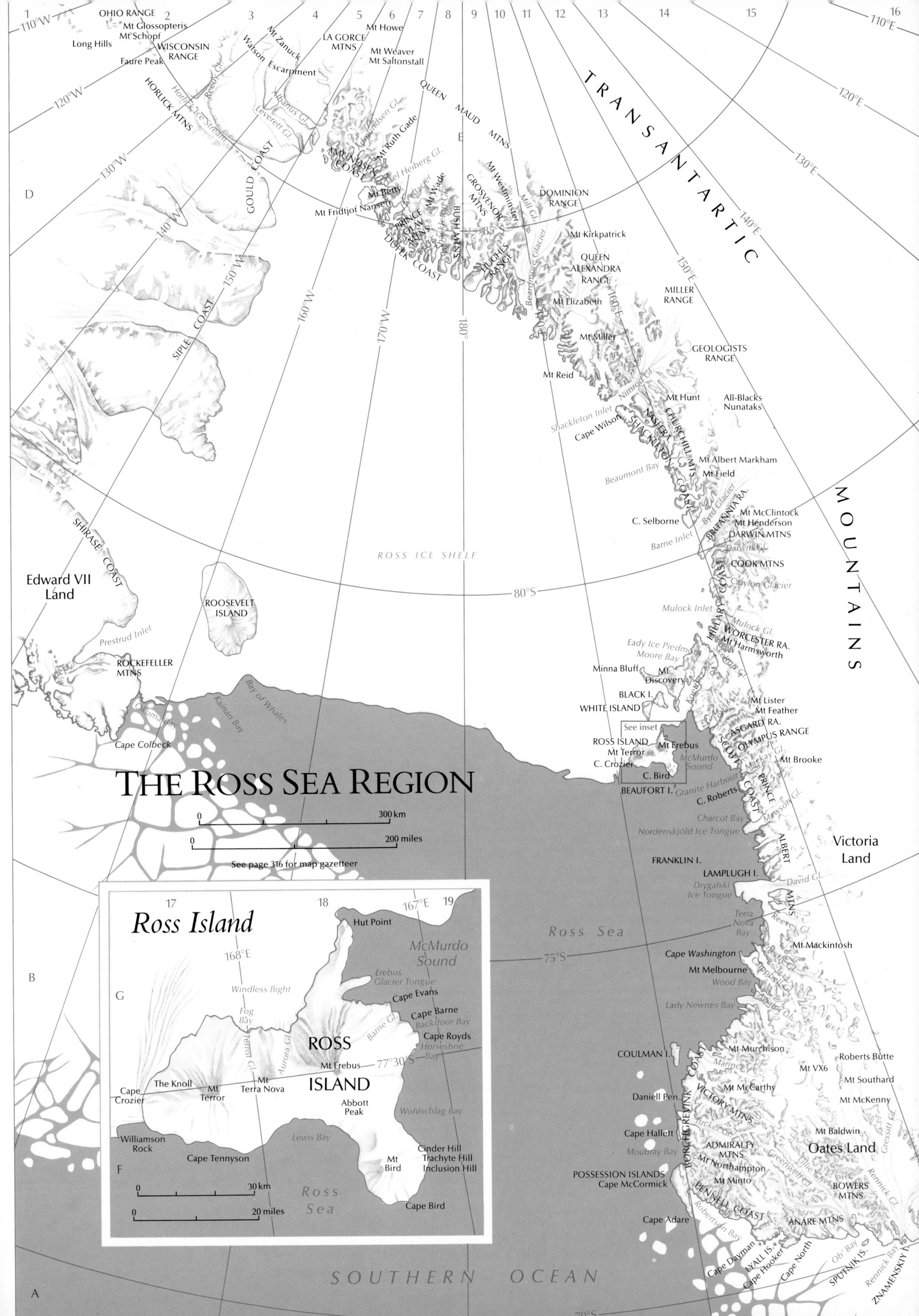
THE ROSS SEA REGION
TRANSANTARTIC MOUNTAINS
ROSS ICE SHELF
Ross Sea
SOUTHERN OCEAN
OHIO RANGE
Mt Glossopteris
Mt Schopf
Long Hills
WISCONSIN RANGE
Faure Peak
HORLICK MTNS
Horlick Ice Stream
Mt Zanuck
Watson Escarpment
LA GORCE MTNS
Mt Howe
Mt Weaver
Mt Saltonstall
QUEEN MAUD MTNS
GOULD COAST
AMUNDSEN COAST
Mt Ruth Gade
Mt Betty
Mt Fridtjof Nansen
Mt Wade
PRINCE OLAV MTNS
DUFEK COAST
BUSH MTNS
GROSVENOR MTNS
Mt Westminster
HUGHES RANGE
DOMINION RANGE
Beardmore Glacier
Mt Kirkpatrick
QUEEN ALEXANDRA RANGE
Mt Elizabeth
MILLER RANGE
Mt Miller
GEOLOGISTS RANGE
Mt Reid
Nimrod Gl.
Mt Hunt
All-Blacks Nunataks
Shackleton Inlet
Cape Wilson
NASH RA.
CHURCHILL MTS
SHACKLETON COAST
Mt Albert Markham
Mt Field
Beaumont Bay
C. Selborne
Barne Inlet
Byrd Glacier
BRITANNIA RA.
Mt McClintock
Mt Henderson
DARWIN MTNS
Darwin Gl.
COOK MTNS
Carlyon Glacier
HILLARY COAST
Mulock Inlet
Mulock Gl.
WORCESTER RA.
Mt Harmsworth
Eady Ice Piedmont
Moore Bay
Minna Bluff
Mt Discovery
BLACK I.
WHITE ISLAND
Mt Lister
Mt Feather
ASGARD RA.
OLYMPUS RANGE
See inset
ROSS ISLAND
Mt Erebus
Mt Terror
C. Crozier
C. Bird
McMurdo Sound
BEAUFORT I.
Mt Brooke
SCOTT COAST
Granite Harbour
C. Roberts
Mackay Gl.
PRINCE ALBERT MTNS
Charcot Bay
Mawson Gl.
Nordenskjöld Ice Tongue
Victoria Land
FRANKLIN I.
LAMPLUGH I.
David Gl.
Drygalski Ice Tongue
Terra Nova Bay
Reeves Gl.
Mt Mackintosh
Cape Washington
Mt Melbourne
Wood Bay
Campbell Gl.
Lady Newnes Bay
COULMAN I.
Mt Murchison
Mariner Gl.
Roberts Butte
Mt VX6
Mt Southard
Mt McCarthy
Daniell Pen.
VICTORY MTNS
BORCHGREVINK COAST
Mt McKenny
Tucker Gl.
Mt Baldwin
Cape Hallett
ADMIRALTY MTNS
Moubray Bay
Mt Northampton
Oates Land
Greenwell Gl.
Gressitt Gl.
POSSESSION ISLANDS
Cape McCormick
Mt Minto
BOWERS MTNS
Rennick Gl.
PENNELL COAST
Cape Adare
ANARE MTNS
Robertson Bay
Cape Dayman
LYALL IS.
Cape Hooker
Cape North
Ob' Bay
SPUTNIK IS.
Rennick Bay
ZNAMENSKIY I.
SIPLE COAST
SHIRASE COAST
Edward VII Land
ROOSEVELT ISLAND
Prestrud Inlet
ROCKEFELLER MTNS
Okuma Bay
Kainan Bay
Bay of Whales
Cape Colbeck
0 300 km
0 200 miles
See page 316 for map gazetteer
Ross Island
Hut Point
McMurdo Sound
Erebus Glacier Tongue
Windless Bight
Cape Evans
Cape Barne
Backdoor Bay
Cape Royds
Horseshoe Bay
Fog Bay
Terror Gl.
Aurora Gl.
Barne Gl.
ROSS ISLAND
Mt Erebus
77°30'S
The Knoll
Mt Terra Nova
Cape Crozier
Mt Terror
Abbott Peak
Wohlschlag Bay
Williamson Rock
Lewis Bay
Cinder Hill
Trachyte Hill
Inclusion Hill
Cape Tennyson
Mt Bird
0 30 km
0 20 miles
Ross Sea
Cape Bird
168°E
167°E

ANTARCTIC TIME CHART

1500-1818 The death of Terra Australis

There have been over 300 expeditions to the mainland of Antarctica, and many more to the subantarctic regions. It has only been possible in this book to cover in detail the most important and interesting ones, so on the following eight pages there is a chronology of all the expeditions in the book, plus some others that have not been discussed elsewhere. Other landmarks in the history of Antarctica are given a place in the chronology, starting with the ancient concept of* Terra Australis, *and finishing in the 1980s, with international discussions about the exploitation of Antarctic resources.

These two pages outline the events that occurred up to 1818. The story of man's relationship with Antarctica up to that time is of the growth of a myth that was then gradually whittled away. Why did geographers develop the idea of *Terra Australis* — the great south land? Why were they reluctant to suggest that the seas of the southern hemisphere extended right to the South Pole?

It was the ancient Greeks who first said that the earth was round and that a large southern landmass must exist to balance the known world of the northern hemisphere. Maps were drawn to depict this massive assumed continent stretching to the South Pole. Although this idea lost favour in Europe for over a millenium, it was revived in the fifteenth century as Europeans began to explore the boundaries of their world and found that the earth was indeed round. Maps again began to show a great south land.

As expeditions of European sailor-explorers pushed further afield, their knowledge of southern waters slowly increased. Bartholomew Diaz and Vasco de Gama showed that Africa extended only to the Cape of Good Hope. Ferdinand Magellan, by entering the Pacific from the east, showed that South America was not connected to a southern continent. Drake showed that no visible landmass existed south of Cape Horn.

But the myth of *Terra Australis* persisted, a triumph of hope over evidence. Expedition after expedition was sent in search of it. Australia was discovered, but the geographers assumed there must be more. French explorers, Jean-Baptiste Bouvet de Lozier in 1738 and Yves Joseph de Kerguélen-Trémarec in 1772, discovered subantarctic islands and both jumped to the conclusion that their discoveries marked the edge of a southern continent.

It was James Cook who finally merged myth with reality. On his voyage of 1772-76 he crisscrossed the southern Indian, Pacific and Atlantic oceans without discovering any new continent. He crossed the Antarctic Circle, but found only ice. He concluded that if any landmass existed, and he thought that it did, then it lay well south of the pack ice and was of no use to the world.

By 1818 several more outposts of the Antarctic region had been discovered, but what lay behind the ice stretching away to the south remained a mystery.

Ancient times
The idea of Terra Australis *begins with the Greeks. Pythagoras in the sixth century and Aristotle in the fourth century BC, argue that the earth is a sphere. Greek geographers then fill this new world with imaginary lands and seas. Their feeling for symmetry leads to the concept of a southern landmass,* Terra Australis Incognita, *to balance the known, northern world. In medieval Europe, however, this classical view of the world is theologically awkward. Flat earth orthodoxy holds sway until voyages of exploration in the fifteenth century.*

1501
The Florentine seaman Amerigo Vespucci makes the first long voyage along the South American coastline, sailing as far as 50°S. A forged letter later suggests that Vespucci reached South Georgia.

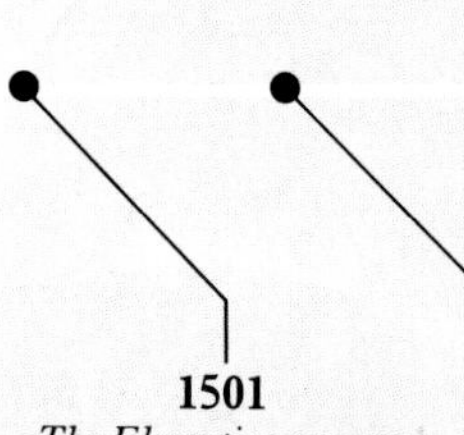

September 1519
Ferdinand Magellan leaves Spain with instructions to follow the coastline of South America and find a western sea route to the Indies. Sailing down the coast he finds the narrow strait that now bears his name and passes through into the Pacific Ocean. To the south stretches Tierra del Fuego which geographers soon seize on as the edge of the long-sought-after southern continent. Magellan continues westwards across the Pacific and, although he is killed in the Philippines, one of his ships completes the first circumnavigation of the globe.

1531
Oronce Fine (Orontius) publishes his map of the world — typical for the time — showing Tierra del Fuego as the northern tip of an immense southern continent centred on the South Pole.

September 1578
Francis Drake in the Golden Hind, *having passed through the Strait of Magellan into the Pacific, runs into a storm and is blown far to the south. Drake's nephew Francis Fletcher describes their falling in 'with the uttermost part of land towards the South Pole without which there is no main nor island to be seen to the Southwards; but the Atlantic Ocean and the South Sea meet in a large and free scope'. This is the discovery of Drake's Passage and shows that Tierra del Fuego is not connected to any southern continent.*

August 1592
The English explorer John Davis in the Desire *discovers the Falkland Islands. Returning northwards along the South American coast with his crew in poor condition, Davis lands on a small island off Puerto Deseado. They kill 14 000 penguins which they dry and salt, and store in the hold. As they sail through the tropics the dried penguins begin 'to corrupt, and there bred in them a most loathsome and ugly worm of an inch [25 mm] long'. The worms eat clothes, boots and timbers — everything except iron — and the men 'fall sick of a monstrous disease'. Of the original 76 crew members only 16 wretched survivors reach home alive.*

January 1616
Willem Schouten and Jacob le Maire discover Cape Horn when they became the first sailors to round the southern tip of South America.

September 1622
The Dutch sailor Dirck Gerritsz, in an account much doubted today, reportedly makes the first sighting of the South Shetland Islands.

April 1675
The London merchant Antonio de la Roché is blown to the south of Cape Horn and makes the first sighting of South Georgia. He shelters in the lee of the island 'with a prospect of great snow-covered mountains falling sheer to the sea'.

December 1687
Lionel Wafer, English surgeon and buccaneer, sails round Cape Horn and, in one of the earliest descriptions of Antarctic icebergs, records 'several Islands of Ice; which at first seemed to be real Land. From these Hills of Ice came very cold blasts of wind.'

January 1739
Jean-Baptiste Bouvet de Lozier discovers Bouvetøya to the south of Africa — an island of 50 sq kilometres (19 sq miles) and the most isolated piece of land on earth. Sailing in the Aigle and the Marie for the French Compagnie des Indies, Bouvet is searching for a fertile southern continent to provide ports for the company's ships. He tries unsuccessfully in bad weather and rough seas to get ashore on this icebound piece of rock. Not knowing if he has discovered a point of the great south land, or only an island, he continues eastwards along the pack ice for over 2000 kilometres (1240 miles) before returning north. Although unrecognised at the time, Bouvet's voyage is a great feat of

January 1772
The French explorer Marion Du Fresne, searching for a southern continent, discovers the Prince Edward Islands and the Îles Crozet — two small uninhabited groups in the southern Indian Ocean. The expedition continues eastwards but Du Fresne is killed by Maoris in New Zealand.

February 1772
Yves Joseph de Kerguélen-Trémarec discovers a group of 300 icebound islands in the southern Indian Ocean — now known as Îles Kerguelen. Kerguélen sails with orders from the French Government to search for the supposed great southern continent. Because of fog and high seas, however, he is unable to land or to chart his islands. Naming them La France Australe, he returns to France reporting: 'The lands which I have had the happiness to discover appear to form the central mass of the Antarctic continent. The latitude at which it lies promises all the crops of the Mother Country . . . wood, minerals, diamonds, rubies will be found . . . If men of a different species are not discovered at least there will be people living in a state of nature . . .'

January 1773
Captain James Cook and the crews of the Resolution and Adventure become the first men to cross the Antarctic Circle. Cook, on his second great voyage of discovery, had left Plymouth six months previously with orders to keep as far south as possible, and to settle the enigma of Terra Australis. He is to spend three years searching for this southern continent, and in failing to find it is to demolish forever the myth of its existence.

December 1773
Captain Cook still on his great voyage in the Resolution and Adventure writes of 'a strong gale attended by a thick fog, sleet and snow, which froze to the Rigging as it fell and decorated the Whole Ship with Icicles. Our ropes were like wire, our sails like plates of metal and the sheaves froze fast in the blocks . . . I have never seen so much ice.' Cook, now in the Pacific Ocean sector, continues along the pack ice for another month reaching 71°S before heading north. He has now been further south than anyone before him and sailed 29 000 kilometres (18 000 miles) through unknown southern seas without sighting land.

January 1774
Kerguélen on a second voyage again sights Îles Kerguelen. After his ecstatic and imaginative report of 1772 he has been given three ships and 700 men and told to colonise his discovery. Faced with the inhospitable reality of the islands he returns to France and a court martial.

January 1775
Cook, into his third Antarctic cruise, discovers South Georgia, an island with 'a terrain savage and horrible, the Wild rocks raising their lofty summits till the clouds, the Vallies buried in everlasting Snow'. Two weeks later he discovers the South Sandwich Islands. Although, after three years in southern waters, Cook has found no substantial land, he notes: 'Yet I believe firmly there is a tract of land near the Pole, which is the source of all the ice spread over this vast Southern Ocean.' By July Cook is back in England having sailed nearly 100 000 kilometres (62 000 miles) in perhaps the greatest sea voyage ever made.

December 1776
Cook on his third voyage, in the Resolution and the Discovery, sights Îles Kerguélen, 'an island of no great extent, which from its sterility I shall call the Island of Desolation'.

1790
The beginning of the American sealing industry on South Georgia. Soon after Cook's discovery of the island, sealers flock to Antarctic waters. Because Europe is locked in war, the sealers are mainly Americans — from the ports of New England.

November 1791
Captain George Vancouver discovers the Snares Islands south of New Zealand. Within 20 years all fur seal colonies are totally destroyed.

1801
In probably the most profitable sealing voyage ever made to South Georgia, Captain Edmund Fanning from New England takes 57 000 fur seal skins. Another 60 000 are taken in the same year by other vessels. The skins are sent straight to China to be processed.

August 1806
The Auckland Islands, 300 kilometres (186 miles) south of New Zealand, are discovered by Abraham Bristow from the London sealing and whaling firm of Enderby and Sons.

July 1810
Frederick Hasselborough, out from Sydney in search of fresh sealing grounds, discovers Macquarie Island halfway between Australia and Antarctica. Within 10 years the fur seal colonies on the island are exterminated.

1819-1894
The coastline takes shape

February 1819
British captain William Smith in the Williams *is on a trading voyage from Buenos Aires to Valparaíso. Rounding Cape Horn he is blown far to the south by a series of storms and discovers the South Shetland Islands. In Valparaíso Smith is offered large sums of money by American sealers to give details of the discovery. He refuses, and in October returns to the islands, lands and claims them for Great Britain. The news spreads fast, and within 10 years the fur seal colonies have been exterminated.*

27 January 1820
Thaddeus von Bellingshausen sights an icefield at 69°S and 2°W 'which seemed to be covered with small hillocks'. Without knowing it, Bellingshausen has made an historic sighting; he is the first person to set eyes on the Antarctic continent. The Russian explorer had been despatched six months previously by Czar Alexander to find southern harbours for the imperial fleet. He has visited South Georgia and been the first to chart the South Sandwich Islands. Bellingshausen continues to skirt the pack ice for another month and makes further sightings before retreating northwards for the winter.

30 January 1820
Following Smith's discovery of the South Shetlands, the Royal Navy sends Edward Bransfield to investigate. With Smith as pilot, Bransfield reaches the islands and continues southeast. He is the first to see the Antarctic Peninsula. His midshipman, Bone, records: 'the only cheer the sight afforded was the idea that this might be the long sought-after southern continent.'

November 1820
The sealer Nathaniel Palmer in the Hero *reportedly sights the Antarctic Peninsula. The 19-year-old Palmer is a member of a large New England sealing fleet in the South Shetlands under Benjamin Pendleton. He has been despatched by Captain Pendleton to investigate the possibility of land to the south. There is doubt today whether Palmer actually saw the mainland, or even left the South Shetlands.*

January 1821
After wintering in Sydney and Polynesia, Captain Bellingshausen returns to Antarctic waters and discovers Peter I and Alexander Islands. He completes his circumnavigation of Antarctica, the first since Cook, and at more southerly latitudes.

February 1821
The American sealer John Davis makes what may be the first landing on the mainland of Antarctica — at Hughes Bay in Graham Land. Davis, from Connecticut, has been searching for seals in the South Shetlands. Not finding many he has ventured south in his Cecilia *where he now lands in 'a large Bay, the Land high and covered entirely with snow'.*

December 1821
Sealers Nathaniel Palmer and George Powell join forces to search for new sealing grounds and discover the South Orkney Islands. They chart the larger islands but are unable to find any fur seal colonies. Six days later, Michael McLeod, a British sealer from Leith, independently discovers the islands.

December 1822
Benjamin Morrell in the Wasp *makes the first recorded landing on Bouvetøya. The American sealer then visits Îles Kerguelen, the South Sandwich Islands and claims to penetrate the Weddell Sea to 70°S. However, the many discrepancies in Morrell's account of his voyage have thrown doubt on all of his achievements.*

February 1823
British sealer James Weddell penetrates the sea now named after him and reaches a record 74°S. There are still clear seas in front of him but, due to the lateness of the season, Weddell decides to return north. The absence of ice to the south leads Weddell to the view, published in his book A Voyage Towards the South Pole, *that there is no large landmass around the pole. No one, with the possible exception of Morrell, is able to enter the Weddell Sea again until Bruce in 1903.*

December 1825
Captain George Norris of the sealing firm Enderby Brothers sights Bouvetøya, lands and renames it Liverpool Island.

February 1831
John Biscoe, employed by the British sealing firm of Enderby Brothers, sights the ice cliffs of Enderby Land — the first sighting of Antarctica in the Indian Ocean sector. Despite the onset of scurvy among his crew, and fierce storms, Biscoe continues to follow the pack ice for hundreds of kilometres. His two ships barely make it to Australia. The next year Biscoe returns to the Antarctic in the region of the peninsula. He discovers Adelaide Island and completes his circumnavigation of the continent. He heads back to England but one of the ships is wrecked and many of the crew desert.

December 1833
Peter Kemp in the Magnet, *searching for new sealing grounds, sights a portion of the Antarctic coast now named after him. Due to thick pack ice he is unable to approach closer and after four days heads northwest.*

December 1833
The Hopeful *and the* Rose *under the command of Henry Rea leave the Falkland Islands to follow up discoveries made by John Biscoe. The* Rose *is crushed in pack ice near the South Shetland Islands and Rea, with the* Hopeful *now badly overladen, abandons the voyage and returns to England.*

February 1839
John Balleny, sailing in the Eliza Scott *and the* Sabrina *for the sealing firm of Enderby Brothers, heads south from New Zealand and discovers the islands now named after him. After landing, he sails west and makes the first sighting of Sabrina Land. The two ships are separated in a storm; the* Eliza Scott *survives with great difficulty, but the* Sabrina *is never seen again.*

January 1840
The scholarly Jules-Sebastian Dumont d'Urville, venturing reluctantly, but on royal orders, into Antarctic seas, notes 'land recognised in an unmistakable manner'. The French explorer sends a longboat onto an offshore island where the tricolour is raised. He names the stretch of coast which he has discovered for his wife, Terre Adélie. D'Urville, in the middle of anthropological exploration of the Pacific, continues along the pack ice for two weeks charting the coastline. He searches unsuccessfully for the South Magnetic Pole before heading north to warmer seas.

January 1840
Lieutenant Charles Wilkes, leader of the United States Exploring Expedition, sights the coast of Antarctica in an area now known as Wilkes Land. 'It had the appearance', he records, 'of being 300 feet [91 metres] in height, forming a sort of amphitheatre, grey and dark, and divided into two distinct ridges of elevations throughout its extent'. Despite leaking ships and a crew on the point of mutiny, Wilkes continues along the pack ice for over 2000 kilometres (1240 miles) sighting land at a number of points. He forms the opinion — still much doubted at the time — that Antarctica is a continent.

January 1841
The Erebus *and* Terror *under Sir James Clark Ross become the first ships to penetrate the Antarctic pack ice. Ross has been sent by Britain's Royal Navy to search for the South Magnetic Pole and to carry out explorations at southern latitudes. He discovers Victoria Land and enters the sea that now bears his name. He discovers Ross Island, Mt Erebus and the great cliffs of the Ross Ice Shelf. He returns to Hobart, but sails south again the following summer and traces the ice shelf further to the east, reaching 78°S — a record that will stand until 1900.*

In 1819 the Antarctic continent had still not been seen by human eyes. After Cook had demolished the myth of a great temperate south land, many geographers even doubted that any large land mass existed at all behind the apparently inpenetrable barrier of pack ice. Then, in January 1820, two remarkable events occurred. Two expeditions, each unaware of the other's existence, and over 2000 kilometres (1240 miles) apart, made the first sightings of the Antarctic mainland.

It is a measure of the unreality of Antarctica to sailors of that time that the first to make the sighting, a Russian admiral, Thaddeus von Bellingshausen, did not recognise what he saw, and indeed failed to record any sighting in his log book. The other sighting, by the British captain, Edward Bransfield, was described as 'the most gloomy that can be imagined.'

It is only with hindsight, of course, and with knowledge of the existence of the continent, that these early discoveries acquire any meaning. To the sailors themselves, they were mere landfalls, not necessarily continental in nature, that could not be properly charted due to ice and bad weather. What was of more importance to them was the discovery in 1819 of the South Shetland Islands, lying to the northwest of the Antarctic Peninsula.

It was the rich fur seal colonies of the South Shetlands that provided the impetus for further voyages and discoveries in the area; and it was almost certainly on the Antarctic Peninsula, in the next few years, that the first landings on the continent occurred.

But by 1830 these sealing grounds were exhausted and the sealers had to search elsewhere. It was they who made the first discoveries on the other side of the continent. John Biscoe in 1831, Peter Kemp in 1833 and John Balleny in 1839 all sighted portions of the coastline in the Indian Ocean sector.

Now nationally organised expeditions took over from the private ventures of sealing and whaling firms in attempts to penetrate the secrets of the ice pack. In 1840 a French expedition under Dumont d'Urville, and the United States Exploring Expedition under Charles Wilkes discovered, within hours of each other, separate sections of the coastline in the area south of Australia. In the loneliest sea in the world, ships from the two expeditions passed by in a fog.

The other great expedition of this period was led by Sir James Clark Ross from Britain. In 1841 he discovered the coast of Victoria Land and the sea now named after him. He entered this sea only to find his way blocked by a great wall of ice up to 60 metres (200 ft) high. It was the Ross Ice Shelf and it was from this area, and from the island also named after Ross, that the great land journeys into the interior were to be made over 60 years later.

After Ross, interest in the Antarctic went into a period of decline. It seemed clear that the region behind the ice was of no commercial value, and for many years the only visitors to the area were sealers picking at the remnants of the subantarctic seal colonies.

But by the 1890s, as northern whale stocks were exhausted, entrepreneurs began to look again to the south. In 1892 whaling fleets from Norway and Scotland arrived in the Weddell Sea. They found few whales that they could catch, but they made significant new discoveries along the Antarctic Peninsula.

Although still sketchy, the outline of Antarctica was beginning to take shape. Most people accepted the idea of a single continental land mass. The great question was now: what lay in the interior?

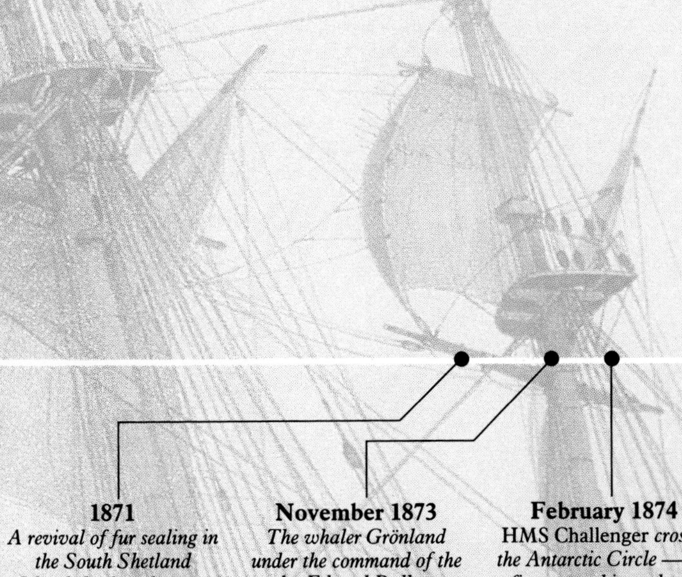

1871
A revival of fur sealing in the South Shetland Islands begins, due to a recovery of seal stocks after the depletions earlier in the century, and an increase in the price of skins. During the next decade every accessible beach in the Southern Ocean is thoroughly searched, leading to another devastation of seal colonies.

November 1873
The whaler Grönland under the command of the sealer Eduard Dallman, becomes the first steamship to visit Antarctic seas. Dallman, in the employ of the German Polar Navigation Company, heads south from the South Shetland Islands and discovers the Bismarck Strait. He continues south along the Antarctic Peninsula to 65° latitude before returning north. It is the first German Antarctic expedition.

February 1874
HMS Challenger *crosses the Antarctic Circle — the first steamship to do so. The* Challenger *is on a four-year scientific cruise of the world, and her scientists have already made a number of landings on subantarctic islands. Although no new land is sighted, the brief visit to the Antarctic provides a wealth of scientific data about the Southern Ocean — especially its great biological richness.*

1881
The first regulations for the control of the Antarctic sealing industry are promulgated. They are introduced by the British Government and apply only to the Falkland Islands and areas of British influence along the Antarctic Peninsula.

November 1892
Carl Larsen, captain of the whaler Jason, *lands on Seymour Island, near the tip of the Antarctic Peninsula, and discovers some specimens of petrified wood — the first fossils found in Antarctica, and evidence of a warmer past. The following season, Larsen sails along the Weddell Sea side of the peninsula, discovering a number of islands and the ice shelf that is named after him. He reaches 68°S before being halted by pack ice.*

December 1892
A fleet of four whaling ships from Dundee in Scotland reaches the Weddell Sea. The fleet searches unsuccessfully for right whales in the area of the Antarctic Peninsula. Captain Robertson on the Active *explores the southern coast of Joinville Island and discovers Dundee Island.*

1895-1922
The age of heroes

In 1895 no one had ventured beyond the coastline of Antarctica, nor even spent a winter in the icy seas that surround it. But that year marked the start of two decades of renewed and enthusiastic activity in Antarctic exploration. Ships were now stronger and, powered with steam, could penetrate the pack ice that lay around the continent.

It was the beginning of an age which brought forth some extraordinary acts of bravery and endurance by legendary figures in Antarctic exploration such as Amundsen, Scott and Shackleton, and the attainment of the South Pole. It was also an era in which the quest for scientific knowledge rivalled that of pure exploration in the bid for private and public sponsorship.

This period of renewed interest had small beginnings. In 1895 the Norwegian whaler, Henryk Bull, landed at Cape Adare in Victoria Land — the first landing on the continent outside the Antarctic Peninsula. Three years later a small group of scientists and sailors in the *Belgica* were caught in the ice off the peninsula and endured the first Antarctic winter. Not all of them survived it in sound mind. A

January 1895
Henryk Bull with a party from the whaler Antarctic *lands at Cape Adare at midnight, 'on a pebbly beach of easy access'. They claim it as the first landing on the continent; it is certainly the first outside the Antarctic Peninsula. One member of the party, Carsten Borchgrevink, has already found lichen on an offshore island — the first sign of plant life within the Antarctic Circle. The aftermath of the voyage is spoiled by an undignified dispute as to which expedition member had actually landed on the beach first.*

July 1895
The International Geographical Congress, meeting in London, decides to make Antarctica the main target of new exploration. This launches an era of government-sponsored national expeditions. Within a short time parties from Britain, Germany and Sweden are being organised.

March 1898
The Belgica *expedition under Adrien de Gerlache finds itself trapped in the pack ice off the Antarctic Peninsula. They spend a year drifting helplessly with the ice and are the first to live through an Antarctic winter. They cut a channel through the ice and finally escape, but the long winter night has caused severe medical problems. One member of the crew dies of a heart attack and two arrive home insane.*

February 1899
Carsten Borchgrevink and the members of the Southern Cross *expedition land at Cape Adare in Victoria Land. They erect prefabricated huts and become the first men to spend a winter on the continent. The next year they land on the Ross Ice Shelf and make a short sledge journey to the south.*

June 1899
Lieutenant Robert Scott crosses Buckingham Palace Road in London, meets Sir Clements Markham, and hears of the plans for a national Antarctic expedition. Two days later he applies to lead the expedition and is accepted.

February 1902
Erich von Drygalski and the members of the official German expedition in the Gauss *sight 'a high vertical wall of ice' and name it Wilhelm II Land. The* Gauss *is held in the ice for 12 months and the party make a number of sledge journeys to the nearby coast. The scientific results of the expedition fill 20 volumes of reports which are compiled over the next 26 years.*

February 1902
The Swedish geologist, Otto Nordenskjöld, and five companions are put ashore by the Antarctic *on Snow Hill Island. They spend two winters on the island and make the first major sledge journey in Antarctica — of 640 kilometres (400 miles). Their ship, however, is crushed in the ice and her crew separated into two groups. They manage to survive the winter and make their way to Snow Hill Island. The whole party is rescued in 1903 by an Argentinean relief ship.*

November 1902
In the first serious attempt to reach the South Pole, Robert Scott, Edward Wilson and Ernest Shackleton leave McMurdo Sound and head south across the Ross Ice Shelf. Two months later, at 82°S, still on the ice shelf and suffering badly from snowblindness and scurvy, they are forced to turn for home. Although failing to reach the pole, Scott's first expedition has covered 5000 kilometres (3100 miles) with sledge teams, and conducted a thorough scientific program.

October 1903
Scott sets out with a small party from McMurdo Sound to climb the Ferrar Glacier (first climbed the year before by Albert Armitage). They ascend 2000 metres (6560 ft) onto the polar icecap and sledge inland for two weeks — the first journey on the icecap.

February 1904
Jean Charcot in the Français *begins his survey of the western side of the Antarctic Peninsula. The small expedition winters in the ship in an inlet on Booth Island. Over two summers they discover the Loubet Coast, Doumer Island and Port Lockroy. They chart the Biscoe Islands and generally extend Gerlache's survey of the western side of the Antarctic Peninsula.*

March 1904
W. S. Bruce and the members of the Scottish National Antarctic Expedition aboard the Scotia, *sight the coast of Coats Land — the first sighting of the continent to the south of the ice-filled Weddell Sea. Bruce is now into the second summer of his expedition, having built his base on Laurie Island in the South Orkneys.*

1904
The birth of modern Antarctic whaling. Carl Larsen sets up the first shore-based whaling station at Grytviken on South Georgia. Within 10 years over 20 stations and factory ships are operating around the subantarctic islands.

January 1905
An Argentinean party in the Uruguay *relieves the remaining members of the* Scotia *expedition at their meteorological station on Laurie Island. The Argentinean Government sends a relief party every year, making Laurie Island the longest continually staffed base in Antarctica.*

March 1908
A party led by Edgeworth David from Ernest Shackleton's Nimrod *expedition begins the first ascent of the 3794-metre (12 448-ft) Mt Erebus on Ross Island. After climbing for five days, they reach the crater of the still-active volcano.*

October 1908
Ernest Shackleton, Frank Wild, Eric Marshall and Jameson Adams begin their attempt to reach the South Pole. In a month they have passed Scott's furthest south of 1903 and on 4 December begin their climb up to the polar plateau. They lose a pony down a crevasse — with a large part of their food supply — but press on south. They reach a point only 180 kilometres (97 nautical miles) from their goal before being forced to turn north due to illness and lack of food. After a tortuous return journey, the four exhausted men reach McMurdo Sound and their waiting ship.

January 1909
Edgeworth David, Douglas Mawson and Alistair McKay reach the South Magnetic Pole after sledging for three months across Victoria Land. David, who is approaching his 51st birthday, has been persuaded by Shackleton to stay the extra summer in Antarctica and lead the magnetic pole party.

June 1909
Jean Charcot on his second voyage to the Antarctic, this time in the Pourquoi-Pas?, *winters at Petermann Island. In the summer months he charts the coast southwards to Adelaide and Alexander Islands.*

September 1910
Roald Amundsen informs the stunned members of his Fram *expedition that he plans to head for the South Pole rather than the north as officially announced. He cables the news to Robert Scott in Melbourne.*

year later, in 1899, Carsten Borchgrevink carried the process another step further when his *Southern Cross* party wintered in a hut on the mainland at Cape Adare.

In 1902 the Swedish expedition under Otto Nordenskjöld made the first major Antarctic sledge journey using dog teams and techniques developed by Arctic explorers. A few months later in the Ross Sea area a British naval expedition under Robert Scott was the first to seriously penetrate the interior in an attempt to reach the South Pole. They also made the first ascent of the polar plateau, the great icecap that covers 98 per cent of the continent.

Meanwhile some of the gaps in the outline of the continent were being filled in. The German scientist Erich von Drygalski discovered Wilhelm II Land, and in 1904 the shy Scottish nationalist W. S. Bruce managed to enter the Weddell Sea to sight the coast of Coats Land. From 1911 to 1914 an Australian expedition led by Douglas Mawson set up base at Commonwealth Bay and made the first venture into George V Land.

While great advances were being made in extending scientific knowledge of the continent, it was the race to the South Pole that excited the world. Ernest Shackleton, one of Robert Scott's companions on his first attempt at the South Pole, launched his own expedition and almost succeeded in reaching the pole in 1908, but for the loss of a pony.

But it was Roald Amundsen, the Norwegian with polar experience second to none, who in 1911 was the first to set foot on the empty ice plain that surrounds the South Pole. His rival, Robert Scott, arrived a month later and died with his companions on the return journey. Amundsen's venture was the more single-minded and better managed, but it was the bravery of Scott's men when all was lost that most moved people of that time.

Shackleton returned to Antarctica in 1914 in an attempt to cross the continent. The expedition was a total failure but became, instead, one of the greatest sagas of endurance and survival in Antarctic history.

Shackleton's death on his third expedition in 1922 marked the end of the 'heroic age'. The continent had been penetrated by men and animals hauling heavy sledges. But the great bulk of it still lay unseen by human eyes, and the future of Antarctic exploration now lay in other directions.

18 January 1912
Robert Scott, Edward Wilson, 'Birdie' Bowers, Edgar Evans and Lawrence Oates reach the South Pole only to discover the Norwegian flag flying there. 'This is an awful place', writes Scott, 'and terrible enough for us to have laboured to it without the reward of priority'. The party turns around for the long sledge journey home.

January 1912
Wilhelm Filchner in the Deutschland *discovers the Luitpold Coast at the head of the Weddell Sea. He decides to build his base on a large tabular iceberg, but disaster strikes when the berg suddenly breaks away from the ice shelf and he has to rapidly salvage all his equipment.*

March 1912
Scott, Wilson and Bowers die in their tent, their fuel exhausted, only 18 kilometres (11 miles) from the next depot. The tent, diaries and the fate of the three are not discovered until November.

April 1916
Ernest Shackleton and five of his men leave Elephant Island in the 6.7-metre (22-ft) James Caird *for South Georgia and rescue. They get there in 15 days, and Shackleton, Tom Crean and Frank Worsley cross the island — the first to do so — to the whaling station at Stromness.*

August 1916
On his fourth attempt, Ernest Shackleton reaches Elephant Island in the Chilean steamer Yelcho *and rescues the 22 survivors of the* Endurance. *They have lasted out the winter sheltering under the upturned boats.*

February 1921
Thomas Bagshawe and M. C. Lester are farewelled at Hope Bay by their colleagues from the failed British Imperial Expedition led by John Cope. They spend the winter alone, sheltering in a makeshift hut built on an old water boat.

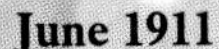

June 1911
Edward Wilson, 'Birdie' Bowers and Apsley Cherry-Garrard set out from Scott's base at Cape Evans to collect emperor penguin eggs at Cape Crozier. For five weeks in the depth of the Antarctic winter they endure unbelievable hardship in what is later described as 'the worst journey in the world'.

14 December 1911
Amundsen with four companions and 18 dogs plants the Norwegian flag at the South Pole after pioneering a new route onto the polar plateau, and a journey of 57 days. Amundsen leaves letters for Captain Scott and returns to his base at the Bay of Whales without mishap.

April 1912
The members of Scott's northern party under Victor Campbell give up hope of being collected by the Terra Nova *as arranged, and prepare for winter. The six men dig a cave out of a snow bank, and with a supply of penguin and seal meat, live in it for six months.*

October 1915
Ernest Shackleton, with a grand plan to cross the Antarctic continent, is forced to abandon his ship, Endurance, *when she is crushed in the ice of the Weddell Sea after a nine-month drift. The 28 men camp on the floating ice for a further five months before taking to the boats and reaching Elephant Island.*

December 1915
The members of Ernest Shackleton's Ross Sea shore party begin their main depot-laying journey. Despite the loss of their ship and its provisions, they faithfully lay the depots for the party from the Endurance *which they expect to cross the continent. Three members die, but the survivors are eventually rescued in 1917.*

January 1922
Ernest Shackleton, aged only 48, dies of a heart attack on board the Quest *and is buried on South Georgia at his widow's request. The expedition continues under deputy Frank Wild.*

November 1911
After six months in Sydney, the first Japanese Antarctic expedition sails south. Led by Lieutenant Nobu Shirase, the party lands at the Bay of Whales and Shirase takes a 'dash patrol' 257 kilometres (160 miles) across the Ross Ice Shelf.

December 1912
Douglas Mawson begins his lone trek across George V Land back towards his base at Commonwealth Bay. Ill and desperately short of food, Mawson has lost his two companions — Lieutenant Ninnis down a crevasse and Xavier Mertz from vitamin A poisoning. Against all odds he makes it home. Despite the tragedy of his own party, six major traverses are carried out by the two arms of the expedition, a new section of the coast is discovered, and radio is used in the Antarctic for the first time.

1923-1990
The mechanised age

Motorised vehicles had been taken to Antarctica before the 1920s. Ernest Shackleton in 1908 and Robert Scott in 1911 had both experimented with motor transport. Mawson had planned to take an aeroplane with him in 1911, but it lost its wings in an accident and was used as a tractor.

The first flights over the continent were made in 1928 by Hubert Wilkins. The results were of limited use, but the flights marked the start of a revolution in methods of Antarctic exploration. In the next decade more of the coastline was identified and mapped than by all previous expeditions put together.

The explorer who most systematically developed the use of aircraft and aerial photography, was the American Richard Byrd. Already a famous aviator, in 1929 he became the first to fly over the South Pole. Byrd also developed the use of two-way radio communication with the outside world, and on his second expedition in 1933-35, used tracked motor vehicles successfully.

The first to fly across the continent was Lincoln Ellsworth in 1935. Ellsworth landed four times during his dramatic 3700-kilometre (2300-mile) flight and showed that planes could successfully land and take off in unknown territory.

One of the problems with aerial surveying

December 1923
Carl Larsen begins a factory ship whaling industry in the Ross Sea. The ships are independent of shore stations and can thus venture further south.

January 1925
The Discovery Committee opens a Marine Biological Station on South Georgia. The committee has been set up by the British Government to collect information on Antarctic whale populations. Between 1925 and 1939 it organises 13 major cruises, first in Scott's old ship Discovery, *then after 1929 in* Discovery II. *It is the first sustained scientific research in Antarctic history.*

1927
The wealthy Norwegian whaler Lars Christensen sends out the first of his Antarctic expeditions. The Norvegia *lands on Bouvetøya and Peter I Øy, claiming them for Norway. Over the next 10 years, Christensen sponsors nine such expeditions, concentrating on the area between 20° and 45°E. More than 3700 kilometres (2300 miles) of coast are discovered.*

November 1928
Hubert Wilkins makes the first flight in Antarctica — from Deception Island in a Lockheed Vega monoplane. A month later Wilkins and Ben Eilson fly 1000 kilometres (620 miles) along the Antarctic Peninsula before turning back. They conclude, wrongly, that Graham Land is separated from the continent. The following year Wilkins returns to Deception Island and tries unsuccessfully to fly across the continent.

October 1929
The British, Australian and New Zealand Antarctic Research Expedition (BANZARE) under Douglas Mawson sets off from Cape Town. Over two summer seasons they discover MacRobertson Land and chart long sections of the adjacent coastline.

November 1929
Richard Byrd and three others take off in a Ford monoplane from his base at the Bay of Whales, and head for the South Pole. They climb the Liv glacier, jettisonning emergency food supplies to gain enough height to reach the polar plateau. After 10 hours in the air they are over the pole. It lies 'in the centre of a limitless plain', wrote Byrd. 'One gets there and that is about all there is for the telling. It is the effort to get there that counts.'

January 1930
A Norwegian expedition under Hjalmar Riiser-Larsen meets Mawson's BANZARE party at Cape Ann. They agree on a dividing line between British and Norwegian efforts. The Norwegians discover and survey new sections of the Dronning Maud Land coast.

1930
The Norwegian whaling captain, H. Halvorsen, discovers Prinsesse Astrid Land. Over the next seven years Norwegian whalers such as Lars Christensen and Klarius Mikkelsen discover sections of the Antarctic coastline.

March 1934
Richard Byrd begins his lone winter sojourn at his advance base 198 kilometres (123 miles) inland from the Bay of Whales. He is the first person to winter in the interior of the continent, but almost dies of carbon monoxide poisoning.

January 1935
The British Graham Land Expedition under Australian John Rymill, arrives at Port Lockroy. During the next two years they survey the western side of the Antarctic Peninsula as far south as Alexander Island, using a sea plane, a tractor and dog teams.

February 1935
Mrs Mikkelsen, the wife of a Norwegian whaling captain becomes the first woman to land on the Antarctic continent, when she steps ashore at the Vestfold Hills.

November 1935
Lincoln Ellsworth from America makes the first successful trans-Antarctic flight on his third attempt. With Herbert Hollick-Kenyon as pilot he sets off from Dundee Island and flies in four stages to the Bay of Whales, running out of fuel only 26 kilometres (16 miles) from Byrd's old base. They are finally picked up by Discovery II.

1937
An International Convention on Whaling is signed by nine nations in London. This is the first serious attempt to regulate Antarctic whaling. Quotas are set and inspectors appointed. The International Whaling Commission is established in 1946, but whale stocks continue to decline.

January 1939
Alfred Ritscher on a secret mission for the Third Reich, photographs 250000 sq kilometres (96500 sq miles) of Dronning Maud Land and drops aluminium darts engraved with swastikas into the ice.

January 1940
The United States Services Expedition under Richard Byrd, establishes Little America III at the Bay of Whales. Another base is set up along the Antarctic Peninsula, and Byrd directs the exploration of the Marie Byrd Land coast by ship, plane and sledge team.

January 1947
Operation Highjump, organised by the United States Navy, brings 4700 men, 13 ships and 23 aircraft to Antarctica. A base is set up at Little America, icebreakers are used for the first time and two groups work around the continent. A large area of the coastline and hinterland is mapped — inaccurately with 70000 aerial photographs.

December 1947
Operation Windmill begins as a follow up to Highjump. Ship-based helicopters put survey teams at key points along the coast. These teams accurately fix the positions of landmarks shown on Highjump photographs, thus enabling some maps to be made.

December 1947
Finne Ronne, the leader of a private American Expedition based on Stonington Island, flies over the southern shore of the Weddell Sea. He is the first to see the mountains marking the western edge of the Filchner Ice Shelf.

February 1950
The first truly international expedition sets up base in Dronning Maud Land. It is a joint Swedish-British-Norwegian venture led by Norwegian John Giaever.

was the lack of ground control. Wilkins on his first flights surmised incorrectly that Graham Land was an archipelago. John Rymill and the British Graham Land Expedition of 1934-37 used a combination of seaplane, tractor and sledge teams to map much of the western side of the peninsula, and to show that there were no channels dividing it into islands.

The end of World War II brought the beginning of a new assault on Antarctica. In Operation Highjump in 1946 the United States sent 4700 men to the continent — over six times the total number who had ever set foot there. Antarctic exploration became a component of government scientific programs and large permanent bases were established, including one at the South Pole in 1957.

While the last 40 years have been dominated by these national expeditions, private ventures (many of them still publicly funded) have continued to visit Antarctica. In 1958 Vivian Fuchs fulfilled a 10-year-old dream when he led the first party to cross the continent. In 1973 David Lewis became the first person to make a single-handed voyage to Antarctica, and in 1981 the English Transglobe Expedition became only the second party to cross it.

Formal national claims had been made to sections of the continent as early as 1908. In 1959, 12 nations, including all seven claimant states, signed the Antarctic Treaty putting all claims in abeyance and making the continent a zone of international scientific co-operation.

Today about 800 people spend each winter in Antarctica and in summer the number increases to over 2000. Nearly all of them are scientists and support staff and certainly, at present, the region remains a peaceful preserve of scientific investigation. But competing national interests have been a strong theme in Antarctic history, and the Treaty is about to come up for review. Now that all nations know that valuable mineral and biological resources exist there, the future of the frozen continent is very much in doubt.

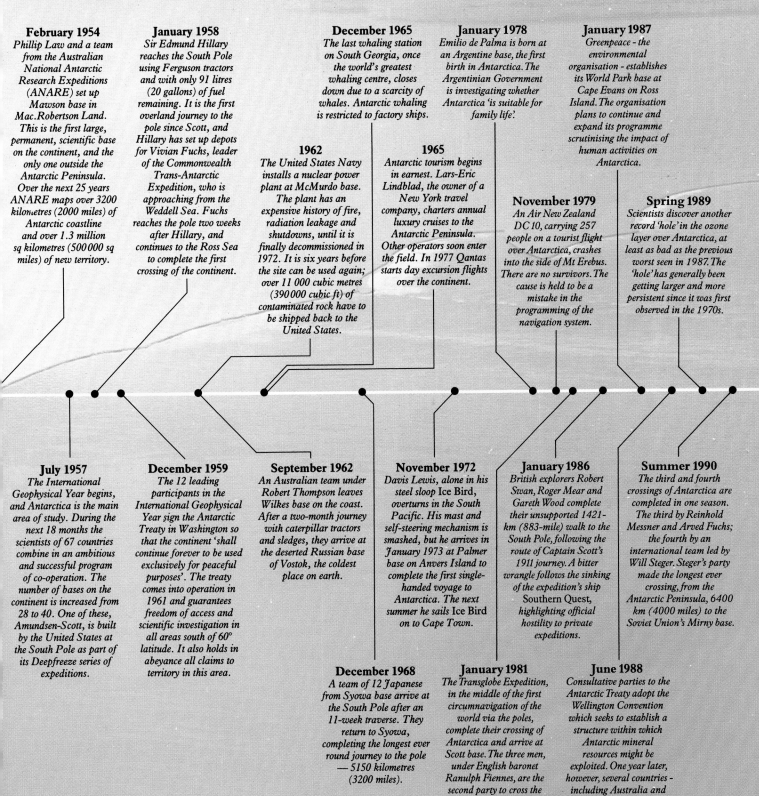

February 1954
Phillip Law and a team from the Australian National Antarctic Research Expeditions (ANARE) set up Mawson base in Mac.Robertson Land. This is the first large, permanent, scientific base on the continent, and the only one outside the Antarctic Peninsula. Over the next 25 years ANARE maps over 3200 kilometres (2000 miles) of Antarctic coastline and over 1.3 million sq kilometres (500 000 sq miles) of new territory.

July 1957
The International Geophysical Year begins, and Antarctica is the main area of study. During the next 18 months the scientists of 67 countries combine in an ambitious and successful program of co-operation. The number of bases on the continent is increased from 28 to 40. One of these, Amundsen-Scott, is built by the United States at the South Pole as part of its Deepfreeze series of expeditions.

January 1958
Sir Edmund Hillary reaches the South Pole using Ferguson tractors and with only 91 litres (20 gallons) of fuel remaining. It is the first overland journey to the pole since Scott, and Hillary has set up depots for Vivian Fuchs, leader of the Commonwealth Trans-Antarctic Expedition, who is approaching from the Weddell Sea. Fuchs reaches the pole two weeks after Hillary, and continues to the Ross Sea to complete the first crossing of the continent.

December 1959
The 12 leading participants in the International Geophysical Year sign the Antarctic Treaty in Washington so that the continent 'shall continue forever to be used exclusively for peaceful purposes'. The treaty comes into operation in 1961 and guarantees freedom of access and scientific investigation in all areas south of 60° latitude. It also holds in abeyance all claims to territory in this area.

1962
The United States Navy installs a nuclear power plant at McMurdo base. The plant has an expensive history of fire, radiation leakage and shutdowns, until it is finally decommissioned in 1972. It is six years before the site can be used again; over 11 000 cubic metres (390 000 cubic ft) of contaminated rock have to be shipped back to the United States.

September 1962
An Australian team under Robert Thompson leaves Wilkes base on the coast. After a two-month journey with caterpillar tractors and sledges, they arrive at the deserted Russian base of Vostok, the coldest place on earth.

December 1965
The last whaling station on South Georgia, once the world's greatest whaling centre, closes down due to a scarcity of whales. Antarctic whaling is restricted to factory ships.

1965
Antarctic tourism begins in earnest. Lars-Eric Lindblad, the owner of a New York travel company, charters annual luxury cruises to the Antarctic Peninsula. Other operators soon enter the field. In 1977 Qantas starts day excursion flights over the continent.

December 1968
A team of 12 Japanese from Syowa base arrive at the South Pole after an 11-week traverse. They return to Syowa, completing the longest ever round journey to the pole — 5150 kilometres (3200 miles).

November 1972
Davis Lewis, alone in his steel sloop Ice Bird, *overturns in the South Pacific. His mast and self-steering mechanism is smashed, but he arrives in January 1973 at Palmer base on Anvers Island to complete the first single-handed voyage to Antarctica. The next summer he sails* Ice Bird *on to Cape Town.*

January 1978
Emilio de Palma is born at an Argentine base, the first birth in Antarctica. The Argentinian Government is investigating whether Antarctica 'is suitable for family life'.

November 1979
An Air New Zealand DC 10, carrying 257 people on a tourist flight over Antarctica, crashes into the side of Mt Erebus. There are no survivors. The cause is held to be a mistake in the programming of the navigation system.

January 1981
The Transglobe Expedition, in the middle of the first circumnavigation of the world via the poles, complete their crossing of Antarctica and arrive at Scott base. The three men, under English baronet Ranulph Fiennes, are the second party to cross the continent, and the tenth to travel overland to the pole.

January 1986
British explorers Robert Swan, Roger Mear and Gareth Wood complete their unsupported 1421-km (883-mile) walk to the South Pole, following the route of Captain Scott's 1911 journey. A bitter wrangle follows the sinking of the expedition's ship Southern Quest, *highlighting official hostility to private expeditions.*

January 1987
Greenpeace - the environmental organisation - establishes its World Park base at Cape Evans on Ross Island. The organisation plans to continue and expand its programme scrutinising the impact of human activities on Antarctica.

June 1988
Consultative parties to the Antarctic Treaty adopt the Wellington Convention which seeks to establish a structure within which Antarctic mineral resources might be exploited. One year later, however, several countries - including Australia and France - still refuse to ratify the Convention.

Spring 1989
Scientists discover another record 'hole' in the ozone layer over Antarctica, at least as bad as the previous worst seen in 1987. The 'hole' has generally been getting larger and more persistent since it was first observed in the 1970s.

Summer 1990
The third and fourth crossings of Antarctica are completed in one season. The third by Reinhold Messner and Arved Fuchs; the fourth by an international team led by Will Steger. Steger's party made the longest ever crossing, from the Antarctic Peninsula, 6400 km (4000 miles) to the Soviet Union's Mirny base.

LIVES OF THE EXPLORERS

Amundsen – Byrd

Many Antarctic explorers devoted their entire lives to the quest for geographical knowledge, often at both ends of the earth. For the sealers and whalers, exploration was part of the job — the first to discover new hunting grounds might make his fortune. But for many of those that followed — the men who trekked across the polar wastes on the great journeys of discovery in the early twentieth century — the motive was often different. They were searching for some other, more personal, conquest. Some were drawn back time and again to the white wilderness to face extraordinary suffering and hardship. The record belongs to Frank Wild, who accompanied five expeditions to Antarctica and spent a total of ten years on the continent or in Antarctic waters. The following pages contain brief lives of the principal figures in Antarctic exploration. Many names must, of course, be omitted from such a brief catalogue. The list is also exclusively male — few women were drawn, or had the opportunity, to make the pilgrimage to the great white south.

AMUNDSEN
Roald
1872-1928

The most successful of polar explorers was born near Oslo in Norway. From the age of 15 he set himself upon a professional career of adventure. He studied medicine but withdrew to go to sea where he worked his way up to the rank of mate. By 1910 he was established as a successful explorer. He had been a member of the first party to winter in Antarctica on the Belgica *in 1898, and had become the first to travel the Northwest Passage in his ship* Gjoa *in 1903-06. He now planned to drift across the North Pole in Nansen's famous* Fram, *but news of Peary's attainment of the pole caused him to secretly change plans and head south. On 14 December 1911 Amundsen and four companions stood at the South Pole, a month before Scott. The expedition was a masterpiece of organisation and concerted purpose. During World War I he made a lot of money from neutral shipping and built the* Maud *to resume his Arctic drift. He completed the Northeast Passage around Siberia — only the second to do so — but made little progress north and left the ship in 1921. Amundsen now ventured into flying, but was soon facing financial ruin before he gained support from Lincoln Ellsworth. Together they flew the airship* Norge *from Spitsbergen to Alaska via the North Pole — the first flight right across the Arctic basin. Amundsen now retired with his reputation at its zenith. Reserved and sensitive, he never came to terms with the British reaction to his secret change of plan in 1910. Mill described him as the most unhappy of all the polar explorers he had met. In 1928, while he was searching for the survivors of an airship accident, Amundsen's plane crashed and he disappeared without trace.*

ARCTOWSKI
Henryk
1871-1958

Born in Warsaw, Arctowski studied chemistry and geology in Paris, Liège and Zürich, and in 1897 joined the Belgian Antarctic expedition under Adrien de Gerlache, as meteorologist and geologist. It was the first group to winter in Antarctica, and Arctowski made the first complete meteorological observations. He was a pioneer in the study of Antarctic climate and was the first to advance the theory that wind could be as harmful as cold. On the liberation of Poland in 1919, Arctowski became Professor of Geology at Lwow University. In 1939 he left for a lecture tour of the United States and remained there after the outbreak of war until his death.

BALLENY
John
Dates unknown

Details of the life of this British sealer and explorer are scanty. His date and place of birth are unknown, but in 1798 he was living in London and the part-owner of a 500-tonne brig. Until 1831 he was the master of various ships involved in coastal trade, then dissappeared from shipping records until 1838 when he was employed by the Enderby sealing firm for a voyage to Antarctica in the Eliza Scott *and the* Sabrina. *Balleny discovered the islands that now bear his name and a section of the Antarctic coast known as Sabrina Coast. But the* Sabrina *disappeared and sank during a gale, and Balleny returned home with only 178 seal skins. For some years he traded between London and Calcutta, but there is no record of his later life or when he died.*

BORCHGREVINK
Carsten Egeberg
1864-1934

Borchgrevink was born in Oslo of a Norwegian father and an English mother. At 24 he sailed to Australia where he taught languages and science, and travelled widely. In 1894 he shipped on board the whaler Antarctic *on its way to the Ross Sea, as a deckhand and part-time scientist, and took part in the historic landing at Cape Adare, claiming to be the first ashore. He also collected the first vegetation to be found within the Antarctic*

Carsten Borchgrevink

Circle. Borchgrevink then travelled to London and, with the support of the wealthy publisher Sir George Newnes, organised another expedition, setting sail in 1898 in the Southern Cross. *He spent the first winter on the continent, at Cape Adare, and made the first sledge journey on the Ross Ice Shelf. At one point, while standing on shore, he was almost drowned by a freak wave. Borchgrevink was opportunistic and given to egotistic exaggeration, and he was not liked in England where the importance of his expedition went unrecognised for over 30 years. He made one more voyage, to the West Indies in 1902 to examine volcanic eruptions, but for the remainder of his life he lived in Slimdal in Norway where he was active in literary and sporting activities.*

BOUVET de LOZIER
Jean-Baptiste
1704-1786

Jean Bouvet de Lozier

Bouvet was leader of the first deliberate incursion into subantarctic waters, and the discoverer of Bouvetøya. He joined the merchant marine at 16, then transferred to the French East India Company in 1731. He began proposing voyages to find a suitable Atlantic base for the company, and in 1738 with two ships he sailed south. On New Year's Day 1739 he sighted land which he named Cape Circumcision, suggesting that it might be part of Terra Australis. *It was in fact one corner of Boyvetøya, an ice-capped extinct volcano, and the most isolated piece of land on earth. Unable to get ashore, Bouvet continued east for over 2000 kilometres (1240 miles) along the ice pack before returning to France. In later years Bouvet was Governor of Mauritius, and in 1748 conveyed French troops to Madras under the nose of a superior English force, an exploit which won him the Cross of St Louis. He continued to agitate for another voyage to southern waters but failed due to lack of influence at court. Bouvet was a fine leader, seaman and planner, and his Antarctic voyage foreshadowed those of Captain James Cook.*

BOWERS
Henry Robertson
1883-1912

'Birdie' Bowers was born in Scotland, the son of a master mariner. At 16 he became a midshipman in the merchant navy, and from 1905 served in the Royal Indian Marine, reaching the rank of lieutenant in 1909.
The support of Markham gained him a place on Scott's second Antarctic expedition and Bowers' organisational ability immediately impressed Scott, who promoted him to the landing party with control over stores. Bowers accompanied Wilson and Cherry-Garrard on the tortuous winter journey to Cape Crozier in search of emperor penguin eggs.
On the polar journey he was a last-minute addition to the final party, travelling without his skis which had been left at the previous depot. Only 162 centimetres (5ft 4in) tall, he had great strength, but died with Scott and Wilson in March 1912, 280 kilometres (174 miles) from their hut.

BRANSFIELD
Edward
c1795-1852

Although for many years he was thought to be the first to sight the Antarctic continent, Bransfield was in fact beaten by Bellingshausen by three days. Very little is known about his life. He was born in about 1795 and was serving in Britain's Royal Navy off Chile in 1819 when the discovery of the South Shetland Islands by William Smith was reported. Bransfield was put in command of Smith's vessel and sent to examine the islands. After reaching the South Shetlands he continued south and on 30 January 1820, during a momentary lifting of the fog, he sighted the Antarctic Peninsula — certainly the first to see that part of the continent. On his return to England he left the navy.

BANKS
(Sir) Joseph
1743-1820

A British naturalist, and patron of the natural sciences, Banks was born into a wealthy Lincolnshire landed family. He is said to have become interested in botany at Eton through the beauty of the local wildflowers, and when, at Oxford University, there was no teacher of botany he paid for one to be sent from Cambridge. He travelled to Newfoundland and Labrador in 1766 collecting specimens, and in 1768-71 he sailed on the Endeavour *(at his own expense and with a staff of eight) on Cook's voyage to the Pacific and eastern Australia. Banks' discoveries of new flora and his skill at self-promotion ensured that the voyage became his triumph as much as Cook's. He planned to sail on Cook's next voyage, to Antarctica, and had the* Resolution *fitted out for himself and an entourage of 15. However, the ship became top-heavy and Cook ordered the fittings pulled out. Banks resigned in a rage. He then became honorary director of the Kew Gardens and developed a worldwide exchange of botanical specimens, introducing over 7000 new plants into Britain. He was president of the Royal Society from 1778 and was created a baronet in 1781. During the 1780s he led the movement to establish a penal colony at Botany Bay in Australia. He was greatly troubled by gout in his later life and he died, full of fame and honours, in 1820.*

BELLINGSHAUSEN
Faddei (Thaddeus)
1778-1852

Bellingshausen was the first person to sight the Antarctic continent. He was born in Estonia and studied at the naval academy in Kronstadt. In 1803-06 he took part in the first Russian round-the-world voyage under Kruzenstern, the father of the Russian Navy. He was dispatched by the progressive Czar Alexander I in 1819 in the Vostok *and the* Mirnyi *on a voyage of southern exploration. He charted the South Sandwich Islands and on 27 January 1820 he saw an 'icefield covered with small hillocks' — possibly the first sighting of the continent even though Bellingshausen was unaware of it. Over two summers he circumnavigated Antarctica, well to the south of Cook, and discovered Peter I and Alexander Islands. He returned to Russia after a voyage of over 90 000 kilometres (55 900 miles). Bellingshausen was a humane and efficient commander but diffident and self-effacing, and he never received full recognition for his achievement. During 1829-30 he was engaged in the Russo-Turkish war and from 1839 was military governor of Krondstadt. He died in that post.*

Admiral Bellingshausen

BISCOE
John
1794-1843

Biscoe was born in Middlesex, joined the Royal Navy in 1812 and fought in the American War until July 1815. He then joined the merchant marine, serving as mate and master on voyages to the West Indies and Asia. In 1830 he was appointed by Enderby Brothers to lead a sealing voyage to Antarctica. In the Tula *and the* Lively *he circumnavigated the continent, being only the third to do so. He discovered Enderby Land, the first landfall in the Indian Ocean sector of Antarctica, and Adelaide Island. On the homeward voyage the* Lively *was wrecked in the Falklands, and most of Biscoe's crew deserted. He arrived back in England with only four men, three boys and little cargo. In 1837 he moved to Sydney and later Hobart. Biscoe was by then in ill health, and in 1842 a public appeal was launched to allow him and his family to return to England. He sailed in 1843, but died at sea.*

BJAALAND
Olav
1872-1961

Norwegian skier and explorer, Bjaaland was born in Morgedal, Telemark, one of the pioneer generation who brought skiing out to the world. In 1902 he won the Nordic ski championship; he was also a skilled carpenter and musician. He asked Amundsen if he could join his expedition in 1910 and was accepted. He was a lithe, dark figure, the only expedition member who could poke fun at Amundsen without giving offence. He led the way up the Axel Heiberg Glacier and Amundsen asked him to lead the final kilometres to the pole. 'So now we have attained the goal of our desires', wrote Bjaaland, 'here it's as flat as a lake at Morgedal and the skiing is good'. On his return Bjaaland continued to live on his farm at Morgedal until his death.

BRUCE
William Spiers
1867-1921

Bruce was born in London, the son of a surgeon. He studied medicine, then in 1892 joined an Antarctic whaling voyage as surgeon and naturalist. In 1895 he took charge of the meteorological observatory on Ben Nevis, then took part in a number of journeys into the Arctic. Bruce refused a post of naturalist on Scott's first Antarctic expedition to lead an all-Scottish venture of his own in 1902-04, exploring the Weddell Sea and discovering Coats Land. On his return he worked on the extensive scientific results of the expedition and in 1907 set up the Scottish Oceanographical Laboratory, mainly with his own money. Bruce made seven visits to Spitsbergen and became the authority on the area. In 1915-16 he managed a whaling station in the Seychelles, but found the tropics distasteful and was glad to return. Bruce was a quiet, private man but also a fierce Scottish nationalist and this proved a continual problem when raising money for his ventures from English sources. He was also uncompromising in his scientific aims and only reluctantly took part in public relations efforts. Bruce died in 1921 after a long illness and his ashes were scattered over Antarctic waters.

BULL
Henryk Johan
1844-1930

Bull was born in Norway and travelled to Australia in 1885. While working for a trading firm, he tried to organise a whaling venture to Antarctica. He was convinced from Ross' 1842 reports that right whales could be caught in Antarctic waters. In 1893, unable to gain support for his plan in Australia, he returned to Norway where the whaling pioneer Svend Foyn agreed to fund a southern expedition. Sailing in the Antarctic *in 1894 Bull saw few whales, but he did make the first landing on the Antarctic continent outside the peninsula, at Cape Adare. The expedition was also the first to find vegetation within the Antarctic Circle. Although commercially unsuccessful, and marred by disputes between Bull and his captain, Kristensen, the voyage sparked a revival of interest in Antarctica. Bull continued in ventures to the far south. In 1906 on a sealing voyage, and at the age of 62, he was shipwrecked on the Îles Crozet and was marooned there until rescued two months later.*

Bull was among the first party to land at Cape Adare.

BYRD
Richard Evelyn
1888-1957

Richard Byrd

Byrd was born into a famous southern family in Virginia, entered the United States Naval Academy at 20, and was commissioned in 1912. He learned to fly in World War I and began his long love affair with the aeroplane. In 1926 he became the first man to fly over the North Pole, and the following year made the third non-stop trans-Atlantic flight. In 1928-30 he led a private expedition to Antarctica, establishing a base at the Bay of Whales and making the first flight over the South Pole. During his second expedition in 1933-35 he almost died from carbon monoxide poisoning while wintering alone at an inland base. Byrd's two expeditions spurred United States' Government interest in Antarctica and he then led three official expeditions. The first was in 1939-41, followed by Operation Highjump, larger than all previous Antarctic expeditions put together, in 1946-47; and Operation Deepfreeze I in 1955-56. Byrd was foremost in harnessing the revolution in transport and communications to polar exploration.

CHARCOT Jean-Baptiste August 1867-1936

Charcot, 'the polar gentleman' as Captain Scott called him, was born the son of a renowned and wealthy French neurologist. Graduating as a doctor, but not wanting to follow in his father's footsteps, Charcot embarked on a career of polar exploration. He built the Français *and organised, with government assistance, a national Antarctic expedition, accurately surveying in 1903-05 the western side of the Antarctic Peninsula. On his return, Charcot's wife divorced him for desertion; at his second marriage in 1907 his new wife had to promise never to oppose his expeditions. Charcot then built the most modern polar ship known to that date, the* Pourquoi-Pas?, *and in 1908-10 extended his work along the peninsula, exploring 2000 kilometres (1240 miles) of unknown coastline. From 1926-36 Charcot made regular oceanographic voyages to the Greenland Sea. In September 1936 the* Pourquoi-Pas? *was wrecked on the coast of Iceland and Charcot died, together with most of the ship's crew.*

Commandant Charcot, his wife and daughter.

CHERRY-GARRARD Apsley George Benet 1886-1959

English explorer and writer, Cherry-Garrard was born the son of a wealthy general. He studied history and the classics at Oxford, donated £1000 to Scott's second Antarctic expedition, and on Wilson's recommendation was appointed assistant zoologist. With Wilson and Bowers he took part in the extraordinarily arduous winter journey to Cape Crozier which he later described in his polar classic, The Worst Journey in the World. *He was a member of the polar support party and was deeply disappointed when Scott sent him back. In World War I he was invalided home, and from then on his health was always frail. Always emotional, Cherry-Garrard was for many years profoundly affected by Scott's tragedy and the values of gentlemanly altruism that he saw becoming increasingly lost in the modern world.*

CHRISTENSEN Lars 1884-1965

Norwegian whaling entrepreneur, Lars Christensen was born into a Sandefjord whaling family. By the age of 23 he had his own small shipping company and moved into whaling in Alaskan and South American waters. By 1920, having inherited a number of family whaling businesses, he held one of the largest concentrations in the history of the industry. However, it is for his contribution to Antarctic exploration that Christensen is best known. From 1927 to 1937 he sent out nine expeditions, including two he led personally, to the Southern Ocean to catch whales and claim land for Norway. Bouvetøya, Peter I Island and Dronning Maud Land were claimed in this way. The coast of Dronning Maud Land was charted for the first time and Christensen also financed the publication of the extensive scientific results of his expeditions. He died in New York.

COOK Frederick Albert 1865-1940

One of the most colourful and controversial of polar explorers, Cook was born in Hortonville, New York. After the early death of his father, he supported himself through medical school by delivering milk. In 1892 he accompanied Robert Peary on an expedition to northeast Greenland, then in 1897-99 he was surgeon on the Belgica *expedition under Adrien de Gerlache, the first to winter in Antarctica. Cook's polar experience and efficient good humour helped the party through the stresses of that winter. In 1906 he claimed the first ascent of Mt McKinley, the highest peak in north America. In September 1909 Cook returned from the Arctic, claiming to have reached the North Pole with two Eskimos on 21 April 1908. Five days later Peary returned from the north saying that he had reached the pole on 6 April 1909 and that Cook had 'handed the public a gold brick'. In the ensuing controversy, Cook's inability to produce his original navigational records, the denial of the two Eskimos that they had ever been out of sight of land, and the growing doubts about his ascent of Mt McKinley, led to the general acceptance of Peary as the conqueror of the pole. In 1923 Cook was convicted of fraud over the sale of oil shares. He spent five years in jail where he became an expert on embroidery and announced that he had discovered a cure for baldness. He spent his last years lecturing and in unsuccessful litigation against those who disputed his North Pole claim.*

Dr Frederick Cook

DAVIS John Dates unknown

The log of this obscure sealer's voyage to Antarctica in 1820-21 was rediscovered in 1952, and he is now credited with being possibly the first person to set foot on the Antarctic mainland. Davis left New Haven, Connecticut, in the Huron *in 1820 and, finding the main sealing grounds occupied or worked out, headed southwest in his shallop* Cecilia *'on a cruise to find new Lands'. On 7 February 1821 he landed at what is thought to be Hughes Bay on the Antarctic Peninsula and commented, 'I think this Southern Land to be a Continent'. Davis's log shows him to have had a keen navigating ability and a lively curiosity. He returned to New Haven in 1822 but nothing further is known of his life.*

DAVIS John King 1884-1967

Davis was born in London and taken to Cape Town by his father before running away to sea in 1900. At 23 he met Shackleton and was appointed chief officer of the Nimrod, *then later captain. He was captain of the* Aurora *during Mawson's Antarctic expedition of 1911-14, sailing the ship along 1770 kilometres (1100 miles) of unknown coast and making a major contribution to the geographical and oceanographic discoveries of the expedition. In 1916, again on the* Aurora, *he organised the relief of the marooned members of Shackleton's Ross Sea Party. His final Antarctic voyage was with Mawson in 1929-30 for BANZARE. Davis was perhaps the greatest of modern Antarctic navigators. He was always determined to maintain his authority at sea in matters affecting the safety of his ship, and in 1929-30 this led to some sharp disagreements with Mawson. From 1920 until his retirement in 1949, Davis was Australian Director of Navigation. He died in a Melbourne boarding house, aged 83.*

DEBENHAM Frank 1883-1965

The son of a pastor from Bowral, New South Wales, Debenham studied geology under Edgeworth David at Sydney University. On David's recommendation, Debenham was appointed in 1910 to Scott's second Antarctic expedition. He took part in both the western geological parties that explored the dry valleys and parts of Victoria Land. During World War I he was severely wounded and shell-shocked in Salonika. After the war Debenham made a career for himself at Cambridge, at first working on the cartography of the expedition, then in 1931 becoming the first Professor of Geography, a position he held until his retirement in 1946. He was also instrumental in setting up the Scott Polar Research Institute at Cambridge in 1926 with the residue of the Scott Memorial Fund. He died in Cambridge.

DRAKE Francis 1540-1596

English explorer and buccaneer, Drake was born in Devon of humble parents. He went to sea at 13 and was soon making voyages to the West Indies. On one raid against the Spanish at Panama, Drake was wounded but came away with extensive booty. In 1577-80 he sailed around the world, the first Englishman to do so, charting new territory and plundering Spanish ships. At one stage, having sailed through the Strait of Magellan into the Pacific, Drake was blown by a storm to 57°S and back into the Atlantic, thus showing that Tierra del Fuego was not connected to any southern continent. Drake's contribution to the defeat of the Spanish Armada in 1588 increased his already great popularity and fame in England. On a voyage to the West Indies in 1596 he developed a fever and died of dysentery.

DRYGALSKI Erich Dagobert von 1865-1949

Drygalski was born in Königsberg, in Germany. In 1891 he led a four-year expedition to Greenland and the resulting publications established his reputation. In 1899 he became Professor of Geography at Berlin, and two years later was chosen to lead the official German Antarctic expedition in the Gauss. *This expedition discovered Wilhelm II Land before being trapped in the ice for 12 months when Drygalski led a 90-day sledge journey to the adjacent coast. The mass of scientific data collected filled 20 volumes of reports and provided work for Drygalski for the next 28 years. In 1906 he became Professor of Geography at Munich and in 1910 took part in Count Zeppelin's expedition to Spitsbergen. He retired from his university post in 1934.*

COOK
James
1728-1779

Captain James Cook

A great navigator and explorer, Cook was a man 'whose competence changed the face of the world'. He was born in Yorkshire, England, the son of a farm labourer. He went to sea at 17 in the North Sea and Baltic trade, then at 27 entered the Royal Navy as a common seaman. Cook was entirely self taught, but he was promoted quickly. His survey of the St Lawrence River greatly helped the British capture of Quebec in 1759 and brought Cook to official notice. In his first great voyage of 1768-71 he completely charted New Zealand and discovered the east coast of Australia. Within a year he was at sea again on a voyage often considered the greatest feat of navigation and seamanship. In a period of three years his ships Resolution *and* Adventure *sailed nearly 110000 kilometres (68000 miles). He went further south than anyone had been before, and established that if a southern continent existed it lay frozen behind the pack ice. In his third voyage of 1776-79 he explored the Arctic coasts of North America and Siberia, but in 1779 in Hawaii, Cook was killed by angry natives in a dispute over a stolen cutter, and his body dismembered. His achievements were many. In his rigorous use of fresh food Cook defeated scurvy as a seafaring disease, he established precise navigation as a common sea skill, and he discovered more about the Pacific, Southern and Arctic Oceans than anyone before him.*

CROZIER
Francis
c1796-1848

Crozier entered the Royal Navy in 1810. From 1821-27 he sailed with Parry on three voyages of Arctic exploration. From 1830 he served on the Portuguese coast then in 1835 he accompanied James Clark Ross to the Arctic. As captain of Terror *in 1839-43, he again sailed with Ross, this time to Antarctica, discovering Victoria Land, the Ross Sea, Mt Erebus and the Ross Ice Shelf. Ross was unstinting in his praise for his deputy. Again on* Terror, *Crozier set off in 1845 with Sir John Franklin on his ill-fated voyage in search of the Northwest Passage. Despite many searches, no trace was found of the expedition until 1859 when the final story was pieced together. The ships had become trapped in the ice in 1846 and when Franklin died, the following year, Crozier took command. In 1848 the ships were abandoned and the men died as they tried to walk to safety.*

DALLMAN
Eduard
1830-1896

In 1873 after an extensive career in Arctic sealing and whaling, Dallman led the first German Antarctic expedition in the Grönland *for the German Polar Navigation Company of Hamburg. This was the first steamer to operate in southern waters and, although no whales were found, Dallman was the first to chart the Bismarck Strait and the adjacent coast of the Antarctic Peninsula. From 1877 Dallman undertook trading voyages through the Kara Sea to northern Siberia, then from 1884 he worked for the German New Guinea Company, helping to annex the Bismarck Archipelago and maintaining shipping services to various Company outposts. He returned to Germany in 1893.*

DAVID
(Sir) Tannatt
William Edgeworth
1858-1934

Edgeworth David

David is now considered to be the father of Australian geological science. He was born in south Wales, graduated in classics from Oxford University and then went to Sydney in 1882 to take up a position as a government geological surveyor. In 1891 he became Professor of Geology at Sydney University and soon developed a worldwide reputation as an authority on ice ages. He went with Shackleton to Antarctica in 1907 and was persuaded to remain for the winter rather than return home as he had first planned. He led the first party to climb Mt Erebus and at the age of 50 sledged 2000 kilometres (1240 miles) across Victoria Land to the South Magnetic Pole. David was a man of gentleness and generosity, and on his return to Australia provided continuing assistance to subsequent Antarctic expeditions. He resigned from the university in 1924 to write a massive study of Australian geology, a work still unfinished at his death.

DUFEK
George J.
1903-1977

Dufek was born in Rockford, Illinois, and educated at the United States Naval Academy. He was a navigator on Byrd's third Antarctic expedition in 1939-41 and on a spectacular flight discovered the mountains of Thurston Island. After action in World War II, during which he sank the last German destroyer lost in the war, Dufek returned with Byrd to the Antarctic as leader of the eastern group on the massive Operation Highjump in 1946-47. He led a naval expedition to the Arctic in 1948, then captained an aircraft carrier during the Korean War. Dufek was the operational leader of the Deepfreeze expeditions of 1955-57, during which five Antarctic bases were constructed and Dufek became the first person to stand at the South Pole since Scott in 1912. After the death of Byrd in 1957, Dufek became the head of the United States Antarctic programs.

DUMONT
d'URVILLE
Jules-Sebastian
Cesar
1790-1842

Dumont d'Urville was born in France and joined the navy at 16 where he developed a wide interest in science and languages. In 1820, on the Greek island of Milos, he arranged the purchased of the classical statue of the Venus de Milo, and the following year he helped found the Paris Geographical Society. In 1822-25 he circumnavigated the world

Dumont d'Urville

with Duperrey, then from 1826-29 he explored the Pacific in the Astrolabe, *successfully searching for the wreck and remains of La Perouse, who had disappeared 40 years previously. After the revolution in France in 1830 he escorted the king from the country, but by 1837 was back to lead a voyage of anthropological study to the Pacific in the* Astrolabe *and* Zélée. *During this voyage Dumont d'Urville ventured into Antarctic seas and in 1840 discovered land which he named Terre Adélie for his wife. A landing was made on a nearby island, the tricolour raised and a bottle of Bordeaux opened. Back in France, d'Urville was promoted to rear admiral but in 1842, with his wife and son, he was killed in a train accident near Versailles.*

ELLSWORTH
Lincoln
1880-1951

Lincoln Ellsworth

Polar aviator and son of a Pennsylvanian mining millionaire, Ellsworth first worked as a surveyor for the trans-continental railway, then as a prospector and engineer on the Alaskan goldfields. During World War I he served in the United States Army Air Corps and in 1924 went to Peru to take part in a geological expedition in the Andes. In 1926, with finance from his father and using an airship, Ellsworth, Amundsen and Nobile made the first flight across the Arctic basin via the North Pole. In 1931 Ellsworth began a long association with Hubert Wilkins and from 1933 to 1939 they took four expeditions to Antarctica. In 1935 Ellsworth and Hollick-Kenyon flew across the continent in three steps from Graham Land to the Ross Sea. They ran out of fuel 26 kilometres (16 miles) from Byrd's Little America base and spent eight days walking on snow shoes and towing an improvised sledge before finding it. This was the most important flight yet made in Antarctica and the landings in bad weather marked a distinct advance in polar flying. Ellsworth died in New York in 1951.

ENDERBY
Charles
1797-1876

One of the early patrons of British Antarctic exploration, Charles was the son of Samuel Enderby, himself a promoter of voyages of discovery and the father of British whaling. On Samuel's death in 1829, Charles succeeded to the family business with his brothers. In 1830 he helped to found the Royal Geographical Society and throughout his life combined his commercial responsibilities with his interest in geography and exploration. He chose his captains largely for their education and interest in discovery. Thus the Enderby-sponsored sealing voyages of Biscoe, Rea and Balleny all added significantly to what was known about Antarctica. They were commercially unsuccessful. In 1839 Enderby established a whaling station on the Auckland Islands which had been ceded to him by the Crown. However, it did not thrive and was wound up in 1852.

EVANS
Edgar
1876-1912

'Taff' Evans was born in south Wales and joined the Royal Navy in 1891. He became a petty officer on the Majestic *where he first met Scott, and he volunteered for the National Antarctic Expedition in 1901. During that expedition, in the summer of 1903, he sledged over 1100 kilometres (680 miles) across Victoria Land with Scott and Lashly. He became a talisman to Scott, who commented on his resourcefulness, his bear-like strength and fund of anecdotes. After the expedition Evans became a naval physical training and gun instructor, then in 1910 was one of the first to volunteer for Scott's second expedition. After a drunken spree in New Zealand where Evans fell into the sea, Scott intervened to save his position in the expedition. Evans was one of the five to reach the pole, but his condition deteriorated rapidly during the return, exacerbated by a badly cut hand. He was the first of the party to die, and was buried at the foot of the Beardmore Glacier on 18 February 1912.*

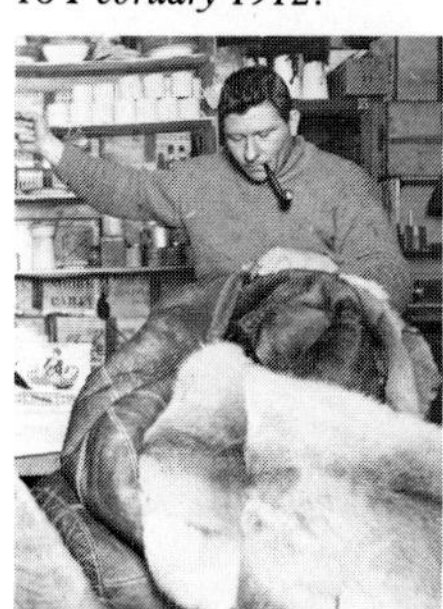
Petty Officer Evans

EVANS
Edward Ratcliffe Garth Russell
1881-1957

Evans was the son of a London barrister. After a rebellious childhood he entered the Royal Navy and took part in the relief of Scott's first expedition in 1902. In 1910, with the aid of Sir Clements Markham, Evans became Scott's deputy on his second Antarctic expedition. Evans had a reputation for boisterous vigour and was given to spectacular, if silly, feats of strength. Scott thought him loyal, but shallow and unsound. Evans led the polar support party that turned back only 275 kilometres (171 miles) from the pole. He succumbed to scurvy on his return, and was carried to safety by his companions Lashly and Crean. As the senior survivor of the expedition he helped propagate the romantic legend that developed around Scott and his men. In World War I he was the youngest commander at sea and won fame for the sinking of two German destroyers. Evans commanded the Australia Squadron from 1929, and the Africa Station from 1933. During World War II he was a Commissioner for Civil Defence and in 1945 he was created a Labour peer, Lord Mountevans.

Lieutenant 'Teddy' Evans

FILCHNER
Wilhelm
1877-1957

Scientist and explorer, Filchner was born in Zürich and grew up with Liszt as a family friend. He was educated at the Prussian Military Academy and at 22 travelled on horse through the Pamir Range of central Asia. He led an expedition to Tibet in 1903-05 then developed a plan for a crossing of Antarctica. This expedition in the Deutschland *in 1910-12 failed in its main purpose, but Filchner reached the head of the Weddell Sea, an area then completely unknown. In 1926-28 and 1934-38 he led two further important expeditions to Tibet. In 1939 Filchner made a magnetic survey of Nepal then spent World War II in India, making no secret of his anti-Nazi sentiments. He died in Zürich aged 80.*

FOYN
Svend
1809-1894

Norwegian whaling entrepreneur, born in Tønsberg, Foyn took to sea at 14 working in the timber trade. In the late 1840s he led the southern Norwegian port towns into Arctic sealing. By the 1860s he had become very rich from his sealing activities and he looked to the possibilities of harvesting blue whales in the North Sea. Because of their speed, these whales could not be caught by the old whaling methods, and Foyn spent five years and £20 000 developing a gun harpoon with an explosive head. This gun revolutionised the industry and by the 1880s was standard equipment on whaling ships. Despite his wealth, Foyn led a spartan life, starting work at five in the morning and not finishing until late at night. In 1893 he funded the voyage of the Antarctic *to search for southern right whales, a voyage that marked the revival of interest in Antarctica. Foyn died before the expedition returned.*

HILLARY
(Sir) Edmund
1919-

Hillary was born in Auckland, and on leaving school followed his father's career of beekeeping. After two years as a flying boat navigator in the Pacific during World War II, Hillary turned to his passion for climbing mountains and joined a number of New Zealand and British expeditions to the Himalayas. In 1953 he took part in John Hunt's Everest Expedition and with Tensing Norkay was the first to reach the summit of the world's highest mountain. In 1955-58 he joined Fuchs' Commonwealth Trans-Antarctic Expedition, organising the depots on the Ross Sea side of the continent for the crossing party. Hillary pioneered a new route onto the polar plateau and, in the first land traverse since Scott's, drove a team of Ferguson tractors to the South Pole to wait for Fuchs. In 1961, during an unsuccessful attempt to climb Mt Makalu in Nepal, Hillary suffered a mild stroke, but in 1967 he returned to Antarctica and led the first ascent of Mt Herschel. Now an author, lecturer and camping consultant, Hillary lives in New Zealand and visits Nepal to build schools and hospitals for the Sherpa people.

Sir Edmund Hillary

HOOKER
(Sir) Joseph Dalton
1817-1911

English botanist and son of a botanist, Hooker graduated as a doctor and at 22 became assistant surgeon and botanist on Ross's expedition to Antarctica. When landing on the newly discovered Franklin Island in the Ross Sea, Hooker slipped and was almost crushed to death between the boat and the rocks. He survived, and his botanical collections during the three-year voyage and later explorations in India, Morocco and North America, established him as one of the nineteenth century's most distinguished natural scientists. His published florae *rank among the finest of botanical literature. Hooker became a firm friend and supporter of Darwin, and in 1865 he succeeded his father as director of Kew Gardens. In his old age, Hooker became a mentor to the new generation of Antarctic explorers.*

HURLEY
James Francis ('Frank')
1885-1962

Frank Hurley

Photographer and adventurer, Hurley was born in Sydney, the son of a trade union official. He ran away from school at 13 and worked as a fitter's handyman and a docker before studying engineering. He bought a camera, and with his father's help became a partner in a postcard business. In 1911, after securing a seat next to Mawson by bribing a train conductor, he persuaded Mawson to take him to Antarctica. Hurley was one of the magnetic pole party who established a sledging record of 66 kilometres (41 miles) in a day. On his return he joined Shackleton's Endurance *expedition. When the* Endurance *was crushed in the pack ice Hurley dived into the water to save his negatives. Weight was now crucial and he was only allowed to keep 120 — the other 400 he smashed. The surviving plates are Hurley's greatest legacy — stark, simple and stirring records of that heroic ordeal. Hurley was an official Australian war photographer in both world wars. He undertook film ventures in New Guinea and central Australia, lecture tours in America, and in 1928 made the first flight from Australia to Athens. In 1929-31 he again joined Mawson on the BANZARE Antarctic voyages. A professional photographer to the end, Hurley died in Sydney.*

JOYCE
Ernest Edward Mills
1875-1940

A third generation British Naval seaman, Joyce was serving off Cape Town during the Boer War when he was selected for a vacancy on the southward-bound Discovery *expedition. He took part in a number of sledge journeys and became friendly with Ernest Shackleton. In 1907 Shackleton was looking out his office window in London and saw Joyce on the top deck of a passing bus. He sent his secretary in pursuit and persuaded Joyce to join his* Nimrod *expedition, where he was put in charge of provisions and dogs. In 1911 Joyce selected the dogs for Mawson's Antarctic expedition, then in 1914-17 led the Ross Sea Party of Shackleton's unsuccessful trans-Antarctic expedition. Stranded, the Ross Sea Party dutifully laid the depots for the crossing party that never came. Joyce was awarded the Albert Medal.*

FUCHS
(Sir) Vivian Ernest
1908-
Fuchs was born of German and British parentage. He trained as a geologist at Cambridge, then from 1929 took part in a number of expeditions to Greenland and east Africa. He spent two winters in Antarctica where, in 1948, he conceived the idea of crossing the entire continent via the South Pole. With grants from a number of governments and private sources, the Commonwealth Trans-Antarctic Expedition finally got off the ground in 1955. After building bases on the Weddell Sea side of the continent, and having depots laid by Sir Edmund Hillary on the Ross Sea side, Fuchs finally made the crossing with Sno-cats in the summer of 1957-58. Arriving at McMurdo Sound after 99 days on the ice, he became the first person to cross Antarctica. In 1958 Fuchs became head of the British Antarctic Survey and retired in 1977. He now lives in Cambridge.

FURNEAUX
Tobias
1735-1781
British naval commander, born near Plymouth, Furneaux entered the Royal Navy as a midshipman at the age of 20 and in the early 1760s served on the French and African coasts and in the West Indies. As second lieutenant on the Dolphin *he sailed with Captain Wallis on his round-the-world voyage in 1766-68. He accompanied Cook, as captain of the* Adventure, *on Cook's great second voyage of 1772-75, circumnavigating Antarctica at high latitude. Once, separated from Cook, Furneaux charted the east coast of Tasmania but, although a fine seaman, he lacked Cook's curiosity and explorer's zeal. Separated from Cook again, off New Zealand, Furneaux lost nine of his crew, eaten by Maoris. In 1777, during the American War of Independence, Furneaux took part in the British attack on New Orleans. He died at home aged 46.*

GERLACHE DE GOMERY
(Baron) Adrian Victor
1866-1934
Gerlache was born in Hasselt, Belgium. As a young naval lieutenant he organised a voyage to Antarctica in the Belgica *in 1897-99, charting new land along the western side of the Antarctic Peninsula. This was the first fully scientific expedition and the first to spend a full winter so far south. In 1901 Gerlache led a zoological expedition to the Persian Gulf, then in 1903 joined Charcot's Antarctic expedition, but resigned in Buenos Aires. He made a number of important journeys to the Arctic — to Greenland in 1905 and 1909, and the Barents and Kara Seas in 1907. He assisted Shackleton in his organisation of the ill-fated trans-Antarctic expedition (1914-17), selling him his yacht which was renamed* Endurance.

GIAEVER
John Schelderup
1901-
Giaever, born in northern Norway, worked as a journalist in the 1920s, then from 1929 took part in a number of hunting expeditions to Greenland. From 1935 he was secretary to the Norwegian Arctic expeditions, and during World War II worked for the liberation of Norway in Britain, America and, later, in Norway itself. In 1948 he became head of the Norwegian Polar Institute, then in 1950-52 led the first truly international Antarctic expedition, the joint Norwegian-Swedish-British scientific expedition to Dronning Maud Land.

HANSSEN
Helmer Julius
1870-1956
Hanssen was born into a family of sealers and fishermen in the Vesterålen Islands in northern Norway. He took his mate's certificate, and in 1897 first met Roald Amundsen. He was second mate on the Gjoa *during Amundsen's traverse of the Northwest Passage in 1903-06, becoming an expert dog driver during their three seasons on the ice. He went with Amundsen to Antarctica and stood with him at the South Pole in 1911. His handling of the dog teams greatly contributed to the success of the expedition. He joined Amundsen again in the* Maud *for the long-delayed Arctic drift, but left the expedition in Alaska after three years. In 1924 he was dog driver on an English expedition to Spitsbergen and later worked as polar advisor to a film company. He was employed for many years with the Norwegian Customs service.*

HASSEL
Helge Sverre
1876-1928
Hassel, Norwegian born, had already served on the Fram *when he first met Amundsen and was asked to join an Arctic drift. He accepted the sudden change of destination and was one of the four Norwegians who reached the South Pole with Amundsen in 1911. Hassel's value lay in his all-round abilities — navigator, sailmaker and saddler. After the expedition he worked for the Norwegian Customs in Grimstad, but on a visit to Amundsen, he fell down dead at his leader's feet.*

Sverre Hassel

KEMP
Peter
(?-1834)
Almost nothing is known of this British sealer who, in 1833, discovered a section of the Antarctic coastline. The original log and chart are thought to have been lost in a London cab, and the only authority at all for the voyage is a map of the world preserved in the Hydrographic Department of the Royal Navy. Kemp was an experienced master, who since 1813 had made over 14 voyages to southern seas. He was employed by Messrs Bennet and Sons to sail in the Magnet *to the southern Indian Ocean in search of new sealing grounds. On 26 December 1833 he sighted an area of the Antarctic coast now named after him. He was held off shore by the pack ice and after four days returned northwards. On the voyage home Kemp fell overboard and was drowned. The details of his Antarctic sightings were confirmed by Mawson a century later.*

KERGUÉLEN-TRÉMAREC
Yves Joseph de
1734-1797
The discoverer of Îles Kerguelen in the southern Indian Ocean, Kerguélen was born of a well-connected old Breton family. Kerguélen entered the French Navy at 16. After service in the Seven Years War he gained his own command, and in 1771 was chosen to lead an expedition in search of Terra Australis. *Sailing south from Mauritius in January 1772 he discovered the island which now bears his name but, unable to land in fog and rough seas, he returned to France. Naming his discovery La France Australe, he claimed that it was 'the central mass of the Antarctic continent'. He was promoted to captain and put in command of a second expedition. Planned as 'the finest voyage ever to be undertaken' it left France in 1773 but proved a disaster. Kerguélen spent 29 days hovering indecisively off the coast of 'La France Australe' but scurvy, the unseaworthiness of his ships and quarrels among his officers forced him back to France. Kerguélen was court-martialled and shown up as a lecherous, petty and ill-tempered leader, who had used the voyage to engage in private trading. He was sentenced to 20 years gaol, but only served four. During the war against England from 1778 he raided enemy merchant ships. The tables were turned in 1781 when, only a day out of port on a private voyage of discovery, his ships were taken over by English pirates. After the French Revolution of 1789 he secured a position in the Ministry of Marine, but under Robespierre spent eight months in prison. At his death he was still planning voyages of trade and discovery.*

LARSEN
Carl Anton
1860-1924
Larsen, born in Norway, left school at 14 to join his father at sea. By the age of 20 he had learned English and Spanish and gained his master's certificate. In 1885 he had his first whaler command. In 1892-94, on a whaling expedition, he found the first Antarctic plant fossils, discovered Oscar II Land and charted new sections of Graham Land. On his return he managed a whaling station in the far north of Norway before joining, in 1901, the Swedish Antarctic Expedition under Otto Nordenskjöld as captain of their ship Antarctic. *After leaving most of the expedition on Snow Hill Island, the* Antarctic *was caught in the ice and crushed. Larsen and the 19 crew spent the winter of 1903 in a stone hut, eating penguins, before rejoining the others and being rescued. In 1904, with Argentinean capital, Larsen established the first shore-based whaling station on South Georgia — the beginning of modern Antarctic whaling. After World War I Larsen tried to start a factory-ship whaling industry in the Ross Sea. He died there on board one of his whalers.*

Carl Larsen

LAW
Phillip Garth
1912-
Phillip Law was born in northern Victoria and studied at Melbourne University where he was appointed a lecturer in physics in 1943. In 1947 he became senior advisor to the Australian Antarctic Expeditions (ANARE) and in 1949 head of all Australia's Antarctic operations. Law made numerous summer voyages to the Australian Antarctic sector and in 1954 set up Mawson base, the first permanent base anywhere on the continent, and the first outside the Antarctic Peninsula. In 1957-58 Law led a voyage that comprehensively traversed the full length of the Australian sector. From 1966-77 he was Executive Vice-President of the Victorian Institute of Colleges. He now lives in retirement in Melbourne.

Lazarev – Rea

LAZAREV
Mikhail Petrovich
1788-1851

Lazarev was born near Moscow of a lesser noble family. At 12 he entered the Naval Cadet Corps and from 1803 spent five years on loan to the British Royal Navy. He served in the Russian Baltic fleet then sailed around the world on the Suvorov. *In 1819-21, as captain of the* Mirnyi, *Lazarev was second in command to Bellingshausen during their circumnavigation of Antarctica. On this voyage they became the first men to sight the continent. Lazarev was a more popular and less taciturn figure than Bellingshausen, and showed himself a splendid seaman with a capacity to take risks. In 1822-25 Lazarev sailed around the globe with a Russian scientific expedition. He then served with the Russian Navy in the Mediterranean and the Baltic before becoming commander of the Black Sea Fleet in 1833. He died on a visit to Vienna, aged 63.*

LEWIS
David
1919-

Adventurer and scientist, David Lewis was born in New Zealand of Welsh and Irish descent. While at medical school he climbed 19 unclimbed peaks in New Zealand's South Island, then at the tail end of World War II became a parachute medical officer. He came third in the 1960 trans-Atlantic single-handed yacht race, then in 1964 gave up his 18-year medical practice to spend three years sailing around the world in a catamaran. Following a legendary Polynesian course, Lewis was the first navigator of modern times to cross the Pacific without instruments. In 1972-73 he made the first single-handed voyage to Antarctica in his 10-metre (33-ft) sloop Ice Bird. *In 1977-78 he again sailed to Antarctica in the yacht* Solo *with a crew of eight. In 1981-82 he lead another expedition to Cape Denison to compare data on wildlife, climate and the ice sheet with that gathered by Mawson. In 1977 Lewis established the Oceanic Research Foundation in Sydney, of which he was still director in 1985.*

David Lewis pushing his boat *Icebird*.

MAGELLAN
Ferdinand
c1480-1521

Ferdinand Magellan was born into a noble Portuguese family. He served in Portuguese fleets in the Indian Ocean and took part in the capture of Malacca in 1511. After a break with the Portuguese court he offered his services to Spain, and in 1519 was given five ships to sail westwards to the Moluccas. Sailing down the coast of South America, he discovered the strait that bears his name and entered the Pacific showing that South America was not joined to any southern continent. But his sighting of Tierra del Fuego to the south strengthened the belief that land of some sort lay at the bottom of the world. Magellan crossed the Pacific, the first to do so, but in 1521 he was killed by natives in the Philippines. One of his ships, the Victoria, *returned to Spain, completing the first circumnavigation of the earth.*

MARKHAM
Clements Robert
1830-1916

Patron of British Antarctic exploration, Markham was born in Yorkshire into a clerical family. At 14 he entered the Royal Navy and in 1850-51 took part in one of the searches for the lost Arctic explorer, Sir John Franklin. He left the navy, spent over a year wandering in Peru, then in 1853 joined the India Office. In 1877 he retired from the civil service, resumed his wide travelling and wrote incessantly — mainly travel books, but also three historical romances. From 1893 he was president of the Royal Geographical Society and made the main aim of his presidency the furthering of Antarctic research and exploration. His choice of Scott as leader, and his insistence on full naval control, determined the final shape of the 1901-04 Discovery *expedition Markham was a man of immense energy, but was also obstinate and unreceptive to new ideas.*

MAWSON
(Sir) Douglas
1882-1958

Douglas Mawson

Douglas Mawson was born in Yorkshire and came to Australia as a boy. He studied geology under Edgeworth David at Sydney University and was appointed a lecturer at Adelaide University in 1905. In 1907 he joined Shackleton's Antarctic expedition and was a

NARES
(Sir) George Strong
1831-1915

Nares was born in Aberdeen into a naval family. He entered the Royal Navy in 1845 and in 1852 took part in the search for the lost Arctic explorer, Sir John Franklin. After service in the Crimean War he specialised in hydrographical work for the navy until his appointment as captain of the Challenger *in 1872. The four-year voyage of the* Challenger *established oceanography as a science in its own right. Nares was a popular and generous commander, sensitive to the needs of his large complement of scientists. In 1874 the* Challenger *became the first steamship to cross the Antarctic Circle, but late that year Nares had to leave the ship when he was appointed to lead an expedition to the Arctic. From 1879 to 1896 Nares was employed in the harbour department of the Board of Trade, becoming a vice admiral in 1892.*

NORDENSKJÖLD
Nils Otto Gustaf
1869-1928

Otto Nordenskjöld, explorer and geographer, was born in southern Sweden to a family with military traditions. His uncle was the discoverer of the Northeast Passage around Siberia. Nordenskjöld took a doctorate in geology and became a lecturer at Uppsala University. He led geological expeditions to Tierra del Fuego in 1895-97 and to the Yukon in 1898. At 32 he led the Swedish Antarctic expedition, wintering on the western side of the Antarctic Peninsula. After the crushing of his ship Antarctic, *the party was divided into three groups, two of which became lost. The whole expedition was rescued in 1903 and the scientific results were arguably the most important from the Antarctic to that date. Nordenskjöld received fame from the expedition but remained in debt for the rest of his life. He took the chair in geography at Göteborg in 1905 and held it until his death. He also led further expeditions — to Greenland in 1909 and to Peru and Southern Chile in 1920-21.*

OATES
Lawrence Edward Grace
1880-1912

The death of 'Titus' Oates has become a byword for Edwardian honour and courage. He was born in London, went to Eton and, after failing to enter Oxford University, joined the cavalry. He fought in the Boer War where he was badly wounded in the leg, then served in Ireland, Egypt and India. A proud, introverted figure, he was becoming unhappy with the army and applied to join Scott's second Antarctic expedition. He paid £1000 for the privilege and was placed in charge of the ponies and dogs. Oates was chosen as a member of the final polar party and developed badly frostbitten feet on the return from the pole. His rapidly declining conditions slowed down his companions. Scott describes Oates' end on 17 March 1912 (his 32nd birthday): 'He slept through the night before last, hoping not to wake; but he woke in the morning — yesterday. It was blowing a blizzard. He said, "I am just going outside and may be some time." He went into the blizzard and we have not seen him since.'

Captain 'Titus' Oates

PALMER
Nathaniel
1799-1877

Palmer was born, the son of a shipyard owner, in Stonington, Connecticut. He went to sea at 14 and was soon captaining small coastal vessels. This was the heyday of the American sealers and in 1819-20 he sailed to the South Shetlands as second mate on the Hersilia. *The next season Palmer returned to the South Shetlands as part of a large fleet from Stonington. Scouting to the south of the main fleet in the 45-tonne* Hero, *Palmer sighted land on 16 November 1820. Thus began the long-running claim, fostered by his biographer Edmund Fanning, that Palmer had discovered Antarctica. Even if Palmer had seen the*

member of the parties under David that made the first ascent of Mt Erebus and reached the South Magnetic Pole. He was invited by Scott to join his next Antarctic voyage but instead organised his own in 1911-14 to Commonwealth Bay, the windiest place on earth. Mawson's lone journey across George V Land after the death of his two companions, remains an epic of polar exploration. After World War I Mawson returned to Adelaide to work on the expedition results. He was appointed Professor of Geology in 1920 and in 1929-31 led two summer voyages to the Antarctic coast to the west of his first base. A tireless promoter of Australia's Antarctic interests, Mawson retired from the university in 1952 and died in 1958, the last leader from the heroic age.

MORRELL
Benjamin
1795-1839

An American sealer and adventurer, Morrell was born the son of a shipbuilder in Rye, New York. He ran away to sea at 16 only to spend two years as a prisoner of war of the British. In 1821 he was first mate on the Wasp *under Robert Johnson on a sealing voyage to the South Shetlands, and had a number of narrow escapes from drowning. The next year, now in command of the* Wasp, *he again headed south in search of seals. His own account of this voyage is open to doubt. Certainly Morrell was guilty of exaggeration, if not complete plagiarism and fraud. He claimed to have landed on Bouvetøya (the first to do so), to have penetrated the Weddell Sea to 70°S, and to have charted the non-existent island of New South Greenland. Some of his positions put him over 200 kilometres (124 miles) inland. He died of fever in Mozambique.*

MURRAY
(Sir) John
1841-1914

John Murray was born in Canada of Scottish parents. Sent to Edinburgh University, he refused to follow set courses, sit examinations or acquire degrees, but merely pursued his interest in natural history. In 1868 he spent seven months on an Arctic whaler and in 1872 was a last-minute replacement on the scientific staff of the Challenger. *On the four-year cruise of the* Challenger *Murray was in charge of bird specimens, but it was the analysis and publication of the full expedition results that became his life's work. He succeeded to the editorship of the* Challenger Reports *in 1882 and when money became tight he contributed his own. For 20 years the Challenger office in Edinburgh was the centre of marine biological study. When, in 1895, the last of the 50 great reports finally appeared, seven of them had been entirely written by Murray. From 1882 to 1894 he also directed a biological investigation of Scottish waters, and in 1906 he surveyed the depths of the Scottish lochs. Murray became wealthy from a phosphate mining venture on Christmas Island in the Pacific Ocean. He died in a car accident.*

NANSEN
Fridtjof
1861-1931

Fridtjof Nansen

Explorer, scientist and politician, Nansen was born in Norway. After early Arctic experience on a Greenland sealer he led the first crossing of the Greenland icecap, in 1888-89. He then devised a startling plan to reach the North Pole by drifting across the Arctic basin. In the Fram, *specially built to lift upwards under ice pressure, he drifted, ice-bound, for three years with the Arctic currents. Although unsuccessful in reaching the pole, a dash from the* Fram *over the ice took him closer to it than anyone before. In his use of dogs, sledges, skis and other equipment, Nansen had a profound impact on later polar explorers, especially Amundsen who used the* Fram *for his own expedition in 1910. Nansen was also an original scientist, becoming Professor of Zoology at Oslo and making a significant mark on histology and later, as his interests changed, in oceanography. From 1905 he became a leading political figure in the newly independent Norway, and from 1919 in the League of Nations. He directed the repatriation of prisoners of war from Russia in 1920, and developed the concept of a passport for displaced people. This became known as the Nansen passport and in 1922 Nansen was awarded the Nobel Peace Prize.*

mainland (which is still disputed), his sighting was nine months after those of Bellingshausen and Bransfield. But Palmer certainly has one discovery to his name. A year later he discovered the South Orkney Islands with the British sealer George Powell. Palmer then spent several years sailing vessels to the West Indies. In 1829 he again ventured to the Antarctic, but the sealing was poor and on the return voyage his ship was boarded by pirates. In the 1830s he grew wealthy from Atlantic trade, and later became involved in the clipper trade with China. He died at the age of 78 in San Francisco after returning from a voyage to the east.

PONTING
Herbert George
1870-1935

Born in Salisbury, England, Ponting followed his father into banking but soon gave it up to travel in the western United States, dabbling in farming, cattle and gold mining. He took up photography in 1900 then sailed to the Far East where he travelled and worked as a war correspondent in the Russo-Japanese and Spanish-American wars. He was a pioneer in the use of photography as an art form, rather than just as a means of recording events, and by 1909 he had established a world-wide reputation. In that year he met Scott and was appointed 'camera artist' to the Terra Nova *expedition, becoming the first professional photographer to go to Antarctica. Ponting's pictures — portraits and landscapes — are perhaps the greatest ever taken of the Antarctic. He also made a film,* 90 Degrees South, *which he remade into a sound version in 1933. His book,* The Great White South, *was reprinted many times.*

Herbert Ponting at work.

PRIESTLEY
Raymond Edward
1886-1974

Raymond Priestley was born in Tewkesbury where his father was the local grammar school headmaster. At 20, and without any degree, he was appointed by Shackleton as assistant geologist to Edgeworth David on the 1907-09 Nimrod *expedition. Returning from Antarctica, he studied under David at Sydney University, then was recruited by Scott for his second expedition. Priestley was a member of the northern party under Victor Campbell who were forced to winter in a small snow cave, living off seal meat. He also led the second ascent of Mt Erebus. In World War I he served in signals and won a Military Cross. After studying agriculture at Cambridge, Priestley followed a career in university administration. He was vice chancellor of Melbourne University from 1935 to 1938 then for 14 years at Birmingham. Antarctica continued to be a consuming interest and he made two visits there in his old age.*

Raymond Priestley

REA
Henry
c1804-?

Rea was a British naval officer appointed to follow up the Antarctic discoveries made by Biscoe. As far as is known he was born around 1804. He had been in the Royal Navy for 13 years when he left England in 1833 in the Hopeful *and* Rose *for the south Atlantic. The voyage was a sealing venture promoted by the Enderby Brothers, but it had also been indemnified by the British Government. At 60°S, the* Rose *was crushed between two icebergs. Although the men and provisions were saved, this disaster and mutinous crew forced Rea back to England. The failure of the voyage greatly embarrassed the Enderbys.*

Ritscher – Worsley

RITSCHER
Alfred
1879-1963

Ritscher spent his early career in the merchant marine before joining the German Navy. In 1912 he was captain of a ship taking an expedition to Spitsbergen. The venture was a disaster, the ship was frozen-in and abandoned, and Ritscher was lucky to return alive. In 1938 he was chosen by Göring to lead a mission to Antarctica. For three weeks, using an aircraft-refuelling mother ship, aerial photographs of 250 000 sq kilometres (96 500 sq miles) of Dronning Maud Land were obtained, and swastika-engraved aluminium darts systematically dropped to further German claims to sovereignty. After World War II Ritscher worked on the publication of the results of the expedition.

ROSS
(Sir) James Clark
1800-1862

Born in Scotland, Ross was considered one of the most dashing and handsome men of his age. He joined the Royal Navy at 12 and in 1827 sailed in an unsuccessful attempt to reach the North Pole. In 1831, with his uncle Sir John Ross, he located the North Magnetic Pole. By 1839

Sir James Clark Ross

he was the most experienced Arctic captain ever, and was appointed to lead a national expedition to Antarctica. In the Erebus *and* Terror *he discovered the Ross Sea and went further south than anyone before. He did not find the South Magnetic Pole, but returned home in 1843 to great acclaim and a knighthood. When he married later that year, one of the conditions set by the bride's father was that Ross forgo any more long polar voyages. Apart from an unsuccessful attempt to relieve Sir John Franklin in the Arctic in 1848, he lived at Aylesbury and edited his Antarctic scientific reports.*

RYMILL
John Riddoch
1905-1968

John Rymill was educated in Melbourne and in 1929 took part in a Cambridge University ethnological expedition to Canada. He studied surveying then joined Gino Watkins' two expeditions to Greenland in 1930-33, and took over as leader when Watkins was drowned. Rymill then planned and led the British Graham Land Expedition of 1934-37 to Antarctica which, through the combined use of aircraft and sledge parties, proved that Graham Land was a peninsula and not an archipelago as previously thought. Rymill was a huge man, and as a leader was thorough and methodical, and never known to give a direct order. After a period in the navy reserve during World War II, Rymill spent the rest of his life as a grazier in South Australia. He died following a road accident.

SCOTT
Robert Falcon
1868-1912

Scott was born the son of a Devonshire brewer with naval connections. He entered the navy training school at 13, graduated to midshipman and lieutenant and served in the Caribbean and the Pacific. In 1899, while torpedo lieutenant on the Majestic, *he met Sir Clements Markham in a London street and applied to lead his National Antarctic Expedition. Under Scott, the 1901-04*

Captain Robert Scott

Discovery *expedition covered 5000 kilometres (3100 miles) with sledge teams and carried out a significant scientific program: Scott, with Shackleton and Wilson, also sledged to a record 82°S. By 1907 Scott was organising a second expedition with one of the aims being to reach the South Pole. Like its predecessor, it was to be along strict naval lines. Scott, now a captain, was a brave but lonely figure. He had a restless inquiring mind, but was also given to self-doubt and vacillation. He and four companions reached the pole on 17 January 1912, only to find that Amundsen had been there a month earlier. All died on the return journey. The heroism of their end, and Scott's moving diaries, began an enduring legend that masked a real failure of organisation.*

WILD
Frank
1874-1930

Frank Wild

Born in Yorkshire, Frank Wild was the son of an itinerant preacher. He went to sea at 16, then at 26 joined the Royal Navy as a seaman gunner. He volunteered to join Scott's 1901-04 expedition and began a career that saw him move from seaman to expedition leader and became the most experienced Antarctic hand of his time. During that expedition he became firm friends with Shackleton who invited Wild to join him on the Nimrod *expedition of 1907-09. With Adams and Marshall they made one of the greatest of all sledge journeys, discovering the Beardmore Glacier and marching to within 180 kilometres (97 nautical miles) of the pole. Under Mawson in 1911-14, Wild was leader of the Western Party and explored 500 kilometres (310 miles) of new coastline. As deputy to Shackleton on the* Endurance, *Wild was left in charge of the 22 men on Elephant Island in 1916, steering them through a winter where they had only boats as a hut, an insufficient diet and rotten clothes. In 1917 he served with Shackleton in the North Russian Force, then went to Africa to plant cotton before being summoned back by Shackleton for the* Quest *voyage. After Shackleton's sudden death in 1922 Wild took command and completed the voyage. He married and returned to Africa, but his cotton farm failed and he took to drink. He died of pneumonia in the Transvaal.*

WILKES
Charles
1798-1877

Charles Wilkes was born in New York, entering the navy as a midshipman in 1818. His natural scientific bent led to his becoming head of the Naval Department of Charts and Instruments where he built the first observatory in the United States. At the age of 40 he was appointed to lead the controversial United States Exploring Expedition after more senior officers had turned it down. Often described as the most unhappy and ill-prepared of Antarctic expeditions, it set sail in 1838 with six ships, returning in 1842 with only two. Despite the unseaworthiness of his ships and a scurvy-ridden crew, Wilkes managed to follow the Antarctic coast for over 2000 kilometres (1240 miles), sighting new land at a number of points. But running disputes with some of his officers led to Wilkes being court-martialled on his return. He was eventually cleared and spent over 12 years working on the official reports of the expedition. He returned to active service in 1861 during the Civil War, but his interception of a British mail steamer almost brought Britain into the war on the side of the Confederacy, and Wilkes was court-martialled again, found guilty and placed on the retired list. Only years after his death was Wilkes finally hailed for his Antarctic achievements.

WILKINS
(Sir) George Hubert
1888-1958

A professional adventurer and explorer, Hubert Wilkins was born the son of a South Australian farmer. He was sent to the School of Mines in Adelaide, then spent four years wandering in Europe and America before working as official Turkish photographer in the 1912 Balkan War, taking some of the earliest film of troops in action. He spent 1913-17 as photographer with Stefansson's Arctic expedition, then enlisted in the Australian Flying Corps. In 1920 he joined John Cope's poorly planned British Imperial Expedition before serving as ornithologist with Shackleton's last expedition on the Quest. *In 1923-25 he led a collecting expedition to central Australia for the British Natural History Museum, then returned to the Arctic for three years, making major exploratory flights north from Alaska with Ben Eielson. Wilkins next headed south in 1928-29 as leader of an expedition financed by William Randolph Hearst, and made the first Antarctic flight. In 1931 he took a submarine, which he had bought from the United States Navy for $1, under the Arctic ice in an unsuccessful attempt to reach the North Pole. He then took a series of expeditions to Antarctica with Lincoln Ellsworth, acting as leader of the support team during Ellsworth's flights. During World War II and afterwards Wilkins was an adviser to the United States forces on cold-climate equipment. When he died his ashes were scattered from a submarine on the ice at the North Pole.*

SHACKLETON
(Sir) Ernest Henry
1874-1922

Sir Ernest Shackleton

Shackleton was born in Ireland, one of 10 children of an Irish doctor and a Yorkshire Quaker. They moved to London when he was 10, and at 17 he was apprenticed to the merchant marine, rising to the position of third officer. He secured a late position on Scott's first Antarctic expedition and through ability and force of personality soon became a leading figure in the party, marching with Scott and Wilson on the southern journey in 1902. Shackleton's breakdown from scurvy led to him being invalided home, and to a fierce resolve to prove himself. After episodes as a journalist, secretary of the Royal Scottish Geographical Society, failed Liberal parliamentary candidate and failed businessman, he secured funds for his own Antarctic expedition. In 1909 with three companions he almost reached the South Pole and returned home to fame and a knighthood. The aim of his second expedition of 1914-17 was to cross Antarctica, but the loss of his ship transformed the venture into the greatest epic of survival of Antarctic exploration. Shackleton's mixture of prudence and inspired risk-taking saved his whole party. In the closing months of World War I Shackleton was put in charge of equipment for the north Russian campaign. He sailed to the Antarctic for the last time in the Quest *in 1921, but died of heart failure. Shackleton was a larger-than-life figure, generous and colourful. 'He lived like a mighty rushing wind', wrote Hugh Mill.*

SHIRASE
Nobu
1861-1946

In 1893 Shirase took part in an expedition to the Karil Islands north of Japan. As a little-known army lieutenant, he fought government and public ridicule to organise a Japanese expedition to Antarctica. He finally gained the support of Count Okuma, a nobleman and former Premier of Japan, and the expedition set sail in the Kainan Maru *in 1911. Forced to retreat to Sydney after their first voyage south, the party landed at the Bay of Whales the following year, where they met members of Amundsen's expedition. A 'dash patrol' under Shirase sledged with dogs 260 kilometres (160 miles) inland to raise the Japanese flag for the first time. Shirase then returned to a tremendous reception in Japan.*

SIPLE
Paul Allman
1908-1968

Paul Siple was born in Ohio and at the age of 19 was chosen from among the Boy Scouts of America to accompany Byrd on his first Antarctic expedition in 1928-30. He served as dog handler and naturalist, beginning a life-long friendship with Byrd and a passion for Antarctica. He followed Byrd south again in 1933-35, this time as chief biologist, and led a 77-day sledge journey across Marie Byrd Land. Siple completed a PhD in geography in 1939 then joined the 1939-41 Antarctic expedition as chief supply officer and leader of the western base. From 1946-63 he worked in Army research taking part in Operations Highjump (1946-47) and Deepfreeze (1955-57). During the latter expedition he supervised the building of the South Pole Station and spent the first winter there as scientific leader. Siple developed a wind-chill index as a measure of cold in different wind and temperature conditions.

WEDDELL
James
1787-1834

James Weddell was the son of a Scottish upholsterer and an English Quaker. He joined Britain's Royal Navy at eight, but soon left to join the merchant marine. From 1805 he made a number of voyages to the West Indies and at one stage was put in irons for striking down a tyrannical captain. He returned to the Royal Navy for the remainder of the Napoleonic wars then resumed merchant voyages to the West Indies. From 1819 to 1822 he made two sealing voyages to Antarctic waters in the brig Jane, *owned by James Strachan. He independently discovered the South Orkney Islands, and penetrated the sea now named after him to 74°15'S — the furthest south that any man had been at that time. His book* A Voyage Towards the South Pole, *published in 1825, is full of Weddell's self-taught scientific curiosity. He continued as the master of various trading vessels, but in 1829 was wrecked in the Azores and was only saved by lashing himself to a rock. His last voyage was to New South Wales and Tasmania in 1830-32. He died in London in relative poverty aged only 47.*

James Weddell

WILSON
Edward Adrian
1872-1912

'Bill' Wilson was born in Cheltenham, the son of a doctor. He became fascinated with nature and drawing and studied natural sciences at Cambridge. He then studied medicine, but in 1898 discovered that he had tuberculosis. Following successful convalescence he volunteered to join Scott's first Antarctic expedition. In 1902, with Scott and Shackleton, he reached 82°S — further south than anyone before — and became Scott's closest friend and confidant. On return Wilson spent five years working on a survey of grouse disease. Shackleton wanted him to join the Nimrod *expedition but, partly out of loyalty to Scott, Wilson refused. On Scott's second expedition Wilson was appointed head of the scientific staff. He led Bowers and Cherry-Garrard on the famous 1911 winter journey to Cape Crozier in search of emperor penguin eggs. Gentle, solitary and self-effacing, Wilson was one unmistakeable religious figure among Scott's men. As example and counsellor, he was the moral centre of both expeditions. He was also a fine painter of watercolours. Wilson reached the pole with Scott in 1912 and died with him of starvation and exhaustion on the return journey.*

Dr Edward Wilson

WISTING
Oscar
1871-1936

Oscar Wisting

Oscar Wisting was Amundsen's closest associate. He worked on whalers around Iceland before joining the Norwegian Navy as a gunner. He was recommended to Amundsen for the Fram *expedition and was one of the four to reach the South Pole with their leader. In 1918 Wisting joined the Arctic drift of the* Maud *and took over as commander when Amundsen left the voyage in 1921. Although completing the Northeast Passage, the expedition failed to make substantial progress northwards and was abandoned in 1925. Wisting became a captain in the navy, then in 1926, with his old leader, he flew across the Arctic basin in the airship* Norge. *When Amundsen disappeared in 1928, Wisting led one of the search parties. In 1936 after the* Fram *had been installed in an Oslo museum, Wisting asked for permission to sleep aboard. The next morning he was found dead in his old cabin.*

WORSLEY
Frank Arthur
1872-1943

Born in Akaroa, New Zealand, Worsley went to sea at 15 becoming a mate, then master, of New Zealand Government schooners working in the South Pacific. In 1914 he was appointed captain of the Endurance *on Shackleton's trans-Antarctic expedition. After the* Endurance *was crushed, and the men managed to reach Elephant Island, Worsley navigated the 6-metre (20-ft)* James Caird *the 1300 kilometres (800 miles) to South Georgia. With Shackleton and Crean he then crossed the island, a feat which until then had been considered impossible. In 1917-18 Worsley won the Distinguished Service Order for operations against U-boats, then served on the north Russian front. He joined Shackleton again in the* Quest *in 1921-22. In 1925 he was joint leader of an Arctic expedition which penetrated to Franz Joseph Land, then in 1935 travelled to the Cocos Island in an unsuccessful search for hidden treasure. Worsley died in England, active to the last, having refused to retire.*

INDEX

This index covers all pages in the book except for the maps that appear on pages 288-91. A separate gazetteer to those starts on page 316. Page numbers in bold type indicate main entries, while those in *italic* refer to illustrations which are indexed separately from text references that appear in roman type.

A

B

C

D

E

F

G

H

I

J

K

L

M

N

O

P

R

S

T

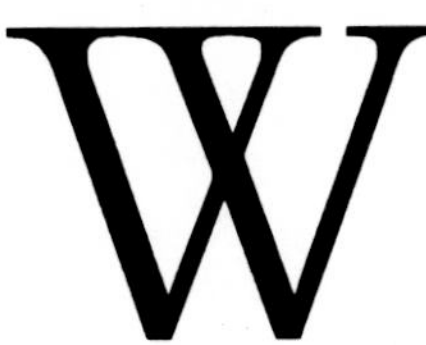

MAP GAZETTEER

The following gazetteer contains all the names that appear on the maps between pages 288 and 291. Some places appear two or three times because they are shown on the general map (288-89), on the detailed map of the Antarctic Peninsula (290), on the detailed map of the Ross Sea region (291), or on the Ross Island inset (291).

ACKNOWLEDGEMENTS

Many people and organisations assisted in the preparation of this book. The publishers would like to thank them all, particularly:

Academy of Sciences of the USSR, Moscow; Akademie der Wissenschaften der DDR, Leipzig; Alexander Turnbull Library, Wellington; Mme M.R. Allart-Charcot; Ian Allison; American Geographical Society, New York; American Geographical Society Collection of the University of Wisconsin, Milwaukee; The American Museum of Natural History, New York; Antarctic Division, Christchurch, particularly R.B. Thomson and K.O. Clegg; Antarctic Division, Tasmania, particularly Dr Patrick G. Quilty; Archiv für Kunst und Geschichte, Berlin; Archive of the Naval Academy of the USSR, Moscow; Archives de France, Paris; Archives Office of Tasmania, Hobart; Ardea London Limited; Asahi Newspapers, Tokyo; Dr Peter Barrett; Richard Barrett; Bayerische Staatsbibliothek, Munich; BBC Hulton Picture Library, London; Beinecke Rare Book and Manuscript Library, Yale University, Connecticut; Bibliothèque Nationale, Paris; Bibliotheque Royale Albert Ier, Brussels; Bildarchiv Preussischer Kulturbesitz, Berlin; The Rt. Hon. The Earl of Birkenhead; Bruce Boutet; Dr J.D. Bradshaw; British Antarctic Survey, Cambridge, particularly Miss Anne Todd; The British Library, London; Paul Broady; Broughty Castle Museum, Dundee; Associate Professor Grahame Budd; Commander M.K. Burley; Sue Burrows; Jim Caffin; Canterbury Museum, Christchurch; Duncan Carse; Jonathan Chester; Debby Cramer; Lieut. Commander Andrew David; W.H. Dawbin; Sara Day; Department of Transport, Pretoria; Deutsche Forschungsgemeinschaft, Bonn; Deutsche Staatsbibliothek, Berlin; Sara Dodds; Dundee Museums and Art Galleries; John Dyson; Edinburgh University Library; Edward Arnold (Publishers) Ltd, London; Brian Enting; Dr David Everitt; Expéditions Polaires Françaises, Paris; Fisher Library, University of Sydney; Arthur Fletcher; Dr R. Ewan Fordyce; Neville Fox-Davies; Anne Fraser; Freie Universität, Berlin; Sir Vivian Fuchs; Commander J.R. Furse; The Geographical Society of Gothenburg, Sweden, particularly Christina Nordin; Göteborgs Universitetsbibliotek, Göteborg, Sweden; Professor Laurence M. Gould; Mrs Jane Grey; Ludwig Harms; The Hearst Corporation, New York; Wally Herbert; The Hermitage Museum, Leningrad; Colleen Hodge; Michael Holford; Dr Don Horning; Robyn Hudson; Hunterian Museum, University of Glasgow, particularly Professor Frank Willett; Hydrographic Department, Taunton, England; Institute for Oceanographic Sciences, Wormley, England; Peter Jacob; Ulf Johansson; Norman Jones; Noel B. Kemp; Vere Kenny; Dr Uwe Kils; Kommandør Chr. Christensens Hvalfangstmuseum, Sandefjord, Norway; B.A. Krutskih, Director of the Arctic and Antarctic Research Institute, Leningrad; Kungl. Vetenskapsakademien Biblioteket, Stockholm; Kungliga Biblioteket, Stockholm; Ing-Gén G.R. Laclavère; Dr R.M. Laws, Director, British Antarctic Survey, Cambridge; The Lenin State Library of the USSR, Moscow; Leningrad Maritime Museum; The Library of Congress, Washington; Alain Lockyer; J.M. Mackenzie, Historical Studies Section, Department of Defence, Canberra; The Maritime Trust, London; Capitán Roberto Manuel Martinez Abal, Director, Instituto Antártico Argentino, Buenos Aires; Mary Evans Picture Library, London; Mauritius Archives Department, Beau-Bassin; The Mawson Institute for Antarctic Research, Adelaide, particularly Mrs E. Sawyer; Dr B.C. McKelvey; Nick McRae; Edwin Mickleburgh, The Staff of the Mitchell Library, Sydney; Betty Monteath; Dominic Mouflier; Musée de la Marine, Paris; Museum für Deutsche Geschichte, Berlin; Y. Nagamoto; National Aeronautics and Space Administration, Washington; National Archives and Records Service, Washington, particularly Alison Wilson; National Archives of Norway, Oslo; National Art Gallery of New Zealand, Wellington; *National Geographic* magazine, Washington; Staff of the National Library of Australia, Canberra; National Maritime Museum, Greenwich, particularly Mrs A.M. Shirley; National Museum, Wellington; National Portrait Gallery, London; Nationalmuseum, Stockholm; New Zealand Antarctic Society, Christchurch; New Zealand Meteorological Service, Wellington; Laraine Newberry; Gustalf Nordenskjöld; Shaun Norman; Norsk Folkemuseum, Oslo; Norsk Polarinstitutt, Oslo; Norsk Sjøfartsmuseum, Oslo; Österreichische Nationalbibliothek, Vienna; W & F Pascoe Pty Ltd, Sydney; Paul Popper Ltd, London; Peabody Museum, Salem, Massachusetts; Public Record Office, Kew, England; The Rank Organisation, London; Jacques Rauffet; Geoff Renner; Mrs Shelagh Robinson; H. Roger-Viollet, Paris; Pedro J. Romero, Director, Instituto Antartico Chileno, Santiago; Royal Geographical Society, London; Royal Scottish Geographical Society, Edinburgh; Royal Scottish Museum, Edinburgh; The Royal Society, London; Mrs E. Rymill; Paul Sagar; Sandefjord Sjøfartsmuseum, Norway; Scott Polar Research Institute, Cambridge, particularly Harry King and Clive Holland; Sir Peter Scott; Tom Scott; Seaphot Limited, Bristol; Oliver Shepard; Shirase Antarctic Expedition Memorial Association, Tokyo; Chitoh Shirase; Sjøfartsmuseet, Göteborg, Sweden; Société de Géographie, Paris; Dr Lauritz Sømme; South African Defence Force Archives, Pretoria; Linda Spain, Staatsarchiv, Amberg; State Library of South Australia, Adelaide; The State Library of Victoria, particularly Ms Mary Cox; The State Russian Museum, Leningrad; Statens Sjöhistoriska Museum, Stockholm; Alfred Stephenson; Stockholms Stadsmuseum, Stockholm; Rod Streeter; Süddeutscher Verlag, Munich; Soames Summerhays; Gunnel Sundbom; Robert Swan; Dr Charles Swithinbank; Tasmanian Museum and Art Gallery, Hobart; Edward P. Todd, Director, Division of Polar Programs, Washington; Trinity House Lighthouse Service, London; Ullstein Bilderdienst, Berlin; United States Naval Academy and Museum, Annapolis; Universitäts-Bibliothek der Humboldt-Universität, Berlin; Universitätsbibliothek, Munich; Universitetsbiblioteket I Oslo; Universitetsbiblioteket, Uppsala; University of Oxford, Department of Zoology; The University of Sydney Archives; Patricia Vestal; Ms Janet Vetter; Paul-Emile Victor; Per Voksø; T.D. Wakefield; Suzanne Walter; Rebecca Ward; Dr John Warham; Rod Westblade; Dr Kim Westerskov; Westfälischen Wilhelms-Universität, Münster; Alwyne Wheeler, British Museum (Natural History), London; Wilkins Memorial Foundation Inc., Montrose, Pennsylvania, particularly Winston Ross; Graham J. Wilson; Ragnar Wold; Robert J. Woodward; Yale University Library, Connecticut; Takehiro Yukawa; Zentralbibliothek, Zürich.

Numerous letters, diaries, articles and books were consulted while researching the text for this book. The publishers acknowledge their indebtedness to all the diverse sources, although it is only possible to list the principal ones here.

Alone Richard E. Byrd (Putnam, New York, 1938); *America in the Antarctic* P.I. Mitterling (New York, 1959); *Americans in the Antarctic* Kenneth J. Bertrand (AGS, New York, 1971); *Animals of the Antarctic – the Ecology of the Far South* Bernard Stonehouse (Peter Lowe, London, 1972); *Antarctic Adventure – Scott's Northern Party* R.E. Priestley (Fisher Unwin, London, 1914); *Antarctic* magazine (various editions) (NZ Antarctic Society, Christchurch); *The Antarctic Manual* J. Murray (Ed.) (RGS, London, 1901); *The Antarctic Ocean* Russell Owen (Museum Press, London, 1948); *The Antarctic Pilot* (Hydrographer of the Navy, Taunton, 1974); *The Antarctic Problem* E.W. Hunter Christie (Allen and Unwin, London, 1951); *The Antarctic* H.G.R. King (Blandford, London, 1969); *Antarctica* Eliot Porter (Hutchinson, Sydney, 1978); *Antarctica – The Last Continent* Ian Cameron (Little Brown, Boston, 1974); *Antarctica and its Resources* Barbara Mitchell and Jon Tinker (Earthscan, London, 1980); *Antarctica, or Two Years Amongst the Ice of the South Pole* Otto Nordenskjöld (Hurst, Blackett, London, 1905); *Antarctica: Glaciological and Geophysical Folio* D.J. Drewry (Ed.) (SPRI, Cambridge, 1983); *Antarctica: Weather and Climate* Neal W. Young (Ed.) (Melbourne, 1981); *Antarctica: Wilderness at Risk* Barney Brewster (Sun Books, Melbourne, 1982); *Argonauts of the South* Frank Hurley (Putnam, New York, 1925); *Australians in the Antarctic* R.A. Swan (MUP, Melbourne, 1961); *Beyond Horizon* Lincoln Ellsworth (Doubleday, New York, 1938); *Blizzard and Fire* John Béchervaise (Angus and Robertson, Sydney, 1963); *British Polar Explorers* E.R.G.R. Evans (Collins, London, 1943); *Captain Scott* Stephen Gwynn (Allen Lane, London, 1939); *Challenge to the Poles* John Grierson (Foulis, London, 1964); *Charcot of the Antarctic* M. Oulie (London, 1938); *Chronological History of the Voyages and Discoveries in the South Seas* James Burney (London, 1817); *Cold* Laurence M. Gould (Brewer, Warren & Putnam, New York, 1931); *The Coldest Place on Earth* Robert Thomson (A.H. & A.W. Reed, Wellington, 1969); *The Conquest of the South Pole* J. Gordon Hayes (Butterworth, London, 1932); *The Crossing of Antarctica*, Sir Vivian Fuchs and Sir Edmund Hillary (Cassell, London, 1958); *Cruise of Her Majesty's Ship Challenger* W.J.J. Spry (London, 1876); *The Cruise of the 'Antarctic' to the South Polar Regions* H.J. Bull (Edward Arnold, London, 1896); *Deutsche Antarktische Expedition 1938-39* Alfred Ritscher (Leipzig, 1943); *Deutsche Sudpolar-Expedition 1901-03* E. Drygalski (Berlin, 1931); *Discovery* Richard E. Byrd (Putnam, New York, 1935); *Discovery II in the Antarctic* J. Coleman-Cooke (London, 1963); *Edward Wilson of the Antarctic* George Seaver (Murray, London, 1933); *Exploring the Antarctic in the Discovery II* J.W.S. Marr (London, 1933); *First on the Antarctic Continent* C. Borchgrevink (Newnes, London, 1900); *Footprints on a Frozen Continent* John G. McPherson (Hicks Smith, Sydney, 1975); *French Explorers in the Pacific* John Dunmore (Clarendon, London, 1969); *The Geographical Journal* (various editions) (Royal Geographical Society, London); *The Great Antarctic Rescue* F.A. Worsley (Times Books, London, 1977); *Great Waters* Sir Alister Hardy (Collins, London, 1967); *Great White South* Herbert Ponting (Duckworth, London, 1921); *Harpooned – The Story of Whaling* Bill Spence (Crescent Books, New York, 1980); *The Heart of the Antarctic* Sir Ernest Shackleton (Heinemann, London, 1909); *Herbert Ponting – Another World* H.J.P. Arnold (Sidgwick, London, 1975); *A History of Polar Exploration* David Mountfield (Hamlyn, London, 1974); *The Home of the Blizzard* Sir Douglas Mawson (Heinemann, London, 1915); *Huskies* Robert Dovers (Bell, London, 1957); *Ice Bird* David Lewis (Collins, Sydney, 1975); *In the Wake* Gerald S. Doorly (Robertson & Mullins, Melbourne, 1936); *Last of Lands...Antarctica* J.F. Lovering and J.R.V. Prescott (MUP, Melbourne, 1979); *Le Français au Pole Sud* J.-B Charcot (Paris, 1906); *The Lichens and Mosses of Mac.Robertson Land* Rex B. Filson (Antarctic Division, Melbourne, 1966); *The Life of Sir Ernest Shackleton* H.R. Mill (London, 1923); *Little America* Richard E. Byrd (Putnam, New York, 1930); *Log Letters from the Challenger* Lord George Campbell (Macmillan, London, 1877); *The Lonely South* André Migot (Hart-Davis, London, 1957); *Mawson of the Antarctic* Paquita Mawson (Longmans, London, 1964); *Narrative of the United States Exploring Expedition* C. Wilkes (Philadelphia, 1845); *National Geographic* magazine (various editions) (National Geographic Society, Washington); *No Latitude for Error* Sir Edmund Hillary (Hodder, London, 1961); *Once More on My Adventure* Frank Legg and Toni Hurley (Ure Smith, Sydney, 1966); *Operation Deepfreeze* George J. Dufek (Harcourt Brace, New York, 1957); *Penguins* John Sparks and Tony Soper (David and Charles, London, 1967); *Physiological Adaptation and Health of an Expedition in Antarctica* D.J. Lugg (AGPS, Canberra, 1977); *Polar Record* (various editions) (SPRI, Cambridge); *The Polar Rosses* Ernest S. Dodge (Faber, London, 1973); *Quest for a Continent* W. Sullivan (New York, 1957); *Relation de deux Voyages dans les Mers Australes et des Indes* V.J. Kerguélen-Trémarec (Paris, 1782); *Report on the Scientific Results of the Voyage of HMS Challenger...* Thomson and Murray (Eds) (London, 1880-1895); *The Ross Sea Shore Party 1914-17* R.W. Richards (SPRI, Cambridge, 1962); *Saga of the White Horizon* Magnus L. Olsen (Nautical, London, 1972); *Scott and Amundsen* Roland Huntford (Hodder, London, 1979); *Scott of the Antarctic* Elspeth Huxley (Weidenfeld, London, 1977); *Scott's Last Expedition* Arranged by L. Huxley (Smith Elder, London, 1914); *Scott's Men* David Thomson (Allen Lane, London, 1977); *Sea Dogs of Today* A.J. Villers (Harrap, London, 1932); *Sea Guide to Whales of the World* Lyall Watson (Hutchinson, London, 1981); *Shackleton* M. & J. Fisher (London, 1957); *Shackleton's Argonauts* Frank Hurley (Angus and Robertson, Sydney, 1948); *Shackleton's Last Voyage; the Story of the Quest* F. Wild (Cassell, London, 1923); *The Siege of the South Pole* H.R. Mill (London, 1905); *The Sierra Club Handbook of Whales and Dolphins* Stephan Leatherwood (Sierra Club, San Francisco, 1983); *Sir Hubert Wilkins – His World of Adventure* Lowell Thomas (RBC, Melbourne, 1962); *Sledging into History* David L. Harrowfield (Macmillan, Auckland, 1981); *South* Sir Ernest Shackleton (Heinemann, London, 1919); *South From New Zealand* L.B. Quartermain (Government Printer, Wellington, 1964); *South Latitude* F.D. Ommanney (Longman Green, London, 1938); *The South Polar Trail* E.E.M. Joyce (Duckworth, London, 1929); *The South Pole* Roald Amundsen (John Murray, London, 1912); *South With Mawson* C.F. Laseron (Harrap, London, 1947); *South With Scott* E.R.G.R. Evans (Collins, London, 1922); *Southern Lights* John Rymill (Chatto & Windus, London, 1938); *Tel fut Charcot* Marthe Emmanuel (Beauchesne, Paris, 1967); *This Accursed Land* Lennard Bickel (Macmillan, Melbourne, 1977); *Through the First Antarctic Night* Frederick A. Cook (Heinemann, London, 1900); *Two Huts in the Antarctic* L.B. Quartermain (Government Printer, Wellington, 1963); *Two Men in the Antarctic* T.W. Bagshawe (Macmillan, New York, 1939); *Voyage au Pôle Sud et dans l'Océanie sur les corvettes 'l'Astrolabe' et la 'Zélée'* J. Dumont d'Urville (Paris, 1843); *The Voyage of Captain Bellingshausen* Frank Debenham (Ed.) (Hakluyt Society, London, 1945); *A Voyage of Discovery and Research in the Southern and Antarctic Regions* Sir James Clark Ross (Murray, London, 1847); *The Voyage of the Scotia* Brown, Pirie and Mossman (Blackwood, Edinburgh, 1906); *The Voyage of the 'Why Not' in the Antarctic* J.-B Charcot (Hodder, London, 1911); *The Voyage of the Challenger*, Eric Linklater (Murray, London, 1972); *The Voyage of the Discovery* Captain Robert F. Scott (Smith Elder, London, 1905); *The Voyage of the Resolution and Adventure (1772-1775)* James Cook (Ed. J.C. Beaglehole) (Hakluyt Society, London, 1961); *The Voyage of the Resolution and Discovery (1776-1780)* James Cook (Ed. J.C. Beaglehole) (Hakluyt Society, London, 1967); *Voyage to the Ice* David Lewis (ABC, Sydney, 1979); *A Voyage Towards the South Pole Performed in the Years 1822-24* James Weddell (Longman Rees etc, London, 1825); *Voyages of Discovery in the Arctic and Antarctic Seas...* R. MacCormick (London, 1884); *White Out* Michael Guy (Alister Taylor, Martinborough, 1980); *The Winters of the World* Brian S. John (Ed.) (Jacaranda, Milton, 1979); *The World Atlas of Exploration* Eric Newby (Mitchell Beazley, London, 1975); *The Worst Journey in the World* Apsley Cherry-Garrard (Constable, London, 1923); *The Year of the Quiet Sun* Adrian Hayter (Hodder, London, 1968); *Zum Kontinent des Eisigen Südens* E. Drygalski (Reimer, Berlin, 1904); *Zum sechsten Erdteil: die zweite deutsche Südpolar-Expedition* Wilhelm Filchner (Ullstein, Berlin, 1922)

The following organisations and individuals provided photographs and gave permission for them to be reproduced. The publishers also acknowledge the work of individuals listed below, used in the preparation of illustrations and diagrams.

Cover: Colin Monteath. **1:** Another day on Windy Ridge, Shaun Norman. **2/3:** Sea ice on McMurdo Sound, Colin Monteath. **4/5:** Weddell Sea ice cliffs, Charles Swithinbank. **6/7:** Mount Erebus by moonlight, Colin Monteath. **8/9:** Midnight at Browning Pass, Victoria Land, Shaun Norman. **10:** b, Colin Monteath. **11:** tl, Lands and Survey Department, Wellington; tr, National Aeronautics and Space Administration, Washington; cr, br, Colin Monteath. **12/13:** Adélie penguins on Paulet Island, Colin Monteath. **14:** bl, adapted from the work of M. J. Rubin *(Scientific American*, September 1962). **15:** tl, tr, Colin Monteath; cr, bl, United States Department of Commerce, National Oceanic and Atmospheric Administration; br, adapted from the work of M. B. Giovinetto in *Antarctic Snow and Ice Studies* (American Geophys. Union, Antarctic Research Series, Vol 2, 1964). **16:** t, Colin Monteath; c, Noel Kemp; bl, Roger Mear; bc, Norman Jones. **17:** t, cr, Noel Kemp; bl, adapted from work of P. Siple in *90 South* (Putnam, New York, 1959). **18:** t, Colin Monteath, lcl, from *Snow Crystals* by W. A. Bentley and W. J. Humphreys (McGraw-Hill, New York, 1931); lcr, Neal Young; rct, rcb, rb, Xie Zichu. **19:** t, Jeff Wilson; c, Neal Young; bl, diagram adapted from work of Claude Lorius, Dominique Renauld, Jean-Robert Petit, Jean Jouzel and Liliane Merlivat in *Annals of Glaciology* Vol. 5; br, Lex Harris. **20:** t, Lex Harris; c, Australian Antarctic Division, collected by Lex Harris. **21;** t, Neal Young; cl, diagram adapted from the work of L. Fitzner, Australian Antarctic Division; cr, adapted from *The Surface of the Antarctic Ice Sheet* in *Antarctica: Glaciological and Geophysical Folio (*Scott Polar Research Institute, Cambridge, 1983). **22:** l, tr, Neal Young; br, Lex Harris, **23:** t, image from Landsat 1, digitally enhanced by CSIRO Division of Computing Research and Neal Young; c, Colin Monteath, b, Andrew Gledow. **24:** t, Colin Monteath; ct, Neal Young; c, Colin Monteath; cb, Neal Young; b, Colin Monteath; br, diagram adapted from work of Ian Allison in *IASH*, Publication No 131. **25:** t, Instituto Antartico Chileno, Santiago; br, bl, Colin Monteath. **26/27:** John and Margaret Bradshaw. **28:** t, Colin Monteath; ct, cb, Shaun Norman; bl, br, Colin Monteath. **29:** tr, cl, Colin Monteath; cr, Chris Hendy; b, Colin Monteath. **30:** t, P. Jacob. **31:** ct, P. Wardill; cbl, US Defence Meteorological Satellite Program; cr, R. J. Francis/ Mawson Institute for Antarctic Research, Adelaide; b, National Aeronautics and Space Administration, Washington. **32:** t, bl, Colin Monteath; c, br, Harvey Marchant. **33:** t, cr, br, Colin Monteath; cl, bl, Harvey Marchant. **34:** bl, Colin Monteath; all others Rodney Seppelt. **35:** cr, br, Harvey Marchant; all others Rodney Seppelt. **36:** t, Paul Broady; c, br, David Everitt; bc, Paul Broady; br, David Rounsevell. **37:** tr, Paul Broady; ct, Rodney Seppelt; cb, J. L. Sagar; bl, David Everitt; br, Paul Broady. **38:** t, Colin Monteath; bl, adapted from the work of N. A. Mackintosh in *Discovery Reports,* 36, 1973; br, adapted from the work of A. L. Gordon and R. D. Goldberg in *Antartic Map Folio Series,* 1970. **39:** t, tc, Dr Uwe Kils; bc, adapted from the work of R. M. Laws in Phil. Trans. R. Soc., Series B, 1977: br, adapted from the work of H. Meguro in *Antarctic Record,* 1962. **40:** t, John Béchervaise; cr, Paul Sagar; bl, br, Colin Monteath. **41:** tl, John Darby; tr, c, b, Colin Monteath. **42:** t, bl, Colin Monteath; c, br, Don Horning. **43:** t, Dr Kim Westerskov; c, John Warham; b, Don Horning. **44:** t, John Darby; c, br, Colin Monteath; bl, Don Horning. **45:** t, b, Colin Monteath. **46:** Colin Monteath. **47:** t, Don Horning; c, b, Colin Monteath. **48:** t, Colin Monteath. **49:** t, Colin Monteath. **50:** t, K. W. Fink/Ardea. **52:** Colin Monteath. **53:** Colin Monteath. **54:** tr, tl, John Darby; c, br, bl, Colin Monteath. **55:** t, John Darby; b, Geoff Renner. **56:** t, Richard Hasler; ct, Colin Monteath; c, cb, J. Chester; b, Colin Monteath. **58:** t, Don Horning; b, Colin Monteath. **59:** c, Don Horning. **60:** Rodney Seppelt. **61:** Rodney Seppelt. **62:** t, Colin Monteath; b, Nigel Wace. **63:** Colin Monteath. **64:** Colin Monteath. **65:** t, Ronald Lewis Smith; b, Commander Chris Furse/Joint Services Expedition. **66/67:** Peaks in the Royal Society Range, Colin Monteath. **68:** Michael Holford/ National Maritime Museum. **69:** cr, bl, National Library of Australia. **70:** Bibliothèque Nationale, Paris. **71:** t, Bibliothèque Nationale, Paris; b, Lauritz Sømme. **72:** t, Musée de la Marine, Paris; b, Bibliothèque Nationale, Paris. **73:** Bibliothèque Nationale, Paris. **74:** State Library of New South Wales. **75:** l, National Art Gallery, Wellington; r, National Library of Australia. **76:** Public Record Office, London. **77:** Mitchell Library, Sydney. **78:** t, J. Chester; b, Mitchell Library, Sydney. **79:** tl, National Museum of New Zealand; c, Mitchell Library, Sydney; tr, National Maritime Museum, London. **82:** Central Navy Museum, Leningrad. **83:** Central Navy Museum, Leningrad. **84:** tl, Mitchell Library, Sydney; tr, Charles Swithinbank; bl, Mitchell Library, Sydney. **85:** br, Central Navy Museum, Leningrad. **86:** t, b, Hydrographic Department, Taunton; c, Public Record Office, London. **87:** t, Hydrographic Department, Taunton; b, Colin Monteath. **88:** t, Peabody Museum, Salem; b, Library of Congress, Washington. **89:** t, Mitchell Library, Sydney; b, Yale University Library. **90:** tl, Mitchell Library, Sydney; tr, Royal Scottish Geographical Society. **91:** t, ct, Mitchell Library, Sydney; c, cb, Tom Scott/Royal Scottish Museum; b, Mitchell Library, Sydney. **92:** tl, Royal Geographical Society; tr, John Béchervaise. **93:** c, b, Royal Geographical Society. **94:** tl, cl, State Library of New South Wales; b, British Library. **95:** tl, Charles Swithinbank; tr, Mitchell Library, Sydney; br, British Library. **96:** t, National Library of Australia; all others Bibliothèque Nationale, Paris. **97:** t, Peabody Museum, Salem; all others Bibliothèque Nationale, Paris. **98:** b, Bibliothèque Nationale, Paris. **99:** t, Ronald Lewis Smith; c, b, Bibliothèque Nationale, Paris. **100/101:** Bibliothèque Nationale, Paris. **102:** t, Tasmanian Museum and Art Gallery; b, The State Library of Victoria. **103:** tr, W. D. Parkinson. **104:** t, United States Navy Academy and Museum, Annapolis. **105:** Mitchell Library, Sydney. **106:** Peabody Museum, Salem. **107:** t, The Beinecke Rare Book and Manuscript Library, Yale University Library. **108:** Yale University Library. **109:** t, Library of Congress, Washington. **110:** tl, National Maritime Museum, London; tr, The Royal Society. **111:** bl, Scott Polar Research Institute, Cambridge; bc, Mitchell Library, Sydney; br, Mary Evans Picture Library. **112:** Colin Monteath. **113:** Scott Polar Research Institute, Cambridge. **114:** National Maritime Museum, London. **115:** t, Colin Monteath; c, b, Scott Polar Research Institute, Cambridge. **116:** tl, tr, Scott Polar Research Institute, Cambridge. **117:** t, br, private collection; br, Mitchell Library, Sydney. **118:** t, Colin Monteath; c, b, The Mawson Institute for Antarctic Research, Adelaide. **119:** c, b, The Mawson Institute for Antarctic Research, Adelaide. **120:** t, b, Department of Zoology, Oxford University. **121:** tr, Department of Zoology, Oxford University. **122:** Department of Zoology, Oxford University. **123:** bl, br, Department of Zoology, Oxford University. **124:** cr, Department of Zoology, Oxford University. **125:** t, c, Department of Zoology, Oxford University. **126:** tl, tr, Norsk Sjøfartsmuseum, Oslo; c, Popperfoto; b, Geoff Renner. **127:** tl, tr, City Museums and Art Galleries, Dundee, Scotland; b, Norsk Sjøfartsmuseum, Oslo. **128:** tl, Norsk Sjøfartsmuseum, Oslo; tr, Colin Monteath; c, b, Mitchell Library, Sydney. **129:** b, Mitchell Library, Sydney. **130:** t, Harlingue-Viollet, Paris; b, Janet Vetter. **131:** t, Colin Monteath; b, Janet Vetter. **132:** Janet Vetter. **133:** Janet Vetter. **134/135:** Norsk Polarinstitutt, Oslo. **136:** t, Colin Monteath. **137:** Norsk Polarinstitutt, Oslo. **138:** t, National Archives and Records Service, Washington; b, Noel Kemp. **139:** Royal Geographical Society. **140/141:** Akademie der Wissenschaften der DDR, Leipzig. **142/143:** Akademie der Wissenschaften der DDR, Leipzig. **144:** t, BBC Hulton Picture Library; c, Alexander Turnbull Library, Wellington; b, Colin Monteath. **145:** Royal Geographical Society. **146:** t, b, Royal Geographical Society; c, State Library of New South Wales. **147:** tl, Royal Geographical Society; tr, Scott Polar Research Institute, Cambridge; c, Alexander Turnbull Library, Wellington. **148:** t, c, bl, Royal Geographical Society; br, Colin Monteath. **149:** t, Scott Polar Research Institute, Cambridge; br, The Maritime Trust, London. **150:** t, John Béchervaise; b, The Mawson Institute for Antarctic Research, Adelaide. **151:** tl, Popperfoto; all others Colin Monteath. **152/153:** Mr Gustalf Nordenskjöld/Gothenburg Geographical Society. **154/155:** Mr Gustalf Nordenskjöld/ Gothenburg Geographical Society. **156:** Mr Gustalf Nordenskjöld/Gothenburg Geographical Society. **157:** t, Mr Gustalf Nordenskjöld/Gothenburg Geographical Society; b, Colin Monteath. **158:** t, Colin Monteath; b, Mr Gustalf Nordenskjöld/Gothenburg Geographical Society. **159:** t, Mr Gustalf Nordenskjöld/Gothenburg Geographical Society; b, Colin Monteath. **160:** t, Hunterian Museum, University of Glasgow; b, Scott Polar Research Institute, Cambridge. **161:** tr, tl, b, Hunterian Museum, University of Glasgow; c, Ronald Lewis Smith. **162/163:** Hunterian Museum, University of Glasgow. **164:** t, Royal Geographical Society; bl, Popperfoto. **165:** t, c, bl, Colin Monteath; br, Royal Geographical Society. **166/167:** Harlingue-Viollet, Paris. **168:** Mme Allart-Charcot. **169:** tl, tr, Mme Allart-Charcot; b, Colin Monteath. **170:** Harlingue-Viollet, Paris. **171:** t, Harlingue-Viollet, Paris; b, Mme Allart-Charcot. **172:** t, Mme Allart-Charcot; b, Harlingue-Viollet, Paris. **173:** t, Geoff Renner; c, bl, br, Mme Allart-Charcot. **174:** t, Colin Monteath; b, The Mawson Institute for Antarctic Research, Adelaide. **175:** tl, Royal Geographical Society; tr, bl, The Mawson Institute for Antarctic Research, Adelaide; br, Shaun Norman. **176:** t, br, The Mawson Institute for Antarctic Research, Adelaide; bl, Royal Geographical Society. **177:** bl, The Mawson Institute for Antarctic Research, Adelaide; bc, br, Mitchell Library, Sydney. **178:** t, Royal Geographical Society; b, The Mawson Institute for Antarctic Research, Adelaide. **179:** t, The Mawson Institute for Antarctic Research, Adelaide; b, Colin Monteath. **180:** t, The Mawson Institute for Antarctic Research, Adelaide; b, Scott Polar Research Institute, Cambridge. **181:** The Mawson Institute for Antarctic Research, Adelaide. **182:** t, b, Scott Polar Research Institute Cambridge; c, Popperfoto. **183:** Colin Monteath. **184:** Norsk Folkemuseum, Oslo. **185;** tl, The Library of Congress, Washington; tr, Mary Evans Picture Library; bl, Norsk Folkemuseum, Oslo. **186:** t, Scott Polar Research Institute, Cambridge; b, Colin Monteath. **187:** tl, private collection; tr, Mary Evans Picture Library; b, Library of Congress, Washington. **188:** t, State Library of New South Wales; cr, Norsk Folkemuseum, Oslo; cl, Library of Congress, Washington; b, The Royal University Library, Oslo. **189:** Wally Herbert. **190:** t, b, Colin Monteath. **191:** tr, tl, Popperfoto; b, Alexander Turnbull Library, Wellington. **192:** tl, Scott Polar Research Institute, Cambridge; tr, c, Alexander Turnbull Library, Wellington; br, bl, Popperfoto. **193:** c, Alexander Turnbull Library, Wellington; b, Popperfoto. **194:** t, Antarctic Division, Christchurch; c, b, Popperfoto. **195:** t, Popperfoto; b, Scott Polar Research Institute, Cambridge. **196:** Scott Polar Research Institute, Cambridge. **197:** t, b, Scott Polar Research Institute Cambridge; c, Colin Monteath. **198:** Scott Polar Research Institute, Cambridge. **199:** t, Colin Monteath; c, Popperfoto; b, State Library of New South Wales. **200:** t, Colin Monteath; b, Desmond J. Lugg. **201:** tl, Desmond J. Lugg; tr, Australian Antarctic Division/D. Parer; b, Australian Antarctic Division/G. Merrill. **202:** tl, Süddeutscher Verlag, Munich; tr, b, Ullstein Bilderdienst, Berlin. **203:** Ullstein Bilderdienst, Berlin. **204:** Ullstein Bilderdienst, Berlin. **205:** t, Geoff Renner; b, Ullstein Bilderdienst, Berlin. **206:** t, Takehiro Yukawa/Shirase Antarctic Expedition Memorial Association; b, Asahi Newspaper Company, Tokyo. **207:** t, br, Asahi Newspaper Company, Tokyo; bl, State Library of New South Wales. **208:** tl, b, Colin Monteath; tr, Popperfoto. **209:** The Mawson Institute for Antarctic Research, Adelaide; bl, Royal Geographical Society; br, Popperfoto. **210:** t, b, The Mawson Institute for Antarctic Research, Adelaide; c, Mitchell Library, Sydney. **211:** tr, Mitchell Library, Sydney; all others The Mawson Institute for Antarctic Research, Adelaide. **212:** tl, Mitchell Library, Sydney; tr, Rod Leadingham. **213:** t, b, Mitchell Library, Sydney; c, The Mawson Institute for Antarctic Research, Adelaide. **214:** t, Mitchell Library, Sydney; b, The Mawson Institute for Antarctic Research, Adelaide. **215:** Mitchell Library, Sydney. **216/217:** Colin Monteath. **218:** Royal Geographical Society. **219:** t, private collection; b, Royal Geographical Society. **220/221:** Royal Geographical Society. **222:** t, Commander Chris Furse/Joint Services Expedition; c, b, Royal Geographical Society. **222:** tl, Commander Chris Furse/Joint Services Expedition; tr, Royal Geographical Society; b, National Library, Canberra. **224:** t, Colin Monteath; b, National Library, Canberra. **225:** tr, c, private collection; b, Instituto Antartico Chileno, Santiago. **226:** tl, Colin Monteath; tr, Dick Richards. **227:** t, Colin Monteath; b, Dick Richards. **228:** Colin Monteath. **229:** tr,

Antarctic Division, Christchurch; bcl, bl, Rod Leadingham; all others Colin Monteath. **230:** Scott Polar Research Institute, Cambridge. **231:** Colin Monteath. **232:** Scott Polar Research Institute, Cambridge. **233:** t, Mitchell Library, Sydney; ct, Colin Monteath; cb, b, Scott Polar Research Institute, Cambridge. **234/235:** Institute of Oceanographic Sciences, Surrey, England. **236:** t, Harlingue-Viollet, Paris; b, Popperfoto. **237:** BBC Hulton Picture Library. **238/239:** The American Geographical Society Collection of the University of Wisconsin–Milwaukee Library. **240/241:** National Archives and Records Service, Washington. **242/243:** National Archives and Records Service, Washington. **244:** t, ct, The Mawson Institute for Antarctic Research, Adelaide; cb, Popperfoto; bl, John Béchervaise; br, Chris Hendy. **245:** tl, Norman Jones; bl, National Archives and Records Service, Washington; all others Colin Monteath. **246/247:** The Mawson Institute for Antarctic Research, Adelaide. **248/249:** National Archives and Records Service, Washington. **250/251:** National Archives and Records Service, Washington. **253:** Colin Monteath. **254:** tl, Scott Polar Research Institute, Cambridge; tr, Colin Monteath; b, Mrs E. M. Rymill. **255:** Scott Polar Research Institute, Cambridge. **256:** t, Charles Swithinbank; b, Scott Polar Research Institute Cambridge. **257:** Scott Polar Research Institute Cambridge. **258/259:** National Archives and Records Service, Washington. **260/261:** National Archives and Records Service, Washington. **262/263:** Colin Monteath. **264:** t, Süddeutscher Verlag, Munich; b, Ullstein Bilderdienst, Berlin. **265:** t, c, Süddeutscher Verlag, Munich. **266/267:** National Archives and Records Service, Washington. **268:** British Antarctic Survey, Cambridge. **269:** t, c, British Antarctic Survey, Cambridge; b, Antarctic Division, Christchurch. **270:** British Antarctic Survey, Cammbridge. **271:** c, British Antarctic Survey, Cambridge; b, Antarctic Division, Christchurch. **272/273:** National Archives and Records Service, Washington.**274/275:** David Lewis. **276/277:** Sir Ranulph Fiennes. **278:** APA/Black Star/John Stetson. **279:** t, APA/Black Star/Will Steger; b, APA/Black Star/Gordon Wiltsie. **282:** David Tranter. **283:** Colin Monteath. **284/285:** Mount Erebus from the pressure ridges, Colin Monteath. **286:** bl, from *Little America* by R.E. Byrd (Putnam, New York, 1930); br, Geoff Renner. **287:** Lands and Survey Department, Wellington. **292/293:** James Cook's ships at Îles Kerguelen, Mitchell Library, Sydney. **294/295:** Dumont d'Urville's ship the *Astrolabe* trapped in the pack ice, Bibliothèque Nationale, Paris. **296/297:** Scott, Oates, Wilson and Evans (l to r) beside Amundsen's tent at the South Pole, Library of Congress, Washington. **298/299:** Byrd's ship the *City of New York* moored in the Bay of Whales, National Archives and Records Service, Washington. **300:** l, Royal Geographical Society; r, Bibliothèque Nationale, Paris. **301:** t, Central Navy Museum, Leningrad; c, National Archives and Records Service, Washington; b, Mitchell Library, Sydney. **302:** l, Harlingue-Viollet, Paris; r, Janet Vetter. **303:** tl, bl, private collection; tr, The Mawson Institute for Antarctic Research, Adelaide; br, National Archives and Records Service, Washington. **304:** t, ct, Popperfoto; cb, The Mawson Institute for Antarctic Research, Adelaide; b, Antarctic Division, Christchurch. **305:** t, Norsk Folkemuseum, Oslo; b, Norsk Sjøfartsmuseum, Oslo. **306:** t, The Mawson Institute for Antarctic Research, Adelaide; c, David Lewis; b, from *Scott's Last Expedition,* (Smith Elder, London, 1941). **307:** t, Mary Evans Picture Library; bl, Alexander Turnbull Library, Wellington; br, Scott Polar Research Institute, Cambridge. **308:** tl, National Maritime Museum, London. tr. from *The Voyage of the Discovery* by R. F. Scott (Smith Elder, London, 1905) bl, Mitchell Library, Sydney. **309:** t, private collection; ct, Royal Scottish Geographical Society; cb, from *The South Pole* by Roald Amundsen (John Murray, London, 1912); b, from *Scott's Last Expedition,* Volume II (Smith Elder, London, 1914).

Position of photographs on the page: t–top, c–centre, b–bottom, l–left, r–right.

Typesetting by Smith & Miles Limited,
433 Kent Street, Sydney, NSW 2000.

Colour separations by Toppan Printing Company.

Printed and bound in 1990 by Dai Nippon Printing Co. (H.K.) Ltd, Hong Kong
for Reader's Digest (Australia) Pty Limited (Inc. in NSW)